# UTAH'S NATIONAL PARKS

*Hiking, Camping and Vacationing in Utah's Canyon Country*

## ZION · BRYCE · CAPITOL REEF ARCHES · CANYONLANDS

## Ron Adkison

WILDERNESS PRESS · Berkeley

First edition August 1991
Copyright © 1991 by Ron Adkison

Front cover photo © 1991 David Muench
Back cover photo by Ron Adkison
Maps and photos by Ron Adkison
Drawings by Nicky Shriver
Design by Thomas Winnett and Roslyn Bullas
Cover design by Larry Van Dyke

Library of Congress Catalog Number 91-28496
International Standard Book Number 0-89997-126-1

Manufactured in the United States of America

Published by    Wilderness Press
                2440 Bancroft Way
                Berkeley, CA  94704
                (800) 443-7227
                Write for free catalog

**Library of Congress Cataloging-in-Publication Data**
Adkison, Ron.
    Utah's national parks : hiking, camping, and vacationing in Utah's
canyon country— Zion, Bryce, Capitol Reef, Arches and Canyonlands /
Ron Adkison. — 1st ed.
        p. cm.
    Includes bibliographical references and index.
    ISBN 0-89997-126-1
    1. Outdoor recreation—Utah—Guide-books. 2. Hiking—Utah—Guide-
books. 3. Camping—Utah—Guide-books. 5. Natural history—Utah—
Guide-books. 6. Utah—Description and travel—1981- —Guide-books. I. Title.
GV191.42.U8A35 1991                         91-28496
790'.09792—dc20                             CIP

# Acknowledgments

Writing a guidebook to the national parks of Utah, a multifaceted landscape encompassing nearly one million acres, was a monumental task. I had hiked in these parks before, and I was sure no more than a year would be necessary to gather all the information that was needed. After working for two full years on this book, I have not much more than scratched the surface of hiking opportunities but learned much of their fascinating and their diverse aspects.

Among those who helped me to gain knowledge of Utah's national parks are the rangers, seasonals, and professionals of the National Park Service. They most graciously allowed me to pick their brains and learn much about the intricacies of the parks, and they shared their vast knowledge, their documents and their libraries. Without their unending help and guidance, this book would never have become a reality.

To the following individuals, and to all associated with the national parks of Utah, this book is dedicated:

Zion National Park: Victor Jackson, Paul Kirkland.

Bryce Canyon National Park: Jack Roberts, Margaret Littlejohn, Ken Kerr, Christopher Rumm, Susan Colclacer.

Capitol Reef National Park: George Davidson, Glenn Sherrill, Ann Corson, Ken Kerer.

Arches National Park: John McLoughlin, Sonja Paspal, Shawn Duffy.

Canyonlands National Park: Larry Frederick, Chas Cartwright, Judy Chrobak-Cox, Judy Perkins, Gary Cox.

Many thanks to my good friend Ken Kukulka. Together we explored The Maze, taking a most unforgettable journey.

Donna Lozier was most generous in typing the bulk of the manuscript, and offered many important and valuable suggestions and corrections.

My wife Lynette Kemp also helped with typing and offered unflagging support, as well as the original idea for the book.

And I wish to extend my gratitude to Nicky Shriver for taking time from her busy schedule to produce some excellent line drawings.

Finally, at Wilderness Press, I must thank Tom Winnett for his assistance and enduring patience throughout the course of the work, and Jeff Schaffer for his guidance on the production of maps for this book.

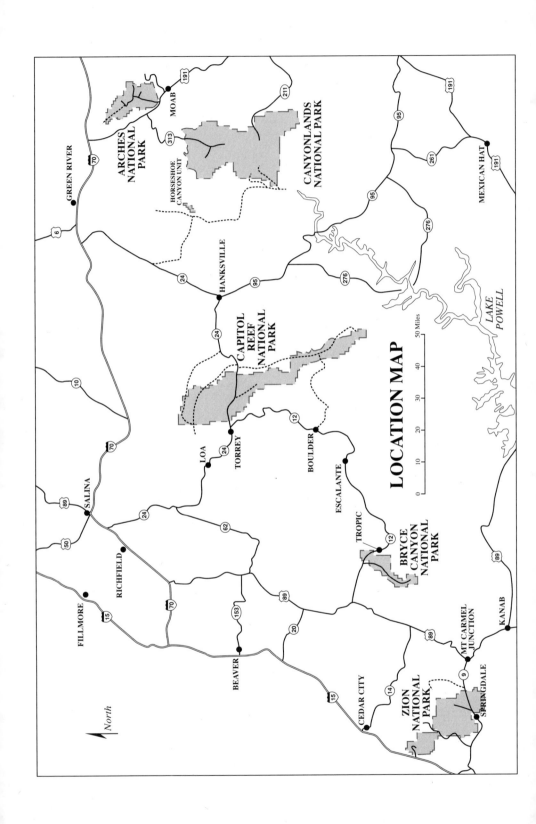

LOCATION MAP

# Contents

# The National Parks of Utah

Stretching across the southern third of Utah are five of perhaps the most magnificent national parks in the nation. These parks embrace some of the finest and most unusual examples of erosional forms on the globe, and they are truly among the wonders of the world. Utah's national parks are a veritable wilderness of stone, and indeed much of the land in each park has been recommended for federal wilderness designation.

Many serious hikers, however, shun national parks, believing that such areas are tourist meccas where a wilderness experience is difficult, if not impossible, to have. That may be true for some of our national parks, but not for Utah's. Even in Zion National Park, where annual visitation averages about two million people (nearly half the total annual visitation to all Utah national parks), the hiker can enjoy magnificent, wild country and a good deal of solitude only a short distance from any road.

The majority of park visitors spend only a day in each Utah park, viewing the scenery from the comfort of their vehicles as they try to see as much country as a one-to-two-week vacation will allow.

For visitors with limited time, these parks indeed have a great deal to offer. Much of the parks' scenery can be enjoyed from park roadways, and numerous short trails, many of them nature trails, offer visitors a chance to stretch their legs, smell the desert's fragrance, feel the wind in their faces, view seemingly endless panoramas and incomparable landscapes, enjoy the delicate blossoms and the perfumes of myriad wildflowers, and observe desert creatures going about their day-to-day lives. Many short trails require no special hiking ability, and some are accessible to handicapped persons in wheelchairs and even to baby strollers.

For an extended stay, each park has one or more excellent campgrounds, and some are available to large recreational vehicles. Each park also boasts a visitor center and interpretive activities that include ranger-led hikes and evening-campfire naturalist programs.

For the backcountry enthusiast, each park also contains broad stretches of pristine wilderness, and in some places, particularly in Capitol Reef and Canyonlands, hikers can roam for days and not see a single soul.

Visitors to the majestic landscape of Utah's

national parks will enjoy a wide range of scenery, including vast plateaus clothed in cool forests of pine, fire, and aspen; magnificent canyons up to 4000 feet deep, soaring cliffs, some of them sheer and smooth from top to bottom, others broken and fluted with great buttresses and columns; cliff-edged mesas, some capped by stone, others topped by velvety grasslands and "pygmy" forests of pinyon and juniper; broad desert valleys and sun-baked desert flats; domes, crags, arches and pinnacles of solid stone, colored in nearly every shade of the spectrum.

Another part of the scenery in Utah's national parks is the diversity of plants and animals, all of them living in delicate balance and adapted to the rigors of the high desert, where rainfall is scant and undependable, and where temperatures can be excessively hot. This desert country of the Colorado Plateau may seem harsh and unforgiving, inhospitable to human life if not to plants and animals, but humans have lived and even thrived here for thousands of years. Park visitors will encounter granaries and cliff dwellings of the Anasazi, rock-art panels dating back more than 2000 years, old homesteads, cowboy line camps, and even farm equipment.

Yes, Utah's national parks have a great deal to offer to everyone, from chapters of natural history and human history to chapters of earth history spanning more than 300 million years. Recreational opportunities are also diverse, ranging from dayhikes to extended backcountry treks, horseback rides (in Zion and Bryce), jeep trips, and river float trips.

# Hiking Utah's Desert Parks

The unique landscapes of rock and sand, canyons and mesas that make up the high desert of the Colorado Plateau offer some of the finest, most remote and most awe-inspiring wilderness hiking in the nation. But to enjoy this magical country to the fullest, and to minimize your impact on the land—and the land's potential impact on you—pretrip planning and an awareness of the special hazards involved in a desert trek are imperative.

Utah's high-desert national parks are arid to semiarid, meaning that an average of 15 inches of moisture or less falls upon the landscape annually. Often an entire month's share of precipitation may fall in a few hours or in a single day. Humidity is very low, and summer heat is intense. Daily temperature fluctuations of 30-50° between daytime highs and nighttime lows are not uncommon. Surface water is scarce, and much of it is highly mineralized and not potable. Many trails are rugged, and some require the use of hands to scramble over steep slickrock—bare, smooth sandstone.

The trails in Utah's national parks sample virtually every aspect of the park landscapes, from wooded mesas and forested pleateaus to open desert flats, cliffs, and deep, cavernous defiles. Many trails follow canyon bottoms, where the hiker may encounter deep sand or be forced to wade through waist-deep waters or even swim across deep pools. Some trails are accessible only to the adventurous wilderness enthusiast with basic rock-climbing ability, while others can be trod by visitors who have never before set foot on a trail. Still other "trails" are mere routes over slickrock, marked only by cairns—small piles of rocks.

Hiking over slickrock can be a joy, but it is not without its hazards. Loosened sand grains can make slickrock somewhat slippery, but usually even steep slickrock provides good traction, even when wet. However, smooth sandstone when snow-covered is extremely treacherous and should be avoided.

Dedicated backcountry hikers use a park's trails merely for access to the vast, untracked backcountry, where one reaps the rewards of self-reliance and perserverance, and enjoys solitude and the discovery of the desert's hidden secrets—as well as self-discovery.

It is in these unfettered hinterlands that introspection is inescapable. A more humbling experience than a trek into the vast, untracked desert is hard to find in our modern world. As modern technology and urban sprawl creep into every corner of our lives, many of us seek the few remaining wild places where nature reigns and our daily troubles seem vastly unimportant.

A trip into Utah's deserts is not a life-threatening survival situation, but one must be prepared to meet the challenges and to confront emergency situations if they arise. In most areas of the national parks in Utah, help is usually not far away. But in more remote areas, such as the North and South districts in Capitol Reef, the North Fork Road in Zion, and the Maze District in Canyonlands, emergency assistance is distant. Proper planning and recognition of hazards and of one's abilities are your best insurance for a safe and enjoyable outing.

Above all, hikers should try to minimize their impact on the fragile desert landscape.

## Hiking Seasons

One can hike in the national parks in Utah during all seasons except in Bryce Canyon, where winter snowpack renders that park accessible only to the cross-country skier or the snowshoer. Many visitors take their vacations during summer, but summers in the Utah desert are very hot, so it is not the most desirable time to visit here, except in the high country of Bryce Canyon and parts of Zion, where summers are pleasantly warm. Hot summer conditions usually invade the Utah desert by mid-June, although in some years summer may begin earlier. Daily high temperatures of 90-100° are common, with occasional spells of 110° heat. Nighttime lows typically dip to 60° or 70°, but areas with abundant slickrock continue to radiate heat long into the night. Usually by late July the thunderstorm season begins, bringing the threat of heavy downpours, high winds, lightning, and flash floods. Some summers, however, are quite dry, while others are uncommonly wet, but thunderstorms usually begin to abate by mid-September.

Autumn is perhaps the most delightful season to visit the Utah desert. Daily maximum temperatures range from the 70s and 80s in September to the 40s and 50s in late November and December. Overnight lows are typically in the 20-50° range. Storms are possible, but usually of short duration. Autumn typically boasts some of the clearest, most stable weather of the year, but snow may fall in October, and the possibility of snow increases as temperatures drop and Pacific storms become more vigorous by late November and December.

Although the chances of snowfall increase during winter, snow cover is generally light and rarely lasts more than a few days except in sheltered recesses. January and February are often the driest months of the year, with daytime highs ranging from the 20s to the 40s, and overnight lows ranging in the the teens and 20s, rarely dipping below zero. But above 7000 feet, and particularly in the high country of Zion and Bryce, temperatures are much colder and snowpack is often heavy.

Spring weather is typically more unstable than winter, with wide variations in temperatures and precipitation. March usually brings an onset of spring weather, but occasional Pacific storms bring winds, clouds, rain, and possibly snow as late as April. Most often, spring storms are characterized by showers, sometimes with sunny periods in between. But the weather is generally delightful during spring, with daytime highs averaging from the 50s to the 70s, and nighttime lows ranging from 30° to 50°.

In general, visitation to Utah's national parks increases during spring, often reaching a peak around Memorial Day, slackening during summer, and then increasing again around Labor Day. Bryce and Zion, however, continue to experience heavy use through the summer months.

## Heat and Safety

Summer is a challenging season in which to hike in the Utah desert, and special precautions must be taken to avoid heat and water-related injuries.

Park literature tells visitors they must drink one gallon of water per day, regardless of the season. But seasoned desert rats know that summer hiking increases that requirement, and they drink at least six quarts of water per day to avoid dehydration. Remember the maxim, "Ration sweat, not water" when hiking in the desert, and drink often, not just when you feel thirsty, and particularly during meals and during the cooler hours.

During summer, rest 10 minutes every hour, and hike only in the morning hours before noon and in the late afternoon, after about 5 or 6 o'clock. During midday, find a shady niche, perhaps in an alcove or beneath an overhanging ledge, and rest until the heat begins to abate and the shadows fall.

As one exercises during the heat of a summer day, one increases the chance that the body may not effectively be able to maintain cooling and circulation. Heat cramps, heat exhaustion, and in the worst case heat stroke may result. *Heat cramps* usually develop in the arms and legs after exertion, causing painful muscle spasm. *Heat exhaustion* is more serious, and occurs as the body diverts blood away from internal organs to the skin so it can be cooled. Symptoms include cool and clammy skin, perhaps nausea and weakness, and rapid, shallow breathing. If you heed the warning signs, heat exhaustion need not be dangerous. As with heat cramps, immediately cease activity, rest or lie in the shade, loosen clothing, and drink water. If one must resume activity, one should begin slowly.

*Heat stroke* is a serious medical emergency, and it can be fatal if not recognized and treated immediately. Heat stroke involves the temporary shutdown of sweat glands, so the body is unable to cool itself through evaporation. Though heat stroke is uncommon, learn to recognize the symptoms, which initially include hot, dry, flushed skin, dry mouth, headache, dizziness and nausea, followed by rapid, shallow breathing, muscular twitching, convulsions, and unconsciousness.

If heat stroke is suspected, one must rapidly cool the victim and seek medical attention immediately. Remove the victim's clothing, and cool by immersion in water or by covering with wet cloths, while fanning continuously to help dissipate body heat. Massage the extremities gently to help increase blood flow and heat loss.

These methods should be continued until medical assistance arrives or, if unavailable, until the victim begins to recover. Rest and care should be provided until the victim is feeling better, and physical activity should be resumed slowly.

Sunburn is possible at any time of the year, and hikers should take the appropriate precautions. Wear loose-fitting, light-colored clothing that will reflect the heat. Though long pants and long-sleeved shirts are preferable and help reduce dehydration, many hikers wear shorts. Sunscreen is then a must. Wear a hat that will shade the eyes and ears, and use sunglasses to avoid the intense glare reflecting from slickrock. Avoid licking your lips if they are dry, as this will cause splitting, and instead apply lip balm.

## Equipment for Desert Hiking

Many hikers are unsure of what type of footwear to use in the desert. Some hikers wear jogging shoes, and these offer no ankle support or protection from thorny plants. Rigid lug-sole boots don't provide adequate traction on slickrock. Instead, consider wearing lightweight, breathable hiking boots. These offer ankle support and have a softer, more flexible sole for better traction. Carry lightweight shoes for wear around camp, giving your boots the opportunity to air out.

Backpack stoves are a necessity on backcountry outings, as open fires are not allowed in Utah's national parks. Even in the desert, it is advisable to carry raingear, as storms can happen at any time, and often develop unexpectedly. Most hikers carry a tent, for protection not only from storms but also from carnivorous insects. Sand flies, mosquitoes, and especially the tiny, black, gnatlike flies called midges constantly harass hikers from early spring through midsummer. Strong insect repellents, preferably a natural product, are effective against mosquitoes, and to a lesser extent provide protection against flesh-eating sand flies, but these products seem to have little effect on midges. The only product that deters midges is a bath oil spray from Avon called Skin-so-Soft.

Most soils are shallow in Utah's national parks, and sometimes backpackers have to pitch their tents on solid rock. Obviously, tent stakes are of little value on rocky sites; hence, free-standing tents are the answer.

## Flash Floods

Many hiking routes are restricted to canyon bottoms, and whether one is simply hiking through a canyon or searching for a campsite, keep in mind the possibility of flash floods. Always camp above the high-water mark, indicated by water stains on canyon walls and debris washed from previous floods. Whenever hiking in a canyon, keep an eye out for escape routes to higher ground. Many canyons in the national parks gather their waters beyond park boundaries, so even during sunny weather in your location, a vigorous, isolated thunderstorm miles away could send a roiling wall of water down your canyon. If you hear an increasing roar up-canyon, signaling oncoming floodwaters, seek higher ground immediately, and do not attempt to outrun rushing waters; it cannot be done. Another rule of thumb in desert country is that one should never camp in a wash, regardless of the weather; heavy rains can develop suddenly and unexpectedly. Floodwaters in many washes typically subside in a few hours to 24 hours.

## Backcountry Camping

When choosing a campsite, observe the regulations of the particular park you're hiking in, maintaining minimum distance from roads, trails, and particularly water sources. Desert wildlife depends upon the few springs and streams for its survival, and if backpackers camp too close, some animals, particularly the shy bighorn sheep, will avoid the water sources. Choose a durable campsite, preferably on bare ground, or on needles and duff in a pinyon-and-juniper woodland.

For various reasons this guide doesn't attempt to direct hikers to specific campsites; one reason is that potential camping areas are far too numerous to mention. Campsites are everywhere, on benches in the canyons, on mesa tops, or hidden in slickrock niches; just look for them and camp far away from others so as not to disrupt their solitude. Don't camp near water, but instead tank up at a spring or a waterhole and move on to a dry camp.

## Water Safety

In all Utah national parks, rangers and park literature recommend treatment of backcountry water sources. If you're out for two or three days, you can carry water from a developed, potable source. Hikers who wish to avoid the added weight of extra water (one gallon = 8.33 pounds) and hikers planning a longer trek where water sources are known to exist along the route must treat their water. The old standby is to boil it for at least one minute. But then it takes a while for the water to cool enough to drink, and one must carry the extra weight of fuel. Iodine or disinfectant tablets may be used, but these are less effective than boiling, and they impart an unpleasant taste to water that usually already has a high mineral content and its own distinct flavor.

The best treatment is the use of one of the pump-type filters that are widely available at outdoor equipment stores. These not only filter out microscropic bacteria and protozoans, but they also remove natural and chemical impurities and much of the mineral taste. Remember always to treat suspected water not only for drinking but even for brushing your teeth.

## Desert Hiking

Plan your trip in advance, including possible sidetrips, and study topographic maps. Leave your itinerary with a friend or relative, and have them notify the appropriate park office if you don't return when expected. It is easy to get sidetracked into exploring hidden canyons and mesas in the Utah desert, but try to stick to your planned route. Careful study of the topographic map before and during your trip will keep you oriented and help you to avoid unnecessary confusion.

Hiking alone in the desert is unwise, but many people do it. If you hike alone, you must take great care not to become lost and to avoid situations which might result in injury. When hiking with a group, set the pace according to the slowest member, and stay together. Don't exceed the limits of your capabilities or those of others in your group. Before climbing steep rock, ask yourself if you are making a wise decision. Don't climb up anything that you may not be able to get back down, and vice versa.

Many hikers who visit Utah's national parks return time and again to this wonderful, magical land, and some develop a desire to tread beyond established trails and explore the untracked backcountry. Some cross-country hiking requires rock-climbing skills and great determina-tion, while other routes are simply a matter of reading the topographic map and setting the right course. At times a compass is necessary, but many routes are straightforward and require no special skills other than a good memory of the landscape and the ability to stay oriented. The land can look quite different when you are traveling in the opposite direction, and the seasoned hiker pays careful attention to the landmarks and frequently takes note of the trail behind, so it will be familiar upon returning.

The geology of Utah's national parks is highly variable, and each rock formation has its own unique characteristics. Hidden within the 40 or 80-foot contours of topographic maps are the intracacies of the landscape that one will observe only while on the ground. While knowledge of the geology is not necessary to enjoy the Utah desert, it is important to cross-country hikers when they plan their excursions. Many rock formations form sheer cliffs, overhanging ledges, or other impassable terrain that may not be apparent on a topographic map. Thus, when planning an off-trail route, it is important to

**Upper Courthouse Wash, La Sal Mountains**

incorporate the geology into the map. Knowledge of rock formations and characteristics is gained mostly through experience, but there are several good geology books on the Colorado Plateau region that are helpful. In addition, each national park in Utah except Bryce Canyon has geologic maps, available through visitor centers, that show all the rock formations in the park. These maps are invaluable in planning cross-country routes, and are of great interest to anyone wishing to learn more about the fascinating geology of these parks.

**Midget faded rattlesnake**

## Poisonous Desert Creatures

The Utah desert does have its share of biting and sometimes poisonous creatures. The aforementioned sand flies, or deer flies, are common in sandy washes, but mosquitoes are much less common, usually found only near water. Midges, however, are ubiquitous in all the national parks, and they inflict an itching bite even more irritating than the mosquito's.

Tarantulas, though large and dangerous-looking, rarely bite unless provoked, but their strong jaws can inflict a painful bite. Their poison is mild, but a bacterial infection can result.

The giant desert hairy scorpion is also threatening in its appearance, but its sting is harmless except for being painful.

Black widow spiders are common but rarely seen due to their secretive nature. Take care when lifting rocks, as these creatures may be lurking underneath, and always empty your boots each morning, as spiders and scorpions are often attracted to them by warmth and moisture.

Finally, poisonous snakes are feared more than any other creature in the desert. The small midget faded rattlesnake occurs in Capitol Reef, Arches, and Canyonlands national parks, where the Hopi rattlesnake is also believed to dwell. In Bryce Canyon is the five-foot Great Basin rattlesnake, and in Zion, the western rattlesnake. Hikers are more likely to encounter a rattler in Bryce Canyon than in any other Utah park, and overall, sightings of rattlesnakes are rare. When a hiker approaches, a rattlesnake will either slither away

and hide, or coil in defense. Many rattle a warning, but some do not. Pay attention to where you place your hands and feet, especially when hiking in brushy or rocky areas. Don't panic if you are bitten; remain calm and still. Exercise only serves to transport the venom rapidly through your body. People rarely succumb to the bite of a rattlesnake, even without the benefit of any first-aid treatment. The traditional cut-and-suck method has been found to have little value, and can actually increase your chances of infection.

A rattlesnake bite results in immediate pain accompanied by swelling. Tie a constricting band above the bite and the swelling, and remove it for 1 minute during every 15-minute period. Remain calm and quiet, and drink plenty of water. A companion should immediately go to the nearest trailhead or ranger station for help or, if you are alone, you should proceed slowly to the nearest location where people are likely to be.

## Reducing Your Impact on the Desert

While the desert appears to be a durable landscape, it is actually delicate and fragile, and plant and animal life can be easily disrupted, even by walking off of established trails for only a short distance. Throughout your travels in the Utah desert, you will surely notice a black, crusty covering on bare ground, primarily on clay soils. This ground cover is an assemblage of lower plants, called a *microphytic* or a *cryptogamic* crust. The crust, made up of mosses, lichens, cyanobacteria (blue-green algae), and fungus in various combinations, is easily destroyed by feet and by vehicle tires, and it may take 25 years to recover. When you walk on this black lumpy crust, you are destroying plants and hastening wind and water erosion. To reduce your impact on this fragile association of crusty plants, stay on the trails or, if you're hiking cross-country, hike in washes or on slickrock as much as possible, or on soils free of cryptogamic crusts.

Another important aspect of the national-park experience in Utah is the historic sites, such as Anasazi structures and rock art. Encountering a cliff dwelling, a granary or a rock-art panel left behind by a long-vanished culture hundreds or even thousands of years ago is one of the special joys of hiking in the Utah desert, and these reminders of ancient desert dwellers lend an air of mystery to the enchanting landscape. Yet with each passing year, vandals destroy parts of these valuable resources and remove artifacts from archaeological sites.

It is our reponsibility to protect these sites, not only for their scientific value but for ourselves and those who come after. Structures are fragile and crumble easily; do not climb on them. Skin oils destroy pigments on pictograph panels, so restrain the urge to touch them. Do not add graffiti to rock-art panels. Leave archaeological sites as you found them, preserving the sense of discovery for those who follow. Every artifact— a kernel of corn or a potsherd—provides an important link to the past.

Once an artifact is removed or disturbed, it becomes merely an object that cannot be related to its context. Even walking around a dwelling or other site may destroy cultural resources. The Antiquities Act of 1906 and the Archaeological Resources Protection Act of 1979 make it unlawful to remove, damage, excavate, deface or alter the material remains of human life and activity over 100 years old. There are also state laws protecting cultural resources. Civil and criminal penalties are enforced, and rewards of up to $500 are provided for information leading to the arrest and conviction of offenders.

There are many ways in which hikers can reduce their impact on the fragile desert. Although techniques of minimum-impact behavior are now common practice among hikers, we occasionally need reminders. Previously mentioned in this chapter are suggestions to camp on durable sites, to avoid camping near water sources or trampling cryptogamic crusts, and to allow ample room between backcountry campsites. In addition, hikers should keep noise to a minimum, as sound carries far in the desert and echoes among rocks and canyon walls. Keep group size as small as possible, and consider splitting your group into smaller parties while hiking and camping. When traveling cross-country, spread out instead of walking single file and concentrating your impact.

Always carry out your trash or garbage. In the arid desert climate, things like orange and banana peels will not decompose; rather, they become mummified. Respect plant and animal life in the desert. Moving a stone, uprooting a plant, or killing an undesirable creature disrupts the delicate balance that desert life has achieved. Above all, remember that you are a visitor in the home of plants and animals, so behave as you would in someone's home and act with respect for all desert dwellers.

# Driving in Utah's National Parks

Most trailheads in the national parks of Utah lie along paved park roads and are accessible to any vehicle, but some lie along remote dirt roads. Dirt roads are often impassable to even 4WD vehicles during and shortly after a heavy rain, when they become a sticky, slippery mess. Some roads follow canyons that are subject to dangerous flash floods.

Drivers of 4WD vehicles should be experienced in rough road travel before attempting most of the jeep roads in Utah's national parks. Since many jeep routes follow sandy washes, vehicles should be equipped with wide, deep-lug tires. Traveling with a group is a precaution in case one vehicle gets stuck or damaged. A winch is useful—but it is often difficult to find an anchor point in the desert.

Everyone traveling off main roads should be sure to have a full tank of gas and perhaps some extra, at least 5 gallons of water, a shovel, extra food and clothing, a tow line, and a tire pump.

Avoid steep downhill grades in sand unless you are certain you can make it back up. If you begin to get stuck in sand, don't spin the wheels, as you will only dig in deeper. You can increase traction by deflating tires to about 20 p.s.i.—but be sure to re-inflate them once you're beyond the obstacle. If deflating tires doesn't do the trick, use your jack to lift the stuck wheels and place rocks, boards, or brush underneath for added traction. Consider carrying boards, burlap bags, strips of carpet, pieces of chain-link fence—anything that might provide traction in deep, soft sand.

Be sure to check road conditions and weather forecasts before driving off main roads, and when in doubt, stop your vehicle and scout ahead on foot; a few minutes of scouting may save you hours of digging out.

# Park Regulations

The mission of the National Park Service is to preserve the natural and historical values within national parks, while providing for the enjoyment of the landscape in a manner that will leave it unimpaired for future generations. We can all assit by following the guidelines established by park managers. Observing these regulations need not hinder our outdoor experiences, and in fact most embody common-sense behavior. Though regulations are the law of the land in our national parks, we should choose to employ techniques of minimum impact not only in the parks but wherever we travel.

Regulations specific to one national park are listed in the following chapters. Below is a list of regulations that apply to all Utah national parks.

- Backcountry use permits are required for all visitors camping in the backcountry or in 4WD campsites. They are free and available at all visitor centers. Rangers will explain pertinent regulations when you obtain your permit.

- Campfires are prohibited except in campgrounds.

- Wood gathering is not allowed, so you must bring your own wood for use in campgrounds, and carry a stove in the backcountry.

- Vehicles must be licensed and street-legal, even those used on backcountry jeep roads. All vehicles, including mountain bikes, are restricted to designated vehicle routes; off-route travel is not permitted.

- Visitors are urged to use toilet facilities where available. Otherwise they must bury human waste in a hole 4-6 inches deep, carefully covering it when finished. Some parks require that backcountry users pack out their toilet paper rather than burn it. Do not bury it, as it will not readily decompose.

- Pets are not permitted in any backcountry roadless area or on hiking trails. They may be transported in vehicles on park roads, including jeep roads, and may be kept overnight in backcountry vehicle campsites and in park campgrounds. Any pet outside of a vehicle must be on a leash less than 6 feet long or otherwise physically constrained at all times. Pets may be left unattended if they are restrained at a location where they will not interfere with wildlife or with travel by other visitors, and secured in a way that will avoid resource damage. Barking and aggressive dogs may not be left unattended, and no pet should be left behind if weather conditions would endanger the animal's health. No pet may be left unattended overnight.

- All trash and garbage must be packed out of the backcountry. Burial of refuse is not permitted.

- Weapons must be unloaded, broken down and cased during transport in national parks. Weapons of any kind are prohibited in the backcountry.

- Observe camping restrictions in regard to water sources and do not use soaps in or near water sources. In most parks, campsites can be established no closer than

300 feet from nonflowing water sources, such as seeps, springs and potholes, and no closer than 100 feet from free-flowing streams. Swimming in potholes is not allowed unless the pothole is continually recharged by flowing water.

- Destruction, defacement, disturbance, or removal of natural and historical objects in national parks is not permitted.

**Devils Garden Campground in Arches National Park**

# Using This Book

## The Hike Descriptions

Here is a brief explanation of the hiking description format. A round-trip hike is one on which you retrace your outbound steps. A loop trip involves no retracing. A semiloop trip retraces part of a route after making a loop somewhere along the course. A shuttle trip is one in which hikers walk from one trailhead to another, requiring the use of two vehicles to establish a car shuttle or some other arrangement.

Low/High elevation figures give you an idea of how much you'll climb and descend.

The "Suited for" classification tells whether a trip is a *Walk* (a short stroll accessible to anyone, even nonhikers), a *Dayhike* (usually a longer or more demanding trip lasting as long as all day), a *Backpack* (a trip on which you spend one or more nights in the backcountry), a *Jeep Trip* (usually accessible only to high-clearance 4WD vehicles), or a *Mountain Bike Trip* (a trip along a jeep road accessible to mountain bikes). Some trips are "suited for" more than one of these.

The "difficulty" rating of a given hike is essentially arbitrary, arrived at by taking into account a variety of factors including length of the hike, elevation change, nature of the trail, and availability of water and shade—all in relation to the average hiker's ability.

"Best Season" is the average optimum season in which to hike the trail, including those months with the greatest probability of fair weather and moderate temperatures. Seasons vary from year to year. In some years spring can be quite moist and cool, and in other years spring can be unusually hot and dry; likewise with the months of autumn. The parks, however, can be enjoyed year-around. Visitors are encouraged to check with the appropriate national park office to determine weather patterns prior to their visit.

"Hazards" indicate things the hiker should be aware of before venturing onto the trail. Only the most pertinent hazards are listed; all hikers are advised to be prepared for a variety of unexpected situations.

Mileage and elevation figures are given in parentheses within each hike description. The mileage figures are not cumulative, but rather give the distance from one point to the next. Elevation figures give the elevation at a particu-

13

lar point. The difference between two consecutive elevations does not necessarily indicate the amount of elevation gain or loss between the two points, as many trails have their ups and downs between points. Elevation figures were arrived at with the aid of topographic maps and an altimeter, and should be accurate within 20 feet.

The "Driving to the Trailheads" sections also list mileage figures, but not elevations. The first figure in parentheses is the mileage from the previous point; the second figure is the cumulative total from a given starting point.

Although this book is not a climber's guide, some trips described herein may require that hikers have some rock-climbing ability.

Most trips described in this book follow trails or easy cross-country routes where the only skill required is walking—Class 1. Some cross-country routes may have sections or pitches that require scrambling or boulder-hopping—Class 2. Especially in narrow canyons, where dry waterfalls or large boulders block a route, a hiker must use relatively large hand and footholds to surmount the obstruction—Class 3. Occasion-

ally, these water-worn obstructions are smooth, sometimes with only minor handholds or small cracks. This type of climbing usually involves steep pitches and dangerous exposure—Class 4.

## Topographic Maps

The topographic maps in this book are parts of USGS quadrangles. The book's maps are on a scale of 1:50,000, which equals 1.25 inches per mile. These maps have been updated by the author, and they show the correct location of roads, trails, and park facilities.

The large numbers next to trails and jeep trails on the book's maps correspond to trip numbers described in the book. The small numbers are trailhead numbers, allowing hikers to quickly locate their trailhead.

The index map for each Utah national park shows the location and number of all the maps for that park.

**Butte and mesa**

# Geology of the Colorado Plateau

Geologists have subdivided the United States into physiographic provinces, each with its own distinct characteristics of landscape, mode of formation, and patterns of geology and geography. The Colorado Plateau physiographic province is one of the most unusual regions on the globe. This 130,000-square-mile region is a vast highland that lies above lower-elevation regions to the south and west, and abuts the higher country of the central and southern Rocky Mountains to the north and east.

Flat-lying rock beds, mostly of sedimentary origin, characterize the plateau. However, geological periods of folding, uplift, and erosion have given the plateau an irregular surface. Great blocks of the plateau have been uplifted along faults, forming the High Plateaus upon which Bryce Canyon and Zion are situated. Folds, anticlines, and synclines in the earth's crust are largely responsible for the incomparable scenery in Capitol Reef, Arches, and Canyonlands national parks. Two erosional forms typify the Colorado Plateau. Mesas (meaning table in Spanish) are remnant segments of the plateau isolated by erosion, generally flat on top, and bounded by steep cliffs. Buttes are smaller, cliff-edged prominences, with or without a flat top, that have been completely isolated and are detached from the main body of a mesa.

Sedimentary rocks are dominant in the national parks of Utah and the Colorado Plateau as a whole, with only a few scattered outcrops of igneous and metamorphic rocks. Most of the sedimentary strata in the region are flat-lying and rest in the same sequence in which they were laid down. Since the climate of the region is dry, little soil and vegetational cover have developed. Moreover, downcutting of the canyons has exposed to full view the full sequence of sedimentary rocks deposited on the Colorado Plateau. Like an open book, geologists are able to read this rock record, learning much about the climate and the environmental conditions that prevailed when the sediments were laid down. The presence of fossils here also increases our understanding of the development of life on the ever-changing earth.

More than 300 million years have elapsed since the rocks exposed in Utah's national parks were deposited. The region included, at various times in the past, sea floors, floodplains, river deltas, swamps, coastal marshes and lagoons, sea coasts, and vast arid deserts. Yet nowhere in the geologic record is there an indication that the region earlier contained the great canyon systems it does today. Around the periphery of the plateau great mountains were uplifted and then eroded away, and other areas of the land in the plateau's interior subsided into basins and low-lying areas that were periodically inundated by seas or freshwater lake systems.

Following regional uplift of the Colorado Plateau about 10-15 million years ago, erosion by the Colorado River and its tributaries stripped away much of the thousands of feet of lithified (consolidated) sediments, exhuming older strata that had been buried by younger sediments for millions of years. Today, weathering—whereby rocks are broken down into their constituent materials—and erosion—whereby these materials are carried away by wind and running water, are the principal earth-shaping processes affecting the land in the Colorado Plateau.

# Formation of Arches

There are two categories of arches in Utah's park lands: those with an opening below or behind the arch, and those without openings, such as the many large arches that are found high on massive sandstone walls in Zion National Park. Arches without openings are not considered in this discussion. Neither are natural bridges because, while arches are common in Utah's national parks, natural bridges are not. They are formed as a direct result of a meandering stream cutting laterally into a narrow fin of rock, eventually cutting a hole through it. Such features are best seen in appropriately named Natural Bridges Natural Monument, in southeast Utah. In contrast, arches that develop openings below or behind them do so in the absence of streams.

Arches with openings are relatively rare in the world. but are quite common on the Colorado Plateau, and they are found in all of Utah's national parks. There are two very common types of arches with openings in Utah's national parks: 1) arches in a thin, vertical wall—or fin—of sandstone; they have an opening entirely

below the arch; and 2) pothole arches, which have an opening behind the arch. Both types of arches owe their existence to chemical and physical weathering by water.

In the first type the process of arch formation begins when groundwater seeps down through a porous sandstone layer, and it encounters an impermeable layer, such as shale. The groundwater then seeps outward along this interface of layers, eventually reaching the face of a cliff. There it dissolves the natural cement that binds sand grains into stone, and then water, wind and gravity remove the sand grains.Thus a small indentation begins to form on the cliff face at the horizontal interface between the two layers. This indentation grows horizontally along the interface and also vertically as rock immediately above the indentation is undercut and destabilized, and breaks away. Over time, more rockfall on a small or a grand scale causes the arch to grow. The indentation becomes larger, forming in the cliff what is called an alcove. If the body of rock behind the cliff is narrow enough, like the fins in Arches and Canyonlands national parks, the alcove will continue to penetrate the rock until it reaches the other side, and an opening forms. If two alcoves form on opposite sides of a fin, the process occurs much more rapidly.

The second type of arch, a pothole arch, is the most common type in Capitol Reef and Canyonlands national parks. A pothole arch begins to form when a pothole close to a cliff face collects water. Although much of the water trapped in a pothole evaporates, some seeps down into the porous sandstone below. When this groundwater reaches an impermeable layer, it seeps outward along the interface to the cliff face, and an alcove eventually forms there, in the same way as described above. The alcove and the pothole above continue to enlarge, and they eventually coalesce, forming a nearly vertical opening called a pothole arch.

# The Rock Formations of Utah's National Parks

Utah's national parks are as diverse as they are beautiful. But what they all have in common are their colorful, magnificently sculpted rocks, which make these parks some of the finest scenic attractions in the world. The effects of erosion on more than two dozen different sedimentary rock formations have made the landscapes of the parks exciting and dramatic.

Following is a very brief description of the sedimentary rocks that compose the core of Utah's national parks.

Beginning about 345 million years ago, salts accumulated to a thickness of more than 5000 feet in a vast inland marine depression in eastern Utah known as the Paradox Basin. These salts are now the rocks of the *Paradox Formation*, and their presence beneath thousands of feet of younger rocks has created an unstable foundation and has had a profound effect in the shaping of the landscapes we see today in Arches and Canyonlands national parks.

Later, the marine sediments that compose the gray and red limestones, shales, and sandstones of the *Honaker Trail Formation* were deposited. These rocks are exposed only in Canyonlands, where they form the broken cliffs in the inner gorges of both the Green and Colorado rivers, from Cataract Canyon upriver for several miles above the rivers' confluence.

Around 300 million years ago, the limestones, shales, and sandstones of the *Elephant Canyon Formation* were deposited just offshore in a retreating sea near the present-day confluence of the Green and Colorado rivers in Canyonlands National Park. These rocks form the broken cliffs just below the canyon rims in the lower reaches of the Green and Colorado rivers.

The next stage of deposition was responsible for the red- and white-banded *Cedar Mesa Sandstone*, the principal scenery producer in the Maze and Needles districts of Canyonlands. The striking Cedar Mesa sandstone is composed of offshore sand-bar and coastal sand-dune deposits. However, the Cedar Mesa also contains red beds, composed of red, stream-deposited sands that interfinger with the white sandstones.

Overlying the Cedar Mesa in Canyonlands are thick deposits of reddish-brown siltstones and sandy shales of varying hardnesses collectively known as the *Organ Rock Shale*. These dark red rocks are contorted and irregular, much like the Entrada Sandstone's Dewey Bridge member in Arches National Park. The Organ Rock forms the monoliths of Land of Standing Rocks in the Maze District and the pillars of Monument Basin in the Island District.

Overlying the Organ Rock Shale is another rock formation that is widespread in Canyonlands but crops out only in the deepest canyons in Capitol Reef, the *White Rim Sandstone*. Despite the thinness of the White Rim, it is a distinct scenery producer in Canyonlands. These rocks form a prominent bench above the inner gorges of the Green and Colorado rivers beneath the Island in the Sky mesa. This sandstone also forms the western rim of The Maze, and resistant caprocks of the White Rim protect the softer beds of the Organ Rock Shale in places, such as on the Chocolate Drops and Nuts and Bolts in the Maze District and the spires of Monument Basin in the Island District.

Following deposition of the White Rim, a dolomitic stratum of marine origin was deposited in south-central Utah and northern Arizona, the *Kaibab Limestone*. This mostly white rock forms the broken cliffs in the Goosenecks of Sulphur Creek and in the Fremont River canyon in Capitol Reef National Park.

Deposition of the red *Moenkopi Formation* beds occurred about 225 million years ago. These rocks are exposed in all Utah national parks except Bryce Canyon. The Moenkopi is composed of deep red, thinly layered sandy shale and silty sandstone, forming slopes, low cliffs, fluted columns, and ledges. Tracks of small reptiles and amphibians are found in the Moenkopi, but most abundant are ripple marks, formed after shallow, wind-rippled water created a corrugated surface on the sediments just below the water surface.

Around 200 million years ago the wide variety of sediments that compose the *Chinle Formation* were deposited. Dinosaur tracks, fossil freshwater fish, fossil plants and leaves, and petrified wood from a coniferous genus found in the Chinle show the evolution of life on the planet.

Like the Moenkopi, Chinle rocks are found in all Utah national parks except Bryce Canyon, where younger rocks predominate. The Chinle consists of sandstones, conglomerates, bentonitic mudstones, limestones, and siltstones. It is a varicolored unit, ranging from red and purple to yellow, green and gray. The gray layer is composed primarily of volcanic ash.

The *Shinarump Conglomerate*, the lowermost layer of the Chinle, forms a prominent white or tan cliff band that discontinuously caps the Moenkopi in Zion and Capitol Reef. This rock consists of lithified coarse sand and stream-polished pebbles. In Canyonlands, however, the Shinarump is absent. Instead, its place in the stratigraphic sequence is taken by the *Mossback member* of the Chinle. The Mossback is similar in composition to the Shinarump, but its dark gray-green color sets it apart.

Around 200 million years ago, vast deserts of drifting sand dominated the Colorado Plateau landscape. One of these windblown sand deposits is the *Wingate Sandstone*, and whenever it is exposed in Capitol Reef, Arches, or Canyonlands, it forms cliffs that have been major barriers to travel. The Wingate most often forms sheer, but sometimes broken and fluted, cliffs as high as 400 feet. These rocks are typically orange-red in color, but are often stained with patches and streaks of *desert varnish*—a dark brown, black, or bluish coating of iron and manganese oxides formed as mineral-laden water evaporates on the rock's surface.

The vast Wingate desert did not extend as far southwest as Zion National Park. Instead, its corollary in Zion is the thin but prominent Moenave Formation, composed of red siltstones and yellow sandstones of floodplain origin.

The thin beds of the *Kayenta Formation* that overlie the Wingate and Moenave range in color from nearly white to reddish-brown, and usually form ledges, low cliffs, and slopes. In Zion, the Kayenta is soft, and consequently it erodes into slopes rather than the ledgy cliffs it forms in Arches, Capitol Reef, and Canyonlands.

The resistant *Navajo Sandstone* was also deposited around 200 million years ago, when once again the region was buried under drifting sands. Perhaps no other rock formation on the Colorado Plateau is as famous as the Navajo. These rocks erode into gigantic cliffs both sheer and rounded, and great domes, for which Capitol Reef was named. The Navajo also composes the great cliffs of Zion Canyon, the Petrified Dunes of Arches, and the domes that cap the Island in the Sky mesa in Canyonlands. The Navajo achieves its greatest thickness, approximately 2200 feet, in Zion.

Cross-bedding, the sweeping diagonal lines most obvious in the hummocky structures of the Navajo, reflects the advance of the ancient dunes across the landscape as northerly winds swept the region.

Overlying the Navajo in Zion is a thin, discontinuous layer of shale and sandstone, the *Temple Cap Formation*. Most of this reddish-brown layer has been removed from the Markagunt Plateau by erosion.

Less than 200 million years ago, the limestones, shales, sandstones, and gypsum of the *Carmel Formation* were deposited. The soft rocks of the Carmel cap much of the Markagunt Plateau in Zion, and outcrop on the eastern flanks of the Waterpocket Fold in Capitol Reef.

The *Entrada Sandstone* is the most widespread rock unit in Arches, and its rocks form most of the scenic highlights of the Park. This formation has been divided into three subunits, each with its own special characteristics. The *Dewey Bridge member* is the lowermost and softest layer of the Entrada, and erosion attacks it vigorously. Dark red in color, the beds of this silty sandstone are often contorted and irregular. Its relatively soft nature allows it to erode more readily than the overlying *Slick Rock member*. The result has been the formation of many fascinating hoodoos, such as those found along The Great Wall, and these rocks form the pedestals for many balanced rocks in Arches.

The Slick Rock member of the Entrada Sandstone is the dominant rock in Arches, and its presence is responsible for the unusual scenic beauty of the Park. This rock is orange or salmon-hued, occasionally nearly white. The Slick Rock member forms rounded to vertical cliffs, domes, and fins—the narrow sandstone walls that dominate the scene in Devils Garden

**Bulging Navajo Sandstone walls embrace the narrow wash of lower Courthouse Wash**

and Fiery Furnace in Arches. This is the rock that Arches visitors encounter more than any other, for the arches they have come to see are formed almost exclusively in it.

The uppermost member of the Entrada, the *Moab Tongue*, could easily be mistaken for the Navajo Sandstone, since it has many of the same characteristics and is similar in color. The Moab Tongue is a white, fairly thin bed of wind-deposited dune sand, and this rock displays the cross-bedding common in wind-blown sand deposits.

Anyone familiar with the Entrada in Arches will hardly recognize that formation in Capitol Reef. Here much of the soft red beds of the Entrada has been eroded away, and only a few low domes crop out in and near the valleys east of the Waterpocket Fold. In Capitol Reef, the Entrada is a soft, thinly bedded formation composed of sandstones and siltstones.

The *Curtis Formation* lies above the Entrada only in Capitol Reef's North District. This gray, limey marine sandstone is prominent on the rim of The Hartnet, and it forms a protective caprock on the monoliths of Cathedral Valley and South Desert.

Another formation unique to Capitol Reef is the *Summerville*, composed of thinly bedded red mudstones and siltstones. Three members of the *Morrison Formation* are found in Arches, and two of these also occur in Capitol Reef. Sand, mud, silt, and volcanic ash make up the various

**Tower Arch is formed entirely within the Entrada's Slick Rock Member**

layers of the Morrison.

The red silty shales of the *Tidwell member* of the Morrison outcrop in a few locations only in Arches National Park. This is a relatively thin layer, and it is most easily identified where the abundant white concreations, composed of silica, have weathered from the formation and now litter surrounding slopes.

The *Salt Wash Sandstone*, though not noted for forming spectacular scenery, nevertheless adds its own distinct character to the landscape wherever it occurs in Capitol Reef and Arches. Light yellow sandstones and conglomerates compose this member of the Morrison, along with some mudstones, siltstones, and limestones. Most of the fossil dinosaur bones found on the Colorado Plateau are located in the Salt Wash Sandstone. A great deal of organic debris is also present. This fossil plant debris is a major source of uranium ore, and the Salt Wash Sandstone contains the world's most significant reserves of this ore. The areas east and south of

Arches were focal points for uranium mining during the uranium boom of the 1950s.

The *Brushy Basin Shale* is famous for its badlands and colorful "painted desert" scenery. One of the most striking rock formations on the Colorado Plateau, it is composed of clay and mud deposits. The formation is nutrient-poor, and the clays on its surface swell rapidly when wet and shrink upon drying. The surface absorbs little moisture and is usually devoid of vegetation.

Similar to the Brushy Basin Shale, the *Cedar Mountain Formation*, exposed only in Arches, consists primarily of soft mudstones that form slopes and beds of conglomerates that form ledges. The mudstones are colorful—mostly light green, gray, and lavender—and in Arches these rocks are difficult to distinguish from the underlying Brushy Basin Shale.

About 135 million years ago were deposited the sediments that compose the thin layer of the *Dakota Formation*—one of the most widespread sedimentary formations in the western U.S. Attesting to its marine origin are the vast amounts of fossil shells in the Dakota's upper layer. One of the best places to see these fossil shells is in the Oyster Shell Reef in Capitol Reef's South District. The Dakota is most common in Capitol Reef, but there are also a few minor outcrops in Arches and atop Zion's highest summit, Horse Ranch Mountain.

**Entrada pillars capped by Curtis sandstone below Lower South Desert outlook**

Sediments forming sandstone and shale were subsequently deposited atop the Dakota, and they are collectively called the *Mancos Formation*. These rocks are among the youngest and the most widespread rocks on the Colorado Plateau. The great buttes and mesas east of Capitol Reef near Hanksville are composed of both shales and sandstones of the Mancos. Shales of the Mancos also dominate the floor of lower Salt Valley and Cache Valley near Wolfe Ranch in Arches. Tropic Shale, a local name for the Mancos, forms the nearly barren hills and slopes surrounding the Paria Valley east of Bryce.

Around 100 million years ago, the *Straight Cliffs* and *Wahweap* formations were deposited in a layer 1000-2000 feet thick. Since the Straight Cliffs sandstone when eroded typically forms a cliff, and since it is interlayered with the less resistant Wahweap, these formations resemble a series of giant stairs on the eastern escarpment of the Paunsaugunt Plateau in Bryce.

The final episode of the Mesozoic era, around 65 million years ago, was the deposition of the *Kaiparowits Formation*. Clays, sands, and gravels that were ultimately cemented into stone form this discontinuous layer, which outcrops just below the Pink Cliffs in Bryce.

About 60 million years ago, lakebed deposits composed of sand, gravel, silt, and limey clay made up the varied layers of the *Wasatch Formation*—the rugged Pink Cliffs for which Bryce is so famous. The varied layers of this formation contain beds both hard and soft. Each bed erodes at a different rate, and this differential erosion has resulted in a fantastic array of pinnacles, towers, and finlike ridges collectively called *hoodoos*. Altogether, the hoodoos and badlands of Bryce's Pink Cliffs are referred to as *breaks*.

Volcanic activity that began about 37 million years ago enveloped much of southwest Utah in a blanket of lava, mostly basalt. The subsequent uplift of Utah's High Plateaus and erosion have since made the volcanic layer discontinuous in this part of the Colorado Plateau. However, these rocks outcrop close to Bryce, forming the steep southern face of the Black Mountains north of the Park, which are visible from most overlooks there. Volcanic rocks also cap the plateaus of Boulder and Thousand Lake mountains to the southwest and northwest of Capitol Reef. Stream-rounded boulders of basalt litter much of that Park, transported there by runoff from melting glaciers on the aforementioned mountains.

Following that volcanic activity, a now-discontinuous sedimentary layer was deposited atop the Wasatch beds, which escaped entombment in the lava. The *Brian Head Conglomerate* is most obvious where it forms the caprock of Boat Mesa, a high prominence rising above the Paunsaugunt Plateau between Fairyland and Sunrise points in Bryce. This formation contains stream-polished pebbles, many of which are volcanic in origin.

Volcanic rocks of more recent origin are exposed in parts of Zion and Capitol Reef. In the North District of Capitol Reef, particularly in the Middle Desert-Cathedral Valley area, there are many curious volcanic intrusions that were emplaced within the sedimentary layers about 4 million years ago. A *dike* is where molten magma is injected into a more or less vertical crustal fracture such as a joint or a fault. Erosion of the softer sedimentary rocks that surround a dike leaves it standing as a thin wall of rock. A *sill* is formed where molten magma is injected into a zone of weakness parallel to the bedding planes of the sedimentary strata.

Volcanic rocks also occur sporadically throughout the southwest and central parts of Zion National Park. These young (Pleistocene and Holocene) basaltic lava flows issued from vents and cinder cones, flooding canyons and forming terraces atop the Lower Kolob Plateau.

Since that time, erosion has been the dominant force in shaping the landscapes of Utah's national parks: deposition, such as the accumulation of alluvium or of drifting sand, has played only a minor role.

| GEOLOGIC TIME SCALE | | | | | |
|---|---|---|---|---|---|
| **Era** | **Period** | **Epoch** | **Began (years)** | **Duration (years)** | **Rock Formation** |
| | Quaternary | Holocene | 10,000 | 10,000 | Products of weathering and erosion |
| | | Pleistocene | 1,800,000 | 1,800,000 | Zion volcanics |
| **Cenozoic** | Tertiary | Pliocene | 5,200,000 | 3,400,000 | Capitol Reef volcanics |
| | | Miocene | 21,700,000 | 16,500,000 | Brian Head |
| | | Oligocene | 35,000,000 | 13,300,000 | High Plateaus volcanics |
| | | Eocene | 49,000,000 | 14,000,000 | |
| | | Paleocene | 64,000,000 | 15,000,000 | Wasatch |
| **Mesozoic** | Cretaceous | | 135,000,000 | 71,000,000 | Kaiparowits<br>Wahweap<br>Straight Cliffs<br>Mancos and Tropic Shale<br>Dakota |
| | Jurassic | | 195,000,000 | 60,000,000 | Cedar Mountain<br>Morrison<br>Summerville<br>Curtis<br>Entrada<br>Carmel<br>Temple Cap (only in Zion)<br>Navajo |
| | Triassic | | 225,000,000 | 30,000,000 | Kayenta<br>Wingate (Moenave in Zion)<br>Chinle<br>Moenkopi |
| **Paleozoic** | Permian | | 280,000,000 | 55,000,000 | Kaibab<br>White Rim<br>Organ Rock<br>Cedar Mesa<br>Elephant Canyon |
| | Pennsylvanian | | 345,000,000 | 65,000,000 | Honaker Trail<br>Paradox |
| Older rock formations not exposed in national parks | | | | | |

# Desert Flora

The national parks of Utah, despite their arid to semiarid climates, high temperatures in summer and bitter cold in winter, lack of dependable precipitation, and poorly developed soil cover, are home to hundreds of species of plants.

Animal forms, though diverse in numbers and species, are infrequently seen due to their mobility and their mostly nocturnal habits. On the other hand, each plant occupies its own niche in the desert, growing only in a habitat that meets its specific environmental requirements.

It is beyond the scope of this guide to catalog all or even many of the hundreds of plant species visitors are likely to encounter in Utah's national parks, but the trail descriptions do identify certain plants at various locations. Anyone interested in learning more about desert flora can obtain one or more of the books listed in the bibliography of this book.

Plants of riparian woodlands and hanging gardens (assemblages of water-loving plants found on canyon walls) are hardy enough to withstand extreme heat, but they could be called drought-escaping plants, since they grow only where a continuous supply of moisture is available, either on the surface or underground.

Most other desert plants have developed various methods for coping with extremes of heat and drought. *Phreatophytes* are plants that have deep, extensive root systems that enable them to tap underground sources of moisture. Once their roots reach the water table, their growth is not dependent on rainfall.

Most desert plants, however, are *xerophytes.* Xerophytes include succulent plants, which have fleshy leaves or stems that enable them to store water for extended periods. Succulent xerophytes include cacti, which have shallow and often widespreading root systems that can take up soil moisture from even the lightest rainfall. Cacti are leafless; their succulent pads are actually stems. These stems swell with stored moisture in spring, and they slowly and economically metabolize that moisture throughout the dry part of the year. When much of the moisture has been used, the stems shrink and become wrinkled, but unlike nonsucculent xerophytes, cacti do not go dormant when stressed by drought.

Nonsucculent xerophytes survive long periods of drought by various means other than water storage. The deep root systems and special cellular structures of some of these plants are able to obtain moisture from the soil long after the rains have fallen. Other characteristics of non-succulent xerophytes that help to prevent moisture loss and excessive heating of plant tissues include:

- vertical orientation of leaves, which reduces the surface area exposed directly to sunlight
- dense matted hairs on leaves and/or stems or a resinous coating
- a grayish pigment on leaves and stems
- very small pores on the leaves
- wide spacing of plants

Some plants conserve energy and moisture by curling their leaves or even dropping them. If there is not enough moisture to support the plant, then all but perhaps a single branch will die back, or the entire above-ground plant may die, all of its energies being diverted to preserving the life-sustaining root system. Many xerophytes have rigid, woody, spiny branches, which, when combined with hairy or resinous foliage, discourage browsing animals from eating them.

In most mountainous regions in the Western U.S., plants are fairly evenly separated into belts, or zones, that vary with elevation, temperature and precipitation. However, the plant communities of the Colorado Plateau are not uniform in their patterns, and likewise the land itself is highly varied, containing deep and sometimes moist canyons, parched mesas and desert flats, vast expanses of naked stone, and sheer cliffs devoid of vegetation and soil.

For example, the pinyon-juniper woodland is one of the most common plant communities visitors will encounter, but this woodland does not grow at any typical elevation; rather, it grows where local environmental conditions are suitable to support it. In Zion National Park, for example, one will find this woodland growing at 4000 feet, while near Canyonlands it is found above 7000. Where a canyon has been eroded into the plateau, one may also find a pinyon-juniper woodland, while above the canyon only a scattering of shrubs may exist.

**Buffaloberry**

# Zion National Park

## Introduction

In the far southwestern corner of Utah, very near where the Colorado Plateau meets the mountains and valleys of the Great Basin, lies Zion National Park, one of the gems of the national-park system.

Within its 147,000 acres are landscapes of incredible beauty and infinite diversity. Sculptured cliffs towering thousands of feet above deeply incised canyons display a kaleidoscope of pastel hues, their color and brilliance changing before a viewer's eyes with the changing light of the day.

As the seasons change, so does the face of Zion. Spring brings the melting of snow atop the plateaus. Where runoff waters reach the brink of the great cliffs, hundreds of waterfalls are born. Bright green leaves adorn the trees and shrubs, and wildflowers explode in incomparable color. Streambeds run bank-full until the searing heat and dryness of approaching summer sap their vigor.

With the onset of autumn, broadleaf trees paint the landscape with brilliant reds and golds that vie with the colorful cliffs for the viewers' attention. The grip of winter blankets the land with its envelope of white, and decorates springs and seeps with icicle curtains.

Not only do the landscapes of Zion change with the passing seasons, but the land itself is in a state of constant change. Most of this change is imperceptible in a human lifetime, but at times the change is dramatic and obvious, as in rockfalls and landslides.

Zion National Park encompasses that part of the vast Markagunt Plateau that forms the Virgin River watershed, southwest Utah's largest tributary to the Colorado River. The Hurricane Cliffs bound the plateau on the west, forming the boundary between two major physiographic provinces: the Basin and Range Province to the west, and the Colorado Plateau stretching eastward to the Rocky Mountains.

The Markagunt is one of the most extensive of Utah's high plateaus, roughly 70 by 30 miles. The southern half of its surface is incised by tributaries of the Virgin River. These tributary canyons, combined with the nature of the sedimentary rock layers through which they have eroded, are responsible for the magnificent scenery that visitors from all corners of the globe come to enjoy.

The North Fork of the Virgin has created a deep and narrow canyon of incomparable beauty. At its widest point, one-third mile separates the canyon walls, and at its narrowest, only 20 feet or so. Imposing buttes and towering crags crown the canyon's cliffs, and from below they appear to be majestic mountain peaks. From the heights of the gently contoured plateau, however, viewers gain a different perspective of them. Up there, one quickly notices that the tops of these buttes and towering crags were at one time parts of the continuous level landscape of the plateau. They are simply now isolated from it by erosion.

Geologists have subdivided the Colorado Plateau physiographic province into a number of distinct units. Parts of Zion and Bryce lie within the Grand Staircase section, near the southern margin of the High Plateaus. True to its name, the Grand Staircase rises in a series of varicolored cliffs and broad plateaus from the north rim of the Grand Canyon to the Pink Cliffs high on the flanks of the Markagunt, Paunsaugunt and Aquarius plateaus. Each "step" contains vast wooded plateaus, and each "riser" exposes varicolored cliffs.

The belt of cliffs forming the "riser" in Zion is the White Cliffs, composed of the Park's dominant sedimentary rock layer, the Navajo Sandstone. The Vermilion Cliffs, composed of the Moenave Formation, outcrop along the flanks of lower Zion Canyon. The youngest rise in this series of steps is the one at the edge of the highest of the southern High Plateaus—the Pink Cliffs of Cedar Breaks and Bryce Canyon.

# Human History of Zion

Mankind has been in the Zion landscape from time immemorial. We know that the Anasazi dwelled here, attested to by their cliff houses in Parunuweap ("water that roars") Canyon, their rock art, the abundance of chipping sites throughout the Park, and caves that bear reminders of ancient fires. Archaeologists also believe that people of the Fremont culture may have lived in the northern reaches of the Park.

Prehistoric people lived here from about 500 until their mysterious departure around 1200. During that time they evolved from hunter-gatherers into farmers of corn, squash, and beans. Following their departure, the land we know as Zion remained largely unoccupied until the arrival of Mormon settlers during the mid-19th century. However, during that time scattered bands of Piutes inhabited the upper Virgin River Valley, camping in areas that were later the sites of Mormon settlements, some of which remain as towns today. The Piutes utilized the Zion region for seasonal hunting and gathering forays, and some bands farmed in the valleys outside the Park. They did not, however, venture very far into the canyons.

It was the Piutes that early travelers and explorers encountered in southwest Utah. They contributed their geographical knowledge of the region, but were of little aid when Mormons later explored the forbidden (according to Piute superstition) depths of Zion Canyon. In 1850 a party of Mormons conducted explorations in the region to survey the possibility of establishing settlements on the Mormon frontier. The party returned with glowing reports of a mild climate and exceptional farmland, and Mormons were soon called upon by their leaders to settle the region.

During the early 1860s, a few Virgin River valley settlers began looking toward Zion Canyon in search of farmland. When Joseph Black visited the canyon during those years, he was impressed not only by the stark magnificence of the landscape, but also by the possibility of its cultivation.

As time passed, more settlers began to look toward Zion Canyon, not only for home sites but for its resources as well. Isaac Behunin is credited with bestowing the name "Zion" upon the canyon. Having endured Mormon persecution from the time the Mormons were driven from New York to their arrival in the proposed State of Deseret (Utah), he recognized the canyon as a final, safe refuge from harassment and persecution—hence the name Zion, "peaceful resting place."

Following the exploration of Zion and

Parunuweap canyons by Major John Wesley Powell in 1872, the virtually unknown region was finally put on the map, and that sparked interest in its unusual and spectacular landscape. But travel was difficult in those days, and only a handful of hardy travelers made the trek to Zion.

During the early years of Mormon settlement along the Virgin River, homes were built of stone supplemented by wood hauled in from northern Arizona. Extensive forests of ponderosa pine were near at hand atop the cliffs of Zion, but were virtually inaccessible. Brigham Young, the Mormon prophet, visited the Virgin River settlements in 1863 and proclaimed that one day a means would be discovered to transport timber from the plateaus to the valley below "like a hawk flies."

After a youthful foray onto the plateau from Zion Canyon near Springdale, young David Flanigan and his three companions explored the forests of the plateau. With the knowledge of Young's prophecy, Flanigan was to set in motion a series of events that would ultimately fulfill Young's declaration and provide much-needed lumber to the Mormon settlements.

Bales of wire were carried to the rim, and David Flanigan, with the help of his brother, began the long trial-and-error process of laying the wire for a lumber cable, attaching it to pulley structures at both the top and the bottom of the cliff. A year later they began sending loads via the cable. The cable fell into disuse for lumber hauling between 1901 and 1904, but soon thereafter, Flanigan purchased a sawmill and moved it to the East Rim Plateau, probably near Stave Spring. During the following two years, 200,000 board feet of lumber were sawed on the plateau and transported over the cable to the canyon bottom. This lumber helped build structures along the Virgin River from Springdale to St. George, including the original Zion Lodge and its cabins. The cable was finally removed in 1930, and with the completion of the Zion-Mount Carmel Tunnel that same year, the cable works became obsolete.

After the turn of the century, Zion gained increased attention, and the idea spread of preserving it for future generations as a showcase of exceptional scenic and scientific value. First, Mukuntuweap National Monument was estab-

**The Draw Works atop Cable Mountain**

lished on June 25, 1909. Soon after the establishment of the National Park Service in 1917, an automobile road, improving upon the old wagon road, was constructed as far as The Grotto. Finally in 1919, a bill was signed by President Wilson that changed the unpopular name of Mukuntuweap National Monument to Zion National Park and enlarged the area to 120 square miles. In 1937 the Kolob Section was established as Zion National Monument, and in 1956 it was added to the Park.

The road to Temple of Sinawava was completed in 1925, as were a number of foot trails. One problem remained—that of linking Zion by road with other scenic wonders in southern Utah and northern Arizona, including Bryce Canyon and Grand Canyon. The 1.1-mile long Zion-Mount Carmel Tunnel, truly a great engineering feat, was completed in 1930, cut just inside the Navajo Sandstone cliff face. Five galleries in it allowed early travelers to stop and enjoy rock-framed vistas of incomparable beauty, but today, stopping inside the tunnel is not allowed, for safety reasons.

## Plants and Animals of Zion

Zion is home to 670 species of flowering plants and ferns, 95 species of mammals, 30 species of reptiles, and 125 species of birds. This vast array of life in Zion helps dispel the myth that a desert is barren and lifeless. True, the region is semiarid, annual precipitation ranging from slightly more than 15 inches in the canyon to an estimated 21 inches atop the plateaus. But despite searing summer heat, Zion more than any other Utah national park has a relative abundance of water. More than a dozen canyons boast perennial streams, many nurtured by springs that issue from the Navajo Sandstone, a thick and porous layer that is a virtual stone reservoir. Not only do these streams provide delightful haunts for hikers, but their presence promotes the diversity of plant and animal life.

Elevations in the Park range from 3666 feet to 8740 feet, so a wide range of vegetation is represented. A *life zone* contains the plant communities that are typically found within its range of elevation and precipitation. For example, the Transition Life Zone in Zion contains the ponderosa-pine and mountain-brush plant communities, and occasionally members of the fir and aspen communities as well. Life zones often overlap altitudinally because particular combinations of soil cover, and exposure to sunlight, create microclimates here and there. Within the altitudinal range of the Park, plant communities range from sparse desert shrubs to cool forests of pine, fir and aspen. Blackbrush, yucca, and various species of cacti, mostly prickly-pear and beavertail cactus, dominate the shrublands in the Lower Sonoran Zone.

The Upper Sonoran Zone is widespread on drier sites, mostly in the lower-to-mid-elevations of the Park. Single-leaf pinyon and Utah juniper distinguish the pinyon-juniper woodland, and are the dominant tree species in this zone, well adapted to heat and drought. Two-needle pinyon and juniper dominate on mid-elevation slopes, and typical shrubs in this zone include buffaloberry, Utah serviceberry, squaw-bush, broom snakeweed, rabbitbrush, and shrub live oak. Little-leaf mountain mahogany, very similar in appearance to black-brush, grows almost exclusively on slickrock in the upper limits of the zone. Gambel oak often mixes into the pinyon-juniper woodland, and it forms oak woodlands in wetter, protected sites in the canyons as well as extensive thickets atop the plateaus in the Transition Zone.

The Transition Zone is dominated by stands of ponderosa pine, frequently mixing with Gambel oak on the plateaus. Dominant shrubs here are greenleaf manzanita, alderleaf mountain mahogany, snowberry, and big sagebrush. Bigtooth maple is common in some areas, its foliage turning red or orange after the first autumn frosts. On well-drained sites, Rocky Mountain juniper is found mixing into the pine forests. Poorly drained sites on the plateaus contain mountain meadows, and even wetter sites have forests of quaking aspen.

The Canadian Zone is limited to well-watered slopes in the Park's higher elevations, particularly near Lava Point and the buttes rising above the Kolob canyons. Ponderosa pine is present, but in lesser numbers than in the Transition Zone. The dominant tree here is white fir, while Douglas-fir occurs in the coolest, most protected sites. These trees are also found on sheltered sites far below on canyon walls where cooler microclimates prevail.

In most of the Park's life zones, riparian vegetation occurs along streams, including the North Fork Virgin River, and in isolated patches along washes where water lies close to the surface. Fremont cottonwood is the dominant tree, and adding diversity to the riparian woodland are velvet ash, boxelder and netleaf hackberry.

Hanging gardens, found growing on moist cliffs throughout Zion, are unusual sylvan oases in desert areas. Due to abundant seeps and springs, they are more widespread in Zion than in any other Utah national park. (For more about hanging gardens, see the "Plants and Animals" chapters for Capitol Reef, Arches, and Canyonlands.)

By late March or early April, an abundance of wildflowers bursts onto the scene, their colorful blossoms vying for the visitors' attention with the colorful canyon walls. As spring changes to summer, more flowers bloom, but their colors are short-lived. Many early summer flowers fade as heat and dryness begin to dominate, and night-blooming flowers then begin to blossom.

Summer thunderstorms initiate Zion's second most prolific blooming season. Even some spring flowers bloom again if summer rains are abundant. Yellow flowers seem to dominate the scene in late summer and fall.

A vast array of birds is found in Zion, representing 271 species, of which 125 remain year-round. Rufous-sided towhees, blue-gray gnatcatchers, and blackheaded grosbeaks are common denizens of forest habitats, while water ouzels, Say's phoebes, great blue herons, and Calliope hummingbirds prefer an aquatic habitat. Roadrunners scurry across open desert, and golden eagles and red-tailed hawks soar on invisible air currents in search of prey. In the fall pinyon and scrub jays congregate in pinyon woodlands, feasting on pinyon nuts.

Reptiles are by far the most frequently encountered animals on Zion's trails. These cold-blooded creatures are especially well-adapted to living in a semiarid environment. Of the 30 species of reptiles occurring in Zion, hikers will most commonly see the eastern fence lizard, likely doing "pushups" on a trailside boulder. Short-horned lizards and western skinks are also common.

Gopher snakes and whipsnakes are common in the drier areas, while the western garter snake prefers to stay close to water. The western rattlesnake is Zion's only poisonous reptile, occurring in canyons and on dry slopes. They are rarely seen, however, and if given half a chance will usually slither away and hide.

Amphibians, of which only seven species occur in Zion, are infrequently seen, since they stay close to water sources and damp areas. Snails are an important part of Zion's aquatic community. Most noteworthy is the Zion snail, a tiny invertebrate about the size of a pinhead. Endemic to Zion, this snail is found only along seeps and springs on the canyon walls of the Zion Narrows.

Fish inhabit many of Zion's streams, including cutthroat trout and bluehead suckers. Fishing is poor, however, in the silt-laden Virgin River.

Common Zion rodents are the desert cottontail, the pocket gopher, and the cliff chipmunk. The latter is particularly noticeable begging handouts from hikers in places such as Observation Point.

One of the most common large mammals in Zion is the mule deer. They range from Zion Canyon to the plateaus. Rarely seen is their chief predator, the mountain lion. Occasionally, a Rocky Mountain elk wanders into the Park from the higher plateau to the north.

Striped and spotted skunks, gray foxes, ringtails, mountain voles, and insect-eating bats also live in Zion, although most of them are seldom seen.

Finally, many hikers are well acquainted with the most abundant of life forms in the Park, insects. Mosquitoes, no-see-ums, and biting flies are real nuisances in spring and early summer and in some locations these annoying creatures persist well into autumn.

## Interpretive Activities

Everyone's first stop in Zion should be at the Visitor Center. Books, maps, backcountry permits for overnight hiking, weather reports, a museum, and schedules of interpretive programs are available there. Park rangers on duty are veritable encyclopedias of information. Zion's Visitor Center is the largest and most complete such facility in all of Utah's national parks, and your experience in the Park will be greatly enriched by a stop.

During the peak tourist season, roughly from late March through early November, Visitor Center hours are 8 A.M.-9 P.M.. Winter hours are 8 A.M.-5 P.M. Evening programs at South Campground's Amphitheater and naturalist programs at the Visitor Center are conducted from spring through fall. Children's programs are conducted twice daily at the Nature Center, near the campground amphitheater, from Memorial Day through Labor Day. Parents can leave their children here and enjoy a short hike in the canyon.

Ranger-guided hikes include the Gateway to the Narrows Trail; up the Narrows to Orderville Canyon; Angels Landing; the Emerald Pools Trail to Middle Pool; the Watchman Trail; the Canyon Overlook Trail; and naturalists-choice hikes.

Springdale, Utah, located at the mouth of Zion Canyon just south of the Park's south entrance, offers a full line of services for Park visitors. Hikers, however, are advised to come prepared, since there is little hiking equipment or backpack food available in town. Springdale has several motels, restaurants, gas stations, and grocery stores. The communities of St. George, Hurricane, Kanab, and Cedar City also have a wide array of services and accommodations. Hospitals are located in St. George, Kanab, and Cedar City.

## Campgrounds

The private Zion Canyon Campground, a short distance south of the South Entrance, offers a spacious, shady campground with tent sites and full hookups for RVs. Hot showers, a laundry, and a market are also available.

Zion has two large campgrounds, one of which remains open through the winter. Watchman and South campgrounds are located between the South Entrance and the Visitor Center. Overnight camping fees are collected at the self-registration station at each campground.

Watchman Campground is Zion's largest, with 246 campsites on a bench above North Fork Virgin River at 3900 feet. Young boxelders, velvet ash, netleaf hackberry, and Fremont cottonwoods shade campers, but are still small enough to allow fine views of the canyon walls, including the fluted cliffs of The Watchman and Bridge Mountain. South Campground, at 3950 feet, is considerably smaller, with 141 campsites. Large netleaf hackberry and Fremont cottonwood provide ample shade for campers at this pleasant riverside campground. These two campgrounds often fill by early- to mid-afternoon during the spring-through-fall peak season, so come early if you plan to camp here.

Lava Point Campground is a stark contrast to the desert-like campgrounds in Zion Canyon. It rests atop the lava-capped mesa of Lava Point at 7900 feet. This is a primitive campground, and since no water is provided, no fee is charged. Its six campsites are shaded by white fir, ponderosa pine, aspen, and Gambel oak. Views from the campsites are limited to the peaceful forest that surrounds it.

Wood gathering in the Park is prohibited, so if you want to build a fire in the grills provided at each campground, bring your own.

Zion has two developed picnic sites. The Grotto Picnic Area is on the shady canyon floor between Red Arch Mountain and The Spearhead. A large parking area serves the spacious picnic area, elevation 4290 feet. The Kolob Canyons Viewpoint (elevation 6300 feet) at the roadend in the Kolob section of Zion also boasts a small but delightful picnic area. Nestled against a hillside in a woodland of pinyon and juniper, this site offers some of the most dramatic views in all of the Park.

Visitors are free to picnic wherever they wish in the Park, but everyone should be sure to pack out all their trash, including orange and banana peels—these biodegradable items will not decompose in the arid desert climate.

Zion Lodge offers a variety of services and accommodations. A motel, motel suites, and western cabins are available for an overnight stay, but guests are advised to make reservations four to six months in advance. The lodge is usually open from about May 15 through about October 3. A restaurant and a gift shop are here. Guided tram tours are available, and arrangements for horseback rides along the Sand Bench Trail and information on the shuttle service for hikers are also available at Zion Lodge.

For further information:

*Park information:*

Park Superintendent
Zion National Park
Springdale, UT 84767
(801) 772-3256

*Information regarding the private Zion Canyon Campground:*

Zion Canyon Campground
P.O. Box 99
Springdale, UT 84767
(801) 772-3237

*Information regarding Zion Lodge*:

TW Services, Inc.
451 North Main
Cedar City, UT 84720
(801) 586-7686 (individuals) or
(801) 586-7624 (groups)

# Hiking in Zion

The trail network of Zion National Park provides a wide array of hiking opportunities to satisfy anyone wishing to park the car and experience this magnificent landscape at a leisurely pace. Ranging from paved 5-minute strolls to backpack trips of several days, Zion's more than 100 miles of trails sample virtually every aspect of the Park. Boasting more than 5000 feet of vertical relief, scenery along Zion's trails includes vast plateaus clad in pine, fir, and aspen; deep and narrow canyons that lie in eternal shadow; sun-baked expanses of open desert;

lofty vista points; pinyon-juniper woodlands; and the green spreads of lava-rimmed meadows.

However, one feature of Zion that makes the Park stand out above all other national parks in Utah is the availability of water. Few trails lack water somewhere along their courses. The length of a backpack trip in some of the drier parks, such as Canyonlands and Capitol Reef, is limited by the amount of water one is able to carry. But hikers in Zion have greater flexibility in planning the length of their stay in the backcountry.

As in all of Utah's national parks, rangers strongly advise that hikers purify all the water they obtain from backcountry sources, as signs at all major springs attest. Some streams, including La Verkin Creek and North Fork Virgin River and their tributaries, are fouled by the wastes of sheep and cattle that graze in their headwaters. So don't take the chance of contracting a miserable intestinal infection; always purify any open water you obtain in the backcountry.

Not only is there a wide variety of scenery awaiting hikers, but the trails themselves vary greatly. Some are faint paths seldom trod by Park visitors, while others are paved and frequently used. Some of Zion's shorter paved trails offer access to wheelchairs and even baby strollers. There are cliff-hanging trails that are intermittently paved where they were blasted into steep cliffs of Navajo Sandstone, providing surefooting on what otherwise would be a sandy, slippery, dangerous trail.

Although 6000-7000 backpackers enjoy Zion's backcountry each year, they represent only a small fraction of the two million visitors who annually vacation in the Park. Hikers can still enjoy solitude amid breath-taking majesty of this beautiful and unique park by following lesser-used trails or hiking in the off-season. Solitude seekers will want to avoid holiday weekends, spring vacation, and the peak tourist season in May and June. The trails of Zion Canyon then receive the heaviest use, though primarily by dayhikers.

As snows fall, melt, and refreeze on winter nights, many of Zion's cliff-hanging trails become treacherous. Winter hikes are still possible, depending upon trail conditions, but lower-elevation hikes, such as the Watchman

Trail (*Trip 2*) and the Petrified Forest Trail (*Trip 1*) are attractive alternatives during the snow season.

The bulk of Zion's 147,000 acres is proposed for wilderness designation. Within the Park are three pristine areas with a total of 126,585 acres.

Common-sense rules of desert hiking apply in the backcountry of this diverse Park, as they do for hiking elsewhere on the Colorado Plateau. Lightning, flash floods, rockfall, and dehydration, to name but a few hazards, are always possible and should not be taken lightly (see the chapter "Hiking Utah's Desert Parks"). Novice hikers who may be uncomfortable hiking the trails on their own, and anyone wishing to gain a better appreciation of the natural history of the Park, can take advantage of naturalist-led hikes on many of Zion's shorter trails. Schedules of guided hikes are posted at the Zion Canyon Visitor Center.

Car shuttles are necessary to complete many of Zion's trails and avoid retracing your route. Hikers with only one vehicle have two options. Inside the Zion Canyon Visitor Center hikers will find a "shuttle board." This allows hikers to coordinate their hike with another party wishing to hike the same trail and establish a car shuttle. Also, a commercial shuttle service is offered by Zion Lodge.

Weather in Zion, though often pleasant, can range from extremes of heat and drought to bitter cold, snow and severe thunderstorms. Annual precipitation ranges from an estimated 21 inches atop the plateaus to 15 inches in Zion Canyon, and recorded temperature extremes range from 115° to 15° below zero.

Two pronounced wet seasons occur in Zion, the first from winter to early spring, and the second, dominated by thunderstorms, from mid to late summer. Each season in Zion is as distinctive as it is beautiful. Whatever time of year you visit the Park, you are sure to return home filled with vivid memories of a unique landscape.

In addition to the standard national-park regulations listed at the beginning of this book, there are a few special restrictions applying to Zion's backcountry:

- Open fires are prohibited in all backcountry areas except in The Narrows,

where small campfires are allowed. Elsewhere hikers should be sure to carry a backpack stove for all their cooking needs.

- Large groups of 12 or more hikers must divide into two or more widely separated groups when camping, to avoid too much impact on backcountry campsites.

- Camping in The Narrows is limited to one night, and is restricted to hikers making the two-day trip downstream from Chamberlain's Ranch.

- Backpackers can camp anywhere in Zion's backcountry within legal camping zones (see below), but are advised to choose a site 100 feet or more from trails and water sources.

# Backcountry Camping Zones

1. *Kolob Canyons*: south of Shuntavi Butte in Timber Creek drainage.

2. *Hop Valley*: north of last fence and private inholding at north end of the valley.

3. *Wildcat Canyon Trail*: from Lava Point to Northgate Peaks Spur Trail.

4. All of Left and Right Forks North Creek.

5. *Huber and Coalpits Washes*: 1 mile north of Utah Highway 9.

6. *Petrified Forest Trail*: beyond transmission lines near the trailhead.

7. *West Rim Trail*: from Lava Point to 1 mile north of Scout Lookout.

8. *East Mesa Trail*: from Park boundary to Observation Point trail junction.

9. *East Rim Trail*: 1 mile beyond trailhead to 1/4 mile above Observation Point Trail junction in Echo Canyon.

Backcountry permits are required for all overnight camping on Zion's trails. They are available at Zion Canyon and Kolob Canyons visitor centers, where hikers can also obtain up-to-date information on trail and weather conditions, and the availability of water.

Self-registration for backcountry permits is available at the West Rim Trailhead below Lava

Point. Hikers planning to hike all the way through The Narrows in one day must obtain a permit, but permits are not required for other day hikes.

# Driving to Zion's Trailheads

A sightseeing drive through Zion National Park can be an enchanting and humbling experience in itself. Such a trip can be a scenic stepping stone enroute to any of the Park's hiking trails, as marvelous roadside scenery gives exciting intimations of even more incredible scenery in the backcountry.

Utah Highway 9 transects the Park, roughly east to west, and it is the primary Park road. Other roads—the Kolob Terrace Road, the Zion Canyon Scenic Drive, and the North Fork Road—branch off Utah 9 and bisect magnificent country while passing numerous trailheads. The Kolob Canyons Section of the Park is accessed via Interstate 15 between St. George and Cedar City, Utah.

Driving directions below for trailheads in Zion follow Utah 9 from west to east. Hikers traveling westbound on that highway should reverse these directions to pinpoint Utah 9 trailheads.

## Utah Highway 9 trailheads for *Trips 1, 2, 12*, and *13*

If you are traveling from the south via Interstate 15, take the Utah Highway 9 exit, 10 miles north of St. George, which is signed for Zion National Park, and proceed 11 miles through the town of Hurricane to La Verkin. From the north, take the Toquerville exit off Interstate 15 and drive southeast on Utah 17 for 6 miles to La Verkin and the junction with Utah 9.

(0.0) Drive east from La Verkin on Utah Highway 9. Beyond the small town of Virgin, a paved road (6.1) branches north at the east end of the town, signed for Kolob Reservoir. Hikers bound for *Trips 17-21* should refer to the road

log below (Kolob Terrace Road). Beyond Virgin the road stays north of the Virgin River while following its canyon upstream, passing lush green hayfields and stock pastures.

(6.5; 12.6) The highway bridges usually dry Coalpits Wash. Just east of the bridge, a dirt road leaves the north side of the highway and descends to a camping area next to the wash. A hikers' gate through the fence here offers hiking access into the wash and an alternative route to the Petrified Forest area (see *Trip 1*).

(1.2; 13.8) The highway bridges the dry course of Huber Wash. A large pulloff just before the bridge offers parking for a cross-country hike up that wash. The Petrified Forest Trail (*Trip 1*) crosses the wash 2 miles upstream.

(1.7; 15.5) Leave the east end of Rockville.

(1.2; 16.7) A large turnout on the north side of the highway. *Trip 1* begins here, but hikers with high-clearance vehicles can pass through the gate and follow the dirt road as it climbs to the Rockville Bench above. One mile up that rough, eroded road, avoid a left-branching road and proceed another 0.3 mile to the **Trailhead 1** parking area near the Park boundary.

Almost immediately the highway curves northeast, entering Zion Canyon. Parunuweap Canyon, a deep gorge through which flows the Virgin River's East Fork, is a deep, gaping chasm, approaching the proportions of Zion Canyon. Permission to cross private land is required to gain access to that canyon. Inquire at the Visitor Center for details if you want to hike there.

The road stays west of North Fork Virgin River as we proceed into incomparable Zion Canyon.

(2.2; 18.9) Entering scenic Springdale, a small town wedged between the towering cliffs of Mount Kinesava and The Watchman. A variety of services is available to meet the needs of most Park visitors, but hiking and backpacking supplies are limited. Scattered homes line the remaining distance to

(1.3; 20.2) the Park boundary and the Park's South Entrance Station. An entry fee is collected here, good for access to the Park for seven consecutive days. We immediately pass the entrance to Watchman Campground on our right.

(0.3; 20.5) The road to South Campground

forks right from the Park road, descending 0.1 mile to roads forking left to the Nature Center and right to the campground. Turn left here, then quickly turn right where a sign indicates the amphitheater, and proceed to a spacious parking area just short of the amphitheater. *Trip 2* begins at **Trailhead 2** where a WATCHMAN TRAIL sign indicates the beginning of the trail.

The highway ahead soon passes roads forking left and right to Park employee residences.

(0.5; 21.0) The Zion Visitor Center turnoff lies on the west side of the highway. A stop here is a must, and particularly for hikers, who need trail and weather information and up-to-the-minute river conditions in The Narrows.

Up-canyon beyond the Visitor Center, the road soon turns abruptly east, bridges the North Fork, and meets

(0.0; 21.9) northbound Zion Canyon Scenic Drive. Hikers bound for *Trips 3* through *11* will turn left here, and refer to the Zion Canyon Scenic Drive road log below, while the rest follow Highway 9 into Pine Creek canyon. The road climbs at once into the lower reaches of the canyon before switchbacking up its north-facing slope.

(3.4; 25.3) Enter the mountain at the mouth of the Zion-Mount Carmel Tunnel. The 1.1-mile-long tunnel, completed in 1930, was an engineering feat of grand proportions. It finally linked the communities along the Virgin River with the isolated Sevier River Valley communities in south-central Utah. On our way through the lighted tunnel, we pass five galleries in which earlier travelers could stop and view the magnificent scenery on the "outside."

(1.1; 26.4) Immediately beyond the tunnel a spacious parking area on the roadway's southeast side offers parking for *Trip 12* hikers at **Trailhead 9**. Beyond the tunnel it seems as if we had entered another world. The red pavement winds eastward, following above the typically dry course of Clear Creek, a Pine Creek tributary.

(1.4; 27.8) After a few minutes of driving, we pass through a second, much shorter tunnel.

The entire area traversed by the highway is excellent for short hikes into any of the north-

west- and southeast-trending branch canyons. Numerous turnouts along the way make good starting points for such forays, and some of them have interpretive signs explaining various aspects of the landscape.

(3.5; 31.3) A northwest-bound paved spur road, signed for RANGER RESIDENCE and TRAILHEAD, leaves the highway here and climbs 300 yards to **Trailhead 10**, where *Trip 13* begins. The pinyon- and juniper-shaded parking area has space for approximately 10 cars. Westbound drivers will find the trailhead turnoff 14 1/2 miles from Mount Carmel Junction.

Drivers bound for *Trips 14-16* will continue east on Highway 9, passing the East Entrance station 100 yards beyond the *Trip 13* trailhead turnoff. The road then ascends the valley of the Co-Op Creek drainage, wedged between mesas that are notably lower in stature than those behind us.

(0.7; 32.2) Upon leaving Zion National Park, red pavement gives way to typical blacktop.

# North Fork Road, *Trips 14-16*

This possibly unsigned road branches north from Utah Highway 9, 1.7 miles east of the Park's east boundary, and 12.8 miles west of Mount Carmel Junction. Eastbound drivers will locate the turnoff 50 feet east of milepost 46 on Highway 9.

(0.0) Driving north on this road, we find the first few miles to be paved, and the remainder a good dirt road.

(0.25) From spring through fall, a roadside sign reminds hikers bound for The Narrows that a permit is required for the trip and that the canyon may be closed to hiking due to dangerous conditions. In winter the only reason to follow this road would be to access ski slopes, but a sign nevertheless warns that the canyon is then closed to hiking.

(5.25; 5.5) To gain access to the trailheads for *Trips 15* and *16*, turn left (west) where a sign indicates the Ponderosa-Zion's Hunting Club.

Almost at once we pass through a gate, ignoring a MEMBERS ONLY sign. Closing it behind us, we pass south of the A-frame cabin with a sign: THE PONDEROSA, HOME OF ZION'S HUNTING CLUB. The roads we follow ahead are public roads across private property. Respect landowner's rights as you proceed. Our road continues generally northwest. Enroute ignore three left-branching, lesser-used roads leading to cabins.

(0.7; 6.2) Turn left onto Buck Road, which should be indicated by a sign. Drivers bound for *Trip 15* should refer to directions below to locate their trailhead. After about 100 feet we must bear right, following a rough and rocky road through charred vegetation.

(0.7, 6.9) Turn left (south) here, where a sign indicates Gooder-Reagan; then after another 100 feet turn right (west) onto West Pine Street, where another sign indicates Gooder-Reagan.

(0.1; 7.0) Bear right just past two summer cabins, avoiding left-forking Palos Verdes Drive.

(0.1; 7.1) Turn right again, and again for a fourth and last time.

(0.1; 7.2) We shortly pass an A-frame cabin. Beyond it bear left where an uphill northbound road forks right. Presently our rough, narrow road declines to a Park service gate (0.1; 7.3), where there is room for one vehicle. However, we can pass through the gate (closing it behind us) to where two cars can be parked just short of the post barricade at **Trailhead 11**, where *Trip 14* begins. The end of this road is quite rough, but low-slung cars can make it if driven carefully.

(0.7; 6.2) Parting company with drivers bound for *Trip 14* via Buck Road, we bear right (northwest) onto signed Ponderosa Road. Climbing to a saddle north of a broad hill, ignore a northeast-bound spur road (0.5; 6.7) just over the top. Descending over the broad plateau, we intersect Beaver Road (0.3; 7.0) and turn right. Avoiding five left-forking roads to summer cabins as we proceed north, we cross the upper reaches of the Echo Canyon drainage, and meet one left fork and two faint right-forking tracks in a

sagebrush-clad opening (0.9; 7.9). The road ahead is badly eroded in places and should be driven only with high-clearance vehicles. Hikers with ordinary cars must begin their hike here.

(0.3; 8.2) Ignore a left fork here, and proceed past another right fork, immediately passing a left-branching track. We finally reach a fence and a locked gate at the Park boundary (0.4; 8.6) at **Trailhead 12**. A green hiker's gate just south of the locked gate marks the beginning of *Trip 15*.

(5.5) Resuming our drive northbound on the North Fork Road, we traverse the slopes of a vast rolling plateau. Dipping into Bull Hollow, we ignore a private eastbound road (6.6; 12.1) into another parcel of the extensive Zion Hunting Resort, and stay left. Quite soon we descend into the upper drainage of Orderville Gulch (0.2; 12.3). Climbing out of Orderville Gulch we ignore another road (0.8; 13.1), that branches right, once again leading into Zion Hunting Resort land.

(3.6; 16.7) At length we reach a bridge over the Virgin River's North Fork, and immediately thereafter meet a junction with the road to Navajo Lake, 16 miles to the right, where our road branches left to the Zion Narrows Trail (so signed). This road proceeds westward on the northside of the river to a gate and a drift fence (0.5; 17.2) delineating the Chamberlain's Ranch property. A sign here reminds us of flash-flood danger, and that we can look forward to a *minimum* 10-hour hike to the Temple of Sinawava. Don't forget to sign in at the trail register here, and be sure to close the gate before proceeding.

The remainder of the road to the trailhead is poor, rough and rutted, but a high-clearance vehicle will have no trouble. Continuing down the final stretch, avoid the spur (0.2; 17.4) branching left to the ranch house and quite soon ignore another road (0.1; 17.5) badly eroded, forking right. Not long afterward the road fords the North Fork (0.2; 17.7) and hikers taking *Trip 16* park in one of the spaces north of the ford at **Trailhead 13**.

## Zion Canyon Scenic Drive,
## *Trips 3-11*

This road should be traveled at a leisurely pace, allowing ample time to park in any of the several turnouts enroute to take a short walk or a longer hike, or to simply soak up the incredible scenery at hand.

(0.0) Junction of Zion-Mount Carmel Highway (Utah 9) and Zion Canyon Scenic Drive, also signed for Zion Lodge. More trailheads lie along the Scenic Drive than any other road in the Park. This part of the canyon is visited by the most people, and not all of them are here to hike. The drive allows those with limited time to experience the atmosphere of the canyon and the magnificence of the Park without ever leaving their cars.

Northbound on the Scenic Drive, we are at once flanked by a gargantuan, rubbly mass of slide debris (see *Trip 3*) that funnels the river here into a narrow, rocky channel. This huge mass of debris detached from the east wall of The Sentinel 4000 years ago and slumped into and dammed the canyon, forming Sentinel Lake, a large body of water that extended upstream to The Grotto picnic area. The dam is also believed to have been responsible for the impoundment of waters in lower Pine Creek along Highway 9.

(1.6) Parking for Court of the Patriarchs at **Trailhead 3**. *Trips 3* and *4* begin here on opposite sides of the road.

(0.9; 2.5) Avoiding a right fork, signed EMPLOYEES ONLY and leading to the Zion Lodge, we quite soon encounter a left turn (0.1; 2.6), signed EMERALD POOLS and HORSE CORRAL. Hikers taking *Trips 5* will park in the spacious **Trailhead 4** parking area on the west side of the road. A spur trail connecting with *Trip 3* allows alternate access to the Sand Bench Trail, and the two trips can be combined into a half-day hike. Opposite this trailhead turnoff is a spur leading to the guest parking area at Zion Lodge.

(0.2; 2.8) Another road forks right toward the lodge, signed GUEST REGISTRATION. *Trip 6* begins from the northeast edge of that parking area at **Trailhead 5**.

Following a grassy bench and paralleling the trail from the lodge, we soon curve into The Grotto (0.6; 3.4), where tall Fremont cottonwoods shade the commodious picnic area. Directly opposite is the **Trailhead 6** parking area, where hikers taking *Trips 7 and 8* will park, while *Trip 6* leaves the picnic area, bound for the lodge.

Continuing past The Grotto, we soon skirt the base of what is arguably Zion's premier monolith, The Great White Throne. We follow the river as it describes a huge semicircle, the Big Bend, around Angels Landing and its companion tower, The Organ. The 2000' walls of the monolith rise abruptly from the canyon floor to the broad mesa that crowns it. Here it is too close for us to fully appreciate its dimensions, but a turnout farther ahead reveals its immense bulk to better advantage.

Numerous shady alcoves, of which Weeping Rock is the largest and wettest, are seen ahead as we proceed through grassy openings and among shady groves of cottonwood, boxelder, and velvet ash. Before the road doubles back along the Big Bend, the signed spur to Weeping Rock Parking Area (1.2; 4.6) forks off to the right. *Trips 9* and *10* begin from the **Trailhead 7** parking area, which tends to become congested. The road ahead curves west beneath two gaping alcoves, passes north of a large turnout, and abruptly turns north where a roomy parking area for southbound drivers only

(0.6; 5.2) offers a grand view of The Great White Throne. Upstream the canyon becomes increasingly narrow, and we soon enter a shady flat. Here we curve westward around another bend in the river and reach

(1.0; 6.2) the large and often congested Temple of Sinawava Parking Area, its namesake crag jutting above the parking area to the north. Popular *Trip 11* begins at **Trailhead 8**, where *Trip 16* hikers terminate their trek.

## Kolob Terrace Road, *Trips 17-21*

This highly scenic road leaves Utah 9 at the east end of Virgin (6.1 miles from La Verkin and 14.1 miles from the Park's South Entrance). This road is paved for much of its length, but has several steep grades and many sharp turns. All its trailheads can be driven to in passenger cars, but short, rough segments of dirt road near Lava Point and Kolob Reservoir dictate careful driving. Even nonhikers will find the drive exceptionally rewarding, as it traverses unique and varied landscapes seen by only a handful of Park visitors. In winter, the upper reaches of this road are closed to all but ski and snowmobile traffic.

(0.0) From Utah 9 our paved road soon passes some outlying residences of Virgin, then begins ascending the drainage of North Creek, the primary watershed in the west-central part of the Park. Passing varicolored slopes of Moenkopi Formation rocks, we bridge North Creek twice and at length begin ascending a sloping, basalt-capped ridge.

(6.3) Our road enters Park lands amid pinyon-juniper woodland. As we approach Grapevine Wash on the upper limits of the ridge, signed Smith Mesa Road (1.1; 7.4) peels off to the left. Presently, hikers bound for *Trip 17* must carefully note their odometer reading in addition to observing landmarks (with the aid of a topographic map) to locate their unsigned trailhead. Soon the road curves north while ascending directly toward the red mass of Tabernacle Dome, flanked on the left by the fluted cliffs of Point 6083, and by Point 5855 on the right. Approaching these points, look for a short spur (0.6; 8.0) branching off to the right (east). Park at **Trailhead 14** 100 feet off the paved road, where there is usually ample space for at least five vehicles, and begin *Trip 17* here.

The road ahead climbs past Tabernacle Dome on the right and a private residence on the left. Soon the grade abates and we leave the Park and enter the broad, grassy expanse of Cave Valley. Soon we strike due north for an ascent to the west slopes of the brush-clad Spendlove Knoll cinder cone. Due west of Spendlove Knoll we re-enter the Park and as the road begins to curve east, a second cinder cone, Firepit Knoll, fills the view ahead. A sign indicating the Hop Valley Trail informs *Trip 18* hikers where to turn (4.5; 12.5) onto the short paved spur to **Trailhead 15**, just north of the road.

The road ahead ascends to a saddle separating the cinder cones, then continues the ascent above spreading Lee Valley. Soon the road descends east into the valley of Pine Spring Wash,

then switchbacks once, climbing steeply among tall pines onto a plateau east of the valley. Upon reaching the plateau, and immediately before the road doubles back to the northwest, the signed Wildcat Canyon Trailhead spur leaves the pavement (2.8; 15.3). This narrow, unpaved spur leads quickly south to the **Trailhead 16** parking area (0.1; 15.4) amid thickets of Gambel oak on the edge of spacious Pine Valley. *Trip 19* hikers will end their hike here.

The road ahead eventually climbs into the expansive meadow of Little Creek Valley, and at its upper end we reach the end of pavement at the Park boundary (3.0; 18.3). Our wide but washboardy road ahead soon climbs into Oak Spring Valley. It then skirts volcanic Home Valley Knoll, enters another grassy spread, and finally meets

(2.3; 20.6) signed Lava Point Road.

Hikers bound for *Trips 19* and *20* turn right here, follow the dirt road across a well-watered spread, and soon pass summer homes tucked back into the forest. We re-enter the Park (0.8; 21.4) and quickly reach a road fork (0.1; 21.5) on a flat ridge amid an aspen-and-white-fir forest.

If you are planning to camp before embarking on *Trips 19* and *20*, or if you would like an overview of the vast plateau and the canyons, turn right and proceed along the forested, basalt-capped ridge to a campground turnoff (0.7; 22.2). The Lava Point Campground (7900') lies north of the main road, offering six pleasant, conifer-shaded campsites along its loop road. You must bring your own water to this primitive campground. No fee is charged here, but there are tables, fire pits, and pit toilets.

Barney's Trail departs from campsite Number 2, descending 0.3 mile via an aspen-and-fir-clad slope to the trailhead access road, 0.7 mile from the West Rim Trail. Lava Point Fire Lookout, open during the summer season, lies 0.2 mile east of the campground turnoff, and offers an exceptional panorama of the Park and much of the Markagunt Plateau.

Turning left at the campground junction,

signed for WEST RIM TRAIL, we immediately bypass a left fork leading to a ranger residence and descend, steeply at times, along the forested north slope of Lava Point. The road is narrow, rough and rutted in places, and should be avoided immediately after a good rain. At length we skirt the edge of a grassy opening beneath Goose Creek Knoll and soon reach **Trailhead 17** (1.4; 22.9) where *Trips 19* and *20* begin. A locked gate here blocks the road eastbound to MIA camp. Parking is available here for about seven vehicles.

Hikers bound for *Trip 21* and Kolob Reservoir should stay left at the Lava Point Road junction, shortly passing the turnoff to Kolob Mountain Ranch and Lodge (0.3; 20.9) above Blue Springs Reservoir, and thereafter passing numerous summer homes. The dirt road leads through bucolic meadows dotted with grazing cattle during summer and early fall.

Upon reaching large Kolob Reservoir (spillway 8188'), avoid the left fork branching toward the dam. Instead we follow the main road as it twists and turns above the east shore of the popular reservoir. At the north end of the reservoir, we reach a signed junction (4.5; 25.4) with our trailhead access road (left), from where the primary graded road continues north, leading to Cedar City in 27 miles.

Turning left, our narrow road follows the north shoreline closely, shortly curving northwest along the Indian Hollow arm of the reservoir. At the upper end of this arm, ignore a left fork that follows around the opposite shoreline, and quickly reach a sign (1.0; 26.4): TO LA VERKIN CREEK IN ZION NATIONAL PARK. Turn right here and park off the road in the aspen grove, just below the gate. *Trip 21* begins here at **Trailhead 18**.

# Kolob Canyons Road,
## *Trips 22 and 23*

This is another supremely scenic drive bypassed by most Park visitors. The road is paved, has a steady grade and many turns, and offers exceptional views into the Finger Canyons of the Kolob, an area that many would argue is the finest scenery in the Park, if not some of the most incredible scenery on the globe. Everyone traveling this road should first stop in the Kolob Canyons Visitor Center and obtain a copy of the Kolob Canyons brochure. In addition to providing ample information on the natural history of the area, the brochure is also a road guide, keyed to numbered stops along the way.

(0.0) The Kolob Canyons Road leaves Interstate 15 at exit 40, 19 miles south of Cedar City and 33 miles north of St. George. The Kolob Canyons Visitor Center (0.3) offers books and maps for sale, backcountry information, and backcountry permits.

Beyond the Visitor Center, the road quickly bends north while climbing the wooded slope of the Hurricane Cliffs, which form the western margin of the Markagunt Plateau. A gate here may be closed periodically between late fall and early spring if rockfall or snowpack blocks the road ahead.

As we head north toward Taylor Creek canyon, we briefly enjoy expansive views across a broad valley to the bulky Pine Valley Mountains. Here on the face of the Hurricane Cliffs we are entering the Colorado Plateau Province, while our views both west and northwest stretch into the Basin and Range Province, which encompasses much of western Utah.

The road ahead curves east into Taylor Creek canyon, and climbs eastward south of the creek.

(2.0; 2.3) *Trip 22* begins on the left (north) side of the road, indicated by a TAYLOR CREEK TRAIL sign, where a spacious turnout offers ample parking at **Trailhead 19**. The road ahead winds upward through the pinyon-juniper-oak woodland, soon curving east into Taylor Creek's South Fork. A spacious turnout (1.3; 3.6) on the right shoulder of our road is encountered just before we curve across the South Fork. It offers parking for picture taking or for a rewarding jaunt up that canyon, via a faint but traceable pathway.

Beyond the South Fork our road curves west and climbs north-facing slopes below Beatty Point, reaching the Taylor Creek-Timber Creek divide at signed Lee Pass, 6060' (0.5; 4.1). From the pass the Finger Canyons of Timber Creek suddenly explode upon the scene, but they can be enjoyed to better advantage from the roadend ahead. The **Trailhead 20** parking area for *Trip 23* lies just south of Lee Pass of the left side of the road.

The road continues southwest 1.4 miles to the roadend, where there is a picnic area and dramatic views into the Finger Canyons.

# Trip 1
## Petrified Forest Trail to Coalpits Wash

**Distance**: 14.4 to 17.0 miles round trip
**Low/High elevations**: 4025'/4450'
**Suited for**: Dayhike or backpack
**Difficulty**: Moderate
**Best season**: Mid-September through March
**Map/Trailhead**: 1/1
**Hazards**: No water is available between the trailhead and Coalpits Wash, at the trail's end.

**Introduction**: This is Zion's longest low-elevation trail. Seldom trod during the summer, it becomes an attractive excursion during the cool months from fall through spring. The grade is gentle as the trail traverses broad benches clothed in woodlands of pinyon and juniper, with an exciting backdrop of soaring, brilliantly hued cliffs. Campsites are abundant beyond the powerlines near the trailhead, and there is ample room for off-trail exploration. A scattering of petrified wood offers a glimpse into the distant past, when ancient streams carried driftwood from far-away highlands, depositing them on a sloping coastal plain.

**Description**: Our trek begins at the hiker's gate at the Park boundary, (0.0; 4025). (If you start below, at Highway 9, then you'll add 2.6 miles to the round-trip distance.) We first follow a northwest-trending jeep road along broad Rockville Bench, its gentle contours contrasting with the brightly colored cliffs of Mt. Kinesava, soaring more than 3000 feet above in a lateral distance of less than 2 miles. Upon the flanks of

that giant crag four prominent sedimentary rock layers are exposed to full view, representing a 50-million-year span of geologic history.

After a gentle ascent, the jeep track passes under a power transmission line (0.5; 4100) serving the town of Springdale, beyond which we enjoy expanding vistas, presently including volcanic Crater Hill, and the hogback crest of distant Pine Valley Mountains, both to the northwest. Branching right onto another jeep track at a trail sign (0.2; 4100), we climb easily around the shoulder of a ridge (0.8; 4220), then curve north, traversing wooded slopes above the shallow gorge of Huber Wash. Our eyes can follow the Shinarump rimrock of the extensive bench as it contours around the flanks of Huber Wash. The finest display of petrified wood in the Park lies ahead, scattered over the bench beyond Huber Wash. Fluted red cliffs bounding Mt. Kinesava rise boldly above to the northeast, while to the northwest, foregrounded by the broad wooded bench, more barrier cliffs soar skyward to the rim of Cougar Mountain.

Soon we cross two dry forks of Huber Wash (0.6; 4160). Vegetation here is typical of the pinyon-juniper woodland, including prickly pear and cholla (the latter more common in the Lower Sonoran Zone, which dominates the southwest of the Park), squawbush, blackbrush, broom snakeweed, big sagebrush, rabbitbrush, cliffrose, and buffaloberry. After climbing moderately out of the wash, the trail crosses another small wash (0.5; 4240), where shrub live oak joins the woodland.

The grade slackens as we trace a northwestward course across the bench, and soon fragments of petrified wood begin to appear alongside the trail. Look for multihued rock fragments that seem out of place among the tan rocks of the Chinle Formation. Some pieces of the petrified wood are large enough that we can actually count growth rings, and in places entire tree trunks have been exposed by erosion. Although broken into sections, they lie where stream sediments buried them 200 million years ago. Restrain the urge to collect petrified wood, remembering that collecting or disturbing natural features is prohibited in national parks.

As we proceed, we gain vistas east of West Temple and the Sundial from a perspective much different from that of most Park visitors. Eventually we notice petrified wood with much less frequency, and soon proceed across a prickly-pear-studded bench, brilliantly colored with delicate flowers in spring.

After crossing a gentle divide, the trail climbs to a minor gap in a west-trending ridge (1.1; 4420) above Scoggins Wash, from which we enjoy a sweeping panorama of the crenulated cliff band that rises beyond the bench to the east and to the north. Beyond the ridge, the trail winds down to, then out of, a dry gully, and descends pinyon-juniper slopes to cross usually dry Scoggins Wash (0.6; 4210), where a few scattered Fremont cottonwoods and tamarisks indicate the presence of subsurface moisture. Presently hiking westward, we follow the Shinarump rimrock above the deepening gorge of the wash. A few scattered fragments of petrified wood persist along our route, among cobbles weathered from the stream deposits of the Shinarump conglomerate. Here it consists of either large sand grains only, or sand mixed with stream-rounded pebbles and cobbles. By now the old jeep road has faded into a sometimes-faint trail indicated by cairns.

Where a north-trending wash crosses the trail (0.6; 4310), a possible cross-country route begins. The small wash can be followed north for 0.8 mile to a prominent gap in the ridge, from which a minor wash then leads down into the upper reaches of Coalpits Wash. This route offers the option of looping back to the end of our trail route, and then following it back to the trailhead. That loop route reaches Coalpits Wash only 0.5 mile downstream from some old oil-well ruins, an interesting spot worth a visit.

Cresting a minor ridge (10.2; 4350), we obtain more fine views that sharply contrast the horizontal aspect of the bench with the vertical cliffs beyond. Presently the trail descends wooded slopes to the banks of a minor wash, soon crosses its west branch, and then climbs briefly to a low gap. Colorful badlands slopes composed of Chinle shales rise above the bench to our right (northwest) while to the southern distance, the rugged crags of the Vermilion Cliffs dominate the scene. A final look over our shoulders reveals the mighty crags of the Towers of the Virgin and, north of them, The Bishopric.

Southwest of the gap we reach another minor wash and a junction (0.8; 4150) with the old Scoggins Stock Trail, branching left into the depths of Scoggins Wash. The trail was used by pioneer cattlemen moving their stock to and from the grassy tablelands of Rockville Bench. The trail ahead proceeds along the bench beneath colorful Chinle hills, finally curving above Coalpits Wash, where the bench becomes increasingly narrow. We reach the rim of the wash, where the bench terminates, and a short but steep descent takes us to the banks of the small stream in that wash (1.3; 4100). A reliable spring 0.1 mile downstream offers fresher water than the somewhat alkaline stream.

A wide variety of cross-country hiking opportunities in the area can keep hikers busy here for several days. Among them are forays over the volcanic landscape to the west, and up and down Coalpits Wash.

Crater Hill, a 5207-foot cinder cone, is responsible for the basaltic lava that dominates the landscape west of the wash. One-half million years ago, lava flows from Crater Hill dammed Coalpits Wash, subsequently forming a short-lived seasonal lake one square mile in extent. Pollen samples recovered from the lakebed indicate that trees similar to ponderosa pine, spruce, and fir may have then inhabited what is presently the hottest and driest region of the Park.

Return the way you came.

# Trip 2
## Watchman Trail

**Distance**: 2.9 miles semiloop trip
**Low/High elevations**: 3970'/4420'
**Suited for**: Dayhike
**Difficulty**: Moderately easy
**Best season**: Open all year, but hot in summer and possibly snow-covered in winter.
**Map/Trailhead**: 2/2
**Hazards**: Steep dropoffs near the trail's end, and springs that require purification before drinking (as do all open water sources in the Park).

**Introduction**: The Watchman Trail is a short but scenic route leading to a rocky bench on the east slopes of lower Zion Canyon, offering unique vistas available from no other trail in the Park. The bench lies below a prominent red spire rising 2500 feet from the canyon floor, dubbed The Watchman by early Mormon settlers. The trail is a fine leg stretcher for guests of Zion Canyon's campgrounds, and its unique views and interesting terrain make the trip a fine choice for the hiker with limited time and energy.

**Description**: Hikers can begin this trip from either of two points. Those staying in Watchman Campground can follow the paved service road northeast from the self-pay station near the campground entrance for 0.3 mile, then follow a trail east for 0.1 mile very near a minor arroyo to a trail register box.

Visitors staying in South Campground, and other hikers, can begin at the amphitheater parking area near the Nature Center. From that trailhead (0.0; 3970) look for WATCHMAN TRAIL sign and stroll past the amphitheater, beyond which we descend to a riverside terrace. The trail strikes northeast across the grass- and rabbitbrush-covered terrace, soon joining a service road, on which we turn right to stroll across a bridge over the river.

Where that road makes a right angle, a WATCHMAN TRAIL sign indicates the beginning of the trail proper (0.2; 3975). Leaving the road, pause long enough to gaze northeast up to imposing Bridge Mountain, rearing 2800 feet above us. Those with sharp eyesight or with binoculars can make out a narrow stone arch on the skyline north of the peak. A host of jagged summits form the rugged skyline above us, from Bridge Mountain in the northeast to Johnson Mountain at Zion Canyon's mouth.

Our trail presently takes us across the wide bench, studded with four-wing saltbush, opposite a group of Park employee residences. The trail from Watchman Campground joins our path from the right (southwest) next to a trailside register box (0.2; 3970). Trail registers located at or near trailheads in the Park should be signed, to help the Park Service monitor use.

From here the trail heads east up a minor canyon and begins ascending beneath imposing cliffs. Our trail takes us upward through the varicolored mudstones and siltstones of the Dinosaur Canyon layer of the Moenave Formation. Proceeding upward toward the next layer in that formation, the Springdale Sandstone, we'll notice undercut ledges created by the differential erosion of a soft rock layer underlying a harder, more resistant one.

After negotiating four switchbacks, we curve into the head of the canyon, where several sluggish springs host lush riparian vegetation, such as Fremont cottonwood, boxelder, and a variety of seasonal wildflowers. These springs give life to the small, seasonal stream that trickles into the canyon below. Presently, we begin a southwestward traverse while enjoying increasingly outstanding vistas of the north-facing canyon wall. Here we notice a change in vegetation, for a comparatively cooler microclimate prevails on this more sheltered slope. Utah juniper and now singleleaf pinyon predominate among shrubs typical of the pinyon-juniper woodland, such as buffaloberry, singleleaf ash, Utah serviceberry, and yucca.

Where it attains the high bench above Zion Canyon, the trail forks (0.8; 4420), forming a scenic loop around the perimeter of the bench. Hikers eager to enjoy unobstructed vistas will bear right for now, returning via the left fork. The trail winds along the Springdale Sandstone-capped rim, soon reaching a junction. A spur to an overlook forks to the right here, quickly leading to the brink of the rim, where a broad panorama unfolds.

Below, at the wide mouth of Zion Canyon, is the town of Springdale, a Mormon settlement dating back to the 1860s. Beyond the town are the aptly-named Vermilion Cliffs, adorned by the landmark Eagle Crags. Those rugged cliffs, composed of Moenave Formation rocks, the same rocks upon which we stand, are one of the "risers" forming southwest Utah's Grand Staircase. Rearing mightily toward the heavens across the wide floor of Zion Canyon are the Towers of the Virgin, boasting a vertical relief of nearly 4000 feet. Our view also extends up the narrowing canyon, encompassing a myriad of colorful, soaring cliffs, crags, and tree-topped plateaus.

Our vantage point is an excellent spot from which to observe some aspects of canyon widening. The canyon becomes progressively narrower upstream, where the river has cut a slot barely 20 feet wide in The Narrows, where the uniform Navajo Sandstone dominates. Below us the canyon is a rather wide valley, with a wooded bottom and rocky slopes that sweep back to broken cliffs.

To return via the loop trail, backtrack from the overlook and turn right. This longer side of the loop follows the rim of the bench eastward, then turns abruptly northwest, where we climb easily amid sandstone blocks, pinyon, juniper, and various shrubs, soon reaching the main trail (0.4; 4420), where we bear right to retrace our route to the start.

# Trip 3
## Sand Bench Trail

**Distance**: 3.9 miles, semiloop trail
**Low/High elevations**: 4230'/4715'
**Suited for**: Dayhike
**Difficulty**: Moderate
**Best season**: September through early June
**Map/Trailhead**: 2/3
**Hazards**: No water; possible encounters with horses from Zion Lodge spring through fall.

**Introduction**: One of many day-use trails in Zion Canyon, the Sand Bench Trail offers incredible close-up views of the awe-inspiring, colorful cliffs of the lower canyon from a sandy bench 600 feet above the canyon's floor. The trailside terrain is clothed in a pinyon-juniper woodland typical of the Park's lower elevations. Much of the tread is deep, soft sand churned up by horse traffic from Zion Lodge. Because of this, few hikers take the route, and save for occasional saddle trains, hikers who choose this trail will enjoy considerable solitude, a rarity on Zion Canyon's popular trails.

This trip can be taken by itself, or it can be combined with the Emerald Pools Trail (*Trip 5*) by utilizing a dusty riverside connecting trail (used by horses coming from the corral near

Emerald Pools trailhead) for a half-day hike passing many of the scenic wonders of central Zion Canyon.

**Description**: From the parking area (0.0; 4250), proceed across the Scenic Drive via a crosswalk; a footbridge sign indicates the trail on the west side of the road. The wide trail follows a bend of North Fork Virgin River, just north of a paved spur road leading to a water tank and various buildings. Following FOOTBRIDGE and HORSE-TRAIL signs, we quickly reach a sturdy bridge over the river (0.2; 4230), where signs indicate SAND BENCH TRAIL and NO CAMPING. Exposures of lakebed sediments deposited in Sentinel Lake nearly 4000 years ago can be seen on the riverbank just upstream.

Beyond the bridge, the trail may be briefly ill-defined. Avoid the faint, boulder-strewn path along Birch Creek to the left, and instead follow the path to the right indicated by a TRAIL sign. After quickly climbing to a bench above the river, the trail then forks. The right fork offers quick access to the Emerald Pools connecting trail, but we take the left fork, soon crossing a small wash emanating from Mt. Moroni, then climbing briefly to junction with the aforementioned connecting trail (right fork) and the Sand Bench Trail (left fork) (0.1; 4265).

The immense amphitheater before us is the Court of the Patriarchs. The Three Patriarchs, a triad of giant Navajo Sandstone crags, soar 2500 feet above us to the northwest. Mt. Moroni is a particularly impressive spire piercing the Utah sky 1400 feet above to the north.

One of the most striking trailside plants present here is sacred datura, or jimson weed. It is easily identified by its large blue-green leaves and its huge, white, trumpet-shaped flowers. It is one of the few plants that bloom in the canyon during the hot summer months. The flowers open in the evening and close in the morning as the sun rises over the canyon wall. The fruit of this poisonous plant is round and spine-covered. Some Southwest Indian tribes used this plant in religious ceremonies.

Tall ponderosa pines are skylined on the rim above the Court, lending a sense of scale to the immense cliffs that surround us. Quickly the trail descends to the cottonwood-shaded course of Birch Creek. The creek is diverted into a pipeline a short distance upstream, for use as the Park's primary water supply. The trail leads us very briefly upstream to a crossing of the often-trickling creek, and from there we climb the north slope of Sand Bench via five switchbacks. The grade slackens above the switchbacks amid a woodland of Utah juniper and singleleaf pinyon. Views behind us reveal the Court of the Patriarchs and the towering crags above in full magnificence. Notice that these crags are separated from one another by narrow and precipitous joint-controlled canyons.

Soon we reach the loop trail (0.3; 4350) and ponder our choice of turning right or left. The right fork takes advantage of the close-up views of The Sentinel and The Streaked Wall, saving more expansive vistas from the rim of the bench for the return trip.

Turning right, we find the tread sandy and the going slow, but views of incomparable cliffs and monoliths should distract us from our labors. Vistas are ever-increasing as we rise moderately among singleleaf pinyon, juniper, greenleaf manzanita, and shrub live oak—the only evergreen oak in the Park.

Isolated Sand Bench is somewhat of a curiosity in Zion Canyon, as there are few benches save for riverside terraces. The bench was formed as an immense slump block detached from the face of The Sentinel about 4000 years ago, subsequently damming the river and forming a short-lived lake—Sentinel Lake—that extended as far upstream as the Grotto Picnic Area. The narrow lake reached a depth of 350 feet and had a surface area of 0.7 square mile. Thus the chaotic jumble of sandstone blocks and sand over which our trail passes is a relatively recent addition to the landscape.

Slogging through the sand to the summit of the trail (0.7; 4715), we welcome the chance to pause and absorb the magnificent panorama. Towering above us to the west is the 1400' wall of The Sentinel, capped by the red rocks of the Temple Cap Formation. Southwest of our vantage point rises the even more striking cliff of the 1600' Streaked Wall, its face decorated by draperies of runoff-deposited desert varnish. Crowning that wall is aptly-named Bee Hive Peak, a cone-shaped dome of Navajo Sandstone.

Our gaze also stretches up and down the canyon, encompassing a parade of striking crags from Deertrap Mountain to Johnson Mountain at the mouth of Zion Canyon. Continuing ahead, we shortly reach a corral, two picnic tables, and a pit toilet (0.6; 4600). A wooded knoll just to the south offers superb vistas over the lower reaches of Zion Canyon, and is but a short scramble from this spot.

The trail ahead curves eastward through the pinyon-juniper woodland and among large, lichen-encrusted Navajo Sandstone blocks. Quite soon the trail forks (0.1; 4640). The left fork slices through the heart of the bench, while the right fork follows close to the canyon rim. Both trails are 0.7 mile long.

The bench trail (left fork) climbs gently, gaining 60 feet, and offers fair views framed by trailside trees. The rim trail (right fork) undulates along or very near the rim of Zion Canyon. Views are expansive from this trail, and short detours to the edge of the rim offer glimpses of North Fork Virgin River 600 feet below. It may be difficult to imagine that such a small stream is responsible for carving this immense canyon, but remember 15 million years have passed since the river began its handiwork.

The two trails rejoin near the rim (0.7; 4700), from where we descend at a moderate grade, soon curving north across a pleasant wooded flat. Finally our trail meanders downhill northwest, soon completing the loop, and we turn right (0.6; 4350) and retrace our steps to the trailhead.

# Trip 4
## Court of the Patriarchs Viewpoint Trail

**Distance**: 100 yards round trip
**Low/High elevations**: 4250'/4290'
**Suited for**: Walk
**Difficulty**: Very easy
**Best season**: All year
**Map/Trailhead**: 2/3
**Hazards**: Negligible

**Introduction**: Zion's diversity of trails offers something for hikers of every ability, and one need not be a dedicated hiker to enjoy the splendors of this magnificent Park. A case in point is the Court of the Patriarchs Viewpoint Trail, an easy five-minute stroll offering views up and down much of the length of Zion Canyon.

**Description**: From the parking area (0.0; 4250) the trail switchbacks uphill at a moderate grade, passing through a thicket of Gambel oak, netleaf hackberry, and Utah juniper, ending after 50 yards where an awe-inspiring panorama unfolds (4290'). Westward, the sky-piercing summits of the Three Patriarchs and their companion peak, Mt. Moroni, soar boldly above the cliffbound amphitheater of Court of the Patriarchs. Behind the Court lies the remote and inaccessible hanging valley of upper Birch Creek.

But there are more lofty crags and magnificent, sweeping cliffs to capture our attention and stir our imagination. Our view stretches up-canyon as far as the lofty perch of Angels Landing; down-canyon, prominent features include The Sentinel, The Streaked Wall, and The Bee Hives.

# Trip 5
## Emerald Pools Trail

**Distance**: 2.1-mile loop trip
**Low/High elevations**: 4280'/4600'
**Suited for**: Walk
**Difficulty**: Easy
**Best season**: All year
**Maps/Trailhead**: 3,2/4
**Hazards**: Steep dropoffs; trail should be avoided when ice- or snow-covered.

**Introduction**: One of Zion Canyon's most-used trails, this very scenic one- to two-hour jaunt tours a shady side canyon featuring a perennial stream with dense vegetation, and four limpid pools reflecting towering canyon walls. Hikers not inclined to undertake the entire loop can follow the mile-long paved trail (accessible to wheelchairs) to the lower pool and a dripping alcove resplendent with water-loving vegetation.

**Description**: The signed trail (0.0; 4280) quickly bridges North Fork Virgin River west of the large parking area, then immediately forks. The right fork, a gently climbing, paved trail, offers the shortest and easiest route to the lower pool, while the left fork offers access to the loop trail and to a riverside spur trail leading to the Sand Bench Trail.

Turning left beneath the soaring heights of Lady Mountain, we stroll south along the shady riverbank, under the spreading branches of Fremont cottonwood, water birch, and Gambel oak. Quite soon we reach a signed junction (0.1; 4300) from where the riverside stock trail (also open to hikers) continues down-river and the loop trail climbs the slope above.

---

Hikers who wish to combine the Emerald Pools Trail with the Sand Bench Trail for an all-day excursion can follow that riverside trail downstream from the junction (0.0; 4300). Heading south, the trail soon passes a corral and becomes dusty. Initially we are shaded by groves of Fremont cottonwood and boxelder that hug the river, but as we climb slightly onto drier slopes, Gambel oak, shrub live oak, and Utah juniper dominate. The river below alternates from a cottonwood-shaded course to an open one lined with bushy tamarisk.

As we pass under the colorful, broken cliffs of imposing Mt. Moroni, we encounter an abundance of the Park's largest cactus, Engelmann prickly pear, adorned with delicate yellow flowers in spring and purple fruit in autumn. Proceeding amid oak and juniper woodland, we'll notice an unusual climbing vine draping trailside trees. Canyon wild grape is common in the shady depths of Zion Canyon, and is particularly abundant along the Weeping Rock Trail (*Trip 9*).

The trail crosses a sagebrush-clad flat as it curves toward Court of the Patriarchs, and is soon joined by an informal trail climbing up from the Court of the Patriarchs trailhead. Quite soon we cross a typically dry wash and join the main trail (1.1; 4265) climbing up from that trailhead, where we bear right onto the Sand Bench Trail, described in *Trip 3*.

---

Resuming our hike along the Emerald Pools Trail, we turn right at the loop-trail junction. A

single switchback ensues, followed by a protracted traverse. The trail quickly crosses slide
debris beneath Lady Mountain, a soaring crag
rising 2500 feet above the trail. Shrub live oak,
Utah juniper, Gambel oak, singleleaf pinyon,
Utah serviceberry, buffaloberry, singleleaf ash,
narrowleaf yucca, and prickly pear are thickly
massed along the mountainside above the canyons. Enroute we'll splash through the runoff of
several verdant springs, their courses banked
with cottonwood, water birch, and boxelder.

Views throughout the traverse are inspiring,
encompassing square-edged mesas topped with
tall pines, sculptured cliffs streaked with curtains
of red, and the gaping cleft of Zion Canyon. The
trail maintains a gentle grade, and is intermittently paved above steep dropoffs.

As the trail curves around a shoulder of the
slope, the manicured grounds of Zion Lodge
come into view, and several outstanding landmarks form a ragged skyline above the canyon.
Among them, from north to south, Angels Landing, The Great White Throne, Mountain of the
Sun, and Twin Brothers. The prominent gothic
arch on the flanks of imposing Red Arch Mountain, just south of The Great White Throne, was
formed in 1880 when an enormous slab of Navajo Sandstone spalled off the cliff and buried
Mormon pioneer Oliver D. Gifford's cornfield.
Altogether, the peaceful floor of Zion Canyon,
with the river threading its way among grassy
openings and groves of cottonwoods, and with a
backdrop of soaring sandstone cliffs, makes a
most attractive picture.

As the trail enters the Heaps Canyon drainage, we are confronted by a gigantic amphitheater, its north wall of Navajo Sandstone
intricately cross-bedded and capped by the
prominent spire of The Spearhead. Below us, the
perennial waters of the canyon nourish a dense
forest of Gambel oak, boxelder, and Fremont
cottonwood.

Where more springs course over the trail
ahead, bigtooth maples arch their branches overhead, their leaves turning a brilliant red after the
first frosts of autumn. As we approach the draw
of the canyon, Douglas-firs appear on trailside
slopes, and soon Heaps Canyon creek comes into
view, pouring off an overhanging ledge between
the middle and lower pools. Immediately below

the overhang, a seepline nurtures a narrow strip
of hanging gardens.

Soon we reach middle Emerald Pool (0.8;
4380), perched near the brink of the pouroff and
rimmed by Douglas-firs, willows, Utah junipers,
and Fremont cottonwoods. The small, still pool
reflects an exciting backdrop of sculptured, pas-
tel-shaded canyon walls. Overhead, tall ponderosa pines form scattered silhouette figures
atop the canyon rim.

Proceeding 50 yards beyond the pool to a
junction, we ponder the option of turning left and
ascending to the upper pool or turning right and
looping back to the trailhead. The upper pool is
the largest and deepest, and well worth a visit.
The trail leading to it crosses a slope littered with
boulders that were spread across the trail by a
major flash flood in 1987. The correct route may
be lost amid a confusing array of use trails, all of
which ultimately lead to the upper pool.

As we ascend the brush slope at a moderately
steep grade, an abundance of creeping
hollygrape at the trail's edge heralds our approach to the upper pool, where the grade abates.
Quite soon we reach the edge of the large pool
(0.2; 4600) where velvet ash, willow, bigtooth
maple, and boxelder, many of them draped by
vines of the canyon wild grape, crowd the edge
and provide a shady canopy for hikers on a hot
day.

Numerous springs and seeps feed the pool,
and after heavy rains or the melting of the snowpack on the plateau above, a noisy waterfall
plunges over the tall cliff behind the pool. Rising
sheer above us one three sides are lofty cliffs of
Navajo Sandstone, stained with desert varnish
from dust and mineral-laden rainwater. Notice
the Douglas-firs clinging to the ledges on the
cliff face south of the pool. That north-facing
cliff is shaded from heat and sunlight, so soil
moisture evaporates more slowly and nurtures a
suitable microhabitat for trees that are more
commonly found atop the plateaus more than
3000 feet above.

After backtracking to the junction near the
middle pool (0.2; 4380), we should bear left if
we intend to complete the circuit. Quickly we
meet a left-branching trail bound for the Grotto
Picnic Area, 0.8 mile ahead. But we turn right,
passing through a narrow cleft between two im-

mense boulders fallen from the cliffs above. Rock stairs then lower us to a junction with another left-branching trail (0.1; 4350), which quickly connects with the aforementioned trail leading to the picnic area.

Our trail immediately leads us under an overhanging ledge just above the lower pool, which is merely a wide spot in the creekbed. Presently wedged between the cliff face and the waterfall emanating from the middle pool, our wet trail leads us past horizontal seeplines resplendent with the growth of hanging gardens. A white, powdery residue of sodium bicarbonate coats the trailside wall, left behind by the evaporation of seeping water.

We are likely to get wet under the dripping wall as we proceed out of the canyon's draw and begin the final leg of the loop. The trail presently traverses southeast across lower slopes of the amphitheater beneath a canopy of Gambel oak and bigtooth maple, their ranks mixed with Utah juniper and singleleaf ash. Inspiring views of canyons, cliffs, and mesa rims accompany us as we descend to the floor of Zion Canyon. Reaching the river, the trail hugs the west bank the remaining distance to the bridge, from where we quickly backtrack to the parking area (0.7; 4270).

# Trip 6
## Zion Lodge to Grotto Picnic Area

**Distance**: 1.2 miles round trip
**Low/High elevations**: 4280'/4320'
**Suited for**: Walk
**Difficulty**: Very easy
**Best season**: All year
**Map/Trailhead**: 3/5
**Hazards**: Negligible

**Introduction**: This pleasant stroll offers an alternative route from Zion Lodge to the Grotto Picnic Area for visitors who would rather walk than drive. It features shady, canyon-bottom vegetation, grassy openings, and close-up views of towering canyon walls. The trail is used primarily by guests of the lodge.

**Description**: The trail begins behind the ice machine at the northeast end of the lodge parking area (0.0; 4280), where a sign indicates GROTTO PICNIC AREA. The trail, nearly level throughout, parallels the Zion Canyon Scenic Drive, passing through grassy openings and groves of Gambel oak, Fremont cottonwood, and boxelder, beneath the abrupt cliffs of Red Arch and Deertrap mountains. Views extend westward into the cliffbound amphitheater below Heaps Canyon, in which the Emerald Pools rest. Approaching the tree-shaded flat of the Grotto, the trail passes a ranger's cabin, then quickly reaches the loop road in the picnic area (0.6; 4290). Opposite the picnic area, trails lead to Emerald Pools, Angels Landing, and the West Rim Trail.

# Trip 7
## Grotto Picnic Area
## to Emerald Pools Trail

**Distance**: 1.6 miles round trip
**Low/High elevations**: 4290'/4480'
**Suited for**: Walk
**Difficulty**: Easy
**Best season**: All year
**Map/Trailhead**: 3/6
**Hazards**: Avoid when ice- or snow-covered.

**Introduction**: This trail offers an alternate, less used means of access to the Emerald Pools trail system (see *Trip 5*), and it can be combined with *Trip 6* to form a pleasant, scenic half-day loop. The trail ascends an open, rocky slope from which views of central Zion Canyon are superb.

**Description**: From the Grotto trailhead parking area (0.0; 4290), cross North Fork Virgin River via a sturdy bridge and immediately turn left, parting company with hikers beginning *Trip 8* and those finishing *Trip 20*. Our trail climbs easily up the rocky slope above the noisy river, passing beneath the broken, red east face of The Spearhead. Soon the trail rises moderately along the boulder-littered slope, passing vegetation typical of the dry lower slopes of the canyon, including singleleaf pinyon, Utah juniper, and shrub live oak. Enroute we enjoy fine views across the canyon to Observation Point, The Great White Throne, and Angels Landing.

Eventually, the trail curves west, continuing the traverse into the Emerald Pools amphitheater. Where the trail forks (0.7; 4420), we have the option of turning left and descending 70 feet in 0.1 mile to the lower Emerald Pool or staying to the right and traversing 0.1 mile to the middle pool. To complete the hike to Emerald Pools, see *Trip 5*.

# Trip 8
## Grotto Picnic Area to Scout Lookout and Angels Landing

**Distance**: 3.8 miles round trip to Scout Lookout; 4.8 miles round trip to Angels Landing

**Low/High elevations**: 4290'/5350', 5790'

**Suited for**: Dayhike

**Difficulty**: Moderate to Scout Lookout; moderately strenuous to Angels Landing.

**Best season**: March through November

**Map/Trailhead**: 3/6

**Hazards**: Steep dropoffs; avoid when snow- or ice-covered and when a thunderstorm is threatening.

**Introduction**: The highly scenic trail to Scout Lookout, built in 1926, was among the first to be constructed in what was then Zion National Monument. One section of the trail, a series of switchbacks called Walter's Wiggles, is an engineering marvel, spanning an otherwise impassable cliff to allow access to a memorable viewpoint 1000 feet above the floor of Zion Canyon.

The route to Angels Landing is rigorous and exposed, in places requiring the use of both hands and feet. Faint-hearted hikers and small children should not attempt this steep trail. It's a dangerous route even during fair weather, and only the foolhardy will attempt it when it is snow- or ice-covered, or when a thunderstorm is threatening. Both trails receive moderate use,

and backpackers hiking the West Rim Trail should remember that camping is not permitted until one is a mile beyond Scout Lookout.

**Description**: From the Grotto trailhead parking area (0.0; 4290) we immediately cross the river via a bridge and part company with hikers taking *Trip 7*. A pleasant riverside stroll ensues, leading to a moderate ascent upon brushy slopes, amid a jumble of boulders from a Cathedral Mountain rockslide.

Paved switchbacks carved into the Navajo Sandstone elevate us into the shady, narrow hanging gorge of Refrigerator Canyon. A pleasant stroll along the floor of the cliff-framed chasm, a delightful spot to rest on a hot day, leads us to more switchbacks. Ascending the 250' wall above the canyon, we negotiate Walter's Wiggles, above which we step out onto the canyon rim amid scattered ponderosa pines.

Nearby, a sign identifies Scout Lookout (1.9; 5350) which has two trailside toilets. Many dayhikers terminate their journey here, satisfied with the superb views into Zion Canyon directly below, and east into the gaping alcove at the mouth of precipitous Echo Canyon, flanked on either side by majestic, soaring cliffs.

---

## Angels Landing

The sentinel monolith of Angels Landing juts outward into Zion Canyon, forcing the south-flowing river to make a great bend around it and its lower satellite rock, The Organ. Hikers with a fear of heights should be content with the exceptional views from Scout Lookout and avoid this trail.

From the signed junction immediately below Scout Lookout the trail follows the pine-clad rim generally south, climbing over a minor rise before attacking the north ridge of the Landing. The route, cut into solid rock very steeply ascends a knife-edged sandstone rib, from which cliffs plunge 500 feet or more on either side. Sloping steps cut into the rock make footing precarious. Short segments of chain bolted intermittently to the rock offer occasional handholds, but many exposed stretches offer no such protection. The route is steepest and most exposed just below the top, but once we surmount the crest we simply follow the narrow ridge among scattered ponderosa pines to the high point on the canyon rim (0.5; 5790) where an incredible, aerial-like view unfolds.

Rock. Fine cliff-framed views extend southward down Zion Canyon, and North Fork Virgin River is not only seen but heard.

Retrace your steps *with caution* back to the Grotto trailhead.

**Sheer face of The Great White Throne**

Seemingly a stone's throw away across the gaping maw of Zion Canyon is the Park's most famous landmark, The Great White Throne. Rivaling some of the world's greatest stone monoliths in size, form, and relief, its sheer cliffs rear abruptly 2200 feet from the canyon to the broad mesa above. Also capturing our attention is the 1000' red-stained wall of Cable Mountain.

The wooden frame of the Draw Works, constructed by ingenious pioneers to transport lumber from the plateau to the canyon bottom, is visible along the edge of that mountain. The trail leading to that mountain and Observation Point can be traced along the canyon wall as it climbs above the verdant growth engulfing Weeping

# Trip 9
## Weeping Rock Trail

**Distance**: 0.5 mile round trip
**Low/High elevations**: 4350'/4450'
**Suited for**: Walk
**Difficulty**: Easy
**Best season**: All year
**Map/Trailhead**: 3/7
**Hazards**: The trail can be slippery in winter when snow- or ice-covered.

**Introduction**: This short but moderately

steep and paved nature trail (too steep for wheelchairs) offers a host of scenic delights and is a must for anyone visiting Zion. Hanging gardens, shady riparian vegetation, and a dripping alcove nurtured by water emanating from the vast Navajo Sandstone aquifer are but a few of the outstanding features along this trail.

**Description**: Immediately beyond the parking area, our trail crosses the bridge over Echo Canyon creek and then forks. Hikers bound for *Trips 10* and *13* turn right here, but our trail begins climbing a grassy slope above the creek, beneath the spreading branches of boxelder and netleaf hackberry. Interpretive signs all along the trail identify and explain trailside vegetation typical of riparian and hanging-garden habitats.

Where the trail passes a hillside seep, we notice an abundance of scouring rush and, in season, the delicate yellow blooms of cliff columbine. The west-facing slope also harbors creeping hollygrape, maidenhair fern, and false Solomon's seal—denizens of moist, shady environments.

As we approach the Weeping Rock alcove, velvet ash and Fremont cottonwood spread arching branches over the trail. Canyon wild grape drapes over many trailside trees along the way. Shrub live oak and squawbush, typically found on drier sites, are also present at this merging of habitats. Views from the trail are also exceptional. The sheer red and gray facade of Cable Mountain looms above us to the south, while the isolated red monolith of Angels Landing and other towering canyon walls rise to the plateau rim in the west.

The hike ends at an overlook platform inside the deep, wet alcove of Weeping Rock (0.25; 4450). For a span of 100 yards along the cliff face above us, a continuous rain of spring water nurtures abundant water-loving vegetation. Cementing agents binding the sand grains of the Navajo Sandstone have been dissolved by groundwater and redeposited on the wall above as tufa formations, lending the cliff a corrugated appearance.

Be sure to stay on the trail to avoid trampling the delicate vegetation, and expect to get just as wet when you exit the alcove as you did upon entering it.

Return the way you came.

# Trip 10
## Weeping Rock to Hidden Canyon, Observation Point

**Distance**: 2.2 miles round trip to Hidden Canyon; 7.4 miles round trip to Observation Point

**Low/High elevations**: 4350'/5100'; 6507'

**Suited for**: Dayhike

**Difficulty**: Moderate to Hidden Canyon; strenuous to Observation Point.

**Best season**: March through November

**Maps/Trailhead**: 3,4/7

**Hazards**: Steep dropoffs, little shade; trail should be avoided if thunderstorms threaten. Snow or ice makes travel hazardous from late fall through early spring.

**Introduction**: This exceptionally scenic trip is most often taken as two separate hikes, but they can be combined for a memorable all-day hike.

The general route of the trail dates back to the time when native Americans inhabited the region, offering them access to the plateaus for hunting and gathering forays. Later, the trail was improved upon by pioneers driving cattle to summer range. The Flanigan brothers used the route while developing their cable draw works on Cable Mountain.

Hidden Canyon is the goal of a moderate hike to a cool and shady hanging canyon, a pleasant retreat on a hot day. The more rigorous trail to Observation Point, although it ascends exceedingly steep cliffs, offers an alternative to the Angels Landing Trail for faint-hearted hikers who wish to revel in what is arguably the finest vista in the Park.

No water is available enroute, so be sure to pack an adequate supply.

**Description**: From the Weeping Rock parking area (0.0; 4350) we follow the trail as it bridges Echo Canyon creek and bear right where the Weeping Rock Trail (*Trip 9*) forks left. We quickly exit the narrow ribbon of riparian growth hugging the streambank, climbing steeply at once upon rubbly slide debris. Above this slope we reach concrete pavement and begin ascending a series of moderately steep switchbacks cut into the cliff face beneath the seemingly overhanging wall of Cable Mountain. Views enroute stretch across Zion Canyon to the sentinel rock of Angels Landing.

At the eighth switchback, the signed trail to Hidden Canyon peels off to the right (0.6; 4850), and from here we have a fine view back down to the shady alcove of Weeping Rock. Turning right onto that unpaved trail, we begin switchbacking at a moderate grade amid pines and firs, directly beneath the sheer walls of Cable Mountain. Above this climb, a traverse leads us into a shady chasm supporting Douglas-fir, white fir, ponderosa pine, and velvet ash. Soon the trail exits the chasm via a low but slippery slickrock wall, where acrophobic hikers may be compelled to turn back.

Beyond that traverse, we curve into the mouth of Hidden Canyon, hanging 700 feet above the floor of Zion Canyon. Numerous potholes have been worn into the slickrock Navajo Sandstone floor of the canyon by abrasive runoff waters. These waterpockets are like those commonly encountered in the same rock unit in Capitol Reef National Park, and they may hold water after substantial rains.

Steps cut into the rock allow passage around some of the potholes, but soon we are forced into the narrow, sandy, rocky wash as giant cliffs close in on either side. The trail apparently ends where we dip into the wash (0.5; 5180) and some hikers may be content to go this far, but to others, this mysterious chasm beckons. Douglas-fir, white fir, and ponderosa pine thrive in this relatively cool, moist microclimate within the confines of the canyon. Great sheer cliffs soar heavenward on either side of the narrow, arrow-straight canyon. A number of small alcoves and other erosional features await those who hike the dry wash upstream, for another 1/2 mile or so. Rock climbing skills are necessary to reach the head of the canyon.

---

Hikers bound for Observation Point will continue on the steadily climbing trail beyond the Hidden Canyon trail junction, switchbacking several more times before curving around a slickrock shoulder and entering Echo Canyon. The trail traverses the south canyon wall above a very narrow slot gorge, but soon declines to the floor of the dry wash, which we follow upstream over slickrock and sand.

After climbing briefly out of the wash, our trail passes above a spectacular inner gorge, 25-30 feet below. This stint shortly leads us into the slot itself, a cool hallway beneath overhanging, red-tinted cliffs. The trail ahead stays north of the wash, meandering into and out of narrow side canyons until finally reaching a signed junction (1.3; 5580), where we part from *Trip 13* hikers and bear left.

The Observation Point Trail, concrete-paved and carved into the steep north wall of Echo Canyon, wastes little time gaining elevation as it switchbacks steadily upon that 800-foot-high wall. The steeply sloping Navajo Sandstone slickrock is dotted with shrubs and trees that have gained footholds on narrow ledges wherever enough soil has collected to support them.

Compensating us for our labors are ever-expanding views into the deep canyons of Echo and Zion, above which rise steep cliffs and tree-rimmed plateaus. Don't let the scenery distract you from the narrow catwalk of the trail, clinging to the face of plunging cliffs. We'll be able to view the canyons in their full magnificence farther on from the comparative safety of Observation Point.

Above the switchbacks a moderately ascending traverse takes us into the realm of the red and tan rocks of the Temple Cap Formation. Not as massive as the Navajo Sandstone below, this formation is more broken and hence supports a thriving woodland of pinyon and juniper.

Soon the pavement ends and, having attained the brush-clad plateau, we meet the northeast-bound East Mesa Trail (1.5; 6500). Camping is allowed throughout the length of that trail (see *Trip 15*). Turning left, we proceed west across a brushy promontory of the plateau where greenleaf manzanita and Gambel oak are massed thickly along the trail.

Curving south, we soon reach the canyon rim at Observation Point (0.3; 6507), where a breathtaking panorama explodes upon the scene. Great cliffs, mostly of Navajo Sandstone, rise as much as 2500 feet from the wooded floor of Zion Canyon, streaked with red tapestries of iron minerals and dark patches of desert varnish, their faces fluted and etched by ages of falling rock and abrasive waters. These cliffs march southward in a parade of rugged crags to the canyon's gaping mouth, framing the distant Vermilion Cliffs.

Outstanding landmarks dominating our view include the sentinel tower of Angels Landing and its eastern extension, the Organ, which together divert North Fork Virgin River. To the south are the Yosemite-like walls abutting Cable Mountain and The Great White Throne.

The alignment pattern of tributary canyons becomes apparent from our vantage point. Most of these canyons, of which Hidden Canyon is a prominent example, have been eroded along joints, or fractures, in the Navajo Sandstone, and trend northwest.

Also obvious are the effects of downcutting in the Navajo. We can see by looking into the narrow depths of Hidden Canyon that downcutting proceeds at a much faster rate in this rock than does widening. These narrow depths are the result of millions of years of abrasive runoff waters cutting like a bandsaw deep into that rock layer.

In addition to the Navajo, three other sedimentary layers of rock are visible, beginning atop the plateaus where the reddish Temple Cap Formation forms small platforms and buttes. Below the tall Navajo cliffs are narrow red ledges of the Kayenta Formation, and finally the Springdale Sandstone ledge of the Moenave Formation crops out far below on the flanks of the lower canyon.

A green ribbon of trees accompanies the rushing waters of North Fork Virgin River all along the canyon floor. Following its course downstream, our gaze stretches past Zion Lodge to the Park Visitor Center. The only other evidence of human influence upon the landscape is the red pavement of the Scenic Drive. Its traffic is, unfortunately, audible from our otherwise peaceful vantage point.

Return the way you came.

# Trip 11
## Gateway to the Narrows Trail, Orderville Canyon

**Distance**: 2.0 miles round trip to the trail's end; 6.4 miles round trip to Orderville Canyon

**Low/High elevations**: 4418'/4490'; 4610'

**Suited for**: Walk to trail's end; dayhike to Orderville Canyon.

**Difficulty**: Easy to end of trail; moderate to mouth of Orderville Canyon

**Best season**: Trail open all year, but may be snow-covered at times during winter. River hiking is best from May through September.

**Map/Trailhead**: 3/8

**Hazards**: Negligible along trail; deep wading beyond trail's end over a slippery river bottom, and the possibility of flash floods and cold water. Check NARROW CANYON DANGER LEVEL sign at the trailhead or the Park Visitor Center, updated daily to reflect changing river conditions.

**Introduction**: The Gateway to the Narrows Trail is Zion's most heavily used trail, and with good reason. Seeping alcoves, luxurious hanging gardens, shady riparian woodlands, a nearly level trail (paved for wheelchair access), and an ever-narrowing and ever-deepening canyon draw visitors from the world over to hike beyond the trail's end and into The Narrows, one of the classic canyon treks on the Colorado Plateau.

Slicing into the heart of the Markagunt Plateau, North Fork Virgin River has carved a canyon 1000-2000 feet deep, and ranging in width from 200 yards at the Temple of Sinawava to barely 20 feet above Orderville Canyon.

To negotiate any part of The Narrows beyond the trail, hikers must be well prepared, and must not underestimate the hazards of wading through a knee-deep river in a narrow flash-flood-prone canyon (see *Trip 15* for more information).

Few trips in Zion are more rewarding than wading the Virgin River through The Narrows on a hot, clear summer day. But forays into the canyon from the Temple of Sinawava are for day hiking only. Hikers planning on a backpack through the length of the canyon must begin at Chamberlain's Ranch, hiking downstream.

Never hike into The Narrows alone, and be sure to have a sturdy staff for balance and lightweight, rubber-soled shoes for traction on the slippery river bottom. Hikers can obtain a pamphlet at the Park Visitor Center explaining the hazards and precautions one should take before entering the canyon.

**Description**: Since this trail is the Park's most popular, expect plenty of company as you stroll up the trail beyond the parking area (0.0; 4418), flanked by the redrock tower of the Temple of Sinawava on one side and the unimposing red spire of The Pulpit on the other. The trail leads upstream, east of the river, in the shadow of tall, broken cliffs. White fir and Douglas-fir stand tall on the canyon walls above us, while the canyon floor is well-shaded by velvet ash and boxelder. Along the way we'll pass interpretive signs explaining canyon widening, hanging gardens (where the Zion Rock Snail, a species endemic to The Narrows, makes its home), a rockslide, and a perpetually wet desert swamp.

Many visitors enjoy picnicking along the rushing river, and some of them may wish to follow a use trail that follows left only 100 yards from the trailhead, quickly leading to the river's edge.

The trail ends where the canyon bends northeast (1.0; 4490), and hikers unprepared for river hiking are advised to go no farther. But those who are prepared simply plunge into the river, either crossing to the opposite bank or following its waters upstream. The river is usually only knee-deep, but depending on recent rains or snowmelt runoff, it can be much deeper, and swift. Even during low water, expect some holes to be waist-deep or even deeper. Use your staff to probe deep holes as you proceed.

The canyon becomes increasingly narrow, and even in summer, little sunlight penetrates into this narrow corridor. Boxelder grows on riverside benches in tandem with white fir, a tree typically found on the plateaus 3000 feet above. The river meanders below Orderville Canyon, and along this stretch we can crisscross it between sandy benches, following short trails between crossings.

Mystery Falls, a 100' cascade backdropped by rugged Mountain of Mystery, is the first of many outstanding features we encounter along the way. As we proceed, we'll pass numerous springs and seeps nurturing verdant hanging gardens that decorate fluted canyon walls that are stained with streaks of red and dark patches of desert varnish.

As we proceed, we should choose our crossings carefully, as the riverbed is strewn with slippery, moss-covered rocks. Black basalt rocks and boulders, eroded from the plateaus far above, are abundant and particularly slick. Approaching Orderville Canyon we are forced into the river more frequently, as the benches are fewer and widely spaced. Orderville Canyon contributes its small stream to the river (2.2; 4620) where it exits a narrow cleft on our right (east).

Strong dayhikers can continue up-canyon about as far as Big Springs (2.1 miles ahead) but many dayhikers go no farther than Orderville Canyon. That canyon is a challenging hike in its own right, but small waterfalls and other obstacles make much of the route passable only to the experienced canyoneer.

On the return trip, wade the river with care.

# Trip 12
## Canyon Overlook Trail

**Distance**: 1.0 mile round trip
**Low/High elevations**: 5130'/5240'
**Suited for**: Walk
**Difficulty**: Easy
**Best season**: All year, but the trail should be avoided when ice- or snow-covered, or if thunderstorms threaten.
**Map/Trailhead**: 2/9
**Hazards**: Steep dropoffs

**Introduction**: This short, self-guided nature trail leads across slickrock to a grand vista point high above Pine Creek Canyon. Views into lower Zion Canyon, 1000 feet below, include some of the most striking landmarks in the Park. The hike should appeal to hikers of varied abilities, and is an especially fine choice for a short stroll if one has limited time or energy.

An interpretive leaflet available at the trailhead or the Visitor Center explains the natural history of the area, and should help hikers to gain knowledge and better appreciate what they encounter along the trail.

Ranger-led walks are frequently conducted along this trail; check the schedule of interpretive activities at the Visitor Center.

**Description**: From the parking area at the east portal of the Zion-Mt. Carmel Tunnel, carefully cross the highway to the beginning of the trail (0.0; 5130), indicated by a small sign.

A series of steps soon leads to a traverse high above the narrow cleft of Pine Creek Canyon. Despite the presence of handrails along exposed stretches, hikers should nonetheless exercise caution throughout the trail's length.

A variety of seasonal wildflowers adorn the Navajo Sandstone slickrock among such trailside shrubs as squawbush, buffaloberry, singleleaf ash, and shrub live oak, and an occasional Utah juniper.

Where we curve into a prominent but narrow side canyon, maidenhair fern appears in the moist and sheltered habitat beneath an overhanging slab. Other denizens of these rocky environs include singleleaf pinyon, littleleaf mountain mahogany (found exclusively on and near slickrock), and Utah serviceberry. More maidenhair fern is encountered ahead, growing along a seepline that dampens the wall of a trailside alcove.

Upon exiting the side canyon, we continue to follow the seepline, and soon pass a lone Fremont cottonwood, further evidence of ample moisture within the sandstone. The slickrock trail ahead winds among tilted sandstone slabs, soon reaching a fenced overlook (0.5; 5255) perched on the rim above Pine Creek Canyon. The Great Arch, that deep, arch-shaped alcove seen from the highway below, invisible from our vantage, lies just below the brink of the cliff. Thousand-foot slopes plunging from Bridge Mountain and East Temple frame a stirring view of the Towers of the Virgin, a host of rugged crags rising nearly 4000 feet above the canyon floor. A plaque at the overlook identifies many of the prominent landmarks that meet our gaze.

One of the five galleries in the Zion-Mt. Carmel Tunnel can be seen on the cliff below. During the three years of construction in the late 1920s, narrow gauge rail cars hauled waste rock from the tunnel to the galleries, from where it was dumped over the cliff into Pine Creek Canyon.

Above us, conspicuous cross-bedding on the face of the Navajo Sandstone, formed as ancient winds swept across a vast sand desert, offer evidence that the world has not always been the same as it is today.

Return the way you came.

# Trip 13
## East Rim Trail to Weeping Rock via Stave Spring and Echo Canyon

**Distance**: 10.7-mile shuttle trip, not including sidetrips to Deertrap and Cable mountains

**Low/High elevations**: 4350'/6730'

**Suited for**: Dayhike or backpack

**Difficulty**: Moderate as a dayhike or overnighter.

**Best season**: May through October

**Maps/Trailhead**: 4,2,3/10

**Hazards**: Stave Spring is the only water source enroute.

**Introduction**: Most hikers take this trip as an overnighter to the Stave Spring environs, then hike the spur trails to Cable and/or Deertrap mountain before backtracking to the East Entrance trailhead. Through hikes to Weeping Rock require a car shuttle of about 14.4 miles. Hiking up Echo Canyon from Weeping Rock to Stave Spring—the only reliable water source— is strenuous, regardless of the load you carry.

Vegetation ranges from pinyon-juniper woodlands to stands of oak and pine, and views from the trail are far-ranging and panoramic.

Much of the ponderosa-pine forest atop the plateau was cut around the turn of the century.

The sawmill that operated here is only a memory, but the draw works still standing on the rim of Cable Mountain offer mute evidence of pioneer ingenuity.

**Description**: The trail begins beyond the locked gate above the trailhead (0.0; 5740) and heads north past a trail register and a mileage sign. We follow a devious northward course through the broad upper reaches of Clear Creek amid an open woodland of pinyon, juniper, and Gambel oak, their sizes dwarfed by a scattering of ponderosa pines.

The White Cliffs, composed of Navajo Sandstone, rise above us to the north, their flanks stained orange-red in places due to the leaching of hematite from the red shales of the overlying Temple Cap Formation. Narrowleaf yucca, big sagebrush, rabbitbrush, prickly pear, and Utah serviceberry are common trailside shrubs, among which many seasonal wildflowers enliven the landscape.

The trail is actually an old road built to access timber atop the East Rim Plateau, and as we ascend Clear Creek canyon over weathered Navajo Sandstone, the tread is quite sandy.

Streams bearing red mud invaded the sandy Navajo Sandstone landscape during the early Jurassic Period, and these waters caused the yet uncemented sands to slump. Now cemented into stone, these slump structures are evident immediately below the Temple Cap in the upper several feet of the Navajo Sandstone.

The Temple Cap sandstones herald our climb out of Cave Canyon, where, upon reaching a switchback, we promptly double back on a higher contour. A reliable spring issues from the canyon 0.1 mile above where we leave its floor.

A mostly gentle climb ensues on sun-drenched slopes hosting a woodland of scrubby pinyons and junipers, but also harboring shrubs such as cliffrose, greenleaf manzanita, Utah serviceberry, and scattered Gambel oak. This 3/4-mile stretch of trail can become uncomfortably hot during summer. Next, we curve northwest around the shoulder of a ridge, then traverse above the White Cliffs, which embrace the abyss of lower Jolley Gulch. Enroute we capture fine views across the wooded reaches of Clear Creek's valley to aptly named Checkerboard Mesa and a host of other forest-crowned tablelands.

After crossing the usually dry wash of Jolley Gulch (2.7; 6080) at the very brink of a dry waterfall, we briefly enjoy cliff-framed views stretching southward before resuming our traverse. Soon we curve into a minor, west-trending gulch, switchback, and shortly thereafter climb northwest onto the gentle slopes of the plateau, presently blanketed by the gray limestone of the Carmel Formation, which forms a gently rolling surface over much of the Markagunt Plateau in Zion.

The limestone tread provides more stable footing as we traverse west beneath the shade of

**The wooded cliffs of Echo Canyon frame the West Rim**

relatively tall ponderosa pines and into a shallow draw. Curving northwest and climbing moderately above the draw, we regain the gentle, well-drained surface of the plateau, clothed not only by ponderosa pines, but by pinyon and juniper as well.

A protracted nearly level stretch of trail ensues across the plateau, where vignettes of the Pink Cliffs and of the vast forests of the Markagunt Plateau help pass the time. Much of the Carmel Formation is masked by vegetation, but gray cobbles in the roadbed attest to its presence.

When we top out on a broad, oak-clad ridge (2.5; 6730), much of the East Rim Plateau stretches out before us far to the north and northwest. Presently we descend slopes clad in pinyon, juniper, Gambel oak, and ponderosa pine, and before long encounter a short spur trail (0.5; 6500) forking left into the draw harboring Stave Spring. A trickle of water issuing from the pipe is our only reliable water source. In 1901, 25,000 barrel staves were probably cut and split nearby. They made up the first load of ponderosa-pine lumber the brothers Flanigan sent down the cable works, primarily to convince skeptics of the feasibility of cabling lumber from the rim to the canyon below.

Campsites near the spring are showing signs of overuse, so backpackers should tank up here and choose one of many potential campsites well away from the spring.

The trail continues descending below the spring, soon passing a reddish outcrop indicating our passage back into the realm of the Temple Cap Formation. Shortly thereafter we meet a signed junction (0.1; 6445) where we ponder our hiking options. The left fork is a spur leading to trails that end at Cable and Deertrap mountains. Some hikers may elect to stay overnight in the area, hiking to either mountain the next day before backtracking to the trailhead. Others may wish to tank up on water at the spring, then spend the night atop the plateau enroute to the two mountains. Still others may wish to hike on through to Echo Canyon and camp among the pines, slickrock, and towering canyon walls of that drainage.

# Deertrap and Cable Mountains

**Distance**: 3.7 miles to Deertrap Mountain; 3.1 miles to Cable Mountain
**Low/High elevations**: 6445'/6910' for Deertrap Mountain; 6445'/6900' for Cable Mountain

Turning left at Stave Spring junction ( 0.0; 6445) onto the signed Deertrap Mountain Trail, we ascend a draw southward, initially across a sagebrush-choked flat. Soon the trail leaves the draw, climbing moderately southwest alternately through thickets of Gambel oak and grassy, wildflower-speckled openings. On the plateau, the grade eases as we stroll west to a signed junction (1.2; 6860) with the trail to Cable Mountain, forking right, and the Deertrap Mountain Trail, continuing ahead. Numerous potential campsites can be found enroute to either mountain, but backpackers must have an adequate water supply.

Those bound for Deertrap Mountain will continue southwest from the junction and descend easily amid oak groves and grassy clearings into the densely wooded valley above and south of Hidden Canyon. Our trail traverses tan Temple Cap Formation rocks as we enter a draw, its gentle contours contrasting with the shadowy, cliffbound nadir below. We cross the dry course of the draw about 200 yards upstream from an ephemeral spring, then climb steeply west on Temple Cap rocks to a broad ridge crowned with Carmel limestone. From here we enjoy fine views stretching south-southeast over a landscape of domes and cliffs embracing the valley of Clear Creek.

Now we follow the descending trail southwest to the head of The Grotto's abysmal canyon, then almost top another limestone-capped knoll (6921'). Deertrap Mountain appears to be little more than a broad, wooded bench slightly below us, and with the inspiring vistas we presently enjoy, some hikers may decide to go no farther. But hikers who wish to gaze over a 2500' precipice into the gaping maw of Zion Canyon will follow the trail over the Carmel-capped knoll, switchbacking down over red Temple Cap rocks, and finally strolling across the rolling bench of Deertrap Mountain to the brink (2.5; 6740) of the great cliffs plunging into the canyon below.

Two of Zion's most rugged hanging canyons, knifed deep into the plateau, can be seen in full profile opposite our viewpoint—Heaps Canyon to the northwest, above the Emerald Pools amphitheater, and Birch Creek due west, above the Court of the Patriarchs amphitheater to the northwest. Farther down-canyon, The Streaked Wall foregrounds one of the Park's pre-eminent landforms, West Temple.

With our eyes we can trace the Sand Bench Trail far below as it climbs to the wooded, slide-formed bench below a broad sweep of sheer, colorful cliffs.

Hikers can easily visualize the once-uninterrupted surface of the Markagunt Plateau, as the rim of the plateau opposite looks essentially the same as where we now stand, save for a greater abundance of tall pines.

To the south and southwest tower the bulky crags of Mountain of the Sun and Twin Brothers and the square-edged platform of mighty East Temple. Perched on ledges and shady niches below them are hanging forests of ponderosa pine and Douglas-fir.

The green lawns and historic buildings of Zion Lodge, seeming to lie at our feet 2500 feet below, contrast its manicured grounds with the raw and magnificent workings of nature that dominate our senses.

We now have the choice of backtracking to the Cable Mountain Trail, following a faint trail south along the rim for more inspiring vistas, or following a well-worn path north along the rim for 1/2 mile. That path reveals a broader view of Zion Canyon, from Springdale, near the canyon's mouth, to Angels Landing in its upper reaches. The viewpoint at the end of the trail on a shoulder of the Deertrap Mountain ridge offers a head-on view of monolithic Great White Throne, its nearly level, brushy crown punctuated by a host of Navajo Sandstone hoodoos.

---

The Cable Mountain Trail, following the course of an old wagon road that led from the plateau-top sawmill to the Draw Works, ascends

gradually northwest from the Deertrap Mountain Trail junction for a little while among ponderosa pine and Gambel oak, then begins a steady descent for the remaining distance to the rim.

Enroute, scattered stumps attest to the extensive forest that thrived here prior to 1904, when timber harvesting began in earnest. Today, only scattered ponderosa pines grow on this part of the plateau, and most of them have grown up since the big trees were cut. Timber cutting disturbed the landscape and created sunny openings, and now the plateau is infested with greenleaf manzanita, alderleaf mountain mahogany, pinyon, juniper, and Gambel oak.

Upon entering a pinyon-juniper woodland growing on a northwest-facing slope, we negotiate a single switchback, from where we enjoy splendid vistas of hoodoo-capped Great White Throne and the Draw Works on the rim of Cable Mountain, with the immense cliffs of Zion Canyon and the forested platforms above them forming the backdrop.

Below the switchback we stroll northwest over brush-choked slopes, concluding the hike at the headframe of the Draw Works (1.9; 6496). While absorbing the sublime vistas of the Big Bend of Zion Canyon, Angels Landing, Echo Canyon, towering cliffs, and seemingly endless plateaus thick with woodlands of pine and oak from our perch atop 1200' cliffs, we can reflect on the ingenious operation of transporting much-needed lumber from the forest-rich plateau to the timberless land below.

The tenacious spirit of early Mormon settlers and the painstaking trial-and-error efforts of David Flanigan led to the realization of the prophecy of Brigham Young that "like a hawk flies," a way would be discovered to transport lumber from the plateau down the great cliffs into Zion Canyon.

Trees felled and milled on the East Rim Plateau helped to build structures in communities along the Virgin River from Springdale to St. George. The original Zion Lodge was built with ponderosa-pine lumber in the 1920s.

The headframe of the Draw Works that remains today, stabilized with cables and on the National Register of Historic Places, is the third such structure, the two before it having been consumed by fire. Do not damage or deface this historic structure in any way, and exercise caution when walking near the cliff edge.

While the time required to transport a load of lumber to the canyon bottom was only 2 1/2 minutes, those planning to hike there will be on the trail for another three hours.

---

Upon returning to the trail junction below Stave Spring, hikers continuing to Weeping Rock will turn left and descend easily across a sagebrush-infested flat. A spur trail, actually an old road closed to vehicles, forks right (0.3; 6390), leading 0.5 mile to an obscure trailhead at the Park's eastern boundary (see *Trip 14*).

Our route proceeds across a gently sloping basin, rimmed by low mesas clad in pinyon and juniper. As the draw steepens and curves northwest, we begin traversing a narrow wooded bench above a precipitous gorge and leaving any potential campsites behind until Echo Canyon, more than a mile ahead.

Pinyon-juniper woodlands dominate alongside the trail, but the shady cliffs above the canyon below us harbor hanging forests of ponderosa pine and Douglas-fir. Views extend down the cleft of Echo Canyon, past the Observation Point Trail to the cliffs abutting the west rim beyond.

The traverse suddenly terminates high above the floor of Echo Canyon (0.8; 6430), a slickrock-embraced chasm dotted with tall ponderosa pines and rimmed by wooded mesas. Now the rocky trail plunges steeply down the upper wall of a side canyon, amid a greater diversity of trees and shrubs, including Douglas-fir, ponderosa pine, pinyon, juniper, cliffrose, greenleaf manzanita, and Utah serviceberry. Soon the trail leads us down a steep, rocky rib above an Echo Canyon tributary thick with pines and Douglas-firs. In autumn Gambel oaks and bigtooth maples splash their red and gold foliage across the landscape, contrasting with the white cliffs above and the somber green conifer forest.

After we enjoy down-canyon views, the descent briefly ends where we cross Echo Canyon's dry wash (0.9; 5610), along which the descent continues. Numerous potential campsites can be found not only up-canyon but atop the numerous rocky, pine-studded knolls that rise north of the wash. The canyon is waterless, but the overwhelming quiet, sheer, crenulated cliffs, the green plateau above us, and tall pines combine to make the area sublimely attractive.

The trail ahead alternates between rock and sand, and although it descends, progress is fairly slow. After jogging into three north-trending draws, our rough, undulating trail finally crosses slickrock where the route is indicated by cairns. Soon after sighting the Draw Works atop Cable Mountain's mineral-streaked walls, we join the trail (1.0; 5580) climbing toward Observation Point and enter the front-country zone, which is closed to camping.

To complete the trek, follow the first part of *Trip 10* in reverse, hiking the final 1.9 miles to the Weeping Rock parking area.

# Trip 14
## East Boundary to Echo Canyon Trail

**Distance**: 0.5 mile one way to Echo Canyon Trail

**Low/High elevations**: 6390'/6450'

**Suited for**: Dayhike when combined with East Rim trails (see *Trip 13*)

**Difficulty**: Easy

**Best season**: May through October

**Map/Trailhead**: 4/11

**Hazards**: Negligible

**Introduction**: This seldom-trod spur trail offers quick access to the Stave Spring environs, allowing jaunts to Cable and Deertrap mountains to be completed in less than a day. Although the drive to the trailhead can be confusing, the easy access to the backcountry of Zion more than compensates for the extra time required behind the wheel.

**Description**: Beginning at a gate on the Park's eastern boundary (0.0; 6450), we follow a long-closed road gently downhill under a canopy of ponderosa pine. Crossing to the south side of the draw, we descend almost imperceptibly among scattered Gambel oaks, soon passing an outcrop of the Temple Cap Formation on the right.

Shortly thereafter we break into the open, cross a sagebrush-clad flat, and gently descend to meet the Echo Canyon Trail (0.5; 6390), *Trip 13*.

From here it will take most hikers little more than two hours to reach either Cable or Deertrap mountains. Stave Spring, a modest but reliable source of water, dampens the draw only 0.4 mile up the trail to the south.

# Trip 15
## East Mesa Trail to Observation Point Trail

**Distance**: 3.2 miles one way to Observation Point Trail
**Low/High elevations**: 6500'/6815'
**Suited for**: Dayhike or backpack
**Difficulty**: Easy
**Best season**: May through October
**Maps/Trailhead**: 4,3/12
**Hazards:** No water; trail should be avoided if thunderstorms threaten.

**Introduction**: Beginning at a remote trailhead on the eastern fringes of the Park, the seldom-used East Mesa Trail follows a broad promontory that juts westward from the rolling shoulders of the Markagunt Plateau toward the rim of Zion Canyon.

Excepting the curious, roughly westward alignment of Echo and Orderville canyons, between which the East Mesa is wedged, all the canyons viewed from this trail follow the jointed grain of the landscape in a north-northwest direction. Woodlands of Gambel oak, juniper, pinyon, and ponderosa pine are thickly massed atop the mesa, and offer ample shelter for the many potential campsites passed along the way. Most hikers however, use this trail for the quick and easy access it provides to the overlook at Observation Point (see *Trip 10*).

**Description**: The East Mesa Trail, actually the faded remains of a long-closed jeep road, begins at a hiker's gate (0.0; 6520) allowing passage through a fenceline along the Park's eastern boundary.

Designed to keep grazing cattle out of the Park, fences have been erected along much of the perimeter of Zion. Nevertheless, the presence of cattle and sheep beyond Park boundaries at the headwaters of La Verkin Creek and North Fork Virgin River have fouled those backcountry water sources, necessitating purification.

Beginning in a woodland of pinyon and juniper, we find taller ponderosa pines mixing into the forest as we progress westward, ascending gently along the plateau. Views enroute stretch far to the north and northwest, where the two-tiered surface of the Markagunt Plateau becomes apparent. Much of the extensive southern tier is exposed to our gaze. This is the plateau in which North Fork Virgin River has cut Zion Canyon. The upper tier, considerably higher in elevation and capped by geologically recent lava flows, is bounded by the Pink Cliffs of the Wasatch Formation, relatively soft Eocene lakebed sediments that compose the cliffs of Cedar Breaks National Monument and those of Bryce Canyon National Park.

Enroute, we can briefly detour north from the trail at points 1.25 and 2.2 miles from the trailhead, to the rim, where exceptional views unfold, overlooking Orderville and Mystery canyons, drainages that are densely forested with pine, white fir, and Douglas-fir, the trend of their courses controlled by jointing in the Navajo Sandstone.

Eventually the trail turns southwest, following the crest of the mesa. Then, just above the south arm of Mystery Canyon, it gently ascends to the summit of our hike (2.3; 6815). Shortly we arc westward over the crunchy Carmel limestone, then begin a steady descent south into a pinyon, juniper, and oak woodland. Approaching the foot of the descent, we circumnavigate the head of a plunging Zion Canyon tributary, and conclude the hike on a shadier slope among ponderosa pines, Douglas-firs, and thickets of Gambel oak, greenleaf manzanita, and Utah serviceberry.

At the junction (0.9; 6500) we have the choice of either backtracking to the trailhead, turning right to Observation Point (0.3 mile), or going left and descending to Weeping Rock trailhead (see *Trip 10*).

# Trip 16
## The Narrows—Chamberlain's Ranch to Temple of Sinawava

**Distance**: 17.5 miles, shuttle trip
**Low/High elevations**: 4418'/5830'
**Suited for**: Backpack
**Difficulty**: Strenuous
**Best season**: Clear days in summer
**Maps/Trailheads**: 5,6,3/13,8
**Hazards**: Wading a river through a deep and narrow slickrock canyon (see Introduction for details).

**Introduction**: The famous Narrows of Zion Canyon is one of the classic canyon hiking trips on the Colorado Plateau. This hike is perhaps the most exciting and challenging trip in all of Utah's national parks. Throughout most of the canyon's 17-mile length, much of your time will be spent wading through knee-deep waters. Depending on water levels, some swimming may be required through deeper holes.

The optimum season for the trip is from early to midsummer. During that time, the river has receded from snowmelt runoff and the probability of thunderstorms is usually low. Temperatures are typically hot by mid-June, and a summer hike through the shady depths of the canyon is refreshing and enjoyable. From about mid-July through mid-September, Utah experiences its monsoon season, when thunderstorms can occur frequently, sometimes daily. These heavy rains increase the probability of rising water levels and flash flooding. The canyon can be hiked during this season, but hikers must be aware of the Danger Level, posted at the Visitor Center and at the Temple of Sinawava trailhead each day. The canyon may be closed to hiking if storms are possible in the North Fork Virgin River watershed.

Autumn brings cooler weather and shorter days, with cold water increasing the chances of hypothermia. At that time of year, hikers must proceed steadily through the canyon, beginning at dawn in order to complete the hike before dark.

Backcountry permits must be obtained for overnight hikes and dayhikes through the length of the canyon. Overnight hikers must begin at Chamberlain's Ranch, hiking downstream. Permits are not required for dayhikes in part of the canyon. Permits will be issued only when weather forecasts are favorable, and no more than 24 hours in advance. Hikers who choose to spend more than one night in the Narrows must bear in mind that weather forecasts are not reliable for more than 24 hours. Conditions can change rapidly, and there are risks that must be considered.

General rules for safety and common sense for canyon hiking are especially important for a backpack in The Narrows, considering the river has such a large watershed. As one hikes through the canyon, observe the high-water mark, usually a dark line on the canyon walls, below which the sandstone is polished smooth and shiny.

*Always be aware of possible escape routes to higher ground*. Changes in the water, from clear to turbid, an increase in the current and in water level, and in the worst case, the roar of rushing waters upstream, are indicators of a flash flood. Seek high ground immediately; you cannot outrun floodwaters. The river should recede within 24 hours after heavy rains have stopped.

Be sure to wear good, rubber-soled boots that provide ankle support and remain lightweight when wet, and a sturdy walking stick to aid balance and probe deep holes. Some hikers use two ski poles instead of a walking stick. When hiking in cold temperatures, consider wearing polypropylene thermal long underwear, since it will keep you warm even when wet. Shorts are best for wading the river, since bare legs offer less friction.

All hikers should carry a pack with extra food and clothing in waterproof containers or plastic bags. Backpackers should likewise protect their additional gear, which should include shoes for wear around camp.

Avoid drinking river water if possible, but if you must, purify it, as the river drains the summer range of cattle and sheep. Instead, draw your water from any of the numerous springs enroute. Some hikers may prefer to carry all their water.

Backpackers may think that hiking downstream sounds easy, but the current will tend to pull your feet out from under you. Don't try to fight the current as you move in the river. When heading downstream, it is best to walk across the river at an angle. Rough water and deep holes can usually be avoided; plan ahead and proceed with caution. Take this hike only if you are in good physical condition and have adequate cross-country experience. A person must be at least 12 years of age and 56 inches or taller to hike in The Narrows.

A car shuttle of about 34.3 miles is required and 10-12 hours of hiking are necessary to complete the trip. When you obtain your backcountry permit at the Zion Canyon Visitor Center, you will be informed about weather forecasts and river conditions, and you will be given a pamphlet full of detailed information about the hazards you will encounter, and the precautions to take on a hike through The Narrows.

**Description**: Our trek gets underway where the jeep road fords North Fork Virgin River (0.0; 5830). Unless the river is low, we'll get our feet wet at once. Beyond the crossing, we follow the road westward, heading downstream on the south floodplain and skirting sloping meadows—part of Chamberlain's Ranch—where cattle and horses graze in summer. The surroundings give little intimation of the deep and narrow cleft that lies ahead. Rolling ridges, clad in pinyon, juniper, oak, and various shrubs, rise north and south of the canyon. In autumn these hills are brilliantly colored with the golds of oaks and the reds of squawbush.

After an easy mile, a right-branching road leading down to a stockpond should be avoided. Shortly we pass through a gate and close it behind us. Passing the old Bulloch Cabin (2.4; 5620), the road soon drops to the banks of the small river, little more than a mountain stream here in its upper reaches. Here (0.5; 5540) we must ford the river or boulder hop to the north bank, continuing down the road.

In the next half mile, we follow the road as it crosses the river several more times. Low Navajo Sandstone cliffs begin to encroach upon the canyon, and ponderosa pines begin to supplant the woodlands that dominate upstream. The road eventually fades, and a trail continues to take us from one side of the river to the other. Camping is allowed in this part of the canyon downstream to Big Springs.

As the cliffs rise higher and the canyon becomes increasingly narrow, the sheltered microclimate thus created supports Douglas-fir, white fir, and bigtooth maple.

Hikers should begin to take notice of the high-water mark. Sticks and branches on ledges above the canyon, wrapped around riverside trees, or high on benches are evidence of past flash floods. Flood waters can reach 8 feet or more above the normal level of the river here in the canyon's upper reaches, and in The Narrows proper below Big Springs, the river may rise as much as 20 feet.

In certain moist, shady locales, the thick growth of maple and fir may remind hikers more of the Pacific Northwest than of the stereotypical parched desert lands of Utah.

Forming the understory in the shady forest are plants one might also associate with a northwest forest, such as red-osier dogwood, pachystima (mountain-lover), dogbane, creeping hollygrape, and false Solomon's seal.

After 6 miles and about 3 1/2 hours of hiking, we encounter the first truly narrow section of the canyon, where the river briefly enters Park lands. Here canyon walls soar 500 feet above us. By this time, we have been wading in the river for some time, and the wade will continue for much of the remainder of the trip. Ahead the canyon becomes even more deeply entrenched between lofty cliffs, and after 7 miles we encounter a 12' waterfall plunging over a resistant sandstone ledge. A short trail through a narrow gap to the left of the falls allows us to proceed.

We reach the confluence with Deep Creek (6.5; 4940) after about five hours. The river is noticeably larger downstream, as Deep Creek increases its volume by two thirds, and its waters are colder and less turbid than the North Fork's.

Thus far, the gradient of the river has averaged 130 feet per mile, but downstream from Deep Creek the gradient slackens to an average of 71 feet per mile. Our progress is slower now in the larger stream, but the slower pace allows us to enjoy the numerous springs and seeps farther downstream. Many of them support hanging gardens, where we may observe a Calliope hummingbird feeding on the nectar of columbines or, where insects gather near seeps, we may glimpse a Say's phoebe feeding upon them.

By noticing the side canyons that join the river, we can gauge our downstream progress. Numerous campsites are perched on benches above the river between Deep Creek and Big Springs. The Narrows is the only backcountry area in Zion where campfires are allowed, so hikers can warm up and dry their clothes before the second day of the trek.

Narrow Kolob Creek canyon enters from the northwest after 10.3 miles and nearly 6 hours from the trailhead. Its waters are impounded in Kolob Reservoir high atop the plateau, and hence its course may be dry during the summer. About 0.5 mile below Kolob Creek is one of the gems of The Narrows. The Grotto, a deep, cave-like alcove where verdant growth is nurtured by constantly dripping water, has been used as a sheltered campsite. The springs across the river offer good water.

Small Goose Creek enters from the northwest at 11.5 miles, about 30 minutes beyond The Grotto. If time allows, Goose Creek, as well as Kolob and Deep creeks, make worthwhile sidetrips. Less than one hour below Goose Creek is gushing Big Springs, 12.2 miles from Chamberlain's Ranch. The most voluminous springs in the canyon, Big Springs' waters maintain a year-round temperature of 50°, spouting out of the canyon wall and pouring over boulders thick with mosses and adorned with maidenhair fern, cardinal flower, monkey flower, and columbine. Big Springs is your last chance for camping in The Narrows.

The following 2.1 miles to the mouth of Orderville Canyon lie in eternal shadow. The canyon is an empty hallway, save for the brawling river, hemmed in by water-worn cliffs that tower nearly 2000 feet overhead. This stretch has the deepest pools, and hikers should proceed with caution. This segment is also the narrowest, with no place to escape from floodwaters, and at times we are funnelled between walls barely 20 feet apart. Here the canyon deviates little from a straight line, and between cliffs that seem to overhang the river only a narrow ribbon of sky

can be seen. Try to find sandbars or shallows to avoid the deeper holes.

At 14.3 miles, after hiking for nearly 3 hours from Big Springs, we encounter Orderville Canyon. This is the first major canyon that enters on the east. From here downstream we join an increasing number of dayhikers, and follow the directions of *Trip 11* in reverse, criss-crossing the river for 2.2 miles to the Gateway to the Narrows Trail, which we follow for the final mile to Temple of Sinawava trailhead.

# Trip 17
## Kolob Terrace Road to the Subway

**Distance**: 7.8 miles round trip
**Low/High elevations**: 4630'/5360'
**Suited for**: Dayhike
**Difficulty**: Moderate
**Best season**: April through November
**Map/Trailhead**: 7/14
**Hazards**: Poor trail and cross-country scrambling, slippery slickrock, and much boulder hopping.

**Introduction**: This day-long trip, much of it without the benefit of a trail, is recommended for experienced hikers only. The route has received increased use in recent years, but the canyon remains wild and relatively undisturbed. Most hikers spend only a day in the canyon, but there are a few poor campsites, and the Left Fork North Creek runs the year around.

Prominent features on the hike include young lava flows contrasting with ancient sedimentary rocks, well-preserved fossil dinosaur tracks, and The Subway, a unique slot canyon.

Summer is a hot time to take this hike, though the shady confines of The Subway offer a modicum of relief on a hot day. Spring and fall are best for this trip.

**Description**: The beginning of the well-worn path (0.0; 5125) is indicated by an ENTERING ZION BACKCOUNTRY sign, beyond which we proceed generally east across the wooded, basalt-capped upland, soon crossing two dry forks of Grapevine Wash. The bench is thickly cloaked in a woodland of juniper and singleleaf pinyon, with an understory of shrub live oak, Utah serviceberry, cliffrose, yucca, and greenleaf manzanita.

Other paths join our route as we proceed, all of them leading to the rim ahead. Upon reaching the canyon rim (0.6; 5050) the basalt tread is replaced by red Kayenta Formation rocks, although they are much obscured by talus blocks fallen from the tall Navajo Sandstone cliffs above us to the north. Hiking with care, we descend the steep talus slope toward the canyon bottom. Numerous use trails, some cairned by past hikers, thread their way down the steep, slippery slope. Choose the path you are most comfortable with.

After 420 feet of descent, we reach the boulder-strewn banks of perennial Left Fork North Creek (0.2; 4630). Above us to the west, a thick basalt caprock bounds the north side of the canyon. Along parts of the cliff are vertical columns, formed as the lava cooled and subsequently shrunk.

It is an unusual sight on the Colorado Plateau to see volcanic rocks in juxtaposition with ancient sedimentary rocks. But in Quaternary and Tertiary times, a great quantity of volcanic material erupted onto the surface of Utah's High Plateaus. In Zion, an abundance of basalt issued from vents and cinder cones, associated with fault zones in the western margin of the Park.

From our canyon-bottom vantage point, we can gaze at a cross-section of 16 different basalt flows that emanated from vents near Spendlove Knoll in upper Cave Valley to the northwest, approximately 260,000 years ago. The flows filled our canyon to a depth of 500 feet, damming the creek and forming a lake. Later, after lake waters breached the dam, the Left Fork North Creek began cutting a new stream channel along the margins of the lava flows.

Once on the canyon floor, we are on our own and must seek the path of least resistance, boulder hopping our way up the canyon from one side of the small stream to the other. Occasional deeper pools in the stream harbor a few large cutthroat trout.

Just short of Pine Spring Wash we cross the East Cougar Mountain fault, where Kayenta

**Left Fork North Creek channeled into a joint**

rocks abruptly give way to rocks of the Moenave Formation. Shortly beyond, Pine Spring Wash enters from the north (0.5; 4780), and shortly thereafter, Little Creek, a perennial stream, also enters from the north (0.2; 4830).

Tall Navajo Sandstone cliffs soon begin to border the canyon to the north and south. Pay attention to a row of pinnacles on the skyline to the north, and as we pass beneath them, begin to look for large, tilted slabs of Kayenta mudstones above the north bank of the creek. A few large gray slabs display numerous fossil dinosaur tracks. These tracks and others like them in the Kayenta Formation are all that remain in the Zion region (since no fossil bones have yet been found) to remind us of the three-toed reptiles that roamed over muddy floodplains 200 million years ago.

Proceeding along the canyon among velvet ash, Fremont cottonwood, Gambel oak, and an occasional water birch, we eventually reach the first obstacle (2.0; 5280), where an undercut cliff and waterfall bars farther progress along the streambed. Search for a trail that bypasses the fall on the south side of the canyon. This trail leads us past seeplines and hanging gardens at the Kayenta-Navajo interface. Once above this waterfall, we continue along the path, bypassing another fall just above it, then quickly regain the streambed.

During periods of low runoff, much of the creek is funnelled into a small, narrow joint in the streambed. Abrasive stream waters will deepen this slot more rapidly than they will widen it. It is likely that The Subway and many of Zion's other slot canyons formed under similar circumstances.

From here on we are forced to walk on the canyon floor, where the stream flows as a sheet over moss-covered slickrock, making footing treacherous. Following the canyon as it curves southeast, we soon reach the entrance to the aptly named Subway (0.4; 5360), a narrow, tunnel-like slot carved into the canyon bottom. This is a strange, empty hallway carved in stone, with only the echo of running water to keep us company. Above the tunnel, the canyon narrows into a mere slit between sandstone walls, then widens beyond, soaring 800 feet to the south canyon rim.

Hikers can proceed upstream, the route still confined to the canyon floor, but a waterfall bars farther progress a short distance beyond The Subway. Some experienced canyoneers follow a route down Russell Gulch from the Wildcat Canyon Trail (*Trip 19*), rappelling over the falls and hiking down the Left Fork to the trailhead on Kolob Terrace Road.

Return the way you came.

# Trip 18
## Kolob Terrace Road to Hop Valley, La Verkin Creek

**Distance**: 13.8 miles round trip
**Low/High elevations**: 5280'/6380'
**Suited for**: Dayhike or backpack
**Difficulty**: Moderate

**Best season**: April through October
**Maps/Trailhead**: 8,11/15
**Hazards**: Expect to encounter cattle on a private inholding in the upper parts of Hop Valley, and purify any water you obtain there.

**Introduction**: Following a highly scenic and less-used route to La Verkin Creek and Kolob Arch, this attractive trail leads through incomparable Hop Valley, a long, green meadow with a backdrop of soaring red cliffs. A number of excellent backcountry camping opportunities exist beyond the private inholding in lower Hop Valley.

This trip is best taken as a backpack, but strong dayhikers can hike to Kolob Arch and back in one long day.

**Description**: The initial segment of the trail, to the jeep road 1.6 miles ahead, was constructed in 1987, thus avoiding the roads formerly used to access Hop Valley. This trail heads generally north from the trailhead (0.0; 6380), descending at first, then rising gently beneath picturesque, pine-dotted knolls of Navajo Sandstone, lying at the foot of the Firepit Knoll cinder cone. Lava flows that issued from the cone have buried much of the sandstone in the area, as well as the valley through which we are presently hiking.

Our sandy trail meanders along the eastern margin of the valley, threading its way among Gambel oaks, sagebrush, prickly pear, and a host of seasonal wildflowers. Prominent landmarks include 7410' Red Butte to the northwest and 7265' Firepit Knoll, its brushy slopes rising above the trail to the east. To the north, a wall of amazingly sheer salmon-tinted cliffs rises above as-yet-invisible La Verkin Creek valley.

As we pass beneath the basalt-crowned rim north of Firepit Knoll, conspicuous Burnt Mountain soon meets our gaze on the distant northwest skyline. Typical of the mesas in Zion, its wooded crown contrasts with abruptly plunging cliffs. Upon reaching a hikers' gate (1.6; 6342) we pass through a fenceline, entering a 400-acre private inholding, through which we will be hiking for the next 2.5 miles. Expect the possibility of encountering cattle beyond the gate, and as you pass through private land, respect landowner rights.

Our route presently follows a rough road that soon curves north past a field cleared of sagebrush. We quickly pass more such clearings before descending amid ponderosa pines and Gambel oaks to the crossing of a small, dry wash, beyond which we climb to a minor ridge with a fork in the sandy road (0.5; 6300).

Bearing right, we begin a steady, moderately steep descent beneath broken, hoodoo-capped cliffs. As we proceed down the oak- and juniper-dotted ridge, we soon glimpse the grassy, narrow spread of Hop Valley. The broken cliffs rising above it frame a memorable view of the tall cliffs rising above La Verkin Creek to the north.

A knee-jarring descent on a series of steep, rocky switchbacks finally gets us to level ground, where we cross a dry, sandy wash (1.0; 5850), then proceed northwest along its east bank. A sluggish stream soon emerges from the sands of the wash, and we continue along the grassy banks to the head of Hop Valley, where an interesting side canyon joins from the east, also boasting a small stream.

The grassy spread of Hop Valley that lies before us is truly one of the gems of Zion. Its exceedingly flat floor, narrowly wedged between 600' cliffs, seems an enigma; there is nothing else in the Park quite like it. Hikers familiar with the backcountry of the Needles District in Canyonlands National Park will recognize its similarity to The Grabens there. But unlike a down-faulted graben valley, Hop Valley was formed initially as a result of erosion; later, its floor was buried in lakebed sediments.

Part of the ridge northeast of Burnt Mountain, the prominent mesa rising 2000 feet above the lower end of the valley, experienced a major landslide approximately 1500 years ago, which dammed the canyon and formed a lake nearly 1/2 mile long. Geologists have found evidence to suggest that the dam was breached only about 200 years ago. Much of the lakebed sediment remains, giving the valley its flat profile.

To proceed through the valley, we follow either the streambanks or cattle trails, eventually passing a branch canyon (1.0; 5740) emerging from the cliffs to the northeast. Shortly thereafter, another canyon enters the valley from the southwest. Next we encounter the heavily wooded, gaping mouth of Langston Canyon

(0.5; 5720), joining the valley on our right (northeast). That canyon is worthy of exploration if time allows, but cliffs and steep dropoffs block progress after a short distance up it.

Climbing to a hikers' gate at the northernmost fenceline (0.6; 5700), we then stroll along the boxelder-shaded bench before descending back to the valley bottom. Camping is allowed north of that gate, and hikers can find a number of pleasant campsites on benches above the valley, where they will enjoy considerably more solitude than in La Verkin Creek.

Presently we hop across the small creek and follow its west bank downstream. Soon we bid farewell to the beautiful valley and climb steeply northwest to a pine-studded hill, beyond which the trail descends gently along a broad bench. This bench is composed of landslide debris fallen from the ridge northeast of Burnt Mountain, the cliffbound mesa that towers overhead.

Soon the trail leads us through several curious depressions pockmarking the slide debris. As the mass of rock broke away from the walls above us and began to slide downhill, a large volume of air was trapped beneath the slide and compressed by the overlying debris. The trapped air escaped by erupting from the slide, and thus the depressions were formed.

Reaching the northern edge of the bench, we begin to descend steadily via switchbacks amid Gambel oak thickets to the La Verkin Creek Trail (1.7; 5350). From here, we ponder our options of either returning the way we came, turning right to reach Beartrap Canyon and Willis Creek, or turning left and hiking down La Verkin Creek canyon (see *Trip 23*). Kolob Arch, a popular destination and justifiably so, is but a mile away via the left fork.

# Trip 19
## Wildcat Canyon and Northgate Peaks Trails

**Distance**: 6.0 miles shuttle trip, plus 2.4 miles round trip to Northgate Peaks overlook.

**Low/High elevations**: 6910'/7460'
**Suited for**: Dayhike or backpack
**Difficulty**: Moderate
**Best season**: May through October
**Map/Trailheads**: 9/16, 17
**Hazards**: Negligible

**Introduction**: This scenic trip leads the hiker from the lava rimrock to the sandstone realm of lofty domes and crags, as seen from the Northgate Peaks Trail and Pine Valley. The lightly used trail features oak-rimmed meadows, a gushing spring, and peaceful, park-like forests of ponderosa pine. Camping is allowed east of Pine Valley and the Northgate Peaks Trail junction.

The trail can be followed in either direction, but starting near Lava Point involves the least amount of ascent. A car shuttle is necessary to avoid retracing your steps.

During early spring, when the Kolob Terrace Road to Lava Point may be blocked by snow, hikers must then begin the hike at the Pine Valley

Trailhead. The lower part of the trail near that trailhead is often used by cross-country skiers during winter, and much of the gentle terrain of the Lower Kolob Plateau is well suited for ski touring.

**Description**: From the West Rim Trailhead (0.0; 7460) we stroll 150 yards down the oak-lined trail to the register box, where we sign in and part company with hikers taking *Trip 20*, turning right onto the signed Wildcat Canyon Trail. The basalt-capped rim of Lava Point rises above us to the northwest, its crest adorned with white-fir forest and the two antennas serving the fire-lookout tower there.

Soon we pass an old grain drill, attesting to an early dry farming venture. Wheat and grass were once raised here to provide feed for livestock. The trail is actually an old road for much of the way. The road provided access to farmland and timber on the plateau. An abundance of Gambel oak attests to early logging ventures throughout much of the Lower Kolob Plateau. As sun-drenched openings were created by the

**An old grain drill alongside the Wildcat Canyon Trail**

felling of trees, the oaks, which prefer dry, sunny sites on the plateaus, quickly grew to dominate the forest.

Lava Point fades from view as we begin a descent into a small side canyon amid Gambel oak and Rocky Mountain maple. Curving into the upper reaches of Wildcat Canyon after 1.3 miles, we glimpse the white cliffs that embrace the rugged lower parts of the canyon to the south. Ahead of us on the canyon's west side, the volcanic rim gives way to rubbly slopes composed of slide debris, decorated by a scattering of white fir, aspen, oak and maple. Reaching the dry wash in the canyon bottom (1.6; 7050), we encounter a variety of colorful wildflowers, including silky lupine, skyrocket gilia, and broom groundsel in autumn. The canyon is thickly clad in a forest of white fir, ponderosa pine, Gambel oak, and Rocky Mountain maple.

As we begin a southwestward ascent across a slope of black basalt boulders, we are treated to fine views down-canyon, the walls framing square-edged buttes and smooth sandstone cliffs. A reliable, unnamed spring (0.3; 7120), overgrown with bracken fern, issues from the broken lava above the trail. This spring is our best source of water along the entire trail, but no potential campsites exist along the trail for the following mile, so backpackers should tank up here.

The wide trail gradually ascends the canyon wall, eventually passing through a broad gap before descending into a lovely meadow (1.2; 7300). Here a westward course leads across the pine- and oak-rimmed spread. Beyond the meadow, a sidehill traverse through oak and pine woods follows, from which we obtain fine views down Wildcat Canyon to a host of redrock spires. Volcanic rimrock foregrounds the twin sandstone domes of Northgate Peaks to the south, and they in turn frame the distant beehive-shaped dome of imposing North Guardian Angel. Our trail ahead, descending almost imperceptibly, crosses the oak- and pine-clad plateau to a signed junction (1.6; 6950), where Northgate Peaks Trail peels off to the left (south).

The Northgate Peaks Trail, sandy in places, follows the nearly level plateau south through a lovely forest of ponderosa pine. Ample opportunities for camping can be found all along the trail here. The trail gains little elevation, and before long we reach the basalt-capped overlook (1.2; 6900), perched on a point of the plateau, with the slickrock domes of Northgate Peaks flanking us on either side. The incredible view that unfolds is well worth the extra effort required to get here.

The gargantuan dome of 7395' North Guardian Angel dominates our southward view over the labyrinth of rugged canyons draining Left Fork North Creek. Russell Gulch, the slickrock-bound gorge below to the east, is a challenging route used by experienced hikers to gain access to Left Fork North Creek and The Subway.

A host of striking cliffs, crags, buttes, and mesas meets our gaze as we look southeast, but towering above them all toward the south is the lofty platform of West Temple. As we face west, the distant hogback crest of the 10,000' Pine Valley Mountains is framed by the sandstone domes of the western Northgate Peak and Pine Valley Peak.

One can't help but notice the prominent cross-bedding on virtually all of the nearby Navajo Sandstone cliffs and domes. Vertical surface fractures aligned at right angles to the cross-bedding (checkerboarding) are obvious, but not as well developed as they are along the Zion-Mt. Carmel Highway between the tunnel and the East Entrance of Zion.

Back at the junction where this spur started, we turn left to complete our journey, strolling through pine forest to the sandy bed of a wash. A seeping spring can be found by following the grassy banks of the wash 0.4 mile upstream, but hikers must remember they can establish campsites east of the Northgate Peaks Trail junction only.

After crossing that wash, the trail ascends gradually through the broad expanse of Pine Valley, finally ending at the oak-rimmed trailhead (1.3; 7000) in the shadow of 7428' Pine Valley Peak.

# Trip 20
## West Rim Trail—Lava Point to The Grotto

**Distance**: 13.8 to 15.2 miles one way
**Low/High elevations**: 4290'/7460'
**Suited for**: Dayhike or backpack
**Difficulty**: Moderate as an overnighter if begun at Lava Point; strenuous as an all-day hike.
**Best season**: May through October
**Maps/Trailheads**: 9,3/17,6
**Hazards**: Steep dropoffs; water is available in only three widely scattered locations atop the rim.

**Introduction**: The West Rim Trail is among the most scenic and lengthy backpack trips in the Park, and it receives moderate use throughout the hiking season. Strong hikers can, however, complete the trip in one long day.

Trailside scenery ranges from the pine forests and aspen-clad draws of Horse Pasture Plateau to the vertical realm of sandstone monoliths in Zion Canyon. Vistas of Zion's remote backcountry and other vast panoramas offer glimpses into the erosional processes that shaped the landscape. Sidetrips to Angels Landing or to the remote niches of Corral and Sleepy hollows should appeal to the adventurous hiker.

A one-hour, 42-mile car shuttle is necessary for the hike from Lava Point to The Grotto, but many hikers begin at either of the two trailheads and hike the trail only part way before returning. An option for round-trip hikers beginning at either trailhead would follow the Telephone Canyon Trail and loop back to the main trail at West Rim Spring.

Backpackers who wish to extend the hike and enjoy more plateau scenery can begin the trip at the lower Wildcat Canyon Trailhead, adding 6.0 miles to the hike (see *Trip 19*) but shortening the car shuttle by 6.7 miles.

**Description**: A destination and mileage sign at the trailhead (0.0; 7460) indicates the beginning of a memorable journey. We stroll 150 yards southeast to a trail register and a junction with *Trip 19*, where we bear left.

Our trail, with a tread of gray Carmel Formation limestone, undulates along the crest of Horse Pasture Plateau, a long, rolling promontory dividing the waters that drain into North Creek from those that drain into North Fork Virgin River. Frequent summer thunderstorms occasionally ignite fires atop elevated terraces such as this, and during our trek we will pass trees charred during past lightning fires.

From the junction, we soon cross a peaceful meadow rimmed by ponderosa pine and Gambel oak. Sweeping vistas of the vast Markagunt Plateau are excellent from the start, and will accompany us for miles to come.

Soon we reach the signed trail to Sawmill Spring (0.8; 7330), forking right. That trail is faint at first, but soon becomes easy to follow as it passes over crunchy limestone and under branches of Gambel oak, ponderosa pine, and Rocky Mountain juniper. Descending into a south-trending draw, the trail enters a beautiful meadow and soon ends at reliable Sawmill Spring (0.4; 7180). Below the spring lies a marshy, seasonal pool, and nearby are the remains of an old wagon frame. Be sure to replace the metal cover over the developed spring after you draw your water supply.

Returning to the West Rim Trail, we turn right and proceed on the level in an open forest of pine, oak, and juniper. The trail ahead rises and declines gently and, 2.5 miles from the trailhead, we enjoy our first glimpse into Left Fork North Creek, but even finer views into that magnificent wild and rugged canyon lie farther ahead. Sweeping slopes of Navajo Sandstone rise gracefully from the canyon's inner gorge to a host of slickrock domes. Prominent among them are North and South Guardian Angels, separated by the deep notch of Guardian Angel Pass, below which lies the presently invisible Subway.

As we proceed, our gaze extends into northwest Arizona and the Basin and Range Province, where the Virgin Mountains form the distant horizon. Eventually, we pass beyond fire-damaged forest and enter an intact woodland of ponderosa pine and Gambel oak. The understory shrubs are typical of the Transition Zone—alderleaf mountain mahogany, greenleaf manzanita, and Utah serviceberry. We shortly reach a dry, well-drained site where the thin limestone soil supports a heavy understory and a woodland of pinyon and juniper. It becomes apparent while hiking Zion's trails that microclimates have as great an influence on where one finds plant species as does elevation.

Gazing east from our rim route, only the very tops of the cliffs give the slightest intimation of the canyons that cut deeply into the plateau. After about 4 miles from the trailhead the trail strikes southeastward along a spur ridge before curving south and descending moderately beneath the spreading branches of oaks, junipers, and pines via a shallow, southwest-trending draw.

Emerging from the draw, we enter the grassy expanse of Potato Hollow, a popular camping area. Pines and oaks rim the meadow, and farther on, we enter a stand of aspens, some of which bear carvings on their silvery trunks dating back to the 1930s. The aspens, oaks, and hillside maples in the hollow combine their red, yellow, and orange autumn colors into a memorable display, reaching their peak of brilliance during October.

Reaching a mileage sign (4.7; 6830) we notice an eastbound path branching left from the main trail. That path leads 0.1 mile to an old stock pond fed by a seeping spring, perched very near the brink of the cliffs that plunge into the rugged depths of Imlay Canyon, a Zion Canyon tributary. Backpackers will find an almost unlimited selection of potential campsites throughout Potato Hollow.

Presently, the West Rim Trail crosses a grassy slope, dips into a wooded draw, and climbs moderately-to-steeply up forested north-facing slopes, from which we enjoy good views over the aspen-rimmed meadow of Potato Hollow to the colorful cliffs above Imlay Canyon. After topping out on a ridge at 7060 feet, we contour into a draw, climb to its head and gain an open ridge (0.8; 7250) above isolated Sleepy Hollow, one of several shallow valleys that score the surface of the plateau.

Descending southeast along the rim, we presently gain a striking overview of Right Fork North Creek, embraced by an array of intricately cross-bedded Navajo Sandstone domes, the monolithic butte of Ivins Mountain, and the for-ested platform of Inclined Temple. These buttes were once a part of the continuous plateau surface, but have since been isolated by ages of downcutting and headward erosion of the canyon network. This rugged canyon frames a distant panorama that stretches past the Pine Valley Mountains to the Beaver Dam and Virgin mountains on the far southwest horizon. These fine vistas accompany us as we continue to descend the narrow rim. Enroute we'll encounter creeping hollygrape, a denizen of the plateaus and shaded sites in the canyons, growing side by side with prickly-pear cactus, a typical dweller of the sun-baked desert far below.

The trail bottoms out in a small saddle, then rises steeply to a ridgetop junction with the Telephone Canyon Trail (0.8; 7285). Hikers who prefer to shorten the trip can follow that left-branching trail through a thick forest of pine and oak for 1.8 miles to the West Rim Spring trail junction. But those who have not yet had their fill of awe-inspiring vistas will not want to miss the longer rim trail, branching right.

The West Rim Trail continues south along the edge of the plateau, passing scattered oaks, pines, and various shrubs. Eventually the trail curves southeast, descending from the rim into a pine-forested draw, then finally curves east along the lower south rim of Horse Pasture Plateau. Two deep and narrow slot canyons fall abruptly away from the trail's edge. The first is an arrow-straight tributary to Heaps Canyon, and soon we pass above the gaping maw of Behunin Canyon.

Enroute some hikers may be tempted to use one of the few trailside campsites perched upon the rim, but these should be avoided since using them would interfere with the backcountry experience of other hikers. Soon Behunin Canyon, flanked by Castle Dome to the west and the brush-clad mesas of Mount Majestic and Cathedral Mountain to the east, opens up just enough to reveal a view deep into Zion Canyon.

After switchbacking one time, we join the Telephone Canyon Trail on the left (north). A signed spur trail (3.2; 6730) also forks left here, proceeding north for 100 yards on a lower contour to West Rim Spring. Barely a trickle of water issues from the piped spring, on the very brink of a 700' cliff. This is the last source of water enroute, and hikers can begin to find potential campsites within 1/4 mile of the trail junction by following the Telephone Canyon Trail north.

The trail ahead quickly begins descending a steeply sloping Navajo Sandstone cliff. For safety, the trail has been paved to provide traction on what would otherwise be a very slippery path. A switchbacking descent follows, clinging precariously to the face of the cliff.

After reaching terra firma in a narrow notch at 6315 feet, we quickly descend northeast into the head of a narrow gorge where the pavement ends. Shortly beyond two dry forks of a wash, a gradual descent east across the base of a sheltered, north-facing slope leads us past not only ponderosa pines but white firs and Douglas-firs as well, trees typically found on the plateaus in the highest reaches of the Park. As we proceed farther into the broadening hanging valley, the mineral-stained cliff below West Rim Spring comes into view. This valley is the last place to camp along the trail, and a number of potential sites can be found among the pines north of the wash.

When pavement resumes, we begin to pass over prominently cross-bedded Navajo Sandstone, while viewing a picturesque array of domes and tree-capped knolls. After dipping into a shallow wash, we cross its dry course via a bridge (1.8; 5550). Camping is not allowed between the bridge and The Grotto trailhead. Ascending a few switchbacks beyond the bridge, we gain a sloping slickrock ridge.

After reaching the apex of the ridge, the trail declines toward more switchbacks, where we are greeted by fantastic views of Red Arch Mountain, Angels Landing, The Great White Throne, and East Temple. The trail continues very near the rim above Zion Canyon, and soon we reach signed SCOUT LOOKOUT (1.2; 5350) and proceed down Walter's Wiggles and Refrigerator Canyon to The Grotto trailhead, following *Trip 8* in reverse (1.9; 4288).

# Trip 21
## Kolob Reservoir to Willis Creek

**Distance**: 8.8 miles round trip to Park boundary in Willis Creek
**Low/High elevations**: 6200'/8170'
**Suited for**: Backpack
**Difficulty**: Moderate to the Park boundary, but strenuous back to the trailhead.
**Best season**: June through mid-October
**Map/Trailhead**: 10/18
**Hazards**: The route crosses private land used for cattle grazing. Avoid this trip during deer hunting season, roughly from late October through November.

**Introduction**: A high-elevation start, aspen forests and oak thickets, expansive vistas, and a seldom-used trail combine to make this route an attractive alternative for reaching the La Verkin Creek Trail, where a variety of scenic delights await exploration.

The hike is downhill most of the way, and hikers unable to arrange a car shuttle to either Lee Pass or Hop Valley trailhead must retrace their steps, regaining 2200 feet of elevation in one long, strenuous day.

The route crosses private land all the way to the Park boundary, and camping there is not allowed. This is grazing land; leave all the gates you encounter as you find them. Respect landowner rights, and pack out your trash. Any water you obtain enroute must be treated before drinking.

**Description**: We begin this lonely trek by first passing through a gate just above the parking area (0.0; 8150), then following the road northwest. Ascending a beautiful, grassy draw flanked by white-boled aspens, we pass several summer cabins and soon top out on a Gambel-oak-clad saddle (0.4; 8170), where a road branches right (northwest); ignore it. Instead, bear left and proceed steadily downhill, the road cutting a swath through a veritable forest of aspen. This is a delightful stretch, where dappled sunlight changes with the whims of the breezes through the fluttering aspen leaves.

Here and there Gambel oaks infiltrate the legions of aspens, and in autumn the aspens combine their brilliant colors in a fiery parade of orange, gold, and yellow.

Below the first switchback west of the saddle, we pass a small stock pond and beyond a low, broad ridge we stroll past a second stock pond (0.8; 7800). Continuing our undulating descent, we enjoy incomparable vistas into the heavily forested canyons of the La Verkin Creek drainage, where wooded mesas and plunging red cliffs foreground views of the Pine Valley, Beaver Dam, and Virgin Mountain ranges. We also gain an interesting "back side" perspective of Horse Ranch Mountain, Zion's highest summit, rising to an elevation of 8740 feet in the west-northwest.

At junctions with less-used jeep roads, plastic ribbon will denote the correct route. After hiking an additional mile, we have descended into a broad, oak-rimmed meadow below Birch Spring, passing some old cabins. Leaving the main road beyond Birch Spring's small stream (1.2; 7320), about 100 yards from the last fenceline, we take a faint track through the meadow, following more plastic ribbon southwest enroute.

The track descends first northwest, then steeply west, high above the gaping depths of Willis Creek canyon, then from a nearly level spot on a ridge our old road suddenly jogs south to continue a steep descent down a secondary ridge. The track eventually fades and we follow a trail into the dry creekbed of a steep canyon. Beyond the creekbed, the trail ascends south to another minor ridge, and we then switchback once down into dry Willis Creek canyon, soon reaching the hikers' gate (2.0; 6200) at the Park boundary. To continue into Willis and La Verkin Creek canyons, follow the last part of *Trip 23* in reverse.

# Trip 22
## Middle Fork Taylor Creek to Double Arch Alcove

**Distance**: 5.5 miles round trip
**Low/High elevations**: 5430'/6050'
**Suited for**: Dayhike
**Difficulty**: Moderate
**Best season**: April through November

**Map/Trailhead**: 11/19
**Hazards**: Numerous stream crossings.

**Introduction**: The trail to Double Arch Alcove is rough but easy to follow, and it involves crossing small Middle Fork Taylor Creek dozens of times. Prime features include two homestead cabins, microclimate areas with vigorous growth of riparian vegetation and evergreen forests, a perennial stream, and wildflower-adorned alcoves at the trail's end.

This area is for day use only, and despite its proximity to Interstate 15, the trail generally receives light use, save on holiday weekends.

**Description**: As at most Zion trailheads, views from this location are spectacular. To the west, the walls of Taylor Creek canyon frame the bulky, 10,000' Pine Valley Mountains; up-canyon to the east the rusty prows of Tucupit and Paria points stand guard over the portals of Taylor Creek's Finger Canyons. Massive Horse Ranch Mountain dominates the northeast skyline, its cliffbound flanks contrasting with the brush-choked dome of its 8740' summit. Atop its crest are Zion's youngest sedimentary rocks, sandstones of the Dakota Formation; and younger still are the Quaternary volcanics that crown the summit.

But the interior of a deep and shady canyon beckons, and we get underway beyond the trailhead (0.0; 5510), descending 80 feet in a woodland of Gambel oak, pinyon, and Utah juniper, and soon reaching the banks of Taylor Creek, a small, high-desert stream.

Ahead of us is a fascinating display of the unique geology of the Kolob Canyons Section of Zion. Here in the Taylor Creek Thrust Zone, two prominent north-south-trending ridges have been formed as sedimentary strata have been thrust westward one over another. The thrusting has pushed older strata westward over younger rocks, and the dip of the beds rises upward toward the west.

As we proceed up the presently broad canyon, we have to hop across the stream time and again. A fine display of seasonal wildflowers keeps us company, and big sagebrush, greenleaf manzanita, squawbush, and Utah serviceberry form an understory of scattered shrubs. The Fremont cottonwoods, those ubiquitous denizens of streams and washes in the Southwest, become increasingly large as we proceed, their deeply furrowed boles and excessively branched crowns casting ample shade and forming a picturesque foreground to the stark simplicity of soaring canyon walls.

Approaching the confluence of the North and Middle Forks of Taylor Creek, we cross back to the north bank and continue eastward, soon passing below the well-preserved structure of Larsen Cabin (1.25; 5620), a homestead cabin built with white-fir logs in 1929. This cabin and another one upstream are the only evidence of attempted settlement in the Finger Canyons of the Kolob, but these cabins are not the only evidence of man's use of the canyons. Trailside stumps we may have noticed previously attest to a turn-of-the-century logging and sawmill operation in Taylor Creek. Lumber from the canyon helped to build the small town of New Harmony, west of the Park at the foot of the Pine Valley Mountains.

From his small cabin, Gustave C. Larsen

**Larsen cabin and Tucupit Point**

probably enjoyed the dramatic view of Tucupit Point, abruptly rising more than 500 feet above the confluence, as much as present-day hikers do. Also visible is Horse Ranch Mountain, where an excellent cross-section of five of Zion's nine sedimentary strata is exposed to full view.

Descending slightly from the cabin, we quickly reach Taylor Creek's North Fork. Backpackers can establish campsites in the North Fork only, and they must be 0.4 mile above the confluence, upstream from where a branch canyon enters from the north.

After crossing the North Fork, we continue up the Middle Fork on an increasingly poor trail. Upstream the canyon becomes much narrower and receives little sunlight. Eventually the trail becomes little more than a boot-beaten path, and we follow it to a bench where we encounter the Arthur Fife cabin (1.1; 5840), built in 1930 in a thick stand of Douglas-firs. Since the cabin was built on a moist, shady site, it is more deteriorated than Larsen Cabin. Great salmon-tinted cliffs soar above the cabin, to both the north and the south, and with the onset of autumn, the bushy maples here glow fiery red as well.

Our indistinct path leads quickly from the cabin down to a nearby vigorous spring issuing from the porous Navajo Sandstone where it interfaces with impermeable Kayenta shales. The stream may be dry above the spring, and we continue to follow the canyon around a prominent southeastward bend, beyond which we leave the canyon floor and quickly climb to the shady hollow of Double Arch Alcove (0.4; 6050), a delightful sylvan oasis decorated with white fir and maple.

Beneath the vaulted roof of this deep recess, cliff columbines grow in profusion, nurtured by moisture seeping and dripping from the alcove's interior. Directly above the alcove lies a shelf upon which Douglas-fir and white fir grow tall and straight, and above that shelf, a smooth cliff soars skyward to a large arch perched just below the rim. Evidence of an opening behind that arch is suggested by a tapestry of streaks left upon the wall below by ages of mineral-laden runoff that must have flowed through the opening above the alcove.

From Double Arch Alcove, retrace your steps to the trailhead.

# Trip 23
## Lee Pass to Willis Creek
## via La Verkin Creek Trail

**Distance**: 21.9 miles round trip to Park
   boundary, not including sidetrips
**Low/High elevations**: 5030'/6200'
**Suited for**: Backpack
**Difficulty**: Moderate as a 2-3 day backpack.
**Best season**: April through October
**Maps/ Trailhead**: 11, 10/20
**Hazards**: Numerous stream crossings in
   upper La Verkin Creek canyon; water must
   be treated before drinking.

**Introduction**: This is perhaps the finest
backpack trip in Zion National Park. A perennial
stream, abundant camping areas, forests of tall
conifers foregrounding even taller cliffs, and
sidetrip options to Kolob Arch, Hop Valley, and
Beartrap Canyon combine to make this an unforgettable and scenically diverse trek.

This trip can be taken at almost any time of
the year, but the trail can be muddy and the creek
swollen after heavy rains and during times of
high spring runoff. Snow can obscure parts of
the trail at times during winter.

Although it's best suited for a backpack,
strong hikers can make the 14.4-mile round trip
to Kolob Arch in one day. The trail receives
steady use from spring through fall, but many
hikers go no farther than the Kolob Arch area.
Hence considerable solitude can be found in the
upper reaches of the canyon.

The forks of La Verkin Creek drain summer
range atop the plateau used by grazing sheep and
cattle, so be sure to purify water from the creek.

Backcountry permits for this hike are available at the Kolob Canyons Visitor Center, located a short distance east of Interstate 15 at the
Kolob Canyons exit.

**Description**: Our hike begins near Lee Pass
(0.0; 6060), a low gap on the Taylor Creek/La
Verkin Creek divide. Dramatic views of all the
monolithic, brilliant red stone promontories separating the Finger Canyons of the Kolob lie
before us to both the north and the south.

The initial segment of the trail descends
steadily for 450 feet mostly along a sloping ridge
dividing two headwaters forks of Timber Creek.
Vegetation encountered enroute is typical of the
pinyon-juniper woodland in Zion, but the variety
and density of the flora reflect greater precipitation than that which falls on most such woodlands on the Colorado Plateau.

Singleleaf pinyon, more commonly occurring in lower-elevation woodlands in southern
parts of the Great Basin, and Utah juniper are the
main evergreen tree species, while the understory includes silktassel, a shrub common to low
elevation coastal slopes in California and found
in isolated locations in the Mojave Desert. This
is the only trail in Zion along which this shrub
will be found.

Reaching the foot of the ridge (1.0; 5600),
we cross a dry branch of Timber Creek and
proceed downstream west of the wash, beneath
a canopy of Gambel oak, Fremont cottonwood,
and boxelder. Timber Creek usually flows intermittently, but its flow increases during the spring
and after heavy rains. A riparian zone, dominated by boxelder and cottonwood, clings to the
wash.

The trail is sandy much of the way, and from
spring through fall mosquitoes, no-see-ums, and
flies will constantly harass us. We proceed past
towering, burnt cliffs of Navajo Sandstone abutting promontories that jut westward into Timber
Creek from the lofty plateau above. The canyons
between them reach back into the plateau like so
many giant fingers, and dayhikers will enjoy
exploratory trips into their cliffbound drainages.

The rounded crowns of the lofty mesas
above are typical of the landscape that forms
from the soft limestones of the Carmel Formation, and are thickly clad in brush and white-fir
forest.

After two miles we pass the tall slickrock
shaft of Shuntavi Butte, rising from the western
shoulder of Timber Top Mountain. Backpackers
are allowed to establish campsites from this
point onward, and ahead potential campsites are
numerous, perched above the wash on terraces
shaded by pinyon, juniper, and oak.

Beyond the final crossing of the wash is a
gently rising traverse on wooded, west-facing
slopes. At a broad saddle, (2.5; 5450) an open
stand of pinyon and juniper allows unobstructed

views over the trough of La Verkin Creek to the fluted cliffs of Neagle Ridge, the square-edged bulk of Burnt Mountain, and the pointed dome of Red Butte. Camp could be established atop this broad ridge, but the tall red cliffs, cool forests, and perennial waters of La Verkin Creek will lure most hikers onward.

Presently the trail curves east, descending wooded slopes at a moderate grade. Approaching the north bank of tumbling La Verkin Creek, we amble past a mileage sign and soon skirt a dilapidated corral (1.3; 5050). There are a few overused campsites nearby which you should avoid. Some hikers will enjoy exploring the creek just downstream, where there are several cascades and slickrock pools.

From the corral on up to the Kolob Arch Trail, our trail follows the north bank of the cottonwood-lined stream, a delightful brook tumbling over boulders and slickrock or sliding gently over sandy stretches. Fine campsites are on either side of the stream, where large cottonwoods, pinyon, and juniper offer ample shade. Sites along the south bank offer more shade and are out of sight of other hikers.

Wedged between the serrated crest of Neagle Ridge to the south and the massive cliffs abutting Gregory Butte to the north, our progress is hindered by the exceeding sandiness of the trail, which hugs the north bank of the creek. During periods of high runoff, parts of the trail may be flooded, requiring brief detours.

Splashing through the runoff of a reliable spring (1.2; 5210) we then enter the shade of tall ponderosa pines and soon cross a gully below a seasonal spring. Several campsites are nearby, but they are much too close to the trail. Choose a site on the opposite side of the creek instead.

Shortly thereafter we hop across a small stream draining a north-trending canyon and immediately reach the spur trail (0.6; 5230) to Kolob Arch. No one should miss this short side-trip to what may be the world's largest free-standing arch.

# Kolob Arch Trail

Most hikers visiting La Verkin Creek either have Kolob Arch as their primary objective or include this trail on their itinerary. The trail is rough and requires some scrambling as it ascends a deep, shady canyon to a tree-framed viewpoint, still far below the arch.

This trail leads north from the junction, quickly passing a hitch rail and a sign declaring it closed to horses. We soon leave the pleasant canyon bottom, climbing its east slope.

After the trail drops back into the canyon, we hop across a small creek twice before climbing above it and following the east slope once again. Then, dropping to the creek once more, we must scramble up the streambed, following an obscure trail. Finally, we cross the creek where the main canyon splits into three forks, and climb quickly to a small bench (0.6; 5400) where the trail ends. Nearby pines and firs frame our view of the gracefully arching wedge of rust-red Navajo Sandstone known as Kolob Arch, perched high on the cliff face seemingly in defiance of gravity. Other cliffs, salmon-tinted and streaked by ages of mineral-laden runoff waters, rise above our viewpoint on three sides, forming an amphitheater of grand proportions.

A sign recommends against travel beyond the viewpoint, lest you damage vegetation and increase erosion. Nevertheless, hikers have worn a path farther into the amphitheater to gain a close-up view of the arch—but you should avoid that path.

Kolob Arch vies for the title of world's largest span with Landscape Arch in Arches National Park. Numerous measurements have been taken at both arches, and each measurement finds slightly different dimensions. Measurements conducted by a team from Brigham Young University in 1984 found that Kolob spanned 292 feet between abutments and stood 177 feet high, while Landscape Arch measured 291 feet in width. Until a standard and accepted means of measurement is developed, we can conclude that these two spans are both the world's largest. But regardless of its size, Kolob

Arch is certainly one of the most unusual and beautiful rock spans on the Colorado Plateau.

---

Resuming our eastbound trek on the La Verkin Creek Trail, we continue along the north bank of the creek, but soon boulder hop to the opposite bank, just upstream from a vigorous spring issuing from a stand of water birch. A short but steep climb ensues, leading up the north-facing slope beneath a canopy of oak and maple to a junction (0.3; 5350) with the Hop Valley Trail, where we part company with *Trip 18* hikers and bear left.

Our trail, signed WILLIS CREEK TRAIL, stays high above La Verkin Creek for only a short time, soon dropping back into the canyon amid a jumble of large boulders, part of the Burnt Mountain slide (see *Trip 18*). Hop Valley's small creek trickles out from that slide debris and rests in a few deep pools alongside the trail.

Presently the trail hugs the stream more closely than before, and the increasingly narrow canyon supports a wide variety of trees. Massive cliffs rise above us in all directions, some sheer, others fluted and broken, some solid in color, others banded in varying shades of red; some dotted with vegetation; others simply naked stone.

This trail is obviously much less traveled than the trail below Hop Valley junction; it is ill-defined and quite rocky in places. Numerous potential campsites will be passed as we proceed. We are forced to hop across the stream several times, and as the canyon becomes narrower we will eventually get our feet wet as we wade back and forth across the stream.

There are two points along the canyon that may confuse some hikers. The first is a north-trending canyon (1.3; 5430), where hikers should be sure to stay to the right. The second is a fork (0.7; 5750) where prominent canyons branch east and northeast. The primary route follows the left (northeast) branch, while a short but attractive sidetrip follows the east branch, Bear Trap Canyon.

---

## Bear Trap Canyon

From this fork in the canyon hikers shouldn't miss the 1-mile round trip into Bear Trap. Soaring redrock cliffs. broken and blocky, support a scattering of trees and shrubs on narrow, soil-covered ledges. A faint path follows the grassy banks of the small stream, crossing it a number of times and often requiring wading. The 1000' deep canyon is nearly as confined as Zion Canyon's famous Narrows.

The route terminates after 1/2 mile where a 15' waterfall blocks the way. There may be a log you can use to climb above the fall, but don't depend on it. Upper Bear Trap is the realm of the experienced rock climber; the rest of us should turn back at the fall.

---

Continuing up the canyon of La Verkin Creek, the trail beyond the mouth of Bear Trap Canyon becomes even more ill-defined. The canyon is very narrow and thick with trees. Look for spring-fed hanging gardens along the way.

Upon reaching a large campsite at the confluence of La Verkin and Willis creeks (1.0; 5770), hikers with an exploratory bent can follow the former northward upstream into a BLM wilderness study area, where few hikers ever tread. In its upper reaches, the canyon branches into many side drainages, fed by springs high on the slopes of 9500' Kanarra Mountain.

Willis Creek may be dry upstream from the confluence. If so, hikers should tank up at La Verkin Creek, then follow the path along the canyon floor. The Navajo Sandstone cliffs diminish in stature as we progress eastward.

As we approach the Park boundary, canyons begin to branch off to the right and left, and the canyon broadens. There are fine campsites nearby in parklike forest of ponderosa pine.

Following the main branch of Willis Creek, the trail soon reaches the hikers' gate at the Park boundary (1.75; 6200), beyond which the trail soon climbs steeply to the plateau above, following dirt roads across private land to the Indian Hollow arm of Kolob Reservoir (see *Trip 21*).

# Bryce Canyon National Park

## Introduction

Bryce Canyon National Park, located on the east edge of the Paunsaugunt Plateau in south-central Utah, is the smallest of Utah's national parks, with an area of only 35,835 acres (56 square miles). But within the confines of this Park is perhaps the most unusual spectacle of erosional forms on earth. Here the optimum combination of rock type and climate has led to the creation of a striking array of pillars, finlike ridges, windows and arches, separated from each other by narrow stone hallways and badlands slopes. These features seem to erupt from the rim of the forested plateau in a colorful, fiery display that at once overwhelms the senses.

Drive to any of the overlooks on the plateau rim and you will be astounded by the profusion of stone pillars at your feet, colored in shades of orange, white, and yellow—colors that assume a wide range of hues with the passing hours of the day. When one has finally recovered from the initial explosion of color and form, other landforms besides Bryce's pillars begin to draw attention.

Bryce is not only a showcase for and a tribute to nature's unique expression; it is a place where one can revel in a clean environment and absorb far-flung vistas seen through 100 miles of the crystalline air of southern Utah, vistas limited only by the curvature of the earth. Indeed, clean air is a precious resource in our world, and the desert Southwest boasts the cleanest air in the nation.

Unlike Zion and Grand Canyon national parks, Bryce preserves no one canyon but many, all tributaries to the Paria River, which in turn contributes its waters to the mighty Colorado. As these canyons have eroded back into the eastern escarpment of the Paunsaugunt Plateau, they have created a series of basins, exposing naked stone to the elements. Hence, as one drives to the various overlooks on the crenulated rim, one is greeted by a new and unique view in each place.

When you visit Bryce, park your car and walk the trails. Revel in the endless panoramas of the unspoiled Utah landscape; breath deeply of the clean, thin air; watch the shadows of late afternoon creep over the rim and fill the canyon amphitheaters to the brim; immerse yourself in the sounds of the wind rushing among hoodoos and rustling among the pines; gaze in wonder at the gnarled, time-etched bristlecone pines that stand in quiet defiance of the harsh elements; and wander among the sculptured hoodoos that only nature, in her finest erosional sculpturing, could have created.

In a region where thousands of square miles of magnificent red-rock landscapes seem to continually overwhelm the senses, the incomparable Pink Cliffs of Bryce stand out above all the rest, and will draw you back time and again to savor some of nature's secrets.

# Human History of Bryce

The rugged breaks of Bryce's Pink Cliffs have been a barrier to humans for thousands of years. There is no evidence suggesting occupation of the Bryce region by ancient cultures. Arrowheads and rock chippings have been discovered, but these most likely date back only a few hundred years, to when Piute Indians inhabited the region.

East of the Park, people of the Anasazi culture established settlements in the Paria River Valley at least 1500 years ago. Their way of life depended heavily on farming, but they supplemented their diet with game and food plants obtained from seasonal forays into the high country of surrounding plateaus. After the Anasazis' mysterious departure from the Southwest around A.D. 1300, Piute Indians came to dominate the region. Primarily a hunting-gathering culture, the Piutes also raised crops and utilized irrigation systems, using methods they possibly learned from past encounters with the more culturally advanced Anasazi.

Today, Piute people live on scattered reservations, but some of the names they bestowed upon the landscape remain as reminders of their all-but-forgotten culture. Piute names that described the landscape and are in use today include *Paunsaugunt*, "home of the beaver"; *Yovimp*, referring to the ponderosa pine (although there are no ponderosas at today's Yovimpa Point); and *Paria*, "muddy water."

Today's visitors stand awestruck as they gaze across the incomparable jumble of hoodoos that dominate the eastern escarpment of the Paunsaugunt Plateau, but early Mormon settlers, whose sole and all-consuming occupation was subsistence farming in the dry Paria River Valley, had little interest in these badlands. The Mormons' expansion from their Salt Lake sanctuary brought settlers to every corner of the rugged State of Utah. The town of Panguitch was established in the Sevier River Valley in the spring of 1864, but Indian conflicts in 1865—the "Black Hawk War"—caused the temporary abandonment of the townsite. A Mormon militia, in pursuit of Navajo raiders, encountered the Paria River in June 1866. They returned with a report that the valley was suitable for settlement.

In 1870 Major John Wesley Powell scaled the Pink Cliffs from the headwaters of the Sevier River. Powell's observations spurred interest in the region, and within the next seven years several of his contemporaries began surveys of the region. Reports from later surveying expeditions, expounding on the scenic wonders of the Bryce area, heightened national awareness of the unique natural beauty of southern Utah.

By 1870, Indian hostilities had abated, and in 1871 Pauguitch was re-occupied by Mormon settlers. During 1874 Mormon pioneers began filtering into the Paria River Valley, settling at the confluence of the Paria and Henrieville Creek. Soon more settlers began to arrive in the valley, among them Ebenezer and Mary Bryce, who homesteaded west of the present-day town of Tropic. They grazed sheep and cattle in the canyon that came to be known as Bryce's Canyon, and they built a road for hauling timber. Bryce was unmoved by the beauty of the canyon; rather, he considered it "awful hard to find a cow that was lost" in the rugged labyrinth of pinnacles and gullies there.

In 1905 the Paunsaugunt Plateau, including the Pink Cliffs, was set aside as Sevier National Forest. In 1917, the Forest Service was granted $350 to construct trails below the rim, trails that hikers tread today. A great deal of publicity followed, and in 1919 the governor of Utah petitioned Congress to establish "The Temple of the Gods National Monument." In 1924 the Utah Parks Company began construction of the lodge and cabins, which were completed in 1930.

Today Bryce Canyon Lodge is a national historic landmark, and is being restored to its original 1930s character.

Congress finally passed a bill creating Bryce Canyon National Monument in 1923, and in 1924 the name was changed to Utah National Park. In 1928 another bill changed the Park to its present name, Bryce Canyon, and nearly doubled the size of the area to 14,480 acres. More land was acquired, and in 1931 the Park increased in size to 30,080 acres. The Park Visitor Center was completed in 1959 and dedicated in June 1960. The Park has since been enlarged to encompass 35,835 acres (56 square miles) of one of the most unusual and breathtaking examples of nature's erosional handiwork on the globe.

# Plants and Animals of Bryce

Bryce's 2500 feet of vertical relief embrace an array of distinctive environments, and each different environment supports a particular assemblage of vegetation. Woodlands of pinyon, Utah juniper, and Gambel oak occupy the lowest elevations in the Park, dominating from 6600 to about 7000 feet in the upper limits of the Upper Sonoran Zone, where precipitation averages a scant 12 inches, summer temperatures can exceed 100°, and winter temperatures occasionally plunge below 0°. These woodlands thrive on the weathered sandstones that form a gentle landscape of shallow canyons and broad, rolling ridges well below the breaks of the Pink Cliffs. Few Park trails pass through this zone, but the Under-the-Rim Trail frequently touches its fringes.

As one approaches the 7000' level on the plateau or in the canyons, open, parklike forests of tall ponderosa pines dominate the scene in the Transition Zone. Nurtured by more than 15 inches of average precipitation, these forest trees are widely spaced, as are their lower-elevation counterparts, the pinyon and the juniper, due to competition for moisture. Rocky Mountain juniper sporadically mixes with the pines in this zone.

Within the Transition Zone broad meadows occupy low-lying areas on the plateau. The tall, thick grasses of these meadows attracted pioneer stockmen, who grazed their cattle and sheep on the plateau during summer. The infestation of sagebrush in the meadows reflects the years of overgrazing that these grasslands experienced.

Conifers are steadily encroaching upon the sloping margins of the meadows, but the low-lying depressions are not conducive to tree growth. These areas are typically wetter, in addition, and cold air flowing downslope collects in these meadows, where winter temperature inversions trap cold air. Here temperatures can be 30° colder than on surrounding slopes, and these cold temperatures can severely retard the establishment of tree seedlings.

As one approaches 8500 feet in the southern reaches of the Park, temperatures are cooler still, and precipitation increases markedly from the 15-inch average at the Park Visitor Center. Here the ponderosa pines are mostly supplanted by conifers that like a cooler, moister environment, but ponderosas continue to persist on drier, sun-drenched slopes up to nearly 9000 feet. The dominant trees of the Canadian Zone are Douglas-fir and white fir. Aspens occupy cool, moist draws and meadow margins in this zone.

Growing on the most barren, inhospitable sites on the rim and in the breaks of the Pink Cliffs are the tenacious bristlecone and limber pines. Remarkably, these trees thrive on nutrient-poor limestone slopes where most other plants cannot exist. They must contend with the harshest environmental conditions anywhere in the Park, harsher still than those that pinyon-juniper woodlands must withstand.

The bristlecone is well adapted to conserve available resources. Needles persist on its branches for 25-30 years, and in drought years the trees add no new growth. When conditions cannot support the growth of an entire tree, it will die back and maintain only enough growth to allow survival; often it seems that only a strip of bark supports a few living branches, while the rest of the tree is merely a wind-polished skeleton of its former self.

But the forests of the plateau and the woodlands of the foothills abruptly end in the canyon amphitheaters, where the hoodoos and the badlands of the Pink Cliffs cannot support forest.

**Bristlecone pine**

Only a few trees and shrubs colonize the Pink Cliffs, the elevation of which would put them within the Transition and Canadian life zones.

As one would expect, plant species from both zones are present there, but elevation plays only a supporting role in determining their distribution. Rather, the broken topography of cliffs, steep slopes, hoodoos, and gullies creates a wide variety of microhabitats that support a range of plants distributed according to their environmental requirements. For example, Colorado blue spruce, found sporadically in the shadiest sites and the highest elevations of the plateau, grows on north-facing slopes and on the most sheltered sites in the Pink Cliffs, sites where sunlight and evaporation are minimal. Douglas-fir and white fir are found scattered throughout the badlands to the foot of the cliffs, below which most canyons support forests of ponderosa pine, and the surrounding ridges host pinyon-juniper-oak woodlands, primarily on sandstone soils.

A variety of shrubs forms an understory among the forest trees. Utah serviceberry and cliffrose are common denizens of the pinyon-juniper woodland, and greenleaf manzanita and sagebrush are found here, as well as above, up to the plateau top. The ponderosa-pine forests host thickets of manzanita and bitterbrush, the

higher-elevation relative of cliffrose and an important food source for mule deer. Most shrubs are tall and spreading, save for the ground-hugging manzanita. Among the tall shrubs present on the rim are curlleaf mountain mahogany and Martin ceanothus. Alderleaf mountain mahogany is a shrub typically found in the canyons below the rim. Oregon grape, or creeping hollygrape, and blue elderberry are also found sporadically in the canyons and on the plateau.

In the Canadian Zone, greenleaf manzanita persists, but primarily on sunny, well-drained slopes. Dominant shrubs in the shady forests of that zone are snowberry, wax currant, and common juniper—a mat-forming shrub.

Meadows of the plateau host their own distinctive shrubs, and they are easily observed from the Park road. Nutka rose and horsebrush occupy the meadow fringes, while shrub cinquefoil and sagebrush stretch into the grasslands. Wildflowers in Bryce put forth a dramatic display of delicate blooms that vie with the Pink Cliffs for the visitor's attention. Yellow flowers dominate the landscape, but the full spectrum of color is displayed here.

Many of the flowers found in the breaks and on the fringes of the meadows also reach into the ponderosa-pine forests of the plateau, and the moist forests of the Canadian Zone host many species of flowering plants typical of high-mountain environments. There are some wildflowers that know no boundaries, and these species are found throughout all elevations of the Park. Wyoming paintbrush and thistle are two notables.

Animal life in Bryce is equally diverse as its vegetation. The Park has 49 species of mammals and rodents, 15 species of reptiles and amphibians, and 170 species of birds, 52 of which are permanent residents.

The largest mammal likely to be seen in Bryce is the mule deer, which ranges throughout the Park. During winter, these animals descend from the snow-clad plateau into the eastern foothills, where they feed on shrubs such as mountain mahogany and bitterbrush, the seeds of pinyons, and the berries of junipers.

During fall the raucous call of pinyon jays filters through the sparse foliage of the pinyon-juniper woodland as they feed on a bounty of pinyon nuts. Other less conspicuous winged denizens of these woodlands include the mockingbird, Say's phoebe, mountain bluebird, black-capped chickadee, gray vireo, blue grosbeak, house finch, sage sparrow, and rufous-sided towhee.

The coyote, rock squirrel, desert cottontail, bobcat, striped whipsnake, and three lizards—side-blotched, northern sagebrush and northern plateau, are all common in the lower elevations.

The diversity of shrubs and grasses on the plateau makes an ideal summer retreat for the Park's mule deer and occasionally their chief predator, the mountain lion. Equally as rare on the gentle surface of the plateau are pronghorn antelope and Rocky Mountain elk, which more typically inhabit the heights of Sevier Plateau north of Bryce.

The meadows and forests of the plateau each harbor distinctive animal life. Yellow-bellied marmots, the threatened white-tailed prairie dog, pocket gophers, and skunks make their homes in and around the plateau's grasslands. Animals specifically adapted to forest environments include the porcupine, spruce squirrel, and northern flying squirrel, while the gray fox, long-tailed weasel, golden-mantled ground squirrel, and a variety of chipmunks are also denizens of the plateau's forests.

Common birds of the meadows include the horned lark, western meadowlark, sage grouse, mountain bluebird, and loggerhead shrike. Forest birds include blue grouse, band-tailed pigeon, Williamson's sapsucker, Steller's jay, gray jay, Clark's nutcracker, brown creeper, and gray junco.

Hikers in the Pink Cliffs are likely to notice three common birds, two of which perform aerial acrobatics at such incredible speeds that they are usually seen only for a fleeting instant. The violet-green swallow and the white-throated swift entertain Park visitors near the rim throughout each day during the summer. While diving for its insect prey, the white-throated swift can attain speeds of 200 miles per hour. The sudden chortling of the common raven always startles hikers on Park trails. Evening visitors to the rim overlooks often see numbers of these jet-black birds roosting among the hoodoos below.

The most common reptile seen on Bryce's trails is the mountain short-horned lizard, an armored reptile that symbolizes the desert to many visitors. Another, less-welcome sight on the trail is the Great Basin rattlesnake, the only poisonous reptile in the Park. These snakes attain a length of 5 1/2 feet, but their coloration allows them to blend well with their surroundings, and they won't always rattle a warning if one comes too close. Hikers traveling cross-country should be especially careful where they place their hands and feet to avoid an unfortunate encounter with this beautiful but dangerous reptile.

All the plants and animals in the Park live in a delicate balance, and to disrupt any part of the ecosystem threatens their well-being and consequently the overall health of the environment. So, while enjoying this unique and exquisite example of nature's handiwork, do all you can not only to preserve it for those who follow, but also to show consideration for the plants and animals that make Bryce their home.

# Interpretive Activities

A variety of interpretive activities is available in Bryce to enhance your appreciation and knowledge of the dramatic and dynamic processes that have shaped the Park in the past, and those that play an important role in the Park today.

Every visitor's first stop in Bryce should be at the Visitor Center. But only 40% of the annual average of nearly one million visitors take advantage of this invaluable facility, where Park rangers can answer your questions and help you make the most of your stay. A slide program, interpretive exhibits, and a myriad of publications will help you gain knowledge of every aspect of the Park. Schedules of interpretive programs, including guided hikes and evening amphitheater programs, are posted here as well.

The Visitor Center is open all year, and during the summer season business hours are 8 A.M.-8 P.M. daily. Interpretive activities are held in the Visitor Center auditorium and at the Nature Center, and evening talks are conducted nightly at both campground amphitheaters, from May through August or September.

Ranger-led walks offer novice hikers an exceptional opportunity to enjoy Bryce's trails, and allow any hiker to learn more about the Park's fascinating geology, flora, and animal and bird populations.

## Campgrounds

Bryce's two spacious campgrounds provide 218 campsites, with spaces for RVs and tent camping. A group campsite is available at Sunset Campground. Campers pay the nightly fee at the self-registration station at each campground entrance, but are advised to arrive early in the day as both campgrounds are typically filled by early afternoon during the summer. North Campground, reached via a spur road just south of the Visitor Center, lies at 7900 feet just west of the plateau rim north of Sunrise Point. It sits in an open forest of ponderosa and limber pines, with a scattering of Rocky Mountain junipers. Short trails lead from the campground to awe-inspiring viewpoints on the Rim Trail. Loop A in the campground remains open all winter. Sunset Campground lies west of the Park road, just south of the Sunset Point Road at 8000 feet elevation. This campground is smaller than North Campground, but it is shaded by a cool forest.

Three picnic areas are available to Park visitors. One is in the forest just south of North Campground; a second is alongside the Park road near Sheep Creek Trailhead (see driving directions below). The last and largest lies between Yovimpa and Rainbow points at the south end of the Park road.

Historic Bryce Canyon Lodge stands at 7978 feet just west of Sunrise Point. Reservations three or four months in advance are recommended for visitors planning to stay at the motel or the western cabins there. The Lodge also offers a restaurant, a gift shop, and daily horseback rides on two Park trails. Just north of the Lodge are a gas station and a general store where showers are available. The Lodge usually re-

**Rustic cabins at Bryce Canyon Lodge**

mains opens from May through mid-October.

A variety of private campgrounds, motels, and restaurants is found along Utah Highway 12 within a few miles of the Park. Tropic, Utah in the valley east of the Park, offers limited accommodations and services.

Kings Creek Campground, on East Fork Sevier River in Dixie National Forest, is reached via a 7-mile dirt road that begins 4.5 miles west of the Utah Highway 12/63 junction north of the Park. Another Forest Service campground lies alongside Utah 12 in Red Canyon, a few miles east of U.S. 89.

Hiking and backpacking equipment is not available near the Park.

*For further information, call or write:*

Park Superintendent
Bryce Canyon National Park
Bryce Canyon, UT 84717-0001
(801) 834-5322

Bryce Canyon Lodge
TW Recreational Services, Inc.
P.O. Box 400
Cedar City, UT 84720
(801) 586-7686

# Hiking in Bryce

The Park highway offers a variety of scenic overlooks where nonhikers can view the landscape without leaving their cars. But most overlooks require at least a short stroll of 100-200 yards, and most visitors leave their cars for a walk to Sunrise and Sunset points, Inspiration and Bryce points, Paria View, or Rainbow Point.

But these visitors are experiencing Bryce from above; to gain the essential Park experience, one must follow the trails into the heart of the breaks, walking among the ranks of pillars, finlike ridges, badlands slopes, and slot canyons. Some visitors, after gazing from the overlooks, come to think that it is all the same, that perhaps the repetition of views is monotonous, and that the canyon amphitheaters offer little more than can be seen from above. But hiking the trails allows an intimate association with the myriad erosional forms and views that change with every bend in the trail.

Bryce's 60 miles of trails offer hiking opportunities ranging from leisurely strolls to backpacks of three or four days. The trail network samples virtually every aspect of Park scenery.

Except for the Rim Trail and the Bristlecone Loop Trail, all the Park's trails descend from the rim and require a stiff climb to regain it. When you combine the ups and downs with the relative lack of oxygen at the Park's high elevations, many of the trails become demanding, even to seasoned hikers.

Some shorter trails into the Bryce Canyon amphitheater are frequently used, including the incomparable Navajo Loop and Queens Garden trails. Somewhat less used trails north of Bryce Point include the longer Peekaboo Loop and Fairyland trails.

South of Bryce Point are the only backpacking trails in the Park: Under-the-Rim and Riggs Spring Loop. These trails receive considerably less dayhiking pressure due to their length and their location far below the rim.

Many of the Park's shorter trails are wide, smooth, and well-maintained. The Under-the-Rim Trail, by contrast, is a typical narrow backcountry path, with many sandy stretches. There are few trails that offer access to wheelchairs. The Rim Trail between Sunrise and Sunset points, 1/2 mile long, is paved with only minor undulations. Stronger handicapped persons can negotiate the one-mile Bristlecone Loop Trail; however, it has moderate grades, is gravelled, and at one point passes close to the rim.

Despite the well-watered appearance of the green forests that mantle much of the Park, the region is semiarid and the air is dry. When hiking any Park trail, always carry adequate water and ample provisions, and wear sturdy shoes or boots.

Bryce is a high-elevation park; summers are generally warm but winters bring deep snow and bitter cold. Average precipitation ranges from 12 inches near the east boundary of the Park, to nearly 15 inches at the Visitor Center at 7900 feet, to as much as 25 inches in the high southern reaches of the plateau.

June is the driest month, August the wettest. The summer months of July and August see frequent thunderstorms, when downpours scour the debris from gullies and washes below the rim, and thunder reverberates among the hoodoos. The months of May through August bring more visitors to Bryce than all other months combined, and this summer season is one of the most delightful times to visit the Park; days are warm, and the forests and meadows are enriched with colorful flowers.

The sky in the late-summer thunderstorm season displays a dynamic interplay of billowing clouds, sunlight and shadow, lightning, heavy gully-washing rains, and sometimes hail. Thunderstorms typically develop by early afternoon, fed by convection currents of hot air rising from the heated landscape. Since most of the Park's trails are exposed and dangerous during thunderstorms, morning hikes are best if thunderstorms are in the forecast.

By autumn, crowds have abated, the days are cool, and the oaks, aspens and maples paint the Park with colors rivaling those of the Pink Cliffs in brilliance and variety.

Snows typically begin to blanket the landscape by November, and in the winter and early spring months, the Park is the realm of the cross-country skier and the snowshoer. Popular snow routes in the Park include the Fairyland and Paria Point roads and the Rim Trail. The Visitor Center offers snowshoes to visitors free of charge, provided they leave their driver's license while they are out breaking trail.

Most Park trails are the domain of the hiker; there are three exceptions. The Horse Trail, which descends into Bryce Canyon from Sunrise Point, and the Peekaboo Loop Trail *Trip 5* are used twice daily by the Park concessioner for trail rides. The Sheep Creek Connector Trail (*Trip 7*) is used as a stock driveway once in early spring and again in autumn. This is a historic route, and a local rancher has retained the right to use this trail in perpetuity.

An annual average of about 2000 backpackers use the Park's two backcountry trails for overnight camping. Most hikers on the Under-the-Rim Trail (*Trip 6*) use one of the connector trails and spend a weekend at one of the trail camps along that route rather than hiking the trail from end to end. The Riggs Spring Loop Trail (*Trip 12*) also has trail camps within easy reach for most hikers. Both trails make fine weekend trips for novice backpackers or families with children. Before undertaking either trail, be sure to check the water availability chart in the Visitor Center while obtaining your backcountry permit—a requirement for overnight camping in the backcountry. On these trails backpackers must stay in one of the designated campsites. Some have reliable water nearby, while others have only seasonal water or are perpetually dry. Park rangers advise hikers to purify all backcountry water before drinking.

Backcountry campsites are limited to six persons per night, with a maximum stay of three nights at any one site, and a limit of 14 days' stay in the backcountry. Group trail camps in the backcountry are limited to groups of 15 people, but rangers encourage smaller groups in order to limit impact on the environment. Groups can register for these sites at the Visitor Center.

Nights are cool in Bryce, even during summer, and thunderstorms can develop rapidly and unexpectedly, so backpackers should carry warm clothing and adequate shelter on any overnight excursion. As in all other national parks in Utah, campfires are prohibited.

There are no toilets on Bryce's backcountry trails. Unlike in more arid parks, hikers are not required to pack out their toilet paper.

# Driving to Bryce's Trailheads

Access to Bryce Canyon National Park is via Utah 63, a paved dead-end road branching south from Utah 12, 47 miles west of Escalante and 7.5 miles west of Tropic.

Most Park visitors, however, travel from U.S. 89, west of the Park. The prominently signed junction of U.S. 89 and Utah 12, in the upper Sevier Valley, lies 44 miles north of Mount Carmel Junction and 61 miles north of Kanab or 82 miles south of Richfield. Utah 63 is 14 miles east of U.S. 89 via Utah 12.

(0.0) Driving south on Utah 63, we immediately pass the Pink Cliffs Village, a large tourist complex west of the road.

(1.3) Ruby's Inn, the most elaborate tourist facility near the Park, flanks both sides of the road as we proceed along the broad plateau, soon passing a private campground (0.3; 1.6) west of the road.

(0.9; 2.5) We enter Bryce Canyon National Park, where Utah 63 ends and the paved, two-lane Park road continues south, climbing gently through a pleasant, open forest of ponderosa pines.

(0.3; 2.8) The signed Fairyland Road branches east.

This paved spur road is closed nightly from 9 P.M. to 8 A.M. and during inclement weather. It is also closed in winter, when it used by cross-country skiers. It proceeds generally eastward as it gently ascends the wide plateau, here densely clad in a ponderosa-pine forest.

(0.0; 3.7) The road ends near the rim, where a loop provides ample parking. *Trips 1* and *2* begin here at **Trailhead 1**.

(2.8) Resuming our southbound drive on the Park road, we soon top a rise, then descend through the forest to the Park Entrance Station (0.8; 3.6) and pay the entrance fee before proceeding—quite soon encountering the Bryce Canyon Visitor Center (0.1; 3.7), reached via a spur road leading to the spacious parking area just west of the road. There backpackers can obtain backcountry permits, updated information on trail conditions and water availability, and weather forecasts.

About 100 yards past the Visitor Center turnoff, we encounter a left-branching road leading to spacious North Campground and a picnic area, which ultimately joins other roads leading to Bryce Canyon Lodge and rejoins the Park road to the south.

(0.3; 4.0) A signed eastbound spur road leading to the general store and the picnic area offers access to the Rim Trail (*Trip 2*) at its midpoint, and hikers bound for *Trip 3* should leave the Park road here.

(0.3; 4.3) A left-branching road leads to a picnic area and North Campground. Bearing right here, the road curves south toward a gas station and Bryce Canyon Lodge, but after another 1/4 mile *Trip 3* hikers turn left, curving upward toward the Nature Center and the general store. Opposite the Nature Center, after 0.2 mile, we encounter a large parking area at **Trailhead 2**, where *Trip 3* hikers will

**Northward view along the Pink Cliffs, Rim Trail**

begin their scenic half-day hike just below Sunrise Point.

(4.0) Continuing south along the Park road, ignore a right fork to the Park residential and maintenance area (0.2; 4.2) and soon thereafter those not staying at historic Bryce Canyon Lodge should avoid the left-forking road (0.5; 4.7) leading to it.

(0.1; 4.8) The eastbound spur to Sunset Point forks off to the left.

Hikers bound for *Trip 4* will leave the Park road here and drive 0.2 mile to the large parking area at the roadend loop at **Trailhead 3**, from where three improved trails quickly lead to Sunset Point and the Rim Trail (*Trip 2*).

Shortly beyond that spur road, we encounter the westbound spur to shady Sunset Campground (0.1; 4.9) forking right.

(0.4; 5.3) Following the road ahead through pine forest, we encounter yet another junction.

Hikers bound for *Trips 5* and *6* will turn left here, and almost at once reach a junction with the Inspiration Point spur road, which ends in a loop just below the plateau rim after 0.3 mile, offering access to the Rim Trail, *Trip 2*. Bearing right at that junction, the road ascends gently, soon skirting the foot of badlands slopes.

(1.3; 6.6) Reaching roads forking right to Paria View and left to Bryce Point, *Trip 6* hikers might consider making a brief detour to Paria View, perched on the rim at the roadend 0.4 mile ahead (southwest). On the Bryce Point Road we climb beneath open hillsides of white dolomite. The road soon curves northwest to the **Trailhead 4** parking area (0.6; 7.2) where *Trip 2* terminates and *Trips 5* and *6* begin.

(5.3) From the junction of the spur road to Inspiration, Paria, and Bryce points, we proceed southwest on the Park road, immediately passing a gate that may be temporarily closed during inclement weather. The road then skirts the edge of the largest meadow the Park.

Beyond the meadow you climb slightly into pine forest. Soon the road leads south, skirting a narrow, southern arm of the same large meadow.

After crossing to the meadow's west edge, we reach the

(2.8; 8.1) Sheep Creek Trailhead, where *Trip 7* hikers will park in the small turnout on the road's east side at **Trailhead 5**. Just after the southbound road curves southwest, we reach the

(0.6; 8.7) Swamp Canyon Trailhead, a small parking area at **Trailhead 6** on the southeast side of the curving road. *Trip 8* hikers begin their descent to the Under-the-Rim Trail here.

The road begins a steady grade ahead, and after an abrupt curve above invisible Trough Spring, we continue our steep ascent. A steep switchback then leads us onto the undulating ridge of Whiteman Bench.

(4.9; 13.6) A picnic area shaded by scattered conifers lies on the west side of the road, and hikers using the Whiteman Connector Trail *Trip 9* should park here, 0.3 mile southwest of **Trailhead 7**, but be careful not to block the picnic site for other Park visitors.

Whiteman Bench continues to narrow ahead as we climb to the plateau rim, soon reaching the Farview Point Parking Area (1.2; 14.8), lying on the east side of the road. A short trail and inspiring views offer ample incentive for a brief stop here before proceeding.

Beyond Farview Point, the road curves through the forest while rounding a broad ridge, then steadily descends to

(1.9; 16.7) Natural Bridge Viewpoint, where drivers should exercise caution as cars are frequently entering and leaving the road here. A stop in the turnout here is a must, as there is an exceptional view of an 85' arch just below the rim. In spite of the viewpoint's name, the span below is an arch, not a bridge.

The road ahead curves around the west slopes of Point 8872, reaching an unsigned viewpoint (0.7; 17.4) where we regain the rim.

Beyond the viewpoint we curve west of another hill and rejoin the rim at

(0.7; 18.1) Agua Canyon Viewpoint. Our view from here reaches into the rather large amphitheater of Agua Canyon, an exciting view of colorful pillars and fluted cliffs surpassed in this southern part of the Park only by the view from Rainbow Point.

Soon the roadway leaves the rim, climbing a gentle grade, once again on forested, west-facing slopes high above the valley of East Fork Sevier River. Shortly we reach

(0.6; 18.7) Agua Canyon Trailhead, where a turnout on the road's east side, **Trailhead 8**, offers marginal parking for *Trip 10* hikers.

The road ahead soon curves southeast, reaching the rim at Ponderosa Canyon Overlook, just short of Milepost 15 (0.4; 19.1). When construction of a new trail over Point 9011 is completed, *Trip 10* hikers will begin their hike to the Under-the-Rim Trail from here, switchbacking northeastward up to that point (9011) and joining the present Agua Canyon Connector Trail, thus avoiding the confusing and faint trail that now climb past a park-service gravel pit near the aforementioned trailhead.

Once again, the road ahead abandons the rim for slopes clad in pine, fir, and aspen to the last overlook (0.7; 19.8) short of Rainbow Point.

Passing a gated service road on our right (1.3; 22.0) that leads down to the pumphouse at Yovimpa Pass, we negotiate the final grade toward Rainbow Point. Where the road executes a horseshoe bend, we pass northwest of Yovimpa Point before curving north and entering the spacious parking area and loop at the roadend just south of

(1.1; 23.1) Rainbow Point overlook. Hikers beginning *Trips 11* and *12* will park here at **Trailhead 9**, while *Trip 6* hikers will end their trek and meet their shuttled cars here.

Trailheads for *Trips 13* and *14* are located east of the rim of Paunsaugunt Plateau, off of Utah 12.

(0.0) To reach the trailhead for *Trip 13*, proceed east on Utah 12 from its junction with Utah 63, heading across the open, shrub-clad plateau. In less than a mile, the highway re-enters Bryce Canyon National Park, and shortly thereafter we breach the Pink Cliffs and begin a steady descent into Tropic Canyon.

Soon the road follows the broad, dry wash of Tropic Canyon, and before long a sign indicating Mossy Cave directs *Trip 13* hikers to

(3.7) **Trailhead 10**, lying on the west side of the road just south of the Water Canyon bridge.

To locate the Cooks Ranch Trailhead in lower Bryce Canyon, continue southeast down the widening drainage of Tropic Canyon, soon emerging from the mountains into broad Tropic

Valley, where the highway soon curves due south.

After entering the small town of Tropic, begin to watch for milepost 21. Note the odometer reading at milepost 21, and proceed south another 0.2 mile, where signed Bryce Way branches west (3.7; 7.4). Turn onto this paved road, proceeding west through a residential area. Leaving the town, the road curves southwest, meeting eastbound 50 South Street (1.0; 8.4) at the end of the pavement.

The road ahead is a good, wide, dirt road, easily traveled by cars except immediately following heavy rains. Soon we encounter a right-branching jeep road (0.4; 8.8), which we ignore, and shortly thereafter an equally good graded road, (0.5; 9.3), which we also ignore, branches left (southeast).

The road ahead curves west while ascending the broad, wooded valley of lower Bryce Canyon. Soon, ponderosa pines begin infiltrating the pinyon-juniper and Gambel oak woodland, and a small but lush green meadow south of the road heralds our approach to the loop at

(1.3; 10.6) **Trailhead 11** where *Trip 14* hikers begin their jaunt into Bryce Canyon.

# Trip 1
## Fairyland Trail

**Distance**: 5.75 miles shuttle trip, or 8.0 miles loop

**Low/High elevations**: 7170'/7980'; 8155' along loop trip

**Suited for**: Dayhike

**Difficulty**: Moderate

**Best season**: May through October

**Map/Trailheads**: 12/1,2

**Hazards:** No water; little shade; steep dropoffs.

**Introduction**: This fine dayhike circumnavigates the amphitheaters of Fairyland and Campbell canyons, passing not only a myriad of striking erosional forms, including Boat Mesa, Chinese Wall, Tower Bridge, and Seal Castle, but also wildflower-enlivened badlands slopes, and stands of trees ranging from bristlecone and limber pines to parklike groves of ponderosa pine and stands of Douglas-fir growing in sheltered niches.

The trail involves considerable climbing, and hikers must either arrange for a pickup or car shuttle to Sunrise Point or else loop back to Fairyland Point via the northern leg of the Rim Trail (*Trip 2*), which adds 2.5 miles and 250 feet of elevation gain to the hike, making the trip an all-day excursion for most hikers.

**Description**: From the viewpoint just beyond the loop at the end of Fairyland Road, hikers enjoy a fine view east to the fantastically eroded Fairyland amphitheater, bounded by the tableland of Boat Mesa on the south and our vantage point on the north. Ponderosa pines and Douglas-firs cling to the badlands slopes and in shaded recesses below, between an incredible cluster of orange and white hoodoos.

Our wide trail avoids that rugged amphitheater by descending a narrow ridge eastward from Fairyland Point (0.0; 7770), at once passing a few stunted aspens and enjoying inspiring views into Fairyland.

After we cross over to the north side of this east-trending badlands ridge, views open up into the depths of Fairyland Canyon and its rugged headwaters amphitheater to the north. Scattered ponderosa and limber pines soon appear next to the trail, as well as a few bristlecone pines, a distinctive tree with dark green needles in bundles of five at the ends of its branches, tufted and resembling a fox's tail.

The concentration of hoodoos in Fairyland Canyon doesn't compare with that in the Fairyland amphitheater, but the red- and white-banded erosional forms there, highlighted by scattered forest, are an eye-pleasing sight nonetheless.

After bending southeast and then switchbacking twice, we descend into a draw and follow it downhill, continuing amid mixed conifer forest and passing boulders composed of Wasatch Formation limestone that litters trailside slopes. After we curve southwest toward the foot of the Fairyland amphitheater, pinyons begin to appear, indicating a warmer and drier environment, yet we are only 1/2 mile below the cool pine forests of the plateau.

The trail soon crosses a dry wash and heads southeast downstream. We then climb easily, winding among towers and cliffs rising above, colored in shades of purple, orange, and white, soon topping out at the eastern foot of an intricately eroded cliff.

Soon Fairyland Canyon's colorful walls briefly frame views of far-away mesas in the southeast before the trail dips into another draw. Trees are widely scattered on the limestone slopes, and the purple blooms of thistle are among the showiest flowers here as they are along much of the trail. Rising above the draw we reach a narrow saddle (1.0; 7200), where we may notice a scattering of boulders composed of the Brian Head Conglomerate, the uppermost rock layer in Bryce. This white rock, laced with dark pebbles, caps much of Boat Mesa above us to the west, and these trailside boulders have surely been eroded from its rim and have tumbled down to the ridge on which we now stand.

The trail ahead continues generally south, soon climbing easily to crest another ridge amid interesting hoodoos before descending into and then climbing gently out of another east-trending draw. Presently ascending badlands slopes toward a wooded ridge, we'll observe a variety of summer flowers decorating nearby slopes, including yellow flax, yellow evening primrose, the yellow tube-like flowers of manyflower gromwell, monardella—a blue-flowered mint—dwarf blue columbine, Indian paintbrush, goldenweed, Oregon grape, and hymenopappus.

After negotiating two switchbacks we gain a timbered ridge and follow it northwest, first along its narrow crest and then on south slopes. Soon we trade the inspiring views of the Fairyland for those of the great amphitheater at the head of Campbell Canyon. Cliffs, multihued slopes, and pockets of forest fall away from the rim above into that broad basin.

Traversing below the ridge amid scattered boulders of the Brian Head Conglomerate, we enjoy far-ranging vistas from northeast to southeast. Far to the north, the volcanic Black Mountains rise above the Paunsaugunt Plateau, bounding the southern rim of the Sevier Plateau. Like the prow of a great ship, Boat Mesa and its southeast ridge loom boldly above us, dividing the Fairyland and Campbell canyon drainages.

A few scattered limber and ponderosa pines and junipers offer scant shade up this sun-drenched ridge. Cryptantha is a common wild-flower here, but particularly noteworthy is the prostrate groundcover of mat penstemon, a plant densely covered with tiny blue flowers. This unusual plant is an excellent deterrent to erosion on the otherwise barren limestone slopes.

Beyond the ridge, our trail traverses into numerous draws emanating from the south slopes of Boat Mesa. Goldenweed and evening primrose add their seasonal color to the perpet-ually colorful slopes passed enroute.

Eventually, our trail descends toward the now-visible floor of Campbell Canyon. The ridge rising south of the canyon has generally smooth contours, and its orange and white slopes, incised by numerous steep gullies, are strikingly beautiful. Westward along that ridge are Seal Castle and Mormon Temple, two prom-inent bluffs that rise just east of a triad of pictur-esque towers.

Two switchbacks lower us to the canyon floor, and enroute we can gaze across the canyon to the opening of Tower Bridge. This intriguing erosional feature consists of a fin of orange limestone pierced by one large and one small opening near its eastern terminus. A bridge of stone connects two prominent pinnacles, form-ing the larger opening. This is not a true bridge by definition, since it was not formed over a watercourse. More accurately it could be called an arch or a window.

On reaching the canyon floor, the signed TOWER BRIDGE spur trail forks left (3.0; 7220), leading to the foot of the arch in 200 yards.

Proceeding up the canyon from that junc-tion, the trail ascends the canyon for 0.1 mile, crossing the wash twice, then climbing moder-ately, at first through forest but later on colorful slopes nearly devoid of vegetation. We soon pass a few erosion-isolated hoodoos, traverse a nar-row ridge, and then briefly contour southwest, outflanking a row of towers on the ridge above before climbing one more switchback leg to regain the ridge.

Gazing southeast from the switchback, we can look across a colorful, yet barren, shallow bowl, beyond which rises the fluted white cliff

of Chinese Wall, pierced by several small win-dows.

The trail ahead contours into a forested, northwest-trending draw, then begins to rise be-neath a thickening forest canopy. The rim pres-ently lies just above to the west, decorated by tall trees, colorful hoodoos, and pinnacle-capped cliffs. Bulky, tree-capped Boat Mesa fills the view to the northeast, rising from Campbell Can-yon via steep layered slopes and fluted cliffs colored in shades of white and orange.

Upon gaining the crest of the forested ridge, we climb moderately to a junction with the Rim Trail (1.5; 7980) on the northeast ridge of Point 8047. From here we can follow the Rim Trail to the right (northwest) for 2.5 miles and loop back to Fairyland Point, or turn south, proceeding toward Sunrise, Sunset, and Bryce points, (see *Trip 2*).If you have a shuttled car at **Trailhead 2** near the general store, follow the Rim Trail south for 250 yards, then turn right (northwest) and proceed 0.1 mile to the large parking area there.

# Trip 2
## Fairyland Point to Bryce Point via the Rim Trail

**Distance**: 5.5 miles shuttle trip
**Low/High elevations**: 7770'/8330'
**Suited for**: Dayhike
**Difficulty**: Moderate
**Best season**: May through October
**Map/Trailheads**: 12/1,4
**Hazards**: Steep dropoffs; no water.

**Introduction**: Parts of the Rim Trail are quite popular among Park visitors, as the route offers exceptional overviews of the Fairyland and Campbell and Bryce Canyon amphitheaters, in addition to vistas of far-away plateaus and mesas that fade into the heat-hazy distance of the Colorado Plateau.

The trail can be easily reached from not only Fairyland and Bryce points, but also from the popular viewing areas of Sunrise, Sunset, and Inspiration points via very short access trails, and many hikers tread only a part of this scenic route, enjoying the grand scenery at a leisurely pace.

To hike all or part of this trail, a car shuttle is required to avoid retracing one's steps, but the advantages of backtracking and viewing the same features as they change with the passage of the sun offer ample incentive for hikers to take a full day to enjoy this view-filled jaunt.

**Description**: The signed Rim Trail heads south from Fairyland Point (0.0; 7770), following close to the brink of the rim above a labyrinth of gullies and a profusion of colorful spires, battlements, and shaded recesses within the Fairyland amphitheater. Unobstructed views to the northeast are dominated by the Table Cliffs, composed of the same rock formations as Bryce Canyon, but offset by uplift and hence resting at elevations 2000 feet higher than the rim on which we stand.

Massive Canaan Peak rises south of the Table Cliffs and broad, wooded benches rise in stairstep fashion eastward from Tropic Valley, while the distant dome of Navajo Mountain

highlights the far southeastern horizon.

Similar views of these features will accompany us along our entire journey to Bryce Point. A short jaunt along the rim brings us to a sign indicating SUNRISE POINT (0.2; 7800), where a less-used trail forks left.

---

# Boat Mesa Trail

This trail offers a possible sidetrip for some and a destination for others. The steep trail ascends a southeast-trending ridge to the 8076' point of Boat Mesa. While laboring up the steep trail, we may pause long enough to notice an abundance of small, mostly black, rounded pebbles littering the trailbed. These pebbles, rounded by abrasion, are a component of the Brian Head Conglomerate, the youngest and most erosion-resistant rock layer in the Park, evident in only a few locations. Boat Mesa

**Tropic Valley and Table Cliffs from Bryce Point**

stands as an island in a sea of softer, rapidly eroding rocks, and over time the subsequent erosion of the Wasatch Formation rocks will likely leave the mesa standing even higher above its surroundings than at present.

Between 37 and 19 million years ago, volcanic activity in the region produced large flows of basalt that capped Utah's High Plateaus. As this basalt was eroded away, streams and rivers reduced its fragments to the size of pebbles, which were later cemented together to form rock. Today, erosion and weathering are exhuming the pebbles from their rocky tomb, and they will continue the downward journey they began millions of years before.

After the stiff climb, we welcome the nearly level surface of Boat Mesa. Vistas extend southward to Bryce Point, viewed over a series of spectacularly eroded, colorful amphitheaters. Northwestward, one can gaze across the undulating surface of the Paunsaugunt Plateau to where it eventually breaks away in ranks of cliff and buttes. Northward, the loftier surface is the Sevier Plateau, seen rising beyond the volcanic battlements of the Black Mountains.

---

From the junction (0.2; 7800) the Rim Trail drops briefly to a saddle, then climbs gently along or near the rim in a southwestward direction, through open stands of ponderosa, pinyon and Rocky Mountain juniper. Where the trail approaches the open brink of the rim itself, we can gaze downward into cool, shady niches, surrounded by myriad colorful battlements and spires. We'll enjoy views southward deep into Campbell Canyon and spy Tower Bridge, the Chinese Wall, Seal Castle and Mormon Temple.

Climbing west, then northwest, we soon pass an intriguing jumble of hoodoos and fins rising to eye level, isolated from the rim by headward erosion. Topping out just north of Point 8155, we can briefly enjoy vistas of the vast and undulating surface and the dense forests and meadows of the Paunsaugunt Plateau, beyond which our eyes scan the lofty summits of the Markagunt Plateau far to the northwest.

Descending tree-clad slopes west of this prominence, we negotiate one switchback while briefly viewing the Park Visitor Center below to our west. The trail regains the rim above the Campbell Canyon amphitheater at an 8000' saddle where a colorful cliff band falls away abruptly into forested slopes that descend to the canyon floor.

Ahead, our trail traverses the sparsely forested west slopes of two rim-top hills above North Campground. Beyond the second, southernmost hill, we regain the rim, passing two use trails, less than 0.1 mile apart, that lead to the campground access road. A third trail forks west, descending past the campground's amphitheater.

Our route usually becomes increasingly crowded as we proceed toward the busy Sunrise Point area, passing yet another use trail heading southwest 100 yards to a Park road opposite the Bryce Canyon General Store. Presently, our rim route climbs to the northeast ridge of Point 8047, where we intercept the Fairyland Trail (2.3; 7980) climbing up out of Campbell Canyon. Visually we can trace that trail northeast until it disappears amid castle-like formations below the rim. Far-ranging vistas extend northeast to the Table Cliffs and to the long hogback of Canaan Peak, east across Tropic Valley, its woodlands broken by hayfields and rangeland, and far to the southeast to the immense dome of Navajo Mountain, resting on the southern border of Utah.

Proceeding south, we traverse the steeply sloping east flank of Point 8047, soon descending easily to a junction with the Sunrise Point Trail. Two very short forks of that trail join at a Y a few feet to the northwest, and that trail in turn leads 0.1 mile to the large but often crowded Sunrise Point parking area opposite the Nature Center and just south of the general store.

Past the southern leg of the Y, a dusty horse trail forks right (southwest) leading past a corral to Bryce Canyon Lodge in 0.2 mile. Immediately beyond that trail, the signed Horse Trail forks left, descending through the forest from the rim. The Park concessionaire, T.W. Services, conducts seasonal horse rides twice daily along this trail, which is the only trail in the Park open to private use by horses. Hikers can use the horse trail, but it is dusty and they must step off the trail, on the downhill side where possible, when saddle stock approach.

A sign here on the Rim Trail indicates QUEENS GARDEN TRAIL and SUNRISE POINT on the south, and we proceed south along the wide, surfaced trail and gently ascend toward 8015' Sunrise Point. Immediately before we reach the point, however, the Queens Garden Trail (*Trip 3*) peels off to the left, descending a narrow ridge southeastward, while a southwest-bound trail leads right for 0.2 mile to the Lodge.

The fenced-in overlook platform atop Sunrise Point (0.2; 8015) is a favorite, easily accessible viewpoint offering a comprehensive overview of the Park from Boat Mesa in the northeast to Bryce Point in the south. In the south, the thickly forested rim falls away abruptly eastward. Its steep orange- and white-layered slopes are lacking well-developed hoodoos, but below these steep slopes is an array of colorful hoodoos and fluted, finlike ridges jutting above badlands slopes.

Below us to the south lies the Queens Garden amphitheater, an unforgettable jumble of brilliantly colorful columns and spires. The Garden's namesake trail can be see threading its way among these wondrous erosional forms, beckoning hikers to descend from the rim and explore its enchanting realm.

After descending slightly from Sunrise Point back onto the Rim Trail, we head southwest on the nearly level, paved trail (handicapped accessible). The half-mile segment between Sunrise and Sunset points is the most popular stretch along the Rim Trail.

Enroute, we'll stroll past spur trails forking off toward Bryce Canyon Lodge, visible through the forest just west of the rim. We'll also pass occasional benches located along the rim for restful viewing of the incredible scenery.

Approaching Sunset Point, we'll notice stunted aspens growing at the foot of the tan cliff below, where they have tapped into a subsurface water source. Since aspens require abundant moisture, their presence almost universally indicates that water lies close to the surface. Below this cliff band under the rim, badlands slopes fall away into an exciting landscape of hoodoos and finlike ridges.

Three paved spur trails fork off toward the

spacious Sunset Point parking area, but we ignore them and follow the paved trail to the fenced-in viewing area at Sunset Point (0.5; 7999), which rests atop a serrated, razor-edge fin. This exceedingly popular overlook is the point from which to view the rugged grandeur of the Bryce Canyon amphitheater in its entirety. Visitors stand awestruck at what is considered the finest display of hoodoos on the planet. Particularly breathtaking is the southward view overlooking the Silent City, an especially dense concentration of orange fins separated by deep fissures, narrow, dark, and mysterious. Your imagination can conjure up a wide variety of images and likenesses in what is arguably the most sublime spectacle in the Park.

Eastward, colorful hoodoos of every description embrace the nearly flat, pine-forested floor of Bryce Canyon. This broad canyon collects seasonal runoff from the rim and transports it to the Paria River near the town of Tropic, visible in the bucolic valley below. Distant vistas also vie for our attention, from the Table Cliffs, to Canaan Peak, to the gray and red sandstone bluffs rising east of Tropic Valley, to the dome of Navajo Mountain, peeking above leagues of wooded mesas over 90 miles distant.

A gentle stroll along the rim connects the unforgettable viewpoints of Sunset and Inspiration points. Contrasting the green pine forests and the gentle terrain of the plateau with the strange beauty and vivid colors of the Silent City and the famous Bryce Canyon amphitheater, this is a memorable segment of the Rim Trail and is surprisingly uncrowded, compared to the previous segment.

From Sunset Point the Rim Trail follows the rim of the plateau first southwest, then south, overlooking the maze of Silent City, a labyrinth of hoodoos and narrow gorges that is astonishing in its symmetry and repetition of form. Controlled by joints—vertical cracks in the rocks of the Wasatch Formation—this is a surprisingly orderly complex of hoodoos, though at first glance it may appear to be as haphazard a congregation of columns as most other erosional forms in the Park. Here narrow chasms separate the ranks of hoodoos, all of which radiate outward from just below the rim, like spokes of a wheel. On the short hike between Sunset and Inspiration points, hikers will likely linger over landscapes they have never dreamed of, conjuring up images of ancient temples falling into ruin, or throngs of human-like figures crowded together and perpetually frozen in stone.

As our route hugs the rim, bound for Inspiration Point, we'll pass numerous trees whose roots have been exposed by erosion. Here are excellent examples of headward erosion, where the tributaries of the Paria River have cut back farther into the plateau with each passing year. Estimates are that the rim is retreating an average of 1 1/2 feet per century.

As we progress we soon parallel close to a service road leading to a water tank visible through the trees a short distance to the west. Approaching Inspiration Point amid ponderosa, limber, and bristlecone pines and a few Douglas-firs, we enjoy occasional tree-framed vignettes of the rolling, forest-clad surface of the Paunsaugunt Plateau, where only occasional outcroppings of Wasatch Formation limestones appear through the green mantle of conifers.

As we pass above the large Inspiration Point parking area, we'll pass a very short spur trail forking right (southwest) to the trailhead, and quickly climb to meet the main trail leading to the parking area on our right, switchbacking up wooded slopes. Here a very short spur forks left to the fenced-in lower overlook, and we proceed just west of the rim for 0.1 mile to meet the longer trail from the parking area. Very soon another spur forks left and quickly climbs to Inspiration Point proper (0.9; 8325), where we can view the scene from another fenced-in overlook.

The central location of Inspiration Point offers a tremendous overview of the Bryce Canyon amphitheater, the largest and arguably the most scenic such bowl in the Park. The view of the pinnacle jumble of Silent City is without equal in the Park, particularly when seen in the pastel glow of a Utah sunrise. Above Silent City we can see the fence-lined rim at Sunset Point and we can gaze northward past Sunrise Point along the Pink Cliffs' broken, colorful landscape stretching toward the broad, open expanse of Johns Valley. Particularly prominent features seen beyond a sea of colorful hoodoos below the rim include the broad tableland of Boat Mesa in the northeast, and east of it rises the curious sloping platform of a point aptly named Sinking Ship.

On the badlands slopes west of Bristlecone Point and north of Bryce Canyon, widely scattered ponderosa, limber and bristlecone pines stand amid the bleached snags of their former companions.

From our viewpoint atop this rocky promontory jutting eastward into Bryce Canyon's amphitheater, we gaze downward past varicolored fins and hoodoos into a southwestern arm of Bryce Canyon, thickly forested with pines, firs, and spruces. Above that branch canyon, a prominent ridge contains the castle-like formation of The Cathedral, and the Peekaboo Loop Trail is seen descending northward just below it.

---

The southern segment of the Rim Trail completes the semicircuit above the Bryce Canyon amphitheater, ending at the parking area above Bryce Point. Choked with brush in frequent sunny openings, this part of the rim, although higher in elevation than previous parts, is the driest. However, views are expansive and this section of the Rim Trail is the least traveled.

Hikers starting from the Inspiration Point parking area have a choice of three ways to access the Rim Trail. First, to gain the quickest access, one can follow a left-forking trail for about 100 feet from the north end of the parking area and turn right on the Rim Trail. Or one can take the main, signed trail and climb quickly to a junction, where one can turn left and switchback easily to lower Inspiration Point or turn right and climb to Inspiration Point proper, 0.2 mile from the parking area.

From the point, return west to the nearby Rim Trail, which quickly curves southeast and undulates along the rim. The small town of Tropic is the sole enclave of civilization visible from the rim, lying near the western edge of Tropic (or Bryce) Valley. Sweeping views extend along the rolling surface of the Paunsaugunt Plateau from the south to the northwest where open meadows notch the forested plateau surface. These historic summer grazing lands first attracted pioneers to this corner of Utah.

From Tropic we can trace the route of Utah Highway 12 as it passes into the canyon between the Table Cliffs and Canaan Peak to the northeast, bound for the towns of Escalante and Boulder, and for Capitol Reef National Park. The Table Cliffs, especially colorful when backlit by the setting sun, are composed of the same rocks as Bryce Canyon, and now-familiar Navajo Mountain continues to dominate the scene on the southeast horizon.

Groundsel is a particularly abundant yellow wildflower along this section in summer and other wildflowers include thistle, the tall Wyoming paintbrush, gilia, and manyflower gromwell. A common shrub here is Martin ceanothus, a low-spreading shrub with oval green leaves and spine-tipped branches. The stunted, twisted habit of many trees along the rim reflects the harsh weather and soil conditions with which they must cope. Pinyon, ponderosa, limber, and bristlecone pines, Douglas-firs, and Rocky Mountain junipers are the forest trees encountered.

As we proceed, we'll enjoy inspiring views into the hoodoo-jumble of the Bryce amphitheater, and spy trails suddenly appearing and disappearing among the colorful upright rocks below.

After 0.7 mile from Inspiration Point, we pass above the narrow Wall of Windows, but from this vantage its openings are difficulty to see. Beyond the Wall of Windows, white hoodoos begin jutting outward below the rim, and ahead we'll pass above other window-like openings while gazing toward the promontory of Bryce Point. Seeping groundwater has dissolved bedrock below the point to create numerous alcoves in the varicolored cliffs. When we reach a notch at the head of a plunging, north-trending gully, we are standing on Peekaboo Fault, one of the minor faults that lace the Park. One of the best places from which to observe the offset strata is on the Peekaboo Loop Trail, beginning at Bryce Point (*Trip 5*).

Beyond this notch our trail curves northeast along the rim amid a sparse forest and climbs easily to a junction with the short, paved Bryce Point Trail, forking to the left (north). Turning right, we descend for 100 yards to conclude our hike at the Bryce Point parking area (1.2; 8300).

# Trip 3
## Queens Garden Trail

**Distance**: 3.4 miles round trip
**Low/High elevations**: 7400'/8000'
**Suited for**: Dayhike
**Difficulty**: Moderate
**Best season**: May through October
**Map/Trailhead**: 12/2
**Hazards**: Steep dropoffs; no water.

**Introduction**: This trail is a popular dayhike into the incomparable Bryce Canyon amphitheater, descending into the realm of hoodoos, castles, and balanced rocks, many of which have been likened to familiar images and given such fanciful names as Gullivers Castle and Queen Victoria.

Many hikers combine the Queens Garden Trail with a leg of the Navajo Loop Trail (*Trip 4*) and loop back to Sunrise Point via the Rim Trail (Trip 2). Others, if they don't mind meeting horses and hiking a dusty trail, can loop back to the trailhead via the mile-long Horse Trail, a route that few hikers tread. The minor inconvenience of possibly encountering horseback riders from the Lodge is more than compensated for by the striking landscapes that trail passes and the exceptional views it offers. Whichever route hikers choose, they will be rewarded by some of the most awe-inspiring scenery the Park has to offer.

**Description**: From the parking area just southeast of the Nature Center and General Store (0.0; 7950), hike past a SUNRISE POINT sign and follow the paved trail southeast for 150 yards to a fork and bear right, quickly reaching the Rim Trail (see *Trip 2*). (The left fork also leads to the Rim Trail.) Immediately beyond this junction, a trail forks right toward Bryce Lodge, and the Horse Trail quickly forks left, descending from the Rim. Ignoring both trails, proceed south along the rim, climbing gently to a junction with the Queens Garden Connector Trail (0.2; 8000) immediately before reaching Sunrise Point. Turning left on that trail, we descend moderately along or near a ridge that plunges eastward from Sunrise Point. We will enjoy ever-changing views as we proceed, including Queens Garden, Bryce Point, and the forested floor of Bryce Canyon to the south. The colorful Campbell Canyon drainage and Boat Mesa lie to the northeast, and distant panoramas include the Table Cliffs, Canaan Peak, and Tropic Valley.

Descending a series of switchbacks, we traverse badlands slopes decorated by ponderosa and bristlecone pines beneath isolated hoodoos, soon passing directly below towering Gullivers Castle and a notch in the ridge framing orange fluted cliffs westward below the tree-studded rim, then reach the signed junction (0.6; 7680) to Queens Garden.

Ahead, the Horse Trail goes south along the ridge, reaching Bryce Canyon after 0.4 mile, and to the left, in 1 mile it reaches the Rim Trail north of Sunrise Point. But for now, Queens Garden beckons, so we turn right and descend to its realm via a series of short switchbacks, which soon lead through a short tunnel.

The trail winds downward among the recesses of the garden, where a myriad of starkly beautiful castles, towers, pillars, minarets, and fins, colored in shades of orange and white, stir the imagination. Dark-green conifers contrast with these colorful erosional forms, growing vigorously in intervening gullies and sparsely on nearby slopes.

Bending into a south-trending draw, we traverse southward around the nose of a ridge and pass through another tunnel before bending northwest back into another draw. Many hoodoos in the Park are "primary wall-type" hoodoos—narrow, finlike ridges projecting outward from the rim. They are a concentration of pinnacles, towers, castles, and spires, and their walls are irregularly fluted. Colors range from shades of white to yellow, and orange. Queens Garden is composed generally of the eroded remnants of these finlike ridges, eroded to the point that the hoodoos are largely isolated from one another by intervening badlands slopes and saddles.

Curving southward out of this draw, we pass through a third tunnel and quickly reach a junction (0.4; 7600). A spur trail forks right here, signed for Queen Victoria, while the main trail is signed for the Navajo Loop Trail. This spur leads northwest up a small draw, dead-ending after 100 yards beneath the namesake of this northernmost lobe of the Bryce amphitheater, Queen Victoria. Bearing a striking resemblance to the 19th century monarch, the "Queen," wearing a crown of whitish stone, watches over her realm from atop the northernmost of four prominent pinnacles rising immediately east of the trail's end.

Returning to the main trail, continue southward, bound for the Navajo Trail, at first descending gently along a dry gully. The trail briefly narrows where two orange hoodoos close in, then continues downhill amid tall conifers and taller hoodoos.

After we stroll south for a few minutes from the Queen Victoria spur trail, a sign carved into a trailside stump points the way to the Navajo Loop Trail. Soon thereafter a sign indicating the Horse Trail marks a junction with a spur trail forking left into Bryce Canyon (0.4; 7400). Hikers now have the choice of (1) continuing straight ahead (southwest), reaching the Navajo Loop Trail after an easy 0.4 mile, (2) turning left onto the aforementioned spur trail to reach the Horse Trail, which loops back to the trailhead in 1.4 very scenic miles, or (3) retracing their steps back to the trailhead.

# Trip 4
## Navajo Loop Trail

**Distance**: 1.4 miles loop trip
**Low/High elevations**: 7475'/7999'
**Suited for**: Dayhike
**Difficulty**: Moderate
**Best season**: May through October
**Map/Trailhead**: 12/3
**Hazards**: Steep dropoffs; no water.

**Introduction**: This popular, short dayhike offers ample rewards for a modicum of effort. Passing the crumbling stone edifices of Silent City, the shadow-filled hallway of Wall Street, the water-carved spans of Two Bridges, and the balanced rock of Thors Hammer (to name but a few of the remarkable erosional features passed enroute) this trip packs more exceptional scenery into a two-hour hike than perhaps any other trail in the Park.

**Description**: From the large parking area at the end of the Sunset Point spur road (0.0; 7995), three paved trails lead east for 125 yards to the rim at Sunset Point, where they meet the Rim Trail going left and right.

Just north of the extensive fenced-in viewing area of Sunset Point, the signed, wide, well-maintained Navajo Loop Trail departs downhill, switchbacking down the first cliff band below the rim, its moist and sheltered microclimate harboring stunted aspens at its base. After about 125 yards, the trail forks. The left fork continues descending, while the right fork quickly traverses toward a U-shaped gap between colorful hoodoos. Wall Street and the Silent City beckon, so for now we'll take the right fork.

Passing through a hoodoo-rimmed notch, we stand above the maze of Silent City, where dark, narrow defiles separate finlike cliffs that are as high as 200 feet. At the notch another wide trail forks right, quickly ending in the tunnel visible ahead. Seen from the tunnel, a myriad of tall, fanciful pinnacles rise out of Silent City, their summits just below eye level. This bewildering semicircular array of pinnacles is laced with many deep, dark, mysterious chasms, their shady depths virtually unknown.

The Navajo Loop Trail then descends a steep, orange-colored slope via 29 short, tight switchbacks. Pinnacles tower higher above as we descend past huge boulders. While we descend this well-designed series of switchbacks into Silent City, the horizontal layering of the colorful strata becomes apparent. But midway down our descent, we notice diagonal striations along the base of the wall east of the slope. These striations, or scour marks, which are parallel to the present-day angle of the slope, were probably formed over time as a gully washed abrasive sediments downslope. The scour marks indicate that the slope has maintained its high angle instead of flattening out, as one might expect, as erosion has cut back into the rim.

Below the switchbacks, the trail enters the dark, narrow passage of Wall Street. The cliffs in Wall Street, as in the rest of Bryce, are not smooth but have wrinkled, corrugated surfaces. Here tall cliffs rise steeply over 100 feet above and stand barely 20 feet apart. Some hikers may feel claustrophobic in this chasm, but its cool, shady depths are attractive on a hot summer day. Here we gain a close-up look at the varicolored layers of the Wasatch Formation, sediments laid down at the bottom of ancient Lake Flagstaff between about 60 and 40 million years ago.

The bottom of Wall Street has been scoured over the years by floodwaters, and as a result the cliffs above overhang our trail in places. As we proceed into Wall Street we'll pass a few tall, vigorous Douglas-firs, their straight trunks free of branches, their crowns reaching for sunlight near the top of the fluted cliffs.

Leaving the confines of Wall Street, we turn southeast to join a larger wash draining the rim. Compared to Wall Street, this wash enjoys considerable sunlight, which encourages a diverse forest here, aided by deeper sediments in which trees can gain a foothold and by a concentration of moisture at the foot of cliffs. The dark-green foliage of Douglas-fir, ponderosa and limber pine, juniper and a few spruces frame the colorful pinnacles rising above us. Manzanita carpets the orange-tinted ground, and scattered boulders fallen from the cliffs above attest to the inexorable forces that are constantly reshaping the landscape.

Ahead our trail rounds the abrupt terminus of a southeast trending ridge and we stroll northeast to a four-way junction (0.8; 7475). Following the signed Navajo Loop Trail past the junction, we climb to the left (northwest) into a tree-shaded canyon bounded by a fascinating array of erosional forms. Soon it appears we are heading into a box canyon with no way out, but the trail finds a narrow passageway among colorful minarets. After we enter this narrow defile, numerous gullies feed the main drainage.

A short distance up one of these side gullies (0.2 mile from the junction) are Two Bridges, pointed to by a sign. A quick stroll up this gorge reveals the bridges, which are composed of one of the more resistant layers of the Wasatch Formation. Drainage in the gully has worn away a softer layer underneath. The span of the larger bridge is about 20 feet high, while that of the smaller bridge is only 4 feet above the floor of the gully.

Above Two Bridges, the Navajo Loop Trail climbs moderately steeply up a gully reminiscent of Wall Street. A series of short switchbacks ensue, and hikers pausing to catch their breath may notice Oregon grape thriving in shady nooks along the way. At the top of this stiff climb, we traverse beneath castle-like hoodoos and notice an especially striking finger-like pinnacle rising above the trail—The Sentinel. We then pass a few windows and gaze northward to prominent Thors Hammer, beyond which stands The Pope, clad in a white "robe," and dozens of other startlingly familiar erosional forms. One final switchback leads us to the junction below Sunset Point, where we bear right to retrace our route to the Sunset Point parking area (0.6; 7995).

# Trip 5
## Peekaboo Loop Trail

**Distance**: 5.0 miles, semiloop trip
**Low/High elevations**: 7440'/8320'
**Suited for**: Dayhike
**Difficulty**: Moderate
**Best season**: May through October
**Map/Trailhead**: 12/4
**Hazards**: Limited water; steep dropoffs.

**Introduction:** This superb dayhike tours the southern half of Bryce Canyon amphitheater, passing numerous springs, traversing shady microclimates hosting such trees as Colorado blue spruce and white fir, winding among a colorful collection of hoodoos, and crossing badlands slopes.

Just before climbing back to the rim, hikers find a picnic table and a drinking fountain in a draw below a perennial spring, a fine place for a rest before the stiff climb.

**Description**: To reach the Peekaboo Loop Trail, we depart from the east side of the parking area (0.0; 8300) and follow a paved trail gently downhill toward the southeast, to where we part ways with *Trip 6* hikers at a signed junction (0.1; 8235) and bear left onto the Peekaboo Connector Trail.

Beyond the junction, the wide, smooth, dirt-surface trail leads through an open forest of ponderosa, limber, and bristlecone pines and Douglas-fir. A series of switchbacks soon follows, and they serve to lower us over the rim where white dolomitic slopes give way to the more colorful, iron-rich strata of the Wasatch Formation.

Soon we descend north-facing slopes via two long switchbacks, and the vegetation begins to reflect a cool and sheltered microclimate. We shortly begin a protracted traverse high above a forested, hoodoo-rimmed canyon. Enroute we pass through a short tunnel bored through a knife-edged ridge, where a resistant orange layer and a crumbly lavender layer of the Wasatch Formation coalesce.

Beyond the tunnel, our gaze stretches into the forested canyons below, including the aptly-named Alligator, a white dolomite-capped hoodoo.

The trail leads across the mud and runoff from an upslope spring, and enroute we briefly spy the fenced overlook of Bryce Point, 400 feet above, atop steep white cliffs. Trees are scattered on these steep slopes, and the few shrubs that are able to grow here include bitterbrush and mountain spray, the latter with dense, fragrant clusters of small white flowers during summer.

Adding to the dramatic overviews of the hoodoo-filled amphitheater, a variety of summer wildflowers will delight our senses as well, including tall Wyoming paintbrush, groundsel, hymenopappus, and gumweed.

Soon the trail curves southwest around a steep ridge that plunges below Bryce Point. Gazing beyond the steep draw that lies before us, we see two prominent white pillars below the rim. Between them is one of many arches and windows that penetrate the finlike ridges of Bryce. A keyhole-shaped window lies just south of the above-mentioned window, and numerous alcoves incise the cliffs under the rim. Soon the Wall of Windows comes into view, where two openings frame the sky beyond.

Switchbacks ensue amid colorful hoodoos crowned by resistant caprocks, and we soon reach a junction (0.9; 7680) with the loop trail.

Taking the right fork, we descend via switchbacks amid multihued hoodoos. Many hoodoos in Bryce have been given imaginative names, and as soon as we proceed through this wondrous landscape, the mind imagines likenesses to known people and familiar features such as castles and temples.

Highlighting the intervening slopes and gullies between the hoodoos are stands of Douglas-fir, limber and ponderosa pines, and Colorado blue spruce. Notice the swollen tips of the branches on some spruce trees. These trees are host to the spruce budworm, a blight on spruce trees throughout the western United States.

We soon reach the comparatively level ground of the canyon floor in a forest of mixed conifers. Ponderosa pine comes to dominate the forest as we descend into a warmer and drier environment, and 0.4 mile from the junction we cross the canyon's wash, seasonally dampened by the runoff from an upstream spring. But we soon leave the wash, traversing northwest into another draw, where the wide trail, dusty from daily horse traffic, climbs a south-facing slope beneath striking hoodoos. The harsh environment of nearby slopes permits little vegetation other than widely scattered shrubs and stunted trees.

After contouring into another draw, the trail ascends northward. During the climb we'll have fine views south beyond eye-level hoodoos into the colorful recesses of the Bryce amphitheater. A few switchbacks ensue, leading us to a short tunnel and subsequently to a hoodoo-decorated traverse, ending on a ridge just west of the orange tower of Fairy Castle. Views from this ridge extend from Boat Mesa in the north, past Sunrise and Sunset points, to Bryce Point in the south— an engaging panorama encompassing one of the finest erosional spectacles to be seen on the globe.

Descending colorful slopes via switchbacks, we reach a forested draw and drop to a singed junction (1.3; 7440). From here a short spur leads north less than 100 yards to another junction. The left fork at this junction joins the Navajo Loop Trail, 1/4 mile west. The right fork leads northeast down Bryce Canyon 0.1 mile to a northbound horse trail, then another 0.1 mile to a northwest-bound horse trail, and another 1.2 miles east to a roadend west of Tropic (see *Trip 14*). But we turn left (west) on the return leg of our loop tour, moderately ascending northwest-facing slopes under a shady canopy of ponderosa pines.

After 0.3 mile we climb two switchbacks, gaining a northwest view of the Navajo Loop Trail. We can trace its course from Bryce Canyon to Wall Street, where it disappears in the shady recesses of Silent City. The hoodoos and narrow defiles of Silent City rise in a colorful procession of orange, gray, white, and yellow rocks toward serrated ranks of fins jutting outward from the forested rim. A pause here also reveals the butte of Boat Mesa to the north beyond the colorful ridge north of Bryce Canyon.

Continuing our journey, we glimpse Inspiration Point's overlook perched on the rim above to the west, and proceed southward beneath a row of striking orange hoodoos, dominated by The Cathedral. Soon we gain the crest of a north-trending ridge and continue deeper into the mysterious realm of multihued, upright rock formations. Ponderosa and limber pines, Douglas-firs, and blue spruces are scattered but still offer occasional respite from the penetrating Utah sun.

Pause to view the prominent, very steep gully plunging from the rim west of Bryce Point. Here the Peekaboo Fault has slightly offset the strata, and the fault is most easily observed in the offset cliff bands below the steep white slopes abutting the rim. Our trail ahead gently rises and falls, passes through a tunnel in a ridge below Wall of Windows and switchbacks down a narrow, spruce-clad gully. A spire-topped window juts outward from the rim to the south, while Bryce Point rises 700 feet above on the southeast skyline. At the foot of this gully, we turn west and steadily ascend another draw beneath Wall of Windows, thrusting its sheer, fluted cliffs to the sky.

Soon we top out between trailside hoodoos, then traverse 600 feet below the rim, splashing through the runoff of a spring enroute. Bending northeast, our traverse terminates as we descend a sparsely wooded draw and reach a signed junction (1.6; 7600) just above a corral and a pipe-fed water trough. Here we can turn right and follow the spur trail south for 150 yards to a fine rest spot, featuring 2 picnic tables, toilets, and a spring-fed drinking fountain, shaded by conifers. The trickle of an upstream spring and the breezes through the trees make this a particularly peaceful locale, seemingly a world apart from the hustle and bustle of visitors at Bryce Point, visible nearly 700 feet above.

Returning to the main trail, we skirt the corral, pass a sign pointing to the rim, and quickly hop across a mossy seep from the spring above. Climbing gently through the forest, we soon reach the terminus of the loop (0.1; 7680) and then backtrack the 1-mile view-filled ascent to Bryce Point.

# Trip 6
## Under-the-Rim Trail: Bryce Point to Rainbow Point

**Distance**: 22.8 miles shuttle trip
**Low/High elevations**: 6800'/9115'
**Suited for**: Backpack
**Difficulty**: Strenuous as a one- or two-day trip; moderate as a three-day trip.
**Best season**: May through October
**Maps/Trailheads**: 12, 13, 14/4, 9
**Hazards**: Widely spaced and mostly seasonal water sources; steep dropoffs.

**Introduction**: This memorable trek is the longer of two backpacking trails in Bryce. True to its name, the route stays far below the rim, touching it only at each end. Consequently, hikers have more distant views of Bryce's famous hoodoo formations, but the route allows a more intimate association with the three distinct life zones present in the Park.

Much of the trail passes below the Pink Cliffs of the Wasatch Formation, and instead of traveling over a firm trailbed that the Wasatch provides, the trail travels over a deep, sandy tread weathered from the underlying sandstone formations.

When you obtain your backcountry permit for the trip at the Visitor Center, be sure to check the water availability chart, listing the condition of springs along the trail. Then you can better plan your hiking days between water sources and choose the appropriate campsites.

**Description**: Most hikers begin their trek at Bryce Point, where they stroll southeast from the parking area (0.0; 8300) down the briefly paved trail 0.1 mile to a junction with Peekaboo Connector Trail and bear right (south) onto the Under-the-Rim Trail. On it we proceed south and east along white dolomitic slopes clad in an open forest of ponderosa and limber pine and Douglas-fir.

The trail then switchbacks down to level ground near a red hill dotted with ponderosa pines at 0.6 mile. An interesting jumble of hoodoos lies below the rim south of this 8000' ridge. Expansive views stretch across the Park northeast to the Table Cliffs, then past Canaan Peak, Bryce Valley and the town of Tropic, southeast down the Paria River, and south across vast wooded plateaus to the horizon in northern Arizona. The forested depths of Yellow Creek lie below to the south. Presently we descend east above a hoodoo-filled bowl and enter a woodland of pinyon and juniper.

After curving into and out of the head of Merrill Hollow, we traverse a narrow ridge, passing above the Hat Shop after 2 miles from the trailhead. This collection of hoodoos is quite different from the finlike wall hoodoos most common under the rim. It consists of a jumble of reddish, finger-like pillars composed of soft, loosely compacted gravel. The "hats" consist of resistant gray caprocks, remnants of a once-continuous layer of stone now left balancing upon each pedestal now that much of the softer material below has eroded away.

The trail then descends westward down well-drained slopes into Right Fork Yellow Creek. The sheltered canyon may have free-flowing water during some summers. The descent leads us below the Wasatch Formation into the realm of the Kaiparowits Sandstone, and at this elevation the vegetation reflects a warmer, drier climate. Pinyon and Utah juniper form a dense woodland on the surrounding hillsides, but as we descend the canyon southeastward to small Right Fork Yellow Creek Campsite (3.0; 6835), we'll see that the cool canyon bottom supports some Douglas-fir and ponderosa pine. This fork of Yellow Creek often has a trickling stream until mid-to-late summer, but be sure to purify water taken from it.

The trail soon crosses to the west bank before swinging away from it and heading south-southwest toward the main stem of Yellow Creek. Soon we cross a hot, open flat choked with sagebrush, buckwheat, four-wing saltbush, and winter fat, an important winter forage for deer. These shrubs indicate we are in the desert scrub plant community, the lowest, warmest, and driest community in the Park, and we are presently at our lowest elevation on the trail, 6800 feet. Much of the route ahead maintains elevations above 7000 feet, and follows closely under the rim, where cool forests prevail.

On a curve westward toward Yellow Creek canyon, we reach a signed spur (0.5; 6800) indicating the Yellow Creek Group Campsite just south of the trail. This pleasant camp, limited to large groups of backpackers, lies under a canopy of ponderosa pine, Gambel oak, pinyon and juniper. Yellow Creek, flowing all summer in some years, trickles nearby.

**Rugged face of the Pink Cliffs
above Yellow Creek**

Continuing northwestward on an easy grade, we proceed through the drab oak, pinyon and juniper woodland. Dull sandstone cliffs rise north and south of the canyon's floor, but to the west and northwest the Pink Cliffs form an exciting backdrop, eroded into an intricately detailed cluster of pillars and columns.

After another mile we hop across usually wet Yellow Creek and in 0.1 mile reach Yellow Creek Campsite, (1.2; 7100), situated above chortling Yellow Creek amid scattered ponderosa pines. Yellow Spring, 1/3 mile northwest, waters a lovely meadow and aspen grove, and supports the flow of Yellow Creek. An outstanding view of the Yellow Creek amphitheater backdrops the campsite, making this one of the most inviting campsites on the trail.

Beyond the campsite we leave the forested valley of Yellow Creek and soon begin a southbound ascent of 400 feet in 1/2 mile, first via a hot, grassy hillside and then climbing steadily into a pinyon and juniper woodland. The trail is sandy and the summer sun intense, but views of the broken Pink Cliffs provide enough stimulus to make the going worthwhile. After topping out on a 7600' saddle near the contact zone between the limestones of the Wasatch Formation to the west and the Kaiparowits Sandstone to the east, we descend gradually toward the southwest beneath the imposing Pink Cliffs.

About 1.2 miles from the saddle, we gain a south-trending ridge at 7600 feet. Trailside ponderosa pines and junipers frame incomparable views of the Pink Cliffs southward to the apex of the Park, 9115' Rainbow Point. East of and below the rim, rolling ridges clad in the dull tones of pinyon and juniper woodland dominate the scene. In autumn the bright yellows of Gambel oaks on these ridges and in the canyons vie with the cliffs for our attention.

Our sandstone-based trail contours westward to another minor ridge before descending steadily into the wooded canyon of Pasture Wash (2.9; 7350). We follow the canyon northwest, cross the dry wash, then climb moderately steeply to a manzanita-clad saddle (0.6; 7700). A prominent spire-topped castle rises 600 feet above to the north, jutting its colorful cliffs southward from the rim.

From the saddle we switchback westward

down the sandy tread. Trailside pinyons and junipers offer little shade, but the Pink Cliffs, the colorful, isolated crags of Swamp Canyon Butte and Mud Canyon Butte in the southwest, and an impressive castle on the western skyline offer exciting views along this stretch. Shortly we find ourselves at a well-signed four-way junction (0.8; 7390) in the tree-covered depths of Sheep Creek. The Under-the-Rim Trail continues straight ahead, bound for Swamp Canyon. The right fork, the Sheep Creek Connector trail (*Trip 7*), climbs north over the rim to the Park road, and the left fork descends Sheep Creek for 0.6 mile, losing 200 feet of elevation to remote Sheep Creek Campsite.

---

Hikers wishing to camp off the main trail might consider Sheep Creek Campsite, a good choice for your first night, where you can camp in comparative solitude amid awe-inspiring surroundings. Farther along the trail, Right Fork Swamp Canyon and Swamp Canyon campsites are much more popular, particularly with hikers descending from the Park road during summer weekends.

From the junction, turn left, descending first southeast and then south, keeping east of Sheep Creek, which is usually dry along this stretch. This trail descends gently amid the pygmy forest, although a few tall ponderosa pines decorate the canyon. Thistle, Markagunt penstemon, Fremont geranium, Colorado rubberweed, paintbrush, wild rose, snowberry, Utah serviceberry, dandelion and yarrow splash their vibrant colors alongside the trail.

A sign indicates the campsite, but a rough trail continues down the canyon about 1/4 mile to the Park boundary. This trail, in conjunction with the Swamp Canyon Trail, is used as a stock driveway each spring and summer, connecting summer range atop the Paunsaugunt Plateau with winter range east of the Park.

The small campsite (0.6; 7200) has room for a few tents among scattered ponderosa pines and junipers. Tree-framed views of the Pink Cliffs form an exciting backdrop to the west.

---

From the Sheep Creek Connector Trail, our trail climbs steadily for 0.2 mile under a ponderosa-pine canopy to a junction with a short spur forking right and leading to the connector trail in 0.2 mile. We bear left instead and climb easily to a 7600' manzanita-clad saddle, then descend into the forest of Swamp Canyon, passing just north of the Right Fork Swamp Canyon Campsite (0.8; 7440). This pleasant campsite rests in a forest of ponderosa pine and Douglas-fir, but hikers must carry water for the stream is usually dry. An easy jaunt westward brings us to the junction with the Swamp Canyon Connector Trail *Trip 8* (0.1; 7480), forking right, while the Under-the-Rim Trail turns left (southwest).

From the junction our trail leads us up densely vegetated Swamp Canyon. The diversity of vegetation in this well-watered canyon is without equal anywhere else in the Park. Swamp Canyon Butte, 8302 feet, and Mud Canyon Butte, 8330 feet, soar skyward boldly on the canyon's east wall, while the 300' band of the orange- and buff-colored Pink Cliffs follows the canyon above to the west. But what captures our attention are the sheer number and variety of understory plants in the canyon. Greenleaf manzanita, curlleaf and alderleaf mountain mahogany, Gambel oak, ceanothus, bitterbrush, serviceberry, blue elderberry, snowberry, Nutka rose, wax currant, Oregon grape, and common juniper are plants adapted to a variety of habitats in Bryce, and they find the shady confines of the canyon an ideal environment.

An equally diverse array of wildflowers splash their varied colors over the canyon floor, including meadow rue, dogbane, yarrow, manyflower gromwell, Markagunt penstemon, Indian paintbrush, thistle, blue flax, gilia, Richardson geranium, groundsel, false Solomon's seal, Colorado butterweed, and green gentian. The gentian is interesting in that it is a "biennial": during its first season of growth it puts forth a rosette of large, light green leaves that hug the ground, but during its second year its energy is channeled into producing a tall, flowering stalk, attaining a height of up to 5 feet, densely covered with small, greenish-white flowers. After the blooms go to seed, the plant dies, but its skeleton may remain erect for several seasons.

The canyon becomes progressively narrow

toward the south, and upon reaching the head of the canyon, we rise moderately to a narrow ridge at 8100 feet, upon the brink of a precipice that plunges into the depths of Mud Canyon. The imposing north face of Noon Canyon Butte lies across the canyon to our south, decorated by a collection of large orange hoodoos. Numerous springs and seeps issue forth from that steep cliff, briefly giving life to the creek in Mud Canyon, which is destined to sink beneath the sandy wash below.

From this vantage we can also observe the consequences of stream piracy (also called drainage capture). Erosion has caused and is causing the rim of the Paunsaugunt Plateau to retreat westward, allowing the tributaries of the Paria River to capture plateau-top drainages. Swamp Canyon and Mud Canyon buttes were at one time on the rim of the plateau, and the present-day drainage of Swamp Canyon was formerly the headwaters of East Creek, which flows north atop the plateau. Headward erosion of Paria River tributaries captured upper East Creek and thus isolated Swamp Canyon and Mud Canyon buttes about 1 mile east of the present location of the rim. The inexorable forces of erosion continue, and we may also notice that Mud Canyon has captured the upper southwest drainage of Swamp Canyon.

Bidding farewell to the diverse assemblage of plants in Swamp Canyon, we presently follow the ridge westward, shortly joining the White-man Connector Trail (1.6; 8200) coming down from the rim (see *Trip 9*). Just upslope (north-west) from this junction is Swamp Canyon Campsite, a pleasant spot for an overnight stay, where we can choose to camp under a shady canopy, enjoying fine views of the cliff-bound crags of Swamp Canyon and Mud Canyon buttes. A small spring usually waters the gully below (northwest of) the campsite. Bear in mind that this is the southernmost campsite on the trail with water; Natural Bridge Campsite, nearly 3 miles ahead, is perpetually dry.

The Under-the-Rim Trail continues south from Swamp Canyon Camp through a broad, nearly level gap between the tree-covered slopes of Whiteman Bench to our west and Noon Canyon Butte to our east. From the gap we descend an old fire road, steeply at first, glimpsing Rain-

bow Point's colorful promontory nearly 5 miles south along the broken line of the Pink Cliffs. One mile from the camp, and 1/4 mile after crossing the dry course of Willis Creek, we reach a sign where the old road forks left. We bear right here onto a trail, continuing our descent. Over-the-shoulder views reveal impressive pinnacles south of Noon Canyon Butte, contrasting mark-edly with its smooth, forested western slopes.

About 0.2 mile south of the old road, we'll exit the Park, entering Dixie National Forest as we continue generally south. Re-entering the Park after 0.4 mile, our sandy trail climbs mod-erately through pine and fir to a minor ridge at 8000 feet, passing outcrops of conglomerate sandstone enroute. We may pause briefly to enjoy views of the Pink Cliffs from Farview Point nearby in the northwest to Noon Canyon Butte. The butte's west slopes, forest-clad, fall abruptly away in a line of colorful cliffs into Noon Canyon to the east.

Ahead we slog across the sandy tread amid sparse forest to a saddle in a ridge at 7900 feet, high above the shady depths of Bridge Canyon. A descent of 350 feet follows, and after reaching level ground and crossing the dry wash in the canyon, we immediately reach Natural Bridge Camp, (3.0; 7550), the southernmost camp on the trail. It's a pleasant site, shaded by a park-like stand of ponderosa pines, and one may be tempted to stay a night, if one has packed enough water.

Ahead our trail takes us briefly through the parklike forest, and past a rabbitbrush-infested clearing backdropped by the spectacular Pink Cliffs, then into lower Agua Canyon. Quite soon we exit the Park while maintaining a southwest course up the broad canyon. Re-entering the Park after 0.1 mile, we soon cross the main wash of the canyon, which may be seeping red, muddy water into midsummer. Now we head south, noticing a host of prominent minarets decorating the cliff-bound amphitheater at the canyon's head.

Our trail then switchbacks upon a fir-shaded north slope to a dry sandstone ridge. Here we meet the Agua Canyon Connector Trail (1.5; 8120), peeling off to the west, bound for the rim above (see *Trip 10*).

From the ridgetop junction, the great wall of

the Pink Cliffs, adorned with fantastic hoodoos, arcs southeast toward Rainbow Point, and to get there we gently descend hot, dry sandstone slopes, thickly forested. Wallflower, evening primrose and goldenweed are seen sporadically as we dip into a tributary of the North Fork Ponderosa Canyon, a much cooler environment. Now we continue over a minor ridge into the North Fork proper. But soon we climb out of the canyon, quickly attaining a 7950' saddle. The prominent Pink Cliffs, rising nearly 800 feet to the rim to our west, have been sculpted by erosion into an impressive wall of hoodoos overshadowing the forks of Ponderosa Canyon.

From the saddle we descend gently and soon cross the multibranched wash of Center Fork Ponderosa Canyon (1.3; 7750). This canyon is perhaps the shadiest, best-watered canyon along the trail. Blue spruce, ordinarily found at timberline in many parts of Utah and the southern Rockies, thrives in this cool, moist canyon. After crossing the broad floor of the shady canyon, we switchback up an equally shady north-facing slope to a pine-clad ridge.

A gentle descent ensues, bringing us to South Fork Ponderosa Canyon. There may be a trickle of water beyond the sign until midsummer in some years. Heading southeast out of the canyon, we quickly attain a low pine-clad ridge where a sign points down the trail (south) to Iron Spring. Quite soon we reach a spur trail (1.1; 7880) to the spring, lying just downslope in an aspen-shaded draw. The sluggish, red-stained flow from this spring is not particularly inviting, so we continue an undulating traverse into the forks of Black Birch Canyon. Its North Fork may have a trickle of water in early to midsummer, but don't count on it. Entering the main fork of the canyon, we see Rainbow Point looming 1200 feet above to our south, the centerpiece of a spectacular horseshoe of towering cliffs, adorned with bold pinnacles.

Crossing Black Birch Canyon's dry wash, our trail bends northeast for 250 yards to signed Birch Spring (0.9; 7950), a piped trickle sheltered by water-birch trees growing in the shady forest of spruce and fir.

One more canyon remains to be traversed before we begin our protracted ascent to the rim. Down into the rugged South Fork we go, descending easily below a row of broken cliffs. After crossing two eroded gullies, we traverse out of the canyon and around a northwest-trending ridge, gaining fine views northwestward along the barrier of the Pink Cliffs. Almost immediately below the cliffs we see that the Wasatch Formation gives way abruptly to the underlying sandstone, which forms the long hogback ridges extending eastward from the cliffs, densely clad in Gambel oak, pinyon and juniper.

After rounding the ridge, we instantly gain far-reaching vistas including the Table Cliffs, the distant Henry Mountains, the sloping, wooded crown of Canaan Peak, the vast Kaiparowits Plateau, and distant Navajo Mountain. Closer at hand in the southeast, the Paria River dives into a canyon surrounded by the White Cliffs, composed of Navajo Sandstone, while domes and crags of this sandstone punctuate the plateau above the river's canyon.

After rounding east-trending Ponderosa Ridge, we welcome the firmer tread of the Wasatch Formation, and we climb steadily but moderately uphill. Passing just below an 8600' saddle, we can briefly leave the trail to climb to that gap for stunning views into the Black Birch Canyon amphitheater.

As we climb the ridge southwest, one switchback brings us to the red hill of Point 8330. From here we can trace the magnificent Pink Cliffs all the way back to our starting point at Bryce Point.

The trail ahead switchbacks upward through fir forest, bringing us to the Riggs Spring Loop Trail (3.2; 8960). Here we have the option of extending our hike by turning left onto that trail, where three trail camps invite us to linger, or turning right, climbing and following signs to Rainbow Point, ignoring the Bristlecone Loop Trail enroute, and soon reach the spacious Rainbow Point parking area (0.3; 9115) and **Trailhead 9**.

# Trip 7
## Sheep Creek Connector Trail

**Distance**: 3.2 miles round trip to Under-the-Rim Trail
**Low/High elevations**: 7390'/7970'
**Suited for**: Dayhike or backpack
**Difficulty**: Moderate
**Best season**: May through October
**Map/Trailhead**: 12/5
**Hazards**: No water

**Introduction**: Backpackers who want to avoid the car shuttling or hitchhiking that is required to hike the entire Under-the-Rim Trail, and simply enjoy a leisurely, carefree jaunt along part of that scenic route, can utilize any one of four connecting trails (*Trips 7* through *10*) that join the Park road with that backcountry trail.

This trip begins among the meadows of the Paunsaugunt Plateau, descends a steep canyon flanked by striking erosional forms, and offers easy access to two backcountry campsites along the Under-the-Rim Trail.

**Description**: The signed trail (0.0; 7941), an old jeep route for 1/2 mile, gently dips into a long, narrow, north-trending meadow, heading east for 0.2 mile along the foot of forested slopes. We then gradually bend southeast, climbing easily along the margin of the southeastern arm of the wildflower-speckled grassland.

Upon reaching a break in the Pink Cliffs at the rim, the old jeep tracks end and the trail begins (0.5; 7970). Look for mat milkvetch, with its diminutive purple and white flowers, and Colorado rubberweed among the sagebrush and bitterbrush at this broad saddle. The trail then quickly descends a draw through an open ponderosa-pine forest. As we descend farther into the confines of that shady draw, with the broken Pink Cliffs flanking us on either side, we may notice blue spruce and Douglas-fir joining the forest.

Quite soon our draw broadens to the south, and we stroll steadily downhill to a signed junction (0.9; 7480). The southwest-bound right fork leads in 0.2 mile to the Under-the-Rim Trail, and southbound hikers headed for Swamp Canyon

and its backcountry campsites take that fork. Hikers bound for Sheep Creek Campsite, however, continue straight ahead through the ponderosa-pine forest, noticing colorful rocks of the Wasatch Formation mingling with the sandstone along the trail, and soon they meet the Under-the-Rim Trail (0.2; 7390).

# Trip 8
## Swamp Canyon Connector Trail

**Distance**: 2.2 miles round trip to Under-the-Rim Trail
**Low/High elevations**: 7480'/8050'
**Suited for**: Dayhike or backpack
**Difficulty**: Moderate
**Best season**: May through October
**Map/Trailhead**: 12/6
**Hazards**: No water

**Introduction**: Whether you're out for one day or two, the Swamp Canyon Connector Trail is perhaps the most scenic way to quickly reach the Under-the-Rim Trail. Not only does the trail descend a spectacular canyon enroute, but it offers quick access to two backcountry campsites and the high valley of Swamp Canyon, a thickly forested draw wedged between the plateau rim and the erosion-isolated sentinels of Swamp Canyon and Mud Canyon buttes. This valley displays the most diverse assemblage of plants in the entire Park.

**Description**: From the trailhead (0.0; 8050) we descend east through pine forest to the head of a sagebrush-infested meadow, then switchback south below the rim past a few small orange hoodoos. Colorful cliffs and hoodoos flank the trail on either side, framing fine views into the cool, forested depths of Swamp Canyon, above which rise the tree-topped orange crags of Swamp Canyon and Mud Canyon buttes.

The last switchback edges close to a small spring issuing from the gully immediately to our west, and from there we proceed south down the ever-widening canyon just east of the gully that drains the spring. Ponderosa pines, Douglas-firs, and blue spruces shade us enroute, and a varied understory blankets the trailside slopes. The flow from the spring quickly sinks underground in summer and is not visible where we hop across the small gully draining it.

After an easy, eye-pleasing downhill stroll we join the Under-the-Rim Trail (1.1; 7480), refer to *Trip 6*, and ponder our options.

# Trip 9
## Whiteman Connector Trail

**Distance**: 2.4 miles round trip from picnic
    area to Under-the-Rim Trail
**Low/High elevations**: 8200'/8708'
**Suited for**: Dayhike or backpack
**Difficulty**: Moderately easy
**Best season**: May through October
**Map/Trailhead**: 13/7
**Hazards**: Negligible

**Introduction**: The easiest of the four connector trails to the Under-the-Rim Trail, this route, actually an old road, descends forested slopes below Whiteman Bench, quickly reaching the conifer-shaded Swamp Canyon Campsite, perched on a high saddle just above the Pink Cliffs.

A small spring offers water to campers here most of the year. Backpackers can hike north down Swamp Canyon to Right Fork Swamp Canyon Campsite, or hike south to usually waterless Natural Bridge Campsite. Due to lack of water, the Under-the-Rim Trail south of the Whiteman Connector receives considerably less foot traffic than it does farther north.

**Description**: A sign opposite the picnic area (0.0; 8708) indicates WHITEMAN CONNECTOR TRAIL .3 MILE. Carefully follow the shoulder of the road, watching for traffic, or follow the ridge just above the road to the east. After about 10 minutes, keep an eye out for the possibly unsigned trail leading southeast from the Park road (0.3; 8690).

From the beginning we enjoy far-ranging vistas, framed by trailside trees, extending northeast to Bryce Point, the Table Cliffs, Swamp and Mud Canyon buttes; east to Tropic Valley and

Canaan Peak; southeast to Noon Canyon Butte; south to the Kaiparowits Plateau stretching toward the North Rim of the Grand Canyon; and finally far southeast to the distant dome of Navajo Mountain.

Our wide trail, actually an old fire road, descends moderately through a forest of mixed conifers. We can notice that the Pink Cliffs are absent below the rim of Whiteman Bench; the contours here are gentle and the slopes are densely clad in forest trees. The Pink Cliffs are far below the rim here, not abutting it for nearly a 2-mile stretch, in marked contrast to much of the rest of the Park.

After 0.3 mile we negotiate a minor switchback and proceed downhill along a draw where the fluttering light-green leaves of aspen contrast with the darker tones of the forest. After following the draw northeast for 0.3 mile, we cross to the opposite side and negotiate the undulating trail for the final 0.3 mile to the Under-the-Rim Trail (0.9; 8200). Swamp Canyon campsite lies just to the left (northwest) of the junction.

# Trip 10
## Agua Canyon Connector Trail

**Distance**: 3.0 miles round trip, to Under-the-
    Rim Trail
**Low/High elevations**: 8120'/9011'
**Suited for**: Dayhike or backpack
**Difficulty**: Moderate
**Best season**: May through October
**Map/Trailhead**: 14/8
**Hazards**: Steep dropoffs and occasional
    poor footing; no water.

**Introduction**: This trail is the least frequently used but perhaps the most scenic of all the connector trails leading to the Under-the-Rim Trail. The nearest backcountry trail campsite is Natural Bridge, and due to that campsite's lack of water and to the absence of other trail campsites south of Agua Canyon, this trail is lightly used.

The trail climbs through fir forest, traverses

a spruce-clad, north-facing slope high above the well-developed hoodoos that jut east from the rim in the Agua Canyon amphitheater, and then descends an increasingly dry ridge to its junction with the Under-the-Rim Trail. Here hikers have the option of either heading north 1.5 miles to Natural Bridge Campsite, or turning right (south) and continuing another 6.6 miles to Rainbow Point.

**Description**: Our dirt road begins at a locked gate (0.0; 8865) east of the Park road, and we follow this dirt road as it switchbacks twice up to a point just above a gravel pit, where we find a trail sign. Thereafter, the road becomes faint as it winds south to the round summit of Point 9011, after nearly 1/2 mile.

From Point 9011 we diagonal northeast down east-facing slopes where the forest inhibits vistas. Our peaceful stroll ends abruptly when we reach the rim of the Agua Canyon amphitheater, where the trail turns east at a right angle. Proceeding east along this rim, we become absorbed by the rugged grandeur of the amphitheater, where an ornate display of varicolored hoodoos excites the imagination.

A broad sweep of contrasting landscapes meets our gaze from the rim. The Pink Cliffs foreground the more distant Table Cliffs, while beyond Tropic Valley the Kaiparowits Plateau gently rises toward the southeast horizon. In the far distance, Navajo Mountain appears as a mere bump on the horizon, but its distance—nearly 100 miles away—belies its massiveness. From the rim, cliffs fall away into Agua Canyon in irregular fashion. Capped by a whitish dolomitic rock, these cliffs are underlain by orange slopes, which in turn drop into a spectacular row of hoodoos that jut skyward from the lower reaches of the bowl. Eventually we drop north off the rim, descending 12 rocky switchbacks through a narrow, scree-choked gully between the cliffs.

Below the switchbacks, we traverse northeast beneath a row of orange cliffs, enjoying more fine views into the amphitheater and the densely forested canyon below. As the trail leads toward the Kaiparowits Sandstone that underlies the Wasatch Formation, look for a thin layer of conglomerate separating the two formations. This is a basal conglomerate composed of rounded pebbles and cobbles derived from ero-

sion of the Kaiparowits Sandstone. This layer was deposited on an erosional surface before the influx of Lake Flagstaff's waters more than 50 million years ago. The colorful Wasatch beds were then deposited over the conglomerate in calm backwaters.

Proceeding east along the ridge, we follow the presently sandy tread and shortly join the Under-the-Rim Trail (*Trip 6*) at a ridge saddle (1.5; 8120), about 1 1/2 miles south of Natural Bridge Campsite.

# Trip 11
## Bristlecone Loop Trail

**Distance**: 1.0 mile loop trip
**Low/High elevations**: 9000'/9115'
**Suited for**: Walk
**Difficulty**: Easy
**Best season**: May through October
**Map/Trailhead**: 14/9
**Hazards**: Steep dropoffs; rim prone to lightning strikes.

**Introduction**: Bristlecone pines are among the oldest and most enduring living things on earth. Specimens in the Great Basin mountain ranges of California and Nevada have clung to life for nearly 5000 years, but in Bryce the oldest known bristlecone is "only" 1700 years old, a mere youngster.

This enjoyable and easy stroll not only passes among ancient, gnarled bristlecone pines but traverses cool fir forests as well. The trail differs from most Park trails in that it traverses the rim rather than descending into the Pink Cliffs below. This trail is also the highest-elevation path in the Park, remaining above 9000 feet throughout. In addition, the route offers unique vistas of the southern reaches of the Park and the rugged Pink Cliffs, and a different and more intimate perspective of the Rainbow and Yovimpa Point high country than the often-crowded overlook at Rainbow Point can provide.

**Description**: At the northeast corner of the Rainbow Point parking area and just north of the picnic area, the Under-the-Rim, Riggs Spring Loop, and Bristlecone Loop trails begin at the destination and mileage sign (0.0; 9115).

The trail leads through the shady forest for 100 yards to a junction where a sign points right to Yovimpa Point and left to the Under-the-Rim Trail. We will be returning via the right fork, but for now we continue along the left branch, briefly skirting the plateau rim. Views enroute extend northwest far to the lofty 11,000' and 12,000' summits of the Tushar Mountains, across the broad forested expanse of the Paunsaugunt Plateau. The trail here is smooth and rock-lined as it descends gently beneath a canopy of Douglas-fir and white fir.

After 200 yards, we part company with *Trips 6* and *12* hikers and bear right onto the central trail, signed BRISTLECONE LOOP. The trail branching sharply to our right (southwest) is a cutoff trail leading 350 yards to scenic Yovimpa Point.

Our trail leads us quickly into a shallow draw, then to a gently descending traverse around the shoulder of a minor ridge. Shortly we reach a fenced overlook (0.4; 9000), perched on the rim and featuring a shelter with log benches. The dramatic vista that presently unfolds reaches into the tree-clad depths of Corral Hollow 1000 feet below, seen beyond plunging white cliffs, boulder-strewn orange slopes, and finally ranks of salmon-tinted pillars standing silent guard over Corral Hollow like so many sentinels gazing across distant, undefiled panoramas.

The trail ahead climbs gently to another overlook with far-ranging panoramas framed by sun-burnished snags. Tenacious limber and bristlecone pines also cling stubbornly to existence on this high, weather-tortured promontory. Both trees have needles in bundles of five, but the bristlecone needles are dark green and tufted at the tips of the branches, resembling a fox's tail. The bristlecones are also quite spindly, and some survive only by virtue of a single strip of trunk bark nurturing a few slow-growing branches.

Presently the trail curves northwest, soon passing north of the small air-quality building, where a camera monitors visibility throughout the day. The desert Southwest boasts the best visibility in the nation, attested to by our view of

Navajo Mountain over 100 miles distant. Bryce lies within a federally designated Class I air-quality area, and thus is "protected" from degradation of air quality. However, some areas within our view are allowed minimal degradation of air quality, and distant coal-fired power plants threaten vistas from the Park. Moreover, vast reserves of gas, oil, and coal lie within the scope of our view, and development of these resources in the future could have serious consequences for the pristine landscapes and clean air we presently enjoy.

Passing a few trailside spruces, we soon leave the rim and re-enter forest, and shortly thereafter reach another four-way junction (0.4; 9090). The right-branching, previously mentioned cutoff trail leads back to the lower segment of our loop in less than 0.1 mile. The left fork leads 50 yards southwest to the Yovimpa Point Trail. To conclude the loop, however, we follow the center fork through shady forest, soon reaching the trailhead and parking area (0.2; 9115).

# Trip 12
## Riggs Spring Loop Trail

**Distance**: 8.7 miles loop trip
**Low/High elevations**: 7440'/9115'
**Suited for**: Dayhike or backpack
**Difficulty**: Moderate
**Best season**: May through October
**Map/Trailhead**: 14/9
**Hazards**: Limited water. Check water availability chart at the Visitor Center.

**Introduction**: At Rainbow Point, near the southern boundary of the Park, the east-facing Pink Cliffs that abut the rim of the Paunsaugunt Plateau curve northeast and blend into the rolling, forested shoulder of Ponderosa Ridge, temporarily ending. But south of Rainbow Point and The Promontory, the Pink Cliffs emerge again from the plateau rim. Here they trend east-to-west rather than north-to-south, and form amphitheaters above the drier, south-draining canyons of Corral and Mutton hollows. The Riggs Spring

Loop Trail descends from the cool fir forests of Rainbow Point into the pine and oak woodlands of those canyons, then climbs back to the plateau rim via Yovimpa Pass.

This trip is an alternative to the Under-the-Rim Trail for hikers who prefer a shorter backcountry excursion. But though shorter the route is long on magnificent scenery, ranging from the forests of the plateau and hoodoos of the Pink Cliffs to the wooded reaches of Bryce's southernmost canyons and far-reaching panoramas stretching into Arizona.

Two of the three campsites along the way have reliable water sources and pleasant, scenic camping. The trail can be completed in a day, but the fine scenery beckons hikers to linger.

Before beginning your hike, don't miss the short stroll to Rainbow Point, which, at 9115 feet, lies at the zenith of Bryce Canyon National Park. Visitors who negotiate the long mountain road to the point anticipate ample rewards for their efforts, and they are richly rewarded with a magnificent overview of much of the Park and its surroundings. Befitting its lofty location, its vistas are arguably the finest in the Park, easily

**Pink Cliffs hoodoos from
the Riggs Spring Loop Trail**

justifying the long drive over the narrow, twisting road.

**Description**: The hike can be taken in either direction, starting at Rainbow Point or Yovimpa Point. We'll begin at Rainbow Point and stroll down the Bristlecone Loop Trail (*Trip 11*) to the Under-the-Rim Trail, where we turn left (northeast), descend a single switchback to reach our signed trail (0.3; 8960), and continue straight ahead, southeast.

From there, we descend easily east for a mile beneath a shady canopy of conifers. Upon beginning a moderate downhill grade along the shady north slopes of The Promontory, we pass beneath the second highest summit in the Park, Point 9091, and continue eastward along corrugated slopes, then curve southeast below the long hogback ridge of The Promontory.

Gazing north along the brightly colored wall of the Pink Cliffs, we can see how abrupt the transformation of the landscape is at the well-defined contact zone between the Wasatch Formation and the underlying Kaiparowits Sandstone. It is here on the eastern slopes of the Paunsaugunt Plateau that the varicolored cliffs, hoodoos and badlands give way to a landscape of long, rolling ridges, trending generally east-west. These ridges are composed of a dull-colored sandstone, and since they are lower and consequently drier than the plateau, they are cloaked in a woodland of pinyon, juniper, and groves of Gambel oak. In autumn, after frosts have signaled the oaks to prepare for winter dormancy, their leaves, when turning a brilliant golden color, attract as much attention as the Pink Cliffs and the far-ranging vistas.

As we round a ridge at 8240 feet, about 2 miles from the trailhead, sweeping vistas justify at least a brief pause in our downhill trek. Even though comparable vistas can be enjoyed from the end of a short stroll at Yovimpa Point, the hiker gains a deeper appreciation for the views if he enjoys them from the quiet solitude of a backcountry trail.

Wooded plateaus below us to the southeast form the foothills of the Paunsaugunt Plateau. Some of these plateaus have been "chained"— cleared of brush and trees by ranchers to increase rangeland for their livestock. Navajo Sandstone cliffs and buttes, part of the White Cliffs and one of the great steps in the Grand Staircase (see "Introduction to Zion National Park") embrace the deep canyon of the Paria River in the southeast. An especially prominent white sandstone butte—Mollie's Nipple—rises above the wooded plateau and White Cliffs in the southeast. Beyond the cliffs is the vast Kaibab Plateau with its thick woodlands, rising ever so slightly toward the southern horizon to end at the North Rim of the Grand Canyon. Beyond the unmistakable hogback dome of Navajo Mountain, over 100 miles in the east-southeast, parched desert buttes rise above the invisible Colorado River and our view fades into the distance of Monument Valley.

Descending below 8200 feet via south- and east-facing slopes, we alternate between pinyon-juniper woodland and ponderosa-pine forest. Above us to the north, colorful slopes and hoodoos abut the sparsely forested ridgeline of The Promontory. Below this minor cluster of hoodoos, yuccas—further indications of a hot, dry environment—compete for space with the manzanita that blankets the slopes between the pines.

After rounding the shoulder of a major south-trending ridge at 8000 feet, our trail leads us north high above forested Corral Hollow. Head-on views of the Pink Cliffs, facing south here as they do in only a few other locations in the Park, are dramatic.

After this traverse begins to head west, a stand of Russian olive (a shrub introduced from Europe and widely planted as a windbreak in the arid west), water birch, and willow crowds the grassy seep of Bullberry Spring (2.7; 7880), just downslope from the trail. But the trail quickly turns northwest and descends gradually into the Right Fork of Corral Hollow, where pine, fir, aspen, maple, and oak grow in profusion in the moister canyon bottom. Tall, salmon-hued cliffs, rising 200-600 feet in bold relief, bound the upper reaches of the canyon on three sides.

Ahead our trail rises to an 8000' ridge, and from there we descend into a draw to reach the Corral Hollow Campsite (0.9; 7920). Shaded by large ponderosa pines, Gambel oaks and junipers, this small campsite adjacent to the trail has room for only one tent, and no water is available nearby.

Beyond the Left Fork of Corral Hollow we gain a low ridge and descend, moderately at first, then gently through a thick stand of young ponderosa pines into the Right Fork of Mutton Hollow, where we soon encounter a signed junction (0.9; 7750). Dayhikers or backpackers bound for Yovimpa Pass may want to take the right-forking trail, a more direct route back to Yovimpa Point. This cutoff trail climbs through a pinyon-juniper woodland, crossing three minor ridges on a westward course, then descends gently to the loop trail. During its 0.8 mile course, this cutoff trail gains 250 feet and descends 160 feet, so it is an easy alternative to shorten our loop by 1 mile. But Riggs Spring beckons, so we bear left, descending Mutton Hollow through a parklike pine forest, enjoying the summertime color of Colorado rubberweed and manyflower gromwell. Finally we cross the east bank of the hollow's dry wash, cross another wash, and reach Riggs Spring Campsite (0.8; 7450). The group campsite lies a short distance down the canyon.

This is a delightful grassy campsite, one of the most pleasant trail camps in the Park, shaded by tall pines. Those who choose to stay overnight will likely be lulled to sleep by the fluttering leaves of nearby aspens. Riggs Spring is fenced off in an aspen grove next to the camp.

From the campsite an old road leads up-canyon. Some of the ponderosa pines in this broad canyon are impressively large, while attractive aspen groves contrast their white trunks with the somber green tones of the forest. After crossing a few gullies that funnel runoff into the main wash, we cross another 3/4 mile beyond the campsite that may have a trickle of water from an upstream spring. Shortly beyond we reach a junction with the cutoff trail (1.0; 7840), eastbound for Mutton Hollow.

The old road continues climbing, presently on a moderate grade above the east bank of a small wash harboring aspens and the only cottonwoods encountered on any trail below the plateau's rim. Diverting our attention from the steady grade are colorful cliffs and hoodoos, decorating the southernmost extension of the Pink Cliffs protected within the confines of the Park. Negotiating two switchbacks above the steepening gully, we soon pass into a grassy area thick with Nutka rose, crossing a tiny stream three times as we switchback up to Yovimpa Pass (0.6; 8355), where steep slopes suddenly give way to gently rounded contours atop the plateau. Here we meet a service road headed northwest down the drainage of Podunk Creek.

Just northeast of the pass, peaceful Yovimpa Pass Campsite beckons hikers to enjoy the only plateau-top trail camp in the Park. Yet the grassy campsite appears to be seldom used. The spring issuing from the well at the pumphouse offers the most vigorous flow in the Park, and is reliable even during the driest years.

Beyond the campsite we soon enter an east-trending draw and follow it toward the rim. Just before reaching a pine-clad saddle atop the rim, our trail veers away from it and instead switchbacks steeply up forested slopes. We then gain the rim, where colorful hoodoos foreground distant panoramas of the Kaiparowits Plateau and Navajo Mountain to the southeast and the densely tree-clad surface of the Kaibab Plateau to the south. Closer at hand are the blazing white sandstone walls of the White Cliffs, and below them, forming the next lower step in the Grand Staircase, are the Vermilion Cliffs. South of Navajo Mountain, stark desert buttes stretch to the horizon, where only the curvature of the earth prevents us from gazing farther into the magical realm of Monument Valley beyond.

Continuing on a steady grade, we leave the rim and proceed through a forest, eventually regaining the rim opposite (west of) the fenced-in overlook of Yovimpa Point. From here we may gaze down below the 500' precipice of the Pink Cliffs and trace our route through the forks of Corral Hollow, enjoying once again the afore-mentioned vistas.

The trail proceeds near the rim, still climbing before leveling off next to the Park road. Here our solitude is disrupted by the roar of traffic as we parallel the road. Soon our hike ends as we pass the short trail to Yovimpa Point and reach the Park road just south of the Rainbow Point parking area (1.5; 9110). Here you may wish to follow the short, easy spur trail to enjoy more vistas at Yovimpa Point.

# Trip 13
## Water Canyon, Mossy Cave

**Distance**: 1.0 mile round trip to cave and waterfall
**Low/High elevations**: 6823'/6960'
**Suited for**: Walk
**Difficulty**: Easy
**Best season**: Mid-April through October
**Map/Trailhead**: 15/10
**Hazards**: Negligible

**Introduction**: Before 1892 Water Canyon was just another dry canyon lying in the rainshadow of the Paunsaugunt Plateau. But farmers in the Paria Valley needed more water for their thirsty fields than the few streams in the valley could provide, so a few valley settlers diverted the waters of East Fork Sevier River into Water Canyon via the Tropic Ditch.

Today the canyon boasts a vigorous stream thanks to the ditch, and its waterfalls and cascades are a delight to hikers treading this short but scenic trail. The canyon has its share of salmon-tinted hoodoos, and a scattering of pine woodlands as well.

Mossy Cave is one of the highlights of the canyon, where a continuous supply of dripping water in a deep, cool alcove supports lush, water-loving vegetation seemingly out of place in a high desert environment.

**Description**: Beginning at the mouth of Water Canyon (0.0; 6823), the trail proceeds west through a sunny opening. Picturesque hoodoos in shades of orange and white highlight the slopes of a ridge that rises 300 feet to the north of the canyon, while to our south, a few limber and bristlecone pines grow on the steep badlands slopes. Small water-loving trees, such as water birch and willows, have found the moist banks of this man-made stream to be an ideal habitat.

Within 200 yards we cross the stream via a sturdy wooden bridge. From here we can see three small windows piercing a prominent salmon-hued hoodoo upslope to our west. The falls in the canyon lie on the opposite side (west) of that hoodoo, and we'll soon be there.

After 0.3 mile we bridge the creek for a

second time, pausing to admire the upstream waterfall. After crossing the bridge, we notice false Solomon's seal enjoying the moist, shady environment along the trail.

A brief climb above the bridge brings us to a signed junction: left to Mossy Cave and right to the waterfall. Turning left, we ascend north-west-facing slopes densely clad in juniper, Gambel oak, and ponderosa pine, climbing steeply before we round a bend and are confronted by the dark, dripping alcove of Mossy Cave. A short traverse leads us to the trail's end in the "cave." This cool, verdant oasis is a delight on the hottest summer days. Here an orange cliff has been hollowed out to make a deep alcove by seeping water that has dissolved the cementing agents that bound the ancient lakebed sediments into stone. Constantly dripping water supports a thick coating of moss in the shady alcove, and we may see the delicate bog orchid thriving in the damp soil nearby. A thick stand of water birch shades the shallow canyon below the cave, while tall ponderosa pines and Douglas-firs grow from the canyon floor to meet the sun above the rim of the cave.

Few hikers bypass the waterfall up Water Canyon, a delightful rarity in this semiarid land. To get there, head upstream (left, north) from the junction, splashing through the runoff of an up-slope spring and reaching the 10' waterfall at the point where the stream bends from south to west. Here the blustering creek is backdropped by a scenic cluster of hoodoos rising to the east and pierced by three small windows. The main trail ends just above the waterfall, but a use trail continues upstream, passing among multihued hoodoos on sparsely forested slopes.

The canyon has a dry look to it. Due to its low elevation and its position east of the Paunsaugunt Plateau, it receives much less precipitation, and the scattered forest reflects the competition for this precious moisture. Strong hikers can follow Water Canyon all the way to the rim, but it is quite steep and narrow in its upper reaches, and the rocks of the Wasatch Formation are often crumbly. A number of side canyons offer interesting explorations.

The upper canyon gives hikers the feeling of discovery that is rare in a heavily trailed national park such as Bryce, and since most Park visitors aren't even aware of the canyon, and those who are rarely travel beyond Mossy Cave or the falls, solitude—a precious commodity in the Park—is virtually assured.

# Trip 14
## Cooks Ranch Trail

**Distance**: 2.8 miles round trip
**Low/High elevations**: 6882'/7475'
**Suited for**: Dayhike
**Difficulty**: Easy
**Best season**: Mid-April through October
**Map/Trailhead**: 12/11
**Hazards**: No water

**Introduction**: Visitors who prefer a peaceful, uncrowded approach to the incomparable Bryce Canyon amphitheater and don't mind driving on an unpaved road will enjoy this forested canyon jaunt along the broad floor of lower Bryce Canyon. This trail offers access to a variety of other highly scenic trails and, in addition, the trail offers backpackers the opportunity to lengthen their trek on the Under-the-Rim Trail. Backpackers must obtain a backcountry permit at the Visitor Center before beginning the hike, and they must expect a difficult hitchhike or a long car shuttle from the terminus of the Under-the-Rim Trail at Rainbow Point.

**Description**: From the loop at the end of the road from Tropic (0.0; 6882), a fenceline delineating the boundary of the Park serves the purpose of barring cattle from Bryce Canyon, the exclusive realm of the hiker. The trail, overgrown and seldom used, heads generally west-northwest while gently ascending the broad canyon. The colorful, broken ramparts of Bristlecone Point loom boldly in the north, while steep sandstone slopes rise south of the canyon, their flanks mantled with a dense blanket of mountain mahogany, oak, pinyon and juniper.

Our trail passes initially through the lowest, driest vegetation zone in the Park. Gambel oak and alderleaf mountain mahogany, with a scattering of pinyon and juniper and ponderosa pine, grow thickly on the canyon's floor but offer minimal shade. Ahead in the west, multihued cliffs and the cool pine forests atop the rim beckon us onward.

About 3/4 mile from the trailhead, parts of the trail have been washed away where we merge with one of the boulder-strewn washes draining Bryce Canyon from the southwest. TRAIL signs help lead the way between concrete remnants of old foot bridges on this obscure 0.1-mile section of the trail. Beyond, we rise gently through a ponderosa-pine forest for 0.3 mile to an unsigned, northwest-bound trail, its tread churned to dust by daily horse traffic. Continuing west, we rise slightly for a long 0.1 mile to another horse trail (1.4; 7300), this one leading north.

If you want to reach the Peekaboo Loop, continue southwest on the trail another 0.1 mile, to where a well-signed southbound spur leads quickly south to that trail (*Trip 5*). The canyon trail continues west from the spur to the Peekaboo Loop, leading ever closer to the colorful breaks bounding the amphitheater. This easy 1/4-mile stroll takes us through an open forest to a three-way junction, where we have a variety of choices to extend our day's hike. The signed Navajo Loop Trail (*Trip 4*) forks left, bound for Sunset Point via Silent City in 0.8 mile. The middle fork is the easternmost leg of the Navajo Loop Trail, also leading to the rim at Sunset Point, in 0.6 mile. The right fork offers access to the Queens Garden Trail via an eastbound trail 50 yards northeast of the junction.

# Capitol Reef National Park

## Introduction

While many Colorado Plateau national parks contain prominent canyons that have been incised deeply into the generally flat landscape, Capitol Reef's 241,671 acres encompass the bulk of the Waterpocket Fold, a 90-mile-long crest of slickrock that, when viewed from most any angle, resembles a low but incredibly rugged mountain range.

The Waterpocket Fold is an immense bulge in the earth's crust—a monocline—in which 14 sedimentary strata were tilted upward toward the west. Three types of crustal folds are common throughout the Colorado Plateau—in an *anticline*, the rock layers are buckled upward, forming an elevated ridge; in a *syncline*, the strata are warped downward, forming a valley or depression; and in a *monocline*, the strata are tilted upward and then level off at a higher elevation, rather than slanting up or down on both sides.

The nature of the Capitol Reef landscape, with its sheer slickrock cliffs, towering domes, and blind canyons, was a major barrier to early east-west travel in the region. Hence the name

"reef," a term applied to many such natural obstacles on the Colorado Plateau.

The Park embraces not only the slickrock spine of the Waterpocket Fold and innumerable slot canyons, but also the extensive desert valleys of South Desert and Strike Valley east of the Fold, and the incomparable Cathedral Valleys, where great red monoliths jut skyward from the desert floor like so many jagged teeth.

South of the Fremont River, the Fold narrows considerably as it winds southeastward toward the Colorado River. East of the Fold in this area are several other "reefs" that wind through the desert valley that the Fold bounds, and each consists of erosional remnants of younger strata that were folded in conjunction with the Waterpocket Fold monocline. East of these minor folds, the landscape abruptly assumes the more uniform character typical of the Colorado Plateau, where still younger strata form broad, cliff-edged mesas that rise steadily one after another, toward the lofty Henry Mountains.

Capitol Reef is a not only a celebration of the unique forces that have shaped the land, but a land that is alive with hardy desert dwellers, both plant and animal, and it is a region rich in history, stretching back more than 1000 years.

Visitors who travel off the beaten track to this isolated Park will be richly rewarded, not only by some of the grandest scenery on the globe, but perhaps by self-discovery and introspection that can be achieved only in a land as empty, still, and majestic as Capitol Reef.

# Human History of Capitol Reef

As in most desert areas, the history of human occupation here is closely linked to the availability of water. In the Capitol Reef area, the Fremont River has been the lifeblood of human existence for more than 1000 years. A very distinctive culture, dubbed the Fremont, left an abundance of evidence that the people lived, and even thrived, in the area. These people occupied the Capitol Reef region from about 700 to 1275. Their culture was markedly different and in some ways more primitive than that of their contemporaries, the Anasazi pueblo builders. Fremont people lived in pit houses rather than elaborate stone structures built high on cliffs. On the flood plain of the Fremont River they grew corn, beans, and squash. The area occupied by this culture lies primarily in Utah, in the Great Basin province, as well as the Colorado Plateau.

A wide variety of artifacts from this culture has been discovered in the Fremont River region. Many of the artifacts evidence the distinctiveness of the culture. Perhaps those most readily observed are their rock-art sites. Although rock art is scattered throughout the region, the petroglyphs along Utah Highway 24, east of the Visitor Center, are the most obvious example. Their rock art is mostly petroglyphs, which to make an image is chipped into stone, rather than painted on as are pictographs. Their panels consist primarily of V-shaped, human-like figures and bighorn sheep.

Among the unusual artifacts discovered are unbaked clay figurines, buffalo-hide shields, unpainted black and gray pottery, and animal-hide moccasins. Necklaces and other adornments, garments, baskets, and even burial sites have also been discovered. Farming implements, including crude digging tools, as well as irrigation ditches and dried corn testify to their practice of farming. They enlarged their diet by gathering wild plant bulbs and seeds, and by hunting.

After occupying the region for hundreds of years, their culture evidently underwent a metamorphosis, and they abandoned their way of life in the Capitol Reef area. Thereafter, the Utes and the Southern Piutes established their dominance in the region. These were nomadic peoples, living and hunting in the High Plateaus during summer, and wintering in the milder climate of the deserts near Capitol Reef. They left little evidence of their occupation, save for an occasional petroglyph depicting horsemen in hunting scenes. The Piute name for the Fold translates to "Land of the Sleeping Rainbow."

As far as is known, the first white men to cross the Waterpocket Fold were members of a Mormon militia who, in 1866, crossed the Fold in search of Piutes herding stolen Mormon stock. Unsuccessful in their attempt to recover their cattle, they did discover that the high valleys at the head of the Fremont were suitable for settlement. Thus the stage was set for an influx of Mormon pioneers, who by the 1880s had established a chain of communities all along the course of the Fremont, many of which survive today.

After Indian conflicts had largely abated by 1870s, a colonization of grand proportions was undertaken by the Mormons in their attempt to establish the Kingdom of God in the remote corners of Utah. One of the most ambitious and arduous frontier journeys began in 1879, when more than 250 people, 83 wagons, and about 1000 head of stock began an epic journey to establish a settlement along the San Juan River, a journey they endured for five months.

Their route from Escalante to the new settlement of Bluff traversed some of the most rugged canyon country on the Colorado Plateau. In places, the party spent weeks blasting and shoring up a passable route over sheer cliffs to reach the Colorado River, where a small ferryboat was built to take the wagons across. To build the remainder of the route to Bluff, taking another two-and-one-half months, required much road work while they negotiated innumerable mesas and traversed rugged canyons.

Those who braved the rugged course of the wagon road relied on Charles Hall and his ferry to cross the Colorado. But within a few years of the 1879 journey, Hall found a new and better crossing upstream, near the mouth of Halls Creek. To reach Hall's Crossing, a new route was established from Escalante, this one crossing the rugged basin embraced by the Circle Cliffs. Once over the cliffs at the crest of the Waterpocket Fold, travelers followed a circuitous route, finally descending into a canyon which was barely wide enough for a mule. This canyon, which would be known as Muley Twist, was followed for less than 2 miles to the valley of Halls Creek, which was traced about 25 miles to the crossing.

In 1880, Nels Johnson established a homestead at the junction of the Fremont and Sulphur Creek, and others soon followed, staking homesteads eastward along the Fremont all the way to its confluence with the Muddy River. Johnson soon began planting an orchard, and other recently arrived settlers did the same. Several va-

rieties of apples, peaches, pears, apricots, walnuts, almonds, and grapes were established, nourished by the good soil, a mild climate, and abundant water close at hand. But no more than 10 families ever occupied Fruita during its more than 50 years of existence.

Travel from Fruita to the settlements east of the Waterpocket Fold was difficult at best, following the narrow Fremont River canyon, for the river had to be crossed innumerable times, a difficult route on foot or horse, and rougher still for a wagon.

But in 1883, improving upon a route long-used by Indians, a group of settlers cleared a route through Capitol Gorge, ultimately linking Fruita with distant Hanksville. Traversing colorful shales east of the Fold, the way became known as the "Blue Dugway." This route was the only road through the Fold for the next 80 years, and it remained a difficult passage through flood-prone Capitol Gorge until the completion of Utah Highway 24 through the canyon of the Fremont in 1962.

**Fruita orchard**

In the 1920s two prominent Wayne County citizens, Ephraim Pectol and Joseph Hickman, began a campaign to acquaint outsiders with the scenic wonders of Wayne County in general (the area is still referred to as "Wayne Wonderland") and the Waterpocket Fold country in particular. Their efforts led to the establishment of the Fruita area as a 16-acre state park in 1926.

Pectol was elected to the legislature in 1933, and at once began pressing for the creation of a national monument in the Fruita area. His persistence led to the creation of 37,060-acre Capitol Reef National Monument in 1937.

During the late 1940s and 1950s, the uranium boom spread across the vast reaches of the Colorado Plateau following the development of the nuclear bomb. Prospectors' primary targets were the Chinle and Morrison formations, and roads were built throughout the region. Many roads in the Capitol Reef area were originally cattle trails, later improved by uranium prospectors. One such road is the Burr Trail in the Park's South District. Fortunately, for the lands that would eventually be protected by the national park, no great quantities of ore were discovered.

Finally in 1971, the bulk of Waterpocket Fold, from the flanks of Thousand Lake Mountain nearly to the Colorado River, was included within the boundaries of the newly established Capitol Reef National Park. Under the provisions of the bill, grazing was to be phased out within Park boundaries, although the right to use historical stock driveways—in Oak Creek, for example—will be retained by local ranchers in perpetuity.

Today, the Fruita Historical District preserves the pioneer heritage of the area. Old farm implements are scattered throughout Fruita, many original homesteads still stand—though now housing Park employees—and the fruit orchards continue to thrive under the management of the Park Service. About 3000 fruit trees, including pear, apple, apricot, cherry, nectarine, peach, and plum, are managed not only for their historical value, but also to provide fruit for Park visitors and area residents.

# Plants and Animals of Capitol Reef

Capitol Reef is home to at least 800 species of plants, which is remarkable considering that the Park has a very dry climate, an average of only 7.21" of moisture falling annually at the Visitor Center. Throughout the 65-mile length of the Park, however, there is a variety of landscapes and soil types (derived from 14 different sedimentary rock layers) and a variety of habitats ranging from perennial streams to deep, shady canyons, badlands slopes, slickrock domes, mesas, and grassy desert valleys.

The highest elevations in the Park, on the eastern slopes of 11,306' Thousand Lake Mountain, are trod by few hikers. There one will find ancient bristlecone pines, twisted and weather-tortured, and stands of Douglas-fir, Rocky Mountain maple, ponderosa pine, aspen, and Rocky Mountain juniper, all growing where the Transition and Canadian life zones predominate (see "Plants and Animals of Zion" for more on life zones).

Most of the Park is in the Upper Sonoran Zone, where pinyon-juniper woodlands, shrubs, and grass communities dominate. Within this zone, however, narrow canyons, stream courses, springs and seeps support a variety of plants that have one thing in common—the need for a constant supply of water.

Communities of riparian vegetation are found in all life zones of the Park, forming green ribbons through this parched desert region along the four perennial streams that flow through the Fold. To a lesser extent, green strips line parts of most of the washes that cut into the Fold's tilted rocks. The reason for their existence along the streams is obvious, for water is continually available. In the dry canyons, where tall cliffs shelter plants from the desert sun, runoff waters are concentrated and held in the sands of the washes.

Riparian trees include netleaf hackberry—a tree that can be mistaken for a cultivated fruit tree—Gambel oak, and boxelder. The wettest sections of the canyons and washes support either Fremont, narrowleaf, or lanceleaf cottonwood; a variety of willows; and the exotic tamarisk, a small tree introduced from Eurasia that today is ubiquitous throughout the Colorado Plateau.

Canyon shrubs include brickellbrush, canyon snowberry, and Emory seep-willow—a willow-like shrub of the sunflower family. A variety of grasses, sedges, and rushes colonizes moist streambanks and swampy areas. Common reed, an unusually tall grass attaining heights of 6-8 feet, is found along the Fremont River and other moist areas, and scouring rush is typical in swampy areas, such as the mouth of Spring Canyon. A common plant in the confines of the Fremont River canyon is showy milkweed, a tall plant with large green leaves and clusters of whitish-pink flowers that mature in summer to form large, cucumber-like fruits. Woods rose forms impenetrable thickets along the banks of the river in places. Numerous wildflowers enliven the rockbound canyons, but their range is not restricted to these places. Scarlet gilia, rock goldenaster, dogbane, and a variety of penstemons are some of the wildflowers commonly found in the canyons.

Within the confines of canyons, another highly specialized plant community thrives in the places where springs and seeps issue from protected cliffs. The hanging gardens in Capitol Reef are not nearly so abundant as they are in such well-watered parks as Zion, but where they are found, the delicate fronds of maidenhair fern and the colorful blooms of canyon columbine, cardinal flower, and monkey flower provide a beautiful contrast to a backdrop of solid rock and parched desert.

The principal trees of the Upper Sonoran Zone form the pinyon-juniper woodland which blankets most of the Park. Two trees dominate in this woodland, Utah juniper and pinyon—the two-needle variety that is ubiquitous throughout Utah's high desert country. Typically these trees grow no taller than 25 feet, and are usually much smaller, forming "pygmy" forests of stunted, twisted, widely spaced trees.

Junipers are far more drought-tolerant than pinyons, and are found in pure stands on the parched eastern flanks of the Waterpocket Fold. A variety of coarse shrubs is typically found in these woodlands, forming a widely scattered understory. Common shrubs are the silver buffaloberry, singleleaf ash, green ephedra, gray Torrey ephedra, Utah serviceberry, Fremont barberry, littleleaf mountain mahogany—a shrub that seems to thrive on slickrock—alderleaf mountain mahogany, cliffrose, big sagebrush, yucca, and rabbitbrush.

No desert would be complete without cactus, and Capitol Reef supports eight species. Prickly pear, of which there are three species in Capitol Reef, is common from the desert valleys to the top of the Fold. Fishhook cactus is also seen with some frequency, but perhaps the most striking cactus is claret cup. When blooming in spring, its vivid scarlet flowers can be seen for some distance in this land of drab-colored vegetation.

Adding color to the landscape, although slightly less conspicuous than the cacti, are myriad wildflowers that splash a rainbow of color along roadsides and trails from spring through fall.

Near the upper limits of the Upper Sonoran Zone, one will find scattered ponderosa pines and Douglas-firs clinging to sheltered, north-facing cliffs in places such as Red Canyon and Grand Wash. Ponderosa pines also mix with the pinyon-juniper woodland atop the Fold in the South District, and in alluvium-filled pockets such as Longleaf Flat and Little Sand Flat in the North District.

East of the Fold the landscapes range from desert valleys to cliff-edged mesas, and seven diverse sedimentary layers are exposed, some of which are most inhospitable for the development of plants. Shadscale is a common shrub east of the Fold, colonizing nearly every rock layer exposed by erosion, as well as the alluvium-filled valleys. Smooth hop-sage, littleleaf horsebrush, and halogeton are all fairly common on the dry desert slopes in the eastern reaches of the Park.

Narrow, grass-dominated desert valleys abut almost the entire eastern margin of the Waterpocket Fold. These grasslands, vividly green with new growth in spring, were winter rangelands for pioneer ranchers, and those areas that lie outside the Park are still used as grazing lands. Due to overgrazing the once-grass-dominated valleys are being invaded by shrubs and are host to some non-native species. Russian thistle, or tumbleweed, and exotic varieties of brome, or cheatgrass, give the valleys a weedy appearance in places.

The dominant native grass is Indian ricegrass; its high-protein, rice-like seeds were an important part of the Native American diet. Hilly areas, dry slopes and the valleys themselves host shrubs that require a deep layer of alluvium. Wavy-leaf oak and sand sagebrush are common denizens of sandy areas, while very alkaline sites, mostly along the washes, host pure stands of greasewood.

Rabbitbrush thrives on wash banks in the valleys, sometimes growing as tall as 6 feet, and is one of the last plants to bloom in the year. After its myriad yellow blossoms have ripened, the seeds are harvested by squirrels and rabbits and stored for winter food. Blackbrush is also a common shrub, forming scattered stands that dominate large areas. Less widespread are Torrey ephedra, threadleaf snakeweed, and winterfat. Flowering plants that are most conspicuous are prickly pear, groundsel, lupine, mule's ears, and badlands bahia.

Though not as diverse in numbers as the plants of Capitol Reef, the animal population of the Park also owes its diversity to the variety of habitats here. The northern plateau and side-blotched lizards are the most common reptiles along Park trails, but hikers in the South District will also encounter sagebrush, desert spiny, leopard, and collared lizards. Short-horned and tree lizards are most common near Fruita and along the Fremont River.

The only poisonous reptile in Capitol Reef is the midget faded rattlesnake, a denizen of the slickrock country from east of the High Plateaus in Utah into western Colorado. They are rarely seen in the Park, they blend well into their surroundings, and they are quite timid.

Capitol Reef is largely bone-dry slickrock, but there is enough water here and there to support a limited number of frogs and toads. The Fremont River is home to the Great Basin spadefoot toad, Rocky Mountain toad, red spotted toad, and leopard frog. The tanks, or waterpockets, and Halls Creek in the South District also support these amphibians, as well as the canyon treefrog.

Some birds range throughout the Park, while others require specialized habitats. The well-de-veloped tree canopy along the Fremont River hosts a wide variety of birds, including yellow and Wilson's warblers, and black-headed grosbeaks. Denizens of the cliffs and canyons include canyon and rock wrens, unmistakable by their descending call. The violet-green swallow and white-throated swift are commonly seen flying at high speed among the cliffs in search of their insect prey.

Ravens range throughout the Park, from the rocky backbone of the Fold to the parched desert flats and narrow canyons. Common nighthawks are observed in the evening and early morning hours, soaring and diving for insects. American kestrels and sharp-shinned hawks are soaring birds also, but their prey consists of unsuspecting rabbits, squirrels, and mice.

A variety of "little gray birds" inhabits most areas of the Park. Among the more common are the song sparrow, black-throated sparrow, and house finch. The pinyon-juniper woodlands host the particularly noisy and colorful scrub and pinyon jays. These birds can be seen in large numbers in autumn if there is an abundant crop of pinyon nuts. The common flicker and yellow-bellied sapsucker are occasionally seen in wooded areas of the Park as well. In the open desert area east of the Fold, the mourning dove, sage thrasher, chukar, western meadowlark, and mockingbird are likely to be observed.

Hikers also may notice many of the rodents that inhabit the Park. In the open desert areas are found desert cottontail rabbits and blacktail jackrabbits, which aren't rabbits at all, but hares. The whitetail antelope squirrel, somewhat resembling a chipmunk, is an unmistakable desert dweller, with its tail curled up over its back. Mice are abundant in the Park, and though they are seldom seen, backpackers will likely hear mice searching for food in their packs overnight. The desert woodrat, or packrat, is another infrequently seen rodent, although their nests are commonly observed beneath overhanging ledges.

The ringtail, mistakenly called a ringtail cat, is a nocturnal mammal that feeds on birds, insects, and rodents, including desert woodrats. Badgers are infrequently seen as they usually are nocturnal, but their large burrows are a common sight in the desert grasslands east of the Fold.

**The Castle forms a rugged backdrop to the Visitor Center**

The mule deer is the most obvious and frequently observed large mammal in the Park, particularly in the Fruita area. Coyotes are secretive and not commonly seen, although their howling and yipping are often heard echoing among the cliffs at night. Mountain lions can be found wherever their primary food source, the mule deer, dwells. Sightings are extremely rare, but a lucky hiker may find the big cat's tracks on a dusty trail or in the mud of a wash.

Almost as rare are sightings of desert (Nelson) bighorn sheep, which became quite rare in the Waterpocket Fold by the 1940s. However, a small herd was re-introduced into the South District in the 1970s, and the hiker there may see a few of these graceful creatures scampering effortlessly over slickrock that would challenge an accomplished rock climber.

The Fruita area, with its perennial water and abundant food sources, hosts perhaps the greatest concentration of animal life in the Park. Guests at the Fruita Campground are advised to store food in their vehicles due to an abundance of striped skunks. The orchards along the Fremont also host a large population of yellow-bel-

lied marmots, an animal more frequently seen in mountainous high country. Gray fox, mink, and muskrat also make their homes in and around Fruita and the Fremont River. One animal not usually associated with a desert environment is the beaver, which thrives in the Fruita area and in lower Halls Creek as well. In a large stream such as the Fremont, beaver build their lodges in the riverbanks rather than building dams and lodges in the stream itself.

## Interpretive Activities

Interpretive activities lay the foundation for better understanding and appreciation of Capitol Reef's human and natural history. A stop at the Visitor Center, located just off Utah Highway 24 at the junction with the Park's Scenic Drive, may answer some questions you have about the Park, and perhaps whet your appetite to learn more about this historic and unique area. The Visitor Center offers books and maps for sale, has many interpretive displays featuring plants, geology, and history, and offers a slide program. Rangers on duty can answer your questions on any aspect of the Park, and they issue free backcountry use permits. The Visitor Center is open 8 A.M.-7 P.M. spring through fall; winter hours are 8-4:30.

Evening programs in the Fruita Campground amphitheater are conducted nightly from spring through early fall, as are ranger-guided walks on many of the Headquarters District trails. Schedules of activities are posted at the Visitor Center and campground. Other programs include all-day hikes, auto tours along Utah Highway 24, and the Harvest Homecoming program at the end of the season. This program is a recreation of pioneer life in Fruita.

Fruit picking in the Fruita orchards is an important part of a visit to Capitol Reef. Visitors are welcome to stroll through the orchards and eat the ripe fruit, but all fruit must be eaten in the orchards. During the announced harvest periods, visitors may pick all the fruit they wish, for a fee.

# Campgrounds

On average, nearly one-half million visitors come to Capitol Reef each year, making it one of the less-used parks in Utah. Most stay only for a day or less, but those who choose to stay overnight have a variety of campgrounds and motels to choose from in and near the Park.

The Fruita Campground lies one mile from the Visitor Center on the Scenic Drive at an elevation of 5440 feet. Loops A and B lie next to the rushing waters of the Fremont River, and are shaded by broadleaved trees. The campsites, spread across a green lawn, feature picnic tables, fire grills (you must bring your own wood, wood gathering is not permitted in the Park), water, and flush toilets. Loop C is a recent addition to the campground, and its young shade trees are much smaller. The campground is also open in winter, but the water is turned off and pit toilets must be used. There is no fee for camping in winter.

The lush, green setting of the campground, surrounded by orchards and historic pioneer buildings, is a startling contrast to the multihued slickrock cliffs and beehive-shaped domes that rear skyward in every direction.

Two other campgrounds are in the Park, in the North and South districts. The Cathedral Campground lies on the flanks of Thousand Lake Mountain at an elevation of 7000 feet, 27 1/2 miles north of Utah Highway 24 on the River Ford Road. No fee is charged at this primitive campground, and campers must bring their own water. There are five campsites nestled in a woodland of pinyon and juniper.

In the South District is Cedar Mesa Campground, a beautiful primitive campground lying on broad Cedar Mesa at 6000 feet, 21 miles south of Utah Highway 24 on the Notom-Bullfrog Road. Five campsites are shaded by a thick woodland, and each has a picnic table and fire grill. You must bring your own water. Views into Red Canyon and the broad mesas east of Waterpocket Fold are superb.

There are several established picnic sites in the Park, but visitors are free to picnic anywhere. The large, shady Chestnut Picnic Area is located on the Scenic Drive between the Visitor Center and the Fruita Campground, along the banks of the Fremont River. Other picnic areas are at Capitol Gorge; beside Utah Highway 24, 0.2 mile west of the mouth of Spring Canyon (4.5 miles west of the Visitor Center); and in the South District beside the Burr Trail road, where one scenic picnic area is atop the Fold at the head of the switchbacks above Muley Twist Canyon, and another near the Park's western boundary, 29 miles from Boulder.

Several other campgrounds, both public and private, lie close to the Park. Three Forest Service campgrounds dot the forested flanks of Boulder Mountain along scenic Utah Highway 12 within 20 miles of the Park. Other USFS campgrounds are located near Bicknell and Loa, and there are several others near Fish Lake, high on the Fishlake Plateau 20 miles northwest of Loa, along Utah Highway 25.

Private campgrounds are in Torrey and Hanksville, and at Rim Rock Resort between Torrey and the Park. There are no services available inside the Park, but motels, gas, and groceries are available in Torrey, 11 miles west of the Visitor Center, and Hanksville, 37 miles east of the Visitor Center, both on Utah 24.

Auto repairs and towing are available in Torrey, Hanksville, Bicknell and Loa. The nearest hospital is 75 miles away in Richfield, and a medical clinic is in Bicknell, 19 miles west of the Visitor Center on Utah 24.

Hikers and backpackers should come to Capitol Reef well equipped, as the nearest source of outdoor supplies is in Richfield, on U.S. 89.

*For more information about Capitol Reef National Park*:

Park Superintendent
Capitol Reef National Park
Torrey, UT 84775-0015
(801) 425-3791

# Hiking in Capitol Reef

Capitol Reef offers some of the finest desert hiking in all of Utah's national parks. For the experienced backpacker wishing to meet the desert on its own terms, the rugged reaches of this 65-mile-long Park beckon. There are trails in all districts for hikers of every ability, although most are a little more rugged than those in other national parks in Utah.

The Headquarters District, bounded by Pleasant Creek on the south and Utah Highway 24 on the north, contains the greatest concentration of trails and, due to easy access from the paved highway and the graded Scenic Drive, the area receives the most use. Here, along the towering west face of the Waterpocket Fold, trails lead into narrow canyons, traverse mesas and cliffs, and wind among lofty slickrock domes. Trails here are mostly rough and rocky, some are quite steep, and parts of trails cross slickrock where rock cairns must be followed. The trails are well-signed, and can be used to access cross-country routes in canyons and atop the wooded crest of the Waterpocket Fold. The Headquarters District, encompassing the rugged Capitol Reef part of the Fold, is slickrock country at its finest.

The South District, bounded by Utah Highway 24 on the north and Glen Canyon National Recreation Area on the south, is accessed via two good dirt roads: The Notom-Bullfrog Road,

**Typical waterpocket**

which branches off Utah Highway 24 east of the Park, and the Burr Trail Road, heading east from the small town of Boulder on Highway 12.

Hiking in the South District is largely confined to the numerous slot canyons that penetrate the resistant rocks of the Fold. Both roads offer access to these east-trending canyons. As in the Headquarters District, there are a few trails here that are fairly easy and are passable to the average hiker. But most hiking routes in this district are trailless, following cairns over slickrock or along washes. Red Canyon, Muley Twist Canyon, and Halls Creek require no particular skills and are thus good choices for the average hiker.

Due to the South District's relative ease of access, an abundance of fine hiking routes, and incomparable scenery, this area is perhaps the hiker's best choice in the Park for an extended desert backpack. But as in other areas of the Park, water limits the hiker's length of stay. Several fairly reliable tanks dot the flanks of the Fold from The Post southward along Grand Gulch nearly to Brimhall Canyon. Elsewhere, the land is bone dry save for an occasional seasonal waterpocket.

For hikers who wish to traverse some of the most isolated and remote desert country in Utah, there's the North District, that part of the Park lying north of Utah Highway 24.

Save for a few very short trails to overlooks, the region is trailless, and access is gained only after a long drive on one of two roads passable only to high-clearance vehicles. There are a few routes here that are only marginally cairned, but to the hiker experienced in the use of topographic map and compass, the country is wide open for exploration.

Again, water is limited, and in the few places where it flows on the surface, the high mineral content makes most sources unpotable. Hikers are limited by the amount of water they can carry, usually a two-to-three-day supply at best. So instead of undertaking a grueling test of endurance, you might make short backpacks in the North District until you become familiar with the few good water sources here.

Canyons such as Deep Creek, Polk Creek, Water Canyon, and Paradise Draw, valleys such as lengthy South Desert and magnificent Cathedral Valley, and mesa rims such as The Hartnet and the rim of Cathedral Valley, remain as wild and unspoiled as ever, and beckon the experienced desert hiker for a day, a week, or more.

The amount of water a hiker carries varies with the time of year. During spring, when there is usually an abundance of filled waterpockets, hikers can use the waterpockets for their cooking and washing needs. Most of the year, hikers should carry one gallon for each day in the backcountry, and in summer at least one-and-one-half gallons.

Most visitors come to Capitol Reef during summer, when the Park experiences its warmest temperatures and thunderstorms can sweep the Waterpocket Fold, dumping heavy rains, often accompanied by lightning and high winds. July and August are the wettest, and hottest, months in the Park. Temperatures typically reach well into the 90s during summer, and occasionally break 100°. The South District is typically warmer than the Headquarters area by at least 5 degrees, and likewise the North District is usually a bit cooler. The months of April through June and September through November are per-

haps the best seasons in which to hike in Capitol Reef and most other Utah national parks. For more information on hiking seasons, refer to "Hiking Utah's Desert Parks."

Only about 900 backpackers tread the Park's backcountry each year, and their average length of stay is two nights. Thus, with an area of 241,671 acres, solitude in this Park's backcountry is the rule rather than the exception. One is most likely to encounter fellow backpackers on trails in the Headquarters District; in the North District it is rare indeed to meet someone in the backcountry.

Wherever you intend to backpack in Capitol Reef, you must first obtain a backcountry use permit, available free at the Visitor Center or by mail. Backpackers are required to camp at least 100 yards from water sources, upon which many desert animals depend, and preferably one should camp no closer than 1/4 mile from tanks, springs, and seeps. Campsites must also be located out of sight and sound of Park roads, trails, and other developed areas.

Groups using the backcountry are limited to 15 persons; larger groups must split up. Open fires are not permitted, except in developed campgrounds. Hikers must carry out all their trash and garbage. Even biodegradable items such as orange and banana peels may not decompose in a lifetime in this arid desert climate. Washing is not permitted in tanks or potholes, and the use of biodegradable soap is required. Do all your washing at least as far from water sources as the camping distances indicated above. Human waste must be buried in soil 4-6 inches deep.

# Driving to Capitol Reef's Trailheads

(0.0) Torrey, Utah, elevation 6843. This small community is the last town encountered eastbound on Utah 24 until Hanksville, some 50 miles distant.

(0.8) Junction with southbound Utah 12. That paved road leads 37 miles around the slopes of Boulder Mountain to the village of Boulder, at the western terminus of the Burr Trail Road. Several National Forest campgrounds are found along that scenic highway.

From the junction with Highway 12, Highway 24 curves northeast, crossing Sand and Sulphur creeks near their confluence. The highway then curves east and presently crosses the red mudstones and siltstones of the Moenkopi Formation in a parched region of low rolling hills broken by the more resistant ledges of the formation.

(2.1; 2.9) Rim Rock Resort, beyond which we bridge Sulphur Creek, where hikers will find a spacious turnout from where they can begin a hike of the full length of that canyon to the Park Visitor Center.

(1.7; 4.6) Enter Capitol Reef National Park.

(1.0; 5.6) Twin Rocks Viewpoint turnout along the south side of the highway. Twin Rocks rise north of the highway, where two large boulders of the Shinarump Conglomerate rest upon pedestals of red Moenkopi Formation rocks.

(2.0: 7.6) The turnoff to Chimney Rock Trailhead lies on the north side of the highway, leading 50 yards to the parking area at **Trailhead 1**, where *Trips 1, 2,* and *3* begin. The highway ahead climbs a grade, soon meeting

(0.8; 8.4) the southbound spur road to Panorama Point and Goosenecks Point, where *Trips 4* and *5* begin.

Initially paved, this spur road heads southeast 0.1 mile to another spur branching right, which quickly ends in a turnaround at Panorama Point.

The good, dirt-surfaced Goosenecks Road meanders southward among red hills and ledges dotted with pinyon and juniper, ending near the rim of Sulphur Creek canyon (10.8; 9.2). *Trips 4* and *5* begin here at **Trailhead 2**.

(8.4) Beyond the Goosenecks Road, descending the long grade on Highway 24 toward Capitol Reef and the Visitor Center, we pass south of a prominent cliff composed of thinly bedded Moenkopi rocks aptly named Mummy Cliffs.

(2.3; 10.7) Junction with the Scenic Drive just beyond the Sulphur Creek bridge. Hikers

bound for *Trips 6-12*, or visitors bound for the Scenic Drive, Fruita Campground, or the Visitor Center will want to leave the highway here and turn right.

# Scenic Drive, *Trips 6 -12*

(10.7) Turning south from Utah 24 near the Sulphur Creek bridge, drivers immediately pass the Capitol Reef Visitor Center on the right. Backpackers must remember to stop here to obtain a backcountry use permit prior to entering the backcountry. A guide to the Scenic Drive, which will greatly enhance the visitor's appreciation of the scenery along that road, is also available at the Visitor Center. Hikers either shuttling a vehicle or beginning *Trip 3*, taking the described route in reverse, are asked to park their vehicles at the south end of the parking area. A highly scenic trail, passing remnants of pioneer life in Fruita, parallels the Scenic Drive for 1 mile from the Visitor Center to the campground.

Beyond the Visitor Center, the Scenic Drive passes among orchards and the dwellings of early Fruita settlers, most of which now house Park employees. The road soon curves south, passing the Chestnut Picnic Area and a group campsite just before bridging the Fremont River. Then the road curves past another pioneer house and a large barn. The Cohab Canyon Trail *Trip 6* begins just beyond the barn, but hikers not staying in the campground must continue on to the parking area in Campground Loop C, since there is no parking available where the trail begins.

Almost immediately past Cohab Canyon Trail the spur road to Fruita Campground Loops A and B forks off to the right (1.3; 12.0).

(0.2; 12.2) Hikers not staying in the campground can park in the amphitheater parking area to begin *Trips 6* and *7* at **Trailhead 3**.

Continuing up the Scenic Drive, drivers soon encounter the self-pay fee station. This is the only location in the Park where fees are collected.

(0.3; 12.5) End of the pavement. The road ahead proceeds to climb Danish Hill. It is wide, but invariably has a washboard surface. The towering barrier of Capitol Reef follows this scenic road all the way to Pleasant Creek.

(1.7; 14.2) Junction with Grand Wash Road. Starting north, this dirt road, not recommended for travel during rainstorms or if thunderstorms threaten, curves east after 0.2 mile and enters the great cleft of Grand Wash. The road ahead twists and turns in the shadow of the fluted orange Wingate Sandstone cliffs, ending at a turnaround at **Trailhead 4** (1.2; 15.4) where *Trips 8* and *9* either begin or end, depending upon which direction hikers choose to travel them.

(14.2) From the Grand Wash Road junction, the Scenic Drive heads south over rolling redrock terrain. The road crosses a dry wash numerous times, and this segment should be avoided during heavy rains.

(4.4; 18.6) The Capitol Gorge Road, the former route of Utah Highway 24, forks left, while the southbound road continues on to Pleasant Creek.

Hikers bound for *Trips 10* and *11* will turn left here, quickly passing a picnic area and soon entering the shadowy defile of the gorge. This road should also be avoided during rainfall or threatening thunderstorms. The road is rough and narrow as it follows the dry wash, and drivers must proceed with great care.

(2.2; 20.8) The roadend at **Trailhead 5**, featuring interpretive displays, a picnic area and toilets, is the starting point for *Trips 10* and *11*.

(18.6) Hikers bound for Pleasant Creek, however, will continue south at the junction, soon dropping to a crossing of Capitol Gorge wash. A sign here indicates whether the road ahead is open for travel. This is a good dirt road, but it is not gravelled as is the previous part of the Scenic Drive, and it also crosses several dry washes which are subject to washouts during heavy rains.

This road proceeds through a pinyon-juniper woodland at the very foot of Capitol Reef, crosses a watershed divide, then descends east to a junction.

(2.2; 20.8) Avoid the left fork, signed AU-THORIZED VEHICLES ONLY, leading to the Sleeping Rainbow Ranch. After establishment of the Park, the owners retained the right to occupy the ranch, and visitors should respect the private property during their travels through the Pleasant Creek area.

(0.2; 21.0) Avoid another, similarly signed left fork and bear right, soon passing some old corrals and ranch outbuildings.

(0.4; 21.4) *Trip 12* begins at **Trailhead 6** just before the road fords Pleasant Creek. Parking space is available on the west side of the road.

Resuming the eastbound drive along Utah Highway 24 from the junction with the Scenic Drive in 10.7 miles from Torrey, we soon enter the Fremont River canyon, where roadside orchards and riparian vegetation contrast with sparse desert vegetation and the cliffs that tower above.

(0.8; 11.5) The old Fruita Schoolhouse lies north of the road. A trail, signed for the campground, begins 0.1 mile east of the schoolhouse on the south side of the highway. This trail, 0.2 mile long, leads south through orchards and shady riparian foliage to the Fremont River bridge on the Scenic Drive, where it meets the trail from the Visitor Center and continues on to the campground.

(0.3; 11.8) Petroglyphs turnout on the north side of the highway. A very short path leads to the foot of sheer cliffs where Fremont culture artists carved several triangle-shaped, human-like figures on the desert-varnished wall.

Eastward, the highway passes the last of the orchards and re-enters a world dominated by towering cliffs and streamside vegetation.

(0.9; 12.7) **Trailhead 7**, where *Trips 13* and *14* begin, signed for Hickman Bridge, is on the north side of the highway just short of a bridge over the Fremont River. The eastern end of the Cohab Canyon Trail (*Trip 6*) lies 250 yards east along the south side of the highway beyond the bridge.

Proceeding east along the highway, we follow the south bank of the river, presently deep within the slickrock domain of the Waterpocket Fold. A number of side canyons branching right and left from the river are worthy of exploration and beckon the adventurous to discover their hidden secrets.

(2.0; 14.7) The hard-to-spot mouth of Spring (or Chimney Rock) Canyon opens into the Fremont River from the northwest. Hikers planning the trek through that canyon (*Trip 2*) should first check river conditions here, then backtrack westward for 0.2 mile and park their shuttled car near the picnic area at **Trailhead 8.**

The highway ahead bends sharply south, soon reaching

the lower Grand Wash Trailhead (0.6; 15.3), where *Trip 9* hikers will find parking space for at least five cars at **Trailhead 9**. Depending upon the hiker's desire, that trip can either begin or end at this trailhead.

(0.7; 16.0) Behunin Cabin south of the highway. Beyond the cabin, the great domes of Capitol Reef steadily recede in stature and we soon pass north of a large pond and skirt the river where it plunges over a scenic waterfall. The landscape becomes more open as we proceed east, and we pass south of the broad mouth of Deep Creek and South Desert before leaving the Park.

(3.1; 19.2) East entrance to Capitol Reef National Park.

(0.7; 19.9) The signed NOTOM ROAD forks south from the highway. Hikers bound for *Trips 15-23* should refer to the Notom-Bullfrog road log below.

For the next several miles Highway 24 continues east along the presently shallow and broad Fremont River canyon among red and gray-colored bluffs and broken low cliffs.

(2.7; 22.6) A small sign on the north side of the highway indicates River Ford. Hikers bound for the North District and *Trips 24-28* must keep a lookout for this easy-to-miss junction. Those hikers should refer to the River Ford (Hartnet) Road log below.

(7.3; 29.9) Northbound Caineville Road, just beyond a bridge over usually dry Caineville Wash. This dirt road is a longer alternative for reaching the North District, but high-clearance vehicles are necessary. Information about this road is available at the Visitor Center.

(20.5; 50.4) Hanksville, and the junction with southbound Utah 95 to Lake Powell and northbound Utah 24 to Interstate 70 and Green River. All services are available for travelers at Hanksville.

# Notom-Bullfrog Road, *Trips 15 -23*

The Notom Road is a graded dirt road, paralleling the Waterpocket Fold for 47 miles to Halls Creek Overlook, passing through a stark yet beautiful desert landscape. The road is dirt-and sand-surfaced, but graded only a few times each year, so it often tends to be rough with a washboard surface. However, it is passable to passenger vehicles. But like most dirt roads in Utah's deserts, it may become impassable even to 4WD vehicles after heavy rains.

(0.0) The signed Notom Road leads south from Utah 24, climbing a steady grade between barren slopes. At the crest of a hill, an unforgettable vista of the Waterpocket Fold meets our gaze in the southwest.

(2.3) Our road then descends to bridge Pleasant Creek and we ignore a left-forking road 0.1 mile beyond.

(1.5; 3.8) Junction with northeast-bound road to Utah 24 on the left, which we ignore. Our road then passes private land in the Notom area, climbs south-southeast to the Notom Bench, and descends through nearly barren hills to

(3.8; 7.6) signed Burro Wash at **Trailhead 10** where *Trip 15* begins. There is no developed parking area at Burro Wash for hikers. From Burro Wash, continue south-southeast to the signed crossing of dry Cottonwood Wash (1.2; 8.8). Good campsites are available here.

Passing through clay hills we soon reach Fivemile Wash (1.0; 9.8), then continue through more barren hills before descending to Sheets Gulch (2.7; 12.5).

(0.7; 13.2) Avoid a signed left-branching road winding east toward the Henry Mountains.

(0.1; 13.3) Avoid the signed right-branching Oak Creek Access Road. This rough dirt road requires a 4WD vehicle to negotiate the 4.5 miles to its end at the Oak Creek trailhead. From that roadend, a cairned route leads down to the canyon floor, and from there hikers can follow a wide stock driveway 3 miles to the Park boundary and beyond. Beyond the access road, we bridge normally trickling Oak Creek, avoid a left fork to the Sandy Ranch, then climb a slope to the top of a broad bench high above Sandy Creek.

(0.8; 14.1) A private ranch road forks right, also offering access into Oak Creek and the Coleman Canyons to the south. Permission to use this road can be obtained from Steve Dalton at (801) 425-3282. Our road drops steadily southeast from the bench, and we soon avoid a right-forking road immediately before crossing unsigned and dry Dogwater Creek.

Beyond the creek, the road heads south through a broad valley known as Sandy Creek Benches. Ahead the valley narrows and sandstone bluffs squeeze us into The Narrows of Divide Canyon, the upper reaches of the presently dry Sandy Creek drainage.

(4.8; 18.9) Signed boundary of Capitol Reef National Park. The valley beyond The Narrows opens up once again, and our road heads southwest along the west margin of the valley.

(2.1; 21.0) Junction with spur road to Cedar Mesa Campground. This good but narrow westbound spur leads 250 yards to its end at the campground, where *Trip 16* hikers begin at **Trailhead 11**. Hikers not staying in the campground should park on the Notom Road at the junction.

Beyond the campground turnoff, the main road eventually climbs to Bitter Creek Divide, 5700 feet (3.5; 24.5), then continues south-southeast down the narrow, grassy valley of upper Halls Creek.

After about 3 miles the road passes among and parallel to a series of low ridges or reefs, known collectively as the Oyster Shell Reef, composed of Dakota Sandstone and Brushy Basin Shale. Here in the Oyster Shell Reef, we may want to pause and explore its slopes, for in the Dakota Sandstone we'll find an amazing abundance of marine fossil shells. Be sure not to remove any shells from this area; leave them for others to marvel at.

Passing west of Oyster Shell Reef, we soon head through a gap eroded into the reef, and clearly see the switchbacks of the Burr Trail Road climbing steeply up the headwall of Burr Canyon in the southwest, one of very few gaps in the entire 90-mile length of the Waterpocket Fold.

(8.2; 32.7) Junction with westbound Burr Trail Road. This signed junction's sign indicates mileages to various points, and includes a dis-

play with a map of the Park and offers varied information about the South District.

(32.7) The Burr Trail Road is generally in the same condition as the Notom Road, and is passable to cars but not trailers or large RVs. From the junction, this road soon enters the narrow slot of Burr Canyon. After 0.9 mile, the road suddenly switchbacks steeply up a broken slope, cresting the Fold after six switchbacks. Here a 150-yard spur road forks left of a picnic area featuring extensive vistas stretching east to the distant Henry Mountains.

(21.; 34.8) A sign identifies LOWER MULEY TWIST CANYON HIKERS PARKING at **Trailhead 12**. *Trip 17* begins on the left side of the road. The Burr Trail Road ahead descends to cross the wash of Muley Twist Canyon, then heads west and north across an open valley to a junction.

(1.1; 35.9) Signed spur to Upper Muley Twist canyon.

This right-forking road, rough but passable to all vehicles if driven carefully, leads through open ground to the parking area (0.4; 36.3) at **Trailhead 13**, immediately above Muley Twist. There is parking space for at least 3 vehicles, where *Trip 18* hikers begin their trek.

**In Lower Muley Twist Canyon**

West of that spur road, the Burr Trail Road climbs steadily upon a wooded slope, reaching a signed picnic area (2.1; 38.0) in a woodland of pinyon and juniper, on the right side of the road. Excellent views across the Fold take in the Henry Mountains in their entirety.

The road continues its climb to the Park boundary at 6600 feet (0.5; 38.5), and from there the road traverses wooded mesas and dips into numerous deep, spectacular canyons. It can be quite narrow and rough in places. Approaching the town of Boulder, the road becomes paved (27.9; 66.4), then reaches Boulder and a junction with Utah 12 (2.6; 69.0). Northbound Utah 12 climbs north toward Torrey, 37 miles from Boulder. The town of Escalante lies about 26 miles southwest of Boulder via Utah 12, perhaps one of the most spectacular paved roads in Utah.

(32.7) From the Burr Trail Road junction, the Notom-Bullfrog Road continues to parallel the Fold, passing a number of deep, narrow canyons that cut west into that slickrock wall.

(1.7; 34.4) A sign identifies Surprise Canyon at **Trailhead 14**, where hikers begin *Trip 19*. There is parking for about 4 cars on the right side of the road.

After a short stint through the grassy, shrub-dotted valley, we reach a junction (0.5; 34.9). A sign identifies The Post and Headquarters Canyon where *Trip 20* begins. Parking at **Trailhead 15** is on the left side of the road, but parking space is limited.

A spur road forks right here, leading down Grand Gulch, the upper end of the long, narrow valley of Halls Creek. This spur road is rutted, subject to runoff damage, and rough in places, but it is passable to carefully driven vehicles. It leads south-southeast, passes a large corral and pit toilet, and ends after 0.7 mile at **Trailhead 16** for Halls Creek and the Lower Muley Twist cutoff trail, *Trip 21*.

(34.9) From the Post, the main road jogs northeast. It presently follows the course of a wash, then stays beside it as it curves southeast once again.

(1.0; 35.9) Eastern boundary of Capitol Reef National Park. The road now crosses public lands administered by the Bureau of Land Management. The road ahead skirts the western margin of another grassy valley. After the dirt road climbs gently out of the valley it eventually curves east above another broad, open valley. After midway around this long curve ignore a set of jeep tracks (6.2; 42.1) forking right, toward the west. From there our road descends along the flanks of the valley and soon we meet a signed junction (1.5; 43.6), where we turn right, heading towards Halls Creek Overlook and Bullfrog Basin.

The road ahead follows a shallow valley toward the south, soon reaching a second junction (1.0; 44.6) with a southeast-bound road, also signed for HALLS CREEK OVERLOOK. Turning right, we follow the lesser-used road west-southwest along a draw south of a minor wash, then climb a broken sandstone slope, soon topping out on the gentle terrain of Big Thomson Mesa. The road ahead is sometimes rough, and shortly we reach a third and final junction (2.5; 47.1), also signed for the overlook. Turning right once again, we find this road to be very rocky and rough, and passable only to high-clearance vehicles.

(0.3; 47.4) The road ends at a small turnaround at **Trailhead 17**, where *Trips 22* and *23* begin.

# River Ford Road, *Trips 24-28*

The River Ford, or Hartnet, Road, requires a ford of the Fremont River, which is usually less than 2 feet deep except after heavy rains and during spring runoff from snow melting on the High Plateaus to the west. The ford and parts of the road beyond require a high-clearance 4WD vehicle. Always inquire at the Visitor Center before fording the river. It is also wise to inspect river conditions on foot before driving into the water. There is often a deep hole where you enter the river, but the condition of the channel can change during high water or flash floods.

Drivers can avoid the ford by following the much longer Caineville Road (see Utah Highway 24 road log at the start of this section for the location of this road and check with the Visitor Center for more information), but it crosses numerous washes, some quite muddy, along its course. Even this road requires the use of a high-clearance vehicle, and due to changing conditions a 4WD vehicle is highly recommended. Both are rough desert roads that receive minimal maintenance.

(0.0) From the small sign indicating River Ford just east of milepost 91 on Utah Highway 24, turn north and descend to the cottonwood-shaded flood plain of the Fremont River.

(0.5) At a signed junction roads fork left and right. Usually the left fork offers the more trouble-free ford. Taking the left fork, we reach the river within 80 yards, where it spreads its usually shallow waters across a wide gravel bed. Proceed slowly into the river. Once beyond the ford, the aforementioned right fork joins our road on the right, and together we briefly follow the sandy roadbed along the river's floodplain. Soon we negotiate a single switchback, then wind among colorful hills. We'll notice number signs all along this road, keyed to a road guide available at the Park Visitor Center. We soon traverse above the rim of a gaping declivity—Dry Wash.

Shortly we dip into Dry Wash and cross it three times, then proceed northwest into the broad basin of North Blue Flats. Enjoying broad vistas and a brief stretch of smooth road, we soon pass Stop 5 (5.0; 5.5), just below signed Rube's Pond, hidden behind a low dam and a tamarisk grove east of the road.

(1.8; 7.3) Stop 6 lies just west of a tamarisk thicket and the runoff from a well and stock water tank. A drilling truck, long abandoned, stands nearby. *Trip 24* to The Notch begins here at **Trailhead 18**. Be sure to purify any water you obtain from the spring. The road ahead continues along North Blue Flats to its upper end, then begins climbing into the colorful yet barren Bentonite Hills.

Descending northwest over the hills, ignore an eastbound spur road (2.5; 9.8), signed for 2 GUYS RESERVOIR. Our road continues climbing into a higher, juniper-dotted valley. Ignore another eastbound BLM spur road (0.5; 10.3), this one signed for ROCK WATER.

(3.7; 14.0) Signed junction with westbound spur road to Lower South Desert Overlook.

*Trip 25* hikers will turn left here, following the fairly good graded road into a shallow draw bounded by low cliffs. Midway along the course of this road we enter the Park, and then climb easily toward the rim of The Hartnet, a long broken ridge bounding the valley of South Desert throughout the North District. A small turnout is at the roadend (1.2; 15.2), and *Trip 25* hikers begin their travels here at **Trailhead 19**.

From that spur road junction we follow the main road roughly north across a broad flat before winding back and forth among broken ledges, crossing two shallow washes.

(2.3; 16.3) Enter Capitol Reef National Park, indicated by a large rock-slab sign near the crest of a broad, grassy saddle. Ahead, we quickly top the rise and soon our road bends west, descending into the long, narrow valley of Hartnet Draw.

(1.1; 17.4) **Trailhead 20** for *Trip 26*. A sign on the road's north side indicates: LOWER CATHEDRAL VALLEY OVERLOOK 1 MILE, NO VEHICLES. This location is also indicated by a Stop 10 sign. Hikers must search for a wide spot in the road in which to park.

West along the rough and rocky road, we cross a prominent south-trending draw, skirt the base of a sandstone-topped bluff, then quite soon cross another prominent wash, this one heading west, where our road begins traveling northwest.

(2.0; 19.4) Our road crosses the course of this wash where hikers undertaking *Trip 27* should find a wide spot in the road in which to park at **Trailhead 21**. Beyond this trailhead proceed northwest up the narrowing canyon of Harnet Draw, following west of the sandy wash. Eventually we cross the wash, and within 125 yards cross it a second time. These crossings are wide and sandy, and the road here is subject to considerable erosion, so they are rough but usually passable. Once again, after another 0.1 mile, we cross the wash.

(0.6; 20.0) A sign immediately beyond this third crossing indicates Stop 11, while another sign, north of the road, identifies Ackland Spring, a developed spring invisible from the road. *Trip 28* begins here at **Trailhead 22**. Find a wide spot in the road to park your car.

# Trip 1
## Chimney Rock Loop Trail

**Distance**: 3.5 miles semiloop
**Low/High elevations**: 6051'/6670'
**Suited for**: Dayhike
**Difficulty**: Moderate
**Best seasons**: April through mid-June; mid-September through November.
**Map/Trailhead**: 16/1
**Hazards**: No water or shade

**Introduction**: This is a fine half-day hike on a good trail in the western reaches of the Park. It offers close-up views of the great barrier cliffs of Capitol Reef, and offers more distant panoramas of the Waterpocket Fold and the high plateaus of Boulder and Thousand Lake mountains. Terrain varies from open flats to a sparsely wooded mesa and a cliffbound canyon. A part of the trail is also used as the starting point for the more lengthy Chimney Rock Canyon hike (*Trip 2*).

**Description**: From the signed Chimney Rock trailhead, (0.0; 6051) we briefly climb northwest up low red hills of the Moenkopi Formation before leveling off in a grassy flat decorated by scattered shrubs, pinyons, junipers, and a variety of colorful wildflowers from spring through early fall. Rising 400 feet above in the southeast is the prominent landmark of Chimney Rock, jutting west from and contrasting with the flat mesa above. A fascinating pillar composed of the Moenkopi, its myriad thin layers are accentuated by weathering and erosion, and they support a single block of tan-colored Shinarump Conglomerate. Such balanced rocks are superb examples of differential erosion, in which rocks of different hardnesses are eroded at different rates. Except for the resistant caprock, Chimney Rock's pillar would be reduced to clay and sand in a comparatively short time.

At the northeast end of the flat, the trail begins a series of steep, short switchbacks that lead upward through the varicolored layers of the Chinle Formation. After this stiff ascent, we reach a signed junction (0.5; 6307) and turn right. To our north the Wingate Sandstone cliffs soar nearly vertically 400 feet above, pockmarked by several arch-shaped alcoves. Boulders fallen from these cliffs obscure much of the Chinle Formation below.

Presently ascending north slopes, we soon reach the brink of the Moenkopi cliff and gaze beyond the spire of Chimney Rock to the distant lofty plateau of 11,000' Boulder Mountain, where dense forests and unseen, lake-dotted cirque basins form a stark contrast to the comparatively barren, rock-dominated landscape of Capitol Reef. The trail hugs the rim of a Chinle-capped mesa, soon passing a very short spur to an overlook; enroute we enjoy far-flung panoramas of the Henry Mountains to the east, foregrounded by the great red cliffs and white domes of Capitol Reef rising in bold relief. A northeast-trending tributary to Spring (Chimney Rock) Canyon slicing deep into the sandstone layers of the reef to our east is part of the popular route down Spring Canyon to the Fremont River (*Trip 2*). Also visible is the dirt road to the Goosenecks Overlook, ending above the deep gorge of Sulphur Creek, south of Utah 24.

Leveling off on the mesa, we pass scattered

**Chimney Rock**

pinyons and junipers, the live trees gnarled, twisted and stunted by harsh desert winds, growing among the picturesque wind-burnished remains of their predecessors. Soon the trail descends corrugated slopes to a low saddle, then skirts the base of soaring Wingate Sandstone cliffs amid a jumble of large boulders. These red sandstone blocks demonstrate *cross-bedding*, an indication that this sandstone was deposited by wind. The trail soon descends and bends west down to the nearby signed junction (1.5; 6171) with the return leg of our loop and the northeast route into Spring Canyon (see *Trip 2*).

Continuing west, we ascend the broad upper drainage of this Spring Canyon tributary, with towering red cliffs rising to our north and tree- and shrub-dotted slopes rising gently to our south.

Scattered pinyon and juniper, hop-sage, mormon tea, rabbitbrush and a variety of seasonal wildflowers keep us company as we gently ascend slopes and cross the small, dry wash several times. Keep an eye out for petrified wood enroute toward the skyline saddle in the west; it is fairly common in the Chinle Formation. Upon reaching the broad saddle, (0.8; 6330) you can make a brief detour to the south to see more fragments of petrified wood.

From the saddle we descend north-facing slopes to a junction with the loop trail (0.2; 6307), turn right, and retrace our panoramic route for 1/2 mile to the trailhead.

# Trip 2
## Chimney Rock Canyon to Fremont River

**Distance**: 10.2 miles shuttle trip
**Low/High elevations**: 6330'/5230'
**Suited for**: Dayhike or backpack
**Difficulty**: Moderate as an overnighter; moderately strenuous as a dayhike.
**Best seasons**: April through mid-June; mid-September through November.
**Maps/Trailheads**: 16,17/1,8

**Hazards**: Usually no water; flash-flood danger.

**Introduction**: Owing to its easy access, this fine canyon route is one of the most popular backpacking hikes in the Park. Scenery ranges from pinyon-juniper flats and mesas to a cliffbound declivity deep within the Waterpocket Fold. Campsites are numerous, and hikers have the option of extending the trek by following Spring Canyon upstream toward its source high on the flanks of Thousand Lake Mountain. Much of the route is trailless, but the wash it traverses is easy to follow. The trip requires a usually easy ford of the Fremont River, and a 7-mile car shuttle or hitchhike back to Chimney Rock.

**Description**: From the trailhead, follow the final 1.5 miles of *Trip 1* in reverse to the signed junction with the route into Spring Canyon, and continue straight ahead, down-canyon. For the following 1 1/2 miles, our wash-bottom route, generally hard packed and littered with sandstone boulders, winds northeast amid cliffs of reddish Wingate Sandstone soaring as much as 400 feet above. The cliffs are often fluted but usually sheer, coated in places with desert varnish of a brown, black, or metallic-blue luster, and streaked in other places where runoff pours over the cliffs after infrequent rains, depositing a veiled coating of leached minerals.

Due to the concentration of moisture, shrubs in this canyon reach atypical proportions. Squawbush, with its glossy green, three-lobed leaves; serviceberry, with its silvery bark and small green, oval leaves, serrated at their tips; singleleaf ash; and water motie, or seep-willow, are much larger than their counterparts growing on adjacent ledges and slopes. Among the wildflowers that adorn the canyon are the profuse blossoms of broom snakeweed, a small shrub that blooms from late summer through autumn, the tall stalks of yellow prince's plume, and the aromatic yellow blooms of a sunflower—badlands bahia.

Numerous tributary drainages offer intriguing diversions to hikers with ample time to explore and discover their hidden secrets. We will pass one moist locale enroute, indicated by the presence of such water-loving vegetation as

Fremont cottonwood and tamarisk.

Passing the remnants of an old stock-drift fence, we reach the broad wash of Spring Canyon (1.5; 5918), littered with sandstone as well as basalt boulders, the latter washed far from their source on volcanic-capped Thousand Lake Mountain. From this confluence, hikers may choose either to hike up the wash to the spring that gives this canyon its name, or to proceed down to the Fremont River.

A fine campsite lies across the wash, perched on a bench covered with grasses and decorated by twisted pinyons and junipers. However, this site would be visible from the route, and should be avoided. Numerous other potential sites can be found throughout the canyon.

**Chimney Rock Trail**

## Upper Spring Canyon

Those who decide to turn left up the wash will pass a variety of campsites atop streamside benches, and as they proceed will alternate between dry, rocky stretches and moister locales. A particularly interesting plant, most common in moist areas, is showy milkweed, featuring large leaves and bearing a cucumber-like fruit in mid-summer.

The cliffs become more broken up-canyon, and colorful Chinle rocks begin to crop out on the floor of the wash as we approach a small, seeping alcove, dense with vegetation, on the north side of the wash. About 0.2 mile beyond it and 1.1 miles from the confluence, an even larger alcove is at the foot of the cliffs to the north. A brief detour into this alcove reveals a lovely pool shaded by overarching Fremont cottonwoods. Above the pool lies the contact between the Wingate and the Chinle, and from this contact zone issues seeping water that gives life to the pool below, its dense vegetation, and a host of animals that rely upon its life-sustaining moisture. Willows, cottonwoods, barberry, tamarisk, seep-willow, singleleaf ash, squawbush, and mormon tea all compete for precious moisture at this idyllic locale.

Hikers must bear in mind the importance of this water source to local wildlife both large and small, and not camp within 1/4 mile of the spring.

The canyon continues northwestward, under great cliffs and multihued slopes, for about 10 miles to 8400' Sand Flat, where the canyon gathers its waters along the flank of Thousand Lake Mountain, within Fishlake National Forest.

Most of us will turn right, downstream at the confluence. The boulder-strewn bed of the wash makes for rougher going. Upon entering a narrow, entrenched gorge, we are soon confronted with the first obstacle of the canyon—two dry waterfalls—the upper one about 8 feet high, the lower, 12 feet. To avoid difficult downclimbing, a route along the bench above (northeast of) the narrows has been cairned by Park Rangers. Before entering the narrows, climb briefly to this bench on the left for an easy passage around the falls.

For the following 6 miles, the meandering wash alternates between damp sections hosting moisture-dependent vegetation and dry sections hosting junipers and a variety of shrubs. One of the most notable wildflowers in the canyon is rough Mule's ears, a small perennial shrub featuring long, green, linear leaves and numerous large, yellow blossoms in summer.

As we proceed down-canyon, we'll pass numerous feeder canyons before bidding farewell to the red sandstones of the Kayenta Formation, beyond which sweeping cliffs of Navajo Sandstone, both rounded and near-vertical, rise as much as 800 feet above to myriad domes and spires. The hiking is generally easy and the canyon loses little elevation, but occasional boulder-strewn sections briefly hamper steady progress.

The canyon alternates between unforgettable narrows and wider stretches where a variety of benches, some open with a ground cover of grasses and shrubs, others shaded by cottonwoods or pinyon and juniper, offer scenic campsites to overnight travelers. Despite the intense heat of summer above the canyon, the soaring cliffs above the narrow canyon allow only a modicum of sunlight into its depths. Seasonal seeps muddy the canyon bottom and may offer enough drinking water, but always purify *any* water obtained in the desert canyons of Utah.

Adventurous hikers looking for a diversion from the main canyon might consider following a major canyon (5.1; 5350) that veers off to the east, ultimately leading toward the broad, wooded tableland of Horse Mesa, rising 1/2 to 3/4 mile east of and 1100 feet above Spring Canyon.

The final 2 miles of Spring Canyon are especially narrow, hemmed in by soaring cliffs and domes of cream-colored sandstone. Our approach to the Fremont River is heralded by dense thickets of riparian vegetation, including the tallest grass in the Park—common reed—as well as stands of tamarisk, cottonwood, and willows. After bushwhacking through this veritable jungle, we reach our second and final obstacle, the ford of the Fremont. Most hikers visit the Park during the months of spring, and they likely will find the river swollen with snowmelt from the heights of the plateaus it drains to the west. Then the river could be waist-deep, or at least knee-deep, and swift. A stick used for added balance is recommended during high water. In summer, though, the river is typically only a foot deep.

Beyond the ford, simply bushwhack up the riverbank to the highway (2.1; 5230) and either reach a second car parked in the wide turnouts near the picnic area 0.2 mile west or hitchhike

back to the Chimney Rock trailhead.

# Trip 3
## Chimney Rock Trailhead to the Visitor Center via Sulphur Creek

**Distance**: 6.2 miles shuttle trip
**Low/High** elevations: 5480'/6051'
**Suited for**: Dayhikes
**Difficulty**: Moderate
**Best seasons**: April through mid-June; mid-September through November.
**Maps/Trailhead**: 16,17/1
**Hazards**: Wading; flash-flood danger; rudimentary rock climbing required to bypass three waterfalls; water not potable in Sulphur Creek.

**Introduction**: A jaunt into Sulphur Creek canyon from either the Visitor Center or Chimney Rock trailhead can be a rewarding trip for almost any hiker, especially on a hot day when wading its perennial waters can be delightful. But to complete the entire trip, one must have the confidence and the ability to negotiate steep rock while bypassing three waterfalls in the canyon.

Sulphur Creek drains the high southern slopes of Thousand Lake Mountain and is prone to flash floods. Never enter the canyon if a thunderstorm is threatening anywhere in the Sulphur Creek drainage. Water from the aptly named creek is not potable, so carry your own. A car shuttle or a hitchhike of 3 miles is necessary if you hike the route end to end.

**Description**: From Chimney Rock trailhead (0.0; 6051) cross Utah Highway 24 and descend into the shallow wash opposite the turnoff to the trailhead. Our trailless route ahead then descends the deepening canyon along the rabbitbrush-lined wash amid red cliffs and ledges of mudstones and sandstones of the Moenkopi Formation. Look for ripple marks on slabs of the Moenkopi, formed by ancient winds rippling the shallow waters along a sea coast more than 200 million years ago.

The gradually deepening canyon winds 1.7 miles to its confluence with Sulphur Creek. Nearing Sulphur Creek, the canyon cuts into the Kaibab Limestone, an intricately eroded white dolomite formation. Two short pourovers (dry waterfalls) will be encountered, but are easily bypassed via brief scrambles. When you reach the tamarisk-lined course of Sulphur Creek (1.7; 5900), a grass- and shrub-clad bench just west of the confluence invites backpackers to linger. Another possible campsite is on the low bench south of here, across the creek.

Turning downstream, we presently enter The Goosenecks, where the canyon describes a series of broad meanders for 1.3 miles. From within The Goosenecks, we can gaze skyward nearly 600 feet to the north rim of the canyon and spy the fenced-in viewpoint of Goosenecks Overlook, accessed via a short trail at the end of a dirt road (*Trip 4*). No more possible campsites will be encountered until we leave the narrow gorge after another 1.3 miles. Vegetation is generally sparse in the rockbound gorge, but grasses, clover, and the willow-like shrub called seep-willow are common.

East beyond the overlook, the Park's oldest rocks—White Rim Sandstone—underlying the Kaibab signal our approach to the first in a series of waterfalls. This 6' fall is easily bypassed via a ledge on the south side. Less than 0.2 mile ahead we're confronted with the highest fall in the canyon, where the creek tumbles and roars over an 8' precipice in the White Rim Sandstone. Once again, a detour around the south side, necessitating downclimbing the Class 3 rock of a narrow chute, allows hikers to proceed. For the following mile, we're wedged in the narrow canyon between broken, sometimes overhanging, convoluted cliffs. where the echoing roar of myriad cascades fills the canyon. Expect to be in the water much of the time here. At times, we must seek out ledges to avoid small cascades. Numerous lovely pools offer ample incentive for a brief stopover.

Eventually, a major Sulphur Creek tributary joins from the southwest, ending in an abrupt 20' dry fall (2.5; 5660). Beyond, the high cliffs steadily diminish in stature, and where the canyon broadens, we'll pass more benches, clad in pinyon and juniper, where possible campsites could be located. About 0.8 mile past the dry fall, we reach the final waterfall, and though it plunges only 5 feet, it represents perhaps the greatest obstacle in the canyon. We can bypass the fall on the north side via slippery slickrock leading to an easy ledge traverse, then downclimb to the creek below, or downclimb Class 3-4 rock on its south side—the least dangerous but scariest passage. Below, the white Kaibab dips underground, and once again the strangely eroded cliffs, ledges and slopes of the Moenkopi dominate the canyon, receding steadily as we hike and wade the final mile to the Visitor Center.

Passing just west of the Visitor Center, hike down to the Sulphur Creek bridge on Utah Highway 24 (1.8; 5500), then follow the highway briefly southeast to the Scenic Drive, and go south down it to our vehicle in the Visitor Center parking area (0.2; 5500).

# Trip 4
## Gooseneck Point

**Distance**: 0.2 mile round trip
**Low/High elevations**: 6349'/6370'
**Suited for**: Walk
**Difficulty**: Easy
**Best seasons**: April through mid-June; mid-September through November.
**Map/Trailhead**: 16/2
**Hazards**: Steep dropoffs at and near the trail's end.

**Introduction**: One of the shortest trails in Capitol Reef, the Goosenecks Overlook Trail offers big rewards for very little effort. This easy trail climbs quickly to the rim high above Sulphur Creek. The trail is suitable for most any visitor, even small children, though they should be closely supervised near the rim.

**Description**: A sign at the roadend (0.0; 6349) gives the length of the trail as 600 feet, just over 0.1 mile, and warns: DANGER—KEEP BACK FROM EDGE—LOOSE ROCK.

The trail climbs briefly to the rim and then winds among the red sandstone and siltstone boulders of the Moenkopi Formation, ending at the fenced-off overlook (0.1; 6370), perched on the brink of broken 600-foot cliffs plunging into deeply incised meanders of Sulphur Creek canyon. Whitish cliffs, broken and deeply eroded, underlie the Moenkopi rocks in the depths of the canyon. These are composed of the Kaibab Limestone, the same rocks that form the north rim of Grand Canyon.

Vistas extend east beyond the great red cliffs and white domes of Capitol Reef to the lofty summits of the Henry Mountains. From southwest to northwest the view is dominated by the extensive, forested plateaus of Boulder and Thousand Lake mountains.

# Trip 5
## Sun Set Trail to Sun Set Point

**Distance**: 0.6 mile round trip
**Low/High elevations**: 6349'/6380'
**Suited for**: Walk
**Difficulty**: Easy
**Best season**: April through mid-June; mid-September through November.
**Map/Trailhead**: 16/2
**Hazards**: Steep dropoffs near the trail's end.

**Introduction**: A slightly longer (than *Trip 4*) but equally rewarding jaunt from The Goosenecks roadend leads to Sun Set Point, a splendid overlook high on the rim above Sulphur Creek Canyon. The point is a favorite late-afternoon haunt of photographers and anyone who enjoys often-dramatic sunsets.

**Description**: Forking left (southeast) from the roadend (0.0; 6349), the signed Sun Set Trail climbs easily into a pinyon-juniper woodland. High above Sulphur Creek canyon, our trail ends (0.3; 6380) on the rim, from where the echoing roar of the creek can be heard but not seen in the depths below. The vistas here, as panoramic as those from Gooseneck Point, feature the slickrock spine of Capitol Reef filling the view from north to southeast, foregrounding the distant Henry Mountains in the southeast, while Thousand Lake Mountain forms a horizontal skyline to the northwest. Such are the incongruities of

the Colorado Plateau, where nearly level mesas are edged by vertical cliffs, and subalpine summits rise like islands in a sea of arid land and barren slickrock. In the foreground to the north, the varied ledges, slopes and fluted cliffs of the Moenkopi Formation, extending toward the sheer wall of Wingate Sandstone cliffs beyond Utah Highway 24, form perhaps one of the most intriguing landscapes in the Park.

# Trip 6
## Cohab Canyon Trail

**Distance**: 1.7 miles shuttle trip, without sidetrips
**Low/High elevations**: 5350'/ 5760'
**Suited for**: Dayhike
**Difficulty**: Moderate
**Best seasons**: April through mid-June; mid-September through November.
**Map/Trailhead**: 17/3
**Hazards**: Steep dropoffs; little shade; no water.

**Introduction**: A classic example of a hidden canyon, Cohab is virtually invisible when viewed from the Fruita Campground; only a minuscule notch in the towering orange cliffs to the east gives any intimation that a canyon lies on the other side. Legend has it that Mormon polygamists, or "cohabs," took refuge in this hidden declivity when pursued by United States marshals in the 1880s after federal law made polygamy a felony.

Today, hikers also seek Cohab Canyon as a refuge—albeit brief—from the pressures of our modern world. The initial climb of the colorful Chinle slopes above the campground is short but strenuous, but most hikers find that the vistas from the top of the climb are well worth the effort. Once in the canyon, hikers have a variety of options, including short spur trails to two overlooks above the Fremont River, a descent of the entire canyon to Utah Highway 24 opposite the Hickman Bridge trailhead, or a longer hike southbound over the top of the Waterpocket Fold via the Frying Pan Trail (*Trip 8*), a rewarding hike leading to Cassidy Arch and ultimately to Grand Wash. Hikers not staying in the Fruita Campground must park their vehicles in the parking area in Campground Loop C.

**Description**: This signed trail begins just north of the turnoff to Campground Loops A and B, on the east side of the Scenic Drive (0.0; 5440). Wasting no time gaining elevation, the trail switchbacks steadily upward, gaining 320 feet in the first 0.4 mile over varicolored Chinle slopes littered with the ubiquitous basalt boulders and cobbles. Vistas improve with every step, including the Fruita Campground, its orchards, and wooded mesas extending toward Boulder Mountain in the southwest, highlighted by the deep gash of the Fremont River.

Near the top of this stiff climb the trail enters a sparse woodland of pinyon and juniper, where plants eke out a living in the nutrient-poor upper layers of the Chinle.

After the switchbacks end, we traverse south beneath sandstone cliffs soaring 200 feet above. Over-the-shoulder views of great white domes, contrasting dramatically with the reddish cliffs and ledges below, and rising 1400 feet north of the canyon of the Fremont, are briefly enjoyed before we turn east, passing through a narrow notch in the cliff (0.4; 5760) and proceeding into the head of northeast-trending Cohab Canyon.

We now descend gently through the narrow upper canyon, accompanied by pinyon and juniper, prickly pear (whose beautiful, delicate late-spring flowers contrast with the cactuses' forbidding foliage of spines and dull green stems), and other shrubs. The soaring canyon walls are colored by layers of red and tan rocks and pitted with myriad potholes. Numerous narrow, joint-controlled slot canyons intersect Cohab Canyon, holding the promise of coolness on hot summer days.

The canyon walls recede as we progress, and the trail soon traverses above a pouroff (dry waterfall), now in the tan-colored layer of the Kayenta Formation.

After 1 mile of delightful hiking we reach the signed trail to the Fremont River Overlooks (0.7; 5630), forking left (northwest) and switchbacking for 250 yards on slickrock to a grass-covered bench at 5770 feet, where trails fork southwest and north to the overlooks. The right (north) fork leads across the open bench for less than 0.1 mile to a fine viewpoint. From the lower (north) overlook, one can gaze below to the neat rows of the Fruita orchards, forming a vivid green ribbon along the Fremont River, a marked contrast to the sheer orange-red cliffs and white domes that thrust 1000 feet or more into the Utah sky above.

Southwest along the deep trench of the Fremont, Miners Mountain on the left and the mesa of Beas Lewis Flat on the right frame a distant view of Boulder Mountain, its sheltered north slopes harboring snowfields that often persist into early summer. Capitol Dome draws our attention eastward down the canyon of the Fremont and beyond to the horizontal surface of Horse Mesa on the horizon, its Navajo Sandstone cliffs capped by the rocks of the Carmel Formation.

From the north viewpoint, return to the nearby junction and stroll southwest past the bizarre shapes of weathered Kayenta Sandstone for 1/4 mile to the higher, westernmost overlook, atop a red knoll 450 feet above the river. The views from here are equally impressive, dominated by the overwhelming presence of the towering domes and cliffs of Capitol Reef, the heart of the vast Waterpocket Fold.

Back on the Cohab Canyon Trail, we continue down the canyon about 150 yards before a very short climb leads us to another signed junction. The southbound trail here, climbing to the right, is the northern end of the Frying Pan Trail (*Trip 8*), bound for Cassidy Arch and Grand Wash. Bearing left, however, we descend gently via the hardpacked sand and clay tread of the good trail, following above the shallow drainage of Cohab Canyon. Our trail leads us steadily downward, and inspiring views of massive white domes rising across the canyon accompany us as we cross a small dry wash, switchback a few times beneath the imposing fluted walls of Pectols Pyramid, and finally reach Utah Highway 24 (0.6; 5350), less than 0.2 mile east of the Hickman Bridge Trailhead.

# Trip 7
## Fremont River Trail
## to Fremont Overlook

**Distance**: 2.0 miles round trip
**Low/High elevations**: 5435'/5900'
**Suited for**: Dayhike
**Difficulty**: Moderately easy
**Best seasons**: April through mid-June; mid-September through November.
**Map/Trailhead**: 17/3
**Hazards**: No shade or water; steep dropoffs.

**Introduction**: From the historic Fruita orchards to the commanding vista point of Fremont Overlook, this fine hike captures the essence of the Capitol Reef experience, contrasting the Fremont River's ribbon of green with parched arid mesas, and the manicured lawns of the campground and the neat rows of the orchards with a chaotic jumble of towering slickrock domes and sheer cliffs. Geologic history is represented by seven sedimentary layers stretching 250 million years into past earth history.

The initial riverside segment of the trail is gravelled, and it is the only handicap-accessible trail in the Park.

**Description**: The signed trail begins at the west end of Campground Loop B (0.0; 5435), and follows the east bank of the river upstream between apple and pear orchards on our left, and wildrose thickets and the unusually tall common reed grass on our right. Wildlife abounds in the orchards of Fruita: mule deer, marmots, skunks, and beavers are particularly common. Park managers have installed protective coverings around the trunks of trees here to save them from cambium-eating beavers, while the abundant mule deer enjoy eating not only the lush grasses in the orchards, but also the trees' leaves and bark. Many of Fruita's orchards are encircled by tall "deer proof" fences. The boulders of the fence across the river and those that litter Johnson Mesa and much of Capitol Reef, especially in the Fremont River canyon, originated from the lava fields atop Boulder and Thousand Lake mountains. Their rounded appearance proves they were brought here by swiftly running streams

and rivers that drained melting high-country glaciers thousands of years ago.

The wide, gravel-surfaced trail, accessible to wheelchairs for 1/2 mile, quite soon passes the campground amphitheater. Wedged between a peach orchard and the tumultuous waters of the Fremont, we soon pass a fenced-in smokehouse and sorghum mill, and reach the path joining on our left from the amphitheater parking area in Campground Loop C (where hikers not staying in the campground can park for this hike and the Cohab Canyon Trail, *Trip 6*). Here another sign identifies our route as the Fremont River Trail, and informative pamphlets describing the trail are available. We then pass one more orchard, this one supporting apricot trees, skirt a grassy meadow on our left, and soon reach a fenceline.

Here the gravel surface ends, the trail narrows, and we soon rise moderately upon northwest-facing slopes below red ledges of the Moenkopi. Climbing past the various layers of the Moenkopi, our trail bends southeast, traversing above a precipitous Fremont tributary canyon. Two switchbacks ensue, leading us above a thin, yellowish rock layer—the Sinbad Limestone—one of the five units of the Moenkopi in the Park. Shortly we reach Fremont Overlook (1.0; 5900). Toward the southwest, the yawning gorge of the Fremont cuts deeply into a wooded plateau, separating westward-rising Miners Mountain on the south from broad Beas Lewis Flats on the north. The most extensive outcrops of the Park's most ancient rock, the White Rim Sandstone, lie exposed in the depths of the canyon.

Much of the western facade of Capitol Reef, the most dramatic part of the vast Waterpocket Fold, can be viewed from northwest to southeast. Eastward, on the face of Capitol Reef, we can see five varicolored rock formations rising from the campground to the skyline—the red Moenkopi, the gray, green and maroon Chinle, the towering orange-red cliffs of the Wingate, the wooded benches of the Kayenta, and finally the whitish cliffs and domes of the Navajo. The rugged aspect of Capitol Reef contrasts dramatically with the orchards and lush greenery of the river bottom. On the horizon from northwest to southwest, the extensive plateaus of Boulder and Thousand Lake mountains, with their cool, subalpine forests, aspen thickets, and flower-filled meadows, look particularly inviting on a blistering hot summer day.

From the viewpoint, we retrace our steps to the trailhead.

# Trip 8
## Cohab Canyon to Grand Wash via the Frying Pan Trail

**Distance**: 5.8 miles shuttle trip, plus 0.8 mile sidetrip to Cassidy Arch
**Low/High elevations**: 5380'/6450'
**Suited for**: Dayhike
**Difficulty**: Moderate
**Best seasons**: April through mid-June; mid-September through November.
**Map/Trailheads**: 17/3,4
**Hazards**: No water; steep dropoffs; little shade.

**Introduction**: The Frying Pan Trail provides a link between Cohab Canyon (*Trip 6*) to the north and Grand Wash (*Trip 9*) to the south, following the wooded, Kayenta-capped upper slope of the Capitol Reef section of the Waterpocket Fold. Some hikers tread only the last segment of the trail from Grand Wash to Cassidy Arch, but this route offers the opportunity to connect with several other Headquarters District trails and combine them into a variety of half-day hikes.

**Description**: To begin, we follow the Cohab Canyon Trail (*Trip 6*), from the Fruita Campground to the signed Frying Pan Trail (1.1; 5640) and turn right (southwest). A series of short switchbacks lead us to a traverse high above Cohab Canyon in a pinyon-juniper woodland. Ahead we pass over a low ridge and descend slickrock into another dry wash via sandstone ledges where numerous switchbacks ease the grade. Southwestward, the wash enters a narrow slot between potholed red and tan cliffs.

Beyond the wash, our trail climbs moderately for 800 feet in 1 mile via slickrock Kayenta ledges of reddish, gray, and olive-green hues,

finally attaining a ridgeline (2.3; 6450) decorated by sandstone knolls and abundant pinyon and juniper. Views from this vantage are superb, including the inspiring landscape of lofty domes north of the Fremont River and beyond to the broad plateaus of Boulder and Thousand Lake mountains. Prominent Fern's Nipple dominates the horizon in the southeast, and a sliver of the high Henry Mountains is framed by sandstone knolls in the east. Farther to the east, broad mesas disappear in the heat-hazy distance of the San Rafael Desert.

From the ridge our trail heads gently downhill along the broad mesa, in 1/2 mile reaching the brink of a plummeting cliff. Grand Wash lies 650 feet below where the dirt road leading to the Grand Wash Trailhead is visible. Crossing ledges of the red siltstones and gray sandstones of the Kayenta Formation, we reach the right-forking trail to Cassidy Arch (1.0; 5980), a 0.4-mile long trail.

---

## Cassidy Arch Trail

The Cassidy Arch Trail heads generally southwest, traversing a slickrock bowl (route indicated by cairns) at the head of a precipitous south-trending gorge. Curving south, we wind toward the top of a 6000' redrock knoll, and suddenly Cassidy Arch appears (0.4; 5990), spanning a narrow defile that plunges into the depths below. Although it spans the head of a steep canyon, this opening was not formed by stream erosion. Instead, it is an example of a "pothole arch." Potholes in solid sandstone are quite common in the rocks of the fold, so common in fact that Major John Wesley Powell bestowed the name Waterpocket Fold upon this great monocline in the late 19th century. Potholes collect water from runoff, and this water helps to dissolve the cementing agents that bond individual sand grains, thus slightly enlarging (by an amount barely perceptible in a human lifetime) the pothole every time runoff from heavy rains and wind scours out the loosened sand.

Potholes formed near the brink of cliffs

allow water to seep downward, and some of it may reach the face of the cliff and break down cementing agents, causing sand grains to fall away or larger slabs to spall off in a process called exfoliation, which may form alcoves. Cassidy Arch may have been formed when a pothole above and an alcove in the cliff below joined to form the arch we see today. Like the majority of arches in Capitol Reef, Cassidy is formed within the Kayenta Formation.

Scattered pinyon and juniper, a variety of shrubs, and a host of brilliant wildflowers decorate the slickrock route to the arch. Cassidy Arch gets its name from Butch Cassidy (Robert LeRoy Parker), whose outlaw Wild Bunch gang reportedly had a hideout in the Grand Wash area in the late 19th century.

---

Back on the main trail, we first contour into a shallow gully, skirt the rim 350 feet above Grand Wash, and then curve north into a deeper tributary of Grand Wash. Views are inspiring into the canyon's defile and beyond to its sheer cliffs and glistening white domes. Pinyons, junipers shrubs, and wildflowers cloak the trailside slopes. Descending gently, we traverse along the brink of a precipice directly above the trailhead, then negotiate a series of steep, rocky switchbacks that lower us to the sandy floor of Grand Wash (1.2; 5380). Here we turn right, up-canyon, and follow the broad wash bottom to the short trail that leads quickly to the trailhead (0.2; 5400).

# Trip 9
## Grand Wash

**Distance**: 2.2 miles shuttle trip
**Low/High elevations**: 5200'/5400'
**Suited for**: Walk
**Difficulty**: Easy
**Best seasons**: April through mid-June; mid-September through November.
**Map/Trailheads**: 17/4,9
**Hazards**: The route is trailless; no water;

flash-flood danger.

**Introduction**: Grand Wash is one of only seven drainages that begin west of the Waterpocket Fold and flow through it. The hike down the wash is a delightful stroll for hikers of every ability, featuring nearly vertical sandstone walls rising 600-800 feet from the wash and ending in great sky-piercing crags. In a short but memorable narrows the canyon floor is barely 20 feet wide. Signs at the upper and lower trailheads warn that hikers should not enter the canyon when there is a threat of thunderstorms.

**Description**: The trailhead (0.0; 5400) lies in the shadow of immense orange Wingate Sandstone cliffs. Here we begin our journey by treading the short trail to the wash bottom, where we proceed down-canyon beneath an imposing dome.

Bear Canyon, a large tributary joining on our right (southeast) soon after we leave the trailhead, stretches up to the crest of the Waterpocket Fold and is worthy of exploration if time and energy allow. Bear Canyon is also the beginning of a longer trip for experienced slickrock scramblers, following a route that leads past Fern's Nipple and ends near Golden Throne, from where the Golden Throne Trail can be followed into Capitol Gorge (see *Trip 11*).

Shortly beyond Bear Canyon we meet the southern terminus of the Frying Pan Trail (0.2; 5380). Unlike many sandy washes in the Park, Grand Wash has a hard-packed surface that allows easy progress. This dry wash is occasionally swept by flash floods, which eradicate any colonizing riparian vegetation. Instead of riparian trees, vegetation in the wash is typical of the Park's pinyon-juniper woodland: singleleaf ash, big sagebrush, squawbush, rabbitbrush, Utah serviceberry, and cliffrose. In addition, a variety of colorful wildflowers in season adorns the nearly barren slickrock canyon.

A number of joint-controlled canyons on both sides of the wash beckon the adventurous as we proceed down-canyon toward The Narrows, and several use trails help shortcut the twists and turns of the canyon.

After 1 mile from the trailhead we enter The Narrows, a claustrophic 1/2-mile stretch where the wash is about 20 feet wide, hemmed in by cliffs soaring abruptly as much as 800 feet from the canyon floor. Stained by desert varnish, prominently cross-bedded, and riddled with solution cavities, these high-angle Navajo Sandstone cliffs begin to diminish in stature as we exit The Narrows, and they become progressively lower as we amble out onto Utah Highway 24 (2.0; 5200) deep within the Fremont River canyon.

# Trip 10
## Capitol Gorge Trailhead to the Tanks

**Distance**: 1.6 miles round trip
**Low/High elevations**: 5360'/5400'
**Suited for**: Walk
**Difficulty**: Easy
**Best seasons**: April through mid-June; mid-September through November.
**Map/Trailhead**: 18/5
**Hazards**: Flash-flood danger.

**Introduction**: Capitol Gorge is a narrow defile cut deeply into the Navajo Sandstone of the Waterpocket Fold, and hikers there feel as if they were in a great, yawning cleft deep within the earth. Capitol Gorge probably formed as running water eroded along a joint, or crack, in the Fold, deepening the canyon but scarcely widening it. Fremont Indians left their mysterious petroglyphs on the canyon walls, and inscriptions of early travelers can also be found along the old highway, or "Blue Dugway," as it was called.

A hike through Capitol Gorge to The Tanks is a delightful stroll for hikers of every ability, and it allows one to contemplate the evolution of slickrock canyons, the mysterious Fremont rock artists, and the pioneers and early settlers who built and used this old "road" through a precipitous, flood-prone canyon.

Although it's primarily a round-trip hike, some hikers, who obtain permission from the landowner in Notom, exit the park east of the Fold and return to the Scenic Drive via lower Pleasant Creek.

**Description**: The trailhead (0.0; 5400) lies in the shadow of immense cliffs of Navajo Sandstone, and from here we proceed along the former route of Utah Highway 24, where only patches of the oiled surface remain. After 0.2 mile we reach the petroglyphs, just beyond the point where the Kayenta beds have dipped underground. One of only two easily accessible Fremont petroglyphs (rock carvings) in the Park, it consists of a group of broad-shouldered human-like figures without arms, wearing headdresses of feathers or curved horns. Unfortunately, here as in many other places in the gorge, modern-day "graffiti artists" have defiled the petroglyphs with their carvings.

Quite soon the old road disappears and we proceed through a memorable narrows, where great desert-varnished cliffs loom above. At 1/2 mile is the Pioneer Register, where travelers following Isaac Behunin's "Blue Dugway" through the Fold left signs of their passing. The earliest carvings on the walls here date back to 1871, when a "J.A. Call" and "Wal. Batemen," presumably prospectors, passed through the gorge hoping to find gold. Many other inscriptions date back to the late 19th century, but are confused among myriad modern-day carvings and bullet holes. Numerous iron rods protruding from the canyon walls are remnants of a telephone line that served early settlements east of the Fold.

After another 0.4 mile through the narrow, tortuous canyon, a sign indicates The Tanks (0.9; 5360), which lie just above the wash at the mouth of an inconspicuous west-trending canyon. These large waterpockets can be reached by scrambling up the slickrock at the canyon's juncture with Capitol Gorge. They hold a great deal of water, particularly after heavy rains and in spring, and are an important source of moisture for Capitol Reef wildlife. A small natural bridge can be seen immediately upstream from The Tanks.

Just 100 yards down-canyon, fascinating Waterpocket Canyon leads off to our right (southeast), draining the apex of the Fold. A trail of sorts leads briefly up the sandy mouth of the canyon, soon disappearing in the slickrock. Adventurous and experienced hikers will find this steep canyon, with its narrows and its numerous waterpockets, an exciting route for attaining the

crest of the Fold. Downstream, the canyon walls diminish in height as Capitol Wash winds its way another 1 1/2 miles to the Park boundary and the private land beyond.

# Trip 11
## Golden Throne Trail

**Distance**: 3.4 miles round trip
**Low/High elevation**: 5400'/6100'
**Suited for**: Dayhike
**Difficulty**: Moderate
**Best seasons**: April through mid-June; mid-September through November.
**Map/Trailhead**: 18/5
**Hazards**: No water, little shade; steep dropoffs.

**Introduction**: Golden Throne is one of the premier slickrock domes in Capitol Reef. This golden-toned butte dominates the view from many remote corners of the Park, its smooth cliffs jutting skyward 600 feet above its surroundings. This scenic trail offers access from Capitol Gorge to the top of the Waterpocket Fold, where hikers gain a head-on view of Golden Throne, and more distant panoramas stretch from the Henry Mountains in the east to the wooded slope of Miners Mountain in the west. For adventurous hikers, this trail is only the beginning of a memorable cross-country trek along the crest of the Fold and into the depths of Bear Canyon and Grand Wash.

**Description**: From Capitol Gorge Trailhead (0.0; 5400), turn left on the rocky trail and climb west beneath an overhanging ledge of Kayenta Sandstone. The trail soon bends into and out of three interesting side canyons high above Capitol Gorge, where inspiring views into the dome-capped heart of Capitol Reef are nothing short of spectacular.

Curving into the third in this series of small canyons, after 1 mile, we gain our first glimpse of Golden Throne. Its sheer southeast face, desert-varnished and stained a golden color by its cap of reddish Carmel Formation rocks, thrusts skyward over 1300 feet above us. Its flat crown, decorated by a pinyon-juniper woodland, forms a striking contrast to its smooth, golden cliffs, a scene typical of the Colorado Plateau, where sheer cliffs seem universally to edge nearly horizontal beds. Golden Throne is a butte, the erosional remnant of a mesa, which in turn is the erosional remnant of a more vast surface called a plateau.

Ahead, gnarled, weather-beaten pinyons and junipers dot the rocky ledges. Many of them are barely clinging to existence, nurtured through only a single strip of bark. With their counterparts that have succumbed to the harsh environment, they provide foreground for constant inspiring vistas of the vertical world of Capitol Reef.

After switchbacking up and away from this side canyon, we cross over a low ridge and contour northwest, greeted by a view of the imposing plateau of Boulder Mountain in the west, foregrounded by the gentle, densely wooded slopes of Miners Mountain. South along the crest of the Fold, the subdued, ledgy landscape composed of Kayenta rocks, tree-clad and punctuated by myriad erosional forms, contrasts with the domes and cliffs that dominate our view east of the crest.

Presently the trail climbs easily, contouring briefly into yet another minor canyon before curving south to its terminus at a fine viewpoint (1.7; 6100). From here we can gaze into the abyss of Capitol Gorge, beyond which the dome-capped Fold frames a grand view of the Henry Mountains to the east. The bronze sentinel of Golden Throne, however, captures our attention, jutting nearly 1000 feet into the Utah sky to the north only 1/2 mile from our viewpoint.

Experienced hikers, not without compass and the *Notom* and *Fruita* 15-minute USGS quads, can easily negotiate a trailless route northwest toward Fern's Nipple via a northwest-trending draw west of Point 7289 on Map 18. Beyond, a descent of rugged Bear Canyon leads to Grand Wash about 0.1 mile below that trailhead, completing a memorable hike of about 5 miles.

# Trip 12
## Lower Pleasant Creek

**Distance**: 9 miles round trip to Park boundary
**Low/High elevations**: 5500'/5920'
**Suited for**: Dayhike or backpack
**Difficulty**: Moderate
**Best seasons**: April through mid-June; mid-September through November.
**Maps/Trailhead**: 18,19/6
**Hazards**: No trail; flash-flood danger; water from creek must be purified.

**Introduction**: Born on the lake-dotted flanks of Boulder Mountain and nurtured by numerous high mountain lakes and perennial tributaries, Pleasant Creek is one of only three perennial streams that flow through the Waterpocket Fold. The creek gathers its waters amid alpine meadows, flows through forests of pine, spruce, fir, and aspen, rushes through the narrow defile it has carved in Miners Mountain, and then enters a beautiful slickrock canyon in the Waterpocket Fold just beyond Sleeping Rainbow Ranch, the only private inholding within the Park.

Pleasant Creek offers two distinctly different hiking opportunities. Its deep upper canyon, west of the Fold proper, is clad in pinyon and juniper, and exposed on the canyon walls are the oldest rocks in the Park—the Kaibab Limestone and the White Rim Sandstone. However, a dirt road and a powerline serving the Sleeping Rainbow Ranch, and little opportunity for camping in its 800-foot-deep gorge, ensure a less-than-pristine hiking experience for 2.5 miles upstream to the western Park boundary. But although the upper canyon lacks primitive appeal, the lower canyon, with its slickrock cliffs and domes as well as numerous potential campsites and perennial stream, offers the quintessential Capitol Reef experience.

The Fremont Indians visited Pleasant Creek and carved their petroglyphs on the canyon's walls. And in 1882 Ephraim K. Hanks, once a Mormon scout and mail carrier, homesteaded here and established the Floral Ranch. A former polygamist himself, Hanks harbored fugitive po-

lygamists tracked by federal marshals in and near his ranch in the 1880s after federal law made polygamy a felony.

**Description**: From the parking area (0.0; 5920) a use trail gets us started on our downstream tour of Pleasant Creek. At times we'll ascend sagebrush- and grass-decorated benches, cross old fencelines, and be forced to hop across the creek via sometimes slippery basalt and sandstone boulders where cliffs impede progress.

Most vegetation in the canyon is typical of the pinyon-juniper woodland: big sagebrush, rabbitbrush, Fremont barberry, and prickly pear and claret cup cactus, both of which boast large, delicate, colorful late-spring blooms. Riparian vegetation fed by the canyon's perennial moisture includes Fremont cottonwoods and the exotic tamarisk, both of which offer fine fall colors to further enhance the beauty of this canyon.

After about one hour the canyon narrows considerably (2.0; 5700), and domes and cliffs rise 300-600 feet above, separating numerous parallel, northwest-to-southeast-trending, joint-controlled canyons. Here the creek twists and turns through the gorge, but trees, shrubs and wildflowers will be found wherever they can establish a toehold in the meager soil cover.

After another hour of hiking, the canyon walls recede (2.0; 5550) and the final 1/2 mile to the Park boundary passes through a widening canyon, exiting the Fold and entering the open desert beyond. The numerous side canyons that intersect Pleasant Creek are interesting to explore, primarily to the north, but each is a box canyon ending in impassable cliffs.

The final 1/2 mile of the canyon offers opportunities to climb intricately eroded slickrock slopes north of the creek onto the east flank of the Fold, where fine views of the vast deserts and the Henry Mountains to the east can be enjoyed. From the Park boundary (0.5; 5500) we retrace our route back to the trailhead.

# Trip 13
## Hickman Bridge Trail

**Distance**: 1.9 miles round trip
**Low/High elevation**: 5330'/5650'
**Suited for**: Walk
**Difficulty**: Moderately easy
**Best seasons**: April through mid-June; mid-September through November.
**Map/Trailhead**: 17/7
**Hazards**: Negligible

**Introduction**: The Hickman Bridge Trail is the most popular and perhaps the most scenic trail in Capitol Reef. This fairly easy half-day hike surveys a variety of Park scenery, ranging from the sandy, cottonwood-lined banks of the Fremont River to arid benches littered with volcanic boulders, to a slickrock canyon bounded by soaring sandstone domes, and finally to the most famous natural-rock span in the Park.

The trail is easy to follow but little shade is available enroute. Eighteen numbered posts along the way are keyed to a trail guide available at the trailhead or at the Visitor Center.

**Description**: From the trailhead (0.0; 5330) we proceed east under a broken red cliff of the Kayenta Formation, following along the north bank of the turbulent river. Presently we find ourselves in a riparian environment, where water-dependent Fremont cottonwoods, tamarisk, and willows thrive.

Our jaunt along the verdant Fremont River oasis abruptly ends and we switchback up southeast-facing slopes, entering the arid environment that predominates in Capitol Reef. Decorated by sparse grasses, the orange springtime blooms of globe mallow, and desert-varnished volcanic boulders, this sun-drenched ascent brings us to the right-forking, northbound Rim Overlook Trail (*Trip 14*) (0.3; 5470), leading to aerial-like vistas high above Fruita. Eastward is a memorable head-on view of Capitol Dome, the namesake of the park, visible since the trailhead.

Continuing straight ahead (west), we steadily ascend an open slope strewn with dark volcanic boulders washed more than 15 miles from their source atop Thousand Lake and Boulder mountains. Soon we descend briefly to the banks of a minor sandy wash. Working our way westward along the south banks of the wash, we reach the tiny opening of Nels Johnson Bridge spanning the wash, named for one of the earliest homesteaders in the Fruita area.

Just beyond the bridge, the trail splits, forming a loop under and around Hickman Bridge. Bearing right (0.5; 5600) we then traverse pinyon-juniper-dotted slickrock above the wash. Soon the trail leads up to and through Hickman Bridge (0.1; 5650), one of the largest spans in the Park, with dimensions of 125 feet top to bottom by 133 feet between abutments. The bulk of the bridge is formed in the tan sandstones of the Kayenta, while its abutments rest on the softer red mudstones of the same formation. Differential weathering in which softer rocks below broke down faster than those above contributed to the spalling off of rock slabs: where the once-supportive basal rocks were removed, it hastened the formation of an alcove and ultimately an arch. Some geologists believe Hickman Bridge to actually be an arch whose opening pre-dated the formation of the shallow wash that presently courses beneath it. If this is correct, it is reasonable to assume that the present-day drainage has, at the least, contributed to the enlargement of the opening.

A favorite of late afternoon photographers, Hickman Bridge frames some of the most inspiring scenery in Capitol Reef, a chaotic jumble of white domes and desert-varnished cliffs etched into the Utah sky that combine to make the scene one of unforgettable, compelling beauty.

After passing through the great rock opening, the trail curves southeast through hummocky slickrock. After about 250 yards, a very short spur trail forks right, offering a fine view of the Fremont River. The main trail then leads northeast to the aforementioned junction (0.2; 5600), whence we retrace our route to the trailhead (0.8; 5330).

# Trip 14
## Rim Overlook Trail

**Distance**: 4.6 miles round trip
**Low/High elevations**: 5330'/6375'
**Suited for**: Dayhike
**Difficulty**: Moderate
**Best seasons**: April through mid-June; mid-September through November.
**Map/Trailhead**: 17/7
**Hazards**: Steep dropoffs; no water or shade.

**Introduction**: Rim Overlook, perched atop the sheer cliffs that soar skyward north of Fruita and Utah Highway 24, offers a commanding, unobstructed vista of the rugged reaches of Capitol Reef. This rigorous trail climbs steadily from the Fremont River, crossing much slickrock enroute, where hikers must follow cairns. Allow ample time to absorb the vista and perhaps to explore the hanging canyons beyond the trail's end.

**Description**: From the Hickman Bridge trailhead, follow *Trip 13* to the junction (0.3; 5470) where our trail forks off to the north, passing among erratic volcanic boulders enroute toward desert-varnished Navajo Sandstone cliffs soaring 500 feet skyward. Quite soon we briefly descend to cross a dry wash and then curve northwest for a climb up along it.

Climbing away from the wash beneath striking cliffs, we reach the Hickman Bridge View Point (0.5; 5670). Pause here to walk out on the sandstone point for an intriguing view of Hickman Bridge, spanning the wash below to the southwest.

Above us to our north, Kayenta rocks, upon which our trail is presently located, give way to what many consider the most notable rock formation in the Park—the Navajo Sandstone—which has a typical ridgeline aspect of hummocky domes, abutted by smooth cliffs featuring a tapestry of desert varnish on their faces.

Ahead we curve into and out of two box canyons, the second of which drains under Hickman Bridge. After climbing moderately out of the second wash, we pass through abundant dune sand, anchored by scattered trees and shrubs.

This sand has collected below the Navajo cliffs, which themselves are former dune sand cemented into stone in ancient times and once again weathering into its parent material.

Ahead we bend into and out of two more dry drainages and cross abundant slickrock, where cairns help guide us. Beyond the fourth draw, we finally reach Rim Overlook (1.5; 6375), precariously perched atop sheer cliffs plunging over 600 feet toward the confluence of Sulphur Creek and the Fremont River. Our dramatic aerial-like view takes in Utah Highway 24, the Fruita Campground, and the scattered Fruita orchards. We can trace the Park's Scenic Drive as it heads southeast through a deep red badlands landscape beneath the sheer west facade of the Waterpocket Fold.

The sloping, densely wooded mesa of Miners Mountain rises west of the Scenic Drive, while the crest of forest-topped Boulder Mountain forms a horizontal horizon beyond. Eastward, the deep, narrow chasm of the Fremont River meanders among the mammoth domes of the Fold, forming a picturesque frame for the vast San Rafael Desert stretching eastward to the horizon.

Other isolated mountain ranges meet our gaze in the heat-hazy distance beyond: the second highest mountains in Utah—the La Sals—punctuate the northeast horizon 110 miles distant, while a sliver of the Abajo Mountains peeks above the crest of the Henrys, 100 miles to the southeast.

From the overlook hikers can either return to the trailhead or strike out north across trailless terrain to Longleaf Flat, a seldom-visited draw that should appeal to solitude seekers. One broad, shallow draw east of Longleaf Flat can be followed 1/2 mile north, leading to secluded but dry campsites amid unforgettable Navajo domes, shaded by pinyon and juniper and a few large ponderosa pines.

A low, sandy ridge west of this draw separates it from the more extensive, dome-rimmed spread of Longleaf Flat, also featuring picturesque ponderosa pines rising above the pygmy forest of pinyon and juniper. Avoid trampling the abundant, fragile cryptogamic crust if you travel toward Longleaf Flat.

# Trip 15
## Notom Road to the Waterpocket Fold via Burro Wash

**Distance**: 11.2 miles round trip to crest of Waterpocket Fold
**Low/High elevations**: 5180'/6500'
**Suited for**: Dayhike
**Difficulty**: Strenuous
**Best seasons**: April through mid-June; mid-September through November.
**Maps/Trailhead**: 19,18/10
**Hazards**: No trail; flash-flood danger; undependable water; upper canyon accessible only to experienced hikers with rock climbing skills.

**Introduction**: Between the trans-Fold canyons of Pleasant Creek on the north and Sheets Gulch on the south, three precipitous, narrow defiles slice into the uplifted strata of the Waterpocket Fold: Burro, Cottonwood, and Fivemile washes. These canyons gather their seasonal waters from rainfall atop the Fold, then flow east to sink into the thirsty desert sands beyond.

Each canyon, including that of Sheets Gulch, offers exciting narrows, challenging scrambling and rock climbing over dry waterfalls and around chockstones, occasional deep pools, and quicksand. The canyons are wild slickrock slots with no trails, and experienced hikers must rely on their skills and good judgment to pass safely through them.

Burro Wash is a fine introduction to narrow slickrock defiles in the Waterpocket Fold. It is a classic slot canyon, one of the narrowest in the Fold—so narrow in places that hikers must actually proceed sideways with their packs overhead. Avoid the canyon if rain threatens, as there is no escape from floodwaters. There are no campsites in the canyon, and even if there were, the canyon is too narrow to accommodate a bulky backpack. Carry ample water and expect muddy pools and perhaps quicksand after recent rains.

**Description**: The hike begins where the Notom Road crosses Burro Wash (0.0; 5180) on public lands administered by the Bureau of Land Management. Here we enjoy memorable views of the Waterpocket Fold, a gentle slope densely clad in pinyon and juniper. The Carmel Formation, which forms the slope, weathers easily and forms an ample soil cover to support this woodland. Crags of the Fold loom boldly on the western skyline, dominated by the imposing butte of Golden Throne. Behind us are rolling red desert flats stretching east to the red slopes of a sandstone-capped mesa. Beyond are the summits of the Henry Mountains.

The initial 2 miles follow the broad, sand- and rock-strewn wash to the Park boundary across Bureau of Land Management land, passable to 4WD vehicles. Passing under a low-voltage powerline after 0.1 mile, the wash penetrates low red hills composed of Entrada sandstone and mudstone. Vegetation is sparse in this hostile environment, but rabbitbrush, sagebrush, bunchgrass, and a few spring wildflowers soften the bleak appearance of the landscape.

Where the wash has cut into deep alluvial deposits along this initial stretch, alternating layers of silt and cobbles tell a silent story of past stages of erosion of the Waterpocket Fold. Occasional cottonwoods, tamarisk, and willows indicate the presence of underground moisture in this otherwise bone-dry desert. Eventually, the wash enters the tilted rock of the Fold proper and becomes narrow and boulder-choked, barring further access to 4WD vehicles.

Another 0.1 mile brings us to the Park boundary (2.0; 5340) and the narrowing, sheltered canyon begins to display an increasingly diverse flora. Beyond the boundary, the canyon trends generally southwest. The canyon floor is dominated by sand, but alternates at times with slickrock stretches containing numerous waterpockets.

After the canyon enters the vertical realm of Navajo Sandstone, we enter a short but amazingly narrow section of the wash, (0.7; 5400). This slot sometimes squeezes down to only 1 1/2-2 feet wide, and we may have to walk sideways, holding packs overhead, to proceed. Chockstones in the slot, another obstacle, must be climbed over.

The following 1.7 miles present another difficult stretch of narrows. After rainy periods we

**Narrows in Burro Wash**

will likely encounter potholes, and possibly quicksand. Sometimes large, smooth chockstones are wedged in the narrow canyon above potholes, and these require persistence and imagination to circumvent. Beyond these narrows, the canyon widens, and pinyon and juniper accompany hikers for the last 1.2 miles to the hummocky, Kayenta-dominated crest of the Fold (2.9; 6550), where fine, seldom-seen vistas reward the few persistent hikers who negotiate the full length of Burro Wash.

Return the way you came.

# Trip 16
## Cedar Mesa Campground to Red Canyon

**Distance**: 5.4 miles round trip
**Low/High elevation**: 5610'/6030'
**Suited for**: Dayhike
**Difficulty**: Moderately easy
**Best seasons**: April through mid-June; mid-September through November.
**Map/Trailhead**: 20/11
**Hazards**: No water; flash-flood danger.

**Introduction**: The least demanding hike in the Park's South District, the Red Canyon route is part trail, part cross-country as it follows an old jeep road and the Red Canyon wash into an immense amphitheater in the Waterpocket Fold, bounded on three sides by towering red cliffs of Wingate Sandstone. The hike passes through 9 of the 14 rock formations in the Park, from the rocks of the Morrison Formation to the Navajo Sandstone.

**Description**: We begin our hike at the end of the campground road (0.0; 5610) in full view of the striking red cliffs at the head of Red Canyon. Proceeding southwest near the rim of a juniper-clad mesa, our closed jeep route passes typical high-desert shrubs—big sagebrush, buffaloberry, and yucca—and an abundance of wildflowers brilliantly decorate the otherwise drab mesa.

Curving west along a ridge capped by Salt Wash Sandstone, hikers are treated to dramatic views of imposing slickrock towers capping the Fold to the northwest, while the gentler, more subdued slopes of the Fold fade away toward the southeast. Notice the gypsum crystals sparkling in the roadbed here, formed as salts were precipitated from supersaturated sea water.

Buckwheat and the yellow spring blooms of physaria soon appear as we next trek northwest above a shallow draw. Our jeep route then descends west, crosses the wash, and ends when we reach the hard-packed sediments of Red Canyon Wash (1.4; 5660) for the second time. We now head up-canyon, following the small wash first northwest, then southwest. As we enter the buff-colored band of Navajo Sandstone, the wash narrows and boulders litter its course. Ahead, monumental cliffs of orange-red Wingate Sandstone loom forbiddingly at the canyon's head. Some tamarisks, a few spindly cottonwoods, and extremely tall clumps of common reed grass are found in moist sections in the upper reaches of the canyon.

Presently we pass beneath imposing buff-colored Wingate pinnacles rising to the west and southeast above the canyon, separated by erosion and weathering from the sheer band of cliffs ahead. We reach the head of Red Canyon, a box canyon (1.3; 6030) forming an immense sandstone amphitheater, floored by varicolored bands of the Chinle Formation and surrounded on three sides by cliffs soaring 1200 feet above, decorated by numerous deep alcoves.

Hikers wishing to extend their stay in this enchanting canyon will find benches here, shaded by pinyon and juniper, upon which to pitch camp and enjoy the changing moods of the landscape with the passing of each hour.

Return the way you came.

# Trip 17
## Burr Trail Road to Lower Muley Twist Canyon

**Distance**: 8.0 miles round trip to The Post Cutoff Trail

**Low/High elevations**: 5275'/5690'
**Suited for**: Dayhike or backpack
**Difficulty**: Moderately easy
**Best seasons**: April through mid-June; mid-
  September through November.
**Maps/Trailhead**: 21,22/12
**Hazards**: Flash-flood danger; no water.

**Introduction**: Separated into upper and
lower segments by the Burr Trail Road, Muley
Twist Canyon south of the road continues its
serpentine course deep within the slickrock confines of the Waterpocket Fold. This lower stretch
of the canyon lacks the intriguing arches found
in its upper reaches, but the canyon is highly
scenic nevertheless. Canyon walls soar as much
as 800 feet above the deeply entrenched defile,
and potential campsites perched on wooded
benches are numerous. The route is trailless, but
navigation is easy on the hard-packed wash bottom.

This hike is suitable for a half-day jaunt, or
it can be extended by following the canyon beyond the junction with The Post Cutoff Trail (see
*Trip 21*).

**Description**: Our hike, downhill all the way,
begins by following a cairned route southwest
from the Burr Trail (0.0; 5650), quickly descending a slickrock slope of Wingate Sandstone.
Upon reaching the dry wash, we turn left, down-
canyon, to the southeast. The ever-changing scenery of this fine canyon lures us onward past
sheer cliffs, fluted walls, pinnacles, domes, deep
alcoves, and boulder-littered slopes. Occasional
benches, most clad in scattered pinyon and juniper, offer pleasant camping areas above the
wash's high-water mark. The wash has a hard-
packed surface, but steady progress is hampered
at times due to an abundance of boulders and the
wash varies between confined narrows and
wider stretches.

After perhaps an hour of pleasant canyon
walking, Muley Twist opens up (2.4; 5450),
where a major tributary penetrating the Circle
Cliffs joins from the west, revealing a fine view
westward to the broad, wooded tableland of
Wagon Box Mesa. Southwest of this confluence
rises a prominent sawtooth ridge composed of
Wingate Sandstone, a part of the great Circle
Cliffs that delineate the western margin of the

Waterpocket Fold. The slopes below this ridge
are composed of the multihued shale of the
Chinle Formation, obscured by an abundance of
boulders and arid vegetation.

From here Muley Twist Canyon bends
sharply east, then south, and scattered groves of
Gambel oak begin to appear. In the mile below
the southward bend, the canyon becomes more
rugged, is strewn with boulders, and is hemmed
in by soaring cliffs. The wash smooths out for
the final 0.6 mile to a signed junction (1.6; 5272)
below a high cliff of desert-varnished and prominently cross-bedded Navajo Sandstone soaring
skyward. Here we ponder a variety of options.
We can retrace our route back to the Burr Trail,
turn left toward The Post and follow cairns indicating the route climbing northwest out of the
canyon, or continue down-canyon toward Grand
Gulch and Halls Creek wash (see *Trip 21* for
details on the last two options).

# Trip 18
## Upper Muley Twist Canyon

**Distance**: 14.6 to 15.4 miles, semiloop trip
**Low/High elevations**: 5730'/6690'
**Suited for**: Dayhike or backpack
**Difficulty**: Strenuous dayhike; moderate
  overnighter.
**Best seasons**: April through mid-June; mid-
  September through November.
**Map/Trailhead**: 21/13
**Hazards**: Flash-flood danger; steep
  dropoffs from Rim Route; no water.

**Introduction**: In the southern reaches of the
Waterpocket Fold, south of Red Canyon, the
Circle Cliffs form the west face of the Fold, and
all the canyons that begin below those cliffs
drain a vast, deeply dissected basin, ultimately
joining the Escalante River to the southwest. Just
east of the Circle Cliffs, Muley Twist Canyon
has carved a deep defile within the Waterpocket
Fold. Rather than draining eastward as most
canyons here do, Muley Twist drains southeast
along a trench cut into the crest of the Fold for

more than 12 miles between steep hummocky slopes of the Kayenta Formation to the west and the soaring cliffs and slickrock domes of the Navajo Sandstone to the east. The relative ease of access makes this beautiful canyon one of the primary attractions in the Park's South District.

Upper Muley Twist Canyon is perhaps the most scenic part of the whole canyon, boasting numerous arches and dramatic vista points. The initial 2.5 miles of the route are open to use by 4WD vehicles—the only designated jeep route in the Park. Beyond the vehicle barricade, dayhikers can continue up-canyon to Strike Valley Overlook for exceptional vistas, or continue past fascinating arches to The Narrows. Backpackers and well-conditioned dayhikers can extend the trek into the upper canyon, where they will have the option of returning via the Rim Route, a lightly cairned route following the crest of Waterpocket Fold.

Potential campsites are available throughout the canyon's length, but no water is available. Much of the route follows the wash, which is very sandy in places, so hiking is often slow and tedious.

**Description**: Two-wheel-drive access ends at the hikers' parking area (0.0; 5740), and from

**Unnamed arch in Upper Muley Twist**

here the jeep route drops quickly to the canyon floor and intersects the wash. The wash alternates between sandy and hard-packed sections as it passes among cliffs and domes of orange-hued Wingate Sandstone. Domes of Navajo Sandstone rise abruptly east of the canyon above broken ledges of the Kayenta Formation.

At 1 1/4 miles our shallow canyon opens up where a minor tributary joins from the west. Then, the canyon narrows as we pass below three pothole-type arches that adorn Dome 6464 to the west, composed of Wingate Sandstone. The northernmost opening is actually a double arch, one standing above the other on the intricately eroded, hummocky east flank of the dome. Meeting the signed, northeast-bound Strike Valley Overlook Trail (no mountain bikes or motor vehicles) (2.5; 5880), we ponder the option of continuing up-canyon or following the Overlook Trail for an inspiring panorama.

## Strike Valley Overlook Trail

Turning right, we soon pass between two Navajo domes, their strata tilted sharply downward toward the east, alternating between sandy stretches and slickrock as we climb northeast through a pinyon-juniper woodland. Finally, we scale slickrock southeastward to the apex of the Fold (0.4; 5960). The narrow valley of Halls Creek, lying between the Fold and the mesas beyond, is known to geologists as Strike Valley, because it parallels the strike, or axis, of the Fold. The overlook provides a superb vantage from which to observe the high angle of the steep, eastward-dipping strata of the Fold, which plummet from our viewpoint into the course of a meandering dry wash. The low ridge of Oyster Shell Reef rises just beyond that wash, forming a broken backbone that divides the expanse of the valley. The western flanks of the mesas east of the valley are draped in skirts of gray Mancos Shale that are virtually devoid of vegetation. Beyond, the mesas rise eastward in stair-step fashion to the flanks of the Henry Mountains.

Just beyond the Strike Valley Overlook Trail, a barrier bars 4WD vehicles and mountain bikes in the canyon. Continuing up the canyon, we reach the southern terminus of the signed Rim Route (1.8; 6000), an obscure cairned route climbing east to the rim of the Fold. Opposite this junction, on the steep, hummocky flanks of a large salmon-hued dome, is aptly named Saddle Arch, the largest span in the canyon. Most of the arches in this canyon, including Saddle Arch, are pothole-type arches (see Cassidy Arch in *Trip 8* for more on pothole arches).

Beyond the arch, the canyon narrows, with glistening white Navajo domes thrusting skyward to our right (east) while Kayenta ledges underlie hummocky, convoluted slickrock Wingate slopes to our left (west). We'll pass at least three more arches on our left and five east-trending canyons during the next 2.4 miles.

As we near the entrance to the Narrows (2.4; 6240), cairns indicate the slickrock route that avoids this impassable section of the canyon. The cairned route ahead, also indicated by orange metal markers attached to nearby trees, crosses much slickrock near the brink of cliffs that plunge more than 100 feet into The Narrows. Exercise the utmost caution along this dangerous route. Views up and down the canyon from this route are superb. Up the canyon, cliffs recede and a pinyon-juniper woodland dominates the gentle slopes at the canyon's head.

Eventually we descend back to the wash and meet the north end of the Rim Route (0.6; 6400). Hikers have two options here: (1) proceed up the canyon, where pinyon- and juniper-shaded campsites abound and a number of hiking opportunities exist, including an ascent of the Fold; or (2) follow the Rim Route while working back toward the trailhead. This route is marked by cairns up to the crest of the Fold, where we turn right (southeast). From there the route is unmarked. It is a rigorous up-and-down scramble over knife-edged domes, where cliffs plunge abruptly as much as 400 feet into the canyon below, while exceedingly steep slickrock slopes fall up to 1200 feet into the grassy expanse of Strike Valley.

We'll enjoy incomparable vistas along the entire route, from the Circle Cliffs in the west to the Henrys on the eastern horizon. The north end of the Henrys is dominated by the Mount Ellen massif, rising to an elevation of 11,506'. South of Mount Ellen are four isolated peaks; 11,371' Mt. Pennell, 10,650' Mt. Hillers, 7930' Mt. Holmes, and 8150' Mt. Ellsworth. The latter two peaks, although part of the Henry Mountains, are also known as the Little Rockies. The prominent slickrock slopes of the Fold march southeastward, becoming progressively lower as they approach the deep waters of Lake Powell, some 40 miles distant.

Upon the Fold, occasional pinyon and juniper, littleleaf mountain mahogany, and greenleaf manzanita adorn sandy-filled depressions in the dominant Navajo slickrock. In spring, red paintbrush, yellow-eye cryptantha, Utah penstemon and haplopappus color the forbidding sandstone crest.

On the descent from the final knob on the rim, the ridge broadens and supports a thick stand of pinyon and juniper. Soon we'll reach either a sign indicating the Canyon Route or an east-west line of cairns erected by Park rangers to ensure that hikers know where to descend into the canyon. From here we follow an obscure trail over ledges and slickrock to the canyon floor (3.0; 6000), where we turn left and retrace our steps for 4.3 miles to the trailhead.

# Trip 19
## Surprise Canyon

**Distance**: 2.4 miles round trip
**Low/High elevations**: 4890'/5120'
**Suited for**: Dayhike
**Difficulty**: Moderate
**Best seasons**: April through mid-June; mid-September through November.
**Map/Trailhead**: 22/14
**Hazards**: Some scrambling and Class 3 rock climbing required to reach the head of the canyon; flash-flood danger.

**Introduction**: Untold dozens of narrow slot

canyons cut deeply into the Waterpocket Fold in the Park's South District. In order to ascend through most of these canyons, some wading and even swimming of deep potholes and some rock climbing may be necessary, making them accessible only to seasoned canyoneers. But the short hikes into Surprise and nearby Headquarters canyons (*Trip 20*) are open to most any hiker, and offer a tantalizing introduction to the slickrock slot canyons of the Waterpocket Fold. To reach the head of either canyon, however, hikers must have experience in slickrock scrambling and must use good judgment to negotiate steep rock safely.

If a thunderstorm is brewing over the Fold, save the hikes in these canyons for another day.

**Description**: From the trailhead (0.0; 4900), where a sliver of Peak-a-boo Rock can be viewed atop the Fold in the northwest, our sandy trail heads southwest, crosses a shallow gully, and proceeds across greasewood-clad flats. Fine over-the-shoulder views extend east across the valley of Halls Creek to sandstone-capped mesas rising about barren Mancos Shale slopes. As we head toward the warped strata of the Waterpocket Fold, here dominated by glistening white Navajo Sandstone, a series of narrow, forbidding chasms gives only a vague suggestion of hidden passageways into the depths of that great barrier.

At 0.2 mile we reach the usually dry, tamarisk-lined wash of Halls Creek. Beyond it we climb over a bunchgrass- and juniper-dotted hill via the sandy trail, after which we descend into the wash of Surprise Canyon where the trail ends, amid dwarf clumps of wavy-leaf oak, at 0.4 mile. Ascending the dry course of the wash, we see that red hills of the Carmel Formation give way to sky-piercing cliffs of Navajo Sandstone, topped by striking pinnacles and crags.

The Navajo cliffs, rising as much as 600 feet nearly vertically from the canyon bottom, are encrusted with green, gray and black lichens, as well as brown, black and metallic-blue desert varnish. After 1 mile, the sandy, rock-littered wash narrows considerably. Cliffs are ever higher as we proceed, and we soon reach an interesting undercut and an extremely narrow cleft, where the canyon squeezes down to an opening mere inches wide.

From here we can either turn back, scramble up Class 3 rock to the left (south) of the cleft, or negotiate a brushy bench route traversing the south canyon wall. We can begin the bench route on the left just below the undercut. Above this obstacle the canyon steepens and becomes choked with sandstone boulders. Climbing steeply over and around the jumbled boulders, we eventually reach the head of the canyon (1.2; 5120), where two tributaries come in from north and south. We could scramble up either fork, but both routes quickly end amid impassable cliffs.

Return the way you came.

# Trip 20
## The Post to Headquarters Canyon

**Distance**: 3.0 miles round trip
**Low/High elevation**: 4860'/5420'
**Suited for**: Dayhike
**Difficulty**: Moderate
**Best seasons**: April through mid-June; mid-September through November.
**Map/Trailhead**: 22/15
**Hazards**: Flash-flood danger; no water; rock climbing necessary to reach the canyon's head.

**Introduction**: This short but fascinating jaunt into a narrow slot canyon is much like the trip into Surprise Canyon—its lower reaches are easily accessible, but to gain its upper reaches rudimentary rock-climbing skills are needed. In the late 19th century, the trailhead was a traditional stopping point for cattlemen driving their herds through the Waterpocket Fold country.

**Description**: Peek-a-boo Rock can be viewed in the northwest from the trailhead, and the mighty Waterpocket Fold, rearing its majestic slickrock skyward, fills the horizon, from the northwest to the southeast, with its menacing sawtoothed profile. We begin our jaunt (0.0; 4900) by following a faint trail along the left side of a fence slicing across the Grand Gulch. This leads across greasewood-clad flats generally southward toward a low sandstone knoll, where the fence temporarily ends; likewise the trail soon disappears and we proceed south-southwest from the knoll.

From there we simply climb cross-country up the low red hill, at 1/2 mile reaching a sign pointing west toward Headquarters Canyon and southeast toward Lower Muley Twist Canyon. A cross-country route leads to the lower Post Trailhead, 0.7 mile to the southeast across the valley via Halls Creek Wash. Hikers can then follow *Trip 21* to Lower Muley Twist. From the sign, cairns lead us quickly downhill to the sandy wash draining Headquarters Canyon, where we turn right and slog through the sand amid red slabs of Carmel Formation rocks. Soon the fence reappears above us and east of the wash, which presently bends west, cutting deeply into towering slickrock.

Before long we enter a narrow slot barely 2-3 feet wide, with sheer walls rising nearly 300 feet above on either side. Beyond the confines of these narrows, Gambel oak and boxelder appear. Ahead we bushwhack through dense vegetation, scramble over or around boulders, and slog through deep sand, but despite these obstacles this mysterious canyon lures us onward.

Eventually the wash abruptly ends below a moderately steep slickrock chute (1.5; 5420). At this point we can either turn back or scramble up the chute. Above, we must negotiate a brief Class 4 climb to circumvent a 6' dry waterfall, but the canyon grows even steeper, requiring Class 3-4 climbing to continue the short distance to the head of this precipitous box canyon.

Return the way you came.

# Trip 21
## The Post
## to Lower Muley Twist Canyon

**Distance**: 16.7 miles, loop trip
**Low/High elevations**: 4620'/5475'
**Suited for**: Dayhike or backpack
**Difficulty**: Strenuous as a dayhike, moderate as an overnighter.
**Best seasons**: April through mid-June; mid-September through November.
**Map/Trailhead**: 22/16
**Hazards**: No water; flash-flood danger, steep dropoffs along Cutoff Trail.

**Introduction**: This superb loop trip, climbing over the slickrock slopes of the Waterpocket Fold, winding down a deep, serpentine canyon, and returning via a broad, grassy valley, samples some of the finest scenery in the Park's South District. Strenuous as an all-day hike, the trip is best taken as a backpack, but the lack of dependable water limits one's stay.

The lower 2 miles of the canyon and Halls Creek valley (Grand Gulch) beyond were traversed by a wagon trail of Mormon pioneers bound for southeast Utah in 1879-80. That is when the canyon received its name, as it was narrow enough to "twist a mule" (see "Human History of Capitol Reef").

**Description**: From the trailhead (0.0; 4851) the trail, lined with white posts, heads west across Grand Gulch, a narrow desert valley clad in grasses and greasewood. It crosses the dry course of Halls Creek wash, and then climbs steeply up onto the lower flanks of the Fold amid red rocks of the Carmel Formation. Ahead, the Fold is dominated by erosion-dissected slopes of Navajo Sandstone, and the skyline is highlighted by a seemingly endless row of pinnacles. Our route is indicated by cairns, and as we rise to the contact between the Carmel and the Navajo formations, we gain a new perspective of the steeply folded strata comprising the Waterpocket Fold.

We gain the crest of a red hill at 1/2 mile, just above the contact zone. The route ahead, not recommended for novice hikers, crosses slickrock, where cairns help to guide the way. As this scenic route ascends the east slopes of the Fold, presently dominated by blazing white Navajo Sandstone, it passes domes and pinnacles, traverses around small draws, and offers excellent vistas of the distant sweep of the Fold, the grassy valley of Grand Gulch, sandstone-capped mesas draped in steel-gray shale, and the Henry Mountains. Even the distant Abajo Mountains can be seen beyond the Henrys, 70 miles east.

Eventually we leave the slickrock and cross a sandy opening sitting astride the Fold (1.5;

5475). Fine camps featuring awe-inspiring views could be located here.

Views of the corrugated, hummocky slopes of orange-hued Wingate Sandstone, rising west of Muley Twist Canyon, are enjoyed as we pass through the opening, where wooded posts lead the way to a small, sandy wash. Leaving the wash, our route descends into the larger wash of Muley Twist Canyon (0.5; 5275) via ledges of the Kayenta Formation. Flowers in the canyon are sparse but colorful, including Wyoming paintbrush, tansy-aster, gilia, penstemon, gold-enaster, and broom snakeweed. We proceed down the canyon amid the corrugated slickrock slopes, ledges, and sheer walls of the Wingate, Kayenta, and Navajo formations. The wash varies from hardpacked gravel to sand and occasional slickrock.

After perhaps 2 hours and 4.75 miles of hiking in the wash, we pass a prominent side canyon joining from the north-northeast, which may harbor waterpockets after substantial rains. Enroute we pass three huge undercut alcoves flanked by the piles of talus that spalled off the cliffs during their formation. About 1 mile past the aforementioned canyon, a major side canyon (5.75; 4890) joins Muley Twist from the west.

Below that side canyon, huge desert-varnished Navajo cliffs loom over either side of the canyon. The wash now meanders among tall cliffs and eventually it curves southeast after meeting one more side canyon (2.25; 4700) entering from the west. Soon Muley Twist bends east for a mile-long descent slicing through the thick Navajo Sandstone enroute to Grand Gulch. This part of the route traces the old wagon route used by Mormon pioneers in the early 1880s, passing through a canyon "so narrow it would twist a mule." The high canyon walls recede as the wash begins to exit the confines of the Fold.

East of the Fold, the wash curves southeast. From this point (1.2; 4640) some hikers ascend the low ridge east of the wash to join an old northbound jeep road. Or you can continue the final 1/2 mile to the confluence of Muley Twist and Halls Creek washes (0.5; 4620). Hikers can either turn down-canyon (south), following either traces of the old road and/or the wash for 3.5 miles (see Maps 22 and 23) to the Halls Creek Overlook Trail at Brimhall Canyon and, perhaps

extend the trip by several days while hiking on to Halls Creek Narrows (*Trip 23*). Reliable but stagnant Muley Tanks, which are naturally occurring water holes, lie west of the wash in the third-west-trending draw south of the confluence with Muley Twist. But most of us will want to conclude the trip, and will turn left, north, along Halls Creek wash.

Follow Halls Creek wash north for about 0.8 mile, then begin looking for old jeep trail climbing a hill to the north along a stretch where the wash is aligned west toward the Fold. This northbound undulating jeep trail avoids the meandering wash, crossing hilly terrain just east of it. But the jeep tracks soon become faint, and we can either (1) proceed mostly cross-country north up the grass- and greasewood-clad valley, or (2) follow the wash—a longer alternative of about 6 1/2 miles to the trailhead. The valley route is more desirable as the hiking is easier than in the wash. On that route hikers are likely to find

**Junction with Post Cutoff Trail**

traces of the jeep trail and use trails that lead toward the trailhead.

Initially, the valley route crosses red hills weathered from the Carmel Formation, which drapes the lower flanks of the Fold to our west. Ahead the valley is largely buried in alluvial deposits, with a procession of red knolls of Entrada Sandstone outlining the eastern edge of Grand Gulch. In Grand Gulch, a few cottonwoods drape their foliage over the banks of the wash, and in other locations there are stands of tamarisk.

Two interesting but brief sidetrips to Cottonwood and Willow Tanks, two of the waterpockets that give Waterpocket Fold its name, are possible as we approach the trailhead. Unless we're hiking in the wash, we probably won't notice the sign indicating Cottonwood Tanks on a bench above the west bank of the wash, 5 1/4 miles from the Halls Creek-Muley Twist confluence via the wash (after perhaps 2 hours of hiking), and 3 1/4 miles (1-1 1/2 hours) via the valley route. Referring to the map, experienced hikers can take an interesting sidetrip to Cottonwood or Willow tanks, both of which hold water year-round.

From the valley east of Cottonwood and Willow tanks, we simply make our way north, soon sighting our vehicles at the trailhead, and conclude our diverse tour of the Waterpocket Fold (5.0; 4851).

# Trip 22
## Halls Creek Overlook
## to Brimhall Double Arch

**Distance**: 4.6 miles round trip

**Low/High elevations**: 4460'/5280'

**Suited for**: Dayhike

**Difficulty**: Strenuous

**Best seasons**: April through mid-June; mid-September through November.

**Map/Trailhead**: 23/17

**Hazards**: Steep scrambling over slickrock and talus; possible quicksand; deep wading and possibly a brief swim of a deep pothole;

water available only from potholes in Brimhall Canyon; flash-flood danger.

**Introduction**: A strenuous and demanding dayhike or overnighter recommended only for experienced desert hikers, this short but memorable trip offers rewards commensurate with the effort it requires. The trail descends steeply from the rim of Big Thomson Mesa into the valley of Halls Creek, then ascends a precipitous defile to an overlook of the arch. This canyon is passable only by the experienced desert hiker. There is no shade except within the confines of Brimhall Canyon, and this part of the Park is extremely hot in summer.

Before beginning the hike, pause to soak in the vistas from the trailhead. Halls Creek Overlook lies at the west rim of the broad, grass- and shrub-clad expanse of Big Thomson Mesa. Magnificent vistas reach eastward beyond distant, higher mesas to the Little Rockies, and northeast to the higher prominences of the Henry Mountains. Colorful shale slopes drape the lower flanks of the Henrys from Mt. Hillers northward, but the sedimentary strata abruptly give way to the igneous rocks that compose Henry Mountains.

A 40-mile stretch of the Waterpocket Fold rising above the narrow valley of Grand Gulch can be viewed, from the northwest near The Post to near its southern terminus above presently-invisible Lake Powell in the southeast. Notice how the Fold becomes progressively lower toward the south. Gazing northwest along the Fold, we can plainly see how steeply the rock strata have been tilted, especially where the Kayenta rocks, featuring distinct layering, overlie the white Navajo Sandstone—the dominant rock of the Fold. In places we can also see part of the Circle Cliffs, which bound the western flanks of the Fold, and far to the southeast are heat-hazy buttes rising beyond the Colorado River in extreme southern Utah near Monument Valley.

**Description**: From the trailhead (0.0; 5280), our rough, rocky trail descends northwest along the cliff face of Big Thomson Mesa, passing through a variety of rock strata: the Dakota Sandstone that caps the rim; the Brushy Basin Shale forming the bench below; the Salt Wash Sandstone forming the rim of the bench; the Summerville Formation; and finally the Entrada Sandstone. But all these strata are largely obscured by conglomeratic boulders fallen from the rim, and are difficult to discern one from another. Enroute, we enjoy expansive vistas of the Waterpocket Fold and Grand Gulch, with the redrock prominence of Deer Point, in the west-southwest, and other crags atop the Circle Cliffs rising above.

After negotiating several steep, rocky switchbacks, we emerge onto a slope clad in blackbrush and more boulders, and cross a low ridge between domes of red Entrada Sandstone pitted with solution cavities. Beyond, our well-defined trail heads across a shrubby bench, soon reaching a sign along cottonwood-lined Halls Creek wash (1.2; 4460). The sign lists several destinations and mileages, but the trail ends; from here on travel is strictly cross-country.

To reach the mouth of Brimhall Canyon, cross the wash and follow a faint path southwest along a bench decorated with grasses, sagebrush, rabbitbrush, juniper and scattered and picturesque, excessively branched cottonwoods.

Brimhall Canyon is the first drainage on our right, 0.2 mile from the sign. Vegetation abruptly changes as we enter the canyon and we see a grove of Gambel oak growing at the base of a steep slickrock slope of Navajo Sandstone at the canyon's entrance. Here runoff from Brimhall Canyon saturates the ground, providing ample moisture for the oaks. In addition, runoff from the slickrock above, which absorbs little moisture, provides even more moisture. This availability of moisture combines with the shade and shelter provided by the steep slickrock slope above to produce a microclimate. Abundant vegetation, some of which grows to atypical proportions due to the canyon microclimate, clothes the lower canyon.

Pause at the canyon's mouth to gaze up into the spectacular, labyrinthine canyon, where tall cliffs of Navajo Sandstone frame the ledgy, broken slopes of the Kayenta Formation and the massive steep slopes of orange-hued Wingate Sandstone beyond, sliced by numerous shallow gullies.

After 1/4 mile the canyon appears to end in a boulder-choked chute below a tall, dry waterfall, but actually the main canyon makes a 90°

bend toward the north here. At this point we must briefly climb the slickrock to our right to continue. Above we traverse more slickrock above a narrow chute, then proceed along the boulder-littered wash. Soon the canyon bends sharply west, becoming very narrow, and we are quickly confronted by yet another obstacle, a deep pool. This pool requires a deep wade, or more likely a brief swim, to continue up the canyon. Exiting the pool, we must climb over the large boulders that choke these narrows.

Ahead, more boulders choke the canyon, further impeding progress. But we soon reach another deep pool lying beneath a 12' waterfall, 0.6 mile up the canyon. From here, scramble up the slope rising above to the right, northwest, taking care among the loose boulders and sand.

Our ascent ends atop a minor ridge (0.9; 4780), where we enjoy a head-on view of Brimhall Arch, lying directly west across the canyon. Brimhall Arch boasts two spans, both arcing over a deep alcove. A shallow gully has developed on the hummocky Wingate slope, its runoff pouring under the arches and helping to enlarge them. Another alcove has developed high above the canyon near Brimhall Arch, and it will perhaps evolve into another arch that may attract visitors in the distant future, perhaps long after Brimhall Arch has been reduced to rubble by the inexorable forces of weathering and erosion.

From our vantage we notice how the massive domes and walls of the Navajo abruptly give way to the softer, broken rocks of the Kayenta, which in turn give way to the hummocky slickrock slopes of the Wingate, upon which the arch has formed. To get a closer look at the arch, we can work our way briefly northwest along this ridge, cross a narrow, minor canyon, and carefully descend ledges of Kayenta rocks to the canyon bottom opposite the arch (0.2; 4700).

Return the way you came.

# Trip 23
## Halls Creek Overlook to Halls Creek Narrows

**Distance**: 27.0 miles round trip

**Low/High elevations**: 3920'/5280'

**Suited for**: Backpack

**Difficulty**: Moderate as a three-day backpack

**Best seasons**: Mid-March through mid-June; mid-September through November.

**Maps/Trailhead**: 23,24/17

**Hazards**: Wading required in Narrows; flash-flood danger; very limited water.

**Introduction**: The most ambitious backpack trip in Capitol Reef, this scenic and lonely trek follows the long, narrow valley of Grand Gulch just east of the Waterpocket Fold to the Halls Creek Narrows, where a perennial stream meanders through a deep, narrow slickrock canyon cut into the Navajo Sandstone of the Fold. Part of the return trip follows a historic wagon road turned uranium exploration road to intercept Halls Creek wash above The Narrows.

The magnificent valley known as Grand Gulch is desert wilderness at its best, a primitive kind of landscape unique to the Colorado Plateau. Here hikers can roam the country at will, for there is no trail to guide the way. Few hikers travel beyond Brimhall Canyon to Halls Creek Narrows, the fewer still continue beyond the Park boundary to the banks of Lake Powell. This area, the lowest-elevation region in the Park, can be quite cold in winter and mercilessly hot in summer.

Once you enter Grand Gulch, you will want to spend some time there; it has a magnetic, alluring quality, and lovers of wilderness find it hard to leave. More than a dozen canyons penetrating the Fold beckon the adventurous to discover their secrets. On a hot day, The Narrows are irresistible; within the shady confines of its deep canyon, hikers will wade its perennial waters for 3 miles, with only a narrow opening above allowing only glimpses of a sliver of sky and the fleeting passage of the sun. Beyond The Narrows, you'll be tempted to follow Grand Gulch to its abrupt end amid the extensive mudflats at Halls Creek Bay, an arm of Lake Powell.

Mormon pioneers traversed this desert wilderness in the early 1880s but they probably viewed the area with no more affection than the sparse grasses to feed their stock could inspire (see "Human History of Capitol Reef").

Today a magnificent wild area such as this offers scope to those who require unspoiled landscapes to recreate the experiences of their forebears and to live, albeit for a brief time, in the natural world, unspoiled and unburdened by the works of man—and to those who simply need to know that such a place still exists.

**Description**: Obtain the required backcountry permit from the Visitor Center. Follow *Trip 22* to the signed junction at Halls Creek wash (1.2; 4460). Upstream, Halls Creek wash meanders for about 3.5 miles to the mouth of Muley Twist Canyon. This seldom-visited section of Grand Gulch is highlighted by a low ridge of red Entrada Sandstone domes rising from the valley floor, and it features extensive grassy benches where exposed and austere campsites could be located.

The topographic map indicates a jeep trail in Grand Gulch, and although traces of it can be seen at times, most of this route has faded from view. We simply follow the wash downstream, or any of the numerous old cattle trails that shortcut the meanders of the wash. Hikers will be happy to know that cattle no longer graze the sparse desert grasses of Grand Gulch. Our pace varies with the surface of the wash—at times sandy or boulder-strewn but more often hardpacked, where walking is easy. Possible campsites, the most desirable of which are perched atop open benches, are almost unlimited through the length of the gulch.

The corrugated, slickrock slopes of the Fold present ever-changing aspects as we proceed, and the many interesting side canyons beckon. One of the more interesting features in the gulch is Red Slide, a huge body of red-rock debris emanating from the crest of the Fold, and soon we reach its north edge (2.0; 4387). This gargantuan rockslide is believed to have smothered the landscape more than 10,000 years ago.

Following the wash ahead, we work our way around the Red Slide for 2 miles. In places the flanks of the slide are decorated by many fascinating hoodoos and balanced rocks, vaguely reminiscent of the "breaks" of Bryce Canyon National Park. Look for the Fountain Tanks near the mouth of the second canyon below Red Slide, usually holding water all year.

For the next 6 miles, we pass between the steep wall of the Fold on our right (west) and a broken cliff on our left, featuring three distinct rock formations: low cliffs and knolls of red Entrada Sandstone near the base of the cliffs; the thinly bedded, multilayered Summerville Formation midway up the cliffs; and a rimrock composed of Salt Wash Sandstone. The Fold is dominated by nearly white Navajo Sandstone.

The wash eventually bends east for 1/2 mile, and instead of following along the base of the cliffs bounding the east side of Grand Gulch, it unexpectedly heads into the deep gorge it has cut into the massive Navajo Sandstone of the Fold. Here we enter The Narrows (7.5; 4100), a fascinating serpentine canyon where great cliffs rise as high as 650 feet above. The stream here is perennial, so expect to be wading in shallow water much of the time.

After we twist and turn in the shady chasm for perhaps two or three hours, the canyon walls recede and we re-enter the open country of Grand Gulch (4.0; 3920). From here we can either follow Halls Creek wash 1 mile south to the Park boundary, and thence another 7.5 miles to the muddy shores of Lake Powell (Millers Creek, about 3 1/2 miles from the boundary usually boasts a small stream), or return via the Hall Divide route. That old wagon road and jeep trail is obscured at first, but it can soon be seen from the wash as it ascends the hillside just east of the first northeast-trending side canyon we encounter after we exit The Narrows.

After we bushwhack through streamside vegetation, the route is easy to follow as it ascends the tilted strata of weathered Carmel Formation rocks. After an initial climb, this old road descends briefly into a shallow wash, where we resume our easy ascent via gullies, slopes, and broken hills, and top out at Hall Divide (1.2; 4201).

High cliffs rise 900 feet above in the east, while hummocky slopes of Navajo Sandstone, displaying fine examples of cross-bedding,

**The mouth of Halls Creek narrows**

dominate the view westward. Unobstructed views extend northwest along the cottonwood-lined course of Halls Creek wash, and from the divide we descend easily toward that wash. The old road ends before the wash, but we simply descend eroded slopes to the wash (0.4; 4100), and then retrace our route for 10.7 miles to the trailhead.

# Trip 24
## North Blue Flats to The Notch and South Desert

**Distance**: 8.4 miles round trip

**Low/High elevations**: 5100'/5400'

**Suited for**: Dayhike or backpack

**Difficulty**: Moderate

**Best seasons**: April through mid-June; mid-September through November.

**Map/Trailhead**: 25/18

**Hazards**: Route finding; no water or shade.

**Introduction**: This interesting trip climbs gently from the open desert of North Blue Flats to The Notch, a broad gap in a long desert ridge called The Hartnet, via a shallow, winding canyon. Route-finding skills are necessary as the route to The Notch is not an obvious one. Just over The Hartnet lies South Desert, a 15-mile-long desert valley paralleling the Waterpocket Fold. This seldom-visited valley offers an excellent desert wilderness experience, and several canyons penetrating the tilted slickrock of the Waterpocket Fold are worthy of exploration. Water is scarce in the North District, and seeps such as Notch Water are much too alkaline to be potable.

As we look northwest from the trailhead, we see a long, low ridge of colorful shale and sandstone obscuring the deep trench of South Desert, which lies between the ridge and the Waterpocket Fold. The broad gap in that ridge is The Notch, which offers direct access into the southern part of remote South Desert. A broad sweep of the Fold, from Golden Throne in the south nearly to the flanks of Thousand Lake

Mountain in the northwest, is seen as a rugged slickrock backbone capped by domes, buttes and crags.

**Description**: From the trailhead (0.0; 5100) we head for The Notch, first hiking west-north-west, cross-country (or possibly following a faint jeep trail) across gentle, nearly barren clay slopes. After about 0.4 mile rabbitbrush and some prickly pear appear near the course of Dry Wash. Shrubs and tamarisk crowd around the banks of the wash where we enter it (0.6; 5080), and we follow its sandy bed upstream, heading toward a group of colorful, red- and gray-banded hills in the northwest. A small wash (1.1; 5120) joins Dry Wash on the left (southwest) about 1/2 mile before Dry Wash enters the aforementioned hills. Turn left and follow this shallow wash west as it passes among colorful yet barren hills composed of Brushy Basin Shale.

After hiking for perhaps 1/2 hour, we skirt the foot of a prominent red- and gray-banded hill and enter the Park (0.8; 5190). Soon we pass through a grassy flat and entering the realm of Salt Wash Sandstone, whose sandstone and conglomerate form low, broken cliffs on either side of the wash.

About 0.7 mile from the Park boundary a tributary wash joins from the north, while our wash narrows as it cuts through solid rock. A cairn at the entrance to these narrows indicates a ledge route on the south side used to bypass the chasm, although it is easily passable. Another cairn indicates the point at which we drop back into the wash, which soon forks where a charred juniper stands above the south bank. Take the right fork, soon reaching yet another fork between a live juniper on the south and a juniper snag on the north side of the wash. The larger fork goes right, but we just take the left fork, which leads us to a small, juniper-studded basin, which in turn leads us to the wide gap of The Notch (1.4; 5400).

From the rim of the ridge at The Notch, composed of the reddish Summerville Formation, we can descend steep, gray badlands slopes of the Curtis Formation west into the valley of South Desert, enjoying a view of the broad slopes of the Waterpocket Fold rising beyond. A small monolith of Entrada Sandstone stands at the foot of our descent, and we can see the serpentine course of Deep Creek wash winding through the South Desert. Descending past the monolith, we pass over red sand dunes to reach the wash of Deep Creek (0.3; 5260). The sluggish seep of Notch Water lies just downstream, below where the wash bends from east to south. Another alkaline seep is about 0.4 mile downstream.

Several prominent canyons cut westward into the Waterpocket Fold west of South Desert, and all the canyons provide worthwhile sidetrips if your time and water supply allow. However, one should use the *Fruita* 7.5' USGS quad in one's explorations. Let your determination and sense of discovery guide you into these almost unknown canyons, some of which extend several miles into the Fold. One can camp almost anywhere in South Desert, but campsites are completely exposed, and the few water sources are much too alkaline to be potable.

# Trip 25
## Lower South Desert Overlook to Little Sand Flat

**Distance**: 12.8 miles round trip
**Low/High elevations**: 5580'/6600'
**Suited for**: Dayhike or backpack
**Difficulty**: Moderate
**Best seasons**: April through mid-June; mid-September through November.
**Maps/Trailhead**: 26,27/19
**Hazards**: No water; little shade; flash-flood danger in the washes.

**Introduction**: Many of the ancient sedimentary strata of the Colorado Plateau contain reserves of coal, oil, gas, or minerals in exploitable quantities. After World War II research into the region's resources began in earnest and exploration ensued. Roads were built into this desert wilderness theretofore known only to a handful of ranchers and desert rats. During 1955-56, Phillips Petroleum invested in an oil-drilling project near the crest of the Waterpocket Fold. They built a road across South Desert to Deep

Creek, and on up past Little Sand Flat to the top of the Fold. There they drilled deeply in search of oil, but they found no great reserves, so they capped the well and abandoned the road.

Today this old road offers access to the beautiful slickrock-encircled, cactus-studded grasslands of Little Sand Flat, a 500-acre expanse in the heart of the Waterpocket Fold. Few hikers make the trip to this isolated basin, but those who do enjoy considerable solitude, and the chance to explore hidden canyons, scale slickrock domes, and revel in a truly spectacular landscape.

The trip traverses a diversity of North District scenery, from fluted red cliffs to open desert, from a starkly beautiful canyon to wooded slopes and to the slickrock realm of the Waterpocket Fold. Lower South Desert Overlook, only a 1/4 mile stroll from the roadend, offers a superb vista of South Desert and the Fold. This short jaunt is a fine diversion for visitors enjoying a driving tour of Capitol Reef's North District.

**Description**: We begin (0.0; 5800) by strolling down the abandoned road through red siltstone hills of the Summerville Formation, its nutrient-poor soils nearly devoid of vegetation save for a few scattered shrubs. Some of the few plants here are noteworthy, for they occur near only a few trails in the Park, mostly in the North District. Smooth hopsage, littleleaf horsebrush, shadscale—a member of the saltbush family—and halogeton—a low-growing succulent introduced from Europe—are the more unusual plants here among scattered basalt boulders.

Soon we reach the brink of the rim at Lower South Desert Overlook (0.2; 5760), where gray rocks of the Curtis Formation are eroded into a medley of bizarre pillars and balanced rocks, giving the gray cliffs a strangely fluted facade. These gray cliffs contrast markedly with the overlying red rocks of the Summerville and with the brick-red Entrada Sandstone on the desert floor below.

Thrusting over 500 feet skyward from the nearly level desert floor, the pyramid of 6118' Jailhouse Rock raises fluted red Entrada cliffs to a pointed caprock of the more resistant gray Curtis rocks. To the northwest of the impressive monolith, the pinnacle of 5989' Temple Rock also punctuates South Desert. Without a resistant caprock, this monolith is more susceptible to erosion and will be much shorter-lived than its neighbor. Both of these monoliths are eroded remnants of the once continuous rock layers that blanketed the region in ancient times.

Adding even more contrast to the starkly beautiful landscape is an immense crest of jagged slickrock—the Waterpocket Fold—which seems to emerge mysteriously and rather abruptly from the lush meadows and cool conifer forests along the slopes of Thousand Lake Mountain, whose flat-as-a-table summit ridge rises to over 11,000 feet elevation.

From the viewpoint, the badly eroded road-bed switchbacks twice, steeply descending through the thin layer of gray rock and soon emerging onto the floor of South Desert (0.2; 5650). The road becomes faint at times from here to Deep Creek, but we persist on the obscure track and soon pass a comparatively small red pinnacle. Basalt boulders are abundant, nearly blanketing the flat landscape in all directions. A few wildflowers brighten the barren valley in

**Jailhouse Rock in South Desert**

spring and summer, including cryptantha, globe mallow, badlands bahia, mule's ears, and broom snakeweed.

Soon our road heads west beneath imposing Jailhouse Rock (0.5; 5580) toward the pointed sentinel of Temple Rock. Between the two monoliths we'll pass some excellent examples of dikes—igneous intrusions of basalt injected into vertical cracks in the horizontal strata. Since the basalt is much harder than the rocks it penetrated, these dikes stand above the softer sedimentary strata like ancient stone walls. This basalt is among the youngest rocks in the Park, dated at approximately four million years of age.

Shortly beyond the dikes our road passes just north of isolated Temple Rock (1.4; 5670) on a northwestward course. Like Jailhouse Rock, its base is enshrouded in red scree weathered from the monolith.

Shrubs increase as we approach the wash of Deep Creek and cross several deep gullies. Especially prominent is greasewood, a typical inhabitant of alkaline soils. Passing north of a few possible cottonwood-shaded campsites, we curve southwest to cross tamarisk-lined Polk Creek wash, (0.7; 5700), which may boast free-flowing, yet alkaline, water even in summer.

Beyond it we continue a southwestward course along the base of a basalt-boulder-covered hill and start cross-country into the Deep Creek drainage, which has left the South Desert and now slices into the Fold. Ahead, multihued strata of the Fold rise steadily westward above us, and the dry wash leads us into the realm of stark red and gray cliffs, ledges and slopes of the Carmel Formation, featuring outcrops of while gypsum. Deep Creek rarely flows, however, since its headwaters are diverted northward on the slopes of Thousand Lake Mountain for purposes of irrigation. About 0.8 mile up the canyon, just as the cliffs north of the wash begin to rise more noticeably, look for a winding draw joining from the south. Leave the wash here, proceed west along a bench above the south side of the wash, and quickly find the old roadbed climbing the south wall of the canyon.

The road rises moderately among deeply eroded hills and low cliffs. The hills are blanketed by cryptogamic crust, and abundant gypsum crystals sparkle in the sunlight.

Cresting a watershed divide, we can pause to enjoy fine views of the northern Henry Mountains in the southeast distance. We then ascend two switchbacks upon a northeast-facing, pinyon- and juniper-clad slope. Avoid a spur road heading south at the second bend in the road. The tall stalks of prince's plume, bearing small but bright yellow flowers, are a common sight along the roadside in early-to-midsummer.

After continuing our westbound climb on basalt-boulder-covered slopes, we finally level out on a broad ridge at 6450 feet amid a pygmy forest. Ahead, prominent domes dominate the view, while to our north we gain an interesting perspective of the colorful east-dipping strata of the Carmel Formation on the flanks of the Waterpocket Fold.

The road ahead follows the ridge west, keeping north of three low hills. We finally cross over the west end of the ridge at the brink of a precipitous canyon, passing the upper layer of the Carmel, which has imparted a golden tone to the underlying Navajo Sandstone. Before us lies the dome-rimmed expanse of Little Sand Flat, grass-clad and studded with cactus, pinyon and juniper. It is a superb, isolated locale in which to establish a base camp, and backpackers will find an abundance of canyons and domes to explore. To get there simply stroll down the road to the fringes of the spread (3.4; 6480), where you can camp and roam at will.

# Trip 26
## Lower Cathedral Valley Overlook

**Distance**: 1.6 miles round trip
**Low/High elevations**: 5840'/6000
**Suited for**: Walk
**Difficulty**: Moderately easy
**Best seasons**: April through mid-June; mid-September through November.
**Map/Trailhead**: 26/20
**Hazards**: Negligible

   **Introduction**: The Waterpocket Fold is the primary scenic attraction in all of Capitol Reef National Park. Its slickrock spine, cut by myriad slot canyons, and its giant crags are an awe-inspiring sight from any angle. However, the North District of the Park contains more than just the Fold; its boundaries embrace desert valleys, fluted cliffs, mesas, and the towering monoliths of Cathedral Valley. Within the broad desert flats of Lower Cathedral Valley are two pyramid-like redrock monoliths jutting nearly 300 feet above the desert floor. Perhaps no other features in the North District evoke as much awe and wonder as do the Temples of the Sun and Moon. This short, easy cross-country jaunt offers an aerial-like view of those great monoliths, plus far-ranging vistas across some of the most remote country in the Utah desert, rewards seldom gained on a hike of such short duration.

   **Description**: Looking north from the trailhead, we see two prominent saddles in a long ridge bounding Hartnet Draw, both about 6000 feet in elevation. From the trailhead (0.0; 5840) we head generally northeast across the flat valley toward the easternmost saddle and soon cross the sandy wash draining Harnet Draw. Low hills bound the draw on all sides, but bulky Thousand Lake Mountain dominates the view westward, its sloping meadows rising into the subalpine forests that decorate its crest.

   A steep scramble brings us to the ridgecrest (0.8; 6000) amid outcrops of Salt Wash Sandstone. Before us is an unforgettable panorama of stark grandeur. Two prominent pyramids rise abruptly from the desert plain of Lower Cathedral Valley—Temple of the Moon and Temple of the Sun—which rise about 200 feet and 320 feet, respectively. Composed entirely of red and tan Entrada Sandstone and distinctly layered, these temples are the erosional remnants of a vast layer of Entrada that buried much of Utah in eons past. The red desert flats of Lower Cathedral Valley have a faint green caste even in summer due to the abundant shrubs that grow there. Normally dry Salt Wash, draining the Middle Desert beyond the Temples, hosts clumps of tamarisk along moist stretches, particularly around Campers Spring.

   Views northward into the remote desert beyond are striking, featuring numerous flat-topped buttes abutting the west edge of the lonely Last Chance Desert. Aptly named Black Mountain looms above Middle Desert in the

**Temple of the Sun (left) and Temple of the Moon**

northeast, its slopes blanketed by black basalt boulders. Thousand Lake Mountain is prominent on the western horizon, and if we climb briefly east up the ridge, we can view the entire basin of Lower Cathedral Valley, bounded by red and gray fluted walls on three sides.

You could return the way you came. An alternative, longer route for retracing our steps to the trailhead involves following the blocky ridge west to the westernmost saddle that we viewed from the trailhead. From the first summit, about 100 feet higher than the saddle, we can gaze northeast across seemingly endless desert to the distant summits of the La Sal Mountains near the Colorado border. Beyond, a steep descent along a knife-edged ridge brings us to the westernmost saddle amid Summerville Formation rocks. The view from here doesn't equal that from the eastern saddle, but it is unforgettable nonetheless.

Take care descending from either saddle; the slopes are steep and the rocks are loose. Simply follow the path of least resistance as you return to the trailhead.

# Trip 27
## Temple Rock/South Desert Overlook

**Distance**: 4.0 miles round trip
**Low/High elevations**: 5980'/6598'
**Suited for**: Dayhike
**Difficulty**: Moderate
**Best season**: April through mid-June; mid-September through November.
**Map/Trailhead**: 26/21
**Hazards**: No water or shade; route-finding skills are required.

**Introduction**: The viewpoint at the end of this route offers what are arguably the finest vistas in all of the Park. The route is trailless, and requires route-finding and map-reading skills as it climbs from Hartnet Draw, and then traverses an undulating mesa to the rim of The Hartnet, where an unforgettable vista of the North District country unfolds.

Most hikers complete the trip in a half day, but there is little shade enroute and one should carry ample water.

Adventurous hikers planning an extended

trek through South Desert, the long, narrow valley that bounds the Waterpocket Fold between its emergence from Thousand Lake Mountain and the Fremont River, might consider taking this trip first to gain an aerial-like overview of the entire area.

**Description**: From the road in Hartnet Draw (0.0; 5980) follow the wash southwest about 175 yards, and soon notice an old roadcut climbing the slope to the south. Leaving the sagebrush- and greasewood-clad flats of the wash, follow this steep roadcut onto the juniper-dotted hillside above, to where it ends midway up the slope amid black boulders. We then pick our own way up the slope, heading briefly southeast to the undulating surface of The Hartnet mesa. Once on the crest, proceed southwest along the rim, paralleling a deep wash below to the southeast.

The rolling ridge ahead of us to the south and southeast is the crest of The Hartnet. After 1 mile of hiking southwest we reach the crest of a hill and are rewarded with fine vistas of the northern Waterpocket Fold. Our destination is a prominent knob at the west end of The Hartnet ridge, toward the south-southwest. Heading for the knob, we pass sandstone outcroppings and knolls amid a pinyon-juniper woodland. Snakeweed brightens our route with its dense yellow blooms in late summer, while cryptantha is a common white wildflower blooming in spring. Watch for mourning doves and cliff swallows, which are fairly common here, while nighthawks will entertain us during the morning and evening hours. Try to avoid the delicate cryptogamic crust as you make your way toward the aforementioned knob, crossing low ridges and shallow drainages enroute.

Upon reaching the foot of the knob, we can either climb to the saddle east of it or contour around to its west ridge to attain the summit, avoiding its steep north slopes. Upon reaching the summit of the knob (2.0; 6598), crowned by boulders of basalt and sandstone and by a USGS benchmark, we are treated to a breathtaking, far-reaching panorama. South Desert, lying at our feet, spreads out before us in its entirety, a barren sun-baked desert valley lying at the foot of the Fold. It abruptly ends in the northwest where cliffs rise steeply to the densely forested slopes of Thousand Lake Mountain.

The Fold, emerging from the rounded slopes of that mountain, is displayed in stark profile, a broken crest of slickrock domes and crags stretching far to the southeast. Myriad yawning chasms emerge from the Fold onto South Desert, most notable of which are Deep Creek and one of its red-walled tributaries, Water Canyon. Polk Creek, born on the flanks of Thousand Lake Mountain, drains the upper end of South Desert, its intermittent flow glistening in the sunlight. Fluted red and gray cliffs abut the entire northeast edge of South Desert and fall away for more than 800 feet below us. Broad Boulder Mountain rises beyond the rugged Fold to our southwest. The old road cutting across South Desert and climbing the Fold to Little Sand Flat is seen to the south (see *Trip 25*). Here the prominent fang of Temple Rock and the buttress-ridden pyramid of Jailhouse Rock are displayed in stark detail. The high peaks of the Henry Mountains lie far to the southeast, while eastward, distant buttes and mesas fade into the heat-haze of the vast desert.

Close at hand, the summit of the knob hosts wind-tortured junipers, buffaloberry and shadscale, and the yellow blooms of prince's plume and broom snakeweed add color here in summer.

Reluctantly leaving the colorful, contrasting panoramas behind, we must take care to retrace our cross-country route back to our car.

# Trip 28
## Ackland Rim Overlook

**Distance**: 1.5 miles round trip
**Low/High elevations**: 6000'/6300'
**Suited for**: Dayhike
**Difficulty**: Moderately easy
**Best seasons**: April through mid-June; mid-
  September through November.
**Map/Trailhead**: 26/22
**Hazards**: Moderate route-finding required.

**Introduction**: One of the attractions of a desert wilderness park like Capitol Reef is that hikers can travel wherever they please; virtually every canyon, ridge and mesa offers the sense of discovery and accomplishment that results from traveling through unknown country.

A case in point is the short cross-country hike to the rim above (northeast of) Ackland Spring. Few travelers along the dirt road in the North District would imagine the vast panoramas and the solitude that the rim offers, but the very few who take the time to gain the rim will find that the views from its scenic crest beckon one to explore for miles in any direction. Backpackers who love desert sunrises will find numerous austere, boulder-sheltered campsites all along the rim; they must, of course, carry water as should dayhikers. Albeit a short trip, it should nevertheless be undertaken only by those possessing route-finding skills. Expect much scrambling among boulders and on slippery slopes.

**Description**: A sign north of the road here (0.0; 6000) indicates Ackland Spring and a short jaunt leads to the piped spring, dripping into a stock tank. This spring dates back to the 1950s, when stockmen grazed cattle here before the area

received National Park status. There is no apparent path, but the most direct way to the rim follows the wash leading northeast from the spring, alternating between sand and slickrock. The wash leads us through Salt Wash Sandstone and past colorful slopes of Brushy Basin Shale.

Upon reaching the dead-end of the wash, we scramble up and around sandstone boulders to attain the nearby rim (0.75; 6300). Our view now includes the great cliff-bound amphitheater of Lower Cathedral Valley, but the Temples of the Sun and Moon are, unfortunately, invisible. However, they can be viewed by walking northwest or northeast along the rim. A dry wash meanders through that desert valley 600 feet below, and two prominent temple-like monoliths rise above an intermediate bench northeast of the valley. Thousand Lake and Boulder mountains and part of the Fold dominate the view to the west and southwest.

Unless you are planning a longer hike along the rim in either direction, carefully backtrack to Ackland Spring.

# Arches National Park

## Introduction

Arches National Park, encompassing 73,379 acres of desert and slickrock in east-central Utah, is one of the most delightful national parks on the Colorado Plateau. The Park is small enough that many of its primary features can be viewed from the road, yet large enough to provide a rewarding backcountry experience for adventurous backpackers. The unique examples of nature's sculpture and architecture are not on a grand scale here, but nevertheless the landscapes in the Park evoke awe and wonder in anyone who gazes upon them.

Arches are natural stone openings found throughout the sandstone formations on the Colorado Plateau, but are quite rare elsewhere in the world. They can be found in virtually every national park in Utah, but in Arches National Park there is a profusion of holes in rock; nowhere else on the globe does the concentration of arches approach that within this small Park.

One of the most common questions asked by Park visitors is: how many arches are there in the Park? The answer depends on the definition of an arch. Openings in Arches National Park vary in size from fist-sized holes to those that span hundreds of feet, but for practical purposes an arch is defined as an aperture that is at least 3 feet from top to bottom and from side to side. Using this criterion, there were 900 known such openings within the Park as of 1989, but certainly more are likely to be discovered.

However, natural arches are only a small part of the overall scene in the Park. Pinnacles, towers, cliffs, deep canyons, broad grassy valleys, and a rainbow of colorful rocks foreground distant views of endless deserts, lofty alpine peaks, wooded mesas, and vast plateaus.

Arches National Park lies on a gently sloping highland, the Salt Valley Anticline, that rises gently from the desert valleys that flank its west, north, and east sides, but the highland rises abruptly along its south edge due to past movement along the Moab Fault. The crest of the gently rising bulge in the earth has long since collapsed and eroded away, forming a trough that bisects the Park, separating two parallel ridges that host the salmon-tinted fins of rock in which the arches have formed. The south part of the Park is more complex, consisting of a profusion of monoliths, towers, brush-clad flats, extensive areas of hummocky slickrock, and two deep, serpentine canyons—Courthouse Wash and Salt Wash.

The fascinating landscape of Arches beckons hikers to explore its secrets. When you visit, park your car and walk the trails or explore the untracked reaches of the backcountry. This land is magical, its images are powerful, and your memories will last a lifetime.

## Human History of Arches

Prehistoric peoples using the Arches area have left evidence that they were here at least as much as 10,000 years ago. These ancient inhabitants, known to archaeologists as Paleo-Indians, were thought to have been hunters of large game animals, some of which have long since vanished from the earth. They used spears tipped with stone points that they threw with the aid of a wooden device called an atlatl. The Folsom projectile point, thought to have been used more than 10,000 years ago, is among the scant evidence remaining of their culture, and one such point has been found close to the Park.

Inhabiting the Southwest from about 7000 to 2500 years ago was a hunting-gathering culture dubbed the Archaic. The only evidence of this culture discovered thus far in the Arches region consists mostly of rock-art panels and fragments of split-twig figurines that were fashioned from willow branches into likenesses of animals.

The Archaic Culture evolved over time into two agriculturally based cultures: the Anasazi, who built pueblos and cliff dwellings in the Four Corners region, and their contemporaries the Fremont, whose cultures came to dominance in the region about 2500 years ago.

The Anasazi occupied much of the southern third of Utah, southwest Colorado, northwest New Mexico, and northern Arizona, while the Fremont occupied northern Utah, and parts of Nevada, Idaho, Wyoming, and Colorado. Arches lies near the Fremont-Anasazi territorial boundary, and peoples of both cultures used the area that is now the Park. Rock-art sites from both cultures are scattered throughout Arches, but most abundant are chipping sites, where these ancient peoples fashioned stone tools and projectile points from chert, a hard stone found in some of the sedimentary formations in the Park. Rock-art panels in Arches typically depict deer, bighorn sheep, human figures, and various symbols of unknown meaning. Most rock-art panels are petroglyphs, chipped into the face of some desert-varnished wall. These cultures relied upon agriculture to sustain them, but they also supplemented their diets by hunting and by gathering wild foods.

The successors of the Anasazi and the Fremont (whose cultures evolved into the Hopi and Pueblo cultures of the Southwest about 700 years ago) also chipped images on stone in Arches. The Utes, from which the state of Utah takes its name, were the Indians that early travelers and explorers encountered in the Arches region. Their petroglyph panel near Wolfe Ranch on the Delicate Arch Trail is the most famous in the Park, depicting mounted horsemen, bighorn sheep, and small animals that presumably are dogs.

In one of the earlier attempts at Mormon expansion on the Utah frontier, the Huntington Expedition in 1854 traveled the Old Spanish Trail from central Utah, passing through Moab Canyon and fording the Colorado near present-day Moab, enroute to Navajo country near the San Juan River. The following year 40 men were called on a mission by leaders of the Mormon Church to establish a settlement known as the Elk Mountain Mission, in Moab Valley. There they built a fort surrounded by stone walls, and attempted to establish friendly ties with the Utes who inhabited the area.

But five months later, in September 1855, members of the Elk Mountain Mission were attacked by a band of Utes, resulting in three deaths. The following day, the missionaries abandoned their fort and returned to Manti, Utah. Permanent settlement of Moab finally occurred in the 1870s, when Indian hostilities had largely abated. Access to the new Mormon settlement was gained via a ferry across the Colorado, which operated from 1880 until the construction of the first bridge over the river in 1912.

Arches National Park encompasses a semiarid region with little water and insignificant arable land; hence the region was largely overlooked by homesteaders, with the notable exception of John Wesley Wolfe, veteran of the Union Army. Wolfe brought his son Fred to Salt Wash, and there they built a small log cabin and began raising food plants and cattle. The ranch was a long day's ride—30 miles—from the nearest supply point at Thompson, Utah. After eight years on the ranch, Wolfe was joined by his daughter and family, the Stanleys. Almost at once John Wolfe, his son Fred, and his son-in-law Ed Stanley began hauling cottonwood logs up from the Colorado River to construct a new house for the Stanleys and their two children. The Stanleys stayed on at the ranch until 1908, when they moved to Moab. Today Wolfe Ranch is a fascinating stop on a drive through the Park, lying next to the Delicate Arch Trailhead. All that remains to remind us of Wolfe's brave and persistent venture are an old wagon, a corral, the Stanley's cabin, and a root cellar.

The Arches region attracted little attention in the years following Wolfe's departure. But in December 1922, Alexander Ringhoffer, a Hungarian immigrant turned miner and prospector, came to Arches in search of wealth. In Klondike Bluffs he found it—not the wealth of minerals but a treasure of fantastic rock formations that Ringhoffer called Devils Garden. He contacted officials of the Denver and Rio Grande Western Railroad during the summer of 1923, expounding on its merits as a tourist attraction. These officials were so impressed by the landscape Ringhoffer showed them that they wrote a letter to Stephen Mather, then the director of the infant National Park Service, recommending the area's designation as a national monument. Thus a political process was set in motion that led to a small area of 4520 acres being set aside as a national monument in 1929.

Later, the efforts of John W. "Doc" Williams, a Moab physician, and Loren L. "Bish" Taylor, publisher of *The Grand Valley Times*, a Moab newspaper, led to the establishment of Arches National Monument in 1938, which increased the area's size to more than 33,000 acres. Finally, in 1971, Arches was declared a national park, and its area was more than doubled to its present size of 73,379 acres.

Until 1958, the only way to reach the monument was via a dirt road to The Windows. This sandy route, often made impassable by floodwaters in Courthouse Wash, followed today's Willow Flats Road (*Trip 5*). It was not until 1958 that the first paved road was opened into Arches, and later it was extended to its present-day terminus in Devils Garden. Consequently, visitation to the new park skyrocketed, and the old campground in The Windows Section was moved to its present location. Today, more than one-half million visitors come to Arches annually to enjoy the unique and colorful landscapes in the Park, an area that is truly one of the jewels of the national-park system.

# Plants and Animals of Arches

The casual observer at Arches sees a landscape dominated by rock and sand, with a few coarse shrubs here and a scattering of gnarled, stunted trees there. But upon closer inspection, one will notice a wide variety of trees, shrubs, and wildflowers inhabiting every space where soil has collected.

The most obvious and abundant plant community in the Park is the pinyon-juniper woodland. This so-called pygmy forest, with its small, drab, gnarled and weather-tortured trees, covers nearly half the Park. It is not true forest, however; the trees tend to be scattered discontinuously throughout their range.

Utah juniper, typically squat and multi-branched, dominates in this zone. Two-needled pinyon, also called nut pine since it often produces a crop of tasty nuts, is found with the juniper in higher elevations, where there is a slight increase in precipitation and temperatures are somewhat cooler. Pinyons are also found near the base of cliffs, where runoff from the slickrock above provides additional moisture and a more sheltered environment. Shrubs typical of the pinyon-juniper woodland include cliffrose, singleleaf ash, squawbush, wavy-leaf oak, littleleaf mountain mahogany, Fremont barberry, and Utah serviceberry.

The desert-shrub plant community is the

**Utah juniper**

second most obvious and common group of plants in the Park. It is dominated by low shrubs that at a distance give a dull gray appearance to the landscape. The shrubs typically occupy sand dunes, sand and clay slopes, and flats. Black-brush is the dominant shrub here, but it also creeps upward into the pinyon-juniper belt. In areas of high alkalinity, blackbrush is replaced by salt-tolerant shrubs, such as greasewood, a spiny shrub with fleshy leaves. Four-wing salt-bush, mat saltbush, shadscale, and pickleweed are also found on alkaline soils.

Other shrubs typical of this plant community include mormon tea, yucca, horsebrush, rabbitbrush, big sagebrush, and prickly pear and fishhook cactus, which also range through most of the Park. Russian thistle, or tumbleweed, is found colonizing disturbed areas, such as along rehabilitated roads. Sand sagebrush and the aromatic desert sage are found in sandier areas within the broad range of this plant community.

The riparian woodland differs from other plant communities in the Park in that its inhabitants require abundant and constant moisture.

Salt Wash and Courthouse Wash both have fine examples of this woodland. Wherever these plants grow, even if the wash appears dry, there must be considerable underground moisture. Fremont cottonwood, sandbar willow, and tamarisk are most abundant in riparian woodlands. These green ribbons of vegetation stand in marked contrast to the sparse shrublands and slickrock that surround them.

Grasslands are an attractive plant community, especially in spring when their fresh green grasses contrast with the drab shrublands and colorful cliffs and fins. Almost devoid of shrubs, the grasslands are dominated by sand dropseed, Indian ricegrass, galleta, and purple threeawn, but there are many others, discernable mostly to the trained eye of the botanist. Salt Valley's grasslands have seen their share of grazing and overgrazing by domestic stock, and the subsequent introduction of non-native plant species. Brome, or cheatgrass, is a particular nuisance to hikers because its pointed seeds work their way into socks and irritate one's legs. Winter fat, a low shrub with small, white-woolly leaves, is found in the Park's grasslands, and is important as winter browse for the area's mule deer.

Hanging gardens are a beautiful and delicate kind of plant community in Arches. The plants of this community require a constant source of moisture. They typically occur in sheltered alcoves or on shady canyon walls where water seeps from the sandstone, most often along a horizontal fracture or just above an impermeable layer of rock. Even more than riparian woodlands, these hanging gardens contrast vividly with the harsh landscape of naked stone upon which they thrive. The lush, water-loving plants found in these gardens include maidenhair fern, scarlet monkey flower, alcove columbine, poison ivy, and giant helleborine orchid.

There is a wide variety of colorful wildflowers in Arches, and they put forth a vivid display throughout the Park, particularly in the spring. There are typically two blooming seasons in Arches: during spring after winter rain and snow; and during fall after the summer thundershower season. Many flowering herbs are quite small and sometimes overlooked, while blooming shrubs are quite conspicuous due to their size and profusion of blossoms. Cliffrose is a particularly fragrant shrub, with numerous white blossoms from spring to early summer. Other white-flowered shrubs include yucca, with a tall stalk adorned with large flowers; Utah serviceberry; and tamarisk, with abundant small flowers that are pinkish-white and quite conspicuous in early to midsummer.

Yellow-blooming shrubs include blackbrush, Fremont barberry, squawbush, rabbitbrush (an autumn bloomer), and a small evergreen shrub called broom snakeweed. This common shrub is typically less than a foot tall, and it has small, narrow, green leaves and a broom-like crown covered by tiny yellow flowers that bloom in summer and persist through autumn.

The aromatic shrub, desert sage, a member of the mint family, boasts lovely purple blooms that contrast with the harsh sand-dune environment it typically occupies.

Cacti in Arches are simultaneously the most forbidding and yet the most beautiful plants in the Park. In May or June some of the loveliest flowers in the Park appear in these thorny plants. Particularly striking are the delicate red flowers of claret-cup cactus. Prickly-pear blooms are yellow or red and fishhook cactus boasts lovely pink blossoms.

The flowering herbs, however, excel in color and diversity. There are the reds of paintbrush and curly dock; the yellows of puccoon, wallflower, prince's plume, and goldenweed; the whites of the delicate evening primrose, twinpod, and pepper-grass; and the pinks of rockcress and milkvetch. These are but a few examples of common flowers in Arches, beautiful and important components of this unique landscape.

Animals, like plants, have adapted to the rigors of high desert living. Many are nocturnal, avoiding the heat of the day and venturing from their homes only at night to seek food and water. Some live out their lives close to water sources or hibernate in anticipation of the next major rainfall. Birds are the most abundant and noticeable creatures in the Park, and are most active during morning and late afternoon hours. Some are residents, while others are migratory, visiting the Park seasonally. White-throated swifts, violet-green swallows, and canyon wrens can often

be seen flying among canyon cliffs. Insects, an abundant food supply for birds along watercourses in the Park, attract the greatest variety of birds, including the song sparrow, red-shafted flicker, blue grosbeak, spotted sandpiper, warbling vireo, house wren, common raven, and Bullock's oriole.

Grasslands are the realm of the soaring raptors such as the red-tailed hawk, sparrow hawk, and prairie falcon. Nighthawks will be seen swiftly carving circles, diving, and soaring in pursuit of insects in the morning and evening hours; their distinctive song is unmistakable. Other birds of the grasslands include the western meadowlark, mourning dove, common raven, and horned lark.

Sparrows and finches are common denizens of the Park's scrublands. Pinyon-juniper woodlands host pinyon and scrub jays, house finches, ash-throated flycatchers, gray vireos, black-throated gray warblers, plain titmouses, and various woodpeckers. There are many more birds in Arches, particularly in spring, when food is most abundant. Their melodious songs and flashes of color are important parts of the Arches experience.

Mammals are numerous in the Park, but most are nocturnal. Surface temperatures are exceedingly high in summer, and most mammals are safely tucked away in their cool burrows. Perhaps the most common large mammal in the Park is the mule deer, but you will probably have to explore off of established trails, or hike in the morning or evening hours, to see Arches' largest mammal. Before 1985, bighorn sheep were rarely sighted in the Park, but a transplant of 30 animals from Canyonlands National Park that same year was an attempt to re-establish a herd in its former range in Arches. Hikers may possibly observe some of these secretive creatures in the southwest part of the Park near The Great Wall west of The Windows.

The eerie howl of coyotes in the evening and at night attests to their presence, but these secretive canines are not readily observed. More commonly seen is the blacktail jackrabbit, usually darting from bush to bush seeking cover to remain unseen to predators such as hawks and coyotes. The long ears of jackrabbits and desert cottontails serve as "radiators" to dissipate body

heat. Other Park animals that visitors may encounter are the rock squirrel, whitetail antelope
squirrel, and bats such as the western pipistrel.
The Ord's kangaroo rat, rarely seen due to its
nocturnal habits, is noteworthy because it rarely
drinks water, but instead obtains moisture inter-
nally through the metabolism of seeds.

Of all the animals in Arches, lizards are
second only to birds among those most commonly observed. The northern plateau lizard,
leopard lizard, western whiptail, desert spiny
lizard, short-horned lizard, collared lizard, and
sagebrush lizard are the most common ones.
Only one poisonous snake is found in Arches,
and it is not particularly common; all other
snakes are harmless. The midget faded rattlesnake is native to the Colorado Plateau of Colorado and eastern Utah. It averages only about 18
inches in length, and is typically straw-colored.
Like other rattlesnakes, it is not particularly aggressive, and would rather be left alone by
human visitors. Other snakes in the Park include
the gopher snake, Mesa Verde night snake, racer,
and common, black-necked, and wandering garter snake, which are typically found near water.

In a land of parched, naked stone, it is difficult to imagine the existence of frogs and toads,
but eight species of these amphibians make their
homes. They are found only in moist areas along
Courthouse Wash, the Colorado River, and Salt
Wash.

## Interpretive Activities

Arches has a wide variety of things to see
and do, whether the visitor stays for only half a
day or for several days. To make the most of your
trip, stop at the Visitor Center, located just beyond the Park entrance station. Books, maps, an
interpretive museum, slide shows, and a knowl-
edgeable staff are available to answer any questions one may have about the Park or the
surrounding area. Backpackers can obtain their
backcountry permit here, and also updated information on weather and backcountry route conditions. Visitor center hours are 8 A.M.-6 P.M.
from mid-March through mid-October and 8

A.M.-4:30 P.M. in winter.

Interpretive activities in the Park include
evening amphitheater programs in the Devils
Garden Campground each night from spring
through fall. Ranger-led walks follow a variety
of short trails. The Fiery Furnace hike is a favorite of Park visitors, and guided hikes there are
conducted twice daily, at 9 A.M. and 1:30 P.M.
Reservations for this popular hike must be made
in advance at the Visitor Center. A schedule of
interpretive activities is posted at the Visitor
Center and at the campground.

Most interpretive activities, however, are di-
rected toward self-guiding trails, and an excellent guide entitled *A Guide to an Auto Tour of
Arches National Park* allows visitors to get the
most from their drive through Arches. Self-
guided trails include the Devils Garden Trail and
the 0.2-mile Desert Nature Trail. Points on both
trails are keyed to pamphlets available at the
Visitor Center.

## Campgrounds

The 53-site Devils Garden Campground, located near the north end of the Park road, is the
only vehicle camping area in the Park. This is
one of the most scenic and delightful campgrounds in all of Utah's national parks. The
campsites, along a 3/4-mile-long road in the
southern reaches of Devils Garden, are encircled
by slickrock fins and shaded by scattered
pinyons and junipers. Various shrubs and wildflowers decorate this natural rock garden, and
the campground's location on a highland offers
tremendous panoramas across endless desert and
mesas that stretch eastward into Colorado.

Campers enjoy scrambling on the slickrock
that rises above the campsites, and they have the
opportunity to follow a highly scenic trail to
Broken Arch (*Trip 17*) or to scramble over slickrock behind the campfire circle to stand in the
opening of Skyline Arch, located midway
through the campground. Another trail, 0.3 mile
long, crosses the fin-encircled opening between
the self-pay station at the campground entrance
and Devils Garden Trailhead; thus, campers

**Devils Garden campground is especially scenic**

need not drive to that trailhead to begin their memorable tour of Devils Garden and its numerous arches. A campground fee is charged, and campers are limited to 14 days.

Three widely scattered picnic areas are in Arches. The first lies beneath shade trees deep in Moab Canyon next to the Visitor Center. The second, opposite Balanced Rock, has little shade but features far-ranging panoramas stretching as far away as the lofty La Sal Mountains. The third picnic area lies in the incomparable Devils Garden area, nestled against sheer slickrock fins just short of the campground entrance.

Moab, only 4 miles from Arches, is a small but bustling community that is the hub of recreational activity in the canyon country of eastern Utah. Moab offers a full line of services to meet the needs of most any visitor to canyon country. Groceries, gas, and limited backpacking supplies are available here, as well as four private campgrounds and 14 motels. Those who prefer a guided tour of the canyon country have 13 outfitters from which to choose. Tours range from float trips on the Colorado and Green rivers to jeep trips on any number of 4WD roads in the area.

Camping in the area ranges from spacious private campgrounds around Moab to primitive camping on Bureau of Land Management lands. Many visitors camp alongside the Colorado River upstream from the Moab Bridge along Utah Highway 128, but these sites are overused

and at times the area can be congested. Other primitive sites can be found throughout the area on Bureau of Land Management lands. Two Forest Service campgrounds located alongside lakes high in the La Sal Mountains offer a pleasant refuge from the searing heat of summer.

*For more information on the Park, lodging, guide services, and campgrounds*:

Park Superintendent
Arches National Park
P.O. Box 907
Moab, UT 84532
(801) 259-8161

Moab Visitor Center
805 North Main Street
Moab, UT 84532
(801) 259-8825

Bureau of Land Management
Grand Resource Area Office
P.O. Box M
Moab, UT 84532
(801) 259-8193

U.S. Forest Service
Manti-La Sal National Forest
125 West 200 South
Moab, UT 84532
(801) 259-7155

# Hiking in Arches

Arches has such a wide variety of trails and backcountry routes that it may be difficult to choose among them. The destinations of most trails in the Park are arches, and these trails range in length from 0.1 mile to the 6-mile Devils Garden trail system. Other trails traverse canyons, slickrock, and grassy desert parks. With more than a dozen developed trails, many only a few minutes walk from the trailhead, and large expanses of untracked backcountry, Arches has something for hikers of all abilities.

Most of the developed trails in Arches are fairly short and should present no major difficulties for novice hikers. Exceptions include the Delicate Arch Trail, and the primitive part of the Devils Garden Trail, which should be avoided by acrophobic visitors. Many trails have cairned sections across slickrock, which can be slippery when wet. Backpackers, however, typically use the Park's short trails as means of access to untracked backcountry, where they are free to roam. Hiking in the canyons is largely restricted to wash bottoms, but in open country hikers are limited only by their ability and the extent of their desire to discover the secrets of the desert.

Arches National Park can be enjoyed year-round, but spring and fall usually offer the most comfortable weather. To learn more about hiking seasons, refer to the chapter "Hiking Utah's Desert Parks." Bugs, flash floods, and extreme heat are some of the hazards hikers may encounter in Arches.

There are no dependable water sources in Arches. The only perennial stream, Salt Wash, is too brackish and fouled by cattle to be potable. No backpacker or dayhiker should enter the backcountry without ample water.

Arches contains 70,000 acres of backcountry that has been recommended as or is potential wilderness. Backpackers are free to camp anywhere they choose in this backcountry, with the following exceptions: Campsites must be located at least 1 mile from any road and 1/2 mile from trails. In addition, campsites must be out of sight of trails, out of sight of arches labeled on USGS topographic maps, and a minimum of 300 feet from nonflowing water sources (springs or potholes) and recognizable archaeological sites, such as petroglyphs. A distance of 300 feet from continuously flowing water is encouraged, and 100 feet is required.

Areas of the backcountry open to day use only include Salt Valley, which is closed to camping below the 5040' contour, Fiery Furnace, and Klondike Bluffs, which is closed to camping due to nesting raptors between January 1 and July 15 each year.

Backpack stoves are required in the backcountry, as no open fires are allowed. During periods of extreme fire danger, the Park may be closed to any type of fire.

Biodegradable soaps are required, and they must be used no closer to water sources than 300 feet. Human waste must be buried in soil 4-6 inches deep, and toilet paper must be packed out—not burned.

Refer to the list of Park Service regulations in the "Hiking Utah's Desert Parks" chapter for standard rules that apply to the use of all Utah national parks.

Backpackers, when they obtain the required backcountry permit at the Park Visitor Center, will be informed of any special restrictions that may apply to their camping zone.

The mountain-bike explosion has come to the national parks of Utah, but bikers must remember that they are restricted to designated park roads, and are not allowed in any backcountry area or on trails. The three 4WD roads in Arches (see *Trips 5,6,* and *18*) and the Salt Valley Road are good routes for mountain bikers.

# Driving to Arches' Trailheads

Arches National Park can be reached by driving 26 miles southeast on U.S. 191 from Crescent Junction on Interstate 70, located 20 miles east of Green River, Utah. The signed turnoff to the Park also lies 4 miles northwest of the north end of Moab, and 2 miles from the Colorado River bridge on U.S. 191.

(0.0) From the turnoff in the depths of cliffbound Moab Canyon, the Park road quickly descends past the residences of Park employees.

(0.2) Entrance Station. Entrance fees must be paid to enter the Park. A Park map and information about campsites are available here.

Just beyond the entrance station lies the Park Visitor Center. From there, the Park road curves upward beneath tall cliffs, then switchbacks twice before reaching a southeast-bound grade.

(1.0; 1.2) Stop Number 1. A turnout here offers superb vistas of Moab Canyon, Moab Valley and the town of Moab, beyond which rise the lofty La Sal Mountains. Ahead the road levels out and winds along the foot of impressive 400' cliffs on our left.

(1.0; 2.2) *Trip 1* begins at the signed Park Avenue turnout along the west side of the road at **Trailhead 1**. Ahead the road curves east, then northeast, passing the signed La Sal Mountains Viewpoint spur road (0.3; 2.5) forking right. Curving around a 500' monolith, our road descends toward other outlying monoliths of the Courthouse Towers.

(0.9; 3.4) The North Park Avenue Trailhead (*Trip 1*, **Trailhead 2**) lies below the prominent slickrock shaft of The Organ. This is the northern terminus of the short but rewarding Park Avenue Trail. The road continues on toward Courthouse

Wash, curving around the 300' fin of Tower of Babel. At the bottom of our descent we cross the bridge over signed Courthouse Wash (1.1; 4.5). Limited parking space at **Trailhead 3** is available here for hikers undertaking *Trips 2* and *3*.

Beyond the bridge a steady grade ensues. Contrasting with the low, rolling landscape of the Petrified Dunes to the east is The Great Wall to our left (west), a colonnade of redrock cliffs cut by numerous narrow, steep gullies and alcoves.

(4.2; 8.7) *Trip 4* begins from the Balanced Rock parking area on the right (east) side of the road, at **Trailhead 4**. A picnic area is opposite this trailhead, as is the start for *Trips 5* and *6*, where a dirt road branches west.

The Park road ahead proceeds northeast, cresting a rise and meeting

(0.2; 8.9) The Windows spur road forking right.

The Windows Road climbs as it heads east beneath Ham Rock, and then it curves south.

(1.1; 10.0) The Garden of Eden spur road forks left, quickly leading to a loop at the parking area. The Windows Road ahead leads south and then southeast, passing a series of deep and sometimes overhanging

**Klondike Bluffs**

alcoves.

(1.0; 11.0)  A turnout on the right side of the road offers a convenient point from which to stroll northeast across slickrock into the Cove of Caves. In addition to several deep alcoves, Cove Arch lies at the north end of the cove, while the northwest opening of Double Arch lies at the south end.

(0.2; 11.2)  Stop 10 offers a fine view of the Parade of Elephants and another starting point for a walk into the Cove of Caves. As the road curves around the Parade of Elephants, North Window and Turret Arch come into view straight ahead. Soon the road splits, describing a large loop at its end.

(0.3; 11.4)  Parking near the end of the loop at **Trailhead 5** for *Trip 7* to North and South Windows and Turret Arch.

As we negotiate the loop we'll see enormous Double Arch and pass another parking area along the north side of the road (0.2; 11.6). *Trip 8* to Double Arch begins here at **Trailhead 6**. Beyond this trailhead, we complete the circuit at the roadend and return to the main Park road.

(8.9)  Junction of the main Park road and Windows Road.

The road presently descends northeast across a broad, gentle bench, soon meeting the

(1.0; 9.9)  Panorama Point spur road, forking right. This 0.2-mile spur leads to a loop and overlook on the rim of lower Salt Valley.

(1.3; 11.2)  Junction with side road to Wolfe Ranch, Delicate Arch Trailhead, and Delicate Arch Viewpoint.

Hikers bound for *Trips 9-11* will turn right here. This road is graded dirt, and is passable to most vehicles, but should be avoided during and shortly after wet weather.

The road descends initially among low hills, and eventually crosses Salt Valley Wash and enters the broad floodplain of Salt Wash. Shortly we skirt the shoulder of an east-trending ridge and meet a spur road leading quickly north to

(1.2; 12.4)  The **Trailhead 7** parking area at Wolfe Ranch. *Trip 9* to Lower Salt Wash and

*Trip 10* to Delicate Arch begin here and *Trip 14* hikers must shuttle a car to this parking area. Beyond this spur road, the main dirt road crosses first Salt Wash (usually wet) and then Winter Camp Wash (seasonal). Heavy rains can flood the road and bar progress beyond these drainages. Ahead the eastbound road is wedged between low hills to our south and a taller hill capped by a rimrock to our north.

(1.0; 13.4)  A sign at the next junction indicates Delicate Arch Viewpoint. The graded road turns left here, cutting through Dakota Sandstone as it climbs around the nose of the aforementioned hill. Curving northwest, the road passes through a varicolored band of Brushy Basin Shale, ending in a loop at

(0.3; 13.7) **Trailhead 8**. *Trip 11* begins here.

(11.2)  Junction of the Park road and Wolfe Ranch Road. To gain access to *Trips 12-20*, hikers will continue up the road, while climbing the flanks of Salt Valley in a northwest direction. Shortly beyond Arches' dominant rock formation—the Entrada Sandstone—the signed Salt Valley Overlook spur road (2.3; 13.5) turns sharply to the right. This spur descends slightly for 0.2 mile to end at a loop where an unobstructed vista into lower Salt Valley unfolds. Continuing up the main Park road atop a base of sparsely vegetated red slickrock, we quite soon reach

(0.3; 13.8)  another right-forking spur road signed for Fiery Furnace.

Turning right, we reach the loop and parking area at

(0.2; 14.0)  **Trailhead 9** at the southern terminus of the fins of the Fiery Furnace. *Trip 12* begins here. Ranger-led walks through the Furnace are conducted at 9 A.M. and 1:30 P.M. daily, roughly from April 1 through September, although these dates may change on a yearly basis.

(1.5; 15.3)  Signed Doc Williams Point, a turnout on the left side of the road offers a panoramic viewpoint.

(0.4; 15.7)  *Trips 13* and *14* begin at the signed parking area at **Trailhead 10** on the right side of the road. This trailhead is on the edge of a broad, almost circular grassland at the northern terminus of Fiery Furnace. The roadway ahead skirts fins of the southern Devils Garden, soon meeting

(0.5; 16.2) the dirt Salt Valley Road on our left. Hikers bound for *Trips 18-20* should skip the following description and refer to the Salt Valley Road log below.

From this vicinity of this junction Skyline Arch punctuates the horizon up ahead, and we curve around colorful fins amid scattered pinyons and junipers to

(0.3; 16.5) **Trailhead 11** for *Trip 15* to Skyline Arch, located on the right side of the road. Shortly we reach the loop near the roadend, and branch right, quickly passing a picnic area, and soon thereafter meet

(0.7; 17.2) the right-branching road leading into Devils Garden Campground. *Trip 17* begins in the campground at **Trailhead 12**, 0.6 mile from this junction, next to the restroom just before the loop at the roadend.

Continuing to negotiate the loop on the main park road, we skirt the edge of a circular grassland and soon reach

(0.3; 17.5) the spacious parking area at **Trailhead 13** for *Trip 16*.

## Salt Valley Road, *Trips 18-20*

This road is an infrequently maintained road passable to passenger cars. It should be avoided by all vehicles, however, for a day or so following heavy rains.

(16.2) Turning south from the main Park road on the descending Salt Valley Road, we immediately pass a gate that is closed during inclement weather, then begin winding down into the vast expanse of Salt Valley. Upon reaching the wash draining Salt Valley, our road describes a tight turn toward the northwest. Soon we pass between low red hills, then enter a narrow section of the wash, a dangerous place to be during heavy rains.

The road ahead soon rises over a hill, then descends onto the broad plain of the valley, and follows a northwestward course through the center of the 2-mile-wide valley.

(7.0; 23.2) A signed junction, and **Trailhead 14**, from which *Trip 18* follows the jeep road that forks left (southwest), offering drivers of 4WD vehicles and mountain bikers access to the fringes of Klondike Bluffs. Fifty yards beyond, the road to Tower Arch Trailhead also forks left, heading first west, then curving southwest to

(1.0; 24.2) a small parking area, **Trailhead 15**, at the foot of Klondike Bluffs. This narrow dirt road is passable to most passenger vehicles heading for *Trips 19*.

Continuing up the valley toward the Park boundary, we encounter

(1.7; 24.9) a small, sandy turnout on the right hand (east) side of the road, **Trailhead 16** just short of the Park boundary. *Trip 20* begins here, indicated by a ROAD CLOSED-SCENIC RESTORATION sign.

# Trip 1
## Park Avenue

**Distance**: 0.9 mile, shuttle trip
**Low/High elevations**: 4240'/4560'
**Suited for**: Walk
**Difficulty**: Easy
**Best seasons**: April through mid-June; mid-September through November.
**Map/Trailheads**: 28/1,2
**Hazards**: Negligible

**Introduction**: An easy downhill stroll in a high desert canyon, the Park Avenue Trail leads the hiker among towering slickrock cliffs and stony battlements, nature's counterpart to a city street between lofty skyscrapers. This trip offers a fine introduction to the great monoliths of the Courthouse Towers, plus views of long-ruined arches and of one of the youngest arches visible from any trail in the Park.

**Description**: Beginning with a splendid view of the La Sal Mountains behind us and the cliffs of the Courthouse Towers ahead (0.0; 4560) follow the paved path that leads 100 yards to the Park Avenue Viewpoint. This point offers an awe-inspiring view into the heart of the Court-

**Park Avenue, the Courthouse Towers**

house Towers, where near-vertical redrock fins and towers dominate the scene.

Most Park visitors go no farther, but for a more intimate perspective, bear left just before the viewpoint and follow the dirt trail into the wash below (Park Avenue). Flanked on either side by towering fins (the fins to your right—northeast—are perhaps the eroded remnants of two prehistoric arches), follow the wash downhill among a scattering of twisted Utah juniper, blackbrush, mormon tea, wavy-leaf oak, singleleaf ash, and cliffrose. True to its name, this route is reminiscent of walking among skyscrapers on a city street. The cliffs and fins of Courthouse Towers, composed of the Slick Rock member, stand upon a thinly exposed layer of the comparatively softer, contorted Dewey Bridge member of the Entrada Sandstone.

Soon the floor of our wash-bottom route is dominated by the whitish slickrock of the Navajo Sandstone. Ahead on the northern horizon looms the giant monolith of the Tower of Babel. At 4537 feet elevation, this impressive tower soars nearly 300 feet above its surroundings.

As we approach the Park road near the end of our scenic jaunt, notice a large pinnacle at the north end of the fin on our left (west). Most likely this pinnacle was once the north abutment of an ancient arch, long since collapsed. Such erosional remnants of arches are seen in many places in the Park, but are particularly abundant in the Courthouse Towers region. Here you'll see boulders littering the gap between the pinnacle and the main fin, further evidence that an arch once stood there.

The Three Gossips, a group of three imposing, boulder-capped pinnacles, rise above to the northwest when we pass a trailside display plaque. Then, at an arrow sign under the shadow of the 250' spire of The Organ, we leave the potholed slickrock of the wash and quickly climb to the Park road opposite the North Trailhead (0.9; 4260).

From the viewpoint at this trailhead, aptly named and isolated Sheep Rock rises to the northwest, separated from the main fin by a rather large void. This is perhaps the finest example of a collapsed arch in the Park. Sheep Rock formed the north abutment of what must have been a huge arch. A tiny arch, known as Hole-in-the-Wall or Baby Arch, has penetrated the wall of the main fin to the left of the void. The angular outline of this opening and the boulders littering its base, not yet removed by the forces of erosion, attest to its youth.

# Trip 2
## Upper Courthouse Wash

**Distance**: 12.0 miles round trip to Park
  boundary
**Low/High elevations**: 4120'/4320'
**Suited for**: Dayhike or backpack
**Difficulty**: Easy as an overnight backpack;
  moderate dayhike.
**Best seasons**: April through mid-June; mid-
  September through November.
**Map/Trailhead**: 28/3
**Hazards**: Flash-flood danger; seasonal
  water only, and that is fouled by cattle
  grazing beyond Park boundaries; possible
  quicksand.

**Introduction**: Of the two main canyons in
Arches National Park, Courthouse Wash is more
easily accessible to the average hiker. The Park
highway divides Courthouse Wash into two distinctly different segments. The upper part of the
wash is a sand-bottomed canyon that meanders
for 6 miles among the soaring, salmon-tinted
monoliths and smooth cliffs of the Courthouse
Towers to the west boundary of the Park.

The hike up the wash is a pleasant stroll,
whether it be for only a day or overnight. Numerous sidetrip possibilities beckon to the adventurous, including a route that leads to a
close-up view of the huge span of Ring Arch.
Water flows intermittently in the wash, usually
during spring and after heavy rains. However,
hikers must be sure to purify this water before
drinking, as cattle graze in the drainage beyond
the Park.

Courthouse Wash drains a rather large watershed, and is prone to flash floods. Check the
weather forecast, keep your eyes on the sky, and
heed the warnings of rangers before entering this
or any other desert canyon. Potential campsites
are numerous on benches above the wash. In the
lower reaches of the canyon, these benches are
open and offer little shade, but in the upper
reaches many benches are shaded by tall cottonwoods.

**Description**: From the turnout just north of
the bridge over the wash (0.0; 4140), follow a

worn trail along the north bank of the wash,
avoiding the dense tamarisk and willow thickets
below. Within one-third mile, we descend
slightly into the broad, sandy floor of the wash
and then follow it northwest upstream. Courthouse Wash generally traces the path of the
Courthouse Syncline, a great downwarped segment of the earth's crust cutting from northwest
to southeast through the southwest corner of the
Park. Runoff has carved through the sedimentary
layers, and that erosion has created the awe-inspiring redrock cliffs that surround us.

The wash itself is broad and sandy, gaining
little elevation as it meanders generally northwest among great cliffs of the Entrada Sandstone, decorated with myriad potholes called
solution cavities. After 1 1/4 miles of pleasant,
scenic hiking, you may be lucky enough to spot
the round opening of Ring Arch, 1/2 mile to the
southwest, penetrating the lower flank of a large
dome. It is difficult to spot due to the near-vertical streambank, exposing nearly 12 feet of alluvial deposits. Spanning an opening 64 feet wide
and rising 39 feet above its base, Ring Arch is
the single largest opening in the Courthouse
Towers region. A smaller opening lies just above
Ring Arch. Since this opening spans a steep and
shallow drainage, it may actually be a bridge, but
more likely it is a pothole-type arch. (See *Trip 8*,
Capitol Reef National Park, for more on pothole
arches.)

Large, dripping alcoves, some supporting
lush hanging gardens, and inviting box canyons
offer scenic diversions along the lower 2 1/2
miles of the canyon. The wash boasts a shallow
flow of water during spring and after heavy
summer thunderstorms, and it is then that hikers
will be forced to cross its meandering course
time and again. Many hikers simply go barefoot
through the broad, sandy wash.

As we proceed we notice that the Moab
Tongue of the Entrada Sandstone begins to cap
the great red cliffs that rise above us. At the
contact zone at the base of this tongue there are
occasional seep lines supporting lush but limited
greenery, in stark contrast to the seemingly
bone-dry desert of sand and slickrock that dominates the landscape. In Section 31, at 3 3/4
miles, Sevenmile Canyon joins Courthouse
Wash from the west, draining a wooded plateau

to the southwest, just north of Canyonlands National Park.

Like the prow of a great vessel, a desert-varnished fin separates Sevenmile Canyon from Courthouse Wash, the latter boasting a more energetic flow of water during wetter times. Courthouse Wash grows increasingly narrow above this junction, and as we ascend, the contact zone between the whitish Moab Tongue and the red Slick Rock member of the Entrada lies close at hand, as we have risen toward the upper surface of the Slick Rock member. Fremont cottonwood, boxelder, and Gambel oak grow thickly beneath desert-varnished and lichen-encrusted bluffs of the Moab Tongue. This hard rock, more resistant to erosion and weathering than the Slick Rock member beneath, boasts the most extensive desert-varnished surfaces in upper Courthouse Wash.

Ahead the wash becomes increasingly narrow, another testament to the hardness of the Moab Tongue. Downstream, erosion and weathering are broadening the canyon where the Slick Rock member dominates. Quicksand is ever-present along wet areas of the wash, but presents no great danger for hikers. However, when occasional stray cattle, wandering in from outside the Park, encounter extensive quicksand, their days of wandering usually come to an abrupt end.

Eventually we pass the last hanging garden. At this point, the Slick Rock member has dipped below the surface, and the Moab Tongue now dominates. Eventually though, erosion will expose the Slick Rock member as the intermittent stream continues its never-ending downcutting into underlying rock layers.

The canyon narrows considerably as we proceed through the sandy wash amid the whitish sandstone cliffs of the Moab Tongue, but the canyon walls rise little more than 200 feet above at their highest. As the wall on our left recedes, the opposite wall begins to overhang the wash. Water seeping through this sandstone wall contributes to the flaking off of thin rock layers, further enhancing the overhang.

At 5.6 miles, in Section 30, we proceed among low, dome-capped cliffs to a rock and sandy northeast-trending canyon. This canyon drains Willow Spring, just off the old Park access road 2 miles upstream. Passing among increasing willows and Fremont cottonwoods, you'll reach the barb-wire fence marking the Park boundary (6.0; 4320), 1/3 mile above the last side canyon. Beyond the boundary, the shallow canyon broadens, and hikers will encounter abundant grazing cattle, some of which occasionally manage to find their way into the Park. That part of the canyon offers little in the way of a wilderness experience, so most hikers terminate at the Park boundary.

Return the way you came.

# Trip 3
## Lower Courthouse Wash

**Distance**: 5.3 miles, shuttle trip
**Low/High elevations**: 3960'/4140'
**Suited for**: Dayhike or backpack
**Difficulty**: Moderately easy
**Best seasons**: April through mid-June; mid-September through November.
**Map/Trailhead**: 28/3
**Hazards**: Flash-flood danger; seasonal water only, and that is fouled by cattle.

**Introduction**: This lower part of Courthouse Wash is shallow compared to the part west of the bridge (*Trip 2*), but it is much narrower and its gorge is deeper as it winds among the Navajo Sandstone cliffs and domes of the Petrified Dunes. The canyon walls do become higher and imposing as one proceeds down-canyon, and several branch canyons offer access into the remote Petrified Dunes. The wash is generally wide and sandy, and when water is flowing hikers may get their feet wet. The danger of flash floods is just as great in this narrow gorge as it is in upper Courthouse Wash (*Trip 2*).

**Description**: We can begin our hike into lower Courthouse Wash from one of two points: from the main Park road where it bridges the wash, 4.5 miles from the Park Visitor Center; or from U.S. Highway 191 where it crosses the lower end of Courthouse Wash, 1/3 mile northwest of the Moab Bridge, where the highway crosses the lazy Colorado. This trailhead, with parking limited to maybe two vehicles, lies on the north side of the highway 2 miles east of the Visitor Center and 2 miles northwest of the north end of Moab.

Beginning at the north side of the bridge over the wash on the Park road (0.0; 4140), follow a boot-worn trail leading quickly into the sandy floor of the wash. At first the canyon walls are rather low, but as we proceed the wash cuts deeper into whitish Navajo Sandstone, and the increasingly higher and rounded, sometimes overarching walls, help shade the intermittent stream and its wide, sandy bed. Many hikers walk barefoot here, especially during the stifling heat of summer.

At times rushes form a green line along wetter sections of the wash, while Fremont cottonwoods, willows, tamarisk, and an occasional Russian olive (a large treelike shrub with silvery leaves, originally from Europe, and most often planted as a windbreak in many arid regions of the west) thrive just above the high-water mark.

When the stream is flowing, we will be forced to cross and recross many times. During the first mile and beyond 3 miles, we'll pass a number of sandy benches lying above the wash in its wider parts. Often shaded by Fremont cottonwoods, these benches allow backpackers a pleasant overnight stay in comparative safety above the high-water line, but as a rule, they must pack an adequate water supply. After 1.8 miles from the trailhead, the stream, when flowing, forms a lovely cascade as it tumbles over slickrock ledges.

At times horizontal seepage lines decorate the 150' cliffs above, supporting hanging gardens with plants such as ferns and wildflowers that require a perpetually moist habitat. About 300 yards below the aforementioned slickrock cascades, notice the third in a series of north-trending feeder canyons. This particular canyon makes a fine choice for an interesting sidetrip, as it penetrates deep into the Petrified Dunes section of the Park. However, hikers will need the Arches National Park topographic map to make their way through the Petrified Dunes area.

Shortly beyond this side canyon a seeping alcove on our left (east) supports numerous Gambel oaks in its moist, shady microclimate.

As we progress among increasingly higher slickrock cliffs we'll likely marvel at the impressive aerial acrobatics of the canyon's numerous white-throated swifts. Their pleasant song and that of the canyon wren will serenade us throughout our journey.

Our trek continues among Fremont cottonwoods and boxelder thriving in the comparatively moist canyon bottom. Streaks and patches of desert varnish, occasional seeps and numerous alcoves decorate the canyon walls.

After 4 miles in the middle part of Section 23, the Navajo Sandstone along the wash gives way to the reddish, ledge-forming Kayenta Sandstone, presently capped by white domes of the Navajo. At 4 1/2 miles we pass a stream-gaging station just below a low slickrock waterfall that echoes among the cliffs, and soon the mouth of the canyon opens up to reveal views of distant cliffs in the southwest across the broad flats of Moab Valley.

In the final 1/4 mile, the drone of traffic echoes off the canyon walls, nearly drowning out the melancholy song of canyon wrens. The Park boundary, delineated by a fenceline, is soon encountered, and we quickly reach the highway (5.3; 3960) and the end of our scenic jaunt.

Just before reaching the highway, however, gaze northeast to the canyon wall at the mouth of the wash, and you'll see the remains of the once magnificent Moab Panel. This display of ancient rock has been described as in the Barrier Canyon Style (from its type locality in Barrier Canyon, part of Canyonlands National Park), but it also depicts figures painted by the Anasazi and the Fremont. Unfortunately, vandals destroyed the panel in 1980, and now only a faint outline of the pictograph is visible.

# Trip 4
## Balanced Rock Trail

**Distance**: 0.3 mile semi-loop trail
**Low/High elevations**: 5030'/5055'
**Suited for**: Walk
**Difficulty**: Easy

**Best season**: All year
**Map/Trailhead**: 29/4
**Hazards**: Negligible

**Introduction**: Guarding the approach to the scenic Windows Section of the Park are three redrock monoliths jutting above a gentle highland. The most famous and distinctive of these pinnacles is Balanced Rock. Determining scale in such a setting is often difficult, but the rock itself, seemingly in defiance of gravity, rises 55 feet above a pedestal that itself rises 73 feet above ground level. Composed of the erosion-resistant Slick Rock member of the Entrada Sandstone, Balanced Rock protects the softer pedestal, composed of the Entrada's Dewey Bridge member.

This pleasant stroll not only offers a close-up view of Balanced Rock, but also yields far-reaching vistas of distant mountains, colorful cliffs, and wooded mesas. Balanced Rock and all other arches named on the USGS topographic maps are closed to rock climbing.

**Description**: This trail crests a hill between a monolith fin to the north (Bubo) and imposing Balanced Rock directly above to the south. Its huge boulder appears much larger from beneath than it does from the trailhead. The whitish rock this pinnacle rests upon is the Navajo Sandstone, well exposed across the plateau to the south and southeast. Scattered redrock pinnacles resting atop the Navajo punctuate the landscape and foreground impressive vistas of the La Sal Mountains, a cluster of 12,000' summits on the southeast horizon.

Other notable views include massive Elephant Butte toward the east-southeast, accentuated by the fascinating Parade of Elephants and the openings of Turret Arch and Double Arch, 2 miles distant.

After descending below the east side of Balanced Rock, the route bends west and climbs to a minor gap (0.2; 5055) between that rock and the third of this impressive triad of pinnacles, to the south. We then descend easily northwest to rejoin the access trail, then quickly return to the trailhead (0.1; 5030).

# Trip 5
## Willow Flats Road

**Distance**: 8.0 miles round trip to Park boundary
**Low/High elevations**: 4610'/5050'
**Suited for**: Jeep trip, mountain-bike trip, dayhike
**Difficulty**: Easy 4WD route; moderate mountain-bike trip or hike.
**Best seasons**: April through mid-June; mid-September through November.
**Map/Trailhead**: 29/4
**Hazards**: No water or shade; high-clearance vehicle required.

**Introduction**: The Willow Flats Road is the original access route to what was formerly Arches National Monument. The road heads generally west across an open highland for 4 miles to the Park boundary, ultimately joining U.S. Highway 191. Although the road is shown as a 4WD route on Park maps, carefully driven high-clearance two-wheel-drive vehicles can negotiate it. The route is suitable for nonmotorized recreation, and is a fine choice for the mountain biker. There are no arches along the route; far-reaching vistas and a chance to leave the crowds are this trip's primary attractions.

**Description**: The initial segment of the Willow Flats Road from the Park highway (0.0; 5030) is a smooth, graded dirt road crossing a blackbrush highland dotted with dark-green Utah junipers, leading to a gate and fenceline (0.7; 4970). Closing the gate behind us, we continue straight ahead where a jeep trail, leading toward the Klondike Bluffs and Salt Valley (*Trip 6*), forks right.

Descending westward, our route crosses the broad expanse of Willow Flats, cloaked in bunchgrass, mormon tea, old-man sagebrush, and the ever-present blackbrush. At 1.2 miles the road passes immediately north of a group of low fins composed of the Entrada's Slick Rock member and then passes shrub-cloaked dunes of red sand. Grand vistas extend far to the southwest, beyond the valley containing U.S. Highway 191 to the pinyon- and juniper-clad mesas that extend northwest from Canyonlands National

Park.

The road ahead crosses a small, dry wash (2.0; 4730) and proceeds through sand flats and dunes. The yellow blooms of cryptantha are a common roadside wildflower during springtime. We follow above the north bank of this wash for 0.4 mile before crossing another small wash, above which the route is briefly sandy. Soon we crest a low rise and dip into a normally dry slickrock wash (0.7; 4650). A short detour downstream on foot reveals the perennial seep of Willow Spring, shaded by dense willows and Fremont cottonwoods. Willow Spring was the site of the base camp for Arches National Monument Scientific Expedition in the early 1930s. This 18-man party spent 3 1/2 months mapping the area within the boundaries of the monument, collecting geologic and archaeological data and naming many of the conspicuous features in the area.

Beyond the wash our route passes more low domes, composed of the Entrada's Moab Tongue, tan in color due to a low iron content. From this point the route becomes rougher and crosses abundant slickrock until it reaches another fenceline (0.6; 4630) at the Park boundary. Until repairs are made in the fence, cattle will continue to cross into the Park and graze on the abundant grasses in Willow Flats.

Ahead the route descends for 2 miles to the sandy bottom of Courthouse Wash, and then climbs gently for another 1.7 miles to U.S. Highway 191, 8 miles northwest of the Park Visitor Center. The section of road beyond the confines of the Park is rougher and requires 4WD.

# Trip 6
## Willow Flat Road to Klondike Bluffs Jeep Road

**Distance**: 19.0 miles round trip, excluding sidetrips

**Low/High elevations**: 4790'/5060'

**Suited for**: Jeep trip, mountain bike trip, dayhike, or backpack

**Difficulty**: Easy to moderate 4WD conditions; moderate as a mountain-bike ride; strenuous as a dayhike.

**Best seasons**: April through mid-June; mid-September through November

**Maps/Trailhead**: 29,33/4

**Hazards**: No water or shade; several deep, sandy stretches.

**Introduction**: This scenic jeep route crosses the open, high-desert terrain between the Willow Flats Road and the redrock jumble of fins and spires known as Klondike Bluffs. The trip can be combined with *Trip 18*, on which one has the option of looping back via the Salt Valley Road or driving to the roadend a short distance from Tower Arch.

The jeepway leads northwest just to the west of the long, broken ridge that flanks Salt Valley, passing scenic delights such as Eye of the Whale arch and Herdina Park—an attractive backpacking destination. Terrain encountered enroute ranges from sandstone bluffs to open shrublands and a sandy, cliffbound wash. This is one of the lesser-used areas of the Park, and hikers have ample opportunity for off-trail exploration, if they do not mind hiking part way on a jeep road and carrying water.

Only high-clearance 4WD vehicles should attempt the route, and they might consider taking the trip in reverse, after following the first 1.8 miles of *Trip 18*, since one particularly steep and sandy grade may not be passable in the uphill direction. The route is an excellent choice for the mountain biker, and well-conditioned riders can combine the trip with the Salt Valley Road for an all-day excursion. The tread varies from occasional slickrock to abundant loose sand, so bike riders may be forced to walk parts of the route at times.

**Description**: From the Park and picnic area (0.0; 5030) at **Trailhead 4** near Balanced Rock, follow *Trip 5* to the first junction (0.7; 4970). Branching north from the Willow Flats Road, the rough jeep tracks wind upward amid Utah juniper, blackbrush, mormon tea, and scattered bunchgrasses for 1/2 mile to the crest of a hill. A pause here reveals expansive vistas, including the La Sal Mountains in the southeast, the rolling Abajo Mountains in the south, the broad mesas in the southwest adjoining the north edge of

Canyonlands National Park, and a fine view north and northwest across Salt Valley to a continuous wall of redrock fins from Fiery Furnace to Devils Garden.

Ahead the road bends northwest toward a broad, erosion-dissected dome composed of the Slick Rock member of the Entrada Sandstone. This broad dome-and-fin complex differs markedly from the narrow, parallel fins that dominate the opposite rim of Salt Valley. As we proceed, aptly named Eye of the Whale arch will divert our attention from more distant panoramas.

(1.7; 5000) From here a spur trail leads 0.3 mile south-southwest, offering a first-hand look at this unusual arch. Unfortunately, vandals have decorated the arch with graffiti carved into the sandstone, but the Park Service has removed much of it. The opposite opening is larger (60 feet wide by 27 feet high, compared to the front—northeast—opening of 35 by 11 feet) and more rounded, opening up into a small, slickrock-bounded amphitheater lying just below to the southwest. The broad roof of the arch would provide adequate shelter during a rainstorm.

Proceeding up the main jeep trail, we quite soon reach a set of tracks (0.1; 5020) closed to vehicles for restoration, heading west toward Herdina Park, a very scenic and remote basin popular with backpackers. Forking left toward Herdina Park, we'll glimpse a large, rounded arch partly obscured by the jumble of fins a short distance to the southwest. Called Beckwith Arch after Frank Beckwith, head of the Arches National Monument Scientific Expedition of 1933-34, this span rises 54 feet above its base and opens 47 feet wide between abutments.

The trail becomes faint after 0.4 mile, but hikers can continue cross-country for another mile into Herdina Park, where they can establish a base camp for many rewarding explorations.

Back on the main route, 2.5 miles from the Park highway, pause once again for more intriguing vistas: east-southeast to Elephant Butte, the highest point in the Park at 5653 feet and the centerpiece of The Windows Section, and southeast to the domineering La Sals. Soon, an over-the-shoulder view reveals the monolithic Courthouse Towers foregrounding the distant Abajo Mountains in the south. Vistas also extends northeast into Colorado, where the long

hogback ridge of the Uncompahgre Plateau forms a gently sloping horizon.

Proceeding generally northwest, we pass broken sandstone outcroppings of the whitish Navajo Sandstone and the reddish-brown Dewey Bridge member of the Entrada Sandstone, as well as extensive areas of alluvial and aeolian sand deposits.

At about mile 3.7 the road ahead begins ascending moderately, and soon a sign warns: SAND AHEAD, IMPASSABLE IN SUMMER. Difficult enough to negotiate when moisture has somewhat compacted the sand, this steep, sandy hill can be a barrier to 4WD vehicles during summer when searing heat and drying winds loosen the sand. 4WD travelers should consider taking this trip the opposite direction, going down the hill instead of up. After 0.3 mile, we top out on this sandy grade (1.5; 5060), and from here a revegetated track, closed to motor vehicles, heads 1/2 mile northeast to the rim above Salt Valley, offering superb vistas of much of Arches and the surrounding landscape.

Our road ahead descends amid more sand dunes where fine vistas northwest include the white-capped fingers and fins of the Klondike Bluffs looming 5 1/2 miles ahead. Our meandering road crosses two minor dry washes before climbing briefly to cross the route of the underground Pacific Northwest Pipeline (0.8; 5060), transporting natural gas from New Mexico to Washington state. About 0.6 mile beyond the pipeline, the route crests a broad, minor rise beginning a gentle, protracted descent.

A large butte 2.5 miles west of the rise dominates that view. This butte displays formations present in lower Salt Valley in the vicinity of Wolfe Ranch: the Cedar Mountain Formation, of early Cretaceous age, caps the mesa, while the mudstones of the Brushy Basin member of the Morrison Formation, of Late Jurassic age, forms the slopes.

After descending from the aforementioned rise, the route reaches the floor of a shallow, sandy wash and curves west-southwest for 1/2 mile. After passing beneath low bluffs capped by the white Moab Tongue of the Entrada, we reach a north-trending wash (1.7; 4740) and follow it up-canyon. The soft sand in this wash slows progress considerably for hikers and mountain bikers.

Ahead, corrugated sandstone walls close in as the wash briefly narrows. Soon, Navajo Sandstone domes displaying intricate cross-bedding crop out immediately to the north. When the Navajo coalesces with the narrowing wash, we leave it, climbing above its northeast bank for a 0.3-mile stint through the woodland. The route then briefly dips back into the wash before climbing out once again. Eroded domes of Entrada Sandstone rise abruptly in the southwest while gentler slopes of the Navajo rise in the northeast. Increasingly common is a crust of cryptogamic soil, helping to anchor the clay soils between shrubs in this area.

After climbing steadily, our route tops a rise, then descends amid brush-anchored sand dunes toward an imposing rank of redrock pinnacles called Marching Men. Reaching a three-way junction (3.0; 4900), we can go right (northeast) for 1.8 miles to Salt Valley Road; go left (southwest) 1.5 miles to the western trailhead for Tower Arch, lying in the heart of the Klondike Bluffs, one of the most scenic collections of fins, domes, and pinnacles in Arches (see *Trip 18*); or return to the trailhead.

# Trip 7
## North Window, Turret Arch, and South Windows Trails

**Distance**: Up to 1.1 miles, loop trip
**Low/High elevations**: 5160'/ 5300'
**Suited for**: Walk
**Difficulty**: Easy
**Best seasons**: April through mid-June; mid-September through November.
**Map/Trailhead**: 30/5
**Hazards**: Negligible

**Introduction**: A network of short but very scenic trails begins at the roadend in The Windows Section of the Park. These popular trails can be arranged into a variety of interesting loop hikes that visit some of the best-known and easily accessible arches in the Park. More experienced hikers may wish to loop back to the trailhead from South Window via the so-called primitive trail, leaving the crowds behind and enjoying broad panoramas.

For backpackers, The Windows is the jumping-off place for cross-country exploration of the Petrified Dunes to the south, a 20-square-mile area of slickrock domes and narrow canyons composed of Navajo Sandstone.

**Description**: The wide trail to The Windows, beginning at 5160 feet, leads southeast across a blackbrush-dotted flat for 0.1 mile and then forks. The right fork climbs gently southeast for another 0.1 mile to a trail that branches right, quickly leading to Turret Arch. The right-fork trail then heads east for less than 0.1 mile to a junction with the left-fork trail, meeting between the North and South windows. Along either route both windows are visible.

If you take the short trail to Turret Arch you'll see that, unlike many arches in the Park, this arch's opening is taller than it is wide, 64 feet high versus 39 feet wide. Two smaller openings penetrate this large, isolated hogback fin. The larger is 12 feet wide by 13 feet high; the smaller is only 8 feet high by 4 1/2 feet wide. From Turret Arch the short trail heads northeast, quickly ending where the principal right- and left-fork trails join. The left-fork trail leads back north to North Window, while the right-fork trail heads south to South Window.

If, back at the junction 0.1 mile from the parking area, you branch east onto the left-fork trail, you'll follow this rock-lined trail easily up over Navajo Sandstone slickrock. Just north of North Window is an arch-like alcove. On the opposite side of the alcove, as viewed from the primitive trail, yet another alcove has formed. This is a good example of how many arches form in the Park. As erosion and weathering continue, an even larger opening will form. Hence this alcove has been dubbed "Arch-in-the-Making."

One-fourth mile from the start of the left-fork trail brings us to the opening of North Window, more appropriately termed an arch since it's based at ground level instead of being perched above. This opening is at the contact of two members of the Entrada Sandstone: the lower half of the abutments of North Window is made up of the basal unit of the Entrada, the

**North Window**

Dewey Bridge member, which forms the base of most arches in the Park. This locale is an excellent spot in which to observe the nature of this comparatively soft rock, featuring a contorted, blocky, irregular surface.

In contrast to this rock unit, the overlying and consequently younger Slick Rock member of the Entrada forms the top of the arch as well as the crest of the large fin through which the arch has penetrated. This rock is quite smooth, exhibiting often sheer, unjointed cliffs.

As the softer Dewey Bridge member weathers and erodes away, the openings are often enlarged. Vistas framed by large North Window (51 feet high by 93 feet wide) are exceptional, reaching east across miles of great redrock mesas and cliffs bounding the invisible gorge of the Colorado River.

The trail proceeds south for about 150 yards to a junction with the right-fork and Turret Arch trails. The left-fork trail is bound for South Window. This junction lies below a large, nose-like protrusion between North and South windows.

After briefly leading south, the left-fork trail

rounds the nose-like fin and quickly reaches the expansive opening of South Window. Penetrating the redrock fin farther above ground than its northern counterpart, this opening would more appropriately fit the "window" designation, although its roof is arched as well.

An interesting trail looping back to the parking area east of The Windows begins at South Window. Designated a primitive trail, the route is nevertheless easy to follow, though its tread is not excessively wide and graded as are the primary Windows trails. It offers expansive vistas and a brief opportunity to escape the throngs of tourists pounding out the main trails in The Window Section. From the foot of South Window, cairns lead the way along a small, east-trending wash. The trail becomes more apparent as it quickly arcs to the north, both windows soon coming into view as we traverse below and east of them.

Wallflower, which has a cluster of yellow flowers borne on a single stalk, is a common springtime blossom here, growing among pinyons, junipers, blackbrush, mormon tea, wavy-leaf oak, singleleaf ash, yucca, and prickly pear, which boasts its own vivid blooms in late spring.

Soon the trail crosses the slickrock opposite a large, tunnel-like alcove. Weathering and gravity will, in the not-too-distant future, cause this alcove and another on the opposite side of the fin to merge, adding another arch to the catalog of openings in the Park. Our easy-to-follow trail descends slightly, and we can gaze east beyond the almost imperceptible gash of Salt Wash's lower canyon to broad Dry Mesa, laced by several mineral exploration roads 3 miles to the east.

Ahead a short stretch across slickrock ensues, bringing us to a gap in the fin between two interesting pinnacles. From the gap, our trail descends quickly west into the broad head of a wash. After reaching the brushy flats below, the trail meanders southwest to the nearby trailhead to complete this pleasant, scenic, albeit short, loop, 0.6 mile from South Window.

# Trip 8
## Double Arch Trail

**Distance**: 0.4 mile round trip
**Low/High elevations**: 5120'/5200'
**Suited for**: Walk
**Difficulty**: Easy
**Best seasons**: April through mid-June; mid-September through November.
**Map/Trailhead**: 30/6
**Hazards**: Negligible

**Introduction**: This easy and highly scenic stroll is suitable for hikers of every ability. Double Arch, above the trail's end, is the second largest natural rock opening in the Park. Its eastern arch spans 160 feet between abutments and rises 105 feet above the ground. The smaller western arch opens into the Cove of Caves, and is 60 feet wide and 61 feet high.

**Description**: From the signed trailhead (0.0; 5150), the wide trail undulates over a corrugated flat, dotted with scattered junipers and the ubiquitous blackbrush. Double Arch lies ahead to the northwest, just to the left of a keyhole-shaped

alcove suspended high on the wall above the flats. Nearby lies a larger, similarly shaped alcove known as Archaeological Cave. In the 1930s evidence that ancient Indians used this cave was discovered by the Arches National Monument Scientific Expedition (see *Trip 5*).

The trail passes the east side of Parade of Elephants, and ends beneath the larger, easternmost span (0.2; 5200). Double Arch is one of the most interesting spans in the Park, and it actually boasts three openings if you consider the opening on top between the two arches. The top, or third, opening may be a pothole-type arch, and the formation of the pothole and the consequent concentration and seepage of groundwater probably led to the formation of alcoves and ultimately Double Arch. A tiny opening at the top of the larger arch is forming along a horizontal joint. This may eventually lead to a partial collapse of the arch's roof, thus further enlarging the span.

Hikers scrambling into the smaller opening will have a fine view of the Cove of Caves and Cove Arch to the northwest.

# Trip 9
## Lower Salt Wash—Delicate Arch Trailhead to the Colorado River

**Distance**: 13.4 miles round trip
**Low/High elevations**: 3970'/4280'
**Suited for**: Dayhike or backpack
**Difficulty**: Moderate
**Best seasons**: April through mid-June; mid-September through November.
**Map/Trailhead**: 30/7
**Hazards**: Flash-flood danger; creek and salt springs not potable; no trail; biting gnats and flies.

**Introduction**: The lower part of Salt Wash, from Wolfe Ranch to the Colorado River, offers one of the most remote wilderness hikes in Arches. There is no trail in the canyon to guide hikers, but following the narrow wash is easy. When the creek is flowing, usually during spring and immediately after heavy rains, hikers must constantly crisscross its intermittent flow. Campsites are scarce, but a diligent search will often reveal a suitable site on a bench above the wash, particularly along the first 2 miles of the canyon and again as one approaches the Colorado River. Biting gnats and flies are a constant annoyance from spring until late summer or autumn. The canyon can be as hot as an oven during summer, and it should then be avoided. Be sure to carry all the water you will need.

The canyon's scenery is much different from that in other parts of the Park. Boulder-littered slopes and steep, broken cliffs composed of the Chinle Formation, the Wingate Sandstone, and the Kayenta Formation rise as much as 1200 feet from the floor of the wash, making this the deepest defile in the Park.

Hiking the initial segment of the route to the portal of the canyon can be a nightmare, since the entire floodplain is covered in a vast thicket of thorny greasewood bushes, sagebrush, and rabbitbrush. Once in the canyon, however, the hiking is much easier; still the wash is more rugged and boulder-strewn than other canyons in the Park.

**Description**: From the parking area at Wolfe Ranch (0.0; 4280), walk back to the main road and turn left (east), following it across Salt Wash to where nearby Winter Camp Wash crosses the road. Leave the road here and proceed almost due south, east of Winter Camp Wash, across the shrubby flats toward the portal of Salt Wash slicing into tall, reddish cliffs of Wingate Sandstone.

After about 0.4 mile from the road, depending upon how many zigzags one makes while avoiding brush thickets, we should intersect the small, sandy avenue of Cache Valley Wash, which we follow southwest for 1/4 mile, more or less, to broad Salt Wash. We now turn downstream (south), and we may notice an interesting small, fleshy plant—iodine bush, or pickleweed—colonizing the alkaline floodplain at the canyon's entrance. This small plant has jointed, fleshy green leaves, similar in appearance to the leaves of junipers.

As we proceed down-canyon, towering, upward-thrusting cliffs of red Wingate Sandstone begin to flank the canyon on either side, rising above talus-littered slopes of reddish Chinle Formation mudstones and shales. We will see such colorful slopes and cliffs, capped by bluffs of Kayenta Sandstone, throughout our journey to the Colorado River. Unlike the sheer cliffs in Capitol Reef National Park, the Wingate cliffs in lower Salt Wash are broken by ledges, but these tall cliffs are spectacular nonetheless.

Ahead we follow the serpentine canyon first left, then right, then back and forth again and again. Quicksand, present in spring or after substantial runoff, should be avoided, but it is usually easy to extract your feet if you sink in it.

Most of the tamarisk has been left behind upon entering the canyon, but our progress will be hampered by the boulder- and cobble-strewn wash, a marked contrast to the smooth, sandy floor of Courthouse Wash. During the first 2 miles, we'll pass beneath several grassy benches clad in scattered sagebrush, greasewood, saltbush, and Utah juniper.

Salt Wash is considered the only perennial stream in the Park, but nevertheless it flows only intermittently most of the time. As we proceed the canyon becomes progressively narrow, and

**Salt Springs in lower Salt Wash**

the ledgy cliffs above are colored brown, black and metallic blue by desert varnish. After 3.6 miles we'll pass a series of springs, one of which gushes forth from a crack in solid rock. We may initially believe we have found an excellent source of fresh water, but one taste reveals the springs to be much too salty.

A variety of wildflowers garnishes the canyon floor from spring into summer. Especially brilliant are the orange blooms of globe mallow, most abundant during June in most years. In autumn a parade of yellow blooms bursts forth, the final bloom of the season, thanks to the rabbitbrush that is so widespread in the canyon.

As we negotiate the final 1 1/2 miles to the Colorado River, the canyon becomes increasingly rock-strewn. Finally we exit the Park 1/4 mile before reaching the wide Colorado opposite Utah Highway 128 (6.7; 3970). Mat Martin Point, its mesa clad in a pinyon-juniper woodland, rears its 1200' walls skyward beyond the river. Unfortunately, there is no beach along the river, just dense thickets of tamarisk, and campsites are virtually nonexistent.

Return the way you came.

# Trip 10
## Delicate Arch Trail

**Distance**: 3.0 miles round trip
**Low/High elevations**: 4280'/4840'
**Suited for**: Dayhike
**Difficulty**: Moderate
**Best seasons**: April through mid-June; mid-September through November.
**Map/Trailhead**: 30/7
**Hazards**: No water or shade; steep dropoffs.

**Introduction**: Park visitors with time enough to hike only one or two short trails should put the trail to Delicate Arch at the top of their priorities. This trip is arguably the most scenic of all the hikes in the Park, since it climbs slickrock slopes, passes hanging gardens thriving in hidden alcoves, and ends at a dramatic overlook of the Park's most famous rock span, a lone, arching ribbon of stone aptly named Delicate Arch.

Vistas enroute are superb, ranging from vast expanses of slickrock to wooded mesas and sheer cliffs and the lofty La Sal Mountains, which form an impressive backdrop of alpine peaks approaching 13,000 feet in elevation.

At the end of the trip is a narrow catwalk of trail, carved into the face of a sheer cliff. Acrophobic hikers might instead consider the shorter trail to Delicate Arch Viewpoint (*Trip 11*) for a fine, but more distant, view of this isolated span of stone.

**Description**: This popular trail begins at the site of Wolfe Ranch (0.0; 4280), the only homestead ever established in what is now Arches National Park. Beyond a cabin our trail crosses, via suspension bridge, the perennial, alkaline stream draining Salt Wash. First it heads across a greasewood-clad flat, then it climbs onto the coarse Salt Wash Sandstone.

Just before a switchback, we certainly don't want to miss a short, left-branching spur trail to a Ute Indian pictograph panel, one of only two rock-art sites easily accessible in the Park. This fine pictograph depicts riders on horseback, bighorn sheep (an important food source to native peoples), and what appear to be two dogs. They are believed to be of relatively recent origin, since horses were not introduced to the area's Ute people until the early 1700s.

Presently a view of South Window captures our attention to the south across Cache Valley. A towering wall of Wingate Sandstone flanks each side of the portal of lower Salt Wash, viewed across the valley to the south.

Beyond a bench our smooth, rock-lined trail soon drops into the jumbled topography of an east-west fault zone. As the trail begins to rise through this corrugated landscape, we soon pass into the red shales of the Tidwell member of the Morrison Formation, where slopes are punctuated by numerous large siliceous outcroppings. Climbing a red-colored hill and leaving the corrugated basin, we can glimpse in the wall to our north a split-level alcove resplendent with the verdant growth typical of seep-fed hanging gardens.

On the slickrock of the Moab Tongue, cairns lead the way and steps cut into the slickrock help us gain elevation on steeper stretches. Above this slickrock grade we level off, passing through a fascinating landscape of low, cross-bedded Moab Tongue Sandstone, and climbing into a shallow draw. Plant life in this slickrock desert finds a toehold wherever sand and silt have collected, enduring extreme heat and drought as well as torrential downpours. Backpackers can leave this draw before the trail begins traversing the cliff, and strike out north across a remote juniper-dotted plateau high above Salt Wash.

Soon our trail traverses the nearly vertical north face of a slickrock fin, clinging to the sheer cliff like a narrow catwalk. We quickly pass beneath small Twisted Doughnut Arch, and when we crest the fin (1.5; 4840), we are confronted with a magnificent, not-soon-to-be-forgotten sight.

Lonely Delicate Arch, with a span between abutments of 33 feet, rising to a height of 45 feet, frames the lofty La Sal Mountains, second highest in Utah, on the southeast horizon. This point is a popular destination with photographers, particularly at sunset. This beautiful arch is justifiably the most photographed feature in the park. But other, distant horizons beg for our attention as well. The extensive wall of the Book Cliffs rises above the vast desert lands on the northern horizon. A number of lofty mesas foreground the La Sal Mountains in the southeast. Closer at hand in the west lies the maze of spires and fins of the Fiery Furnace, seen across a white slickrock tableland composed of the Moab Tongue Sandstone. Take notice of that rock's jointed nature, a result of stresses imposed by the upward-bulging Salt Valley Anticline. In each one of the north-south-trending joints soil has collected, supporting thick vegetation.

A small bowl lies below Delicate Arch, and below it invisible cliffs plummet into the depths of Winter Camp Wash. Farther south lies Cache Valley, its floor rising gently southward past stark hills of Mancos Shale, which grades into the red shales of the Chinle Formation. Above, ledgy cliffs of Wingate Sandstone rise steeply to a broad tableland composed of the Kayenta Formation, sparsely clad in shrubs and pygmy forest. The latter three rock units will be familiar to visitors of Capitol Reef National Park, but they are prominent in Arches only in the lower Salt Wash area.

Towering Elephant Butte, the high point of the Park, rises above the Kayenta tableland, and our view also includes the distant opening of South Window. Colorful greenish slopes of the Cedar Mountain Formation and Brushy Basin Shale dominate our view into Salt Valley to the southwest. We may also notice that an alcove is forming in the fin to our west, directly opposite the small alcove we passed before reaching Twisted Doughnut Arch. From Delicate Arch, return the way you came.

# Trip 11
## Delicate Arch Viewpoint

**Distance**: 0.8 mile round trip
**Low/High elevations**: 4400'/4600'
**Suited for**: Walk
**Difficulty**: Moderately easy
**Best seasons**: April through mid-June; mid-September through November.
**Map/Trailhead**: 30/8
**Hazards**: Slickrock scrambling, steep dropoffs.

**Introduction**: Park visitors without the time or energy to hike to Delicate Arch can nevertheless enjoy a fine view of that beautiful span from an unusual perspective by following the short trail from the Delicate Arch Viewpoint parking area above Cache Valley. The trail crosses much slickrock, and a sheer cliff plunges 200 feet from the trail's end, so caution is advised and parents must closely supervise children.

**Description**: From the north side of the loop at the roadend (0.0; 4450), this trail heads generally northeast, winding amid scattered junipers and mormon tea. A variety of shrubs and spring wildflowers is near as we climb a boulder-littered hill atop Salt Wash Sandstone. We'll ascend through the red rocks of the Tidwell member, then ascend slickrock slopes of the Moab Tongue, following cairns as we do.

Our route ends (0.4; 4600) at the brink of sheer cliffs that plunge 200 feet into Winter Camp Wash, its cottonwood-lined course disappearing into the slickrock to the northeast. A prominent sandstone monolith, dubbed Rock Setee, juts above the wash, while above the north walls of the canyon lies a slickrock bowl stretching to the skyline, decorated by isolated stone pinnacles and solitary Delicate Arch, 0.4 mile away. This graceful, aptly named span is considered the symbol of the park, and it is seen on roadside signs and covers of numerous Park publications. After enjoying this unusual perspective of Delicate Arch, we backtrack to the car.

# Trip 12
## Fiery Furnace

**Distance**: 0.75 mile, loop trip
**Low/High elevations**: 4650'/4800'
**Suited for**: Dayhike, ranger-guided
**Difficulty**: Moderately easy
**Best season**: April through September
**Map/Trailhead**: 29/9
**Hazards**: Much slickrock scrambling, no
   water.

**Introduction**: This ever-popular ranger-guided hike offers a tantalizing introduction to the incredible Fiery Furnace, a labyrinth of narrow passageways and towering redrock fins. Going on one of the guided walks, conducted at 9 A.M. and 1:30 P.M. each day from spring through September, offers fascinating insights into the natural history of the slickrock maze.

Hikers are advised not to enter the Fiery Furnace on their own, since in its maze of dead-end defiles one can easily become disoriented. But to experienced desert hikers, the Fiery Furnace offers challenge, solitude, and a number of hidden arches awaiting discovery.

Anyone entering Fiery Furnace (or hiking on any of the Park's trails) should wear sturdy, rubber-soled shoes, as the route crosses much slickrock where traction is necessary for safe footing.

**Description**: The ranger-led walk explores narrow, shaded chasms between nearly vertical and sometimes overhanging slickrock walls,

some towering nearly 200 feet. Hidden grottoes, arches, and even a small natural bridge carved by running water are also explored.

Hikers will climb slickrock and negotiate narrow, sandy wash bottoms that see little sunlight even during high summer. "Moki stairs" have been cut into the slickrock in places to aid passage over steeper stretches. You'll visit Surprise Arch, located in a narrow fin between two slot-like chasms, possibly formed with the aid of running water in the westernmost of the watercourses, which flows beneath the span during runoff. But it also may have been formed by typical arch-forming processes—jointing and slab failure.

One particularly notable arch visited on the hike is Skull Arch, an eerie sight with its empty "eye sockets" peering down at visitors in a deep, shady canyon.

# Trip 13
## Sand Dune and Broken Arches

**Distance**: 1.2 miles round trip
**Low/High elevations**: 5180'/5320'
**Suited for**: Walk
**Difficulty**: Moderately easy
**Best seasons**: April through mid-June; mid-
   September through November.
**Map/Trailhead**: 31/10
**Hazards**: Negligible

**Introduction**: Not only does this pleasant jaunt offer access to two lovely arches, but the trail boasts far-flung vistas and allows the hiker to observe a curious distribution of desert plants. Each plant in this high desert country has certain environmental requirements, and their distribution depends on local environmental conditions. On this short hike, we'll notice that grasses and certain shrubs thrive in deep, well-drained soils, but as one approaches slickrock and the soil cover becomes shallow, shrubs such as black-brush come to dominate. And growing at the very foot of the fins of Devils Garden and Fiery Furnace, where bedrock lies just below the surface, are pinyon and juniper.

**Description**: From the trailhead (0.0; 5180) our sandy trail strikes out northeast, below and impressive array of salmon-hued slickrock fins. Blackbrush, Indian ricegrass and mormon tea dominate the vegetation in the broad flat between Devils Garden to our north and the fins of Fiery Furnace above us in the south. After skirting the south edge of the flat for 100 yards, we reach the trail to Sand Dune Arch on our right and the longer trail to Broken Arch on our left.

Turning right, we plunge into the fins via a narrow crack. We work our way southeast up the small, sand-floored joint flanked by tall, steep-walled fins, reaching the small dune beneath the arch that gave this span its name 200 yards from the junction. This small opening, 30 feet long and only 8 feet high, is formed entirely within the Entrada's Slick Rock member. This is a delightful locale, and it receives little sunlight. Narrow joints, found on the opposite side of the arch, would be good scrambling terrain for experienced hikers.

Return 200 yards to the aforementioned junction and bear right (north) onto the sandy red trail that leads 0.4 mile across the flat. In 0.1 mile we cross a faded set of jeep tracks trending northeast-southeast across the flat, marking the underground route of the Pacific Northwest Pipeline.

Ahead, Broken Arch lies on the north margin of the flat, beyond which rises a maze of tall, colorful fins. A variety of grasses, prickly pear, blackbrush, mormon tea, four-wing slatbush, and winterfat—an important winter browse for mule deer—are all found in this grassland environment. After a gentle stint across the flat, we arrive at a junction (0.7; 5180). The left fork climbs through the fins to a campground in 1/2 mile (see *Trip 17*). But we bear right, curving northeast along the foot of the fins. Notice the pinyons and junipers crowding the sandy flats at the foot of those fins. Since virtually all rainwater runs off the slickrock, flats like these at the foot of the cliffs receive considerable moisture in addition to what falls on them. Also, it is likely that slickrock lies not far underground, capturing much of this moisture in subsurface potholes. Hence these trees have found a suitable habitat, and grow thickly and to atypical sizes. By contrast, the flat we previously traversed does not

support any trees; its deep soils are unable to hold adequate moisture in the root area.

Finally we dip into a slickrock gully and climb briefly to the arch (0.1; 5200). Broken Arch's opening is 43 feet high and 59 feet wide. Capped by white, wind-deposited Moab Tongue Sandstone, it is largely composed of the Slick Rock member. The arch penetrates an east-west-trending fin standing well above the aforementioned gully. This arch isn't actually broken, but there is a deep notch in the caprock atop the arch. The base of the arch is littered with the buff-colored boulders fallen from the Moab Tongue that caps the fin.

Vistas through the rock-framed opening are far-ranging, stretching from the lofty La Sals in the southeast to the Uncompahgre Plateau—site of an ancient mountain range that supplied much of the sediments for the Arches region—on the northeast horizon. From Broken Arch we retrace our route to the trailhead.

# Trip 14
## Clover Canyon to Upper Salt Wash and Wolfe Ranch

**Distance**: 8.25 miles shuttle trip
**Low/High elevations**: 4280'/5180'
**Suited for**: Dayhike or backpack
**Difficulty**: Strenuous
**Best seasons**: April through mid-June; mid-September through November.
**Maps/Trailheads**: 31,32,30/10,7
**Hazards**: Slickrock scrambling; flash-flood danger; miles of bushwhacking; route finding; water not potable.

**Introduction**: This is a demanding cross-country hike not recommended for novice hikers. But the rewards of finding your own way and bushwhacking through tangled thickets are great. The slickrock-bound canyon of Salt Wash is one of the most beautiful areas of the Park, but an area very few hikers ever explore. To complete the trip, plan on shuttling a car to Wolfe Ranch, and bear in mind that the waters of Salt

Wash are not drinkable, so carry all the water you will need.

**Description**: Our journey begins at the Sand Dune-Broken Arch Trailhead (0.0; 5180) (*Trip 13*). From here we follow the trail 100 yards to a junction and turn left toward Broken Arch. Upon intersecting the old pipeline road after another 0.1 mile, we have two options: (1) follow this old road east and then northeast, outflanking Clover Canyon entirely; or (2) for a more appealing, primitive experience continue north about 100 yards to the head of Clover Canyon and follow its inconspicuous headwaters wash northeastward.

Where the small wash cuts into the off-white-colored Moab Tongue, the gorge deepens and we'll be forced to detour around a few dry waterfalls and snag-choked narrows. Beyond those obstructions the wash broadens and its gradient slackens. At times the watercourse runs across sparkling, heat-reflecting sandstone as we descend.

After 1 1/2 miles the Moab Tongue is squeezed into the vicinity of the wash, while reddish shale hills of the Tidwell member of the Morrison Formation flank us to the north and south. At about 2 miles graceful Fremont cottonwoods begin to embrace the wash in damp-grassy stretches, and the clover from which the canyon takes its name becomes quite abundant along sheltered banks.

Soon we reach an orange sign (2.6; 4630) that indicates a gas pipeline lies south of the wash. We then cross its dynamited swath, which cuts across the wash toward the northeast, and quite soon reach the brink of an overhanging, 100-foot pourover (dry waterfall) that may mark the end of the hike for some. Here the wash plummets over the cliffs, which form a natural amphitheater, embracing the lower canyon on three sides. These overhanging walls are virtually impassable. Lower Clover Canyon, densely clad in cottonwoods and other riparian vegetation, winds eastward to Salt Wash, visible 1 mile below to the east.

There are two feasible routes into Salt Wash from this point. Rock climbers may choose to traverse slickrock for 0.3 mile, first southeast and then south, into a Clover Canyon tributary. The traverse ends just above a slot-like dry wa-

terfall dropping 25 feet into the canyon below. The dry fall can be descended with the aid of a rope, but then one must cope with over 1 mile of dense vegetation in lower Clover Canyon to reach Salt Wash. For hikers, there is an easy route into the wash, made possible by the works of man. We can follow the old pipeline road just north of the pourover. It leads us first east, then north, above the cliffs, for 0.6 mile to the swath under which the pipeline lies.

This swath bisects the slickrock in a northeast direction, and a scramble down that swath via loose rock leads us to Salt Wash (0.9; 4410), 250 feet below and 0.2 mile from the rim. We cross the saline stream and climb the east bank to the terrace above. We can either follow the wash downstream, battling quicksand and tangled willows and tamarisk, or go south on the terrace east of the wash. But this route is not without its obstructions. The beautiful slickrock walls that flank the canyon shed enormous quantities of water during summer deluges. When all this runoff reaches the deep, red alluvium in the canyon bottom, myriad narrow, vertical-walled channels, or arroyos, are formed.

As we proceed south through the greasewood-clad terrace, sometimes following cattle trails, we most often won't be aware of these deep channels until we reach them. Thus, we will be forced to detour upstream along them until we find a suitable point for entry and exit, only to resume our terrace-top stroll and be confronted with one deep channel after another.

However, this is a wild, magnificent canyon, and the slickrock scenery more than compensates for the inconvenience of numerous detours. Smooth, rounded slopes of slickrock rise steadily on either side, topped by a nearly vertical band of tan-colored sandstone and ending abruptly along broad mesas. Along much of the west walls of the canyon, hanging gardens thrive, resplendent with water-loving vegetation—a marked contrast to the sun-baked slickrock desert that dominates the landscape for miles around. Campsites can be located anywhere along the stream terraces.

After hiking about 1 1/2 miles downstream, we come to the mouth of Lost Spring Canyon. Embraced by slickrock walls comparable to those in Salt Wash, this canyon, with its intermittent stream from the northeast, makes a fine sidetrip for hikers with extra time to spend, and reveals many surprises.

The mouth of that canyon presents no obstacles, and soon we are on our way south. In about 1/2 mile, we enter the Park, but soon walls close in from the east, the terrace pinches out, and we are forced into the bed of Salt Wash. Tamarisk and willow quickly begin to form nearly impenetrable thickets, and these plus an abundance of quicksand and sticky mud make the final 3 1/2 miles to Wolfe Ranch a grueling, challenging hike. Those who cursed the presence of cattle upstream on Bureau of Land Management lands will be thankful for the narrow corridors these animals have blazed through the thickets—but even so our packs will likely be hung up on the tangled branches time and again.

The stream must be crossed numerous times, but we should pause and enjoy the superlative scenery, for there is great beauty around us, and all is not tamarisk thickets and quicksand. Finally, the sandstone walls, lush hanging gardens, and intriguing alcoves diminish, and mudstone and shale hills begin to enclose the canyon's mouth. Immediately past the mouth, about 1/2 mile from the Wolfe Ranch Trailhead, Freshwater Canyon joins from the west. This intriguing canyon, with its freshwater spring, is an interesting sidetrip, or a fine dayhike from Wolfe Ranch.

Thrashing through the last of the tamarisk thickets and climbing up to the east bank of the wash, we bushwhack one final time to reach the 100-foot-long suspension bridge across Salt Wash and stroll to our shuttled car at Wolfe Ranch (4.75; 4280).

# Trip 15
## Skyline Arch

**Distance**: 0.4 mile round trip
**Low/High elevations**: 5160'/5200'
**Suited for**: Walk
**Difficulty**: Easy
**Best seasons**: April through mid-June; mid-September through November.

**Map/Trailhead**: 31/11
**Hazards**: Negligible

**Introduction**: This very short walk is usually bypassed by hikers bound for longer routes or the promise of solitude in the Park's backcountry. But the hike to Skyline Arch offers anyone willing to walk a close-up view of a large opening high a sheer sandstone cliff.

Skyline Arch is a familiar landmark to visitors staying in the Devils Garden Campground; and drivers on Interstate 70 near Thompson can view the arch from 10 miles away, the only opening in the Park visible from that highway.

Features in the Park are ever-changing, but most changes that visitors can experience are relatively minor. The blowing of sand and the transport of silt, sand and rocks by flash floods are the most commonly observed geological processes. But features such as arches may take many human lifetimes to develop, and rarely do we witness events that dramatically reshape the land. One such even went unobserved in November 1940, when a large block of sandstone fell from the opening of Skyline Arch, nearly doubling the size of the span.

**Description**: Within sight of our destination, our short jaunt begins (0.0; 5160) by climbing gently north, alternating between sand and red slickrock, passing scattered junipers and pinyons, blackbrush, mormon tea, cliffrose and singleleaf ash. Yellow cryptantha is a particularly noticeable trailside wildflower during spring.

Quickly climbing past a prominent fin rising on our left, we'll notice it is composed of a rock of a slightly different character than the Skyline Arch cliff ahead. The base of this fin is composed of the easily eroded, contorted beds of the Dewey Bridge member of the Entrada Sandstone. In color, it is a deeper red than the Slick Rock member, and instead of forming smooth domes and sheer cliffs, it tends to form irregular cliffs and is often honeycombed by solution cavities.

After we are squeezed between low domes, we break into the open in a blackbrush-clad flat, then dip into an erosion-widened joint to reach the trail's end (0.2; 5200), where fins tower above us to the north and south. Here we enjoy a neck-stretching look at Skyline Arch, directly above to the north, high up on smooth cliff. The jumble of angular boulders at its base are remnants of the huge slab that fell from the opening in 1940. The angular nature of the boulders indicates their recent origin: weathering has yet to round their edges very much.

# Trip 16
## Devils Garden Trail

**Distances**: 1.8 miles round trip to Landscape Arch; 4 miles roundtrip to Double-O Arch; 5.2 miles round trip to Dark Angel; or 7.0-mile loop trip, visiting all the arches and returning via the prim itive trail.

**Low/High elevations**: 5180'/5530' to Double-O Arch and Dark Angel

**Suited for**: Dayhike

**Difficulty**: Easy to moderate

**Best seasons**: April through mid-June; mid-September through November.

**Map/Trailhead**: 31/13

**Hazards**: No water; little shade; steep dropoffs; some scrambling over slickrock required beyond Landscape Arch and on primitive loop trail.

**Introduction**: Devils Garden is the most heavily used area in Arches, and the reasons soon become apparent after you leave the trailhead. The area is a wonderland of standing rocks, views are far-reaching and panoramic, the first mile of the trail is wide and gravelled, and most of all, there are more readily observed arches in Devils Garden (at least nine) than in any other area of the Park.

But despite the heavy use, this is one hike no one should miss. The so-called primitive trail offers hikers the chance to see more of Devils Garden, including Fin Canyon, and offers a modicum of solitude for only a little extra effort. The primitive trail does require some steep slickrock scrambling, and should be attempted only by experienced hikers. The trail beyond Landscape

Arch to Double-O Arch and Dark Angel is also considered a "primitive" trail and, although it crosses slickrock as well, it is easily negotiated by novice hikers.

**Description**: A large sign at the trailhead (0.0; 5180) lists mileages to the seven arches accessed by the main trail, and our wide, gravelled trail wastes no time plunging into Devils Garden via an erosion-enlarged joint between towering, salmon-hued fins. Trees and shrubs colonize every available space where sand and clay, derived from the fins above, has collected.

After 0.1 mile, we reach a sandy flat embraced by rock walls, where sand sagebrush, four-wing saltbush, yucca, mormon tea, and Indian ricegrass mass their ranks next to the trail. Shortly thereafter, we reach the spur trail (0.3; 5200) to Tunnel and Pine Tree arches forking off to the right. This smooth trail quickly descends in 50 yards to a junction, from which trails lead right (south) to Tunnel Arch, and left (north) to Pine Tree Arch. Turning right at the junction you go 100 yards up a blind draw to a fine view of Tunnel Arch. Piercing the large, thick fin to the west high above the ground, this window-like opening is one of the better-proportioned in the Park, appearing as a nearly round tunnel. The span measures 22 feet high by 27 feet wide. A smaller, even more tunnel-like arch pierces the fin above and to the left of Tunnel Arch.

To reach Pine Tree Arch, head north from the junction, hugging the fins to the left while skirting a broad flat, then entering a blind draw. We won't get a glimpse of the arch until we reach it, but in less than 0.2 mile we're there. The angularity of the opening indicates that in the not-so-distant past, blocks have fallen from its roof and enlarged the opening. Unlike many arches in the Park, the opening is at ground level. From the right perspective, the arch frames twisted pinyons and junipers in addition to the extensive Book Cliffs and nearby Crystal Arch to the northeast, and an array of domes and fins closer at hand. This span stretches 46 feet between abutments and rises 48 feet from roof to floor. Above the opening, a series of stress fractures has developed which will lead to the inevitable enlargement of the arch. Both Pine Tree and Tunnel arches lie within the Slick Rock member of the Entrada Sandstone.

---

Back on the main trail at a point 0.3 mile from the trailhead, we continue between more massive fins, soon passing a lone pinnacle—all that remains of an eroded fin. But just before reaching that spire, a look to the north reveals a tiny opening in a cliff, the beginnings of another arch. Soon the trail breaks out into the open and crosses a broad flat. We might spy new arches being formed and the broken remnants of former arches in the fins to our left.

One-half mile from the previous junction, the improved segment of the trail ends, and the primitive loop trail forks right and left (0.5; 5230). Bear left, quite soon reaching a point just east of Landscape Arch, visible nearby in the west. This is a lovely, fragile-looking ribbon of stone, and with such an easy access trail, it is *the* arch that most visitors to Devils Garden come to see. Landscape Arch is an old-timer, with only a mere ribbon of stone framing its huge opening. Its fragile appearance and its old age are apparent; it is possible the span will "soon" collapse. It could happen at any time, but when you com-

pare the first known photograph of the arch, taken in 1896, its appearance has changed very little. Viewed from behind, the arch frames a fine picture of distant landscapes. The arch was dubbed Landscape in 1934 by Frank Beckwith, director of the Arches National Monument Scientific Expedition.

The first fatality in what was then Arches National Monument occurred in the spring of 1950, when a 19-year-old youth from New York City scaled the arch via its north abutment. From the top of that abutment, he attempted to descend to the arch itself, but he lost his footing and fell to his death while several tourists looked on in horror. He had failed to obtain permission for the climb, which was a last-minute decision, and his lack of experience and good judgment led to his demise.

Only three successful ascents of Landscape Arch have been recorded; in 1939, 1949, and 1957. Today, climbing on any of the Park's named features is forbidden, but climbers are free to practice their sport elsewhere in the Park with permission from the Park Service. The Entrada Sandstone, which dominates the Park, appears to be solid, but this rock is quite brittle, and only climbers who are well-skilled in climbing

**Jointed fins and pinyon-juniper woodland in Devils Garden**

sandstone should attempt such ascents in the Park—or elsewhere on the Colorado Plateau.

Many have claimed Landscape Arch to be the largest natural rock span in the world, but others claim that title for mighty Kolob Arch in Zion National Park. Kolob Arch was measured by two different groups from Brigham Young University in 1983 and 1984. After the measurements were published, both teams also measured Landscape Arch, also in 1984. The teams used different methods of measurement, and as one might expect, they arrived at different dimensions for each arch. The presently accepted dimensions of Landscape Arch are that the arch rises 106 feet, with a width of 291 feet, while Kolob Arch estimates (more difficult to measure since it rests high on a vertical wall and is inaccessible) range from 177 to 230 feet high and 292 to 310 feet wide. It has been suggested that a standardized method of measurement be used to measure rock spans on the Colorado Plateau, but until then the controversy remains. Facts and figures aside, let us simply enjoy this exceptionally beautiful arch and marvel at its uniqueness.

Beyond Landscape Arch we must briefly follow cairns over slickrock as we climb a passageway between fins, passing very close to Wall Arch (68 feet wide by 41 feet high) after 0.1 mile. This slickrock ascent soon levels off on a juniper- and pinyon-decorated notch.

In this notch we meet a left-forking spur trail (0.5; 5400) bound for Navajo and Partition arches. On this spur we proceed across a shady bench and in 100 yards we reach a fork—left to Partition, right to Navajo, two markedly different spans, both well worth visiting.

---

The spur to Partition Arch, an interesting 0.2-mile stroll, passes through a narrow, wooded bench leading to the nearly round opening of the arch, penetrating the uppermost part of a tall fin. The top of the desert-varnished fin rises about 30 feet above the arch, but standing in the opening we are on the edge of a cliff plummeting 100 feet or more to the east. Hence, viewed from the vicinity of Landscape Arch, Partition Arch seems inaccessible high on that sheer wall. The opening stretches 26 feet from side to side and rises 28 feet from its base. A smaller arch lies

about 15 feet south, on the same wall, separated by a stone "partition." Its opening, also nearly round, is 8 1/2 feet wide and only 8 feet tall. The arch nicely frames views of Devils Garden and the distant Uncompahgre Plateau, across the border in Colorado.

Back at the junction, to visit Navajo Arch we turn left, heading into a wooded draw between low fins. Passing an intriguing honeycombed wall, we continue under an overhang to alcove-like Navajo Arch, reached in 1/4 mile. A low fin rises immediately behind (west of) Navajo Arch and the fin it penetrates. Between the two fins is a narrow, sand-floored joint, aligned northwest to southeast, as are all fins and joints in Devils Garden. The arch is 41 feet wide at its base and 13 feet high, a nearly perfect half-circle.

---

Back on the main trail at a junction 1.3 miles from the trailhead, we proceed briefly across benchland before curving to the rim above Salt Valley. We'll enjoy fine, expansive vistas from northwest to southeast, stretching across a vast, empty landscape. Our route then turns northwest and crosses much slickrock, at times passing atop narrow fins where faint-hearted hikers may wish to turn back. We may scramble west a short distance for broad views into Salt Valley and beyond. Traversing above the abyss of magnificent Fin Canyon, we enjoy a head-on view of parallel ranks of narrow, salmon-hued fins, rising northwest and southeast above the dry wash of the wooded canyon.

Just 0.4 mile from the previous junction is another: left to Double-O Arch, and right for only a few yards to an overlook on the rim above Fin Canyon. True to its name, large Black Arch lies in the dark, mysterious folds of the canyon. Straight ahead from the junction our trail begins climbing, passing a few small arches and tunnels where scattered wallflowers enliven the stark trailside landscape with their vivid yellow blooms in spring.

Continuing our hike over slickrock, we make our way between fins and through groves of pinyon and juniper. Suddenly, while we're crossing over a jointed fin, Double-O Arch comes into view; its smaller opening is partly obscured by woods.

Finally, descending northwest along the top of a slickrock fin, we curve west among large pinyons and reach the foot of the large oval opening of Double-O Arch, piercing the north end of a narrow, desert-varnished fin. The top of the opening is a fine arching ribbon of stone, and a prominent tower rises north of the arch abutting the north end of the fin. The arch was named in 1927 by Hugh Bell, then a reporter and photographer for a Cleveland newspaper. He left an inscription on each of three arches in the Park that he also named, but Double-O is the only name that has survived. One of his other inscriptions can be found under Tower Arch in the Klondike Bluffs. The "Double-O Arch" inscription can be seen in the smaller opening in the fin. The two oval arches measure 71 feet wide by 45 feet high, and 21 feet by 9 feet. The best view, framing the fins of Devils Garden, can be obtained by scrambling around to the southwest side of the fin.

Shortly beyond the arch, the singed loop trail (0.7; 5420) forks off to the right, while another trail continues west (left) bound for Dark Angel. On the left fork cairns mark the route at times, which leads across blackbrush-dominated slopes amid pinyon and juniper. Attaining a northwest-trending slickrock ridge, we at once enjoy broad vistas into Salt Valley, backdropped by a broken redrock ridge and the jumbled Klondike Bluffs. Eventually we reach the foot of the tall, desert-varnished spire of Dark Angel (0.6; 5450), a solitary, remnant of an ancient fin, and the end of the trail.

However, this is only the beginning of a memorable adventure for backpackers into an area where wooded flats, fins, hidden arches and Anasazi rock art await discovery. Hikers should attempt to avoid trampling the cryptogamic crust, instead staying on slickrock or in drainage gullies as much as possible.

From Dark Angel, backtrack 0.6 mile to the loop trail, and turn left (northwest) onto the Primitive Trail. We briefly drop into a woodland at the head of a draw that trends northwest. Yucca, cliffrose, alderleaf mountain mahogany, Utah serviceberry, mormon tea, and Indian ricegrass keep us company as we proceed, soon curving northeast and descending the dry wash between towering fins.

Watching for cairns on this ill-defined route, we soon pass through a short narrows. When the canyon opens up, an arch is visible in the fins a short distance to the north. Widely spaced cairns lead us briefly toward that arch across slickrock before curving back into the main wash. Ahead we bypass a few dry falls before heading southeast over a low rise and descending in that direction toward Fin Canyon, below in the south. Massive vertical, sometimes overhanging cliffs embrace the joints we are descending, and we must negotiate a very steep slickrock slope to proceed.

As we approach Fin Canyon, the route suddenly veers away from a narrow joint and heads north over a low slickrock fin. Proceeding over the fin, we then reach a series of narrow ledges that we must traverse above a defile to reach the floor of Fin Canyon.

About 0.2 mile downstream is an arrow sign point in both directions indicating our route. From here we climb moderately southeast on well-defined trail. Fins in the lower canyon diminish in stature toward the east, and are now capped by the cream-colored Moab Tongue Sandstone.

As we climb generally southeast on blackbrush-clad slopes, the view back across aptly named Fin Canyon is exciting, even awe-inspiring. Ranks of parallel fins and sharp pinnacles form a sawtoothed horizon.

This climb tops between trailside domes, and then we head south along the west edge of a brushy flat, then rise easily once again west of a group of low, eroded fins. Crystal Arch, seen through Pine Tree Arch earlier in our journey, lies among these fins east of the trail. Hiking southeast again, we may see hikers treading the improved trail in the southwest, and we soon curve southwest under an overhanging cliff, where Landscape Arch soon appears to the west. A brief stint on the sandy primitive trail brings us to the improved trail (2.1; 5230), and we turn left to retrace our route 0.8 mile to the trailhead.

# Trip 17
## Devils Garden Campground to Broken Arch

**Distance**: 1.3-mile loop trail
**Low/High elevations**: 5180'/5230'
**Suited for**: Walk
**Difficulty**: Moderately easy
**Best seasons**: April through mid-June; mid-September through November.
**Map/Trailhead**: 31/12
**Hazards**: Some slickrock scrambling.

**Introduction**: This loop hike is a fine leg-stretcher for guests of the Devils Garden Campground. Open grasslands, broad vistas, narrow passageways between slickrock fins, and access to at least two beautiful arches are among the highlights of this short but memorable jaunt.

**Description**: The trail is signed for Broken Arch, and it begins next to Campsite 41 and a restroom just short of the loop road at the east end of the campground (0.0; 5180). The sandy trail initially follows a northeast course beneath a low red dome. After we stroll 0.2 mile, the trail bends east, and we pass a multibranched juniper standing upon buttressed roots. Gaze north from here, and you'll see Tapestry Arch, stained with a tapestry of desert varnish, penetrating a white, sandstone-capped fin 100 yards to the north. A sandy path leads to the span, measuring 30 feet high by 50 feet wide. Immediately behind the arch is another fin, demonstrating the closely spaced jointing of these outlying fins in southern Devils Garden.

Resuming our jaunt on the main trail, we presently curve southeast, bound for the slick-rock landscape ahead. Soon we mount slickrock and pass beneath two solitary sandstone pinnacles, then enter a thick stand of pinyon and juniper. Enroute we'll obtain fine vistas northward across open desert to the escarpment of the Book Cliffs. Where the trees thin out we begin passing among white domes and enjoy vistas stretching southeast across cliffs and mesas to the 12,000' peaks of the La Sals.

Rounding another bend we reach the north portal of Broken Arch (0.7; 5200). Here we briefly scramble over slickrock to pass through the arch, then quickly descend to the small wash on its south side, where we pick up the trail coming from the Park road and Sand Dune Arch (*Trip 13*).

Our route proceeds southwest beneath the parallel fins defining the southern terminus of Devils Garden. One tall fin has been dubbed Mammoth Rock because it is similar to that prehistoric pachyderm. Beyond the broad, grassy expanse stretching southward are the jointed fins of the northern Fiery Furnace area.

At a junction of trails (0.1; 5180) we bear right where a sign points to the campground, and there we part ways with *Trip 13* hikers. Our trail skirts another tall fin and an interesting split-level alcove, then enters a narrow joint amid a striking array of sandstone fins. The trail, presently indicated by cairns, ascends the joint and in spring we'll enjoy the yellow blooms of biscuitroot here. After topping out on a rocky notch at the joint's head, we descend slickrock and sand to the campground, now visible below to the northwest. The trail terminates at the campground road (0.5; 5180) next to Campsite 52. The trail here is indicated by a FOOT TRAIL sign. From there we simply follow the campground road, either returning to our campsites or, if not staying in the campground, walking 1 mile back to the Devils Garden Trailhead parking area.

# Trip 18
## Salt Valley to Klondike Bluffs via the Jeep Trail

**Distance**: 6.6 miles round trip
**Low/High elevations**: 4860'/5180'
**Suited for**: Jeep trip, mountain-bike trip, or dayhike
**Difficulty**: Easy 4WD and mountain-bike route; moderate hiking route.
**Best seasons**: April through mid-June; mid-September through November.
**Map/Trailhead**: 33/14

**Hazards**: No water; little shade.

**Introduction**: Park visitors driving a high-clearance 4WD vehicle will enjoy fast and easy access to the rugged Klondike Bluffs and Tower Arch via this easily traversed jeep road. Only one rugged stretch, climbing out of Salt Valley, presents any difficulty, and that is minor.

This trip is also a good choice for the mountain biker; a strong rider can complete the trip in less than an hour. This road, when combined with Salt Valley Road and the jeepway described in *Trip 6*, makes a grand, all-day tour of the north half of Arches.

**Description**: Branching left (southwest) from Salt Valley Road (0.0; 4980), this track is passable to high-clearance vehicles for 0.8 mile. The roadway crosses across nearly level grass and shrubland to the western margin of the valley, where broken sandstone rises abruptly to an extensive northwest-southeast-trending ridge. There, at the foot of a steep grade, is a wide spot on the right side of the road where one may park to begin a mountain-bike ride or a hike, or shift into 4WD if driving.

From here, we rise steeply on the rocky roadbed, immediately passing onto broken slopes of Navajo Sandstone. As we ascend the grade, we'll be rewarded by sweeping vistas across the broad grasslands of Salt Valley to the broken sandstone fins of Devils Garden and beyond to towering La Sal Mountains. After reaching comparatively level ground, we skirt the foot of an imposing buff-toned dome and climb once more to the crest of the prominent ridge (1.1; 5180). From here views of the Klondike Bluffs and an array of fins in the southwest foreground a striking panorama of contrasting high-desert landscapes.

After a rather steep descent over slickrock ledges amid a pinyon-juniper woodland, the grade eases as we make our way across salmon-tinted dunes and reach a signed junction (0.7; 4900) with the southeast-bound jeep trail to Balanced Rock (*Trip 6*). The spectacular pinnacles of the Marching Men, a platoon of red fingers reaching up an obvious incline toward the east, loom boldly immediately to the north across wind-blown sand dunes. These pinnacles are arguably the most scenic attraction in the Klon-

dike Bluffs area, where there is no shortage of striking erosional formations.

From the junction we descend southwest, staying north of a low band of cliffs, composed of the Slick Rock member, to cross a broad, sandy wash (0.3; 4850). Then the sandy jeep trail climbs steadily as it passes through a pinyon-juniper woodland while skirting just west of the alluring fins of the Bluffs. The route bends sharply to the left and right several times, until we at last reach the roadend at a TOWER ARCH sign (1.2; 5100), its opening visible in a slickrock recess to the east.

A 0.4-mile foot trail offers quick access to the arch and the remote interior of this slickrock labyrinth. At first the route descends the top of a narrow, sloping fin to an arrow sign below. It then crosses a small wash before curving north to the main foot trail just south of Tower Arch. Visitors who drove to the trailhead will have plenty of energy for exploration of the Bluffs; experienced hikers may wish to continue into the slickrock maze and reap the rewards of off-trail exploration.

# Trip 19
## Klondike Bluffs Trail to Tower Arch

**Distance**: 3.0 miles round trip
**Low/High elevations**: 5120'/5220'
**Suited for**: Dayhike or backpack
**Difficulty**: Moderate
**Best seasons**: April through mid-June; mid-September through October.
**Map/Trailhead**: 33/15
**Hazards**: No water; little shade.

**Introduction**: The jumble of white-capped redrock fins and towers known as the Klondike Bluffs, rising above the desert floor east of U.S. Highway 191, are the first exciting features visitors enjoy enroute to Arches National Park. This remote area, in the far northwest corner of the Park, is a miniature version of Devils Garden and, when "discovered" by a miner in 1922, the Klondike Bluffs were in fact dubbed Devils Garden. Later, that name was applied to the area on the opposite side of Salt Valley, and the bluffs take their name from the cold and windy winter conditions in the region. This fine half-day hike leads to outstanding Tower Arch, and hikers should enjoy considerable solitude compared to the situation on most other Park trails. This is an ideal area in which to spend a day or more exploring hidden canyons and searching for arches.

The area is closed to overnight camping from January 1 through July 15 each year to protect nesting raptors.

**Description**: The abrupt east flank of the Klondike Bluffs, some broken cliffs and some towering fins loom boldly 400 feet above the juniper-studded trailhead. Our trail will lead us around the Bluffs to their west side, where a maze of cracks and joints offers access into the heart of this slickrock massif. At once our trail (0.0; 5120) crosses a red-sandy flat dotted with junipers, blackbrush and cliffrose, and then it climbs steeply up a band of Navajo Sandstone. This rock unit underlies the Entrada Sandstone in Arches, occurring as a narrow, discontinuous band of rock in the ridge bounding the southwest margin of Salt Valley. Its most prominent exposure in the Park occurs south of the Windows Section as a vast region of "petrified dunes."

Topping out on a bench and proceeding south along the 5200' contour, we may notice three prominent rock units above us: the Navajo Sandstone, and the Dewey Bridge and Slick Rock members of the Entrada. This exposure contrasts the differing erosional characteristics of each unit, the Dewey Bridge member being the softest. This layer underlies many of the Park's arches. Erosion can undercut it, leaving little or no support for the Slick Rock member above. Consequently, fractures develop and slabs spall off of fins and cliffs, leading to the development of alcoves and ultimately arches.

Rockcress and Indian paintbrush enliven the otherwise drab, bushy bench in spring, but we soon leave it, climbing over a band of Navajo Sandstone and shortly topping out along a broad ridge (0.5; 5220), just below the contact zone where the Navajo Sandstone and the Dewey Bridge member meet. Expansive views, unobstructed by fins or trees, stretch from the extensive wall of the Book Cliffs in the northeast to

the lofty 12,000' summits of the La Sal Mountains in the southeast. Devils Garden and its vast array of redrock fins punctuate the rim of Salt Valley east of our viewpoint and from south to southwest, and beyond legions of vast mesas are the rolling ridges of the Abajo Mountains in the south. This is a pleasant place to rest and soak in the vast, contrasting landscapes, seemingly untouched by the works of man.

Now we descend west on a gentle-to-moderate grade, entering a pinyon-juniper woodland. The imposing Klondike Bluffs jut skyward north of the bowl we are descending, but to the south is a jumble of balanced rocks and above them is a striking parade of pinnacles called the Marching Men.

Descending beyond the reaches of the buff-colored Navajo Sandstone, we pass into a large amphitheater-like basin, embraced on three sides by upthrusting slickrock. At the bottom of our descent (0.5; 4950), we cross two dry, sandy washes, then climb loose red sand to an arrow sign atop an exposure of the contorted Dewey Bridge member below a solitary, desert-varnished fin composed of the Entrada's Slick Rock

**Tower Arch and its namesake tower**

member. Note the contrast between these two rock units; the lower is soft and irregular, while the upper is hard and smooth. Walking around to the opposite side of the small fin from the sign, we see how the comparatively soft Dewey Bridge member is eroding away from beneath the fin. This erosion often results in slab failure above, and is often a contributing factor to the development of Arches.

Presently on a northwest course, we enter the realm of the Klondike Bluffs, where upright, salmon-hued slickrock fins and spires flank our route on either side. Ahead we descend slickrock between imposing fins, and soon spy a striking double arch in an alcove on our right. We then quickly pass the opening of a former arch, pass the ill-defined trail from the jeep road on our left (Trip 18), and soon reach the foot of the large oval span of Tower Arch (0.5; 5200). A tall shaft of salmon-tinted slickrock rises behind the span, capped by a huge knob of white sandstone. This tower is one of the most imposing landforms in the Klondike Bluffs area, soaring above the maze of slickrock fins that dominate the scene.

Scramble up a slickrock to stand amid the massive abutments of the arch and enjoy a sandstone-framed picture of the shrub-dotted parallel fins of the bluffs, with distant mesas to the southwest delineating the horizon. This arch of stone and its abutments, formed entirely within the Slick Rock member, are thicker both vertically and horizontally than many in the Park.

When government surveys were conducted in the mid-1920s in the Arches region for possible designation as a national monument, the name "Devils Garden" was mistakenly placed on the Windows Section, and later it was applied to the area that still bears the name. When Arches gained National Monument status is 1929, the original Devils Garden (Klondike Bluffs) was not included within its boundaries, and it was overlooked during the surveys. Not until 1938, when Arches was enlarged to encompass more than 30,000 acres, did Klondike Bluffs become a part of the Monument.

Many of the Park's features were first named in 1933-34 by member of the Arches National Monument Scientific Expedition, including Tower Arch, apparently an apt title. Hikers who look closely will find two inscriptions, one each on the base of the north and south abutments. Alexander Ringhoffer is indisputably the "discoverer" of the Klondike Bluffs area, or at least the first person to help bring the area to the public's attention. The inscription beneath the south abutment reads: "DISCOV'D BY M. AND MRS. ALEX RINGHOEFFER AND SONS 1922-23." This inscription has led to controversy, since the name "Ringhoffer" is misspelled and the date 1922-23 is ambiguous. It is unknown who actually carved the inscription, but apparently Ringhoffer did not attempt to name the arch. The first title given to the span is indicated by a much smaller inscription near the foot of the north abutment, which reads: "Minaret Bridge. H.S. Bell 1927." This title was unknown to Beckwith when he named the arch in 1934, and moreover the opening is not a bridge, since it does not span a watercourse. One title Bell bestowed on a Park feature—Double-O Arch—survives to this day.

Like trail's end in Devils Garden, this spot is only the beginning of a memorable adventure for experienced hikers out for one day or several. Slickrock fins, shady niches, hidden arches, and more await discovery by anyone possessed by the spirit to wander.

# Trip 20
## Eagle Park

**Distance**: 7.4 miles round trip to Park boundary

**Low/High elevations**: 5020'/5340'

**Suited for**: Dayhike or backpack

**Difficulty**: Moderate

**Best seasons**: April through mid-June; mid-September through November.

**Map/Trailhead**: 34/16

**Hazards**: No water, little shade.

**Introduction**: Remote Eagle Park, a broad grassland encircled by fins and knobs of Entrada Sandstone, is far enough removed from the busy Park road and the bustling Devils Garden area that hikers should enjoy relative solitude here. There is ample opportunity for off-trail exploration in this open area, and diligent hikers may discover one or more of the arches that decorate Eagle Park's fins. The highland that stretches southeast toward Devils Garden from Eagle Park is wild slickrock country dotted with pinyon and juniper, and cross-country travel there is delightful. Hikers can also gain access to the remote northern reaches of Devils Garden via that gentle highland.

**Description**: Our foray into remote Eagle Park begins at the road-closure sign (0.0; 5020), where which we follow the old jeep road that once offered 4WD access into Eagle Park. Deep ruts eroded into the jeepway are the seedbed for the ubiquitous and exotic Russian thistle, or tumbleweed. As we proceed, we'll enjoy fine vistas up and down the broad, grassy spread of Salt Valley. Broken crags of the Klondike Bluffs, a jumble of white-sandstone-capped spires and cliffs, form a scenic backdrop on the opposite side of the valley.

Approaching an elongated sandstone ridge, we mount the whitish sandstone of the Kayenta Formation as the trail bends east. The way is ill-defined at times, but if we keep an eye out for pinyon and juniper saplings, part of a Park re-vegetation project, we'll stay on track. Bending sharply northwest, we begin a moderately ascending, protracted traverse beneath low bluffs of Navajo Sandstone.

Spring offers the most dramatic floral display here, and hikers will then enjoy the colorful blossoms of prickly-pear cactus, astragalus, pepper-grass, rockcress, puccoon, wallflower, twinpod, and dock.

We reach our high point (1.8; 5340) in a pinyon-juniper woodland atop a northwest-trending ridge among outcrops of bare sandstone, then proceed north-northwest across much slickrock. This descent is obscure, but the Park Service has delineated the route with logs, helping us to maintain our course without damaging delicate trailside vegetation and the cryptogamic crust.

We soon enjoy our first glimpse of the broad oval spread of Eagle Park, backdropped by a series of parallel, salmon-tinted slickrock fins. Exiting the woodland after a brief descent, our trail strikes a northward course across the grasslands of this peaceful park. Sheep grazed on the grasslands before the spread was added to the Park, and diligent hikers may find inscriptions left on rocks by sheepherders passing their long months in this remote locale.

Views from our open vantage stretch southeast to the lone sandstone shaft of Dark Angel, 4 miles distant on the outskirts of Devils Garden.

We soon climb easily and level off between low domes, then proceed across brushy flats before passing above a minor drainage trending northeast into a thick woodland, embraced by a jumble of redrock domes. Finally topping out, we pass close to an unpromising oil well drilled in the 1950s (1.1; 5230). Ahead, the trail drops steadily to the Park boundary (0.8; 4940) at the edge of Long Valley, where it meets an old jeep road. The Park boundary lies near the Yellow Cat Mining District, a region of desert flats, hills, and washes that was a rich and important source of uranium ore, found in the 1950s in the Morrison Formation, which dominates this region north of the Park.

Hikers who have persisted to the Park boundary must eventually retrace the route back to the trailhead.

# Canyonlands National Park

## Introduction

When one tries to visualize Utah's canyon country, images of towering mesas and buttes, sheer and colorful cliffs, and yawning defiles appear in the mind's eye. Canyonlands National Park's 337,570 acres have all that and more. Within the vast and remote reaches of this magnificent park are two great rivers and the gaping canyons they have carved, broad and open desert flats, wooded buttes and mesas, a maze of serpentine canyons, extensive grasslands, woodlands of pinyon and juniper, a rainbow of colorful rocks, and more than 100 square miles of slickrock fins, buttes, and spires. Canyonlands is far removed from civilization, and to get to any one of its three districts one must travel far from primary highways. The Park receives much less use than any other national park in Utah, only slightly more than 200,000 visitors each year. If one desires to avoid the crowds encountered in most national parks and enjoy some of the most majestic scenery on the Colorado Plateau, Canyonlands beckons. The Park consists of three separate districts—four if one includes the rivers. Each district is distinctly different from the others, so Canyonlands is more like three parks than one.

## The Island in the Sky District

The lofty, wedge-shaped Island in the Sky mesa juts south into the vast Canyonlands basin toward the confluence of the Green and Colorado rivers. Two arms of this highland, rising more than 2000 feet above the river canyons, diverge near the southern terminus of the mesa. The western arm extends northwest to curious Upheaval Dome, then breaks away abruptly into deep and narrow canyons that yield seasonal runoff to the Green River's Labyrinth Canyon. The southern arm, aptly named Grand View Point, projecting 5 miles from its base at the Island in the Sky, ends abruptly where cliffs plunge 400 feet from its rim, but an erosional outlier of the mesa, 1/2-square-mile Junction Butte, rises beyond. Not only is 6400' Junction Butte the apex of the Island District, it is one of the most prominent landmarks in all the Canyonlands basin.

The Park road traverses the entire mesa system of the Island in the Sky, and turnouts located along the roadway offer far-ranging panoramas of hundreds of square miles of rugged canyons, plunging cliffs, vast desert basins, mesas and their isolated buttes, and lofty mountain ranges. Vistas are what the Island is noted for, and visitors will not be disappointed as they gaze over the entire length and breadth of Canyonlands National Park and beyond.

# The Needles District

Many visitors consider The Needles to be the most beautiful district in the Park. The vast reaches of this large district contain a maze of serpentine canyons and tens of square miles of banded slickrock spires, fins, cliffs, buttes, bluffs, and knolls, all colored in shades of white and red and composed of one of the older rock formations in Canyonlands—the Cedar Mesa Sandstone. Vertical relief in this jumble of standing rocks varies from a few feet to as much as 800 feet.

A number of canyons cut far back toward the heart of The Needles, and many of them are corridors through which foot trails and jeep trails pass. But only one canyon has carved a drainage completely through The Needles District and beyond Park boundaries—Salt Creek. Salt Creek is the principal drainage in the district, gathering its seasonal waters high on Salt Creek Mesa and winding north and northwest for more than 20 miles to the Colorado River.

North of The Needles proper is a landscape of entirely different character. There is still much slickrock; but the relief is minor, save for a few abyssal defiles. The shape of the land is relatively uniform, with only low knolls and knobs of Cedar Mesa Sandstone jutting above it. But there are also broad reaches where there is no slickrock, occupied by brushy flats, scattered pinyon and juniper woodlands, and wide, grassy pockets that lend a bucolic tone to the landscape.

Stretching west from The Needles to the brink of the Colorado River canyon is a unique landscape called The Grabens, a series of closely spaced, narrow, parallel valleys trending northeast-southwest. The valleys are clad in grasses and scattered desert shrubs, and are embraced by broken cliffs, composed primarily of Cedar Mesa Sandstone, which rise as much as 400 feet from the valley floors. These unique graben valleys are the result of the subsidence of blocks of the earth's crust along a series of faults.

From the rim of the Colorado River, broken cliffs and ruined walls plummet 1000 feet or more into the narrow gorge the river has carved. The oldest rocks in Canyonlands are exposed here in the depths of this great canyon

# The Maze District

Many people have gazed out from overlooks in the Island and Needles districts of the Park into the labyrinth of colorful slickrock canyons and tall pillars of red rock in the Maze District, but very few have braved the treacherous jeep roads and long hiking trails to reach that remote and beautiful landscape. It is difficult to imagine an area as remote as The Maze; the nearest town is more than 100 miles away. The Maze is truly one of "the last best places" where the persevering and self-reliant will reap the rewards of their labors in one of the most rugged wilderness areas in the nation.

In general, the Maze District encompasses a vast bench between the escarpment of the Orange Cliffs on the west and the rim of the Green and Colorado rivers on the east. The Maze proper is only a part of the landscape within the Park's boundaries in this district.

The Standing Rocks are a series of spectacular red-rock monoliths resting on a broad highland bisected by a jeep road and dotted with several scenic but primitive vehicle campsites. South of the Land of Standing Rocks, erosion has once again exposed the red- and white-banded Cedar Mesa Sandstone, but not on such a grand scale as in The Maze. This area, known as The Fins, lies at higher elevations than The Maze, and along the western margin The Fins directly abut the Orange Cliffs. As the name suggests, the area is composed of intricately jointed fins. They trend east-west, and are incised by only three short but prominent canyons. Access to this dry section of the Park is gained on the west by following first the Golden Stairs Trail and then the jeep road, and on the east by cairned hiking route beginning at the roadend near The Doll House—a castle-like cluster of Cedar Mesa spires rising above the Colorado River canyon rim near the Land of Standing Rocks.

South of The Fins are the blackbrush benches and rugged canyons of Ernies Country, and beyond, Range and Teapot canyons march south to the Park boundary. No water is available in Ernies Country except, perhaps, from seasonal potholes. Consequently, this section of the Park is visited by a very few hardy backpackers willing to accept the challenges of this harsh desert environment.

The region west of the Maze District and the Orange Cliffs is a vast plateau that slopes gently west into the sandy expanse of the San Rafael Desert. Much of that landscape is administered by the Bureau of Land Management. Numerous deep, labyrinthine canyons have been eroded into the plateau. Some trend southwest toward the Dirty Devil River, a muddy Colorado tributary, while others flow northeast and contribute their seasonal waters to the Green River.

Among the most prominent of the tributaries of the Green is Horseshoe (formerly Barrier) Canyon, a magnificent defile some 30 miles long. In 1971, 3200 acres in the middle reaches of Horseshoe Canyon were set aside as a detached unit of Canyonlands National Park. This unit protects a beautiful slickrock defile, but it was actually set aside for the primary purpose of protecting a series of four magnificent pictograph panels, painted high on the canyon walls as much as 2000-3000 years ago. Access to Horseshoe Canyon is much easier than to most of the Maze District, and hikers of average ability can easily negotiate the dayhike into this remote corner of the Utah desert.

# Human History of Canyonlands

The history of Canyonlands National Park is as fascinating as its magnificently sculptured stone landscapes. This history encompasses 10,000 years of ancient Indian cultures, explorers, cowboys, outlaws, uranium prospectors, government agencies, and modern-day tourists.

The most ancient peoples to use the Canyonlands region, called Paleo-Indians, hunted bison, mammoth, and other creatures, many of which have become extinct. The discovery of large projectile points, the abundance of large game animals, and a lack of evidence of permanent dwelling sites have led archaeologists to believe that these were nomadic peoples, constantly on the move in search of herds of large game. A Clovis projectile point discovered near Canyonlands is believed to be more than 11,000 years old. Their culture dominated the region from about 11,000 years ago to about 7000 years ago. Their descendants, known to archaeologists as the Archaic culture, thrived until about 2500 years ago. They were also nomadic, hunting game and collecting wild plant foods.

The most readily observed evidence of the Archaic culture is their unique rock art, dubbed Barrier Canyon Style from the type location in Barrier (now Horseshoe) Canyon. Many archaeologists believe that these rock-art panels are at least 3000 years old. They all depict large, ghost-like figures, painted on the rock surface (pictographs) rather than chipped or carved into it to make petroglyphs.

As the Archaic culture developed, people adopted a more sedentary lifestyle and became farmers of corn, beans, and squash. As farmers, they required permanent dwellings; they built pueblos and cliff houses, and small circular stone structures in which they stored cultivated grains. This culture, known as the Anasazi, thrived in the Four Corners region for more than 1000 years.

Contemporaneous with the Anasazi were the people of the Fremont culture. Although they built no such permanent structures as the Anasazi, they left ample evidence of their use of Canyonlands, primarily in the form of their distinct rock art. Many rock-art panels in the Salt

Creek Archaeological District in The Needles are of Fremont origin, including the Peekaboo Panel and Four Faces. Unlike Barrier Canyon Style art, their panels depict abstract images and hunting scenes.

The Needles District contains a greater concentration of Anasazi ruins than any other Park district. They consist mostly of grain-storage structures, but there are a few dwelling sites thought to have been occupied by small family groups. In addition to the ruins, chipping sites are occasionally encountered by hikers in the backcountry. These sites are often located near a lofty vantage point where an ancient craftsman chipped out blanks that would later be fashioned into projectile points and tools.

We can only speculate about the reasons that people of the Anasazi and Fremont cultures abandoned the region. Some archaeologists suggest conflicts with newly arrived Indian cultures, while others believe they may have simply depleted the available resources, or possibly a drought during the 13th century caused the end of their agricultural way of life. Another theory suggests that disease may have invaded peoples living in the close quarters of the pueblos. But the Anasazi did not simply vanish from the earth; rather it is believed that these peoples migrated south, and that the modern-day Hopi and Pueblo cultures of the Southwest are descendants of the Anasazi.

Thus, by 1300, the Anasazi and Fremont cultures gave way to the more primitive hunting and gathering cultures of the Navajos and Utes. These peoples were encountered by early explorers in the region, but they left little evidence of permanent occupation. They, like those before them, did leave carvings in stone, including their additions to the petroglyph panel at Newspaper Rock State Historical Monument near the Needles District.

The first white men to actually see and describe the region that would later become a national park were members of the 1859 Macomb Expedition. Their route barely entered a corner of what would become Canyonlands, but they were able to gain an overview of the Canyonlands basin as they descended from Hatch Point to Indian Creek. They terminated their exploration on the rim of the Colorado River canyon, several miles upstream from the confluence of the Green and Colorado rivers.

Another explorer gained much fame for his explorations of the Green and Colorado rivers—Major John Wesley Powell, a one-armed veteran of the Civil War. The epic journeys of the Powell Expedition in 1869 and 1871 from Green River, Wyoming, through the Grand Canyon gained

**Ruins of an Anasazi granary**

**Kirk cabin, relic of homesteading days in upper Salt Creek**

much knowledge of the region known then as "the great American desert" and filled in the last blank spots on the map of the United States. In their wooden boats, they were the first to intentionally float the rivers, including the rapids of Cataract and Grand canyons.

Enroute, members of the scientific expeditions mapped the course of the rivers, and climbed canyon walls and mesa rims to gain overviews of the region, taking compass and barometric measurements. But the expedition was beset with perils—treacherous rapids and overturning boats, rations that were spoiled and in short supply. Within the Grand Canyon, three of the 10-member party abandoned the river on foot, later to be killed by Indians. Many of the names they bestowed upon the land are still in use today: Labyrinth, Stillwater, and Cataract canyons, Buttes of the Holy Cross, Bonita Bend, and Orange Cliffs, to name but a few in the Canyonlands region.

During the time of Powell's travels, and into the 20th century, the Colorado River upstream

from the confluence with the Green was known as Grand River. Grand County, Utah, Grand Junction, Colorado, and the Grand Mesa in western Colorado have taken their names from that river.

In the 1870s cattle ranchers began drifting into Canyonlands country. In 1885 the Dugout Ranch was established on Indian Creek, and in 1886, cattle began to graze on the Island in the Sky. The Dugout Ranch still stands along Indian Creek near the Needles District, one of the last vestiges of early cattle ranching in the Canyonlands region. Many of the trails in Canyonlands were blazed by ranchers, and are still in use today. The Murphy brothers of Moab built the Murphy Trail in the Island District. The Shafer brothers, also Moab locals, built the Shafer Trail in that district, and in the 1940s and 1950s, Howard Lathrop and the Holemans wintered their sheep herds in the Island in the Sky.

Despite the presence of a few ranchers in the Canyonlands region, much of the area remained unexplored and almost inaccessible. But by the end of World War II, one of the effects of that great conflict had made people focus on the Colorado Plateau. Bulldozers, airplanes, and prospectors began carving exploration roads and landing strips throughout the region. Their goal was uranium; its source was the Chinle and Morrison formations. Only the Chinle is exposed in Canyonlands, far below the mesas. The prospectors improved upon old cowboy trails, including the Shafer and Flint trails, and the road over Elephant Hill. They blazed the White Rim Road, and laced the White Rim bench with myriad bulldozer trails, many of which still scar the land. They also blazed routes to The Maze and The Land of Standing Rocks, and for the first time made much of Canyonlands accessible to vehicles.

The uranium boom ended in the 1950s, but even today uranium ore is still extracted from the sedimentary formations of the Colorado Plateau outside of Utah's national parks.

By the 1950s Bates Wilson, then superintendent of Arches National Monument, began explorations of the Canyonlands country. Discovering ancient ruins and rock-art sites in the dramatic landscape of The Needles, Wilson realized the need for protection of the region, and he played an important role in the establishment of Utah's largest park, Canyonlands. In 1959 and 1960 Wilson led study groups into Canyonlands by jeep and on foot. It soon became obvious to Wilson and other National Park Service planners that the entire Canyonlands basin held excellent potential for national-park designation.

In 1961 Interior Secretary Stewart Udall accompanied Wilson on an 11-day trip into The Needles. Based on Udall's enthusiasm for the area, combined with the assistance of Utah Senator Frank Moss, Canyonlands National Park was established in 1964. At that time it encompassed only 257,640 acres, but in 1971 the Park was enlarged to its present size of 337,570 acres, of which 287,985 acres have been recommended for wilderness designation. Late in 1971, the Horseshoe Canyon unit was added to the Park for protection of the superb rock art panels there.

For a park of such great size, Canyonlands attracted a surprisingly small number of visitors until the 1980s, when a dramatic increase in visitation occurred. In 1980 only 56,965 visitors had come to Canyonlands, but by 1988 visitation had skyrocketed to 214,217. Nevertheless, Canyonlands remains the least visited national park in Utah.

# Plants and Animals of Canyonlands

Canyonlands is a vast arid region ranging in elevation from 3720 feet in Cataract Canyon to 6987 feet atop Cedar Mesa in the Needles District. Attesting to the region's aridity are a mean annual precipitation of 8.05 inches at the Island in the Sky and 8.63 inches at The Needles. No records are available from the Maze District proper, but precipitation there is probably equally scant. At first glance the landscape appears to be a barren expanse of rock and sand, but in nearly every place where even the slightest amount of soil has collected, plants grow. They are, however, typically sparse due to competition for the meager moisture and nutrients available. In Canyonlands 429 species of plants have been identified.

In southeast Utah the pinyon-juniper woodland typically occupies only the highest mesas, where the soil is shallow and rainfall is greater than in the canyons and open desert. But in Canyonlands, seemingly regardless of elevation, pinyon and juniper will be found wherever there is much slickrock. They obtain their moisture by growing near, and sometimes in, slickrock, extending their roots into cracks and joints in the bedrock where moisture collects.

Some of the most common shrubs that have the same habitat requirements as pinyon and juniper are singleleaf ash, long-flower snowberry and green ephedra, all of which are important browse plants upon which the Park's bighorn sheep depend, as well as littleleaf and alderleaf mountain mahogany, buffaloberry, Utah serviceberry, cliffrose, squawbush and Fremont barberry.

Desert-scrub communities dominate the vegetation in the Park, and the distribution of their species is determined not only by soil depth but by soil composition and mineral content. Blackbrush is ubiquitous in the Park, growing at most elevations except in the inner gorges of the rivers. It prefers mostly clay soils that do not generally exceed 2 feet in depth.

Beneath the shallow soil cover lies bedrock, and moisture trapped there nurtures this hardy, slow-growing shrub, which is also an important food source for bighorn sheep. Sandy sites in the scrublands host sand sagebrush, wavy-leaf oak and three species of yucca—Harriman, narrowleaf, and the large Datil yucca. The lower elevations of the Park, where there is poor soil cover and very little moisture, have only a scattering of coarse shrubs. These shrubs are a dull gray, and blend with their surroundings when viewed from a distance, lending a barren appearance to the landscape. Shadscale and Torrey ephedra are the dominant species.

Growing near some of the Park's grasslands and upon benches in washes, particularly in the Needles District, are some of the largest shrubs in the Park, occasionally forming impenetrable thickets. The gray, fragrant foliage of big sagebrush distinguishes one of the most common of these shrubs. Rabbitbrush is also quite common, colonizing disturbed sites along washes and roadsides. There are several species of this shrub in Canyonlands, but the plant typically has green stems, long, narrow, green leaves, and clusters of yellow flowers that bloom in autumn. Growing on the most alkaline sites one finds greasewood, a thorny shrub with fleshy leaves, and four-wing saltbush. The latter takes its descriptive name from the shape of its fruit and the salty taste of its foliage.

Grasslands are widespread throughout the Needles District and on the Island in the Sky mesa. The Island is rather unusual in that one would expect a pinyon-juniper woodland to be the dominant vegetation community on the 6000-foot mesa, but due to deep soils these broad spreads of grass lend a soft and velvety appearance to the cliffbound Island.

The Grasslands occupy the areas of deepest soil cover in the Park, and most shrubs, despite their deep root systems, are unable to gather enough moisture to survive in these sites. Grasses typically have shallow, spreading root systems that take advantage of even the lightest rainfall. However, nearly 100 years of grazing in the grasslands of Canyonlands have had a serious impact upon native grasses, particularly in the Needles District in places such as Chesler Park, upper Salt Creek, and The Grabens.

Wherever overgrazing or other disturbance has occurred, exotic plants, such as cheatgrass and Russian thistle, or tumbleweed, have altered the makeup of the Park's grassy spreads.

The canyons host their own unique assemblage of plants. Where subsurface moisture is available in the canyons and along the rivers, a narrow ribbon of green riparian foliage grows vigorously. Fremont cottonwood is the dominant tree, most often quite large, with a spreading crown and roundish leaves that flutter in the slightest breeze.

Also present, primarily in the Needles District, is lanceleaf cottonwood, a hybrid between the narrowleaf cottonwood of the Rocky Mountains and the Fremont cottonwood of the Southwest. These trees offer shade to desert-weary travelers, and they are a sure sign of moisture. They take up gallons of water from the evening through the morning hours, and if one is unfortunate enough to be dying of thirst, one can dig into the sand of a dry wash near a cottonwood tree and likely find water.

Only one other native riparian tree occurs in Canyonlands, the willow, of which there are three species. The exotic tamarisk, introduced to the Southwest more than 100 years ago from Eurasia as an ornamental and for erosion control, has been so successful in its new habitat that it is rapidly spreading up each tributary of the Green and Colorado rivers and vigorously supplanting the native cottonwoods and willows.

Also common in moist sites in washes, and occasionally at the foot of sheltered cliffs, but less water-dependent than riparian vegetation, are forestiera, or desert-olive, a willow-like shrub with small green, olive-like fruit, and a small but large-leaved shrub, buckthorn. Despite its name, this shrub bears no thorns. Wild rose forms thorny thickets in some moist canyons, and Gambel oaks grow in sheltered sites, usually near the foot of the cliffs.

Perhaps the most unusual trees found in these arid, high-desert canyons are Douglas-fir and ponderosa pine. They do not form forests but form only isolated stands in the most sheltered sites in the upper elevations of the canyons.

Even in a land so dominated by naked stone, heat and drought, the canyons nevertheless host verdant oases called hanging gardens. Hanging gardens occur wherever constant moisture issues from a canyon wall or a cliff, most often where a permeable sandstone layer overlies an impermeable stratum. Where only marginal moisture is available in a hanging garden, mosses and occasional maidenhair fern thrive, but where moisture is plentiful, these plants are joined by waterlovers such as scarlet monkey flower and miniature columbine.

The fragrance and delicate color of wildflowers are integral parts of the Canyonlands experience. Here in the high desert, wildflowers are typically widely scattered, but they include not only flowering herbs but showy shrubs as well. In some of the higher reaches of the canyons and in the pinyon-juniper woodland one may find the climbing vine clematis, or virgin's bower, easily recognized by its creamy white flowers in spring and fluffy white seed heads in autumn. Other particularly common wildflowers include a variety of milkvetches, jimson weed, groundsels, tansy-aster, evening primrose, goldenrod, Wyoming paintbrush, longleaf phlox, yellow sweetclover, penstemons, pepper-grass, and a low, clump-forming shrub that is ubiquitous throughout most of the Park. Broom snakeweed is identified by its narrow leaves, and a profusion of tiny yellow blossoms that bloom in late summer, but the dried flowers often persist through much of the year.

Various cacti, including claret-cup, pricklypear, and fishhook cactus, are also found throughout most elevations of the Park. Their delicate blooms are among the largest and most showy in the Park. There are dozens of other beautiful wildflowers throughout Canyonlands, and the visitor will find lists of currently blooming plants at both the Island and Needles visitor centers to aid identification.

Just as many plants are restricted in their range by environmental requirements, so are many of the animals that make their home in Canyonlands. Some animals range throughout the Park, and some visit the area only seasonally,

particularly birds. Desert animals have adapted to the rigors of life in this arid region by their efficient use of resources, and their mobility permits them to escape the searing desert heat. For example, Ord's kangaroo rat is primarily nocturnal and rarely drinks water. Instead, this desert rodent obtains moisture through metabolism of its primary food source—seeds. Lizards and snakes, being cold-blooded, warm themselves on rocks during the day, but retreat into the shade of a boulder or burrow when they become too warm.

**Animal tracks on dune sand**

Some animals in the Park are predators, feeding either on other animals or on insects, while others depend on plants for food and shelter. Blacktail jackrabbits and desert cottontails have developed an interesting means of coping with desert heat: their long ears are laced with myriad blood vessels, which help them to dissipate body heat, as well as helping them to detect predators.

Many birds are restricted to specialized habitats in Canyonlands, but others, such as the turkey vulture, raven, and golden eagle, soar on thermal updrafts throughout the Park in search of prey or carrion. On the mesas, in grasslands, and in pinyon-juniper woodlands birds such as the scrub and pinyon jays, horned lark, mountain bluebird, blue-gray gnatcatcher, kestrel, Audubon's warbler, mourning dove, and western meadow lark are common.

Cliffs and canyons host their own distinct avifauna. Few hikers in the canyons have not heard the melancholy, descending call of the canyon wren, but these tiny birds are not readily observed. The rock wren perches on rocky ledges and also has a distinctive song. Soaring at high speeds among the cliffs, the white-throated swift and the violet-green swallow evoke envy in all who have ever desired to fly. Cliff swallows build their mud-and-plant nests in rows, usually beneath an overhang or in an alcove, not unlike Anasazi cliff dwellings and granaries.

The rivers host their own distinctive varieties of birds, but these are seen primarily by floaters and the handful of hikers who make the long treks to canyon bottoms. Great blue herons, a variety of geese and ducks, spotted sandpipers, western grebes, cinnamon teals, and occasionally, white faced ibises visit the Park's rivers.

Lizards are also frequently observed denizens of the desert. Gray and red-colored leopard lizards and green-colored collared lizards are common in the lower elevations of the Park. These reptiles feed on their smaller relatives as well as insects. Collared lizards are fascinating to watch when they run swiftly on their hind legs. Other common lizards include the fast-running whiptail, the small side-blotched and tree lizards, and the western fence swift.

Snakes are not particularly common in Canyonlands, but there are two species some hikers might encounter. The gopher snake is the larger, attaining a length of up to 5 feet. These large snakes are harmless, and help to control the rodent population. One snake hikers may not wish to encounter is the midget faded rattlesnake. This straw-colored snake rarely exceeds 2 feet in length. They are not aggressive and are uncommon, but their rattle is small enough that it may not be heard by hikers. This rattler is usually found near grasslands and shrublands, but it can range throughout the Park.

Most rodents and mammals in the Park are either nocturnal or active in the early morning and evening hours. At least seven species of bats inhabit the Park, frequently seen around dusk as they emerge in search of insects. Although beavers, porcupines, and badgers are rarely seen, evidence of their handiwork abounds. Through-

out the Park hikers will find the large burrows of the badger and trees stripped of their bark by the porcupine. Along the river bottoms, beavers cut saplings from which they, like the porcupine, dine on the inner bark. The rivers are much too large for beavers to build dams and lodges, so instead they build their homes in riverbanks.

Bobcats and coyotes range throughout the Park, and it is possible that mountain lions visit the area in search of their primary food source, mule deer, which are widespread in Canyonlands, ranging from the rivers to the mesas. Perhaps the most exciting large mammal to observe in the Park is the desert bighorn sheep. They range throughout Canyonlands, but the largest and most stable herd lives in the Island District, where there are an estimated 130-180 animals. Though infrequently seen, bighorns may be observed below the rim of the Island in the Sky mesa, where they will amaze you by their agility on seemingly sheer cliffs. In the Needles District they can be found in the lower reaches of the canyons and along the inner gorge of the Colorado River.

Encroachment upon bighorn range by humans is their greatest threat to survival. It is imperative that Park visitors not approach bighorn sheep, but instead observe them from a distance. Bighorn-sheep observation forms are available at the Park visitor centers, and if you observe a sheep, the sighting should be reported to the Park staff, to help researchers gain more knowledge of the bighorn's activities.

Another large mammal that may evoke awe and excitement is one that few visitors would expect to find in the desert. Black bears, though uncommon, range throughout the high mesas and in the Abajo Mountains near the Needles District, and occasionally enter upper Salt Creek. To date, however, there have been no conflicts between visitors and these wild bears.

When you visit Canyonlands, take the time to observe the plants and animals, and some of their unique relationships with one another and with their environment. A national park is an excellent setting in which to observe nature free of human manipulation, and we must do our best not to disrupt the delicate balance among plants, animals, and a healthy, undisturbed environment.

## Interpretive Activities and Campgrounds in Canyonlands

Canyonlands is still a young park and interpretive activities are not as well-established as in most other national parks in Utah. However, each district has a visitor center, and in Moab one can purchase books and maps, and obtain backcountry use permits at Park headquarters. An entrance fee is collected at visitor centers in the Needles and Island districts, allowing entrance into the Park for seven consecutive days.

The Island in the Sky Visitor Center is the newest such facility in the Park. Rangers on duty can answer your questions about the district, issue backcountry use permits for backpackers and jeepers using any of the eight campsites on the White Rim Trail jeep road, and help visitors make the most of their stay in the Park. The Visitor Center also offers interpretive exhibits, and books and maps for sale, as well as free brochures on various aspects of Park natural history, self-guided trails, and campground information. Business hours are 8 A.M.-4:30 P.M..

Guided walks are conducted on the Mesa Arch Trail (*Trip 4*) several times a week. Self-guided trails in the Island District include the Neck Spring Trail (*Trip 2*), the Mesa Arch Trail, and the Crater View Trail (*Trip 15*). Evening campfire programs are held from spring through fall at the campfire circle at Willow Flat Campground. Schedules of interpretive activities in the district are posted at the Visitor Center.

The Willow Flat Campground is the only camping area available to visitors on the Island mesa. This pleasant campground, at an elevation of 6050 feet, features 12 sites set on a bench above the mesa rim, shaded by a thick woodland of pinyon and juniper. Views are excellent from the campground, including distant panoramas of the Canyonlands basin and close-up view of the sheer Wingate Sandstone cliffs that bound the mesa and the Navajo Sandstone domes that crown its rim. Wildflowers decorate the site from spring through fall, including cryptantha, yucca, and broom snakeweed. Campers must bring their own water, and there is no fee here. Visitors are advised to arrive early, especially during the Easter, Memorial Day, and Labor Day holidays, as the campsites are on a first-come basis.

Only 14.6 miles from the Island Visitor Center is Dead Horse Point State Park, which offers a fine view of the Colorado River gorge, a 23-site campground with water, a visitor center and a picnic area. A fee is charged to enter the Park and to use the campground.

There are eight designated campsites on the White Rim Trail jeep road, and campers must obtain a backcountry use permit to use them. This jeep road is becoming increasingly popular, particularly on holiday weekends, but users can make advance reservations for campsites. Most sites lie on the open White Rim bench below the mesa except for popular Lathrop Camp, located at the mouth of Lathrop Canyon alongside the Colorado River, and the Potato Bottom, Hardscrabble Bottom, and Upheaval Bottom campsites, located alongside the Green River.

There are two established picnic sites on the Island. One is at the end of the road at the Upheaval Dome Trailhead, in a pinyon-juniper woodland beneath the contorted rocks of the dome. The other lies 1 mile short of the Grandview Point roadend at the Gooseberry and White Rim Overlook Trailhead. This site is open, and rests on the slickrock edge of the mesa. Only a scattering of pinyons and junipers shade the sites, but vistas are far-ranging and panoramic.

The Needles Visitor Center is housed in a trailer alongside the Park road, and offers limited visitor facilities. Books, maps, weather and trail conditions, and backcountry use permits are available here. Business hours are 8 A.M.-4:30 P.M..

Campfire programs in the Needles District are conducted several nights a week at the campfire circle in Squaw Flat Campground A. Self-guided trails in the district include Roadside Ruin (*Trip 20*), Cave Spring (*Trip 21*), Pothole Point (*Trip 24*), and the Slickrock Trail (*Trip 25*). Guided hikes also follow these trails, plus parts of the Squaw Flat trail system. Schedules of activities are posted at the Visitor Center.

There are two campgrounds in the Needles District, along the west edge of Squaw Flat. They also serve as trailheads for most of the trails in

**Island in the Sky Visitor Center**

the district. Squaw Flat Campground A features 16 sites nestled against a long slickrock ridge, shaded by pinyon and juniper. Views from the campground are magnificent, stretching over the grassy expanse of Squaw Flat to the comb-like ridges of The Needles and a host of colorful slickrock buttes, including Woodenshoe Arch, North Six-shooter Peak, lofty Cathedral Butte and forested Horse Mountain.

Campground B, with 10 campsites, is similar in setting to Campground A in that most sites are set back against the slickrock and are shaded by pinyon and juniper. But panoramic views are lacking, providing campers with a more intimate association with the immediate surroundings of low domes and slickrock knolls. Water is not available at either campground, and no fee is charged. Water is available near the ranger residences, however, which lies along a signed spur road beyond (southwest of) the Visitor Center (see driving directions). Each site includes a picnic table and fire grill, and there are chemical toilets in each campground.

The Needles Outpost, located on a spur road near the Park boundary, offers ample facilities and services for Park visitors and is usually open from mid-March through October. The privately owned facility offers a general store, gasoline, propane, snack bar, showers, firewood, maps and books. A fee campground with water is available. Also available are jeep rentals, and arrangements can be made there for guided jeep tours and scenic flights.

There are several backcountry campsites on 4WD roads in the district, but a backcountry use permit is required to use them. Three are located in the depths of Salt Creek, and three others are located in highly scenic surroundings in The Grabens area, accessible via Elephant Hill.

There are two picnic areas in the Needles District. One lies alongside the Scenic Drive near the Pothole Point Trail, on a slickrock highland offering expansive vistas. The other is at the Elephant Hill Trailhead at the head of a box canyon, shaded by a woodland of pinyon and juniper.

In the Maze District, the Hans Flat Ranger Station serves as visitor center for both Canyonlands and Glen Canyon National Recreation Area. It is open, as are the other Canyonlands visitor centers, 8 A.M.-4:30 P.M., seven days a week. This ranger station, housed in a trailer, offers books, maps, some interpretive displays, and backcountry use permits. Hikers bound for The Maze can obtain their permits here, as well as jeepers who are bound for backcountry campsites.

There are no established campgrounds in the Maze District, but there are several backcountry vehicle campsites in the Land of Standing Rocks and at Maze Overlook. None of these campsites offers water, and campers must first obtain a backcountry use permit. There are also vehicle campsites in Horseshoe Canyon. The only interpretive activity in the Maze District is guided hikes in Horseshoe Canyon, conducted every Saturday 9 A.M.-3 P.M. from spring through the end of September. Participants meet at the Horseshoe Canyon Trailhead (see *Trip 37*, and driving directions).

For those who prefer guided jeep tours in Canyonlands or float trips on the Green and Colorado rivers, there are 13 guide services from which to choose in Moab. Moab also offers a variety of services to meet the needs of all Park visitors, although backpacking gear is in short supply. Moab, Monticello, and Green River, Utah, all offer groceries, gas, and lodging, plus several private campgrounds. Other campgrounds are available on nearby national-forest land, and visitors are also free to camp wherever they choose on national-forest and Bureau of Land Management lands, but everyone should attempt to minimize their impact on our priceless and irreplaceable public lands.

*For more information:*

Moab Headquarters Office
Canyonlands National Park
125 West 200 South
Moab, UT 84532
(801) 259-7164

or

Monticello Office
32 South 1st East
Monticello, UT 84534
(801) 587-2737

or

Call the Needles District at (801) 259-6568; or the Maze District at (801)259-6513.

*For information about Needles Outpost, contact:*

Mark and Christine Davis
P.O. Box 1107
Monticello, UT 84535
In season call (801) 259-2032

Note: Except for the Moab and Monticello national-park offices, other phones, including the one at Needles Outpost, are mobile radio phones, and reception is spotty at best. Visitors who are unable to make contact with district visitor centers are advised to call Moab Headquarters for information.

# Hiking in Canyonlands

## The Island District

Out of an annual average of the slightly more than 100,000 visitors who come to the 150,000-acre Island District, only about 400 backpackers have explored the backcountry of the Park annually in recent years. This low number of backpackers makes the backcountry of the Island the least used in all of Canyonlands National Park. Most visitors to the Island District use the Park for only a day, driving the Park road to scenic overlooks and perhaps hiking some of the short but rewarding mesa-top trails.

Except for short, day-use trails atop the Island in the Sky mesa, most trails are very rugged and demanding. Virtually all the district's backcountry trails plunge steeply over the great cliff band that nearly encircles the mesa and, although these trails are downhill all the way, they are rough and rocky, and descend 1000 feet or more to the White Rim bench far below. The trails are shadeless and mostly waterless, and are quite rigorous on the return trip to the mesa. But there is much to see and discover in the district's backcountry. Arches are common in the Navajo Sandstone near the mesa rim, and chipping sites and Anasazi granaries can be found by diligent hikers.

Most campsites in the backcountry are located in open desert basins or canyons below the rim. One exception is on the Syncline Loop Trail, where hikers can enjoy the shade of pinyons, junipers, and cottonwoods. Backpackers must remember to obtain a backcountry use permit at the Island Visitor Center before embarking on any backcountry excursion. Especially during spring, tiny biting gnats will annoy you wherever you travel in the Island District, and mosquitoes can be a nuisance along the rivers.

Only the Syncline Loop Trail (*Trip 15*) offers any surface water, and during dry years that water may not be reliable. Unless the hiker can make arrangements with a friend to supply water at points along the White Rim Jeep Trail, one is limited to the two or three days' supply of water one can carry.

Cross-country travel over the broad desert basins below the mesa is a delight to experienced hikers. The terrain above the White Rim is fairly gentle, and the hiker searching for solitude in unspoiled desert surroundings will find it here.

Novice hikers and those who simply don't have the time or energy required to follow the longer trails below the rim have eight short but highly rewarding mesa-top trails from which to choose (*Trips 1, 4-5, 8-10* and *13-14*). These trails sample all aspects of the mesa landscape, from arches to buttes, from grasslands to pinyon-juniper woodlands, Anasazi granaries, and the sweeping panoramas for which the Island is famous. Since backpackers must located their campsites out of sight of trails and 1/2 mile from trailheads and developed areas, the trail listed above are largely restricted to day use.

The White Rim Trail jeep road has become increasingly popular in recent years. It offers a number of backcountry vehicle campsites, a pseudo-wilderness experience far from the average Island tourists, and, in places, challenging driving conditions. The trip requires a high-clearance 4WD vehicle and an experienced driver. Most drivers follow the jeep trail in a clockwise direction, beginning at the Shafer Trail and ending on the Mineral Bottom Road. There are only two very rugged stretches enroute: the first lies beyond the Murphy Campsite where the road descends Murphy Hogback, and the second lies between Potato Bottom and the Hardscrabble Campsite. To get the most from a

trip along the White Rim Trail, plan on spending at least three days to complete the drive.

Since mountain bikes are not allowed on Park trails, bikers might consider riding on parts of the White Rim Trail. But like hikers, they are limited by the amount of water they can carry.

## The Needles District

The greatest concentration of trails in Canyonlands lies within the Needles District. This is a hiking district, and most of the annual average of about 85,000 visitors to The Needles are hikers. Of that number, nearly 3000 camp out in the backcountry each year, further attesting to the area's popularity as a backpacking destination. But there is so much backcountry here in The Needles that finding solitude is rarely a problem.

As in most Utah national parks, there are short trails near the primary Park road that are suitable for novice and casual hikers. But like most other trails in the district, some involve following cairns over slickrock and climbing ladders on steep cliffs.

The longer trails aren't particularly strenuous, but one does encounter much up and down hiking. These trails follow washes; cross grassy valleys, brush-clad flats and pinyon-juniper woodlands; and climb up and over slickrock divides. Many trail sections are simply cairned routes over slickrock, and hikers will occasionally encounter steep slickrock where they must scramble and use friction.

The greatest concentration of trails is in the vicinity of Squaw Flat Campground A, and these trails are among the most popular of all of Canyonlands. From the network of trails one can construct a variety of rewarding and highly scenic loop trips in the heart of The Needles. In addition to the incomparable scenery, the availability of water is an important factor contributing to the area's popularity.

Except during the driest times, hikers will usually find pools, if not running water, in upper Squaw Canyon, in Lost Canyon, in upper Elephant Canyon near Druid Arch, throughout much of Salt Creek, and in parts of Davis and

Lavender canyons. Most other trails, except during the wettest times, are usually dry. Only one trail in the district descends to the Colorado River (*Trip 35*), where there is an abundance of water, but one should drink river water only as a last resort. Be sure to purify any water in the backcountry. In general, dayhikers and backpackers should always carry an adequate water supply.

Despite the number of backpackers who use the backcountry, solitude is easy to find. The intricate nature of the terrain allows one to easily find a private campsite, even close to popular trails. Most potential campsites lie on benches above washes, and many are shaded by pinyon and juniper, sometimes nestled under an overhanging ledge.

Hikers aren't the only ones who use the district's backcountry. There are more 4WD trails in the Needles District than in any other national parks in Utah. Most follow washes and are easy driving, but the Elephant Hill Jeep Trail traverses more open terrain, and the initial stretch up and over the hill presents a challenge to the most seasoned driver. Several vehicle campsites along the district's jeep trails attract more than 3000 4WD enthusiasts each year.

Another attraction of the jeep trails is that they are open to use by mountain bikes; however, most are too sandy to ride on. The exceptions include the Elephant Hill Jeep Trail (*Trip 36*) and the jeep route to Colorado River Overlook (*Trip 19*). Bikers must remember they are restricted to roads only; off-road travel on mountain bikes or 4WD vehicles is not permitted.

There are several restricted-use areas and special regulations in the Needles District that hikers must be aware of.

- Camping in Chesler Park is restricted to three designated camping zones, with a maximum limit of 50 people per night.

- The Joint Trail (*Trip 33*), Colorado River Overlook (*Trip 19*), Confluence Overlook (*Trip 26*), and the upper 2 miles of Elephant Canyon (*Trip 32*) are restricted to day use.

Rock climbing is prohibited in three canyons within the Salt Creek Archaeological District: Salt Creek, Horse Canyon, and Lost Canyon.

For a list of regulations specific to Canyonlands National Park, see page 216.

## The Maze District

The Maze District is *terra incognita*; few people know of it, and fewer still have made the long trek, either in a jeep or on foot, to get there. The Maze is the domain of accomplished backpackers who enjoy pioneering their own way in untracked slickrock wilderness. Except for the trails leading from The Doll House to the Colorado River/Green River Overlook, Surprise Valley, and Spanish Bottom, which are passable to anyone in good physical condition, The Maze proper (the area lying north of the Land of Standing Rocks) is accessible only to experienced hikers with rock-climbing experience and with no fear of heights.

Except for the aforementioned trails in The Doll House area of the district, there is only one designated trail, and that is hardly a trail at all. The 1-mile-long Maze Trail, leading from Maze Overlook to the South Fork Horse Canyon, is a rugged cairned route requiring downclimbing on very steep and exposed pitches of slickrock. No one but experienced hikers should attempt this easiest of routes into The Maze.

There are no other trails in The Maze, but there are a number of cairned routes leading out of the labyrinth. One must search diligently for these routes, as they are usually cairned only where they begin to leave the canyons. Hikers attempting to pioneer their own routes must do so on a trial-and-error basis. All The Maze canyons are exceedingly sandy, and hiking there is slow and tedious. On any trip into The Maze, the wise backpacker will carry a rope to lower or hoist packs over the Class 3 or 4 pitches required to enter or exit the labyrinth.

Many hikers in the district have the desire to reach either the Green or Colorado rivers. But the only route that doesn't encounter pouroffs or require rock-climbing skills is the 1 1/4-mile trail from The Doll House to Spanish Bottom.

Water is found in relative abundance in The Maze, usually originating as seeps in a wash and flowing into pools. During dry periods, there is less flowing water but the pools persist. Many pools are full of algae, tadpoles and water bugs, and some may have a slimy film on the surface. But with purification, most water sources are potable; they are mineralized and have a distinctive taste. Hikers in The Fins and Ernies Country, however, will find those areas to be mostly dry; so, travel there is restricted by the amount of water one can carry. There is usually no water available enroute to The Maze via the North Trail, however, so hikers should first check on water availability at Hans Flat, then pack at least enough water to get into The Maze.

Campsites in The Maze are limited only by one's imagination. Slickrock shelves, mesas, or pinyon- and juniper-clad benches above washes are found throughout the area.

Perhaps the greatest nuisance to hikers in all Canyonlands districts is bugs. During warm weather hikers will be tempted to wear shorts, but the wise hiker will always bring a pair of long pants. In the washes, carnivorous sand flies will attack your legs and arms with a vengeance. In addition, tiny biting gnats and mosquitoes will harass you from spring until midsummer. A good insect repellent will usually give hikers a brief respite from these annoying insects.

During recent years, use of 4WD vehicles and mountain bikes on the jeep trails of the district has increased markedly, and so has dayhiking on district trails and routes. A little more than 5000 visitors come to The Maze yearly, and only slightly more than 10 percent of that number travel overnight into the backcountry.

There are no special restrictions regarding the use of The Maze backcountry, except for the Park regulations listed below. However, whether you're spending the night in the backcountry or in one of the vehicle campsites, you must obtain a backcountry use permit at the Hans Flat Ranger Station.

Horseshoe Canyon, a detached unit of the Park lying northwest of the Maze District, offers easy hiking via a long-closed road and a sandy wash. Not only is the canyon beautiful in its own right, but it offers easy access to some of the finest rock-art panels on the Colorado Plateau. The canyon is restricted to day use, from the end of the jeep road at the barricade near Water

**Moqui stairs on the Maze Trail**

Canyon southward to the Park boundary beyond the Great Gallery pictograph panel.

The optimum seasons for hiking in Canyonlands National Park are much the same as in other Utah national parks. See *Hiking Seasons* in the "Hiking Utah's Desert Parks" chapter.

While most hikers try to limit their impact while traveling through the Park's backcountry, many will be lured off the main trails to gain a better view of an arch, a rock-art panel, some Anasazi ruins, or a particularly beautiful wildflower or animal. When traveling off-trail, try to walk over slickrock or in drainage courses as much as possible to avoid damaging the cryptogamic crust and other coarse but fragile desert plants.

Although most backcountry water sources are safe to drink after purification, some water has a high mineral content and a distinctive taste. In particular, springs issuing from the Moenkopi Formation are too mineralized to drink even after purification, and boiling further concentrates the minerals. Some filters help to eliminate much of the mineral taste. Hikers planning a trip to the Green or Colorado rivers may think it is unnecessary to pack water, since there is an unlimited supply at the rivers. But, unless one is dying of thirst, one should avoid drinking river water, which is not much different from drinking mud. The rivers are exceedingly silty, and contain natural contaminants, agricultural chemicals, and uranium-mining tailings. Remember these rivers flow for hundreds of miles before reaching Canyonlands, and they are the dumping grounds not only for natural runoff but for the agricultural and industrial developments throughout their courses.

Following is a list of Park regulations specific to Canyonlands National Park:

- Campsites in the backcountry must be located 1/2 mile from trailheads and developed areas (such as campgrounds and visitor centers), out of sight of backcountry foot trails and 4WD roads, and 300 feet from non-flowing water sources (such as springs, potholes, and seeps), recognizable archaeological sites, and backcountry trail junctions. Camping no less than 100 feet from flowing water is required, and 300 feet is recommended, except for the Green and Colorado rivers, where one may camp closer.

- Group size for overnight camping in the backcountry is limited to 12 persons-15 persons in vehicle campsites.

- If one must use soap, then biodegradable soaps are recommended for washing in the backcountry. The use of soap is restricted to no less than the camping distances from water listed above. Swimming in pools and potholes is allowed only in pools which are continuously recharged by flowing water.

- Human waste must be buried in soil four to six inches deep and at least 100 feet from water sources. Toilet paper must be carried out.

- Backcountry use permits are required for all overnight camping, including 4WD campsites, in the Park's backcountry.

# Driving to Canyonlands' Trailheads

## The Island in the Sky District, *Trips 1-15*

The trails of the Island District are easily reached via the paved Park road, which branches off from Utah 313 near Dead Horse Point State Park.

(0.0) Prominently signed Utah 313 branches southwest from U.S. 191 about 20.5 miles south of Crescent Junction and Interstate 70, and 9 miles northwest of Moab. Signs list mileages to Dead Horse Point State Park and Canyonlands National Park, and warn that no services are available ahead. Park visitors should be sure to have a full tank of gas and an ample water supply. Initially the road ascends the drainage of Sevenmile Canyon, but eventually we leave the canyon floor and execute two tight switchbacks, then climb onto a broad plateau.

(8.2) A graded Bureau of Land Management road forks right, leading to Dubinky Well, and to Interstate 70 in 70 miles. We soon climb steadily to the higher mesa to the south and meander through a thick woodland. Another graded Bureau of Land Management road forks right (3.7; 11.9) just beyond a cattleguard. The road is signed HORSETHIEF POINT 12, and MINERAL CANYON BOAT RAMP 15. This road offers access to the Green River at a put-in point for river trips, and is also the terminus of the White Rim Trail jeep road. Drivers should not attempt to reach the river via that road without a high-clearance vehicle.

The grade finally abates as we reach the edge of the mesa's grasslands and meet (2.3; 14.2) the left-branching road to Dead Horse Point. The state park there offers a campground with water, and an exceptional view into the canyon of the Colorado River. Our paved road becomes noticeably wider as we continue south from that junction.

(4.4; 18.6) Cross a cattleguard and enter Canyonlands National Park. A short distance ahead is a turnout and large Park sign.

(1.3; 19.9) A signed spur road on our left leads to the Shafer Trail jeep road and the White Rim Trail jeep road. Beyond it we descend gently, soon reaching the parking area at the Visitor Center (0.9; 20.8), at an elevation of 5900 feet. Visitors are asked to pay the entrance fee inside before proceeding farther. A sign just beyond the Visitor Center lists various destinations and mileages.

The mesa becomes increasingly narrow as we descend past the Visitor Center, soon reaching a prominently signed spur road (0.5; 21.3) forking left and ending in 0.1 mile at the **Trailhead 1** parking area, the starting point for *Trips 1* and *2*.

Continuing the descent beyond that spur road, we pass through a gate that may be closed during inclement weather, then reach the end of the downhill grade at the narrow isthmus of The Neck at 5800 feet. Beyond it, we begin steadily climbing past the signed Shafer Trail Viewpoint (0.7; 22.0) and eventually top out on the rolling grasslands of Grays Pasture.

(0.9; 22.9) Signed Lathrop Trailhead on the left side of the road. *Trip 3* to the White Rim begins here at **Trailhead 2**. There is parking space for about 4-6 vehicles in the small turnout.

Our road continues to bisect broad Grays Pasture. From the south end of the pasture, the road executes several S-curves as we gently ascend a sparsely wooded part of the mesa.

(4.0; 26.9) Signed Mesa Arch Trailhead lies on the left side of the road. Hikers bound for *Trip 4* will leave the road here and proceed 100 feet to the parking area at **Trailhead 3**. Quite soon we reach a signed junction (0.2; 27.1) where hikers bound for *Trips 5* through *9* will bear left toward Grand View Point, while those bound for *Trips 10* through *15* will turn right toward Upheaval Dome.

Branching left onto the Grand View Point mesa, the road initially skirts the base of a row of low knolls but soon climbs to the mesa top beyond (1.0; 28.1).

(1.5; 29.6) Hikers bound for *Trips 5* and *6* will find a narrow dirt road branching right. A small sign about 100 feet down that lane indicates MURPHY POINT, ROUGH ROAD, 1.7 MILES. This road is very narrow, with a slightly high center, but it can be negotiated by low-slung cars in dry weather. It proceeds southwest, skirting the edge of the largest grassland on Grand View Point.

(0.4; 30.0) *Trip 6* begins at **Trailhead 4**, at the MURPHY TRAIL sign, and vehicles have but a small space in which to park. The road ahead immediately becomes much rougher, and a sign warns against passenger-car travel beyond this point. High-clearance is a necessity, and 4WD would be desirable. The road ends at a small turnaround (1.2; 31.6) at **Trailhead 5** near the end of Murphy Point, where *Trip 5* begins. Park visitors without a high-clearance vehicle may enjoy a walk or a mountain-bike ride along this scenic road.

(29.6) Resuming our drive on the Park road, we begin to approach the eastern rim of the sparsely wooded mesa, and soon reach a short spur road (0.7; 30.3) forming a small loop on the left side of the mesa. Proceeding south on the main road, we drive along the narrowing mesa.

(1.9; 32.2) Reaching a spur road branching left to a signed picnic area, hikers bound for *Trips 7* and *8* will turn off here and proceed midway through the picnic area for 0.1 mile to the **Trailhead 6** parking area, with only four parking slots for hikers.

The main road ahead leads to a magnificent vista point offering the most comprehensive views of Canyonlands National Park available from any point in the Park. No visitor to the Island District should miss the drive to Grand View Point. The road ends in a one-way loop (1.0; 33.2) just short of the viewing area and the beginning of *Trip 9* at **Trailhead 7**.

(27.1) Visitors aiming for *Trips 10* through *15*, Willow Flat Campground, or the picnic area at the Upheaval Dome Trailhead will turn right at the aforementioned junction just south of the Mesa Arch Trailhead. The road initially leads southwest but soon curves northwest through Willow Flat, another broad grassland on the mesa.

(0.3; 27.4) A signed spur road to the campground branches left. This road is wide, with a gravel surface, but can be rough due to infrequent maintenance. Initially, the road heads west toward a prominent cluster of Navajo Sandstone domes as it descends gently across the grassy expanse of Willow Flat. But upon reaching a gated service road, it turns abruptly south and descends steadily amid a pinyon-juniper woodland to a left-branching spur to the campground (1.0; 28.4). The road continues downhill for another 200 yards to a spacious parking area at the roadend. A short but immensely rewarding jaunt to the rim just beyond at Green River Overlook offers a sublime, cliff-framed view of the Green River in Labyrinth Canyon, the White Rim and the vast bench above it flanking both sides of the river, The Maze, Orange Cliffs, the prominent dome of Cleopatras Chair, and Ekker and Elaterite buttes. A stop here, particularly at sunrise or sunset, is a must for all visitors to the Island District.

(27.4) Resuming our drive northwest on the Park road, we notice the flat-topped slickrock bluff of Aztec Butte looming ahead on the northern skyline, and soon reach the spur road leading to the parking area and **Trailhead 8** for *Trip 10* (0.4; 27.8).

(1.4; 29.2) A small signed turnout on the left shoulder of the road offers limited parking space for *Trip 11* hikers at **Trailhead 9**. Soon we regain the top of the mesa, winding in and out of several minor draws.

(1.7; 30.9) The ALCOVE SPRING TRAIL-HEAD, indicated by a small sign, directs *Trip 12* hikers to the small parking area at **Trailhead 10** on the northeast side of the road.

(0.4; 31.3) The prominently signed trailhead for Whale Rock lies on the right side of the road at the foot of that dome, where *Trip 13* hikers begin their short but rewarding slickrock jaunt at **Trailhead 11**. Already on the flanks of Upheaval Dome, we soon curve into upper Syncline Valley and shortly thereafter reach the loop at

(0.8; 32.1) the roadend at **Trailhead 12**. There is ample parking space here for *Trips 14* and *15* hikers.

## The Needles District, *Trips 16-36*

The Needles District of Canyonlands National Park, although it lies just across the Colorado River from the Island in the Sky, requires a long, roundabout drive over mesas and down deep canyons to gain access. The only road into The Needles is Utah Highway 211, a paved two-lane highway branching west from U.S. Highway 191, 40 miles south of Moab, and 14 miles north of Monticello.

(0.0) The prominently signed junction with Utah Highway 211 lies near the southern end of Dry Valley between the erosional outliers of Navajo Sandstone of Church Rock to the east and George Rock to the west. A sign a short distance west of the junction indicates that there are limited services, including gas and camping, 34 miles ahead.

The road strikes a southwesterly course across broad flats then begins to rise above the flats, eventually topping out on Photograph Gap. Presently the road descends steadily into the broad sagebrush-clad valley of Harts Draw. Rising above the southern margin of the valley onto the wooded slopes of Harts Point, we'll ignore a prominent left-branching graded road (9.6) leading into the Abajo Mountains and a right fork immediately thereafter, staying on the pavement. But, the road soon begins descending a steep grade toward an unnamed canyon. Shortly we negotiate two sharply curving switchbacks and then reach the canyon bottom. Soon, Indian Creek, usually boasting a small flow of water, joins from the south, its course thickly clad in large Fremont cottonwoods.

After the road curves northwest, we reach the signed turnoff (2.5; 12.1) to Newspaper Rock State Historical Monument. There is a superb rock-art panel boasting a profusion of historic and pre-historic petroglyphs just off the road. A picnic area lies opposite the petroglyph parking area, where visitors can relax in the deep canyon beneath the shade of large, spreading cottonwoods.

The road ahead follows above Indian Creek wash in a northwestern direction. The road makes many twists and turns and must be driven slowly, which allows visitors ample opportunity to enjoy the majestic desert scenery. Eventually, we emerge from the confines of upper Indian Creek canyon and its broad intermediate valley spreads out before us. Soon a cluster of ranch buildings come into view near the wash south of our road. That is the headquarters of Dugout Ranch, a cattle operation that has survived in the Canyonlands country since 1885. Soon, at San Juan County Road 104 (7.0; 17.1), a left-turn sign indicates the turnoff to the ranch, and hikers undertaking *Trip 16* will want to leave the pavement here, just before reaching a pond that lies along the north side of the road.

Turning south onto San Juan County Road 104, the gaping canyon of North Cottonwood Creek spreads out to the south, a broad gash cutting far back into the wooded plateau beneath the Abajo Mountains. This is a good dirt road, and is passable to most vehicles during dry weather, but should be avoided during, and for a day or so after, heavy rains. A high-clearance vehicle is desirable as the road is rocky in places. If in doubt about road conditions, check with the Needles Visitor Center when you obtain your backcountry permit for upper Salt Creek. Permits can also be obtained at the Monticello Office.

Quite soon, our dirt road leads us past the ranch house, and within one-half mile we cross usually-dry Indian Creek wash. Beyond this easy crossing we emerge into the broad lower reaches of North Cottonwood Creek.

(3.5; 20.6) Reaching a junction bear right where the sign indicates ROAD 104 and BEEF BASIN. Shortly we pass through a shady cottonwood grove, then ford small North Cottonwood Creek (0.3; 20.9). For the following two miles we continue along the canyon floor, but then we begin climbing at a moderate grade to gain a broad wooded bench. We work our way ever higher above the deepening canyon, curving in and out of several minor drainages.

Eventually the road curves westward high above the deep defile of Stevens Canyon. Then the road curves northwest, traversing an exceedingly steep and crumbling slope

**In the Great Gallery, Horseshoe Canyon**

beneath soaring cliffs and through the runoff of a small spring. Beyond this narrow stretch of road we emerge onto the broad wooded expanse of Salt Creek Mesa, heading for bulky Cathedral Butte, a cliff-bound monolith jutting 1000 feet skyward from the high tableland. The road soon passes above a small stock reservoir and, as we curve around to the west side of the butte, be sure to ignore a right-branching, northwest-bound jeep road. That road follows a point of the mesa for two miles to a superb overlook of upper Salt Creek, but requires 4WD to negotiate it.

Quite soon, however, we enjoy our own dramatic vista into the slickrock maze of upper Salt Creek. Where we regain the mesa just beyond (west of) Cathedral Butte, we meet a minor spur road branching right to a primitive camping area (12.5; 33.4). (If you reach a left-branching road, you've gone 100 yards too far.) Turn right onto that spur road and park in the pinyon-juniper woods at its end after 100 yards at **Trailhead 13**. There is no sign indicating the trail into upper Salt Creek, but *Trip 16* hikers should have no trouble following the cairns along the mesa rim to begin their journey.

Resuming the drive into the Needles District, we enjoy magnificent scenery as we progress northwest. The splintered pinnacles of North and South Six-shooter peaks loom ahead of us; their spires are merely erosional remnants of the Wingate Sandstone that completely covered the region millions of years ago prior to uplift and the subsequent erosion of the canyons. But, to our north the Wingate cliffs form an impassable barrier and, when combined with the red ledges of the overlying Kayenta Formation and domes of Navajo Sandstone, vertical relief from the road to the mesa rim approaches 1000 feet.

One-half mile beyond the Dugout Ranch, we pass above a reservoir and continue skirting the foot of the cliffs as we proceed into the increasingly broad Indian Creek valley. Extensive irrigated hay fields, spreading out south of the road, are bright green even during the searing heat of summer.

(3.6; 20.7) A small sign indicates Lavender Canyon. *Trip 17* gets underway here at **Trailhead 14** where the jeep road forks left, southwest, along the edge of a hayfield.

Soon our road strikes out into the valley, leaving the great cliffs farther behind. Eventually we bridge Indian Creek, then climb above it, soon crossing a cattleguard and quickly reaching a sign indicating a left-branching junction, (3.2; 23.9). The small sign facing eastbound drivers indicates Davis Canyon where a dirt road branches left, southeast. *Trip 18* begins here at **Trailhead 15**.

The road ahead leads us northwest along the southern margin of the immense Indian Creek basin. A sign indicating a right-branching spur road is encountered just before we reach a northbound dirt road (2.7; 26.6) leading into Lockhart Basin. Thereafter, we pass through grassy pockets just north of low, flat-topped buttes and bluffs.

Soon the road dips into a minor wash, then climbs to a rise just south of a prominent red slickrock butte. From the top of the rise the slickrock spires of The Needles suddenly explode upon the scene, beautifully colored in bands of orange, red, and white. Now our road descends a broad grassy expanse, soon entering Canyonlands National Park (2.7; 29.3) at a fenceline and cattleguard. We continue the gentle descent and before long, encounter a paved, northbound spur road (1.4; 30.7) leading 0.6 mile north to Needles Outpost, where gas, camping, showers, groceries, and meals are available.

Shortly thereafter we bridge the usually dry wash of Salt Creek, then rise gradually to the Needles Visitor Center, simply a trailer alongside the road (1.1; 31.8). We are required to pay the entrance fee inside the Visitor Center, where maps, books, and information as well as backcountry permits, are available. *Trip 19* begins at the southwest end of the parking area, **Trailhead 16**, where a sign indicates Colorado River Overlook.

Beyond the Visitor Center we curve south, ascending a slight grade and soon reaching the prominently signed ROADSIDE RUIN TRAILHEAD on the left (east) side of the road (0.3; 32.1). *Trip 20* hikers begin their short stroll here at **Trailhead 17**. The road ahead continues the gentle ascent southwest toward the massive, convoluted red monolith of Squaw Butte, towering nearly 400 feet above us. Soon we encounter a signed junction (0.5; 32.6), where those of us taking *Trips 21-23* will turn left.

This left-branching road is signed for RANGER RESIDENCES and SALT CREEK, and turning here we follow a slickrock bench, ignoring a signed service road after 1/4 mile. Soon we descend toward Squaw Canyon.

(0.7; 33.3) Visitors taking *Trips 21-23* will turn left (east) at the signed junction with a wide dirt road. This road typically has a rough washboard surface as it crosses brushy flats mantled in greasewood, sagebrush and rabbitbrush beneath low sandstone knolls. Passing the Split Top Group Campsite, we quickly reach the Salt Creek Jeep Trail (0.8; 34.1) branching right (south). Drivers bound for *Trips 22* and *23* will begin their journeys here at **Trailhead 18**, while *Trip 21* hikers should bear left, soon reaching the roadend and parking area of **Trailhead 19** alongside Squaw Canyon wash (0.2; 34.3).

Visitors heading to other trailheads or the campgrounds in The Needles need not retrace their route back to the Park road. Returning to the junction with the paved road beneath Squaw Butte, they can turn left, skirting the cottonwood-lined wash of Squaw Canyon. Ignore a signed service road after 0.2 mile, and continue on past the ranger residences, soon reaching a pumphouse and the only developed water source in the district (0.5; 33.8). Those among us who stop here to tank up on water will enjoy a fine view of uniquely beautiful Woodenshoe Arch on the southern skyline. The road ahead winds along the foot of slickrock bluffs, climbs above the wash and soon passes the Woodenshoe Group Campsite, then shortly re-joins the Park road (0.7; 34.5).

The most direct route into The Needles follows the right fork of the paved Park road at the Ranger Residence-Salt Creek spur road junction (32.6).

This road climbs a grade north of Squaw Butte. The butte is atypical of Colorado Plateau buttes, since it does not have the usual square-edged profile. Rather, its bulky mass is irregular, featuring slickrock buttresses, towers, and balanced rocks on its flanks. Curving around the butte, we intercept a minor drainage and follow it onto a higher bench, where a fine view of Woodenshoe Arch unfolds. A turnout on the left hand side of the road offers an unobstructed view of the arch. Like a giant clog, Woodenshoe Arch rests atop a knife-edged ridge of Cedar Mesa slickrock, its crest punctuated by several prominent towers. Quite soon we reach the previously described road (1.4; 34.0) branching left to WATER (in 0.7 mile) and to the SALT CREEK JEEP TRAIL.

Staying on the right at that junction, we curve northwest above Squaw Canyon, soon emerging onto the open grasslands of expansive Squaw Flat, and finally reaching a junction with the Scenic Drive, leading straight ahead to trailheads for *Trips 24-26*, and another road forking left (west) (0.5; 34.5), to the campgrounds and Elephant Hill, and to trailheads for *Trips 27-36*.

The Scenic Drive offers far-ranging vistas of the Canyonlands basin, and passes through grasslands, minor canyons and much slickrock enroute to the canyon rim viewpoint overlooking Big Spring Canyon

Initially, the road follows a northwestern course across broad Squaw Flat. Upon leaving Squaw Flat, we enter a landscape dominated by hummocks and knobs of red- and white-banded Cedar Mesa Sandstone and incised by numerous shallow drainages.

(1.7; 36.2) A picnic area lies on the left (west) side of the road. Soon thereafter, a sign indicates POTHOLE POINT, and hikers bound for *Trips 24* will leave the road here and park in the paved turnout at **Trailhead 20** on the road's west shoulder (0.4; 36.6). The road ahead winds in and out of a few minor draws and, just beyond a sign warning the ROAD ENDS 1000 FEET AHEAD, *Trip 25* hikers will park in a turnout on the right side of the road (1.3; 37.9), where **Trailhead 21** is indicated by a FOOT TRAIL sign. The road then curves west and quickly ends in a loop at **Trail-**

**head 22** (0.1; 38.0) high above Big Spring Canyon, where *Trip 26* hikers begin their trek into the backcountry.

Since the majority of trails in the Needles District begin at Campground A and Elephant Hill, most hikers will bear left at the junction with the Scenic Drive (34.5). This road curves toward the western margin of Squaw Flat, quickly reaching the road forking right to Campground B and Elephant Hill (0.25; 34.75).

To reach Campground A and the Squaw Flat Trailhead, continue straight ahead. The road skirts the foot of slickrock knolls on the right, while passing numerous scenic campsites. Shortly after the road curves west, we reach the large parking area for Squaw Flat Trailhead A next to the campfire circle on the south shoulder of the road (0.9; 35.65). *Trips 27, 28, 29,* and *31* begin at **Trailhead 23**. *Trip 30* hikers going to or from Campground B will find their signed trail opposite the parking area. The campground road ends in a loop at the foot of the towering butte a short distance ahead (0.15; 35.8).

Those of us bound for Campground B and Elephant Hill will turn right at the aforementioned junction, proceeding west.

(0.25; 35.0) The spur to Campground B forks left, while the road to Elephant Hill continues straight ahead. To reach Squaw Flat Trailhead B turn left and enter the campground, soon avoiding a left-branching spur road leading to more campsites. The small **Trailhead 24** parking area is located just short of Campsite 26 at the loop at the roadend, on the right side of the road (0.4; 35.4).

If you're heading for Elephant Hill, continue straight ahead beyond the Campground B turnoff, soon reaching the end of the pavement. This is a good dirt road passable to passenger cars except during or immediately following heavy rains. It is fairly smooth, but can be rocky and sandy in places. There are sharp curves, a few minor grades, and some narrow stretches that dictate careful driving.

The road climbs easily, dipping into a minor wash, then climbs out of it to curve northwest, passing an old, built-up jeep trail climbing the

slickrock just west of a wide turnout on the shoulder of the road.

We soon curve southwest, where the presently narrow road climbs to an open bench. Then the road descends steadily, switchbacking twice into Big Spring Canyon. After following above the wash and heading south, we soon cross the wash. The road ahead curves westward and gently ascends a wooded branch canyon where the roadbed becomes intermittently sandy. Approaching the head of this box canyon, we soon reach the **Trailhead 25** parking area next to picnic tables and pit toilets (2.7; 37.7). *Trips 32-34* begin at the south end of the parking area where a sign lists various destinations. *Trips 35* and *36* follow the signed ELEPHANT HILL JEEP TRAIL as it climbs steep slickrock to the ridge on the western skyline.

## The Maze District, *Trips 37* **and** *38*

Although the Maze can be seen from The Needles and Island districts of Canyonlands National Park, a very long and circuitous drive must be made to reach that district, the most remote region in all of Utah's national parks.

The signed turnoff to the Maze District lies on the east side of Utah Highway 24, about 21 miles north of Hanksville, and 24 3/4 miles south of the Interstate 70/Utah Highway 24 junction west of Green River. The turnoff is easy to miss, but to pinpoint its exact location, look for the signed turnoff to Goblin Valley State Park. The road to The Maze lies one-half mile south of that turnoff.

A high-clearance vehicle is advised on this road, as portions of it can be buried in drift sand. A 4WD vehicle with high-clearance may be necessary to reach the North Trail Trailhead. To drive the Flint Trail into the Land of Standing Rocks or to Maze Overlook, a high-clearance 4WD vehicle with a short wheelbase is required. Standard size pick-ups will have great difficulty negotiating the Flint Trail switchbacks.

Before venturing out this road toward The Maze, be sure to have several gallons of water, extra gasoline, a tow rope and preferably a winch, and basic survival gear in case you get stuck or damage your vehicle.

At the junction with Utah Highway 24 (0.0), a large sign lists various destinations and mileages: ROOST FLATS-32; PARK RANGER-46; FLINT TRAIL-60; THE MAZE-80; UTAH HIGHWAY 95-100. Proceeding southeastward across the vast sandy, grass and shrub-dotted San Rafael Desert, we soon cross sections of drift sand as we rise gradually over the desert floor. Ignore a left fork leading to a gravel pit (2.0) and shortly thereafter we avoid right and left branching roads (0.8; 2.8). The road ahead jogs east beyond Jeffery Well, climbing to a gap flanked by towering buttes. The road descends gradually back onto the desert floor beyond the gap, skirting the foot of Big Top, a massive butte soaring skyward to the south.

(8.1; 10.9) Bear right where another good, graded road branches left, signed for Dugout Spring. Beyond this junction we continue our gradual ascent of the sloping San Rafael Desert, but soon we climb moderately to gain a higher bench.

(5.0; 15.9) Avoid a right-forking road leading to a ranch house atop the bench, beyond which we continue winding ever higher.

(8.5; 24.4) A signed junction indicates the Horseshoe Canyon Foot Trail is reached via the left fork, while Hans Flat Ranger Station lies ahead via the right fork. *Trip 37* hikers will turn left here, winding steadily downhill onto the sandy floor of Antelope Valley. Descending northeast through grassy and shrubby Antelope Valley, we reach a signed junction (5.0; 29.4) indicating HORSESHOE CANYON and turn right. This spur road is more narrow than the main dirt road, and has rocky, eroded, rough and washboard stretches. Although best suited for high-clearance vehicles, passenger cars can nevertheless make the drive, but should be driven with caution. The road gently climbs the eastern flank of the valley, then ascends moderately over rocky sections to the mesa top on the rim of Horseshoe Canyon (1.7; 31.1). *Trip 37* hikers begin their memorable trek just beyond the information sign at the spacious **Trailhead 26** parking area.

Those of us bound for The Maze, however, will ignore the road to Horseshoe Canyon (24.4) and proceed straight ahead, continuing the gradual ascent of the plateau.

(7.0; 31.4) A signed junction directs us to bear left where a right fork leads to Ekker Ranch, one of the oldest operating cattle ranches in the Canyonlands region.

(2.7; 34.1) A lesser-used road, signed for GRANARY SPRING, branches off to the left. Bearing right, we soon enter beautiful Twin Corral Flats, beyond which we climb into a pinyon-juniper woodland. Another left fork is passed (10.5; 44.6) and immediately beyond it, a sign indicates our entrance into Hans Flat. The road ahead becomes quite sandy and rough, and shortly we enter Glen Canyon National Recreation Area, then encounter a bulletin board and the trailer housing Hans Flat Ranger Station (0.7; 45.3), high on the plateau at 6580 feet in elevation.

Backcountry permits for backpacking or camping in the vehicle campsites in the Maze District are available inside, or, if the station is closed, visitors may fill out their own permits available from the dispenser at the bulletin board. The ranger station offers books and maps for sale, and is your sole source of information in the area on the recreation area and the national park. Albeit far from civilization, there is a radiophone at Hans Flat, and visitors should report emergencies to the ranger station here.

The 4WD route to Horseshoe Canyon (22 miles) forks left here, but we follow the road southeast, indicated by a FLINT TRAIL sign. This road becomes exceedingly rough, crossing much slickrock as we proceed. A high-clearance two-wheel drive vehicle is a necessity, and a 4WD vehicle would be desirable. Signs along the way indicate there is no camping alongside the road.

(0.9; 46.2) A spur branches left, leading 400 feet to a dramatic overlook of Millard Canyon.

(1.4; 47.6) Another spur branches left, signed for French's Spring.

(0.2; 47.8) *Trip 38* hikers will turn left off the main road where a sign points to North Point and Panorama Point. The Flint Trail lies 11.5 miles south on the very rough main road. Our road is even narrower and rougher, and is passable to high-clearance two-wheel drive vehicles for only a short distance. Hikers without the benefit of 4WD must look for a parking space near the junction.

The road descends the North Point mesa, passing steep, eroded sections of slickrock. But soon, the grade abates and we undulate over the narrow mesa to **Trailhead 27** (1.0; 48.8), indicated by a small NORTH POINT TRAIL sign. Parking is available among the pinyons and junipers opposite the sign on the north side of the road.

# Trips 1-15: Island in the Sky District

# Trip 1
## Shafer Canyon Viewpoint Trail

**Distance**: 0.4 mile round trip
**Low/High elevations**: 5760'/5820'
**Suited for**: Walk
**Difficulty**: Easy
**Best seasons**: April through mid-June; mid-September through October.
**Map/Trailhead**: 35/1
**Hazards**: Steep dropoffs; little shade.

**Introduction**: This is the shortest Island District trail, and is passable to most any Park visitor. The viewpoint offers an exceptional aerial-like view typical of the Island mesa overlooks, including views of the Shafer Trail and the rugged canyon of the Colorado River.

**Description**: While *Trip 2* hikers will turn right at the trailhead, our brief stroll begins via the left-forking (eastbound) trail (0.0; 5820). After descending slightly among widely scattered Utah junipers and pinyons, we quickly reach level ground and follow the rocky promontory to the trail's end (0.2; 5760) at a distinctly cross-bedded knoll of Navajo Sandstone.

Early-season hikers will enjoy the yellow blooms of hymenopappus enlivening the sandy point, growing among scattered blackbrush.

Since the promontory juts east into the gaping maw of South Fork Shafer Canyon, our vista is unobstructed and far-reaching. Great cliffs encircle the head of the canyon, composed of the Glen Canyon Group of sedimentary rocks—the Navajo, Kayenta, and Wingate—and plunge 1000 feet into the declivity below. Descending a break in the cliff band that bounds all of Island in the Sky mesa are the steep switchbacks of the Shafer Trail jeep road, where four-wheel drivers typically begin their excursion down to the White Rim Trail jeep road, seen traversing the broad bench far below. A narrow band of White Rim sandstone forms the rim of the bench.

Perhaps the most unusual microhabitat in all of the Island District lies along the foot of the Navajo Sandstone cliff south of our viewpoint. While pinyon-and-juniper woodland dominates in the canyon and atop the mesa, a seepline at the foot of the Navajo Sandstone cliff nurtures a stand of Douglas-firs, the only stand of these trees in the arid Island District. Even during summer, hikers will notice that this north-facing cliff receives only a modicum of sunlight.

**Shafer Trail switchbacks are classic**

# Trip 2
## Neck Spring Loop Trail

**Distance**: 5.3 miles, loop trip
**Low/High elevations**: 5520'/5960'
**Suited for**: Dayhike
**Difficulty**: Moderate
**Best seasons**: April through mid-June; mid-September through October.
**Map/Trailhead**: 35/1
**Hazards**: Steep dropoffs.

**Introduction**: This is a fine dayhike, surveying much of the varied scenery and environments found on and near the Island in the Sky mesa. Not only will hikers enjoy an intimate association with the Island mesa landscape, but far-reaching views help to put the Island into perspective in the larger scheme of Canyonlands. The hike also allows a glimpse into the bygone days of cattle and sheep ranching on the mesa, when the trickling waters of Neck and Cabin springs offered some of the few watering sources for grazing stock.

**Description**: Our day trip begins at the south end of the parking area (0.0; 5820), branching right (west) from the Shafer Canyon Viewpoint Trail (*Trip 1*). We start a counterclockwise loop by first dropping quickly west away from the rim to the Park road, crossing it via a crosswalk, and resuming our trail walk west, following cairns across a pinyon- and juniper-studded bench.

Soon, an old road joins our trail (0.2; 5700), descending from the north, and at one time offering access for ranchers to the springs that lie ahead. Our trail then descends steadily for a short time, after which we reach the floor of a shallow basin at the head of Taylor Canyon, the primary drainage of the Island in the Sky mesa. The trail ahead winds south through the basin, first passing below the narrow isthmus of The Neck and then beneath a colorful Navajo Sandstone cliff.

Colorful seasonal wildflowers adorn the floor of the basin, and cryptogamic soil is well developed, so hikers must be sure to stay on the trail. In a pinyon-juniper woodland we curve into a shady alcove with a mossy seepline. A few minor ups and downs ensue, and we soon contour into another, deeper alcove, where seeps nurture abundant water-loving vegetation. A sheer cliff of Navajo Sandstone, streaked with red iron minerals and darkened by desert varnish, soars 200 feet behind the alcove. Cars on the road above can be heard but not seen, and we will soon be out of earshot of tourist traffic.

The trail ahead curves into more alcoves, and finally we reach the largest alcove thus far, crossing the often-damp wash below it (1.35; 5660) that drains Neck Spring. Wildrose, Gambel oak, and even small Fremont cottonwoods crowd the banks of the wash. Immediately beyond the crossing a short trail forks left, climbing amid Gambel oak and juniper to an old watering trough, a remnant of the days of cattle and sheep grazing on the mesa.

Our trail descends north, closely following the wash downstream before contouring northwest above it, continuing our circuit around the scalloped headwaters of Taylor Canyon. The trail ahead undulates over sandy slopes amid scattered pinyon and juniper, blackbrush, and clumps of ground-hugging wavy-leaf oak. Tall lupine, haplopappus, and scarlet gilia enliven the sandy hillside in season, from which we obtain fine views over cliff-bound upper Taylor Canyon and behind us to the narrow gap of The Neck.

About midway between Neck and Cabin springs, a 40-yard spur trail leaves the main route on our right, leading to a superb view into the rugged maw of Taylor Canyon. There is an abundance of cryptogamic soil here, so stick to the trail. The main trail ahead follows a ledge of the Kayenta Formation as it jogs into two more alcoves. Soon, as we approach the deep amphitheater from which Cabin Spring issues, we pass a dilapidated fence, then the remains of an old log cabin, likely a cowboy line shack.

As we hop across the damp wash draining Cabin Spring (1.5; 5600), we may notice an abrupt change in the trailside flora. Fremont barberry, wild rose, rabbitbrush, Gambel oak, and a thick turf of grasses all thrive along the moist banks of the wash. It is likely we will see the tracks of bighorn sheep, mule deer, and coyote here, as they take advantage of this perennial spring, one of the few springs near the mesa top.

The trail ahead climbs moderately, quite

soon passing an old log corral, then climbs up a draw to the west before mounting a slickrock slope of Navajo Sandstone. Cairns guide us to the rim of the mesa, where we curve south and stroll along the rim high above the oak-clad draw below Cabin Spring. We shortly reach a long water trough (0.5; 5880), where the trail begins to curve eastward. Water pumped up from Cabin Spring filled the trough for ranchers' stock prior to the Park's establishment.

A pleasant mesa-top stroll east ensues, alternating stands of pinyon and juniper with the grasslands of Grays Pasture and long stretches of slickrock where the route is indicated by widely spaced cairns.

Eventually we cross the Park road (1.0; 5760), then go north on an old roadbed, east of the Park road in a pinyon-juniper woodland. This easy downhill stint allows us to enjoy far-flung vistas, stretching west beyond gaping Taylor Canyon to the distant San Rafael Swell on the far horizon, seen beyond 50 miles of mesas and desert incised by innumerable invisible canyons. When our trail reaches the Shafer Trail Overlook (0.5; 5820), we enjoy broad views of the Shafer Trail jeep road switchbacking down the cliff into South Fork Shafer Canyon.

Descending easily to The Neck, we pass an old log drift fence once used to contain cattle and sheep on the Island in the Sky mesa, then climb gently amid scattered pinyon and juniper to complete the circuit at the trailhead (0.25; 5820).

# Trip 3
## Lathrop Trail—Grays Pasture to White Rim Trail Jeep Road

**Distance**: 11.2 miles round trip
**Low/High elevations**: 4400'/6125'
**Suited for**: Dayhike or backpack
**Difficulty**: Strenuous
**Best seasons**: April through mid-June; mid-September through October.
**Map/Trailhead**: 35/2
**Hazards**: Steep cliffs; trail steep, rough,

and rocky in places; no water or shade.

**Introduction**: Offering some of the most expansive vistas from any trail in the Park, this trip samples the entire spectrum of Island District scenery, from the grassland of Grays Pasture to the sparse desert shrubs of the White Rim bench. And with a sidetrip down the Lathrop Canyon jeep trail, one can experience the Island from top to bottom. Old uranium exploration roads and mine shafts, long unused, add historical flavor and an interesting diversion for history buffs, but the grand and mostly unspoiled scenery will delight all backcountry enthusiasts. Dayhikers will enjoy the first 2.2 miles of this hike to the mesa rim, where exciting views across the Colorado River canyon unfold.

**Description**: Our trail departs southeastward from the trailhead (0.0; 6000), crossing the extensive grasslands of Grays Pasture. After about 250 yards our trail joins an old road from the north, and we follow its overgrown course as we rise almost imperceptibly toward the grassy ridge ahead. There are enough wildflowers here to color the landscape from spring through fall, including hymenopappus, evening primrose, Uinta groundsel, globe mallow, aster, yellow cryptantha, bladderpod, and broom snakeweed.

As we slowly gain elevation, a blue-gray shrub soon appears—winterfat. With small and narrow hairy leaves it is an important food source for mule deer and bighorn sheep. As we top a rise (1.1; 6125), vistas are outstanding, taking in a vast sweep of east-central Utah. Scattered low domes atop the Island in the Sky mesa foreground distant views of the San Rafael Reef in the northwest and the Book Cliffs in the north, while our gaze stretches east beyond the canyon of the Colorado to wooded mesas, slickrock domes, and the lofty La Sal Mountains, usually streaked with snow until late spring or early summer.

Atop this rise, the road curves east toward an old metal shack, but we follow the sandy trail and drop easily across a bench enroute toward the mesa rim. Soon we follow cairns across Navajo Sandstone slickrock, and are surrounded by whitish knolls that display prominent crossbedding, formed as ancient winds drifted sand to great depths across a vast prehistoric desert.

Before long, more fine vistas unfold, now including the Colorado River far below in its gaping canyon, The Needles, and the flat-topped butte of Airport Tower, detached from our mesa by ages of erosion. The trail ahead leads across more slickrock before dipping into a narrow draw. After exiting the draw we follow a course across a blackbrush-clad flat. This shrub requires fairly shallow soils underlain by bedrock, where the plants' roots can slowly absorb the moisture concentrated there. Soon we reach the edge of the flat (1.1; 5880), where the trail begins steadily descending. Dayhikers out for only a short stroll may wish to turn around here, content with a leisurely hike and panoramic vistas.

To continue, follow the trail as it descends east via ledges. Presently just below the rim, our trail follows the ledges first south and then northwest while searching for a break in the Wingate Sandstone cliffs below. Ahead of us is the head of Lathrop Canyon, where huge alcoves decorate the Navajo Sandstone cliffs under the rim. Far below us we glimpse sections of old uranium-exploration roads contouring through the Chinle and Moenkopi formations. Finally, we curve northwest toward a gaping alcove and negotiate boulder-covered slopes, switchbacking down into the chute carved into the cliffs by ages of runoff from the small amphitheater above. Just enough moisture seeps from the alcove to support grasses and thickets of buckthorn at its base.

As we curve into the draw below, our route follows Kayenta ledges, switchbacking downhill at a moderate grade, but after we reach a rock-strewn debris cone the grade becomes steeper. Despite all the rocks boulders, this is one of the smoother trails below the rim in the Island District. Approaching the bottom of the canyon, we intercept a badly eroded uranium-exploration road (1.3; 4950) and follow it east (downhill), then quite soon switchback west on a lower spur road. Enroute we'll pass a large boulder bearing various inscriptions, including the date 1952, when the uranium boom was in full swing. Shortly we pass above a pourover formed on the black ledge of the Chinle Formation's Mossback member, one of the uranium prospectors' primary targets.

The road ahead leads us down a badly eroded switchback to the alkali-encrusted wash below.

Soon thereafter, at a point just above the wash, we reach another spur road (0.5; 4720), this one branching left. The sign here warns of the dangers of exploring abandoned mine shafts, and we would be wise to heed it. The shafts here penetrate the contact zone between the red Moenkopi Formation and the Mossback ledge of the Chinle above.

To proceed, we follow our road as it dips down to cross Lathrop Canyon's wash, where we'll see tamarisk growing in moist stretches, and we may even encounter a trickle of water. The road ahead contours through red rocks just above the wash, but after several minutes of easy walking the road curves around a minor ridge. Just beyond, leave the road (0.8; 4575) and descend cross-country southeast into a shallow wash, first through a narrow draw and then onto open flats, soon intercepting the White Rim Trail jeep road (0.8; 4400) at the rim of the basin.

From here it is but a short jaunt south on the White Rim Trail jeep road to a nearby spur road that leads 3.5 miles into lower Lathrop Canyon and the Colorado River. There are few places to establish a campsite down that canyon, so backpackers should camp out of sight of the road on the White Rim bench and make the trip down Lathrop as a dayhike. The Lathrop Campsite, for vehicles only, lies next to the river and is the most popular vehicle camp on the White Rim Trail jeep road.

# Trip 4
## Mesa Arch Loop Trail

**Distance**: 0.5 mile, loop trail
**Low/High elevations**: 6040'/6180'
**Suited for**: Walk
**Difficulty**: Easy
**Best seasons**: April through mid-June; mid-September through October.
**Map/Trailhead**: 36/3
**Hazards**: Steep cliffs behind Mesa Arch.

**Introduction**: This easy and popular self-guided nature trail passes a typical array of mesa-top vegetation and leads to Mesa Arch, a small but beautiful span formed in the Navajo Sandstone at the very rim of the mesa. The arch is a photographer's delight, as it frames a dramatic picture of the rugged Colorado River canyon and the lofty summits of the La Sal Mountains.

A pamphlet available at the trailhead describes the diverse plant life found along the trail, and hikers unfamiliar with desert flora will gain from it a better appreciation of hardy desert plants.

**Description**: Our short, popular jaunt begins at the edge of the Grays Pasture grasslands (0.0; 6120), from where we have a fine view of Aztec Butte to the west and the peaks of the Henry Mountains on the southwest horizon, 60 miles distant. Almost at once an arrow sign points the way along the left-branching leg of the one-way loop and, taking that fork, we see pinyon and juniper quickly supplant the grasslands. Cryptogamic crust is well-developed along the trail, so we must stick to the trail to avoid damaging this soil-stabilizing crust.

Many trailside shrubs are identified by small signs corresponding to the trail pamphlet, including blackbrush, prickly-pear cactus, mormon tea, and littleleaf mountain mahogany. Each of these plants has certain site-specific environmental requirements, so they grow in different microhabitats alongside the trail.

The trail curves around the north side of a low sandstone bluff, climbing slightly and then descending onto a sandy bench to a junction (0.25; 6040). Mesa Arch lies but 30 yards away, reached via a short spur trail. The arch is unusual in that it is on the very rim of the mesa and is formed in Navajo Sandstone. Navajo rocks are usually too massive for the formation of true arches, but a vertical joint has formed in the bluff here, isolating a fin of rock in which Mesa Arch has formed.

This beautiful span frames a glorious view of precipitous Buck Canyon, the great declivity carved by the Colorado River, Washer Woman Arch and its companion spire Monster Tower, bulky Airport Tower toward the southeast; and finally the great, sky-filling summits of the La Sal Mountains on the eastern horizon.

Returning to the junction, we take the left fork of the loop, climbing over a low bluff, then dropping back to the trailhead (0.25; 6120).

# Trip 5
## Murphy Point Trail

**Distance**: 1.4 miles round trip
**Low/High elevations**: 6080'/6160'
**Suited for**: Walk
**Difficulty**: Easy
**Best seasons**: April through mid-June; mid-September through October.
**Map/Trailhead**: 37/5
**Hazards**: Steep dropoffs at the trail's end.

**Introduction**: This view-filled jaunt offers some of the finest views of the Green River and The Maze country obtainable from any vista point in the Park. It is a pleasant jaunt, but the route is obscure and sometimes uncairned as it crosses slickrock to a commanding viewpoint on the rim of Murphy Point. Nevertheless, the route is straightforward, and almost any hiker will enjoy this mostly trailless jaunt.

**Description**: From the roadend (0.0; 6160) the trail, easy to follow at first, descends slightly onto Murphy Point, a wooded slickrock promontory that juts southwest from the Grand View Point mesa.

Soon, where we mount Kayenta slickrock and cairns are widely scattered, our trail vanishes. We may encounter remnants of an old jeep road leading toward the rim. Of three points jutting out from the rim, our basic route ends at the central point on the mesa's southern rim (0.5; 6080). Hikers may wish to walk to all the points, however, for an all-encompassing vista. The westernmost point (0.2; 6080) offers perhaps the finest views of the Green River, but all of the overlooks take in a vast sweep of Canyonlands country, from the Abajo Mountains and The Needles in the southeast to the slickrock wonderland of The Maze, the Orange Cliffs, and the Henry Mountains to the southwest, and across miles of vast deserts to the San Rafael Swell on the western horizon. The broad reaches of Soda Springs Basin spread out below in the northwest, bounded by the White Rim below and the barrier of Wingate cliffs above.

Hikers who have previously viewed the White Rim from viewpoints along the east edge of the mesa will notice that its cliff band is wider and thicker on the Green River side. The shallow sea along which this sandstone was deposited had its terminus near where the Colorado River is today, so the deposits had less time to accumulate there than farther west, where the sea persisted for ages.

As in all of the basins below the Island mesa, mineral-exploration roads dating back to the 1950s are very numerous when viewed from above, but many are difficult to locate on the ground.

This viewpoint is a superb location from which to view a desert sunset. Eventually we must reluctantly pull away from the incomparable view of isolated buttes, gaping declivities, vast plateaus, and island mountain ranges, and retrace our steps to the trailhead.

# Trip 6
## Murphy Trail

**Distance:** 9.75 miles, semiloop trail
**Low/High elevations**: 4880'/6200'
**Suited for**: Dayhike or backpack
**Difficulty**: Moderately strenuous
**Best seasons**: April through mid-June; mid-September through October.
**Map/Trailhead**: 37/4
**Hazards**: Steep trail; steep dropoffs; no water.

**Introduction**: This fine circuit tours the full range of Island landscapes, from the mesa top to the great cliffs that bound it to the desert basins of the White Rim. The trail is quite steep as it plunges over the mesa rim, and part of the route in the basin below follows a wash without the benefit of a trail. But the route offers access to the White Rim Trail jeep road, which can be followed in either direction to reach several remote basins, infrequently visited by hikers. Although the trip is best suited as a backpack, stronger hikers can easily complete the circuit in a day.

**Description**: From the trailhead (0.0; 6200)

**The Murphy Trail below the rim**

our sandy trail descends south over the mesa. Approaching the rim, we are likely to be entertained by the aerial stunts of white-throated swifts flying on air currents rising from the cliffs below. Winding among slickrock, we soon reach the rim, where a brief pause reveals fine views into the inner gorge carved by the Green River, seen beyond the broad White Rim bench below. As our eyes are lured beyond the Green's Stillwater Canyon, The Maze, and Ekker and Elaterite buttes meet our gaze—an intriguing landscape seen by many but known only to a few hardy backpackers and jeepers.

Presently our trail, littered with rocks and crossing much slickrock, begins to switchback steeply down over Kayenta ledges to a break in the great Wingate cliffs below. This trail was constructed in the early decades of the 20th century by the Murphy brothers of Moab to provide access to winter range for their stock in the basins below. They spent 11 days carving the trail out of the cliffs. When it was done, six hours were required to move 100 head of cattle single-file down the narrow trail.

Part way down, we cross a wooden bridge spanning a gap in the sheer cliff, but soon the trail becomes smoother as it passes onto steep Chinle slopes below. Views continue to encompass a wide range of canyon and mesa scenery, but we can enjoy them only if we pause, because the trail requires constant attention.

Finally we reach a signed junction (1.5; 5240) where we have two routes to choose from. For now, we bear left into the wash, saving the right-branching trail for the return trip.

Without a trail to guide us, we nevertheless follow an easy route along the wash or on ledges above it, where the footing is better. The red rocks of the Moenkopi dominate the basin, and in places there are excellent exposures of ripple-marked slabs. Part way down the wash is a small corral built of stone slabs and juniper posts. Eventually we join the White Rim Trail jeep road (2.5; 4880) and turn right, rising gently at first, then climbing steeply to surmount the broad ridge of Murphy Hogback. Soon thereafter we pass the first of three vehicle campsites, situated on a bench of White Rim Sandstone. Views into The Maze loom ahead, and behind us are the soaring orange-red cliffs we must climb to regain the rim of the mesa. All hikers are encouraged to use the pit toilets at these and other campsites on the White Rim Trail jeep road, but backpackers must look elsewhere for campsites of their own.

Not long after we stroll past Campsite B a sign indicates the Murphy Trail (1.5; 5270), but some hikers may wish to continue toward Camp-site C, where a superb view unfolds, including the Green River, Turks Head, and Candlestick Tower—an eroded remnant of the mesa now isolated by ages of erosion.

From the trail junction, we follow the gentle surface of broad Murphy Hogback on Chinle Formation rocks. This wide route follows a for-mer stock driveway that was later improved by uranium prospectors. The hogback ridge is lit-tered with chert pebbles—the hard stones that ancient cultures fashioned into tools and projec-tile points—as well as scattered fragments of petrified wood.

Along this stretch the hiking is easy, allow-ing us to thoroughly enjoy the views of cliffs, canyons, and mesas that surround us. As we reach the foot of the great Wingate cliffs, we can leave the route and stroll west to the hogback's rim, where vistas of the Green River and the western Canyonlands basin are seen to better advantage.

At the foot of the cliffs the pathway curves east-southeast staying along the base of the cliffs. Enroute is a particularly interesting pillar of purplish Chinle stratum, curiously capped by a slab fallen from the Wingate cliffs above. Finally we complete the loop at the signed junc-tion (2.75; 5240), and then retrace our strenuous 1.5-mile route to the mesa above.

# Trip 7
## Gooseberry Trail to White Rim Trail Jeep Road

**Distance**: 6.0 miles round trip to White Rim Trail jeep road
**Low/High elevations**: 4740'/6270'
**Suited for**: Dayhike or backpack
**Difficulty**: Strenuous
**Best seasons**: April through mid-June; mid-September through October.
**Map/Trailhead**: 37/6
**Hazards**: No water; poor trail; steep dropoffs.

**Introduction**: The Gooseberry Trail is the shortest way to reach the White Rim Trail jeep road on foot, but its route is very steep and rocky, and the footing is poor. Once below the cliffs, hikers have the option of following the White Rim to various glorious overlooks or exploring remote desert basins.

**Description**: Our trail departs from the park-ing area (0.0; 6270) on a cairned route across potholed Kayenta slickrock, reaching the mesa rim within 175 yards. We may wish to pause here to enjoy the expansive vistas that stretch across the Colorado River canyon. As we gaze north-east along the square-edged mesa, we see the erosion-isolated buttes of Monster Tower, The Washer Woman, and Airport Tower, and still farther north we see Dead Horse Point, the Pot-ash millsite, and a vast expanse of Navajo Sand-stone domes that separate the Canyonlands Basin from Moab/Spanish Valley. A broad bench, edged by the White Rim, lies below us, and beyond is the vast basin carved by the Col-orado, a redrock landscape that rises in a series of benches eastward to the tall Wingate cliffs and wooded mesas on the eastern skyline.

Presently the trail plunges below the rim, taking advantage of a precipitous chute carved by erosion into the barrier cliffs. A variety of plants inhabit this sheltered, north-facing chute, including a scattering of pinyon and juniper, Indian ricegrass, singleaf ash, broom snakeweed, mormon tea, Utah serviceberry, buckwheat, haplopappus, and resinbush.

The trail becomes exceedingly steep as it passes through the Wingate cliff band, but soon we enter Chinle slopes, winding among boulders into the head of the wash below. We follow its course cross-country down the remaining distance into the broad basin below, finally joining the White Rim Trail jeep road 0.3 mile north of the Gooseberry vehicle campsite. Here we are (3.0; 4740) just above the point where our wash pours over the White Rim Sandstone. Huge slabs of White Rim Sandstone litter the red slopes below the rim, and balanced rocks protect the underlying Organ Rock Shale in places. Redrock benches and slopes drop in stepladder fashion into the canyon below.

Hikers can now retrace their steps. Those wanting a campsite will find broad benches within 2 miles of the wash, both north and south along the jeep trail. These benches spread eastward from the jeep trail, and although they are exposed, with no shade, they offer fine views up and down the Colorado River, with a backdrop of lofty cliffs and mesas. Backpackers should make the extra effort to camp out of sight of the jeep trail.

# Trip 8
## White Rim Overlook Trail

**Distance**: 1.8 miles round trip
**Low/High elevations**: 6100/6270'
**Suited for**: Walk
**Difficulty**: Easy
**Best seasons**: April through mid-June; mid-September through October.
**Map/Trailhead**: 37/6

**Hazards**: Steep dropoffs at the trail's end; no shade or water.

**Introduction**: The Island in the Sky is famous for its far-ranging vistas, and hikers need not trek any great distance from the mesa-top roadway to enjoy them. The White Rim Overlook provides perhaps the finest view in the Park of the 2000-foot-deep canyon of the Colorado River, and distant, awe-inspiring panoramas of Utah's rugged canyon-and-mesa country.

**Description**: From the trailhead/picnic area (0.0; 6270) we ignore the Gooseberry Trail (*Trip 7*) forking left across the slickrock, and instead take the signed right fork, a wide trail descending just south of a broken Kayenta Sandstone rim. Drought-tolerant Utah junipers form a widely scattered woodland of small, twisted trees, their ranks joined by only an occasional pinyon. Only a few wildflowers adorn the thin, sandy soil along the trail, but the yellow blooms of haplopappus and broom snakeweed stand out among the coarse gray shrubs.

Far-ranging vistas of the canyon country accompany us all along the trail, which, after 1/2 mile, mounts slickrock where cairns help guide us. Approaching the end of the rocky promontory, we pass beneath a short but prominent pinnacle, and reach land's end at White Rim Overlook (0.9; 6100). This is the one of only two points on a trail in the Island District from which one can see the Colorado River, but only vignettes of its tree-clad banks are visible over 2000 feet below us in the river's inner gorge.

The sandy swath of the White Rim Trail jeep road follows the edge of the broad Moenkopi bench below the mesa, and the Gooseberry Campsite can also be seen alongside that road to the north. The White Rim Sandstone forms the edge of that bench, and here in the eastern part of the Park it is quite narrow and thin, pinching out entirely toward the north beneath the promontory of Dead Horse Point.

The large buildings of the Potash mill can be viewed up-canyon, lying at the end of Utah Highway 279 southwest of Moab. Downstream, the Colorado is a wild river not crossed by another road for 80 miles south of Moab. Scattered Navajo Sandstone domes dot the surface of the Island mesa, but abruptly plunge into the basin below via the Wingate cliffs and a step-like series of softer rocks—the Chinle and Moenkopi. Save for the White Rim, the entire landscape is composed of red slopes, cliffs, canyons, and mesas. This is truly redrock country at its finest.

Our view also reaches into the depths of Monument Basin below the White Rim, where dozens of slender pillars rise from the declivity below. They are composed of the Organ Rock Shale member of the Cutler Formation, a thinly bedded and relatively soft rock. Some pillars are capped by remnants of the White Rim Sandstone, protecting the chimney-like rocks from rapid erosion. But much of the vista encompasses far-away landmarks such as the La Sal and Abajo mountains, and the vast array of sandstone pinnacles in The Needles to the southeast and The Maze to the southwest.

Return the way you came.

# Trip 9
## Grand View Trail

**Distance**: 1.8 miles round trip
**Low/High elevations**: 6220'/6260'
**Suited for**: Walk
**Difficulty**: Easy
**Best seasons**: April through mid-June; mid-September through October.
**Map/Trailhead**: 37/7
**Hazards**: Steep dropoffs at the trail's end.

**Introduction**: True to its name, the Grand View Trail offers perhaps the most all-encompassing panorama of the Canyonlands basin in the entire Park. This is a good and popular trail that follows the narrow mesa among scattered trees and shrubs, ending at a prominent slickrock point that offers a commanding vista. No special skills are required to follow this justifiably popular trail, and it offers great rewards to anyone willing to park the car and walk a short distance among awe-inspiring surroundings.

**Description**: From the spacious parking area (0.0; 6250) we should first stroll the few feet down to Grand View Overlook, where an orientation display helps us to become familiar with prominent landmarks seen across the vast sweep of desert that lies before us.

The signed Grand View Trail strikes southwest just short of the overlook, following the increasingly narrow promontory of Grand View Point, the southern arm of the Island in the Sky mesa. A sparse woodland of pinyons and junipers dots the slickrock of the point, their squat and gnarled forms tortured by the elements but clinging tenaciously to life. The undulating trail is embraced by broken slabs and boulders composed of Kayenta Formation rocks and, where we cross slickrock, cairns lead the way. Vistas enroute are superb, stretching across the vast Canyonlands basin to far-away mountains looming like hazy mirages on the horizon.

We reach trail's end (0.9; 6240) where large boulders are stacked upon the point, and scramble up them for an all-encompassing vista. From our vantage, we cannot see the Colorado River, but we do see the immense canyon system it has created. In the west the Green River flows placidly through Stillwater Canyon, and beyond it vast desert basins and gaping canyons rise steadily to the Orange Cliffs. Three prominent mountain ranges, the Henry, Abajo, and La Sal, as well as Boulder and Thousand Lake mountains—part of Utah's High Plateaus—rise above an endless sea of slickrock desert. Prominent Junction Butte, once part of the immense plain that existed here prior to the downcutting of the canyon network, now stands alone, filling our southward view.

Parts of the White Rim Trail jeep road and a maze of uranium-exploration roads are seen below on either side of the point. The White Rim Sandstone forms a narrow but prominent band around the intermediate basin below the mesa. Eastward is striking Monument Basin, where a host of redrock spires, composed of the Organ Rock Shale, reach skyward from the depths of the deep canyon below the White Rim. Foregrounding the massive Abajo Mountains in the southeast are the aptly-named Needles, a profusion of slickrock spires, and to the southwest is the terra incognita of The Maze.

# Trip 10
## Aztec Butte Trail

**Distance**: 1.5 miles, semiloop trail
**Low/High elevations**: 6050'/6298'
**Suited for**: Walk
**Difficulty**: Moderately easy
**Best seasons**: April through mid-June; mid-September through October.
**Map/Trailhead**: 36/8
**Hazards**: Short but steep slickrock scrambling near the trail's end.

**Introduction**: Aztec Butte is one of the more prominent Navajo Sandstone domes on the Island, and the short but scenic jaunt to its nearly flat summit reaches an all-encompassing panorama. The trail also leads past a few Anasazi granaries, offering glimpses into a long-since vanished culture that thrived in the region hundreds of years ago. These ancient structures crumble easily, so treat them with care and do not climb in or upon them.

**Description**: From the trailhead (0.0; 6100) our gaze stretches across rolling grasslands, stands of pinyon and juniper, and a scattering of low-profile slickrock domes, all foregrounding the ever-present La Sal Mountains on the far northeast horizon. Our trail descends gradually toward the foot of one of those domes among a variety of desert trees, wildflowers, and shrubs. Yucca soon appears in drift sand next to the trail as we reach the foot of the dome and turn north, passing a right-branching trail 60 yards from the trailhead. That trail skirts the eastern foot of the dome, and can be used on the return trip.

Shortly we curve into a draw flanked by low slickrock domes and follow it northeast. As we rise gently through the shallow draw, singleleaf ash and Utah serviceberry join the trailside shrubs, and we soon mount a broad saddle on the edge of Willow Flat's grassland, where the eastern leg of the loop trail joins our trail from the south.

At the foot of Aztec Butte, the most prominent dome in the area, we continue following cairns as we scramble up the moderately steep slickrock slopes of the dome. Erosion along the

bedding planes of the Navajo Sandstone has formed small ledges that offer better footing. But we quickly mount smoother slickrock and climb two steep pitches, connected by a marginal trail. Novice hikers may be intimidated by climbing steep slickrock, but good rubber-soled shoes offer a grip on the coarse sandstone.

After surmounting the summit area of the butte (0.6; 6298), we stroll northeast to the rim, where we find a low stone wall, ruins of an Anasazi granary. Vistas from the butte are superb and far-ranging, stretching across the vast grasslands of Grays Pasture to the distant La Sal Mountains in the northeast and to the two-tiered barrier of the Book Cliffs far to the north. Closer at hand, the prominent gash of Trail Canyon lies 1000 feet below, bounded by soaring red Wingate Sandstone cliffs that are capped by scattered slickrock domes. Seasonal waters draining that canyon are destined for the Green River, a silent waterway lying in the great canyon it has carved far below in the west.

Views southeast extend as far as the forested Abajo Mountains, and lying below them are the fins and spires of the Park's Needles District. South of the La Sals on the distant eastern horizon, our gaze reaches 90 miles to a few towering summits of the San Juan Mountains in Colorado. There is abundant cryptogamic soil on the flat summit of the butte, so stay on the trail to avoid damaging it.

Although these vistas are magnificent, there is even more to see. Head north past the ruin (about 3 feet high and 6 by 8 feet in dimension) and look for a faint trail just below the rim. Follow it west, quickly reaching a small, shady alcove and an arch. The ruins of another small Anasazi granary lie within the alcove.

The trail ahead follows a narrow ledge first west, then southwest, passing two more alcoves with ruined walls of ancient granaries. Curving around to the northwest face of the butte, we reach yet another alcove (0.1; 6290), featuring four small arches. Within the alcove are two well-preserved granaries, built of tightly fitted sandstone slabs. One of these ancient structures is cemented with red mortar, and if one looks closely, finger marks in the mortar are evident. Do not climb in these structures; they are fragile and easily damaged.

Our alcove-framed view is probably much the same as the view when the Ancient Ones traveled here hundreds of years ago, as little has changed in this seemingly timeless land. Only the paved Park road serves to remind us of the modern world in which we live. Perhaps they waited here for deer and bighorn sheep to hunt for food; for west of us game trails crisscross the bench below.

More fine views stretch west from our sheltered vantage point. The square-edged mesas and sheer, colorful sandstone cliffs typify the essence of the canyon country. Far to the northwest, beyond endless wooded mesas, are the uplifted flanks of the San Rafael Reef, its tilted strata rising to the highland of the San Rafael Swell. Utah's High Plateaus form the western horizon beyond the swell, rising to upwards of 11,000 feet in elevation.

To return to the trailhead, continue south along the trail from the granaries, taking great care as the narrow trail immediately skirts the abutment of a small arch, clinging to the edge of a steep dropoff. The trail then quickly regains the top of the butte and loops around the rim to rejoin the primary trail, on which we backtrack down steep slickrock to the saddle below (0.4; 6100). To avoid retracing our entire route, bear left at the broad saddle, following an alternate trail along the margin of the plateau's grasslands, stretching away to the east, and below a low dome rising above to the west.

This trail rejoins our former route in a shallow draw below the trailhead, where we bear left and backtrack to our cars (0.4; 6100).

# Trip 11
## Wilhite Trail—Island in the Sky to White Rim Trail Jeep Road

**Distance**: 12.0 miles round trip to White Rim Trail Jeep Road
**Low/High elevations**: 4250'/5965'
**Suited for**: Dayhike or backpack
**Difficulty**: Strenuous
**Best seasons**: April through mid-June; mid-

September through October.
**Map/Trailhead**: 38/9
**Hazards**: Steep dropoffs; no water; little shade.

**Introduction**: The Wilhite Trail, built by a uranium prospector of that name, is perhaps the most demanding trail in the Island District. The trail is exceedingly steep as it descends a gap in the Wingate cliff band, and once in the broad expanse of Holeman Spring Basin it fades out entirely and hikers must make their own way across the desert to the White Rim Trail jeep road. But the rewards of forging your own route and the solitude one enjoys more than compensate for the effort expended.

A wide range of cross-country hiking opportunities becomes apparent once one descends below the rim, and hikers seeking a pure desert hiking experience will find this route much to their liking. Strong hikers can make the round trip in one long day, but the terrain lends itself to exploration, and travelers will surely want to linger in the lonely basins below the mesa.

**Description**: Our trail departs southwest from the trailhead (0.0; 5840) on a cairned route that quickly descends gullies to the sandy floor of the wash draining Willow Seep. Shortly we intercept a faded road, on which we bear left, briefly heading downstream before climbing steadily toward the broad ridge ahead. The contours of the ridge are gentle, with little bedrock exposed to view in the immediate area, but the seasonal color provided by cryptantha, milkvetch, groundsel, broom snakeweed, and aster enlivens this mostly featureless stretch of trail. Soils are also deep enough here to host a scattering of pinyon and juniper, as well as mormon tea, cliffrose, yucca and blackbrush.

Where we top out on a broad ridge (0.6; 5965) views suddenly open up over Stillwater Canyon, revealing the Orange Cliffs topped by the Navajo Sandstone dome of Cleopatras Chair, The Maze, and the red monoliths of Land of Standing Rocks, while closer at hand are Candlestick Tower in the south and sandstone domes encircling Upheaval Dome in the northwest.

On the ridge's crest, the old road jogs northwest (right), but we follow a faint trail, indicated by cairns, just under a low sandstone rim and then down onto the pinyon- and juniper-clad bench below. After descending ledges of Kayenta Formation rocks, we soon begin following a northwestward course just south of an increasingly narrow draw to the brink of the cliffs that plummet into Holeman Spring Basin. Ages of runoff from that draw have worn a gap into the cliffs below. Traversing a ledge toward the head of that precipitous chute, we then pass a trailside boulder on which "Wil Hite Trail" has been painted, presumably by the man who blazed the trail

About 1 1/2 miles into our hike we begin switchbacking in earnest down a boulder-choked chute where Utah serviceberry and squawbush are common trailside shrubs. The wide trail descends moderately at first, but eventually it narrows and becomes very steep and rocky. We must proceed with care, but our attention may be diverted from the trail at times by white-throated swifts swooping and soaring among the reddish-brown cliffs.

Passing below the Wingate cliff band, our trail enters steep, rock-strewn slopes of the Chinle Formation, and we continue our knee-jarring descend through the varicolored layers of that formation. Finally the grade abates as we dip into a wash (2.0; 4800), climb easily onto a broad bench and very soon pass the "Raven 5" uranium claim. The rimrock forming the edge of the bench here is composed of the Chinle's Moss-back member, eastern Utah's counterpart to the Shinarump Conglomerate that crops out in Zion and Capitol Reef. The Mossback was one of the uranium miners' primary targets in the 1950s, before the area became a national park.

Soaring above us in all directions are barrier cliffs abutting the edge of the Island mesa. Most are sheer and offer no passable route back to the top. Below, Holeman Spring Basin descends westward in a series of step-like benches encompassing an area of about 6 square miles. The wash below cuts deeper into the Moenkopi beneath the bench, and ledges hosting scattered shrubs and junipers offer attractive campsites, but backpackers should remember to camp out of sight of trails, and there is abundant opportunity to establish an isolated campsite in the basin ahead.

From the wash at the bottom of the switchbacking descent, the trail first contours west along the broad bench, but soon it curves south, following an increasingly narrow ledge beneath a soaring reddish cliff of Wingate Sandstone. Eventually, we reach a break in the rim below us (0.8; 4880), but before descending we can pause and enjoy the view across the basin to the distant landmarks of Buttes of the Cross and the broad band of the Orange Cliffs. Candlestick Tower stands watch over the basin to the south, and to our northwest the basin is bounded by the tableland of Steer Mesa.

Presently cairns lead us past a prominent red boulder and onto the steep and rocky slop below, and we soon reach level ground on the basin's red floor. Cairns channel us into a shallow, dry wash, which we then follow downstream. The cairns have disappeared, but we simply follow the ever-deepening wash. As we proceed, more washes join on the left and right, and we must catalog them in our memory so we can be sure to follow the correct one to find our way back to the trail on the return trip.

The wash cuts deeper into the basin as we continue, and eventually tamarisk begins to line the alkali-encrusted wash. Toward the lower end of the basin, the wash opens up as it begins to dissect more gentle terrain. Ahead of us we can now see the White Rim Trail jeep road skirting the edge of its namesake rim, and behind us convoluted cliffs and towers are prominently outlined against the sky.

Upon reaching the jeep trail (2.6; 4250) you have several options. (1) Return the way you came now. (2) First explore Holeman Spring Basin or equally large Soda Springs Basin—7 miles southeast via the White Rim Trail jeep road or 3 miles cross-country over the low, broken ridge below Candlestick Tower. (3) For a fine view of Valentine Bottom on the Green River, follow the White Rim Trail jeep road in either direction for less than 1 mile.

## Trip 12
### Alcove Spring Trail to Taylor Canyon

**Distance**: 10.8 miles round trip to end of
   Taylor Canyon Jeep Trail
**Low/High elevations**: 4250'/5700'
**Suited for**: Dayhike or backpack
**Difficulty**: Moderate
**Best seasons**: April through mid-June; mid-
   September through October.
**Map/Trailhead**: 39/10
**Hazards**: Steep dropoffs; no water; little
   shade.

   **Introduction**: This route is a good choice
for backpackers in the Island District. The descent from the rim into Trail Canyon is slightly
more gradual than the descent on most other
district trails, and once in the depths of Trail

Canyon hikers are free to explore its broad basin
and lonely canyons, where there are innumerable
potential camping areas, although most are exposed. A longer loop trip, utilizing the trail over
Upheaval Dome, and explorations of Trail and
Taylor canyons are among the many hiking possibilities along this route.

   **Description**: From the trailhead (0.0; 5700)
our trail quickly descends to the mesa rim, where
we enjoy a striking view north into the depths of
cliffbound Trail Canyon and to the dome-studded edge of the Island in the Sky mesa beyond.
From our vantage point we can gaze north and
notice how the cliff strata dip slightly downward
toward the west. These rocks were deformed by
the folding associated with the creation of Upheaval Dome, and we are now along the outer
edge of the syncline that encircles the dome.

   Our route ahead descends an old roadbed
over steep slickrock below the rim, and soon the
deep cave from which Alcove Spring issues

**Alcove Spring trickles from a deep alcove on Upheaval Dome**

comes into view. Ages of seeping water have dissolved the cementing agents binding the Navajo sand grains, creating the immense cave.

After a shortcut over steeply sloping Kayenta slickrock, we rejoin the road, heading toward the alcove. But then our road begins descending ledges away from the alcove. However, a use trail can be followed from the road (0.4; 4950) and into the alcove, where there is only a seasonal seep of water.

Below Alcove Spring we switchback steadily downhill via ledges of Kayenta bedrock, through a prominent gap in the Wingate cliff band, and finally onto the upper red and gray strata of the Chinle Formation. A number of lizards and an occasional white-throated swift will likely be the only company we have during our moderately steep descent.

Once on the basin floor, our trail leads northeast across a blackbrush-studded bench to the lip of Trail Canyon, where we descend into the wash via a break in the ledge. Upon reaching the broad wash bottom (1.0; 4530) of Trail Canyon, we simply follow its entrenched gorge downstream. Rubbly slopes embrace the wash, and above, the soaring red, desert-varnished Wingate cliffs, now sheer, now fluted, are our constant companions. The course of the wash straightens toward the northwest as we continue into the canyon's lower reaches. Shortly before we intercept Taylor Canyon, the two prominent slickrock shafts, Moses and Zeus, stand atop the eroded remnants of a promontory that juts west from the mesa into the drainage of Taylor Canyon.

Soon we are funneled into the larger wash of Taylor Canyon, and turn left, downstream. Its headwaters canyons, reaching back into the Island like the fingers of giant hand, are seldom visited and they beckon exploration.

Within 1/4 mile we reach the terminus of the Taylor Canyon jeep trail at the Taylor Canyon vehicle campsite (4.0; 4250). This road follows the broad wash most of the remaining 5 1/2 miles to the White Rim Trail jeep road. The wash is sandy, and occasionally hosts tamarisk along its course. Big Draw is an inviting side canyon, branching northeast from the road one mile west of the roadend. Its upper reaches, however, are impassable where it pours over a steep, narrow chute in the Wingate cliff.

Those who follow Taylor Canyon to Upheaval Bottom on the Green River can return via Upheaval Canyon and the Syncline Trail (*Trip 15*) for a highly scenic two-to-three-day loop hike of about 21.5 miles, surveying the full range of Island in the Sky landscapes.

# Trip 13
## Whale Rock Trail

**Distance**: 1.2 miles round trip
**Low/High elevations**: 5710'/5850'
**Suited for**: Walk
**Difficulty**: Easy
**Best seasons**: April through mid-June; mid-September through October.
**Map/Trailhead**: 39/11
**Hazards**: Sections of scrambling over steep and exposed slickrock.

**Introduction**: To appreciate the dimensions of unusual Upheaval Dome, and in the process enjoy a slickrock scramble from the mesa to a broad sandstone dome, the short trip to Whale Rock offers ample rewards for a little effort. Although parts of the route along the steep slickrock slopes of the dome are exposed, handrails offer a sense of security for novice hikers.

**Description**: Our gravel trail (0.0; 5710) initially heads north, and quite soon we skirt the foot of a low slickrock hill, then begin climbing west toward the hogback crest of Whale Rock. Handrails help steady acrophobic hikers, and mortared cairns guide the way over the rock.

Upon reaching the crest, our route curves south, finally climbing past a display featuring an aerial view of Upheaval Dome and soon thereafter reaching the trail's end atop Whale Rock (0.6; 5850). Looking out, we soon realize that Whale Rock is part of the Upheaval Dome structure. Concentric rings of slickrock ridges and narrow, wooded draws nearly encircle the dome, but from our vantage point we cannot see into the dome's crater. But we can see down the cliffbound course of Upheaval Canyon, its sheer orange walls framing a memorable view of the

Green River and distant mesas stretching far
away toward the San Rafael Swell, some 40
miles west. South beyond the grasslands and
woodlands of the mesa, the pinnacle of Candlestick Tower stands silent guard over the redrock
wilderness of Stillwater Canyon.

Still farther south and southwest are the
landmarks of Ekker and Elaterite buttes and the
slickrock jungle of The Maze. The peaks of the
Henry Mountains, 60 miles away, peek above
the tilted strata of Upheaval Dome, and the ever-
present La Sals dominate our view eastward over
the dome-studded expanse of the Island mesa.

The gaping declivity of Trail Canyon, below
us in the north, slices deeply into the mesa like
a great wound in the earth. Its sheer reddish cliffs
and myriad branch canyons are a delight to adventurous backpackers.

Return the way you came.

**In Labyrinth Canyon on the Green River**

# Trip 14
## Crater View/Upheaval Dome Overlook Trails

**Distance**: 1.8 miles round trip
**Low/High elevations**: 5650'/5800'
**Suited for**: Walk
**Difficulty**: Moderately easy
**Best seasons**: April through mid-June; mid-
   September through October.
**Map/Trailhead**: 39/12
**Hazards**: Steep dropoffs

**Introduction**: This short but rewarding trail
is one of the most popular hikes in the Island
District. It tours the south rim of unusual Upheaval Dome, offering not only dramatic views
into its jumbled and eroded interior but also
far-ranging vistas over canyons and mesas to
lofty mountain ranges.

**Description**: As you begin this short hike,
pick up the *Crater View Trail Guide* pamphlet
available from the dispenser at the trailhead. It
describes the rock strata you will encounter and
discusses how the dome may have formed. Com-
bining the pamphlet along with the interpretive

displays along the way makes this short trip an
informative, self-guided trail.

As we leave the trailhead (0.0; 5760) we may
see ravens, pinyon jays, or white-throated swifts,
while a variety of lizards scurry across the trail
or sun themselves on a trailside rock. As we rise
beyond the junction with the Syncline Loop
Trail (*Trip 15*) after 80 yards, we cross the slickrock of some tilted Kayenta Formation ledges.
Pinyon and juniper stud the broken shelves of
rock, as do shrubs typically found in this plant
association, such as cliffrose, squawbush and
littleleaf mountain mahogany.

As we approach the crater rim, we come to
a junction (0.2; 5760) where a sign indicates that
one viewpoint lies 60 yards to the right via a spur
trail, while another can be reached by walking
1/2 mile on the left-branching trail. Those who
turn right will quickly mount slickrock and
shortly reach the rim of the crater, where an
exciting view unfolds. The floor of the crater,
encircled by sheer cliffs of Wingate Sandstone,
lies 1000 feet below, where the gray and red beds
of the Moenkopi, Chinle, and White Rim formations are tilted and warped in a chaotic jumble
of badlands hills and small peaks. Across the
crater on the opposite wall, we can see that the
beds of Kayenta rocks—those lying between the
Navajo Sandstone domes on the rim and the
sheer, reddish Wingate cliffs below—have been
warped in a wave-like fashion. Interpretive displays on our slickrock viewpoint discuss various
theories of the formation of the dome. Though
geologists know much about the structural geology of the Colorado Plateau, the formation of

Upheaval Dome continues to puzzle them.

The longer trail ahead on the left undulates over slickrock, and where this cairned route descends steeper stretches, steps have been cut into the bedrock to provide better footing. Soon we descend moderately steeply where the trail has been carved into Navajo Sandstone, but before long the grade abates and then we cross a pinyon- and juniper-studded flat and soon reach a fenced overlook (0.7; 5650), from which we enjoy an all-encompassing view of the Upheaval Dome crater. The unobstructed panorama from southwest to north takes in a vast sweep of Colorado Plateau scenery, from the Henry Mountains, to Thousand Lake Mountain near Capitol Reef National Park, the San Rafael Reef, and the Book Cliffs. Down the cliffbound wash of Upheaval Canyon the tilted rocks of the dome in the foreground contrast dramatically with the undeformed vertical cliffs and broad platforms of Buck and Bighorn mesas, which flank the canyon. Upheaval Dome is a superb vantage point from which to enjoy a desert sunset. As shadows begin to fill the crater, the orange light of sunset paints the crater's walls in brilliant pastel shades that are unforgettable.

# Trip 15
## Syncline Loop Trail; Upheaval Canyon to the Green River

**Distance**: 7.8 mile loop (plus an optional 7.5 mile round trip to the Green River)
**Low/High elevations**: 4230'; 3950'/5760'
**Suited for**: Dayhike or backpack
**Difficulty**: Strenuous as a dayhike, moderate as an overnighter.
**Best seasons**: April through mid-June; mid-September through October.
**Maps/Trailhead**: 39,40/12
**Hazards**: Trail steep and/or rough in places; only seasonal water available in Syncline Valley; little shade.

**Introduction**: This route is perhaps the finest short backpacking trip in the Island District.

It traces a circular route around unusual Upheaval Dome, and offers an abundance of campsites, seasonal water, and sidetrip opportunities. The trip can be extended by following the wash of Upheaval Canyon to its mouth at the Green River, or can be combined with the Taylor Canyon jeep trail and *Trip 12* to form a fine two-to-three-day loop.

Hikers following only the Syncline Loop Trail are advised to take in reverse the trip described below. But if the Green River or Taylor Canyon is your goal, the described route offers the shortest and fastest means of access.

Description: Following the signed Crater View Trail (*Trip 14*) west from the roadend (0.0; 5760), we quickly encounter the Syncline Loop branching right and left. Turning left, we soon top a rise and begin a gradual descent via the syncline valley of Upheaval Dome. The valley's floor is composed of broken reddish slickrock of the Kayenta Formation, while domes of Navajo Sandstone flank us on either side. Hikers on the popular Crater View Trail are frequently seen on the skyline ridge to the north, but we'll likely see few hikers on our trail.

Fine views extend northwest, where the cliffs embracing Upheaval Canyon frame distant mesas, the far-away San Rafael Swell, and the eastern flanks of Utah's High Plateaus, their lofty environs hosting snowfields until late spring or early summer. Vegetation in this shallow valley consists of pinyon and juniper, and the shrubs commonly associated with this woodland, such as squawbush, singleleaf ash, mormon tea, and cliffrose.

Upon reaching the west end of the valley, we begin a switchbacking descent in the shadow of towering sandstone domes. As we continue down boulder-littered slopes, views now include the Green River. Our route skirts the warped strata of Upheaval Dome while enroute into the deep canyon below. Where the switchbacking abates, the trail descends a steep ridge into a minor draw, which leads us to the east side of Knoll 4854. Here we switchback once again, descending a steep and sheltered chute carved into the Wingate Sandstone.

Below this chute we finally reach the canyon floor (2.0; 4480) and then follow a cairned route down-canyon to our right. The increasingly deep wash has cut into layers of the Chinle Formation, which vary in color and hardness. We continue between its colorful banks, finally reaching a trail sign (1.1; 4230) where another wash joins from the north.

To complete the loop, we must bear right and follow the course of that north-trending wash.

---

To reach the Green River, turn left, following the inner gorge of the now-larger wash of Upheaval Canyon. Benches perched above either side of the wash offer potential campsites, but they are shadeless. Views are exceptional, however, including the square-edged mesas that embrace the canyon and the dome-capped rim of Upheaval Dome.

Farther down-canyon, as the wash begins to meander, cairns indicate pathways that shortcut the meanders. Eventually the canyon opens up onto its broad floodplain, and we now stroll across nearly level ground north of the wash. The trail, often obscured by drifting sand, crosses alkaline ground hosting greasewood and four-wing saltbrush, but soon tamarisk and cottonwoods appear, and we then intersect the White Rim Trail jeep road (3.5; 3950).

The Upheaval Campsite, for vehicles only, lies just up the road. But to reach Upheaval Bottom on the Green River, stay south of the wash and follow a path that meanders through a dense thicket of tamarisk, willow, and cottonwood. There seems to be a maze of trails here, but all ultimately lead to the river in about 1/4 mile.

The waters of the Green are silent and smooth as it flows between the towering cliffs and mesas of Labyrinth Canyon. A variety of birds serenade us with their varied songs along this riverside oasis. There is also evidence of beaver activity here, and the silence is interrupted only by the wind rustling the trees and the buzzing of hornets, wasps, and bees. There are potential campsites in the riverside thickets, but they offer no views of the magnificent surroundings. Be sure to purify the river water if you must drink it.

In addition to a sidetrip up Taylor Canyon, 1/2 mile to the north by road, another scenic diversion beckons. We can follow the White Rim Trail jeep road south for 3 miles to a narrow promontory jutting west toward the Green River from the flanks of Bighorn Mesa. Here the Fort Bottom Trail begins at the end of half-mile westbound spur road. The trail is rough and rocky as it leads west along the promontory, passing a circular Anasazi ruin once thought to have been used as a lookout—hence the name Fort Bottom. Beyond the bluff on which the ruin stands, the route descends steeply to an old log cowboy cabin near the banks of the river.

---

Back at the aforementioned junction along the west edge of Upheaval Dome, we bear left, first following Upheaval Canyon northeast, then east to where the wash soon forks. We follow a trail climbing steep slopes with the aid of rock steps to the bench above, where we encounter a signed junction (0.2; 4320). Those who wish to explore the unique interior of Upheaval Dome, featuring a moonscape of strangely contorted and colorful strata, can take the right fork, which leads slightly more than 1 mile, via the wash, into the eroded center of the dome.

Forking left and heading into Syncline Valley, we descend easily toward the vegetated banks of an intermittent stream, which we follow up-canyon along an undulating, boulder-strewn trail. Cottonwoods, pinyon and juniper and a variety of wildflowers, including the conspicuous blanketflower in spring, adorn the canyon bottom.

Ahead of us a cliff blocks the canyon, but a steep and rocky trail takes us around the left (west) side of that obstacle, to where we climb above the last cottonwoods and a few netleaf hackberry trees onto a sunny slope. At one point on the stiff climb, a cable offers a handhold where we cross the face of a low cliff on a built-up section of trail. The trail ahead is rather exposed, requiring some boulder hopping and the occasional use of hands.

Above this stretch, we enter the realm of steeply tilted Kayenta slickrock, above which rise domes of Navajo Sandstone. Presently the canyon vegetation is dominated by pinyon and juniper woodlands, but the damp canyon bottom hosts the greatest diversity of plants in the Island District. Cottonwoods, some quite large, thrive along the canyon's wash. Dogbane, or indian hemp, is a white-flowered plant with fairly large, oval green leaves. Water birch grows in tandem with false Solomon's seal and snowberry.

As we proceed up the semicircular canyon of Syncline Valley, we'll probably notice a host of potential campsites on benches above the canyon floor. Our canyon eventually bends south, to be joined by a dead-end, east-trending canyon, where alcoves and wet seeplines can be seen on its Navajo Sandstone slickrock. Presently our canyon narrows considerably between high cliffs, and cairns help guide the way. By now much of the lush greenery has been supplanted by pinyon and juniper, but a few water birches persist in the narrows.

Soon we climb steeply via slickrock ledges, where numerous potholes may hold water after a good rain. The trail ahead undulates over steeply tilted ledges, dipping into and back out of the wash several times, but the hiking is easy, with only minor ups and downs. Eventually, our trail approaches the Park road, then swings away from it, and we must negotiate a few more tilted ledges of the Kayenta Formation before finally joining the Crater View Trail, on which we turn left and stroll the short distance back to the trailhead (4.5; 5760).

# Trips 16-36: Needles District

# Trip 16
## Upper Salt Creek—Cathedral Butte to Salt Creek Jeep Trail

**Distance**: 28.2 miles round trip
**Low/High elevations**: 5380'/7050'
**Suited for**: Backpack
**Difficulty**: Moderate as a backpack of three or four days.
**Best seasons**: April through mid-June; mid-September through October.
**Maps/Trailhead**: 41,42,47/13

**Hazards**: Route is rugged and uncairned, very brushy and difficult to follow in places. Scattered surface water in places, but must be purified before use.

**Introduction**: This is the most ambitious and remote wilderness trek in the Needles District. The 1000-foot descent into Salt Creek is steep and rugged, and once in the canyon, hikers must pay careful attention to the vague route, as it follows brush-choked benches above the deep arroyo draining the canyon. But hikers will be rewarded for their efforts as they soak in the dramatic atmosphere of the slickrock-embraced canyon. Every erosional feature possible in the Cedar Mesa Sandstone, from domes, towers, spires, and balanced rocks to arches, alcoves, bulging cliffs, and sheer walls greets the hiker at every bend in this splendid canyon. Adding to the flavor of the Salt Creek experience are glimpses into the past human activities in the area.

Lee Kirk homesteaded upper Salt Creek in the 1890s, and his remote cabin still stands as a well-preserved relic of the Old West. The Anasazi also used the area, and evidence of their occupation of the canyon can be found if you look for it. Big Ruin, the largest in Canyonlands National Park, lies on a cliff in Salt Creek, consisting of 32 dwelling and granary structures. The Four Faces pictograph consists of Fremont-style rock art next to a cluster of Anasazi granaries. There are many other ruins and rock-art panels in the canyon, and discovering them is a very rewarding aspect of a hike into Salt Creek.

Salt Creek is a wonderful canyon to explore; but do not disturb or deface archaeological sites in any way. Do not touch rock-art panels or climb on the ruins. They have survived here for centuries, and it is our responsibility to preserve them.

**Description**: Our trek gets underway along the rim of Salt Creek Mesa. From the end of the spur road (0.0; 7050) we briefly follow a cairned trail southwest along the rim among pinyons and junipers. The rim of the mesa is formed by the resistant, basal Mossback member of the Chinle Formation, and due to our location high on the Monument Uplift, the Chinle occurs 2000 feet higher here than where it outcrops along the Park road in Indian Creek canyon.

**You may find corn, potsherds and perhaps a metate in upper Salt Creek**

Searching for a break in the low cliff, our trail follows the rim, then abruptly plunges over the edge, steeply descending a boulder-strewn north-facing slope. The trail executes several very steep, rocky switchbacks that funnel runoff waters. Black pebbles polished by ancient streams have been weathered from the conglomerate boulders that litter the trail. In addition, there are large sandstone blocks, and altogether the knee-jarring descent offers poor footing and we are forced to proceed slowly.

During this descent, we probably won't notice the progressively older strata we are passing through, as they are largely obscured on the slope; however, red bands of Moenkopi rocks and Organ Rock Shale seen on the opposite wall of the draw help us gauge our progress. After 1/2 mile we reach a bench and the grade abates.

Enjoying a respite from the plunging descent, we stroll north, presently upon Cedar Mesa rocks, and are soon confronted with another rugged descent. Once again we drop very steeply over slickrock, into the canyon below. At the bottom, the going is much easier as we follow either the small wash or slopes above it.

Eventually we emerge from the confines of the canyon onto a broad flat covered with sagebrush, four-wing saltbush, and winterfat. But we soon dip into a sandy wash that we follow down-canyon, to its confluence with the broad, sandy wash of East Fork Salt Creek. Shortly thereafter we enter the Park, then make our way up the sandy bank of the wash to a bench above, where we find a sign that indicates Canyonlands National Park (2.0; 6050).

Finally, the trail is smooth as we stroll northwest across a nearly level bench west of the wash. Sagebrush and four-wing saltbush form a nearly impenetrable thicket on this and other benches throughout the canyon. Among the trailside wildflowers decorating the bench with their seasonal blossoms are the tiny white flowers of pepper-grass, the bright orange blooms of globe mallow, the purples of tansy-aster, and heronbill, a mat-like goundcover. That plant takes its name from the shape of its ripened fruit.

After 1 1/4 mile from the Park boundary, we emerge from Gambel oaks and cottonwoods onto a broad, swampy meadow rich in wiregrass, common reed, and wild rose, and rimmed by a thick growth of tamarisk. The trail fades from view at the meadow's edge, but we simply make our way through the swampy spread, and will likely get our feet wet as we proceed northeast toward the slickrock at its east margin, where we will likely encounter a well-worn path leading quickly up to a campsite above a minor draw. Ignore this path and continue north along the foot of the slickrock, and soon the trail becomes apparent. The path leads us through a corridor in a grove of tamarisk and then beneath an undercut cliff, soon edging close to a small stream.

About 2 miles from the boundary we emerge from the slickrock above a small cascade and the confluence of Salt Creek's East Fork with the main branch of the canyon, which extends headward to the southwest. The canyon bottom remains choked with willows, tamarisk, and scattered Fremont cottonwoods, not only below us but throughout much of its length. Hence the trail follows benches above the increasingly deep arroyo.

Presently we stroll north above the wash and soon reach Kirk Cabin (2.2; 5920), a well-preserved structure built of hand-hewn ponderosa pine and Douglas-fir logs.

Large Kirk Arch offers a window to the western sky above the opposite side of the canyon, and our view extends down-canyon for a mile or so into a jumble of bulging, colorful cliffs, domes, and towers. Looking into the draw below Kirk Arch, we can see a stand of tall conifers on a sheltered slope. It is believed that this is the site from which Lee Kirk obtained logs for his cabin. We may stop here and rest, appreciating the workmanship and the struggle required to build the cabin in this lonely spot, but we may not camp here, for camping is not permitted within 300 feet of historical or archaeological sites.

Beyond Kirk Cabin, the hiking is smooth and generally easy, but as we reach the mouth of Big Pocket (a broad draw cutting back into the mesa for 1 1/2 miles), the trail reaches the edge of a steep and unstable cutbank high above the arroyo of Salt Creek, and apparently ends (1.5; 5830). The brush is a tangled mass at this point, but if we backtrack from the arroyo's edge for just a few feet, we'll find a trail-of-sorts leading through the brush, and shortly we'll intercept the main trail, dip into a minor draw and continue beyond a point of slickrock that juts out into the canyon.

Farther on, we drop steeply into a deep arroyo and climb the sandy bank opposite. The path is vague here, for the arroyo is occasionally swept by flash floods. Beyond the arroyo the route is obscure as we proceed generally north over patches of slickrock, but the route becomes more obvious as we begin to approach Wedding Ring Arch. The arch lies high on the wall east of the trail. This narrow ribbon of stone is formed in a jointed fin, and its opening is not obvious due to the cliff that rises immediately behind it. During much of the hike we have views of one or more arches. One span can be seen to the north, and another large opening can be seen on the southwest skyline when we are between Kirk and Wedding Ring arches.

Within 0.4 mile beyond the arch we dip into a usually dry stretch of Salt Creek wash and begin to follow benches on its west side. We'll pass several interesting draws and side canyons along this pleasant stretch, and also notice ample potential campsites, although they are far from water. Proceeding along the sagebrush-clad bench, we cross the shallow wash after another mile, then continue north on the opposite bench.

But soon the trail turns abruptly west, and to avoid a slickrock promontory jutting into the canyon we soon dip into a moist stretch of wash and follow it downstream for about 200 yards.

The point where we exit the wash is obscure; just beyond where a low rock wall east of the wash ends, we climb over slickrock and leave the wash, picking up a faint path above its east bank. Presently we follow a bench toward the mouth of an east-trending draw.

Where another promontory juts into the canyon, we once again cross back to the west bank, just above a lovely slickrock cascade. Down-canyon the wash is choked with riparian vegetation due to the abundant moisture here. Our trail follows the bench past several wooded draws trending southwest, and shortly we curve north-northeast, dipping into a small wash. Beyond it we follow the brush-clad bench beneath a northeast-trending slickrock ridge and, as our route and the wash below begin to curve around that ridge, we pass directly above Upper Jump (5.0; 5600). Here the waters of Salt Creek pour over a resistant, undercut ledge of the Cedar Mesa Sandstone.

Beyond Upper Jump the canyon becomes increasingly narrow, meandering among soaring slickrock cliffs that rise 500 feet above. The trail follows a bench south of the wash as it bends west. Farther on, our trail becomes a narrow, winding pathway among thickets of brush. Another path may be seen following the wash, but the bench trail offers the easier hiking.

The trail ahead soon bends northeast as we skirt the foot of another sandstone promontory. Soon the bench blends into the slope, and our presently rocky trail curves around the nose of

**Park boundary, Salt Creek**

that ridge where the canyon once again bends west. Shortly thereafter we are forced into the wash, (1.2; 5630), and make our way through willows and some tamarisk and Fremont cottonwood. There may be an intermittent flow of water here.

In the wash ahead we negotiate a few minor meanders and, at the next pronounced bend, where the wash curves from southwest to northwest, we reach the mouth of Salt Creek's West Fork (1.2; 5500). A sidetrip along its 7-mile course is worthwhile if time and energy allow.

Our route then follows several pronounced meanders while passing a few short but interesting west-trending draws, where some may wish to establish campsites. Eventually we emerge from the wash, reach the south end of the Salt Creek Jeep Trail (2.5; 5380), and either terminate our hike and backtrack to Cathedral Butte (usually a hike of two days) or continue on down Salt Creek. Angel Arch, a major scenic attraction in this part of Salt Creek lies only 2.4 miles ahead (see *Trip 22*).

# Trip 17
## Lavender Canyon

**Distance**: 30 to 35-plus miles round trip

**Low/High elevations**: 5090'/5680'

**Suited for**: Jeep trip or backpack

**Difficulty**: Strenuous as a three-to-four day backpack; easy 4WD route.

**Best seasons**: March through May; mid-September through November.

**Maps/Trailhead**: 43,45,41/14

**Hazards**: Sand flies; limited water in upper canyon; much sand; flash-flood danger.

**Introduction**: Although most visitors drive up the canyon in a 4WD vehicle, Lavender Canyon is nevertheless a fine hike. There are sandy stretches, but much of the wash is damp and hard-packed, and walking is easy. The lower reaches of the canyon are broad and open, displaying the typical canyon-country scenery of sheer cliffs and square-edged mesas. The head

of the canyon is a stark contrast, however, where bulging walls of Cedar Mesa slickrock, a labyrinth of narrow canyons, and several arches make the area immensely scenic and offer enough diversions to keep hikers busy for several days.

**Description**: Leaving the paved highway (0.0; 5150) we immediately cross a cattleguard, then proceed across Dugout Ranch lands while skirting a hayfield. Views extend south up to the broad canyon of Lavender to the wooded mesas and buttes rising to the skyline beyond. The road turns left and then right as we follow a fenceline, and enroute we enjoy fine views west-northwest toward North and South Six-shooter peaks, two great slickrock pinnacles that are erosional remnants of the Wingate cliffs that flank Lavender Canyon ahead and the east margin of Indian Creek valley behind us.

Soon we reach a gate (1.0; 5120) and turn left. Within 1/4 mile the road becomes sandy as we dip into Indian Creek wash, quickly climb above it, and shortly join the wash of Lavender Canyon, which we follow upstream.

Soon the north end of Bridger Jack Mesa towers 1000 feet above us in the east, rising in a succession of colorful ledges, slopes, and sheer cliffs to a crown of scattered Navajo Sandstone domes. Another, unnamed mesa rises to our west, separating Lavender Canyon from Davis Canyon (*Trip 18*).

In places the canyon boasts a flow of water, but springs issuing from the Moenkopi Formation are typically very alkaline and not potable. Hikers should carry enough water to make it to the head of the canyon, where fresher springs issue from the Cedar Mesa Sandstone. In the moist stretches the wash is usually hardpacked and the hiking is delightful, but some dry, sandy sections will slow our progress.

In the lower reaches of the canyon, the wash has cut down into the Moenkopi Formation, and here we can see the gypsum veins that lace the formation. Gypsum forms when supersaturated sea water evaporates quickly in an arid environment. Above the slopes and ledges of the Moenkopi Formation is the prominent black ledge of the Chinle Formation's lower member, the Mossback, a prime target of 1950s uranium prospectors.

After 8 miles from the paved road, cotton-woods begin to appear, and in the wettest areas of the wash are common reed, wiregrass, and willow. As we approach the Cedar Mesa Sand-stone, numerous branch canyons fork right and left. We pass three jeep roads leading into more prominent canyons, and soon rounded cliffs begin to embrace our route, squeezing the wash into an increasingly narrow passageway. Approaching the Park boundary, we can view a beautiful "jughandle" arch decorating a cliff north of the wash, and soon thereafter we leave the wash, cross a cattleguard, and enter Canyonlands National Park (9.5; 5400). After signing in at the register box alongside the road, we drop back into the wash, and within 1/4 mile we can see another arch on the skyline west of the canyon, Caterpillar Arch.

Following the wash between soaring cliffs, we soon reach a fork (0.5; 5400) where jeep roads branch right and left. The larger, left-fork canyon is Lavender Canyon proper, while the right fork is a narrow tributary canyon. Lavender features flowing water, Cleft Arch, and other highlights that make the 8 1/2-mile round trip up it very worthwhile.

Bearing left at the junction, we proceed south into the cliffbound declivity, alternating between sandy and rocky parts of the wash. Pinyon, juniper, Gambel oak and a variety of shrubs are found growing wherever they can establish a toehold in this slickrock canyon. There is a good chance of finding flowing water in the wash during the first 3 miles from the junction.

About 2.75 miles from the previous junction, we may find a small flow of water emanating from a prominent south-trending canyon. Soon thereafter large Cleft Arch comes into view up the canyon, and a spur road (3.3; 5600) soon forks right into a minor draw just north of the arch.

For a closer look at this large opening, follow the tracks on foot up that wash toward the west; its banks are brushy so it's best to stay in the wash. After 0.2 mile, another draw joins from the northwest, but we stay in the left fork. One can explore the canyon for only a short distance ahead, as cliffs and overhangs bar farther progress. Above us to the south is the opening of Cleft Arch, formed in a large alcove on a thick fin of Cedar Mesa Sandstone that projects east into Lavender Canyon. The arch has a somewhat angular opening, and boulders lie near its base. The opening is not yet as large as the alcove it penetrates, and it appears to be a rather youthful arch, with ample room to grow even larger. These short canyons and many other branching from Lavender Canyon are fun to explore, but they all end abruptly in great cliffbound amphitheaters.

Proceeding up the final stretch of Lavender Canyon, we follow the wash directly beneath the south side of Cleft Arch and shortly reach another fork (0.6; 5650), where jeep roads branch right and left. Not far above us the Cedar Mesa slickrock ends and reddish slopes and ledges, thickly-clad in pinyon and juniper, rise to the broad mesas above, but one must search by trial and error for a route through the steep slickrock to attain the highlands.

If we bear right at this junction, we'll soon come to the loop at the end of the rough jeep road (0.3; 5680). A use trail leads across the wash and follows a bench along the opposite bank, but soon drops back into the wash and fades from view. This remote canyon is interesting to explore, and numerous fins projecting into it from the cliffs above separate the drainage into numerous minor draws.

Returning 0.3 mile to the junction, we can also follow the rough left fork for nearly 1/2 mile, to where boulders bar further progress for vehicles. One can hike up this brushy fork for nearly a mile, to where it abruptly ends in soaring cliffs.

To explore the right fork of Lavender Canyon, backtrack for nearly 4.2 miles and bear left (west) up that sandy fork. After almost 1 mile jeep tracks lead 150 yards into a west-trending canyon. The road in the main fork winds among soaring, desert-varnished cliffs and passes a scattering of Douglas-firs growing in the most shady, protected sites. From the roadend (2.5; 5580) one can continue up the increasingly narrow canyon on foot for about one mile. Various draws branching west may invite us to linger, exploring their hidden environs and perhaps discovering some of their delightful secrets.

# Trip 18
## Davis Canyon

**Distance**: 23 miles or more round trip
**Low/High elevations**: 4900'/5420'
**Suited for**: Jeep trip or backpack
**Difficulty**: Easy but quite sandy 4WD route; moderate as a backpack of two or more days.
**Best seasons**: March through May; mid-September through November.
**Maps/Trailhead**: 44,45,47,41/15
**Hazards**: Flash-flood danger; sandy route; unreliable water.

**Introduction**: The trip up Davis Canyon is a shorter version of *Trip 17* to Lavender Canyon. The route follows a jeep road into the canyon to the Park boundary, beyond which numerous sandy spur roads explore the hidden reaches of a half-dozen branch canyons. The route is hard-packed much of the way, but is excessively sandy within the Cedar Mesa Sandstone at the head of the canyon.

But despite the sand and the possibility of encountering an occasional vehicle, the trip is a fine choice for the backpacker who enjoys exploring hidden canyons far from the crowds of hikers pounding out the dusty trails in the heart of The Needles.

**Description**: Leaving the highway at the Davis Canyon sign (0.0; 4900), we quickly rise on a graded dirt road to a gate. The redrock monolith of North Six-shooter Peak looms boldly west of us as we proceed on the rough road.

We soon reach a fenceline and a left-branching spur road to a corral, but we bear right, shortly passing a spur leading to a campsite on BLM land beneath a lone Fremont cottonwood. The road is rocky and rough, undulating across open, hilly terrain. After crossing the wash draining the broad basin of Bogus Pocket, we enjoy a striking head-on view of North Six-shooter Peak, then wind around benches west of Indian Creek wash.

Beyond a second gate, we skirt another cottonwood-shaded campsite, then round a bend

where the broad drainage of Davis Canyon spreads out before us. Above in the southwest is the spire-topped cone of South Six-shooter Peak, not as tall as its companion spire to the west but a spectacular sight nonetheless.

Finally we reach the wide wash draining Davis Canyon (2.6; 5030) and begin to follow it south up-canyon. Our road alternates between the wash and the brushy flats that embrace it. The canyon is flanked by low red ledges of Organ Rock Shale and Moenkopi Formation rocks, but the head of the canyon is the domain of Cedar Mesa slickrock. To our east the canyon is bounded by sheer cliffs of Wingate Sandstone, but westward the only remnants of that formation cap the slickrock fingers of the Six-shooter peaks.

Numerous broad valleys reach west for as much as 2 miles from the wash into the mesas beyond. The canyon becomes increasingly narrow upstream, and where saline runoff waters evaporate in the intense desert sun, the wash is encrusted with alkali. About 7 miles from the highway, we may encounter a seasonal flow of water. The wash ahead becomes narrow and much rockier, and our road frequently avoids these rough sections by climbing above.

After passing the wash of a south-trending tributary canyon, we climb to a sandy bench shaded by tall cottonwoods. Soon the road becomes much narrower as we negotiate several tight turns and short, steep pitches among thickets of sagebrush, rabbitbrush, and greasewood. After topping out on a brushy flat 7.6 miles from the highway, the sandy road drops very steeply back to the wash. Those driving into the canyon should inspect this steep pitch before proceeding; don't try it unless you're confident that you can make it back up.

The lush growth here is nurtured by the waters of Eight Mile Spring, issuing from the alcove east of the wash ahead, the only source of fresh water in the canyon. The canyon ahead is embraced by the bulging slickrock walls of the Cedar Mesa Sandstone and, as we approach the Park boundary, we'll pass a spur road leading into a west-trending canyon. Soon we reach the signed Park boundary, leaving Bureau of Land Management lands behind as we climb out of the wash and cross a cattleguard along a fenceline

(6.0; 5300). After signing the register, we quickly dip back into the exceedingly sandy wash and continue up-canyon. After 1/4 mile, a closed jeep route forks right into a west-trending canyon, and those so inclined can follow the sandy wash on foot for about 1 mile. Shortly thereafter, another jeep route, this one open to vehicles, forks south, paralleling the Park boundary and leading 1.1 miles up a sandy box canyon.

The main canyon is increasingly narrow as we proceed, and cliffs and bulging walls loom ever higher. Vegetation is largely confined to the narrow banks of the wash and slickrock niches. Pinyons and junipers grow to atypical proportions, nurtured by the rainwater that runs off of the Cedar Mesa slickrock.

About 1 1/4 miles from the Park boundary, roads branch right and left up the two main upper forks of Davis Canyon. If you choose to follow the sandy right fork southwest, you'll reach yet another fork after 1/3 mile. Here a right-branching wash can be driven west for another 1/3 mile and then walked another 1.5 miles to the head of a west-trending branch canyon.

The left fork of the main right-fork route follows the main canyon for another 0.6 mile, then encounters boulders choking the narrowing wash that bar further progress to vehicles. Once again, we can continue up-canyon on foot—into three rockbound amphitheaters at the canyon's head.

Those wishing to explore the left fork of Davis Canyon can return to the aforementioned junction and follow the sandy road to its end after 1.5 miles. Beyond the roadend, the upper canyon beckons, and we can hike up its increasingly narrow wash for 2 miles. This is the most remote and seldom-visited canyon in the Davis Canyon system.

# Trip 19
## Colorado River Overlook Jeep Road

**Distance**: 14.6 miles round trip
**Low/High elevations**: 4750'/4920'

**Suited for**: Jeep trip, mountain-bike trip, or backpack
**Difficulty**: Easy 4WD trip; moderate two-day backpack or mountain-bike trip.
**Best seasons**: April through mid-June; mid-September through November.
**Maps/Trailhead**: 46,48/16
**Hazards**: No water; road has some sand and rough and rocky sections between Salt Creek and the overlook.

**Introduction**: This jeep road is the mountain biker's best choice in the Needles District for an enjoyable day's ride. Strong riders, however, can make the round trip in a few hours. The route is also among the easier 4WD roads in the district, but rough and rocky sections dictate careful driving. Even dayhikers or backpackers will enjoy the route, as there are continuous panoramic vistas and miles of untracked slickrock awaiting exploration. The initial 2.7 miles of the road are passable to high-clearance two-wheel-drive vehicles, but 4WD is required beyond the crossing of Salt Creek. As with any other jeep road in the Park, avoid the route during and for a day or so after heavy rains. The overlook is a worthy destination, offering a panoramic, 360° view of the Canyonlands country and the river that created it.

**Description**: Our trip begins at the southwest end of the Visitor Center parking area (0.0; 4920), whence the signed dirt road proceeds generally north. Quite soon we reach a gate, which may be closed during inclement weather, and ignore a road forking right. Beyond the gate we descend gradually into a slickrock-rimmed grassland from which we enjoy expansive vistas ranging from Junction Butte in the northwest to the cliffs bounding Hatch Point and the La Sal Mountains in the northeast.

Soon we pass a signed service road on the left, then curve northeast among the sandstone knobs that punctuate the cheatgrass-dominated flatland. Before long the road curves back northwest, where rabbitbrush and greasewood are overtaking the grasslands. From about the one-mile point onward, the road ahead is a narrow lane through the shrublands, staying just southwest of the intermittently damp wash of Salt

Creek.

After a tamarisk-lined wash draining Squaw Flat crosses the road from the southwest, our route becomes sandy. About 0.9 mile beyond that wash we reach the crossing of Salt Creek (2.7; 4750), and those with only high-clearance two-wheel-drive vehicles must not attempt to go any farther.

A closed jeep route forks west here, and we can walk along its course (no mountain bikes) for 200 yards to Lower Jump, where Salt Creek, when it is flowing, pours over a resistant ledge of Cedar Mesa Sandstone into the lower canyon 150 feet below. Below the pouroff are the softer rocks of the Elephant Canyon Formation, which have eroded into a deep alcove. Just beneath the lip of the pouroff, water from a dripping spring falls through the air far into the canyon bottom. Other seeps emerge from the contact of the porous Cedar Mesa rock and the impermeable upper layer of the Elephant Canyon Formation.

Beyond the crossing the road climbs steadily north. Presently the route is sandy with a high center, and soon we climb rough slickrock, then top out on a blackbrush-clad flat encircled by

**The Colorado River from the Needles overlook**

more slickrock. Magnificent vistas greet us from this highland, stretching out across the vast Canyonlands basin. Atop the flat we leave the Park (0.7; 4900) for a short time, re-entering it (0.3; 4890) after the road curves northwest.

Before long we briefly leave Park lands again (0.2; 4850), then descend to cross two dry, sandy forks of a wash, presently on Bureau of Land Management lands. But soon we re-enter the Park (0.6; 4820), then climb to a brushy hill, atop which the road is briefly smooth. Ahead we cross more rocky sections, then reach a very steep and extremely rough but short downhill grade. The road then continues, with minor ups and downs, across rough patches of slickrock. The final 1/4 mile is a smooth stretch, and the road ends at a loop among slickrock knobs (2.8; 4880). From here we can feel the presence of the river below, but we cannot yet see it. A sign warns of the unfenced overlook ahead, and from the roadend we make our way on foot over the slickrock for a short distance to the rocky knobs at the end of the point.

The river runs smooth and silent in the canyon 1000 feet below, its banks discontinuously lined with tamarisk and willow. It has cut into the gray and red rocks of the Honaker Trail Formation, which forms ledges above the river—some of the most ancient rocks exposed in the Park. On the opposite rim of the canyon, only 1/2 mile away, lies a broad bench of Cedar Mesa Sandstone that stretches away to the White Rim in the northwest. This bench lies in the Park's Island District, and beyond it rise the bulky highlands of Junction Butte and Grand View Point. Great cliffs and mesas embrace the river upstream, beyond which we see only the very summits of the lofty La Sal Mountains. North Six-shooter Peak is a prominent landmark on the eastern skyline, and in the southeast rises the long hogback crest of the Abajo Mountains. The serrated outline of The Needles to the south is a striking and exciting backdrop to the knobby slickrock terrain that surrounds us. Westward is the landmark of Elaterite Butte, and behind it the Orange Cliffs. Below that butte only the top of the slickrock wilderness of The Maze can be seen, punctuated by the white-capped pillars of the Chocolate Drops.

# Trip 20
## Roadside Ruin Trail

**Distance**: 0.3 mile loop trip
**Low/High elevations**: 4940'/4960'
**Suited for**: Walk
**Difficulty**: Easy
**Best seasons**: April through mid-June; mid-September through November.
**Map/Trailhead**: 46/17
**Hazards**: Negligible

**Introduction**: This very easy self-guided nature trail traverses open terrain among slickrock knolls north of the spires and buttes of The Needles. Enroute are broad vistas, common desert plants, and a well-preserved Anasazi grain-storage structure. This is the most easily accessible of untold dozens of granaries in Canyonlands. A leaflet available at the trailhead keyed to numbered posts along the trail describing the vegetation you encounter has an informative description of the Anasazi culture.

**Description**: From the trailhead (0.0; 4950) follow the rock-lined trail to the left among slickrock and a wide variety of shrubs and wildflowers. Soon the trail dips into a minor draw, where we find a spur trail forking left. This spur quickly leads to the granary, a typically round structure built into a sandstone wall and fashioned from slabs mortared together.

The trail ahead climbs out of the draw and loops back to the trailhead, from which we enjoy sweeping vistas of slickrock bluffs, buttes, cliffs, and a variety of unusual erosional features southward up the course of Salt Creek.

# Trip 21
## Cave Spring Trail

**Distance**: 0.6 mile loop trip
**Low/High elevations**: 4920'/4970'
**Suited for**: Walk
**Difficulty**: Moderately easy
**Best seasons**: April through mid-June; mid-September through November.
**Map/Trailhead**: 46/19
**Hazards**: Steep dropoffs; two ladders that must be descended to pass up and down cliffs.

**Introduction**: In the Salt Creek drainage, the primary watershed of The Needles, numerous "pockets" extend away from the wash back into the slickrock that surrounds it. Some of these pockets are quite large, containing isolated basins more than one square mile in extent, while others are only minor draws.

From the late 19th century until the 1970s, cattle from the Dugout Ranch grazed the grassy pockets of The Needles country. Some of the larger pockets were able to withstand intensive grazing, and they remain as grasslands today. But in the small Cave Spring pocket, for example, cattle congregated around the precious water there, and the grassland sustained irreparable damage. Now this pocket is infested with unusually large shrubs, and the Cave Spring Trail carves a swath through the shrubby pocket. Parts of the trail offer expansive vistas, and it passes a pictograph panel and well-preserved cowboy camp.

**Description**: One of the four self-guided trails in the Needles District, the Cave Spring Trail is described by a leaflet available at the trailhead. The trail forms a loop, and arrow signs guide us along the right-hand leg of the loop as we leave the trailhead (0.0; 4920).

From the trailhead we proceed northwest into the brush-clad pocket, thickly overgrown with greasewood, four-wing saltbrush, sagebrush, and rabbitbrush. Small signs along the way identify these and other trailside shrubs. Soon we pass beneath an overhanging ledge, offering brief but welcome shade on a hot day. Shortly thereafter, we exchange the sandy tread for slickrock, which we climb easily to the gentle highland above. Curving south over its prominently cross-bedded surface, we then pass numerous soil-filled potholes hosting shrubs such as yucca, singleleaf ash, and mormon tea, plus pinyon and juniper. Seasonal wildflowers, including cryptantha and haplopappus, further enliven the smooth bedrock alongside the trail.

Enroute we enjoy distant views contrasting

such features as the alpine peaks of the La Sal Mountains with the desert crag of North Sixshooter Peak, and broad, slickrock-embraced grassland with the cottonwood-lined wash of Salt Creek.

After 0.4 mile we reach the first ladder, which we climb down into a narrow joint. Shortly thereafter we reach a second, longer ladder, allowing passage over a plunging cliff. Below the ladder we proceed into another brush-infested pocket and pass beneath the roof of an alcove, then finally reach the deep alcove from which dripping Cave Spring issues. Its seeping waters nourish a small hanging garden of maidenhair fern and mosses. Waters collected in the porous sandstone above the vaulted ceiling of the cave issue from a seepline at the contact zone with an impermeable layer below. This seeping water has, over the ages, dissolved the cement binding the rock together, forming a horizontal zone of weakness that eventually led to the alcove's formation.

Near the spring is a Fremont pictograph, and the alcove's ceiling is blackened by the soot of countless past campfires. Not only did the Anasazi and the Fremont people come here to drink the spring's waters, but cowboys came to establish a line camp here in this land of little moisture.

As we continue beneath the overhang, we pass among squawbush and sacred datura, then stroll through an old cattle drift fence. A trailside feed bin appears as we approach the fenced mouth of another alcove, wherein lies a remarkably well-preserved cowboy camp. Tables, cabinets, old cans, pots and pans, an old stove, and leather harnesses remind us of the bygone days when cowboys maintained their lonely vigil over their herds of cattle. Enjoy this historical site, but do not disturb it in any way.

A seep dampens the wall behind the camp, but cowboys must have relied upon Cave Spring for water. The trail ahead proceeds through unusually tall brush as it quickly curves around a slickrock promontory to end at the trailhead (0.6; 4920).

# Trip 22
## Salt Creek Jeep Trail

**Distance**: 20.3 miles round trip, plus 2.6 miles round trip to Angel Arch trailhead
**Low/High elevations**: 4950'/5500'; 5950' at Angel Arch
**Suited for**: Jeep Trip
**Difficulty**: Moderately easy 4WD trip
**Best seasons**: April through mid-June; mid-September through November.
**Maps/Trailhead**: 46,47/18
**Hazards**: Flash-flood danger; water sources potentially fouled by vehicles; jeep trail is rough and rocky with possible quicksand during wet periods; requires careful driving by an experienced driver; high-clearance 4WD vehicle is necessary.

**Introduction**: Salt Creek, the main stream of the Needles District, drains the flanks of Salt Creek Mesa south of the Park, meandering through a slickrock defile and across open desert flats, and finally plunging into a precipitous gorge to enter the Colorado River.

Since much of the canyon bottom is rocky and hard-packed, the trip is attractive to the backpacker who doesn't mind the presence of vehicles. Dozens of branch canyons are worthy of exploration, and one will find intermittent water in Salt Creek, but that water may be contaminated by vehicles. Not only is the trip highly scenic in its own right, but numerous arches and Anasazi ruins high on the canyon's walls combine to make the trip very rewarding.

**Description**: The Salt Creek Jeep Trail initially heads south from a road junction (0.0; 4950) and very soon drops to a sandy crossing of Squaw Canyon wash. Thereafter we climb to a bench thickly clad in greasewood and reach an interpretive display beneath a sandstone knoll that describes the Salt Creek Archaeological District. Another sign warns that the route ahead is for 4WD vehicles only. Here we pass through an open gate (may be closed during inclement weather) and soon enter the sandy wash of Salt Creek and proceed up-canyon. The canyon is broad in its lower reaches, and the slickrock cliffs, buttes, and knolls rise well beyond the confines of the wash.

Upon reaching a signed left-branching jeep trail (2.5; 5000) leading to Horse Canyon shortly beyond the mouth of its wash, we part company with *Trip 23* takers and continue along the course of Salt Creek, avoiding a deep pothole almost at once. The road then skirts the wash, and ahead it crosses it several times.

About 1/2 mile from the junction we are squeezed into the narrow drainage and drive through water usually about 2-feet deep for about 0.2 mile. Not far beyond the water we can see Peekaboo Arch ahead, and, as we round the bend beneath the arch, we encounter a very short spur leading to popular Peekaboo Campsite just south of the wash. All around this beautiful site are cliffs, domes, and pinnacles of the red- and white-banded Cedar Mesa Sandstone. The camp is available for the use of four-wheel drivers only, and owing to its ease of access and short distance from the main Park road, it receives the heaviest use of any backcountry camp in the Needles District. There are five campsites at Peekaboo, some in tamarisk groves next to the wash, others perched on a hill and shaded by the spreading branches of stately Fremont cottonwoods. Picnic tables, fire grills, and pit toilets constitute the facilities here. As at the other two camps up-canyon, no potable water is available. Peekaboo Arch and the intriguing Peekaboo pictograph panel lie directly above the camp (see *Trip 29*).

Beyond the camp our jeep road skirts the wash while following a bench around a pronounced bend in the canyon, leading us to the opposite (south) side of the arch. Less than 1/2 mile beyond Peekaboo Camp, a bench rising west of the wash has a stand of cottonwoods consumed by fire, the result of a visitor burning toilet paper. When traveling through Salt Creek canyon, use the pit toilets when available; otherwise visitors are required to pack out their toilet paper.

The route ahead follows the meandering canyon, first left, then right, and back again. Generally the wash is rocky and rough, but in places its bed is sandy. The jeepway crosses the wash numerous times, 163 times, in fact, throughout its length.

Numerous canyons branch off from the wash to right and left; the longest and most interesting ones to explore trend southwest from the main canyon, cutting far back into the slickrock wonderland. Drivers who proceed carefully, with an eye toward the colorful canyon walls, may notice an occasional Anasazi granary beneath the overhanging roof of an alcove or on ledges above.

**In lower Salt Creek**

We must proceed slowly as we negotiate water-worn slabs and cross areas of loose rocks. The canyon walls close in and become increasingly higher as we continue. Some of the shaly red and gray beds of the Cedar Mesa Sandstone form bands of broken rock on the canyon walls, and may be mistaken for ruins.

A variety of wildflowers decorate not only the wash but the benches above as well. Wyoming paintbrush, tansy-aster, yellow sweetclover, evening primrose, hairy goldenaster, scarlet gilia, and various cacti all provide a beautiful if seasonal floral display. Cottonwoods, willows, and some tamarisks will be found in moist sites along the wash, as will common reed and wiregrass. On the benches above are thickets of tall greasewood and four-wing saltbush, denizens of alkaline soils. And growing on and very near slickrock we find pinyon, juniper, and typical shrubs of that plant association, such as Fremont barberry, singleleaf ash, and Utah serviceberry.

Eventually we reach Angel Arch Camp (7.1; 5360), consisting of three sites on the east side of the jeepway. This site, beneath a tall cliff, has fire grills, picnic tables, and a pit toilet. Shortly beyond we encounter the signed spur road (0.2; 5370) to Angel Arch.

---

Angel Arch is the largest and arguably the most beautiful span in Canyonlands. The road not only offers fine views of the arch but also offers access to a 3/4-mile trail that allows visitors to stand beneath the towering span.

This jeep road forks left, immediately climbing a steep, narrow grade into the branch canyon above. The road ahead is sandy and rocky as it crisscrosses the wash. Great cliffs and alcoves, domes and spires rise above us, embracing this box canyon on three sides.

As we approach the roadend Angel Arch comes into view, high above the canyon to the south. One final but very rough stretch of slickrock is encountered just before we reach the small turnaround and pit toilet at the roadend (1.3; 5500).

The signed Angel Arch Trail is a well-used path, following the dry wash upstream beyond the roadend amid riparian vegetation. Soon magnificent Angel Arch comes into view once again, and we leave the wash after 200 yards to climb steep slickrock southward toward a sandstone knoll. The grade leads steadily uphill, and the arch looms ever closer.

As on most routes in the Cedar Mesa Sandstone, cairns lead us over slickrock on a roundabout route as we negotiate ledges and dip in and out of alcoves. Finally, after a steep scramble over loose rock and a friction pitch, we stand within the towering opening of Angel Arch (0.75; 5950).

True to its name, Angel Arch, when viewed from a distance, bears a balanced rock on the fin above that resembles an angel with wings folded. The entire fin which the opening penetrates is beautifully streaked with desert varnish, and the edges of the opening are smooth save for the top of the span, which has angular edges where great

chunks of sandstone have fallen and weathering has not yet rounded the opening into the classic arch shape.

---

Back on the main jeep road, it is but a short distance south to the roadend. Beyond the Angel Arch spur road, our road soon dips steeply into Salt Creek wash, then climbs quickly but steeply to the opposite (west) bank. At the top of the rise we find Bates Wilson Camp (0.2; 5380), named for the first superintendent of the Park, a legendary individual who played an important role in the establishment of Canyonlands as a national park.

There is but one campsite here, with a picnic table and fire grill. The site, shaded by tall cottonwoods, rests on a bench just above the wash. Beyond Bates Wilson Camp the road very soon curves back to the east bank of the wash and, after about 300 yards, ends in a tight turnaround. Travel up-canyon is on foot only. See *Trip 16* for details on upper Salt Creek.

# Trip 23
## Horse Canyon Jeep Trail

**Distance**: 18.2 miles round trip, plus 1.4 miles round trip to Tower Ruin
**Low/High elevations**: 4950'/5320'
**Suited for**: Jeep trip
**Difficulty**: Moderately easy 4WD route; strenuous hiking route due to deep sand.
**Best seasons**: April through mid-June; mid-September through November.
**Maps/Trailhead**: 46,47/18
**Hazards**: Flash-flood danger; deep, loose sand in wash; usually no water.

**Introduction**: Horse Canyon is an extremely sandy tributary of Salt Creek that cuts far back into a slickrock wonderland of cliffs, spires, domes, arches, and Anasazi ruins. This trip is a shorter version of the Salt Creek Jeep Trail, and it offers many scenic delights, including a sidetrip to Tower Ruin and two short foot trails to Castle and Fortress arches, plus the opportunity to explore numerous hidden branch canyons. The deep sand in the wash makes the route impassable to mountain bikers and unattractive to hikers.

**Description**: From the beginning of Salt Creek Jeep Trail (0.0; 4950), we follow *Trip 22* up the lower canyon of Salt Creek to the signed junction with the route into Horse Canyon, (2.5; 5000), and bear left, climbing a greasewood-clad bench to avoid small pouroffs in Horse Canyon wash. After 1/2 mile we enter the sandy wash and proceed southeast up-canyon, and before long we reach the short spur road forking left to a view of Paul Bunyan's Potty (1.0; 5050).

A very short trail leads about 100 yards through the sagebrush to the foot of the canyon wall, from which we gaze skyward through the large opening of the arch. True to its name, the arch resembles a gargantuan toilet seat. This is a classic example of a pothole-type arch, formed as wind and water enlarged the pothole on the cliff above (see *Trip 24* for more on pothole formation) while an alcove was forming on the wall below. Ultimately, pothole and alcove coalesced, and Paul Bunyan's Potty is the result, a gaping hole through the vaulted ceiling of the deep alcove.

Beyond the spur road we crisscross the wash and soon encounter another spur (1.0; 5100) forking left and signed for Tower Ruin.

---

Tower Ruin is a magnificent example of an Anasazi cliff dwelling, and this short sidetrip shouldn't be missed. The road leading to it is fairly smooth. It travels northeast across flats studded with greasewood and bunches of Indian ricegrass, ending in a turnaround (0.7; 5120) at the foot of a 400-foot slickrock butte.

The ruin can be seen from the roadend, but for a better view follow the trail for 200 yards around the base of the tower that presumably gave the ruin its name. The trail ends below the ruin, which sits in an alcove midway up the cliff above. It is a tall, square stone structure constructed of carefully fitted slabs. Six wooden poles once supported the roof of the structure. Another smaller structure, left of Tower Ruin, was probably used for storing grain.

As we amble back toward the roadend, we may see another arch across the canyon to the southwest. All the arches in Horse Canyon have formed just above the contact between a hard, mostly white sandstone layer above and the softer red layer of the Cedar Mesa Sandstone below. Weathering and erosion of the softer layer have left the overlying sandstone unsupported in places, resulting in the formation of alcoves, and in some cases arches.

---

When we resume our sandy drive up-canyon, the road alternates between the wash and stream terraces. Pinyon, juniper, and sagebrush clothe the small benches above the wash, and as we proceed farther into the realm of slickrock, great cliffs, some sheer, others overhanging, begin to jut skyward wherever we look. About 1.6 miles from Tower Ruin junction, just after a 1/2-mile stint on a sandy, brushy bench, an arrow sign indicates the correct direction in which to proceed in a wide section of the wash. Those wishing to view aptly named Gothic Arch can scramble quickly up the slickrock chute at the mouth of a branch canyon to our right (southwest) and proceed for about 1/2 mile up that draw to a good view of the span, high on the ridge to the west.

About 1/2 mile beyond the arrow sign, as the wash begins to head south-southwest, we pass beneath an overhang that may be impassable to high-profile vehicles. Gambel oaks begin to occupy sheltered sites beneath canyon walls as we head deeper into the slickrock maze. Several branch canyons may entice us to park our vehicle and explore their rockbound reaches, but most are quite sandy. We may see several arches penetrating thin sandstone fins high above the wash.

Approaching the head of the canyon, we eventually reach the Castle Arch Trail (4.5; 5300) on the west side of the jeepway. The trail is about 0.4 mile long, with an elevation gain of 100 feet. This path initially climbs a hill above Horse Canyon, then drops into a brushy branch canyon. The way passes among charred snags of pinyon and juniper, where big sagebrush and Gambel oaks are vigorously revegetating the area.

Following the small wash, we pass beneath an undercut wall, and beyond it we have a fine view of the arch at the canyon's head. The trail ends near the foot of the wall below the arch. Castle Arch is an old-age span: the edges of its opening are rounded, and only a thin ribbon of stone spans the top of the arch.

All around the amphitheater at the head of the draw are bulging walls, ledges, sheer cliffs and prominent domes resembling castles. The red- and white-banded slickrock is lichen-encrusted and streaked with the dark mineral deposits of desert varnish.

---

Resuming our drive up-canyon, we follow the increasingly narrow and rocky wash, and quite soon, just short of the roadend, we reach the signed trail to Fortress Arch (0.1; 5320) and the roadend.

---

This well-used trail is slightly longer than the one to Castle Arch, and gains nearly 200 feet in 0.4 mile. Here the main canyon divides and the Fortress Arch Trail heads up the right fork, traversing at first, then dipping into the wash after 200 yards. There are scattered cairns in the wash as we follow it up-canyon. Here the vegetation is much more abundant and diverse than in the lower reaches of Horse Canyon, owing to the well-developed soil cover here.

After 0.2 mile the canyon forks again, and the trail leads us southwest into the fork on a sidehill ascent. The route ahead climbs gently, winding over slickrock beneath the canyon walls. Soon Fortress Arch comes into view, formed high on the canyon wall just above the contact between the softer red layer of the Cedar Mesa below and the resistant white sandstone above.

Near the head of the draw, smaller draws begin to branch off on both sides. Presently we scramble over slickrock, climb a steep slope, negotiate steep slickrock, then traverse to the trail's end beneath the arch. The opening has a classic arch shape, but it is formed midway up a streaked cliff, and hence is more likely to be classified as a window rather than an arch.

If you want to stand within the opening, you need rock-climbing skills to scale the steep cliff at the canyon's head. As we stroll back down the trail, distant views stretch to North Six-shooter Peak and the conical summits of the La Sal Mountains, framed by the colorful bulging walls of Horse Canyon. The upper canyons are spectacular and interesting to explore. They are generally rocky and the hiking is easy compared to the sandy wash of lower Horse Canyon.

# Trip 24
## Pothole Point Trail

**Distance**: 0.6 mile, semiloop trail
**Low/High elevations**: 5070'/5090'
**Suited for**: Walk
**Difficulty**: Easy
**Best seasons**: April through mid-June; mid-September through November.
**Map/Trailhead**: 48/20
**Hazards**: Negligible

**Introduction**: This interesting, self-guided nature trail is easy enough for novice hikers, but is also fascinating enough to attract the seasoned hiker. Along the short, cairned slickrock trail on will find myriad potholes.

**Description**: Before beginning this pleasant stroll, pick up a leaflet at the trailhead (0.0; 5070) describing potholes and the small creatures that dwell there. The trail proceeds west initially over corrugated slickrock among a scattering of pinyon, juniper, and various shrubs. After 150 yards the trail forks, and the two forks form a loop. Following the loop in a clockwise direction, we now bear left, crossing slickrock pockmarked with innumerable potholes and passing a number of minor knolls that cap this unimposing ridge.

Most of the potholes are small and shallow, just beginning to fill with sand and clay. Hikers visiting in early spring may find them filled with water and teeming with small crustaceans, such as tadpole shrimp and fairy shrimp, snails, worms; and possibly spadefoot-toad tadpoles. All these creatures and more depend on the pothole environment, where they must complete

**Big Spring Canyon, Junction Butte and Island in the Sky**

their life cycles very quickly in the ephemeral pools.

Larger potholes with deeper soils host a few shrubs, and still larger ones host many shrubs and an occasional pinyon or juniper. All of them have a "bathtub ring" of desert varnish, formed as mineral-laden waters evaporate in the desert sun and leave behind a coating of minerals such as manganese oxide.

Potholes form from the combined action of wind and water. When water collects in a minor depression, the cementing agents that have bound the sand grains into rock there are weakened and dissolved. Once the water has evaporated, wind helps remove the loose sand, thus deepening the depression. Rainwash from downpours also helps to remove loosened sand. As this yearly cycle repeats itself, over time the pothole becomes increasingly large in depth and breadth.

Our trail eventually leads us to a fine viewpoint just above the Scenic Drive, where we gaze upon a host of cliff-edged mesas, the La Sal Mountains, and the rugged Needles. Presently the trail begins to curve back toward the trailhead, passing a very short spur to a viewpoint on a trailside knob that offers a sweeping vista of Canyonlands country. Approaching the trailhead, our cairned route passes between a mushroom-shaped rock and an overhanging ledge. Both are good examples of differential erosion, where the softer, stream-deposited red beds have eroded and weathered at a faster rate than the overlying sandstone.

Once we conclude the loop, we turn left and stroll back to the trailhead (0.6; 5070).

# Trip 25
## Slickrock Trail

**Distance**: 2.4 miles semiloop, plus 0.6 mile round trip to viewpoints

**Low/High elevations**: 4880'/5050'

**Suited for**: Walk

**Difficulty**: Moderately easy

**Best seasons**: April through mid-June; mid-September through November.

**Map/Trailhead**: 48/21

**Hazards**: No water or shade; steep dropoffs.

**Introduction**: This short jaunt is a delightful stroll over Cedar Mesa Sandstone slickrock, featuring panoramic vistas of canyons, cliffs, mesas, and mountains throughout its length. It's an introduction not only to plant life on the slickrock but also to the type of hiking one encounters in The Needles, where most "trails" are simply cairned routes over solid stone.

**Description**: Heading northeast from the trailhead (0.0; 4960) we quickly drop to a trailside box where we can pick up a leaflet with a map and a brief description of the trail. Then we cross a minor wash and wind upward through the slickrock, following cairns amid pinyon and juniper. Topping a rise, we meet the first viewpoint spur trail (0.25; 5050), leading 50 feet northeast to a grand vista stretching from Junction Butte in the northwest to the great orange cliffs that abut Hatch and Harts points and to the La Sal Mountains in the northeast. The gorge of Little Spring Canyon lies below, and to the south are the fins, domes, and spires of The Needles. Prominent North Six-shooter Peak stabs the sky toward the east, and beyond rise the wooded slopes of the Abajo Mountains.

After returning to the main trail, we continue over slickrock, following cairns to avoid walking through small, soil-filled depressions with cryptogamic crust. Some of the larger potholes have blackbrush, yucca, and mormon tea where ample soil has collected over the ages. Soon we reach the loop trail forking left and right (0.25; 5030) and, taking the loop in a clockwise direction, we continue our slickrock stroll above the declivity of Big Spring Canyon on the left.

On the lower walls of the canyon, the Elephant Canyon Formation is exposed, a mostly red rock forming ledges and low, broken cliffs. At the contact zone with the overlying Cedar Mesa Sandstone (the same rock on which we are walking) on the cliffs below we can see alkali-stained seeplines and a few small hanging gardens.

As we proceed north, cross-bedding in the sandstone is apparent alongside the trail, for the light-colored bands of the Cedar Mesa were deposited as wind-blown sand. The sandstone is pockmarked with potholes (like the waterpockets of Capitol Reef) and stained with desert varnish. A common shrub here and on slickrock throughout the Needles District is littleleaf mountain mahogany.

By the time we reach a small trailside sign, another viewpoint spur trail forks off to the left (0.6; 5010). This is the longest spur on this trip, 0.3 mile round trip. Initially, this route descends southwest, and then it turns north while following ledges and winding over slickrock to the viewpoint at 5000 feet. Big Spring Canyon's intermittently damp wash lies 600 feet below. On the canyon walls, more seeps and hanging gardens can be seen. Our view encompasses a vast panorama of cliffs, mesas, and canyons. Prominent among the landmarks are the fins of Ernies Country and the Orange Cliffs, Elaterite Butte and Ekker Butte in the west and northwest. Closer at hand, across the canyon of the Colorado River, are isolated Junction Butte and the vast Island in the Sky mesa. The pointed summits of the La Sal Mountains rise on the northeast skyline, while the spires of North and South Six-shooter peaks are prominent landmarks in the southeast. And of course, the banded stone fingers of The Needles form the striking slickrock landscape behind us to the south.

Returning to the main trail, we very soon reach another spur (0.1; 4920) that leads only 50 yards to yet another glorious viewpoint, where a fine panorama of slickrock knolls, blackbrush-infested flats, cliffs, mesas, mountains, and canyons meets our gaze.

Our route ahead curves around the rim of the canyon, and at length we reach the fourth and final spur route (0.4; 5000), to another fine viewpoint. Following this spur, we descend slickrock, traverse a ledge, and then scramble to a knoll from which we have a fine view of Little Spring Canyon. There are no towering spires here, as there are in The Needles, but a host of jointed knolls instead. Again, our gaze includes the cliffs, canyons, and mesas seen before—landmarks that should presently be familiar and thus are a good means of orientation in this tangled country.

To complete the circuit, we proceed generally southwest over slickrock and across ledges while enjoying constant panoramas. Soon we close the loop (0.25; 5030) and bear left at the junction to retrace our steps to the trailhead (0.5; 4960).

# Trip 26
## Confluence Overlook

**Distance**: 10.2 miles round trip
**Low/High elevations**: 4810'/5100'
**Suited for**: Dayhike or backpack
**Difficulty**: Moderate
**Best seasons**: April through mid-June; mid-September through November.
**Maps/Trailhead**: 48,51/22
**Hazards**: No water; little shade; steep dropoffs.

**Introduction**: This is a memorable all-day hike or overnighter leading over brushy flats, through shallow washes, and among slickrock knolls to a magnificent overlook of the joining of two great western rivers—the Colorado and the Green—and the 1000-foot-deep gorges they have carved deep into the Utah landscape.

**Description**: The signed trail leads past the barricade at the roadend (0.0; 4900) and at once begins descending slickrock ledges of Cedar Mesa Sandstone into the broad, sandy wash of Big Spring Canyon, reaching it just upstream from a seep nurturing lush grasses and tall, spreading cottonwoods. Once we are in the wash, cairns lead us a short distance upstream to a minor branch canyon, which we begin to ascend, at times quite steeply, to a slickrock notch above and west of the canyon, framing a fine picture of distance Junction Butte. A pause here offers more good views behind us, including the broken canyon walls of Big Spring canyon and the round shoulders of the Abajo Mountains on the far horizon.

The trail west of the notch traverses into the head of another minor canyon, where we must climb a short ladder before scaling the natural slickrock steps above. As in many areas of The Needles, the sandstone has weathered along its bedding planes, forming a stairway of minor ledges.

Above this climb we amble over the corrugated slopes of a blackbrush-clad basin, crest a minor ridge, and then traverse ledges before dipping into a small Elephant Canyon tributary. Our route follows this wash down-canyon, rimmed by low bluffs of banded sandstone.

Soon washes join our canyon from left and right, and we then leave the confines of the canyon, crossing over grassy slopes to the wide, sandy wash of Elephant Canyon. The canyon here is a striking contrast to its spire-rimmed upper reaches. Here its drainage is wide and open, and a stroll up or down its course makes a rewarding diversion.

We soon leave Elephant Canyon and begin to ascend a southwest-trending branch canyon. This canyon splits into three forks near its head, and here we ascend moderately steeply via a minor ridge that divides the two left forks. Topping out on a slickrock divide, we proceed west, descending slightly at times above another small canyon. Views now reach back into the heart of The Needles, where a bewildering array of colorful, slender sandstone spires forms a saw-toothed backdrop to the comparatively gentle terrain we are traversing.

The irregular outline of a redrock tower lies ahead, and we proceed toward that landmark, first descending several short but steep friction pitches, then following a sandy drainage lined with clumps of wavy-leaf oak, a common denizen of sandy soils. This stint leads us past and just south of the redrock tower, beyond which we top a drainage divide.

A broad, blackbrush-infested basin now spreads out before us, and we presently descend shrubby slopes on a gentle grade, soon intersecting the jeep road (3.2; 5000) (*Trip 36*) in Devils Lane, which heads north and south. Views enroute are superb, stretching beyond the invisible declivity carved by the Colorado River to the hinterlands of The Maze, the Land of Standing Rocks, the Orange Cliffs, and the landmark buttes of Bagpipe, Elaterite, Ekker, and Buttes of the Holy Cross.

Our trail crosses the jeep road, meanders over a blackbrush-clad hill, and dips into a minor northwest-trending draw, reaching the jeep road (0.7; 4900) once again in the arrow-straight valley of Cyclone Canyon. Cyclone Canyon is a graben valley—a downdropped block of the earth's crust—and its sunken, flat bottom is thickly clad in grasses. Before the establishment of the Park, visitors to valleys such as this would have encountered cattle herds from Dugout

Ranch.

A sign here points to the Confluence Overlook spur road, and we stroll north on the jeep road, quickly reaching its junction with the spur, which we follow west along the course of a shallow west-trending draw flanked by slickrock bluffs. After passing three south-trending draws and then winding northwest, we finally bend southwest, ascending nearly to the head of the fourth draw, where the road ends (0.8; 5030) next to a pit toilet and a CONFLUENCE OVERLOOK sign.

The overlook is close at hand now, but to get there we pass the rock barricade at the roadend, stroll past a picnic table, and follow the wash a short distance southwest up-stream, then climb west via ledges to the ridge above. Enroute, a sign warns that the overlook is unfenced, and indeed we should exercise extreme caution there. Now the trail descends gently via brushy slopes and slickrock ledges to the cluster of boulders below on the canyon rim (0.4; 4900).

We won't see it until we reach the very brow of the rim, but suddenly the canyon opens up to our view and there it is—The Confluence. Here the silty, gray-green waters of the Green River, born on the western flanks of the Continental Divide 400 miles north in Wyoming's Wind River Range, exit the confines of Stillwater Canyon and join the dark brownish waters of the Colorado River 1000 feet below.

The Colorado gathers its waters from the Continental Divide as well, 300 miles distant in Colorado's Rocky Mountain National Park. The rivers contain the silts of the rock formations through which they have flowed, which give each river its own coloration, which varies dependent upon runoff. The grayish and sometimes reddish waters of the Green don't immediately mix into the waters of the Colorado, but rather blend slowly for a mile or so downstream.

During low water, a broad, sandy beach adorns the riverbank where, in 1869, the legendary Powell Expedition established a base camp from which to survey their surroundings. Game trails follow the Green River upstream, just above the thickets of riparian woodland that hug its shores.

The mesas above the rivers are all capped by the red- and white-banded Cedar Mesa Sandstone, and we can visualize a once-continuous landscape prior to the downcutting of the rivers and their tributaries. As we gaze into the canyons below, we see the bluffs of Cedar Mesa Sandstone breaking away abruptly from the rims, below which the red and gray ledges and broken cliffs of the Elephant Canyon Formation are found. Near the canyon bottom is one of the oldest rock formations in all of Utah's national parks—the Honaker Trail Formation, consisting of thinly layered red cliffs and gray and reddish ledges. This band is littered with boulders fallen from above and is nearly devoid of vegetation, presenting a picture of the quintessential desert-canyon landscape. It's not unusual to see rafts floating on the gentle waters below, bound for the roaring whitewater of Cataract Canyon.

Camping is not permitted along the overlook trail, so overnighters must backtrack before searching for a campsite, which must be located out of sight of jeep trails and foot trails.

# Trip 27
## Squaw Canyon Loop Trail

**Distance**: 7.4 miles, loop trip
**Low/High elevations**: 5100'/5500'
**Suited for**: Dayhike or backpack
**Difficulty**: Moderate
**Best seasons**: April through mid-June; mid-September through November.
**Map/Trailhead**: 49/23
**Hazards**: Seasonal water; much slickrock scrambling requiring the use of both hands and feet at times; steep dropoffs.

**Introduction**: The Squaw Flat trail network offers a wide variety of highly scenic trails through the heart of The Needles. Most trails receive steady use from the spring through fall, but the intricately eroded nature of the terrain allows ample opportunities for solitude. These trails can be combined into a variety of loop trips that can last for several days, provided either that you carry an ample water supply or that surface water is available on your route.

This trip ascends the drainage of Squaw Canyon, alternating from open grasslands to woodlands of pinyon and juniper, climbs over a slickrock divide, and returns via the wooded drainage of Big Spring Canyon. Hikers will usually find water in the upper reaches of Squaw Canyon except after extended periods of drought.

**Description**: The trail leads south from the parking area in Campground A (0.0; 5150), skirting a sandstone knoll and a bulletin board, and after only 50 yards trails fork left to Squaw and Lost canyons and right to Big Spring Canyon. This loop trip can, of course, be traveled in either direction; since the following description takes the loop clockwise, we will bear left.

The trail cuts a southeast-bound swath through a grassy flat studded with four-wing saltbush and a variety of seasonal wildflowers. Spires of The Needles loom ominously ahead of us, while to the northeast bulky Squaw Butte foregrounds distant views reaching as far as the great peaks of the La Sal Mountains.

Upon entering a stand of pinyon and Utah juniper at the foot of a low sandstone slope, we quickly pass through the narrow band of trees and then mount slickrock, climbing from cairn to cairn via the step-like bedding planes of the Cedar Mesa Sandstone. After topping out on a minor slickrock ridge, we wind among potholes while enjoying expansive vistas over The Needles and the broad Indian Creek basin—a panorama of cliffs, mesas, mountains, slickrock, and grasslands. An unusual profile of Woodenshoe Arch can also be seen atop a slickrock ridge just north of east from our viewpoint.

The trail ahead negotiates slickrock slopes enroute to the minor wash below, through which we stroll among pinyon and juniper, and then we climb easily to another low sandstone ridge, where we now can see the broad, grassy valley of Squaw Canyon, bounded by slickrock knolls, domes, buttes, and spires. An intermittent green ribbon of riparian vegetation along its wash contrasts with the drab tones of the desert vegetation that surrounds it.

Our trail undulates along the west flank of the canyon, then enters an isolated stand of spindly lanceleaf cottonwoods and reaches a signed junction on the banks of the dry, grass-lined

**Typical Needles trail cairned over slickrock**

wash (1.2; 5110). Here we part company with hikers following *Trip 29* and briefly join those completing *Trip 28*. Hikers just beginning *Trip 28* will also accompany us up the canyon for the next 1.7 miles.

At the junction on the east bank of the wash, we bear right, hiking up-canyon above the wash through a rabbitbrush-fringed grassland. Prickly pear and fishhook cactus are particularly attractive when blooming in spring, and in autumn the blooms of rabbitbrush and broom snakeweed put forth a memorable floral display. The wash banks are thick with wiregrass, which isn't really a grass but a rush that is widespread throughout western North America, typically found in moist, saline areas along streams and in swamps and marshes.

Small cottonwoods also take advantage of subsurface moisture along the wash, and intermittent stands hug its banks, as do willows, tamarisk, and clumps of desert-olive. Wyoming paintbrush is a tall, red wildflower blooming in summer and often persisting into fall, when tansy-aster and the yellow blossoms of helilanthella are in full bloom.

Beyond the wash-side stroll, the sometimes dusty trail leads into drier terrain. Soon we pass beneath an overhanging cliff, offering ample shade during the morning hours. After the trail dips into the wash, we resume our trek on its west bank but then shortly cross back to the east bank just below a deep but stagnant pool rimmed with horsetails. Up-canyon, amidst riparian vegetation, a host of wildflowers enlivens the landscape, including the colorful blooms of scarlet gilia, hairy goldenaster, and evening primrose.

Soon our route ascends the wash, and where a cottonwood-clad drainage enters from the east we may find a few waterfilled potholes after substantial rainfall. The trail takes us in and out of the wash as we trek deeper into the slickrock wilderness.

Parting company with *Trip 28* hikers at a signed junction (1.7; 5200), we bear right, crossing the wash just below a thicket of willows, cottonwoods, and desert-olives. There may be a seep and potholes at or just above the junction, but this is the last water we'll encounter on this trip. Our trail follows above the west bank of the wash along a sagebrush-clad bench. The head of the canyon, bounded by tall cliffs and buttes of the red- and white-banded Cedar Mesa Sandstone and streaked with a tapestry of desert varnish, looms ahead, a seemingly impassable barrier to further travel. Avoiding that barrier, our route soon begins to ascend a side canyon. Up this canyon we'll see a small arch on the southwest skyline. Part way up this canyon, we cross its small wash, then scale slickrock, and then traverse a pothole-covered bench beneath a soaring red, tower-capped wall.

At a signed junction (0.9; 5440) at the southwest end of the bench we meet *Trip 31* hikers on the final leg of their loop. A profusion of knobs, towers, and hummocky slickrock foregrounds distant views of North Six-shooter Peak, the cliff-edged mesas of Harts and Hatch points, and the seemingly ever-present La Sal Mountains.

Bearing right at the junction, we follow cairns as we rise over steep slickrock, using

friction to scale a narrow, water-carved chute, and finally climbing manmade steps to the slickrock divide high above Big Spring and Squaw canyons at an elevation of 5520 feet.

A well-earned pause atop this ridge reveals panoramic vistas encompassing much of the Canyonlands basin and many of its outstanding landmarks. From northwest to north we gaze beyond nearby cliffs and towers to Ekker Butte, Candlestick Tower, Junction Butte, the White Rim, and the vast cliff-edged mesa of Island in the Sky. Big Spring Canyon stretches away to the north below us, but its wash is soon lost from view amid a jumble of slickrock. At the canyon's head is a cliffbound double amphitheater. The redrock fin separating the two amphitheaters has a deep, rounded notch that is likely the remains of an ancient arch.

The Cedar Mesa Sandstone in this area is much less jointed than it is toward the west near Elephant Canyon and Chesler Park. This massive sandstone here forms the towers, buttes, cliffs, and knife-edge ridges that surround us. In the canyon below, the landscape is a slickrock expanse of knolls cut by shallow draws that branch from Big Spring Canyon.

From the divide cairns lead us on a traverse of buff-toned slickrock below which we then descend steeply, using friction on the steepest pitches between cairns. Having carefully completed the descent, we emerge onto the floor of the basin at Big Spring Canyon's head, and the trail leads us through a pinyon, juniper, and Gambel-oak woodland.

The trail ahead alternates between the floor of the rocky wash and just above its east bank. Several branch canyons fork right and left. Backpackers in search of campsites may wish to follow one of these draws, in which they can enjoy the quiet and solitude of this slickrock desert.

As we continue, the canyon opens up somewhat, and we join (2.9; 5120) the southwest-bound trail (*Trip 31*) to Elephant Canyon. Here we meet *Trip 31* hikers in the beginning stages of their loop, but we bear right at the junction, climbing from the wash toward the campground. To complete the circuit, follow the initial 0.7-mile segment of *Trip 31* in reverse, reaching the trailhead in another 30 minutes or so.

# Trip 28
## Squaw Flat to Lost Canyon

**Distance**: 8.9 miles, semiloop trip
**Low/High elevations**: 5100'/5520'
**Suited for**: Dayhike or backpack
**Difficulty**: Moderate
**Best seasons**: April through June; mid-September through November.
**Maps/Trailhead**: 49,47/23
**Hazards**: No water except for a few seasonal pools in Squaw and Lost canyons; steep slickrock; steep dropoffs; one ladder.

**Introduction**: This fine circuit combines the initial segment of *Trip 27* with a jaunt into lesser-used Lost Canyon, an isolated declivity that boasts some of the most abundant riparian vegetation in The Needles. The route features many potential campsites, the exhilaration of scrambling over much slickrock, the possibility of good water sources, and several opportunities for sidetrips.

**Description**: From the Squaw Flat Trailhead (0.0; 5150) follow the left-forking trail described in *Trip 27* to the signed junction in upper Squaw Canyon (2.9; 5200), and bear left toward Lost Canyon. The trail at once climbs the steep, sandy bank of the wash, then curves into a shallow draw, which we ascend via natural stairsteps in slickrock. After reaching the head of the draw, we follow cairns south over a tancolored band of Cedar Mesa Sandstone.

Traversing narrow ledges and scaling slickrock slopes, we top the drainage divide (0.5; 5520) beneath a striking tower soaring 400 feet above. Lost Canyon is hidden from view by the slickrock maze below. Descending from the divide, we carefully make our way down slickrock slopes, using friction at times, and finally drop into the small wooded canyon below, which we follow east-northeast down-canyon. Passing through thickets of sagebrush, we soon reach the floor of Lost Canyon (0.6; 5180) and follow its wash downstream amid rich riparian vegetation. Soon the trail begins crisscrossing the wash and climbing over brushy benches above it. The trail is sandy, so progress is slow. A seasonal seep

and potholes may be found where the serpentine wash executes the first prominent bend from east to west.

Numerous short branch canyons invite exploration, and potential campsites are numerous and varied. Finally, as the canyon begins to open up, we reach a signed junction (2.1; 5100) and ponder our options. The trail that crosses the wash is the one used by *Trip 29* hikers to reach Peekaboo Arch in lower Salt Creek, 2.8 miles away via the eastbound segment of that trail. The trailhead lies 2.6 miles away via the left, westbound fork. To attain either goal, see the *Trip 29* description below. To reach the campground, reverse the initial 1.6 miles of that trip, ascending the wooded draw to the west, climbing a ladder and scaling slickrock to a broad saddle. Then descend into Squaw Canyon and from the signed junction there, reverse the initial 1.2 miles of our hike to Campground A.

# Trip 29
## Squaw Flat Trailhead to Peekaboo Arch

**Distance**: 9.4 miles round trip
**Low/High elevations**: 5120'/5360'
**Suited for**: Dayhike or backpack
**Difficulty**: Moderate
**Best seasons**: April through mid-June; mid-September through November.
**Maps/Trailhead**: 49,47/23
**Hazards**: No water; little shade; steep dropoffs; two ladders.

**Introduction**: Arches are among the rare and unusual landforms that evoke awe and wonder in anyone who gazes upon them. Even more rare are ancient Indian pictographs, their meanings lost to the passage of time. This fine hike leads to a beautiful arch and a Fremont pictograph panel, but enroute hikers will enjoy panoramic vistas and the exhilaration of ambling over miles of slickrock high above wooded defiles. Beyond the trail's end in Salt Creek canyon, the promise of water and a profusion of intriguing branch canyons beckon hikers to linger.

**Description**: From the trailhead at Squaw Flat Campground A (0.0; 5150) follow *Trip 27* to the signed trail junction (1.2; 5110) in Squaw Canyon. Turning left at the junction, we easily ascend an open hillside, contour into a shallow draw thick with pinyon and juniper, and then climb out of the draw via a short but steep, rocky pitch. The trail ahead winds amid open woodlands as we approach the base of a 500-foot-high slickrock butte. The trail abruptly ends when we reach slickrock, but cairns lead us quickly toward a saddle on the drainage divide ahead. Some exposure and the need to search for footholds on the slickrock can be a bit scary for novice hikers.

Topping out on the saddle (0.8; 5290), we may wish to pause long enough to absorb the breathtaking panorama before us. From the vast array of spires and buttes in the foreground to the distant landmarks of Elaterite and Ekker buttes and Island in the Sky, and the Abajo Mountains in the southeast, our gaze sweeps across much of the vast Canyonlands basin. As we look toward the east into a tangle of slickrock buttes, bluffs, and cliffs, it becomes apparent that the Cedar Mesa Sandstone is more massive and less severely fractured here than it is in the heart of The Needles farther west.

Cairns lead the way down the east side of the saddle, first over red slickrock slopes, then onto a white sandstone ledge, which we follow east to a 6-foot ladder. A traverse of the next lower ledge ensues, but soon we begin to descend steeply via smaller, narrow ledges, carefully using the natural footholds that are so abundant in the cross-bedded sandstone.

Upon reaching the canyon floor, the now-sandy trail winds down-canyon. A few large Fremont cottonwoods ahead herald our approach to Lost Canyon, and soon we reach a signed junction (0.8; 5100) in the canyon's wash. Here we part ways with hikers following *Trip 28* through Lost Canyon and continue straight ahead, immediately crossing the wash and climbing to the opposite bank, then hiking briefly up-canyon. Soon we begin to negotiate a series of low slickrock ledges while ascending a minor draw to the sandstone ridge at the head of

**Ladders in The Needles allow passage over bulging slickrock**

the draw.

Beyond the climb we follow a ledge as it wraps around the head of a small but cliffbound canyon. Cairns lead the way as we then pass through a narrow notch, which frames a fine view of the slickrock shaft of North Six-shooter Peak and a unique "back side" perspective of Woodenshoe Arch. From there we drop below the smooth red beds and reach the white sandstone layer below, after which we pass very near the brink of a pouroff before climbing steeply, requiring the use of friction, over the next in the series of minor ridges.

The cairned route ahead traverses the head of another draw beneath cliffs rising more than 100 feet, and approaches the shoulder of yet another rocky spur ridge. But instead of hiking around it, we pass through it via a small arch. A traverse above a final draw ensues, its floor below heavily choked with sagebrush. Soon we descend along a redrock ridge, from where we can now gaze into the cottonwood-lined course of Salt Creek, the Needles District's principal drainage.

Dropping away from the ridge, we quickly enter a minor draw and follow it down to a pouroff. Here we must descend a tall ladder wedged into a very narrow joint. Bulky frame backpacks must be lowered over the ladder by rope, for there is simply no room to spare. Below the ladder we boulder hop our way down to a cactus-studded bench just above an unusually wet stretch of Salt Creek. The creekside bench takes us around a bend in the cottonwood-clad canyon, and soon we conclude our excursion at the opening of Peekaboo Arch (1.9; 5120), just beyond a fine Fremont pictograph panel.

The arch is an interesting and relatively rare geological phenomenon, but the primary attraction here is the Peekaboo Pictograph Panel. The rock art is painted in white, featuring several silhouette hand prints, two rather large, round, human-like figures, and a row of white splotches, believed to have been blown onto the surface of the rock. Perhaps the artist used a segment of common reed grass, typical throughout moist areas of Salt Creek canyon. An unusual feature in addition to the Fremont-style pictograph is a Barrier Canyon-style shield-like figure, believed to have been the work of a pre-Anasazi and pre-Fremont culture.

The arch is a product of differential weathering and erosion of a narrow, fin-like slickrock ridge isolated by erosion along a pronounced bend in the canyon. There are actually two openings; the larger, lower arch is about 12 feet wide and 10 feet high. It formed at the contact of a hard sandstone layer above and softer shaley beds below. As the softer beds eroded away, the sandstone was left above unsupported, probably creating a small alcove on either side of the fin due to slab failure. Eventually the two alcoves joined, and the arch was born. A prominent vertical joint rises above the larger arch, ending at the smaller, higher opening. That opening formed at the intersection of vertical and horizontal joints, and weathering and erosion along those zones of weakness probably played an important role in its development.

Below the arch just to the north lies Peekaboo Camp, alongside the Salt Creek Jeep Road (see *Trip 22*). Since backpackers are required to camp out of sight of jeep roads in the Park, consider exploring one of the dozens of seldom-visited side canyons that branch off from Salt Creek all along its course.

# Trip 30
## Squaw Flat Campground Loop

**Distance**: 1.2-mile loop trip
**Low/High elevations**: 5120'/5300'
**Suited for**: Walk
**Difficulty**: Moderately easy
**Best seasons**: April through mid-June; mid-September through November.
**Map/Trailhead**: 49/24
**Hazards**: Steep dropoffs.

**Introduction**: Visitors staying in Campground B who would rather get to the Squaw Flat Trailhead in Campground A by walking than driving can use one of these two trails to access the Squaw Flat trail network. Even those hikers who simply desire a leisurely stroll over the slickrock above the campgrounds can use parts of these trails or combine them into an enjoyable loop, as in the following description.

**Description:** To begin this short but exciting loop trip, and to reach *Trips 27* and *31* in Big Spring Canyon, we take the right-branching trail that departs from the roadend near campsite 26 (0.0; 5120). Hikers on *Trips 27* through *29* can take the left fork, reaching Squaw Flat Trailhead A after 0.3 mile.

The right-hand trail proceeds into a shallow draw, then begins a gentle ascent. Soon the vegetation abruptly ends where we mount slickrock and climb its step-like surface through red and white bands of the Cedar Mesa Sandstone. As we level off amid potholes on a bench above, a broad sweep of canyon country opens up.

Presently we ascend the bench on a sometimes gentle, sometimes moderate grade, climbing onto the next higher band of red rock beneath an imposing slickrock butte that forms the prominent backdrop to Campground A. Soon we climb briefly to a narrow notch, topping out next to a spindly pinyon. Beyond, the trail descends first via built-up steps, then through a narrow gully, and finally over steep slickrock, where we must use friction to descend narrow ledges to a signed junction (0.3; 5250).

Those who are not aiming for the longer trails ahead now have the option of turning left, where the sign indicates Campground A, and looping back to the trailhead via the cairned campground connector trail. But to continue into Big Spring Canyon, we now ascend steeply sloping slickrock, above visible Campground A, and with the aid of handrails we soon surmount an undulating slickrock ridge, which we briefly follow south before descending toward Big Spring Canyon via ledges and gullies. That shallow canyon cuts a swath through a scenic jumble of jointed slickrock and mushroom-shaped rocks. Up-canyon, the buttes, spires, and slickrock bluffs of The Needles form a colorful and magnificent backdrop.

Shortly we leave the slickrock and follow a soil-covered ledge generally southward, to where we intersect *Trips 27* and *31* (0.3; 5250). Those who wish to return to the campground can bear left at this junction and soon reach Campground A (0.3; 5150). A sign opposite the Squaw Flat Trailhead A indicates a trail leading to Campground B, and we walk across the road and join that trail, strolling through a narrow band of grassland, then dipping into a sandy draw. Then the trail quickly begins ascending slickrock above the campground, climbing to a notch in the ridge above the group campsite and joining the aforementioned cairned route branching west to the initial segment of our loop. More fine vistas greet us from the notch, including Woodenshoe Arch and North Six-shooter Peak in the middle distance and the mesas of Harts and Hatch points and the La Sal Mountains on the far horizon.

Descending north, we bid farewell to distant panoramas as we soon leave the slickrock ridge and begin winding among large, multibranched pinyons and a few junipers, shortly passing below campsite 26 and quickly reaching the Campground B Trailhead (0.3; 5120).

# Trip 31
## Squaw Flat Trailhead to Elephant and Big Spring Canyons

**Distance**: 9.8 miles semiloop trip
**Low/High elevations**: 5120'/5560'
**Suited for**: Dayhike or backpack
**Difficulty**: Moderate
**Best seasons**: April through mid-June; mid-September through November.
**Map/Trailhead**: 49/23
**Hazards**: No water; much slickrock scrambling; steep dropoffs; little shade; two ladders.

**Introduction**: Spire-rimmed canyons, slickrock divides, and narrow, shady joints in the heart of The Needles are among the many highlights that hikers will enjoy as they travel this scenic route. Possible sidetrips to Druid Arch, Chesler Park, and Squaw and Lost canyons offer ample incentive to extend this trip into a backpack of two or more days.

**Description**: Heading south from the parking area (0.0; 5150), we stroll 50 yards to a signed junction and bear right toward Big Spring Canyon. The trail skirts the edge of a grassy pocket beneath a low sandstone ridge, but quite soon we mount slickrock, then pass through a cave-like gap. Beyond the gap cairns lead us along a wide ledge just above the pinyon-juniper-fringed grassland, but we soon climb over the ridge, descending a short but steep friction pitch just over the top. Shortly thereafter, we meet the signed trail leading north to Campground B (0.3; 5250), but we bear left and descend easily through a shallow draw embraced by slickrock ridges and knobs, and finally descend to a junction (0.4; 5120) next to a lone cottonwood and the small dry wash of Big Spring Canyon. The return leg of our loop follows the trail on the left, but for now we bear right, crossing the wash, and soon thereafter turn west into a draw clad in pinyon and juniper.

Approaching the head of the draw, we mount slickrock while scaling a narrow joint. After topping out on the sandstone ridge above, we double-back south, following ledges just below and east of the ridgeline. The tall spires and sheer cliffs of The Needles lie before us, while behind are sweeping views of canyon-country cliffs and mesas, including the lofty prominences of the La Sal and Abajo mountains.

The route ahead leads solely over slickrock. Soil-filled pockets and ledges host a variety of shrubs and the ubiquitous pinyons and junipers. After nearly 1 mile of high traverse, we cross the ridge via a 5375-foot saddle, then drop northwest into a rockbound tributary of Big Spring Canyon. A prominent tooth-like row of spires thrusts 400 feet skyward at the canyon's head, and some backpackers may wish to head toward them in search of campsites.

After dipping into a draw just above a chute in the wash, we then stroll over a hill and drop into another draw, which we follow southwest up-canyon. Reaching the head of the draw, we curve around the shoulder of a fin emanating from the spires to the south. A tiny arch has formed at the base of the fin, the opening penetrating a soft, friable red layer of the Cedar Mesa Sandstone.

**Pinnacles tower over a branch of Elephant Canyon**

Presently we descend into a wooded draw and shortly reach a junction (2.3; 5360) with the trail from Elephant Hill, where we join hikers following *Trips 32* through *34*. Now follow the *Trip 32* description to the second trail junction in scenic Elephant Canyon (1.4; 5275) and turn left up the side canyon. Skirting clumps of wavyleaf oak, we tread southeast up-canyon toward a colorful, cliffbound butte. The trail follows the wash only briefly, however, and we then climb the slope south of the wash but quite soon drop back to its banks. There may be some water here after substantial rainfall, but the wash is usually dry. A small arch can be seen high on the north wall on the canyon, where a row of 400' spires stab at the Utah sky. These pinnacles are seen in the distance from Campground A, and our route is leading us along their "backside."

As we approach the amphitheater at the canyon's head, we mount slickrock and follow cairns toward the ridge above. Just short of a saddle on that ridge, we must climb a 12' ladder and steps carved into slickrock to attain the redrock crest (1.0; 5560). From here we briefly enjoy a fine view down the spire-rimmed canyon we have traversed, then we plunge over the other side via another ladder. Now our cairned route follows ledges as we descend above the head of another pinnacle-rimmed canyon, briefly enjoying views stretching as far as North Six-shooter Peak. Look for a gray limestone layer just below either ladder. It contains chunks of jasper, the red form of the hard mineral chert, a rock the Anasazi used to fashion sharp tools and projectile points.

Our slightly undulating traverse passes east beneath a towering, desert-varnished wall, and we enjoy fine vistas of the La Sal Mountains foregrounded by the rugged upper reaches of Squaw Canyon. Soon we abandon the bench and climb into the shady confines of a north-trending joint, first ascending a log with steps cut into it, then hopping to the top of a trailside boulder. Proceeding into the narrow crack, we tread over logs wedged into its inches-wide opening below us.

Beyond the joint, we stroll across a beautiful, tree-dotted amphitheater beneath tall cliffs, then head into the northern outlier of the same joint. This rift is too narrow to allow passage, however, so we hop across its narrow gap and follow a ledge around the slickrock promontory, now high above Squaw Canyon. Traversing into the head of a northeast-trending draw, we reach a junction (1.1; 5440) and join *Trip 27*.

Before turning left and following the latter half of the *Trip 27* description 3.6 miles to the trailhead, we may wish to pause to enjoy the expansive view toward the northeast—a wilderness of slickrock, cliffs, mesas, and tall mountain peaks.

# Trip 32
## Elephant Hill to Druid Arch

**Distance**: 10.4 miles round trip
**Low/High elevations**: 5120'/5800'
**Suited for**: Dayhike or backpack
**Difficulty**: Moderate
**Best seasons**: April through mid-June; mid-September through November.
**Map/Trailhead**: 49/25
**Hazards**: Steep dropoffs; slickrock scrambling; seasonal water only in upper Elephant Canyon.

**Introduction**: One of the largest and most intriguing arches in Canyonlands is at the head of Elephant Canyon, in the heart of The Needles. This is an unforgettable hike, traversing slickrock, passing through narrow joints between slickrock spires and fins, and ascending a deep, sandy wash where colorful slickrock pinnacles and domes soar hundreds of feet skyward. Like most trails in The Needles trail network, this route can be combined with a variety of other scenic trails to extend your stay for several days.

**Description**: The signed trail wastes no time climbing south from the trailhead (0.0; 5120), as we ascend through a narrow joint, then climb slabby slickrock, leveling off on the bench above. Here we stroll over sandstone and pass pockets of vegetation including pinyon, juniper, cliffrose, mormon tea, blackbrush, Utah serviceberry, littleleaf mountain mahogany, and wavyleaf oak. Tall, banded slickrock buttes tower above us in the west, but our view from northeast to south encompass a dramatic panorama of the vast Indian Creek basin and the soaring sandstone spires of The Needles.

Our trail leads us ever-closer to the ranks of tall spires, and after a mile or so we reach a row of jointed fins and proceed through one of the wider joints, then descend gently through a blackbrush-clad opening. The trail ahead rises gently to a signed junction (1.5; 5360), where we are joined by *Trip 31* hikers on their loop from the campground.

Turning right (west), we mount slickrock, descend through a short joint, and then stroll through a small basin studded with blackbrush and scattered pinyons and junipers, with a backdrop of tall spires. Beyond the basin we descend through a longer and much narrower joint. Steep and rocky switchbacks ensue, leading us to the sandy wash of Elephant Canyon and another signed junction (0.6; 5200). Ample opportunity for camping can be found down-canyon, but the Elephant Hill Jeep Trail crosses the canyon 2 miles to the north, and backpackers must remember to locate campsites out of sight of jeep trails.

Hikers bound for *Trips 33* and *34* will continue straight ahead, climbing the sandy wash bank, but we turn left (south) and begin hiking up the sandy, rocky wash. The trail ahead alternates between the wash and its banks. Bulging walls of slickrock project into the canyon, above which rise tall, red- and white-banded fingers of stone.

Soon we notice a prominent canyon branching off toward the southeast, and upon reaching it find another trail junction (0.8; 5272), where we will bid farewell to *Trip 31* hikers and bear right, continuing up Elephant Canyon. The ensuing stretch is much the same as the last, following either the rocky wash or its wooded banks upstream.

As we approach a minor southwest-trending canyon, we reach yet another junction (0.5; 5300), where we may briefly encounter *Trip 33* hikers coming down from Chesler Park enroute back to their trailhead. Our route ahead follows the wash south, mostly over slickrock, as we proceed farther into the increasingly narrow canyon.

We may soon begin to encounter potholes containing a seasonal supply of water. After 1 1/4 miles, where we reach a sign indicating Druid Arch, we leave the confines of the wash. Just upstream is a deep pothole that might hold water, but in dry years it could be empty. We now begin scrambling over slickrock while ascending a minor gully, shortly reaching a narrow ledge about 100 feet above the gorge. Our route follows the ledge up-canyon, but ends where we encounter a short steel ladder and a handrail that allow safe passage over the bulging slickrock. Above that obstacle we climb a steep gully, finally leveling off very near the head of Elephant Canyon.

The cairned route apparently ends here (1.8; 5800) beneath towering Druid Arch, but some hikers proceed a bit farther for a close-up view, although the route ahead is hazardous. The arch bears a resemblance to a huge, long-legged pachyderm, but its name was probably derived from its likeness to stone monuments at Britain's Stonehenge. ("Druid" refers to a religious order endemic to Britain.)

The arch is formed in a narrow fin projecting into the amphitheater at the canyon's head. Its two openings are tall, narrow, nearly vertical slits, probably formed along vertical joints, many of which lace the rocks of the fin, splitting the rock into a number of large slabs. A thin, red, shaley bed lies beneath the openings, but this stratum does not appear to have played a role in the development of the spans. The fin is composed of a hard, buff-toned sandstone layer of the Cedar Mesa, and has a dark-brown patina of desert varnish. Both openings are also coated with desert varnish, and this coat of minerals takes a long time to develop. The top of the larger span, formed above a horizontal joint in the fin, is angular and does not bear a coat of varnish, indicating the relatively recent enlargement of the arch.

The headwaters amphitheater of Elephant Canyon is pure slickrock, where tall cliffs—some sheer, others bulging—rise to a skyline of domes, towers, and pinnacles, some soaring a full 600 feet above the canyon floor. Gazing down-canyon, our view stretches beyond ranks of tall spires to the distant mesa of Island in the Sky and the prominent monolith of Candlestick Tower.

# Trip 33
## Elephant Hill to Chesler Park

**Distance**: 10.5 miles semiloop trip

**Low/High elevations**: 5120'/5640'

**Suited for**: Dayhike or backpack

**Difficulty**: Moderate

**Best seasons**: April through mid-June; mid-September through November.

**Maps/Trailhead**: 49,50/25

**Hazards**: No water; slickrock scrambling; claustrophobic hikers may wish to avoid the Joint Trail.

**Introduction**: The spire-rimmed, nearly circular grasslands of Chesler Park encompass more than 600 acres of gentle, open terrain that is a delightful change in a region dominated by seemingly endless expanses of slickrock and deep, yawning canyons.

This trip makes a grand circuit of Chesler Park, touching the east edge of The Grabens—an area of narrow, shallow, grassy valleys—and returning to the park via the Joint Trail, a route through an exceedingly narrow defile that is perhaps the most exciting trail in Canyonlands.

Chesler Park is the most popular destination in the district, and backpackers are restricted to three designated camping zones located in the east half of the park.

**Description**: From the Elephant Hill Trailhead (0.0; 5120) we follow the first 2.1 miles of *Trip 32* to the first trail junction in Elephant Canyon. Following the sign pointing to Chesler Park, we climb the sandy bank of Elephant

**Spires guarding the entrance to Chesler Park**

Canyon's wash, then dip into a minor wash and ascend its opposite bank.

Our route ahead climbs broken ledges while heading into a shallow draw. Soon the trail zigzags upward over ledges and among boulders, emerging onto a bench backdropped by towering spires. Chesler Park lies beyond the spires in the southwest, but to get there our trail must first find a passable route between them. We skirt their base as we stroll easily across the bench, enjoying fine views of a profusion of slender stone fingers thrusting skyward.

Reaching a signed junction (0.7; 5540), we turn left and ascend a boulder-filled gully formed in a joint between two soaring spires. The 100' climb is short but steep, but from the top our gaze stretches north over miles of slickrock.

Once over the 5640' top, the trail descends gradually among low sand hills, and soon the broad, grassy expanse of Chesler Park spreads out before us.

It has become necessary to regulate camping in Chesler Park to reduce impacts on its fragile ecosystem. Backpackers must camp in designated camping zones, and spur trails leading to the three zones open to camping are indicated by

wooden posts with a triangle symbol. We soon encounter the first spur trail, and it leads into the sandstone-rimmed pocket to the west. Backpackers are allowed to camp wherever they wish within the camping zones, but are advised to choose a durable site out of view of the trail, preferably on shallow soil near the foot of sandstone outcrops.

Upon reaching a junction (0.2; 5550), we ponder our options. The trail that turns left (southeast) offers access to the other two camping zones in Chesler Park. This trail climbs a sandy rise, then skirts the east edge of the park, joining our trail 1.3 miles to the south. About midway along that trail, a spur to a camping zone beneath the rocks at the park's edge forks left. Just beyond is a fine viewpoint on the rim high above slickrock-bound Elephant Canyon. From there the trail turns southwest and descends gradually to a junction just east of the nest of spires that rises like an island in the middle of Chesler Park. Another camping zone lies along the west foot of those spires. Hikers following this trail along the east edge of Chesler Park can shorten *Trip 33* by 3 miles, taking another trail into Elephant Canyon and then returning to the trailhead.

But to circumnavigate this sea of grass and reach more remote potential campsites, bear right at the junction, following the trail used on the return leg of *Trip 34*. Initially this trail is wedged between the grassy park and a row of tall spires soaring 400 feet above in the north, but later we proceed into rocky terrain and leave the grassland behind. Enroute we enjoy fine views across the spread, views that reach out to wooded mesas in The Grabens area of the Needles District and to the Orange Cliffs and Henry Mountains on the far horizon.

The trail ahead winds into and out of several draws, passes over blackbrush-clad slopes, and before long reaches a short, narrow joint. Beyond the joint our route undulates over slickrock and soon reaches another signed junction (0.9; 5450). We part company here with *Trip 34* hikers and bear left (south-southwest) toward the jeep road in the graben valley below. That valley is flanked by ranks of pinnacles, and above it to the west is the grassy, brushy expanse of Butler Flat. Beyond are more spires and the broad slopes and high, wooded mesas in the far southwest reaches of the Needles District.

The trail descends into a rocky draw, then levels off in an open flat. Soon we intercept a jeep road (0.6; 5260) along the banks of Chesler Canyon's wash. Southbound, our sandy road quite soon crosses the wash, climbs a hill, and becomes rough and rocky as it descends to a junction (0.2; 5280).

Presently we turn left where a sign indicates CHESLER PARK TRAILHEAD, skirting grass- and brush-clad hills and sandstone knolls while following Chesler Canyon southeast upstream. Here cheatgrass dominates among remnant bunches of native grasses, the result of decades of grazing by the Indian Creek Cattle Company.

Reaching the roadend (0.5; 5350), we encounter pit toilets, a picnic table, and the beginning of the Joint Trail, one of the most exciting routes in the Needles District. The trail at once climbs a hill east of the roadend, drops into and crosses a sandy wash, and then climbs steadily toward the jumble of slickrock that lies ahead. Soon we enter a cavernous tunnel eroded into an east-trending joint. Beyond this rockbound hallway we turn abruptly north, following an increasingly narrow joint that is barely 2 feet wide in places. Some hikers may feel claustrophobic within the confines of the joint, and with a backpack it is a tight squeeze at best.

But eventually we exit the joint and climb a rock stairway to a signed junction (0.6; 5550). For a grand view of Chesler Park, take the right fork along a brushy draw, then scale slickrock with the aid of steps cut into the smooth rock, to a commanding viewpoint atop a slickrock knoll at 5600 feet. From north to east, the pinnacle-rimmed grasslands of Chesler Park spread out before you. Westward are such landmarks as the Orange Cliffs, the splintered crown of Elaterite Butte, and the slickrock wilderness of The Maze. The Doll House is the prominent cluster of pinnacles rising above the southeast corner of The Maze.

Returning from that 0.1-mile diversion, we follow the eastbound trail as it skirts the south margin of Chesler Park. This trail rises gradually, winding along the foot of the soaring pinnacles to the south. Soon the trail curves northeast toward the cluster of spires that punctuate the spreading grassland, and then reaches a spur trail leading to the camping zone along the pinnacles' west margin. There is a historic cowboy line camp midway along the foot of this slickrock island, including some old inscriptions on the rock behind it. Rangers ask that backpackers not camp in this historic site or disturb it in any way.

Strolling past the spur trail, we soon reach a junction (0.8; 5620) with the aforementioned trail along the east edge of Chesler Park and bear right toward Elephant Canyon. Our route proceeds northeast, passes through a fin-rimmed gap, and levels off on a flat below. Presently, the trail dips into the head of a draw, which we briefly follow southward downhill, but soon we leave it to wind northeast along a narrow slickrock ledge while searching for a way into Elephant Canyon below. The traverse ends amid potholed slickrock, and we now descend into another draw, sometimes using friction to descend on steep sandstone. But soon it becomes too steep, and we then traverse first east, then south, descending via discontinuous ledges and finally reaching the trail in Elephant Canyon (1.1; 5300) after 30 minutes or so of rugged hiking.

To complete the circuit, follow the first 3.4 miles of *Trip 32* in reverse, and you should be back at the trailhead within two hours.

# Trip 34
## Elephant Hill to Devils Pocket

**Distance**: 10.9 miles, semiloop trip
**Low/High elevations**: 5120'/5800'
**Suited for**: Dayhike or backpack
**Difficulty**: Moderate
**Best seasons**: April through mid-June; mid-September through November.
**Maps/Trailhead**: 49,50/25
**Hazards**: No water; slickrock scrambling; little shade.

**Introduction**: Following a fine loop trail around the most striking pinnacles in all of The Needles, traversing the graben valley of Devils Pocket, and skirting and edge of magnificent Chesler Park, this trip is perhaps the most scenic trek in the Needles District. It is also one of the least used district trails, making it a fine choice for those who prefer relative solitude amid awe-inspiring scenery.

**Description**: Beginning this memorable journey at the Elephant Hill Trailhead (0.0; 5120), follow the description of *Trip 32* for 2.1 miles to the trail junction on the sandy banks of Elephant Canyon. Now climb the opposite bank, following *Trip 33* for 0.7 mile to the next junction, in the shadow of towering spires.

Our trail forks right at this junction and winds northwest through the headwaters basin of a minor canyon. Pinyon and juniper grow twisted and stunted in the basin but are abundant. Comb-like ridges of spires surround us on three sides, while an opening toward the northeast allows views of the cliff-edged mesa of Harts Point and the lofty peaks of the La Sal Mountains.

The trail ahead, crossing much slickrock where cairns show the way, undulates as it traverses numerous headwaters basins of Elephant Canyon tributaries beneath tooth-like pinnacles. Views are panoramic and ever-changing as we proceed. At one point we pass through a tunnel-like joint where backpackers are forced to either crawl or drag their bulky packs behind them.

After 1 1/2 miles, when we finally reach the northern-most point of our trek, we turn west through a joint beneath a solitary spire, then enjoy views west across a landscape of slickrock knolls and balanced rocks to the distant Orange Cliffs, Ekker Butte, and Buttes of the Holy Cross, and northwest to Candlestick Tower, Junction Butte, and Grand View Point. After traversing the basin ahead, we leave it and enter a south-trending joint, emerging into yet another basin. Descending a slickrock chute via a natural stairway, we soon turn west and proceed along the banks of a minor, wooded wash, shortly reaching the end of a jeep road (2.7; 5320) at Devils Kitchen Camp.

The trail heads south-southwest from the signed trailhead at the roadend, and is initially quite sandy as it crosses two minor washes. But soon we reach the open, overgrazed graben valley of Devils Pocket. Cheatgrass dominates the pocket's grasslands, and there is also some Russian thistle, or tumbleweed, as well. These two exotic plants are common throughout overgrazed or otherwise disturbed grasslands on the Colorado Plateau. There are remnants of the native bunchgrass, however, as well as shrubs such as winterfat and four-wing saltbush. Yellow beeplant is a particularly obvious wildflower that blooms during spring and often persists into summer.

Some of the most striking, slender fingers of stone in all of the Needles District soar heavenward 500 feet above the head of the valley, and the valley becomes wider as we proceed. Two prominent gaps notch the comb-like ridge ahead of us, and the eastern notch allows passage over the ridge. But to get there, we first exit the grassland and follow a sandy, joint-controlled gully south between low sandstone walls.

Beyond the gully an easy grade through a grassy pocket ensues, but we soon mount slickrock and climb steeply up a debris-choked, joint-controlled gully. Enroute we may pause to enjoy spire-framed views of the distant Island in the Sky. Steep switchbacks then lead up the final pitch to the 5800' notch. Lying before us in the foreground are more jumbled pinnacles and slickrock, but in the distance the terrain changes to slopes and broad mesas thick with pinyon-juniper woodland, where only a few stone fingers can be seen.

Once over the top, we descend into a chute, but soon climb out of it via a steep joint. From there we traverse around a bend and reach a junction (1.5; 5450) with a trail to the jeep road and Chesler Canyon to the right, and the eastbound trail to Chesler Park to the left. To return to the Elephant Hill Trailhead, we simply follow the first 3.9 miles of *Trip 33* in reverse.

# Trip 35
## Elephant Hill to Lower Red Lake Canyon and the Colorado River

**Distance**: 18.6 miles round trip
**Low/High elevations**: 3900'/5320'
**Suited for**: Backpack; or jeep trip and back pack; or jeep trip and dayhike.
**Difficulty**: Strenuous
**Best seasons**: April through mid-June; mid-September through November.
**Maps/Trailheads**: 49,50,51/25
**Hazards**: No water (avoid drinking river water); little shade; very hot in Lower Red Lake Canyon during summer; high-clearance 4WD required if driving.

**Introduction**: This route combines a hike along the Elephant Hill Jeep Trail with an infrequently used foot trail that offers the only access to the Colorado River in the Needles District. Scenery enroute is diverse, ranging from slickrock highlands to the narrow, grassy valleys of The Grabens, to a starkly beautiful desert canyon, and finally to the sandy shores of the Colorado River. Carry plenty of water, and do not drink river water except as a last resort, and then only after purification.

**Description**: From the Elephant Hill parking area (0.0; 5120) we begin the short but steep grind over Elephant Hill via the jeep road. This road is quite narrow and extremely rough. Sections of pavement in the rockiest areas allow easier passage for 4WD vehicles and also minimize undercarriage damage. The second switchback is such a tight turn that vehicles must proceed out onto a slickrock platform and very carefully turn around in order to proceed up step-like slickrock to the top of the hill.

Topping out among slickrock knolls, we presently enjoy far-away views stretching west to the Orange Cliffs. Now the route descends over bumpy slickrock to a series of steep, very rough switchbacks leading into Elephant Canyon. The second of the three switchbacks here is so tight that vehicles must back down in order to continue. Below this descent we follow a sandy draw down-canyon to the dry wash of Elephant

Canyon, which we also follow downstream toward the north, crossing it three times.

We soon reach a junction (1.5; 5000) with a one-way loop road and bear left, soon crossing a minor wash, then ascending a very rugged but short grade. Descending the opposite side, we reach the north limits of the Devils Pocket graben, a shallow canyon rimmed by desert-varnished sandstone walls, featuring the typical, square-bottomed U-shape of a sunken graben valley. Midway up the sandy pocket, the road climbs part way up the west wall and once again becomes very rough and rocky. Soon we enter a narrow cleft barely wide enough for the narrowest vehicles, then descend the south-trending wash draining the graben to a junction (2.0; 5320).

Splintered fingers of stone reach skyward at the head of Devils Pocket to the south, and the left-branching spur road leads 0.1 mile east to Devils Kitchen Camp and the Devils Pocket Loop Trail (see *Trip 34*). The camp offers several scenic campsites for four-wheel drivers, situated in the rocky coves just north of the road, with two pit toilets.

We bear right at the junction and undulate up and down, mostly down, on the rough road along a shallow draw. Emerging into the long, narrow graben of Devils Lane, we reach a junction (0.6; 5180) with a two-way jeep road. The northbound road branches farther north, one fork leading back to Elephant Hill and the other curving around into Cyclone Canyon and branching toward Confluence Overlook. The southbound road follows the long valley of Devils Lane into Chesler Canyon, passing a spur road to the Joint Trailhead (see *Trip 33*) and continuing on past Bobby Jo and Horsehoof Arch campsites toward the Park boundary and Beef Basin, 8 miles south.

But we turn right (north) in Devils Lane, quite soon reaching a FOOT TRAIL sign. Turning left (west) onto this faint trail, we proceed on the level across Devils Lane to a small grove of netleaf hackberry trees growing at the foot of the valley's west wall. From there a quick climb leads us onto a narrow slickrock shelf, which we follow generally south to a broad gap, then drop into the head of a shallow canyon to the west. Views extend west as far as The Fins in the Maze District, across the Colorado River, but from our vantage point there isn't the slightest intimation of the river's 1000-foot-deep gorge.

Proceeding into the juniper-clad draw below, we soon reach a steep point in the wash where boulders block the way. The trail skirts this obstacle while descending ledges at first, then dropping steeply via rocky slopes to the mouth of the canyon. We then stroll west across the grassy valley of the 3-mile-long Cyclone Canyon graben and intersect the jeep road (1.0; 4850), *Trip 36*. There is only one break in the broken cliffs bounding the west side of Cyclone Canyon, a canyon that is a continuation of the one we previously descended. Crossing the jeep road, we reach a spur that quickly leads to the head of that canyon and a trail sign indicating LOWER RED LAKE COLORADO RIVER 4.

This trail begins by following an old, closed jeep road into the dry wash below. We follow the wash downstream, but soon its course steepens and becomes choked with boulders, forcing us onto slopes to the north. Now the trail, traversing exposures of the Elephant Canyon Formation, becomes rather steep and rocky.

After 1/2 mile we emerge from the canyon onto the broad expanse of Red Lake Canyon, the widest graben encountered thus far. Unlike the grabens passed previously, this one contains a broad, sandy wash, but water was not the sculptor here; the subsurface flow of salt deposits created voids that led to the collapse of blocks of the earth's crust, forming the grabens of Canyonlands.

We can now see how past overgrazing has severely impacted the grasslands of Red Lake Canyon. What were once thick native grasses have now been reduced mostly to a sparse covering of cheatgrass and tumbleweed, although some native grasses persist. Soon, after skirting the east margin of the expansive valley, our trail curves northwest, crossing the wide, sandy wash. As in Cyclone Canyon, the broken cliffs that abut this valley are collapsing inward toward the void created by the subsidence of the graben. Boulders litter the slopes below the 400-foot-high cliffs, and we can see huge slabs tilting toward the valley, seemingly ready to fall to the ground at any moment.

Our trail angles northwest across the valley, but instead of following the wash toward the portal of the lower canyon as one might expect, we begin a very steep 200' ascent up the valley's west wall, climbing above the softer rocks of the Elephant Canyon Formation and back into the domain of Cedar Mesa Sandstone. This grind levels off in a small hanging valley amid a jumble of boulders fallen from the cliffs above.

After we cross the sandy wash in the draw and begin climbing the final few feet to the low ridge above, we can see an arch on the fin above and west of the ridge. This arch has formed at the contact zone between the massive Cedar Mesa Sandstone and the thinly layered and comparatively softer Elephant Canyon Formation. Another arch, with an angular outline attesting to its youth, formed in the lowest layers of the Cedar Mesa, stands below the rim of the draw toward the southwest.

Once atop the ridge (1.2; 4800) we gaze into the yawning declivity of Lower Red Lake Canyon, its wide sand- and rock-strewn wash embraced by broken cliffs of Elephant Canyon Formation rocks. Descending northwest from the ridge, we drop steeply at first, briefly level off, and then descend once again amid a jumble of sandstone boulders.

The trail then proceeds to contour through sparse shrubs on a ledge composed of the Elephant Canyon Formation. This formation makes layered red cliffs and reddish and gray ledges, such as the one our trail follows, while other layers form slopes. Soon we'll see why our trail has thus far avoided the canyon: there are two impassable pouroffs on resistant gray ledges of Elephant Canyon rocks in the canyon below. It is possible, however, to follow game trails from the valley and into the canyon. These trails contour above the pouroffs and then descend into the canyon's wash below.

Our trail, presently traversing a gray dolomite ledge among sandstone boulders fallen from the cliffs above, passes only a scattering of sparse desert growth. Soon we begin to rise gently as we curve around a north-trending promontory, from which we can gaze across the declivity of Lower Red Lake Canyon into the boulder-choked portal of Lens Canyon. This is yet another graben valley, and the strata exposed in the cliffs that flank its void are prominently offset in relation to other horizontal beds due to collapse of a block of the earth's crust.

As we curve southwest, the broken and starkly barren gray walls of the yawning canyon below frame a cluster of Cedar Mesa Sandstone spires on the western skyline. This is the Doll House in the Park's Maze District. Presently we see our trail far below on the canyon floor, but to get there we must descend a series of steep switchbacks, taking great care on the poor footing offered by the rocky trail. At the bottom of the knee-jarring descent, we contour momentarily above the dry wash, but soon we are forced into its sandy, rocky course. But as we continue down-canyon, the trail noticeably avoids the wash, crossing it infrequently from one bank to the other. Legend has it that Butch Cassidy's Wild Bunch and other denizens of the Robber's Roost country to the west used this route to transport stolen horses and cattle. Numerous game trails, seen most clearly from above, show that this is an important route for mule deer and bighorn sheep traveling to and from the river. The trail becomes increasingly sandy as we continue descending on an imperceptible grade. Light gray slopes of the Honaker Trail Formation compose the lower 400 feet of the canyon walls, but the low cliffs and ledges there are largely obscured by debris fallen from above.

The canyon's lower reaches are broad, wide benches sparsely clad in desert growth flanking either side of the wash. As we approach the mouth of the canyon, we leave the benches behind and are presently flanked by the warped, off-white-to-gray strata of an intrusive plug of gypsum, a part of the ancient Paradox Formation, the oldest rocks exposed in Canyonlands. The dome of the plug has been removed by erosion, and as the wash describes a bend from north to south, we travel through the center of the plug. Beyond the bend, the wash curves west below a high bench studded with charred cottonwoods. At this point, particularly during the morning or evening hours, we can feel the moist coolness of the river and begin to smell its rank, alkaline waters.

We now have two choices of routes to reach the river: we can either follow a sandy trail up to the bench and on to the river, or continue down the wash. Finally, we reach the sandy banks of the broad Colorado River (3.0; 3900), clad in thickets of exotic tamarisk. The river has an ocean-like smell typical of alkaline waterways in the Utah desert.

On the opposite bank is a broad bench called Spanish Bottom, its shores thick with tamarisk, willow, and cottonwood. Unfortunately, much of the vegetation there was charred in 1988 by a fire—not a lightning fire, but a toilet-paper fire. The Park Service is attempting to re-establish native vegetation there, but of all the trees, the tamarisk fared far better than native species and likely will vigorously re-vegetate the area. The fire jumped the river and consumed many of the cottonwoods on our side as well. Now, Park regulations require all backcountry campers to pack out their toilet paper rather than burn it.

A starkly barren and broken cliff soars skyward to a row of Cedar Mesa Sandstone domes behind Spanish Bottom, in the Maze District. We can see the steep trail descending that wall from Surprise Valley and The Doll House Trailhead, the most remote trailhead in all of Utah's national parks.

Here we may feel as if we were in the depths of the earth, on top of a mountain range turned upside down: the only direction from the interior of the canyon is up. There are fair campsites in the trees on the riverbank, and on the sandy beach near water's edge. But the river could rise abruptly and with no warning due to heavy rains anywhere along the course of the Green or the Colorado upstream. The amount of sand beach is largely dependent upon the volume of the river. During autumn, there is typically a beautiful sandy beach stretching south on our side of the river. Hikers can follow the beach and the riverbank south to the first bend, from which one can hear the muffled roar of the first rapid in Cataract Canyon. It is possible to continue down to those rapids, where the river is funneled between large boulders.

# Trip 36
## Elephant Hill Jeep Road Tour

**Distance**: 9.4-mile semiloop; with two sidetrip options adding 28.5-plus miles round trip.

**Low/High elevations**: 4820'/5750' at southern Park boundary.

**Suited for**: Jeep trip or mountain-bike trip

**Difficulty**: Moderate mountain bike tour and 4WD route, with two difficult stretches over Elephant Hill and Silver Stairs.

**Best seasons**: April through mid-June; mid-September through November.

**Maps/Trailhead**: 49,50,51,48/25

**Hazards**: No water; little shade; very rugged slickrock and sand along parts of the route.

**Introduction**: This fine trip follows jeep roads into The Grabens section of the Needles District, and offers access to three backcountry trails and numerous cross-country routes. The trip can be hiked or can be driven by *experienced* four-wheel drivers in a high-clearance vehicle. But perhaps the best way to travel the route is on a mountain bike, and due to the deep sand encountered along other jeep roads in the Needles District, this trip is one of the mountain biker's finest choices for a backcountry ride. However, parts of the route are also quite sandy and extremely rocky, and bike riders will have to walk part of the time. There is no water enroute.

A variety of sidetrip options, including spur roads to the Joint Trailhead and the southern Park boundary and Beef Basin, and to Confluence Overlook and Cyclone Canyon, combined with layovers in three vehicle campsites, can keep trippers busy for a number of days.

**Description**: Beginning at the Elephant Hill Trailhead (0.0; 5120), follow the jeep road for the first 4.1 miles of the *Trip 35* description into Devils Lane, where the road forks. The left (south) fork offers access to the Joint Trail and, farther on, Bobby Jo and Horsehoof Arch campsites. This road is sandy as it heads southwest along the floor of the Devils Lane graben. Broken cliffs embrace this long, narrow grassland,

but rising above it on the east side is a splintered row of towering pinnacles and balanced rocks.

Approaching what appears to be the head of the valley, we negotiate a very rough slickrock hill between slickrock spires, gradually descend along the south extremity of Devils Lane, and bend southeast upon reaching the dry wash draining Chesler Canyon. We follow this wash up-canyon, crisscrossing its sandy course amid low slickrock knolls, then reach the terminus of a foot trail (2.75; 5260) on our left (north), where the wash abruptly bends south. Following the description of *Trip 33*, we continue along the jeepway, climbing a minor hill and descending to a junction (0.2; 5280) with a spur road to the Joint Trailhead. To reach that trailhead, continue to follow *Trip 33* along Chesler Canyon for 1/2 mile to its terminus at 5350 feet.

The jeepway beyond the junction climbs into another, much narrower graben, rimmed by low sandstone walls and spires. Before long the route is squeezed between clusters of pinnacles rising nearly 200 feet above, and after 1 mile it passes Bobby Jo Camp, nestled against the slickrock on the west side of the road. Shortly thereafter the 1/4-mile spur road to Horsehoof Arch Camp forks right (northwest). Beyond, the route descends in 1/2 mile to a crossing of Butler Wash, then for 2 3/4 miles it ascends a long graben valley to the Park boundary, 4.5 miles from the Chesler Canyon junction. The region between Butler Wash and the Park boundary is much more open and more heavily wooded than The Needles. In this area a variety of fine off-trail hiking routes beckons the adventurous to explore the hidden graben valleys to the west and intriguing Butler Wash to the southeast.

Beyond the Park boundary the jeep road enters Bureau of Land Management lands, and after 1.75 miles one encounters a very steep and exceedingly rough ascent into Bobbys Hole. This pitch is best taken downhill (in the opposite direction) by drivers entering Canyonlands National Park from the south. A fine loop can be made by following first the road up Cottonwood Canyon (see driving directions for Trip 16) to Cathedral Butte and into Beef Basin, then following the jeep road into Bobbys Hole and into the Park, ultimately ending at Elephant Hill.

Turning right in Devils Lane, we immediately pass the trail leading into Cyclone Canyon and part company with *Trip 35* hikers, following the sandy jeep tracks northeast. Before long the route leads onto a rocky bench, and we presently leave the grassy confines of Devils Lane. Views from this bench are outstanding, stretching west beyond the invisible gorge of the Colorado toward distant landmarks near the Maze District such as The Fins, Orange Cliffs, Gunsight Butte, Sunset Pass, and Bagpipe, Elaterite, and Ekker buttes.

Upon the bench is a short, right-branching spur offering a splendid panorama of The Needles and the Indian Creek basin, and soon thereafter we attain the summit of the bench and the Silver Stairs, a rugged slickrock descent even more difficult than Elephant Hill. Mountainbike riders will likely be forced to walk over this slickrock stairway from the summit gap to the sandy flats below.

Quite soon we reach a one-way road branching right (1.6; 5180) and leading back to Elephant Hill. Here we have the choice of either returning via that road or continuing on toward Confluence Overlook and Cyclone Canyon.

From the junction just north of the Silver Stairs, those who choose to go on will leave the *Trip 36* loop and follow the left fork generally north, descending gradually into another shallow graben valley. Vistas enroute encompass a grand panorama of the Canyonlands basin, but they begin to fade as we continue to descend into the wash.

Shortly, *Trip 26* hikers may be seen following the trail across our jeepway (1.2; 5000) while enroute to Confluence Overlook. While hikers can follow the most direct route into Cyclone Canyon, the road takes a circuitous route around a slickrock highland, soon following the course of the wash beneath low canyon walls, first north, then northwest, around the north terminus of the highland. The jeepway then turns southwest, ascends easily to a narrow gap, and immediately thereafter reaches a junction (1.4; 4900) with the Confluence Overlook spur road. For a superb overlook of the joining of the Green and Colorado rivers, follow the last 1.1 miles of the *Trip 26* description along the road and trail to the viewpoint.

Cyclone Canyon is the deepest, longest, and perhaps the most beautiful graben valley traversed by jeep road in the Needles District. A trip down this cliffbound lane is not only a scenic delight; it also offers access to a trail leading to the Colorado River and to cross-country routes into the Red Lake Canyon, Aztec Canyon, and Upper Red Lake grabens.

Proceeding generally southwest into Cyclone Canyon, the jeep tracks, somewhat sandy, cut a swath through grasslands once dominated by tall, native bunchgrasses. After decades of grazing, however, this valley and most others in the Needles District are infested with exotic cheatgrass and Russian thistle (tumbleweed).

This valley is not arrow-straight as it may at first appear; rather it curves gradually toward the southwest. After 0.1 mile, we pass the southwest-bound trail used by *Trip 26* hikers on our right (east). Our route follows an often-imperceptible downhill grade, but we descend more noticeably at times, where the valley drops in a series of gently sloping steps. Unjointed cliffs flank the narrow cleft of the flat-bottomed valley, composed of the tan-colored basal strata of the Cedar Mesa Sandstone. Dark streaks and patches of desert varnish hang like curtains on the soaring walls, hiding the rock's true colors.

The formation of Cyclone Canyon and other grabens in the area is not the result of erosion; rather, they are blocks of the earth's crust downdropped between shallow faults. The void created by the subsidence of a graben has caused the cliffs bounding it to collapse inward, and in places we will see giant slabs and boulders leaning into the void, seemingly ready to fall at any moment.

Finally, we reach the only break in the valley walls (2.6; 4850), a break traversed by the trail described in *Trip 35*. The right fork of the trail, initially a jeep road, leads about 4 miles to the sandy banks of the Colorado.

The jeepway ahead descends to the lower southwest end of the valley, then climbs out of it over broken terrain onto a minor bench. From there, a steep descent of 200 feet via a southwest-trending draw leads to the roadend (1.1; 4820) near the banks of Chesler Canyon wash. From here it is but a 1/4-mile stroll northwest down into the broad valley of Red Lake Canyon. Other routes into the numerous graben valleys nearby soon become apparent. Aztec Canyon, Upper Red Lake, and the wild and remote Twin Canyons lure exploration by the experienced, adventurous backpacker.

To return to Elephant Hill, we must backtrack for 6.3 miles to the junction of the one-way road beneath the Silver Stairs. Quite soon the eastbound jeepway drops steeply into a minor canyon, then quickly levels off while following its wash eastward. This is a beautiful canyon, flanked by slickrock bluffs.

Upon reaching the mouth of this canyon after 1.1 miles, we intercept the broad, sandy wash of Elephant Canyon. Bicyclists will be disappointed, for they must walk their bikes through deep sand along the wash to conclude the loop along the banks of Elephant Canyon (2.2; 5000). They can then mount up here, and ride much of the 1.5 miles back to the Elephant Hill Trailhead.

# Trips 37-38: Maze District

# Trip 37
## Horseshoe Canyon

**Distance**: 7.5 miles round trip
**Low/High elevations**: 4700'/5300'
**Suited for**: Dayhike
**Difficulty**: Moderate
**Best seasons**: April through mid-June; mid-September through November.
**Map/Trailhead**: 52/26
**Hazards**: Flash-flood danger; limited water.

**Introduction**: The Horseshoe Canyon Detached Unit of Canyonlands National Park drains Barrier Creek, an intermittent stream tributary to the Green River. The canyon cuts a 400-foot-deep gash into the vast, gentle plateau that slopes west from the rim of the Orange Cliffs into the sandy expanse of the San Rafael Desert. As with most canyons on the Colorado Plateau, you won't know it's there until you reach the rim

of the narrow declivity, where suddenly a gaping wound in the earth's crust unfolds before you.

Great bulging walls of off-white-colored Navajo Sandstone embrace a canyon of incomparable beauty, where the leaves of cottonwoods flutter in the slightest breeze, where lizards and squirrels hurry between sheltering rocks and shrubs, where mule deer browse in the morning and evening, and where a small stream flows now over sand, now over slickrock, only to be lost in the thirsty sands of the wash below. This is Horseshoe Canyon, former stomping ground of ranchers, outlaws, prospectors, and ancient Indians.

Excavation of archaeological sites in the canyon indicates that peoples of the Anasazi and Fremont cultures used this area, and artifacts predating those cultures suggest that people of an earlier culture, called the Archaic, were in the canyon as well. Four mysterious rock-art panels depicting ghost-like figures, many of them life-size, are the major attraction in Horseshoe Canyon, and they represent a unique style of rock art. This canyon has the greatest concentration of this style of rock art, which has been called Barrier Canyon style after the former name of Horseshoe Canyon.

It is not only our legal but also our moral responsibility to preserve these enduring pictographs. Do not deface these exquisite sites in any way, and be sure not to touch them, as skin oils can deteriorate pigments on the rock surface.

Camping is allowed only at the two vehicle campsites in the lower canyon and north of the vehicle barricade at the mouth of Water Canyon. Backpackers who wish to camp here must hike either up or down the canyon beyond Park boundaries to establish campsites.

Plan on spending the better part of a day in Horseshoe; the mysterious rock-art panels demand the extra time required to appreciate them and ponder their meaning. Rangers conduct guided walks along this trail at 9 A.M. on Saturdays from spring through early fall.

**Description**: Our journey into the beautiful, mysterious depths of Horseshoe Canyon gets underway at the information sign at the trailhead (0.0; 5300). A leaflet available from the dispenser here offers insights into not only the human history of the area but also the workings of nature in a desert canyon. The initial segment of the route into the canyon follows a long-closed road constructed to access oil-drilling sites on the plateau to the east. It descends south gradually among Navajo Sandstone slickrock and passes outliers of the reddish, discontinuous layer of the younger Carmel Formation, much of which has been stripped from the plateau by erosion.

Views stretch across the gently rolling plateau, clothed in grasses and scattered shrubs and junipers. The deep gash of Horseshoe Canyon lies below us, flanked by domes and rounded slickrock cliffs. Quite soon we skirt a locked gate that bars vehicles, and proceed along the wide roadbed at a moderate downhill grade. Soon we switchback past an old water tank and trough, remnants of the days when ranchers ran their cattle in the canyon before its establishment as a national park. Our road then curves momentarily east, then north past another gate, still high above the cliffbound canyon. Down-canyon, we see that reddish ledges of the Kayenta Formation begin to crop out below the desert-varnished Navajo cliffs. We also see the road climbing steeply up the opposite wall of the canyon, providing access into the canyon for 4WD vehicles coming from Hans Flat.

After descending three final sandy switchbacks, we reach the broad, sandy wash (1.5; 4700), then make our way up-canyon through deep, loose sand, soon passing the jeep road climbing the east wall of the canyon. After 0.4 mile we pass the first vehicle campsite in the canyon and, 100 yards beyond, a very short spur trail branches left, climbing the wash bank to the first pictograph panel in the canyon, the High Gallery. A sign here explains the particulars of the rock-art panels in the canyon. This pictograph is a simple one lacking much detail, consisting of several human-like figures and hand prints painted with red mud.

Not only does the superimposition of Fremont-style pictographs over the Barrier Canyon style in Horseshoe Canyon point to the pictographs' antiquity, but the downcutting of the wash below the remnant streambanks here has left the panels high on the canyon walls. Erosion during the past 2000 years or so has removed the footing that Archaic culture artists

**Hikers won't see this pictograph in Horseshoe Canyon—vandals have destroyed it**

may have once stood upon while creating the panels.

Resuming our walk up the canyon, we shortly reach a right-forking spur road to the second vehicle campsite. Behind the camp on the canyon wall is another more extensive panel, called the Living Site, or Horseshoe Shelter. This pictograph, also painted with red mud, but in different shades, has much more detail, depicting the ghost-like figures typical of the Barrier Canyon style, as well as figures of animals.

Continuing up-canyon, we soon reach the mouth of southeast-trending Water Canyon. There is a good spring about 1 mile up that narrow defile. We then pass through a vehicle barricade and follow the dry wash between soaring canyon walls. The stretch ahead leading to the third pictograph panel allows us time to appreciate the wilderness character of the canyon and its inhabitants. We'll likely see violet-green swallows dipping and darting for insects along the canyon walls, and perhaps hear the distinctive call of the mourning dove or the canyon wren. Wildflowers help to soften the rough edges of the canyon, and some of the delicate blooms we are likely to notice are cryptantha, yellow beeplant, globe mallow, Wyoming paintbrush, basin bahia, evening primrose, Uinta groundsel, and the climbing vine of clematis. Fremont cottonwoods and willows inhabit moist sites in the canyon, and we also encounter rabbitbrush, Fremont barberry and a variety of grasses edging close to the wash.

About 2.6 miles from the trailhead, the wash curves west toward a deep alcove in the canyon wall. Here is the Alcove Site, but in order to reach it we must scale the cutbank in the eroded remnants of the old stream terrace above. Once again, Barrier Canyon style ghost figures dominate the panel, but vandals have destroyed much of it. Even early visitors to the canyon defaced the panel, attested to by a 1904 inscription. This ancient rock art has survived for perhaps thousands of years, only to be perhaps destroyed by modern vandals.

The best is saved for last, and we amble up-canyon in anticipation of the aptly named Great Gallery. This extensive panel comes into view after the fourth west-trending bend in the canyon beyond the Alcove Site. We leave the wash (2.25; 4800) and proceed through the brush to reach the foot of the panel, also high above the present wash level.

The intricate detail and 6-7-foot size of the figures on this long panel are extraordinary. This is perhaps the finest rock-art panel on the entire Colorado Plateau. The ghostly figures have tapered bodies lacking appendages. The heads of many figures have eyes that seem to stare back at you, and the largest figure, called The Holy Ghost, has large, hollow eyes in its skull-like head. Dog-like animals and bighorn sheep are also painted in great detail. An unusual aspect of the ghost figures that dominate Barrier Canyon style rock art is the presence here of two men with spears near a cluster of bighorn sheep. Although out of character with the rest of the panel, the men appear to have been painted by the same artist as the rest of the panel. There are also tiny birds on the panel, and many other intriguing details that demand we linger to study them.

We can continue up-canyon for 2 more miles to the Park boundary, beyond which lie Bureau of Land Management lands. Deadmans Trail, an old stock trail into the canyon, climbs the eastern cliffs to the canyon rim and Park boundary, 0.4 mile up-canyon from the Great Gallery, ending at a jeep road on the plateau after a total distance of 1.5 miles from the Great Gallery.

# Trip 38
## North Point to The Maze

**Distance**: 25.8 miles round trip to The

Maze, not including sidetrips
**Low/High elevations**: 4540'/6560'
**Suited for**: Backpack
**Difficulty**: Moderately strenuous as a backpack of three or more days.
**Best seasons**: Mid-April through mid-June; mid-September through October.
**Maps/Trailhead**: 53,54,55/27
**Hazards**: Flash-flood danger; usually no water between the trailhead and The Maze; very steep and dangerous descent into The Maze; no trails in The Maze.

**Introduction**: The Maze is more remote and difficult of access than any other region in Utah's national parks. For the serious backpacker who wants solitude, challenge, and adventure, there is no better choice for a backcountry trek than The Maze. The hike along the North Trail and the jeep road to Maze Overlook presents no major difficulties and is passable to the average backpacker. However, The Maze is the sole realm of the accomplished slickrock desert hiker. The 1-mile Maze Trail is definitely not for novice hikers, and should not be attempted by anyone with a fear of heights or anyone lacking basic rock-climbing skills. A rope may be required to lower bulky backpacks over some of the steeper pitches and, for most routes climbing out of The Maze, a rope is essential for hoisting packs. And you should have an internal-frame pack.

The hike to The Maze is usually devoid of water, but hikers will be delighted by its relative abundance in the canyons of The Maze. Be sure to pack enough water to reach The Maze, then purify water you obtain there.

There are enough cairned routes in this district of hidden canyons and remote mesas to keep experienced hikers busy for several weeks. If you come to The Maze with a sense of adventure and only with ample desert hiking experience, you will be rewarded with memories of a backcountry experience that will last a lifetime.

**Description**: Our epic journey gets underway (0.0; 6550) in a thick woodland of pinyon and juniper on the mesa of North Point within Glen Canyon National Recreation Area. The North Trail leads us south over the Navajo-Sandstone-capped tableland, but soon we begin descending via a series of benches and reach the more level terrain of a broad basin. The trail curves west as we leave a draw, traversing above cliffs that plummet into the depths of North Trail Canyon below. Steep and rocky switchbacks ensue, leading us down a 300-foot break in the Wingate Sandstone cliffs.

Upon reaching the rock-strewn wash, the way becomes obscure but, as on many "trails" in the Utah desert, we simply follow the wash down-canyon. Almost at once we descend through a slickrock chute, then make our way through brush and among boulders. Great cliffs of Wingate Sandstone and Navajo Sandstone rise abruptly to the skyline on either side of the canyon. Presently within the Chinle Formation, the canyon becomes increasingly broad as we continue. Soon its towering walls begin to frame distant wooded mesas and the splintered crown of Elaterite Butte, a landmark that will guide us for miles to come.

The wash in its upper reaches is choked with shrubs and boulders, and we crisscross it numerous times, sometimes going above it to avoid rugged stretches. By the time we encounter the Black Ledge, a low cliff band forming a bench and composed of the Chinle's basal member, the Mossback, we leave the wash and climb easily to the bench amid sparse desert growth. But soon we descend steeply over the crumbling ledge into the wash below (2.7; 5300), where we encounter the red ledges of the Moenkopi Formation. Look for two historic inscriptions on trailside boulders at the head of the descent. These boulders are composed of the Mossback member of the Chinle, which was one of the uranium prospector's primary targets. One bears the date 1953, which was the peak of the uranium boom; the other, possibly carved by a cowboy, reads: JESS LARSEN, DEC 1-21.

The route ahead follows the wash for much of the next few miles, but occasionally traverses just above it. Its bed is filled with sand and gravel, but it is mostly hardpacked, and the walking is easy. Pinyon, juniper and various shrubs cloak the broad benches above us, and the soaring Orange Cliffs provide an exciting backdrop. The distant La Sal Mountains, Island in the Sky mesa, and isolated Ekker and Elaterite buttes are

**Camp in North Trail Canyon**

constantly in view. The scenery from North Trail Canyon to Maze Overlook is the kind we appreciate on a grand, panoramic scale.

Except for a few lizards, an occasional antelope ground squirrel or a blacktail jackrabbit, birds are among the most frequently observed wildlife. We'll likely see ravens, violet-green swallows, turkey vultures, kestrels, and mourning doves. The tiny canyon wrens and rock wrens, however, are more likely to be heard than seen.

About 5.2 miles from the trailhead, West Fork Big Water Canyon enters from the southwest, offering a splendid view of the Orange Cliffs up its broad drainage. Our route ahead briefly follows the wash as it bends north, but we soon climb up to a bench, shortcutting a broad meander, then cross to the north bank and proceed northeast. Shortly, we exit the wash for the last time, climb to a grassy bench, and pass a lone juniper.

Presently our route follows a faded road above the wash, first east, then north. We soon abandon the drainage to stroll easily over a minor hill and pass the remains of an old boiler. Quite soon thereafter we reach an orange marker and the jeep road (3.6; 5050), left-bound for the remote Millard Canyon Benches and right-bound for Elaterite Basin and the Flint Trail jeep road. Bear right onto the jeep road, dipping in and out of minor gullies and in 1/2 mile joining another jeep road bound for Maze Overlook.

One may find water in a seasonal spring by first following the jeep road south along Big Water Canyon for 0.7 mile, then east 1/4 mile toward the wash via a spur road. A unique phenomenon can be observed in the White Rim Sandstone that flanks the canyon, particularly on its east side. Here a thick, tarry oil—elaterite—can be seen seeping from the sandstone on hot summer days. These "tar sands" contain commercial quantities of oil, but the oil would be difficult and costly to extract. Nevertheless, the potential exists for development of these reserves in outcrops of the White Rim to the southwest.

Proceeding northeast (left) on the jeep road, bound for Maze Overlook, we soon descend toward the wash of Big Water Canyon. Just before reaching the wash, we descend a short but steep slickrock pitch that scrapes the undercarriage of every vehicle passing through. The road then climbs steeply up the opposite bank to a broad bench above. Looking back, we enjoy a superb panorama of the Orange Cliffs and the wooded mesas above them. Presently we leave the ribbon of pinyon and juniper that hugs the wash below and begin a protracted, sometimes undulating traverse along the broad White Rim bench, ultimately curving all the way around imposing Elaterite Butte and several other smaller, flat-topped buttes.

Soon we reach the signed boundary (1.6; 5000) of the Maze District, and after another 175 yards, a cairned route heads northwest from the road across potholed White Rim slickrock, bound for the rocky defile of Horse Canyon, 1 mile north. This is but the first of more than a dozen cairned routes awaiting exploration in the Maze District.

The road ahead proceeds among low hills beneath Elaterite Butte, and panoramic vistas accompany us the remaining distance to Maze Overlook. Vegetation is sparse, including low shrubs such as blackbrush, shadscale, and yucca, and wildflowers including phlox, resinbush, and Mojave aster. At one point about 1 1/2 mile into the Park, we approach the brink of a pouroff, high above a branch of Horse Canyon. Below the pouroff, where the White Rim Sandstone makes contact with the red beds of the underlying Organ Rock Shale, we'll notice numerous seeplines hosting sparse hanging-garden vegetation.

We continue our jaunt along the bench, following it northeast, then southeast, around a jutting promontory, and then climb an easy grade to the rim ahead, where the road forks right and left at Maze Overlook (3.8; 5180). The incredible vista that unfolds is well worth the time and effort required to enjoy it. Before hiking over to the Maze Trail, find a spot, perhaps on a roadside boulder, and take time to absorb the panorama. Northward, the Orange Cliffs and North Point mesa jut east into Canyonlands basin, and beyond is the isolated bulk of Ekker Butte, an erosional remnant of the once continuous, flat-lying plateau. Prominent in the middle distance to the northeast is the broad mesa of Island in the Sky and the detached landmark of Junction

Butte, another erosional outlier. The distant skyline is punctuated by the peaks of the La Sal Mountains, 40 miles from our vantage point as the raven flies. The forested hogback ridges of the Abajo Mountains, also 40 miles distant, form the horizon to the southeast.

But the color and form of the landscape in the foreground captures our attention. This is The Maze, our goal, and we should study it carefully. This vast landscape of cliffs, domes, and canyons, all colored in bands of red and white, seems to stretch away to the very foot of the Abajo Mountains, but becomes progressively higher toward the east. That highland of fins and spires is The Needles country, and it is a separate entity, set apart from us by the yawning gorge of the invisible Colorado River.

We can see little of the canyons of The Maze; rather, we see the rolling slickrock ridges and bulging cliffs above the canyons. Several prominent landmarks rise above the slickrock labyrinth, composed of younger rocks now isolated by ages of erosion. The intriguing Land of Standing Rocks is a highland separating The Maze from the similar Fins country to the south. On this highland are tall pillars of a soft red rock, the Organ Rock Shale of the Cutler Formation. Some of the standing rocks are capped by a still younger formation, a white sandstone we have encountered earlier and one that forms the rim of the overlook on which we stand, the White Rim.

But perhaps the most striking of all landmarks juts skyward from the center of The Maze. The tall, slender, fin-like walls of the Chocolate Drops are an important landmark for navigation in The Maze. Petes Mesa, an irregular redrock highland, juts above the slickrock labyrinth to the east, but is mostly hidden from view once we are within the canyons below.

There are two vehicle campsites at Maze Overlook. One lies on the bench below, at the end of a right-forking spur road. At this junction we turn left and stroll across the White Rim tableland in an open pinyon-juniper woodland. The spur to the second campsite is soon encountered, but we stay left and shortly reach the signed parking area (0.2; 5130) and the beginning of the signed Maze Trail. Cairns quickly lead us to the rim of the mesa, where another sign warns that the trail ahead is hazardous, and indeed it is. Inexperienced and unprepared hikers should go no farther, but to those with ropes and basic rock-climbing skills, The Maze beckons.

At once we scramble over the White Rim Sandstone and onto the red rocks of the Organ Rock Shale. Cairns lead us initially east below a row of redrock pillars capped by blocks of White Rim Sandstone. These are the Nuts and Bolts, another important landmark that is used in conjunction with the Chocolate Drops to relocate the route back to Maze Overlook.

At the bend beyond the Nuts and Bolts, pause long enough to observe the canyons below. We can see a part of the South Fork Horse Canyon, and can look upstream to the mouth of Pictograph Canyon. Even though The Maze is lightly used, there are camping restrictions designed to preserve the pristine scenery as seen from the overlook. Camping is not allowed in any part of the canyons visible from the rim.

Our route ahead curves around a bowl, descending via redrock ledges. Below us are bulging, rounded cliffs of Cedar Mesa Sandstone, and there appears to be no way down. Once we reach the Cedar Mesa Sandstone, the "fun" begins. We'll descend steeply sloping slickrock, then drop into a narrow crack that is much too confined for a bulky-frame backpack. Smaller, internal-frame packs are best for a trek in The Maze. Below the crack, a steep, exposed descent of a rounded slickrock slope ensues. A minor crack on the rock's face offers footholds for the pitch.

Then, winding downward, we encounter another slickrock slope, but this one has steps cut into it to allow easier passage. Now, with the worst behind us, we make our way over slickrock and among boulders to terra firma on the sandy slope above the wash, then follow the trail into the South Fork just below a large, deep pool (1.0; 4530).

Once in the South Fork Horse Canyon, The Maze is yours to explore. The canyons are quite sandy, so hiking there is taxing. Four lightly cairned routes lead out of the canyons, three lead to the Land of Standing Rocks, and another leads to the rim of Jasper Canyon, with a fork heading northeast to Petes Mesa, and a southbound fork to the jeep road at Chimney Rock. The washes

**Deep pool in South Fork Horse Canyon**

are only sporadically cairned, and the routes leading out of the washes are usually cairned only where they leave the washes to climb slickrock.

The South Fork offers one of the more direct routes into the Land of Standing Rocks and the jeep road there, 8.3 miles up-canyon. There are four fairly reliable springs in the upper reaches of that canyon upstream from the Maze Trail, and there are numerous potential campsites on benches above the wash. Hikers will notice an obvious lack of tamarisk in these canyons, but a profusion of tamarisk stumps. This exotic tree is quite successful at supplanting native vegetation, and Park rangers have been attempting to control the spread of tamarisks by cutting them back and in some cases spraying the stumps with herbicide to retard re-growth. But this is a vigorous tree, and many stumps we'll see are growing back.

The way up the South Fork follows the wash as it twists and turns to the right and left. Typical of washes in the Cedar Mesa Sandstone, it is quite sandy and hence hiking is slow and tedious. Initially, we enjoy good views of the Chocolate Drops towering above, but they soon fade from view as we head deeper into the slickrock labyrinth. Two seeping springs are encountered within the first mile above the Maze Trail. Most springs in The Maze originate as seeps in the wash, often at a bend in the canyon, and these often drain into pools where hikers can obtain water. The water is mineralized and has a distinctive taste, but is potable after treatment.

Soon a prominent side canyon opens up to the west, offering a rock-framed view of Elaterite Butte, rising into the sky nearly 2000 feet above. Beyond this branch canyon, you can camp wherever you wish, but try to camp out of sight of the wash.

At this elevation, below 5000 feet, the canyons have a microhabitat that supports a diversity of vegetation. Contrasting with the sparse desert growth on the mesas above, Maze canyons support a vigorous woodland of pinyons and Utah junipers. These trees dot the benches above the wash, as do various shrubs including buffaloberry, Utah serviceberry, Fremont barberry, mormon tea, singleleaf ash, and yucca.

Countless minor canyons branch off to the right and left, and these might be confusing to some hikers. They are all interesting to explore, but they end abruptly amid impassable cliffs. Well within the canyon, all is slickrock, and we may feel as if we'd been swallowed by the gaping jaws of the earth. As we gaze upward to the cliffs, some sheer, other bulging, and all of them topped by domes and spires, we may see some of the numerous arches, mostly the pothole type, that have formed in the Cedar Mesa Sandstone. Distinctive bands colored in shades of red and white, coupled with varied resistances to erosion, give the Cedar Mesa an irregular but beautiful appearance.

Approaching the head of the canyon, hikers will encounter two more seeping springs. Shortly beyond, 6.6 miles from the Maze Trail, the canyon forks. To reach the jeep road at the west end of the Standing Rocks highland, one can follow the left fork south as it climbs steadily. Another spring 1/2 mile up that fork offers hikers their last chance to tank up (if it is flowing) before climbing into the bone-dry country beyond.

This lightly cairned route tops out on a ridge of the red Organ Rock Shale at about 5050 feet and about 1 3/4 miles beyond the fork. The jeep road lies just below the ridge to the south, and one must pick a route to it, since the cairns have largely disappeared. The roadend at The Doll House is another 6 miles by road toward the east. Hiking options in the Land of Standing Rocks are numerous, but most hikers, after a day or so, must return to the canyons for water. Options for loop trips back into The Maze include two routes into Pictograph Canyon, the first descending northwest from The Plug, the other beginning near Chimney Rock. Another highly scenic but waterless route follows the broad ridge north from Chimney Rock almost to Petes Mesa, and then descends a branch canyon back to the South Fork.

From the foot of the Maze Trail, we can also follow the South Fork down-canyon to where, after 0.75 mile, another prominent canyon enters on the right (east). If you want to reach Horse Canyon or simply explore the lower South Fork, bear left at this confluence. This part of the canyon is broad and sandy, with occasional cottonwoods along its banks. There is a good spring and a deep pool about 1 mile down-canyon, at the second major bend in the wash.

At the juncture of the South Fork and the aforementioned eastside canyon, we can follow that possibly damp wash for 1/3 mile, to where we have two routes from which to choose. There are likely to be a pool and a seeping spring at this fork in the canyon. The largest pictograph panel in The Maze lies about 1 mile up south-trending Pictograph Canyon. That canyon also offers a few springs, potential campsites, and a choice of two cairned routes into the Standing Rocks country.

Heading south into that canyon, we mount step-like slickrock, and briefly enjoy fine views up to the Chocolate Drops and the Nuts and Bolts. The wash is firm and hiking is easy where it is damp, but sandy stretches impede steady progress. Camping is allowed anywhere beyond the canyon's mouth. After the first major westward bend in the canyon, we pass beneath the Harvest Scene pictograph, also known as the Bird Site.

This extensive panel represents the Barrier Canyon style of rock art, believed to have been painted by a pre-Anasazi/Fremont culture known as Archaic, and is perhaps 2000-3000 years old. This intriguing panel features large, human-like figures typical of the Barrier Canyon style, but many of them have arms and legs. It differs from the images of Horseshoe Canyon, which depict ghost-like, supernatural figures. Here we see figures stooping to harvest plants, and one large figure holds a plant, apparently a wild grass, in an oversized hand. The two stooping figures hold tools, and may be carrying baskets, which would explain their hunchback profile. Several small animals and birds also adorn the panel.

This canyon is wider than the South Fork, and vegetation is more abundant. Fremont cottonwoods arc their branches over the banks of the wash, and are typically found growing with willow and the broadleaved shrub buckthorn.

Utah junipers are abundant on the benches above the wash, and these benches and the banks of the wash host a variety of shrubs and wildflowers.

The main wash is obvious, but a number of side canyons branch off throughout the length of the canyon. About 2.5 miles from the canyon's mouth, a prominent branch canyon forks left (southeast). Hikers can follow this canyon for 1 mile to where, not far past a spring, a cairned route climbs the cliffs to the canyon rim, ultimately leading to the jeep road at Chimney Rock. Like most routes out of The Maze, the climb is steep and exposed.

We may also continue the trek up the main branch of the canyon, where we may find flowing water, or at least a small, stagnant pool. About 1.2 miles beyond the aforementioned branch canyon we encounter another, but it offers no apparent route out of its cliffbound defile. So instead we bear left and proceed up the main wash, with colorful, bulging cliffs rising 400 feet above us.

The canyon becomes increasingly narrow, and potential campsites are much less numerous than behind us. Eventually, the chocolate-brown monolith of The Wall comes into view, and if we persist almost to the head of the canyon, we'll reach a rugged and demanding cairned route 5 miles from the canyon's mouth that climbs above a southeast-trending branch canyon to the Standing Rocks mesa between The Plug and Lizard Rock—a narrow, wall-like outlier composed of Organ Rock Shale. A rope is required to hoist packs on this route, and friction pitches on very steep slickrock walls are encountered.

———————————

By far the easiest route to the Land of Standing Rocks begins back at the mouth of Pictograph Canyon. From the grassy banks of the wash, we can gaze east into a maze of branch canyons and colorful cliffs and domes for only a short distance. Like all such canyons in The Maze, they look much the same, and hikers can easily become confused and disoriented. Many of these canyons have arches, and all are fun to explore. Only one, however, offers a route out of The Maze.

We can find that route by following the main wash up-canyon toward the southeast, but we would be wise to tank up on water at the canyon fork before proceeding any farther. Alternating between the trees, shrubs and grasses of benches and the water-loving vegetation of the wash, follow this main canyon upstream for 0.75 mile, ignoring three prominent northeast-trending branches that fork off to the left. Upon reaching the mouth of an east-trending side canyon, we'll find cairns that lead us about another 0.75 mile into its depths, beyond which we mount slickrock and follow a circuitous cairned route via ledges to the broad rim above, 2 1/2 miles from Pictograph Canyon.

Views from this highland are outstanding, encompassing much of the vast Canyonlands basin including notable landmarks such as Island in the Sky, The Needles, the Abajo and La Sal Mountains and, behind us, The Maze, Chocolate Drops, and Elaterite Butte. The hummocky, tree- and shrub-dotted highland upon which we stand stretches to the southern horizon, punctuated by more than a half-dozen redrock monoliths in the Land of Standing Rocks. Prominent among them is Lizard Rock, the largest, and the slender spire of Chimney Rock, the smallest. Below us to the east is the gorge of Jasper Canyon, accessible only via a long and arduous route into the lower canyon via a ridge northeast of Chimney Rock. Scattered cottonwoods indicate the presence of moisture deep within that shady defile.

Presently we have a choice of two routes. We may follow this broad highland south via a lightly cairned route to the jeep road near Chimney Rock, 3 miles. Or, we can proceed northeast, just below the Cedar Mesa-Organ Rock Shale contact, traversing slickrock slopes into a draw that offers easy access onto the brush-clad tableland of Petes Mesa, where the route ends. Petes Mesa, capped by the red rocks of the Moenkopi Formation, is an erosional outlier of the benchland we traversed enroute to Maze Overlook. The distance from the ridgetop to the rim of Petes Mesa is less than two miles. The mesa is an open, rolling highland, and from various points on its rim it is possible to gaze more than 1000 feet below into the Green River's Labyrinth Canyon.

# Bibliography and Suggested Reading

## Geology

Baars, Donald, *The Colorado Plateau, A Geologic History*. Albuquerque, New Mexico: University of New Mexico Press, 1983.

Barnes, F.A., *Canyon Country Arches and Bridges*. Salt Lake City: Wasatch Publishers, 1987.

Barnes, F.A., *Canyon Country Geology*. Salt Lake City: Wasatch Publishers, 1978.

Collier, Michael, *The Geology of Capitol Reef National Park*. Salt Lake City: Lorraine Press; Capitol Reef Natural History Association, 1987.

Doelling, Hellmut H., *Geology of Arches National Park*. Salt Lake City: Utah Geological and Mineral Survey, 1985.

Hamilton, Wayne L., *The Sculpturing of Zion*. Springdale, Utah: Zion Natural History Association, 1984.

Harris, Ann, and Esther Tuttle, *Geology of National Parks*. Dubuque, Iowa: Kendall/Hunt Publishing Co., 1983.

Hintze, Lehi F., *Geologic History of Utah*. Provo, Utah: Department of Geology, Brigham Young University, 1975.

Lindquist, Robert C., *Geology of Bryce Canyon National Park*. Bryce Canyon, Utah: Bryce Canyon Natural History Association, 1977.

Lohman, S.W., *The Geologic Story of Arches National Park*. Washington, D.C.: U.S. Government Printing Office, 1975.

Rigby, J. Keith, *Northern Colorado Plateau*. Dubuque, Iowa: Kendall/Hunt Publishing Co., 1976.

Stokes, William Lee, *Geology of Utah*. Salt Lake City: Utah Museum of Natural History, University of Utah, and Utah Geological and Mineralogical Survey, Department of Natural Resources, 1986.

## History

Barnes, F.A., *Canyonlands National Park, Early History and First Descriptions*. Salt Lake City: Wasatch Publishers, 1988.

Crampton, C. Gregory, *Standing Up Country, The Canyon Lands of Utah and Arizona*. Salt Lake City: Peregrine Smith Books, 1983.

Frost, Kent, *My Canyonlands*. New York: Abelard-Schuman, 1971.

Houk, Rose, *Dwellers of the Rainbow, Story of the Fremont Culture in the Capitol Reef Country*. Torrey, Utah: Capitol Reef Natural History Association, 1988.

Jones, Dewitt, and Linda S. Cordell, *Anasazi World*. Portland, Oregon: Graphic Arts Center Publishing Co., 1985.

Markoff, Dena S., and Laurie Simmons, Roselyn Stewart, Merrill Ann Wilson, *The Outstanding Wonder, Zion Canyon's Cable Mountain Draw Works*. Springdale, Utah: Zion Natural History Association, 1978.

Matlock, Gary, *Enemy Ancestors, The Anasazi World with a Guide to Sites*. Northland Press, 1988.

Powell, Allan Kent, *San Juan County, Utah, People, Resources and History.* Salt Lake City: Utah State Historical Society, 1983.

Powell, J.W., *The Exploration of the Colorado River and its Canyons.* New York: Dover Press, 1961.

Schaafsma, Polly, *The Rock Art of Utah.* Cambridge, Mass.: Harvard University, Peabody Museum of Archaeology and Ethnology, 1971.

Weaver, Donald E., *Images on Stone, The Prehistoric Rock Art of the Colorado Plateau.* Flagstaff, Arizona: Museum of Northern Arizona, 1984.

Woodbury, Angus M., *A History of Southern Utah and its National Parks.* Salt Lake City: Utah State Historical Society, 1950.

## Plants and Animals

Andersen, Bernice A., *Desert Plants of Utah.* Utah State University, Cooperative Extension Services.

Buchanan, Hayle, *Living Color, Wildflower Communities of Bryce Canyon and Cedar Breaks.* Bryce Canyon, Utah: Bryce Canyon Natural History Association, 1974.

Davidson, George, editor, *A Guide to Capitol Reef Rocklife.* Salt Lake City: Paragon Press, 1982.

Elmore, Francis, H., *Shrubs and Trees of the Southwest Uplands.* Tucson: Southwest Parks and Monuments Association, 1976.

Nelson, Ruth Ashton, *Plants of Zion National Park, Wildflowers, Trees, Shrubs and Ferns.* Springdale, Utah: Zion Natural History Association, 1976.

Peterson, Roger Tory, *A Field Guide to Western Birds.* Boston: Houghton Mifflin, 1961.

Trapp, Carolyn, *The Cacti of Zion National Park.* Springdale, Utah: Zion Natural History Association, 1969.

Welsh, Stanley L., and N. Duane Atwood, Sherel Goodrich, Larry C. Higgins, editors, *A Utah Flora.* Provo, Utah: Brigham Young University, 1987.

## General

Abbey, Edward, *Desert Solitaire, A Season in the Wilderness.* New York: Ballantine Books, 1968.

Bezy, John, *Bryce Canyon, The Story Behind the Scenery.* Las Vegas: KC Publications, 1988.

Eardley, James A., and James Schaak, *Zion, The Story Behind the Scenery.* Las Vegas: KC Publications, 1988.

Hirschmann, Fred, *Bryce Canyon National Park.* Bryce Canyon, Utah: Bryce Canyon Natural History Association.

Hoffman, John F., *Arches National Park.* San Diego: Western Recreational Publications, 1985.

Johnson, David W., *Canyonlands, The Story Behind the Scenery.* Las Vegas: KC Publications, 1989.

Olson, Virgil J., and Helen Olson, *Capitol Reef, The Story Behind the Scenery.* Las Vegas: KC Publications, 1986.

Trimble, Stephen, *The Bright Edge, A Guide to the National Parks of the Colorado Plateau.* Flagstaff, Arizona: Museum of Northern Arizona Press, 1979.

# Hiking Checklist

The equipment for hiking Utah's desert country is little different from that used in any wild region. Especially on backpack trips, many of us tend to forget something, but even for a dayhike, skim the following list to be sure you haven't forgotten an "essential" item.

-First aid kit (should include bandages, antiseptic, snake-bite kit, constricting band, Ace bandage)
-Pocket knife
-Sunglasses
-Sunscreen
-Topographic maps (learn to read them)
-Compass (know how to use it in tandem with a topo map)
-Flashlight (with fresh batteries and spare bulb)
-Extra food and water (even on short hikes)
-Matches (waterproof or in waterproof container)
-Candle(s)
-Toilet paper
-Day pack and/or backpack
-Sleeping bag
-Foam pad or air mattress
-Tarp or ground sheet
-Sturdy tent, preferably free-standing
-Lightweight shoes for camp
-Insect repellent
-Lip balm
-Small, lightweight digging tool for toilet needs
-Pump-type water filter (First Need or Katadyn) or water purification tablets
-One quart water container(s)
-One-gallon water container(s), preferably collapsible
-Paper or plastic bags for packing out refuse
-Biodegradable soap
-Small towel
-Toothbrush
-Lightweight backpack stove and extra fuel
-Cooking pot(s)
-Spoon and fork
-Can opener
-Aluminum foil (can be used as windscreen for stove or as candle holder)
-Potscrubber
-Enough food for your trip, plus an extra day's supply (include high energy foods)

-Electrolyte replacement for plain water (Gatorade or Gookinaid, or similar product)
-Camera, film, lenses, filters
-Binoculars
-Reliable rain parka or poncho
-Rain pants
-Windproof garments
-Waterproof cover for pack
-Thermal underwear, preferably polypropylene
-Parka, preferably fiberpile
-Lightweight, light-colored clothing (use the "layering" method)
-Pants and shorts
-Extra socks
-Wool shirt or sweater
-Hat, wide-brimmed
-Extra underwear
-Sewing kit
-Watch
-Notebook, pens or pencils
-Backcountry use permit

# NOTE

On the individual maps, the larger numbers are trip numbers and the smaller numbers are trailhead numbers.

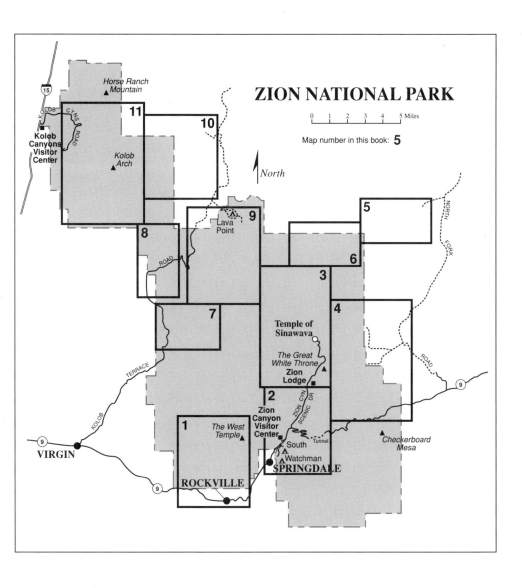

ZION NATIONAL PARK

0 1 2 3 4 5 Miles

Map number in this book: 5

North

Horse Ranch Mountain

Kolob Canyons Visitor Center

Kolob Arch

11

10

9

Lava Point

8

5

6

ROAD

3

7

Temple of Sinawava

The Great White Throne

Zion Lodge

4

TERRACE

2

Zion Canyon Visitor Center

1

The West Temple

South Watchman

SPRINGDALE

Tunnel

Checkerboard Mesa

KOLOB

VIRGIN

ROCKVILLE

NORTH FORK

ROAD

9

9

9

# MAP 1

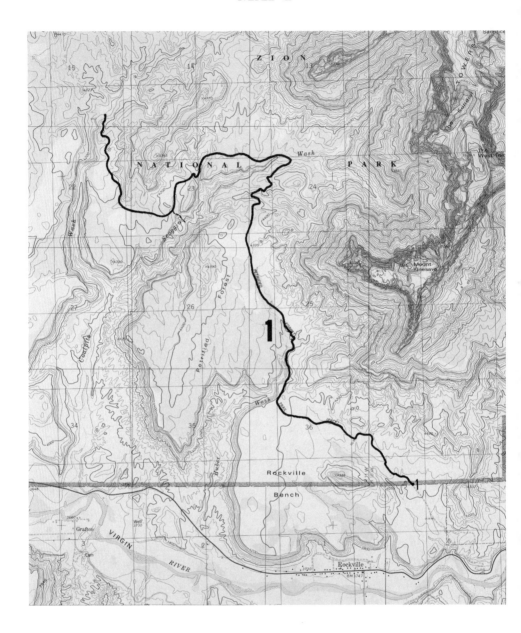

# MAP 2

see MAP 3

see MAP 4

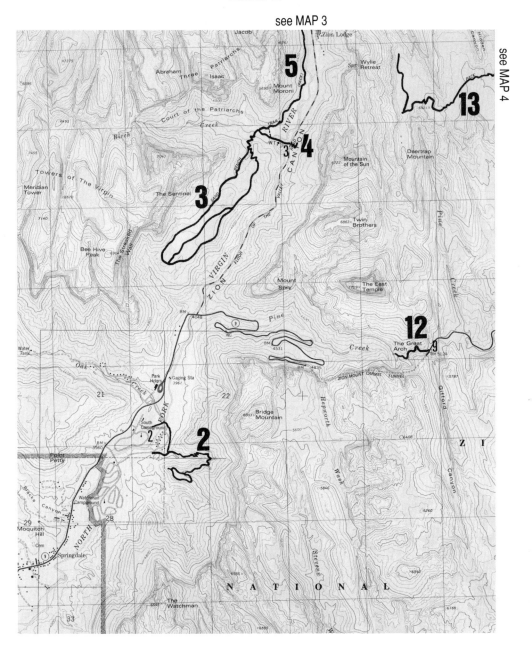

# MAP 3

see MAP 6

see MAP 9

see MAP 4

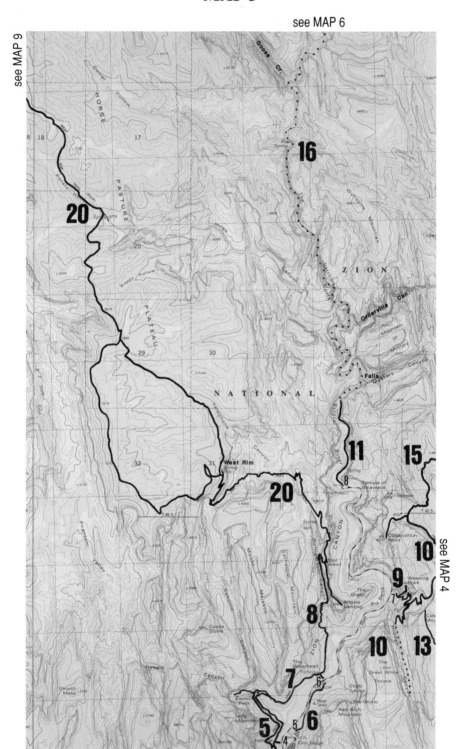

see MAP 2

# MAP 4

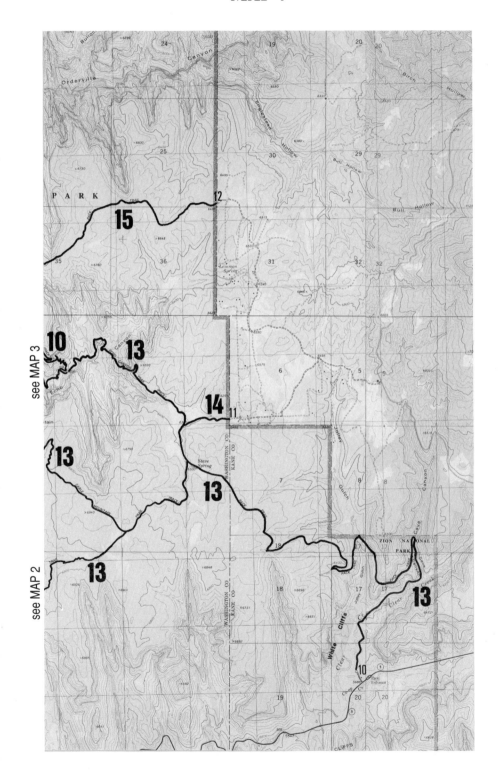

see MAP 3

see MAP 2

# MAP 5

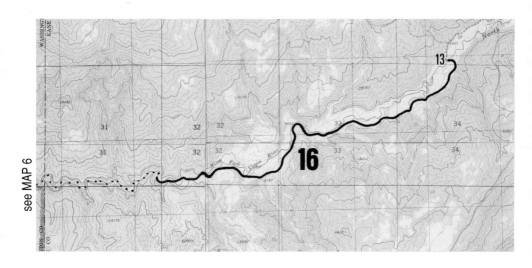

see MAP 6

# MAP 6

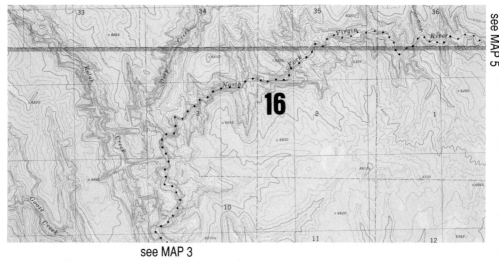

see MAP 5

see MAP 3

# MAP 7

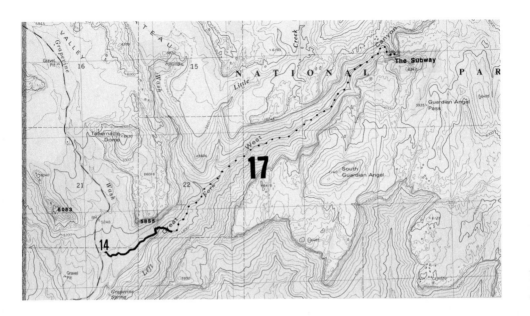

# MAP 8

see MAP 11

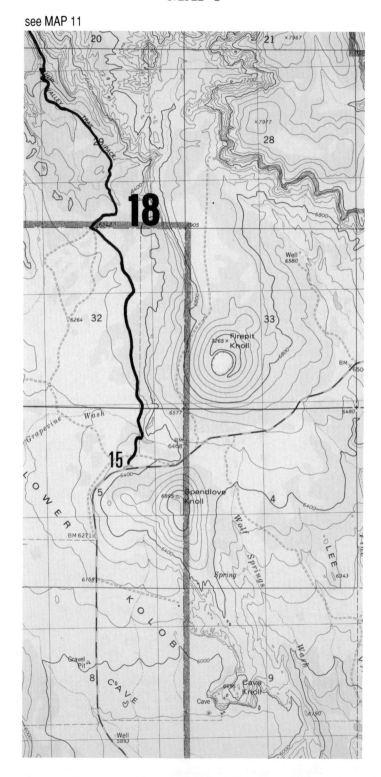

# MAP 9

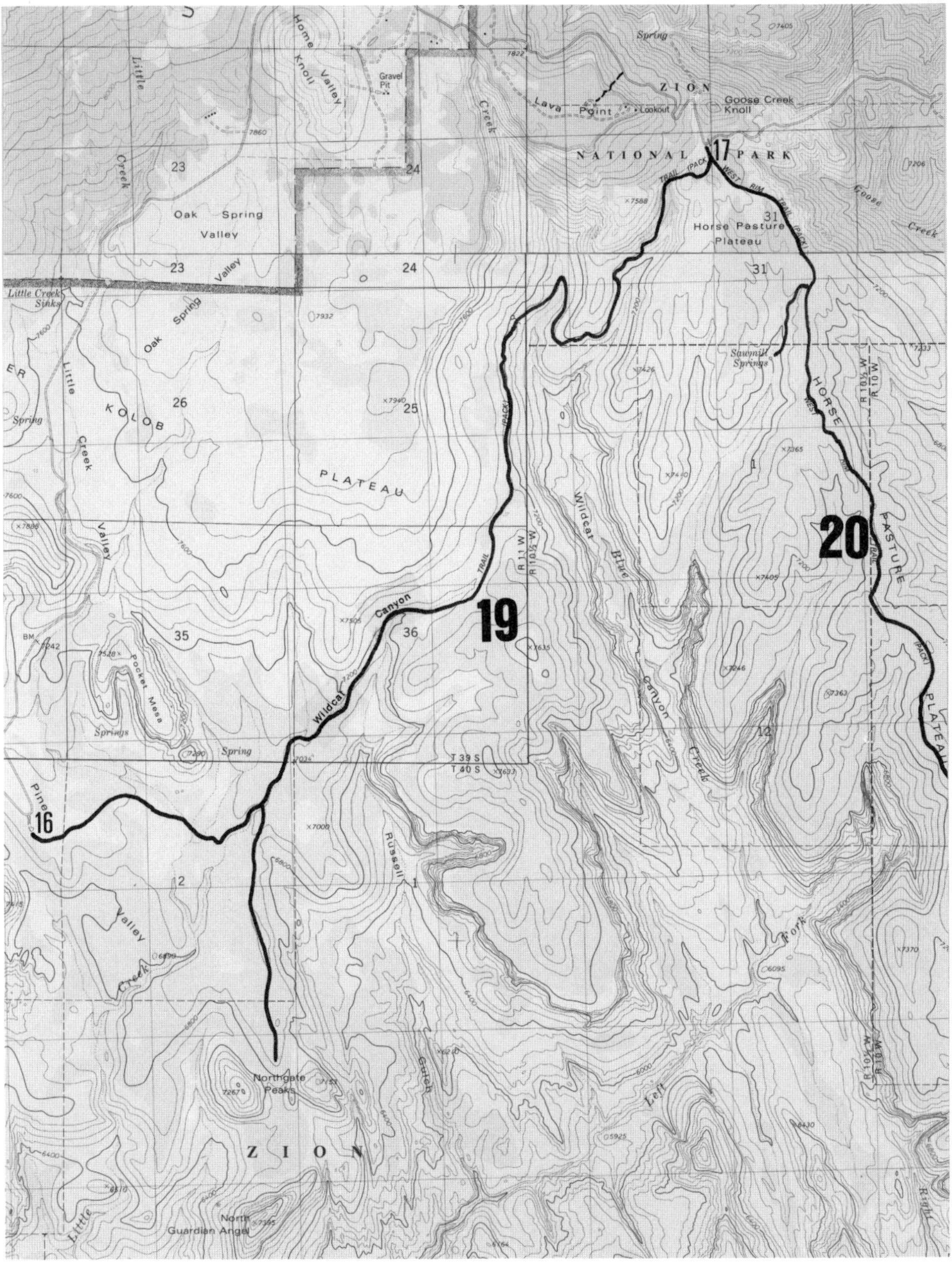

see MAP 3

# MAP 10

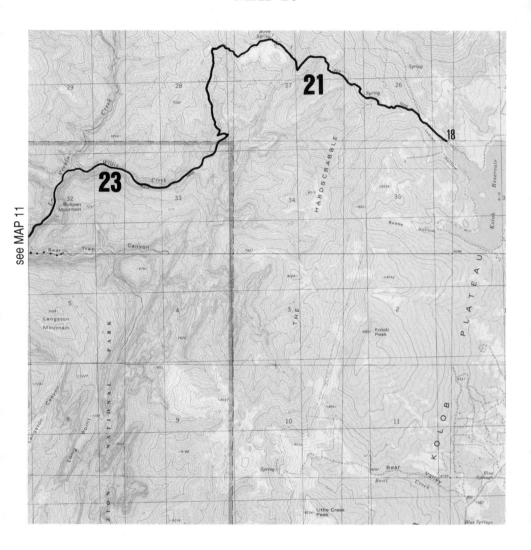

**21**

**23**

**18**

# MAP 11

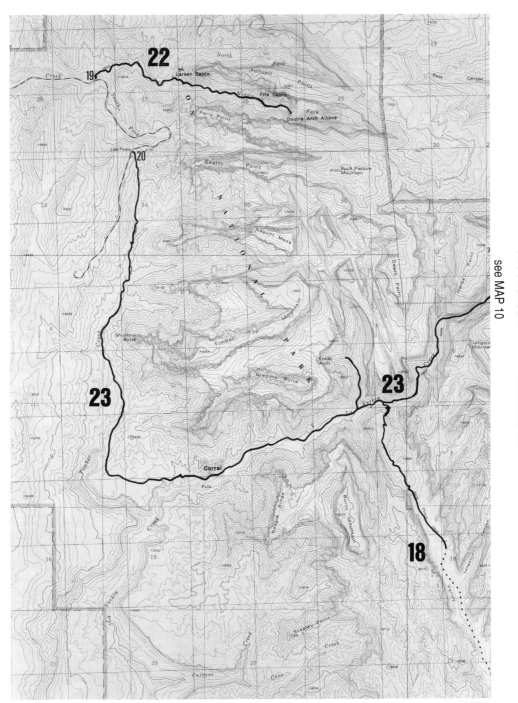

see MAP 10

see MAP 8

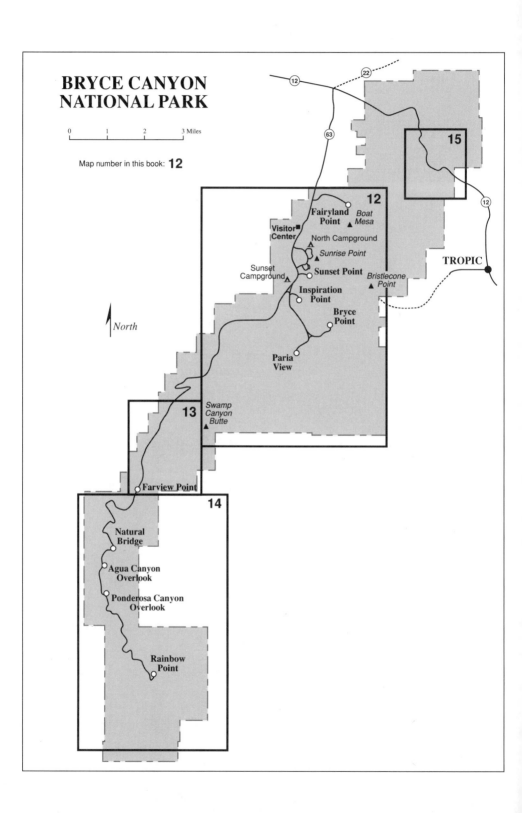

# BRYCE CANYON NATIONAL PARK

0    1    2    3 Miles

Map number in this book: **12**

**12**

**15**

**Fairyland Point**

*Boat Mesa*

**Visitor Center**■

North Campground

*Sunrise Point*

Sunset Campground

**Sunset Point**

*Bristlecone Point*

**TROPIC**

**Inspiration Point**

**Bryce Point**

*North*

**Paria View**

*Swamp Canyon Butte*

**13**

**Farview Point**

**14**

**Natural Bridge**

**Agua Canyon Overlook**

**Ponderosa Canyon Overlook**

**Rainbow Point**

# MAP 12

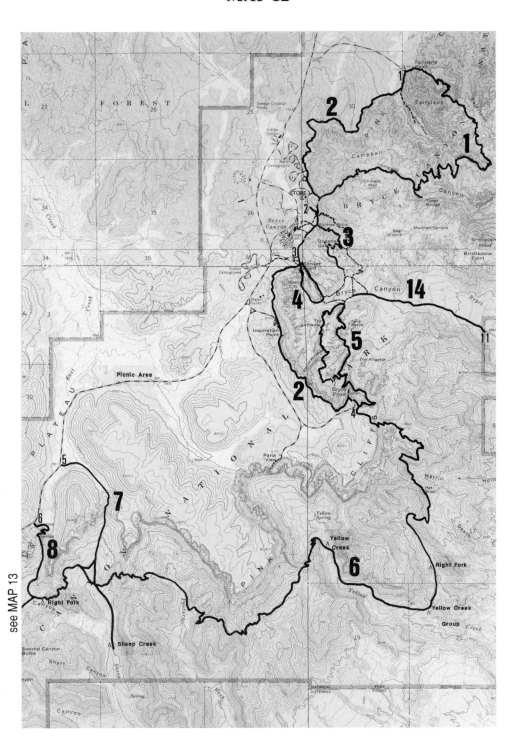

see MAP 13

# MAP 13

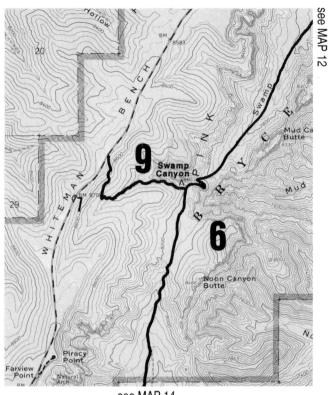

see MAP 12

see MAP 14

# MAP 14

see MAP 13

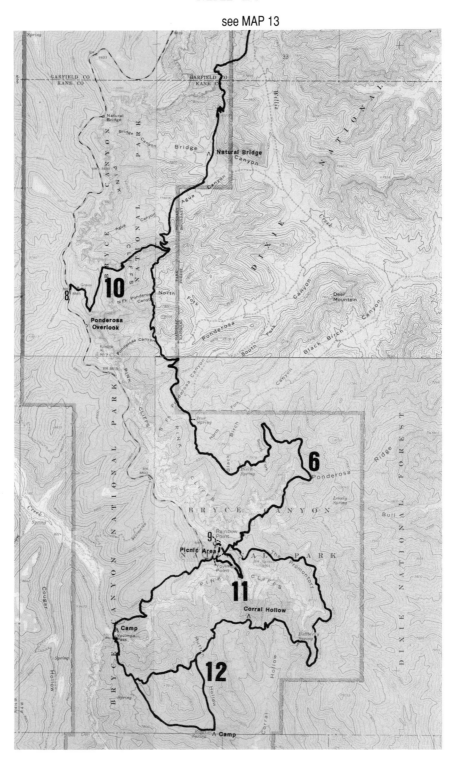

# MAP 15

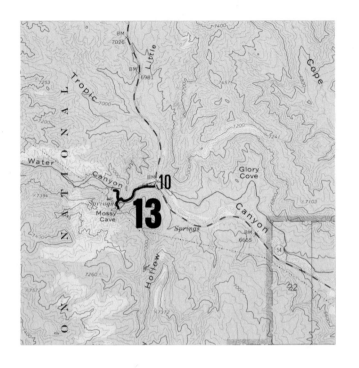

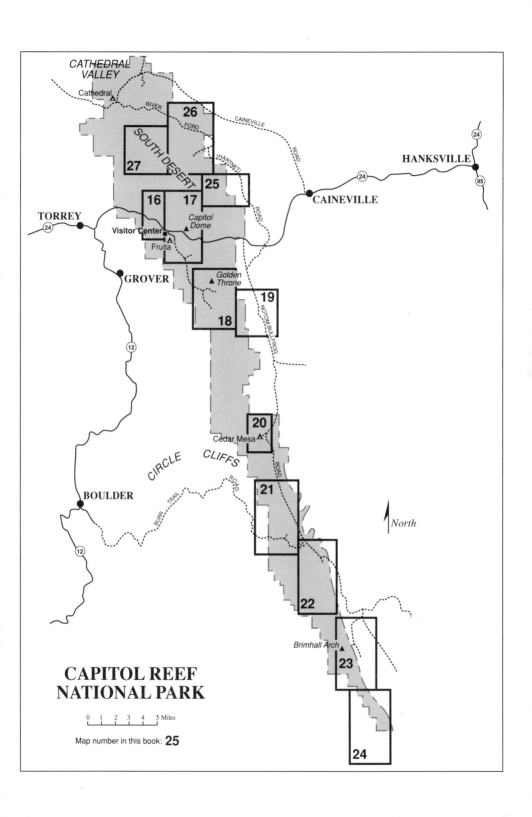

CATHEDRAL
VALLEY

Cathedral

RIVER FORD

CAINEVILLE

SOUTH DESERT

[HARTNET]

**26**

**27**

**25**

**16**

**17**

Capitol Dome

Visitor Center

Fruita

**TORREY**

**GROVER**

Golden Throne

**18**

**19**

NOTOM-BULLFROG ROAD

**HANKSVILLE**

**CAINEVILLE**

CIRCLE CLIFFS

**BOULDER**

BURR TRAIL

ROAD

Cedar Mesa

**20**

ROAD

**21**

North

**22**

Brimhall Arch

**23**

**CAPITOL REEF
NATIONAL PARK**

0  1  2  3  4  5 Miles

Map number in this book: **25**

**24**

# MAP 16

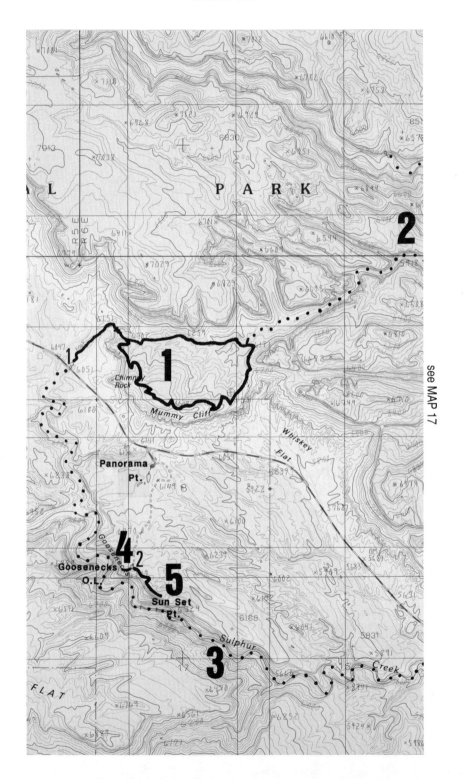

see MAP 17

# MAP 17

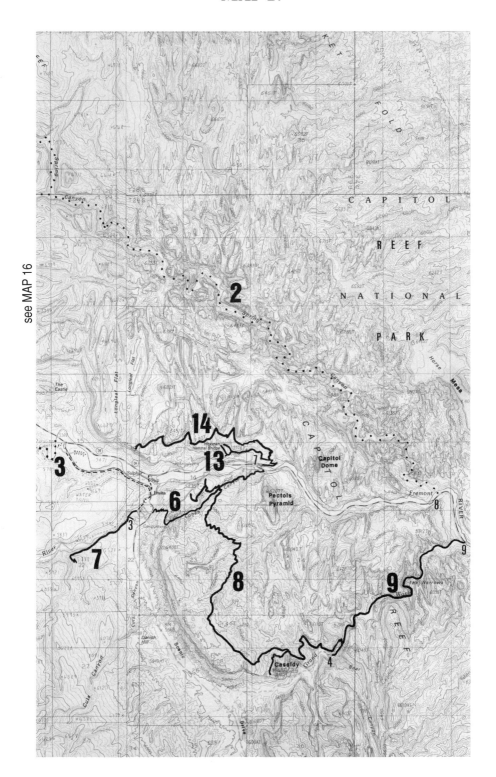

see MAP 16

# MAP 18

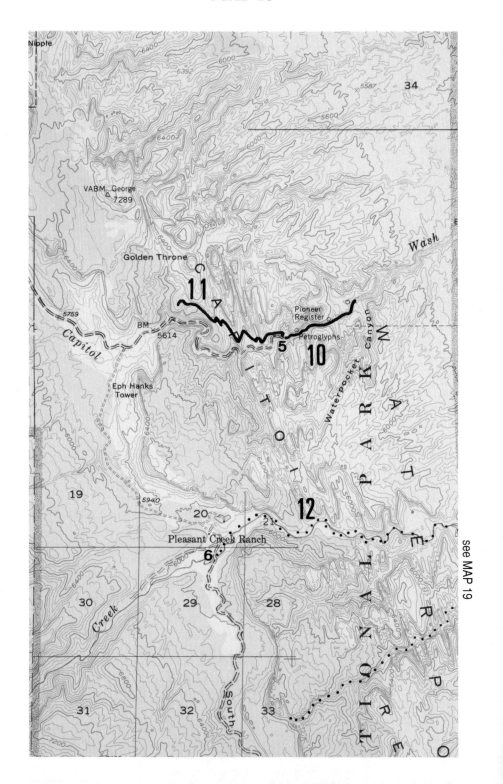

see MAP 19

# MAP 19

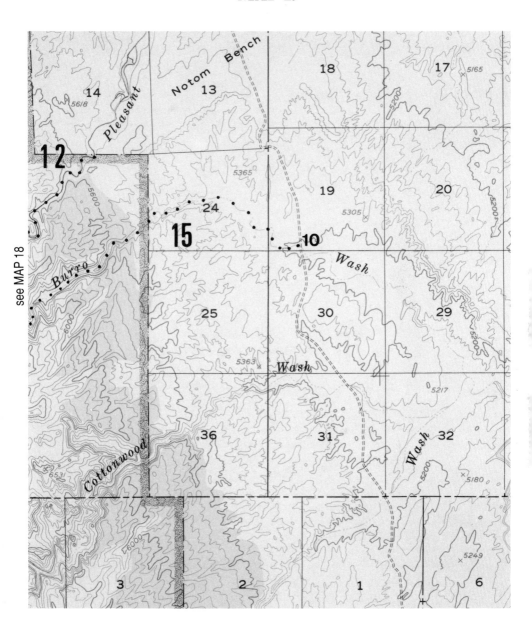

# MAP 20

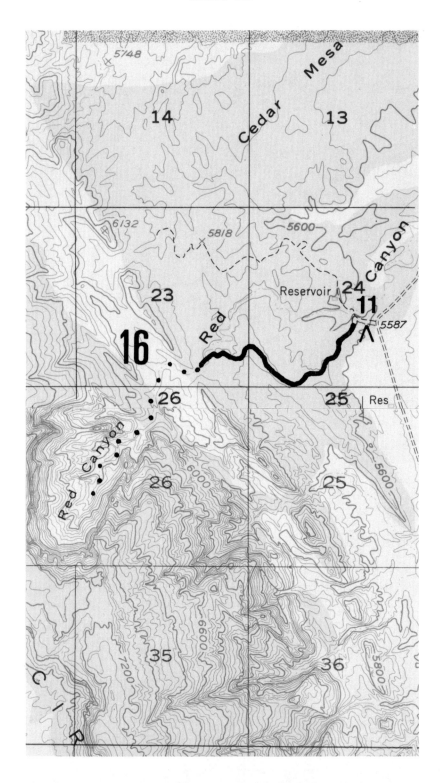

# MAP 21

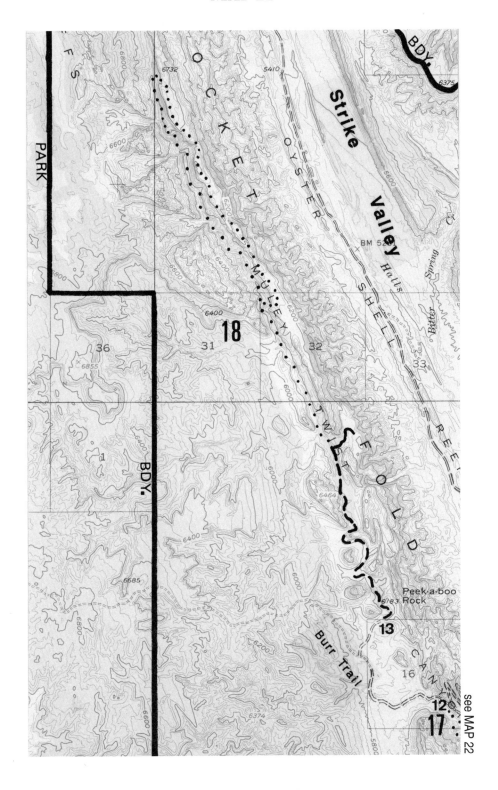

see MAP 22

# MAP 22

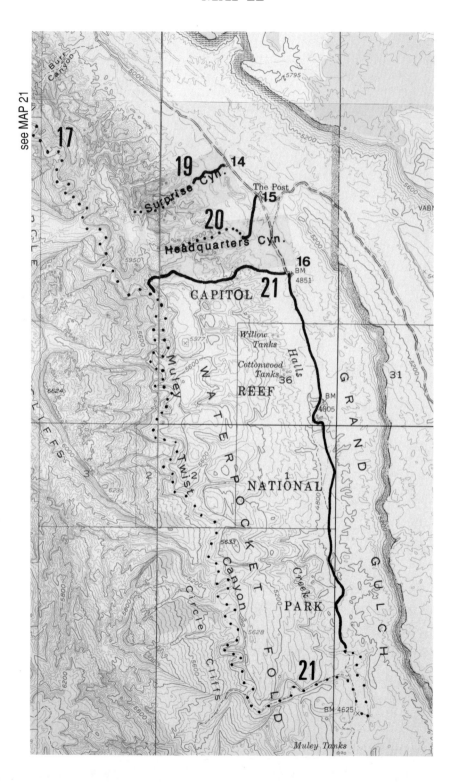

see MAP 21

# MAP 23

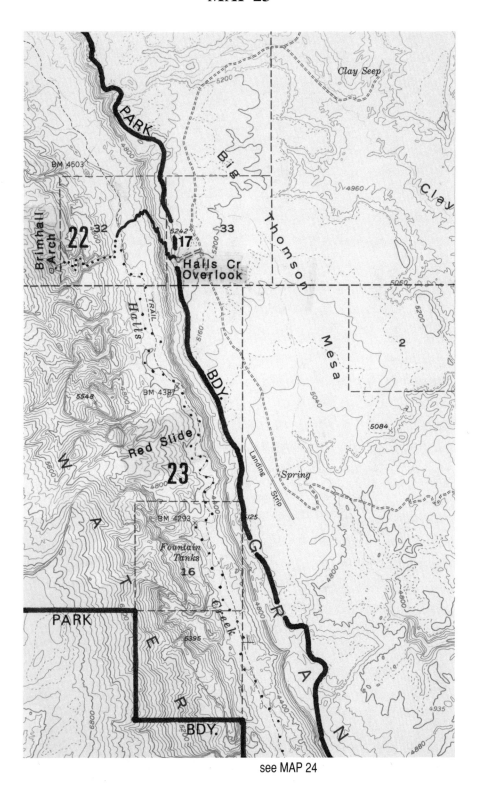

see MAP 24

## MAP 24

see MAP 23

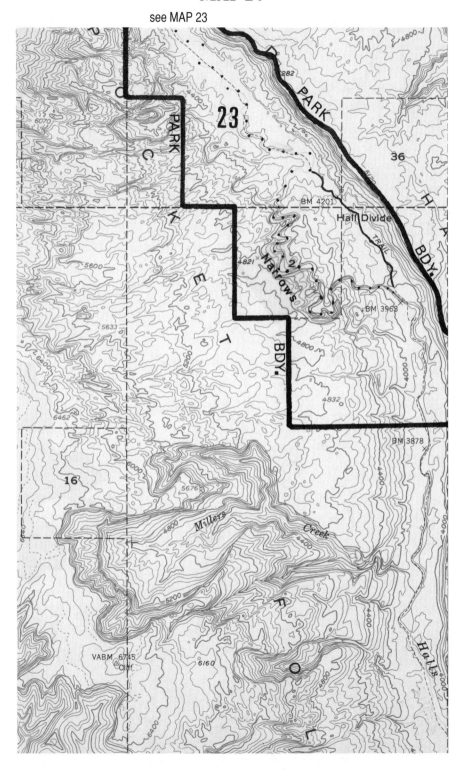

# MAP 25

see MAP 26

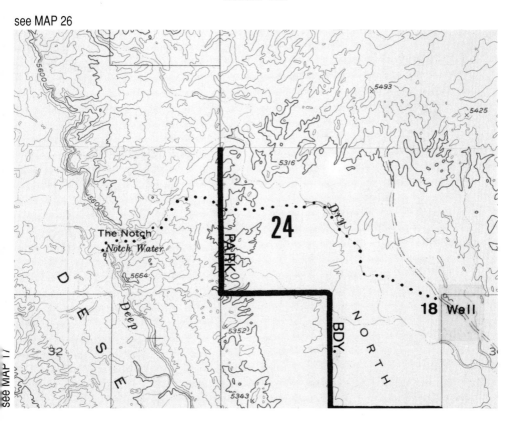

see MAP 17

# MAP 26

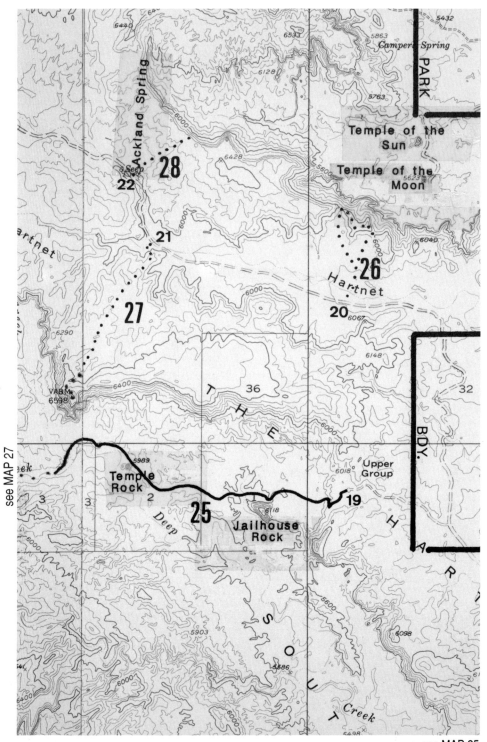

see MAP 27

see MAP 25

# MAP 27

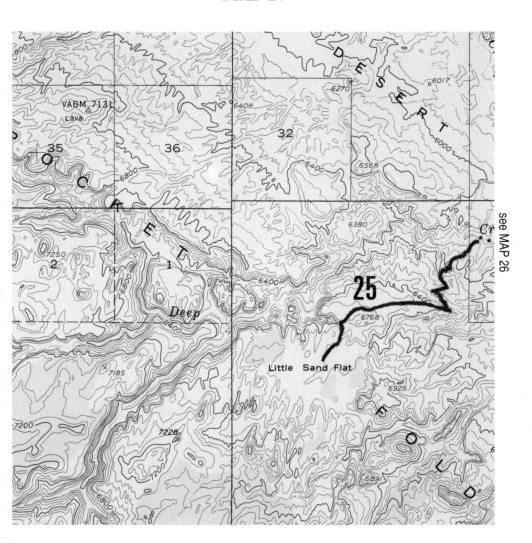

see MAP 26

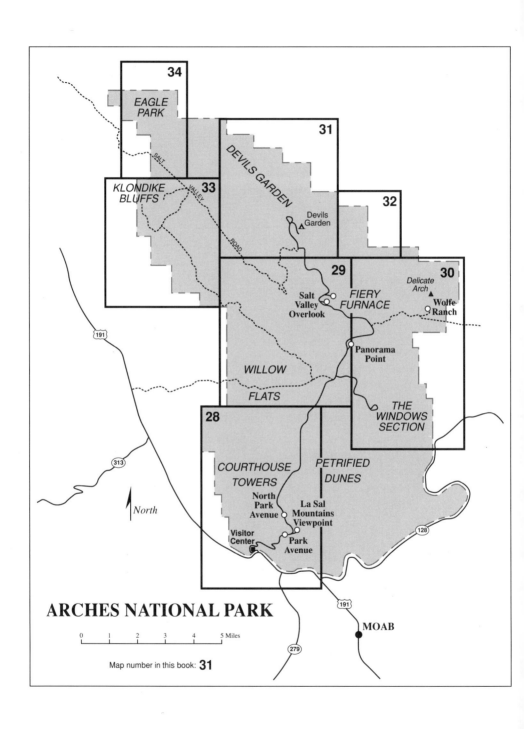

**34**

*EAGLE PARK*

**31**

*DEVILS GARDEN*

**33**

*KLONDIKE BLUFFS*

**32**

▲ Devils Garden

**29**

Salt Valley Overlook

*FIERY FURNACE*

*Delicate Arch* ▲

**30**

Wolfe Ranch

Panorama Point

**191**

*WILLOW*

*FLATS*

*THE WINDOWS SECTION*

**28**

*COURTHOUSE TOWERS*

*PETRIFIED DUNES*

**313**

↑ *North*

North Park Avenue

La Sal Mountains Viewpoint

Visitor Center

Park Avenue

**128**

# ARCHES NATIONAL PARK

0   1   2   3   4   5 Miles

Map number in this book: **31**

**191**

**MOAB**

**279**

# MAP 28

see MAP 29

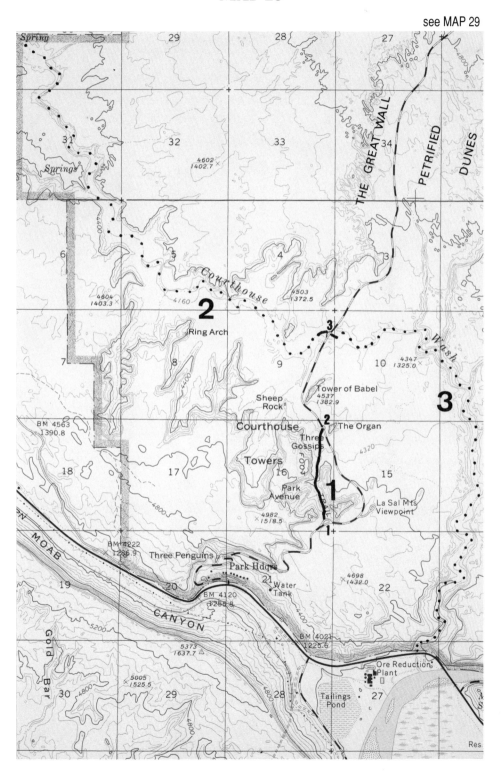

# MAP 29

see MAP 31

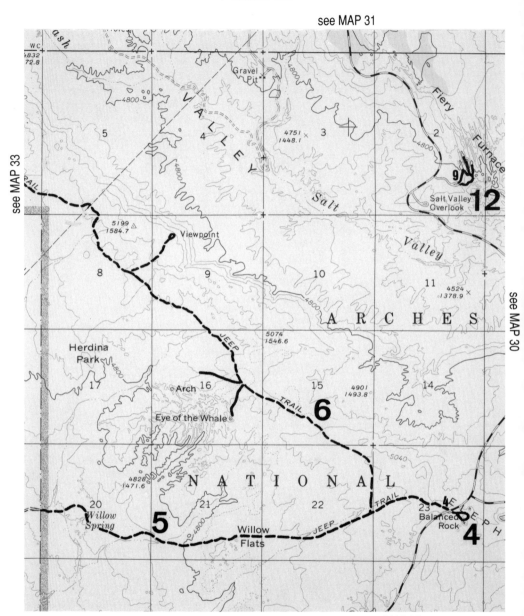

see MAP 33

see MAP 30

see MAP 29

# MAP 30

see MAP 32

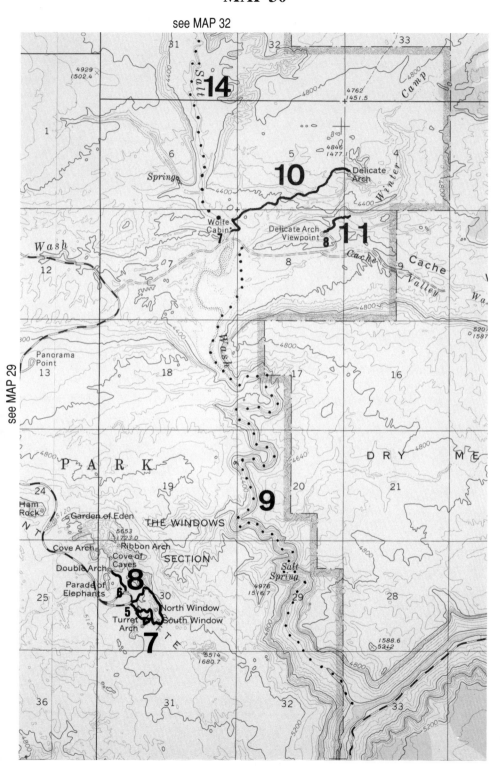

see MAP 29

31
32
33
**14**
Salt
4929
1502.4
4400
4800
Camp
4762
1451.5
1
6
5
4846
1477.1
4
Springs
**10**
Delicate
Arch
4800
4400
Winter
4400
Wolfe
Cabin
**7**
Delicate Arch
Viewpoint
**8**
**11**
Wash
7
8
Cache
9
Cache
Valley
12
Wash
5207
1587
300
Panorama
Point
13
18
4800
17
16
4640
D R Y
M E
P A R K
19
20
21
24
**9**
Ham
Rock
Garden of Eden
THE WINDOWS
5653
1723.0
N T
Cove Arch
Ribbon Arch
Cove of
Caves
SECTION
Salt
Spring
Double Arch
**8**
Parade of
Elephants
**6**
30
North Window
4976
1516.7
29
28
25
**5**
Turret
Arch
South Window
**7**
T E
5514
1680.7
1588.6
5212
4800
36
31
32
33
5200

# MAP 31

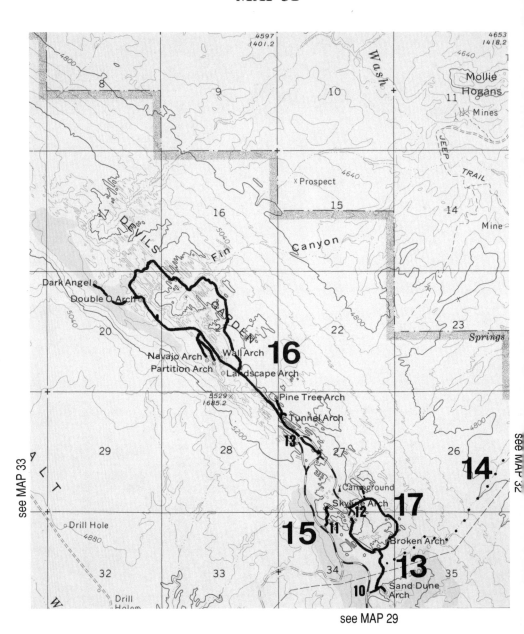

see MAP 33

see MAP 32

see MAP 29

# MAP 32

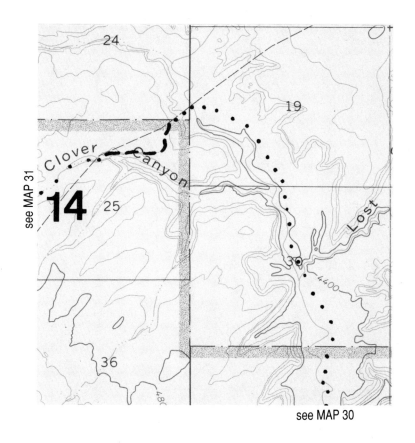

see MAP 31

see MAP 30

# MAP 33

see MAP 34

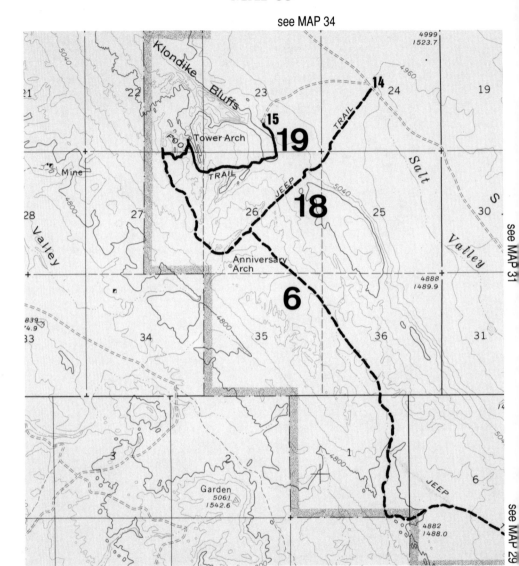

see MAP 31

see MAP 29

# MAP 34

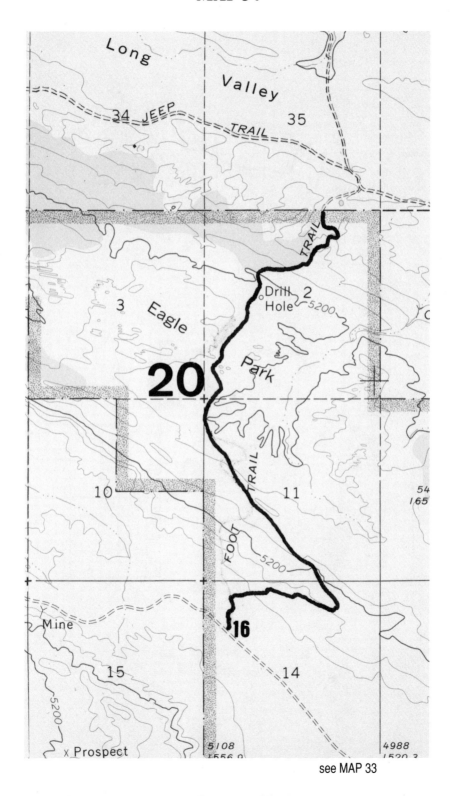

see MAP 33

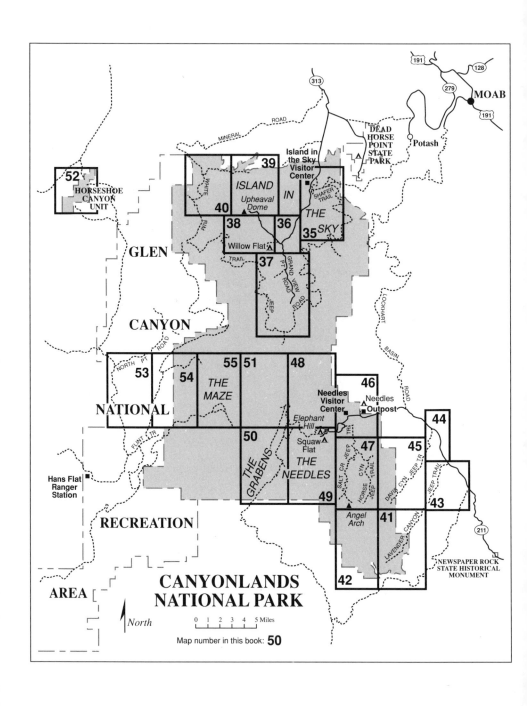

**CANYONLANDS NATIONAL PARK**

North

0 1 2 3 4 5 Miles

Map number in this book: **50**

# MAP 35

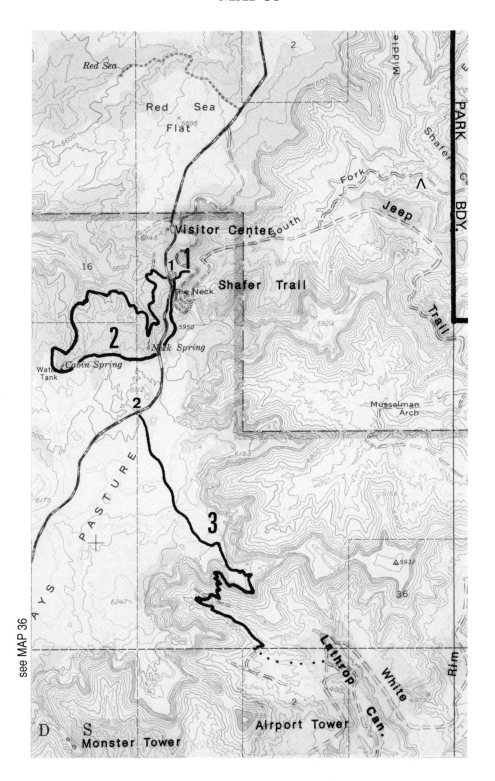

# MAP 36

see MAP 35

see MAP 38

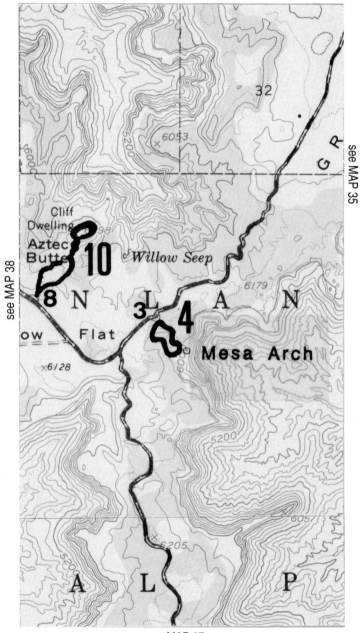

32

6053

Cliff
Dwelling
98
Aztec
Butte
10
Willow Seep
6179
8 N L A N
3 L 4
6 Mesa Arch
ow Flat
6128
5200
6057
6205
5200
A L P

see MAP 37

# MAP 37

see MAP 36

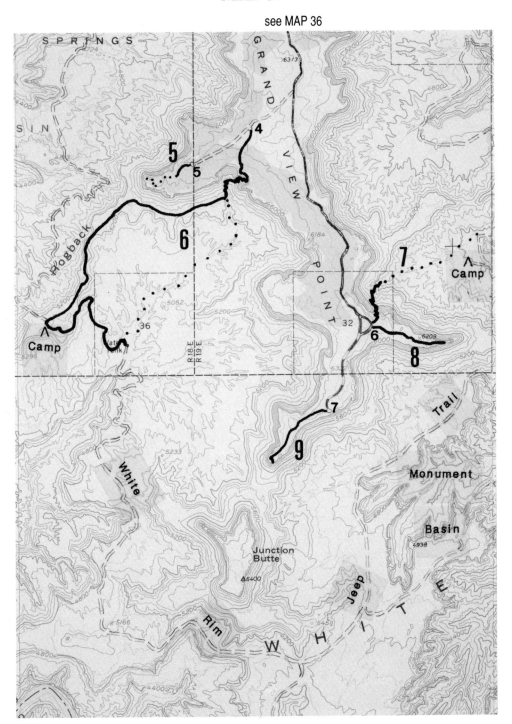

# MAP 38

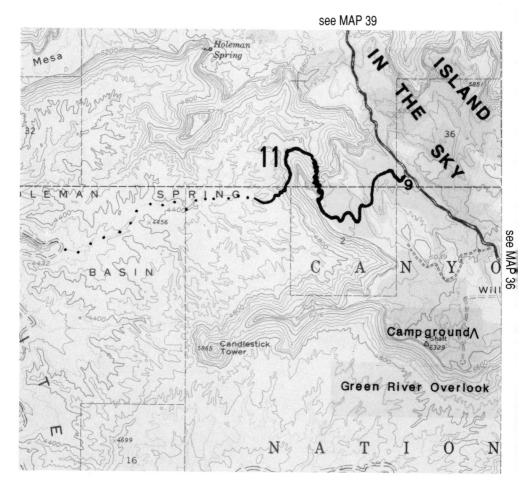

Mesa

Holeman
Spring

ISLAND

IN

THE

SKY

11

LEMAN    SPRING

9

BASIN

CANYO

Will

Campground ∧
Shaft
6329

Green River Overlook

NATION

Candlestick
Tower

# MAP 39

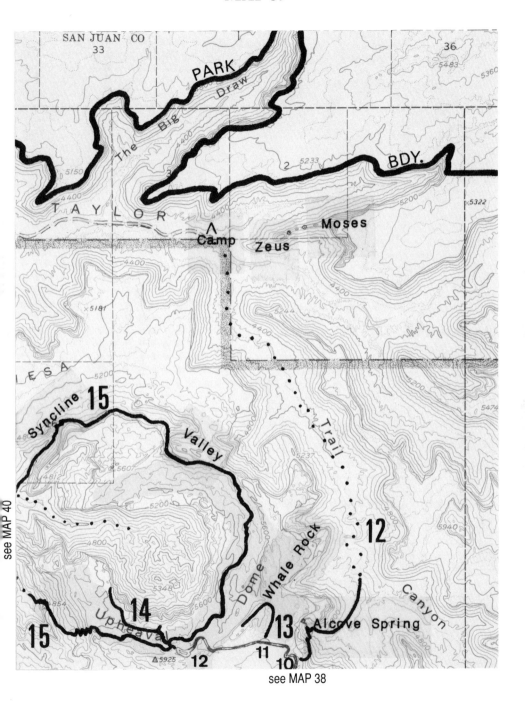

see MAP 40

see MAP 38

# MAP 40

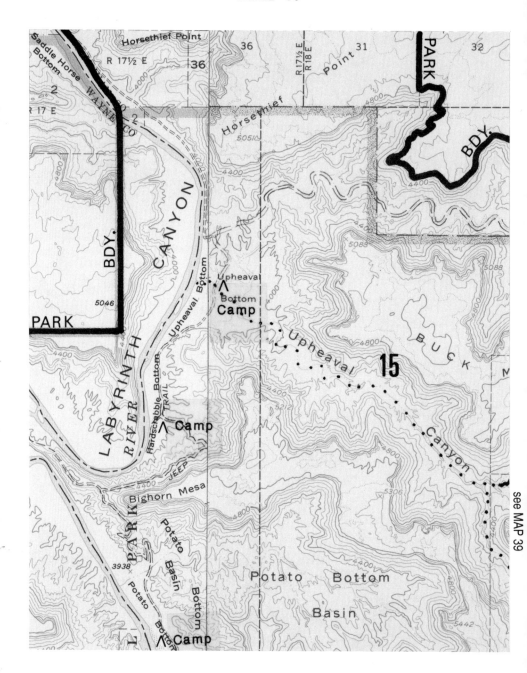

see MAP 39

# MAP 41

see MAP 45

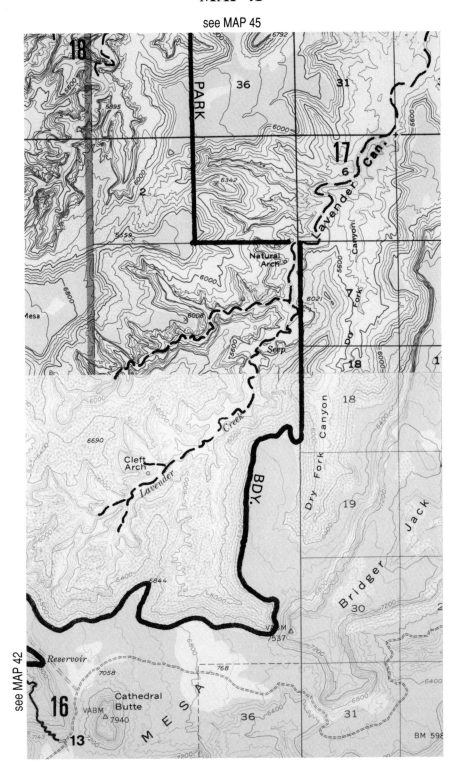

see MAP 42

# MAP 42

see MAP 47

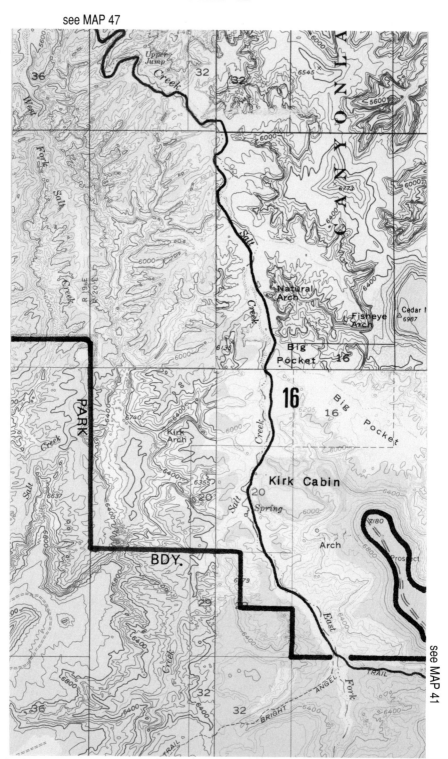

see MAP 41

# MAP 43

see MAP 44

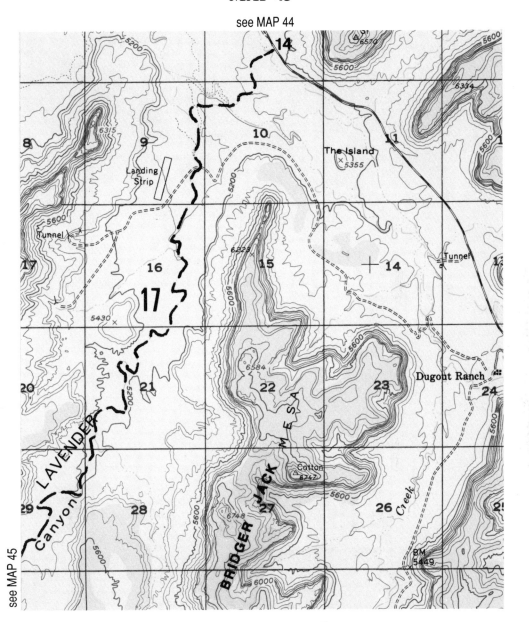

see MAP 45

# MAP 44

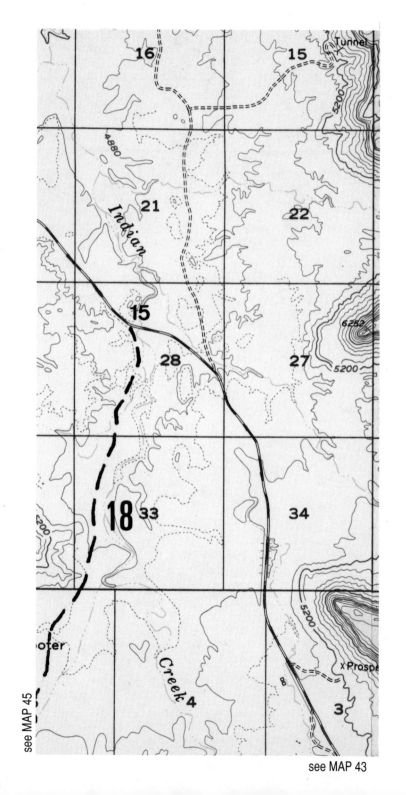

16

15

Tunnel

5200

4880

Indian

21

22

15

6252

28

27

5200

18 33

34

5200

5200

ooter

Creek 4

x Prospe

3

see MAP 45

see MAP 43

# MAP 45

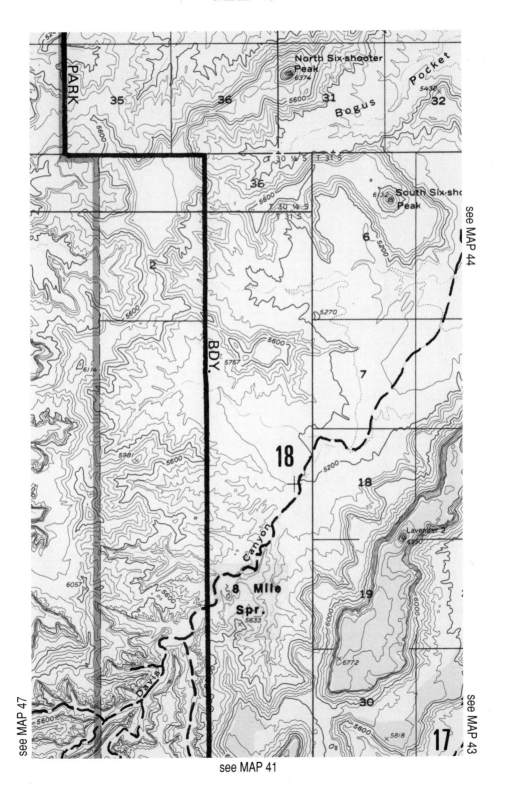

see MAP 44

see MAP 43

see MAP 47

see MAP 41

North Six-shooter Peak
6374

Bogus

Pocket

5438

PARK

35

36

31

32

36

South Six-sho
Peak

6132

5600

6

5200

2

5270

5600

5757

5600

BDY.

7

5981

5600

18

5200

18

6114

Lavendar 2
6950

6057

Canyon

8 Mile

Spr.

5633

19

6772

6000

30

5600

5818

17

Davis

# MAP 46

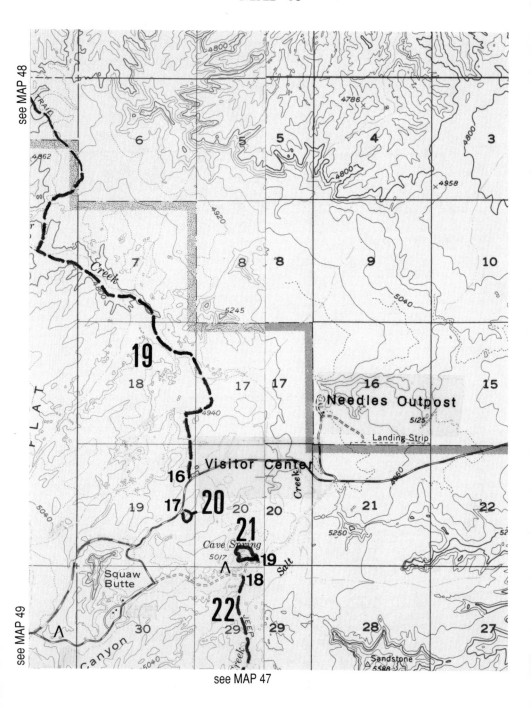

see MAP 48

see MAP 49

see MAP 47

6  5  5  4  3

7  8  8  9  10

**19**

18  17  17  16  15

Needles Outpost

Landing Strip

16  Visitor Center

19  17  **20**  20  20  21  22

**21**

Cave Spring  19

Squaw
Butte  18

**22**

30  29  29  28  27

Sandstone

Creek

Salt

Creek

FLAT

Canyon

TRAIL

JEEP

# MAP 47

see MAP 46

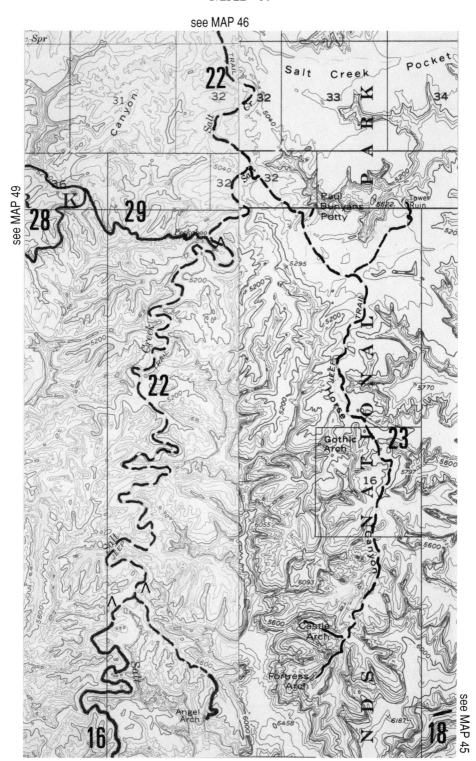

see MAP 49

see MAP 42

see MAP 45

# MAP 48

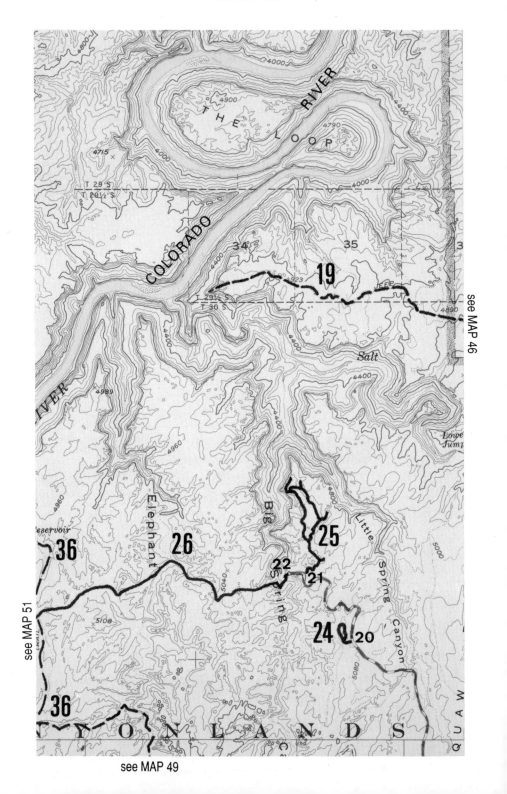

THE LOOP

RIVER

COLORADO

4900

4790

4715 ×

T 29 S
T 29½ S

34

35

19

923

JEEP

T 29½ S
T 30 S

4890

see MAP 46

Salt

RIVER

4989

Lower
Jump

4960

4400

25

Little Spring Canyon

Reservoir

36

Elephant

26

4960

22

21

see MAP 51

5108

5040

24

20

5080

QUAW

36

Y O N L A N D S

see MAP 49

# MAP 49

see MAP 48
see MAP 46
see MAP 50
see MAP 47

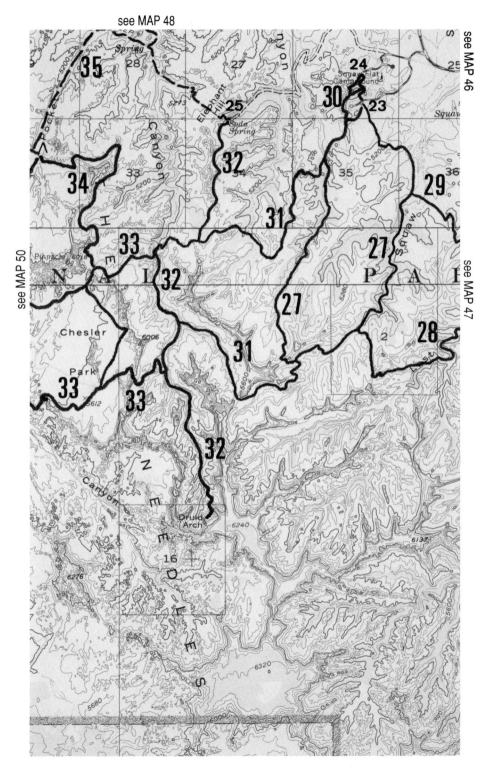

# MAP 50

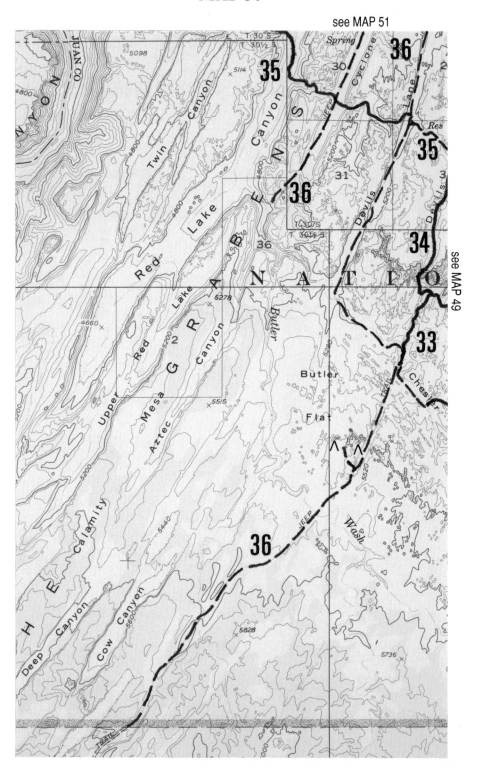

see MAP 51

see MAP 49

# MAP 51

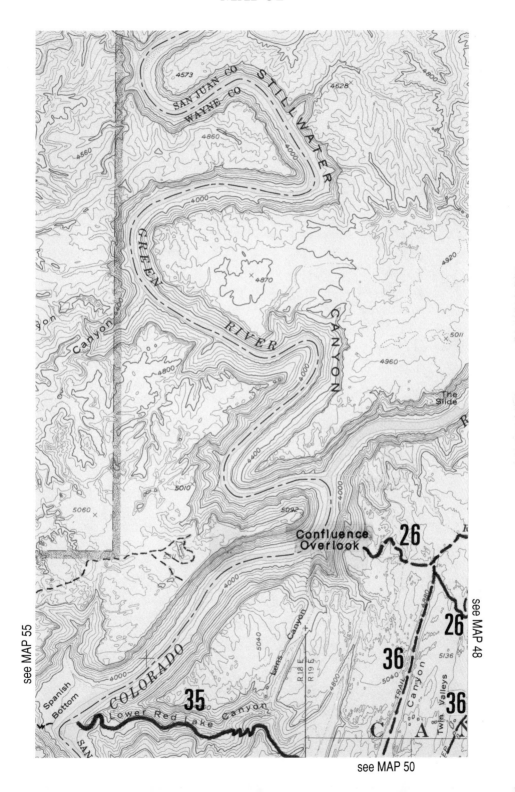

see MAP 55

see MAP 48

see MAP 50

# MAP 52

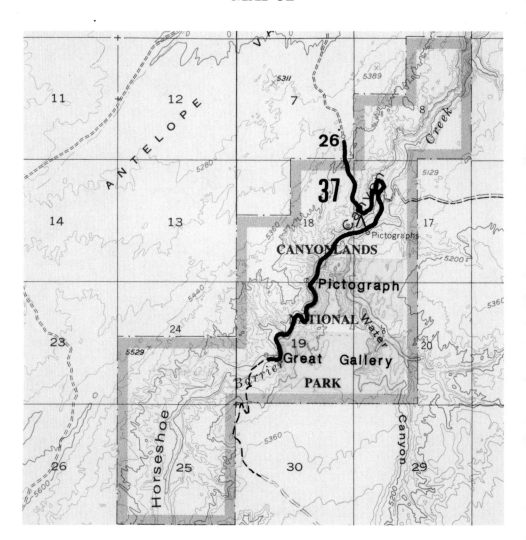

# MAP 53

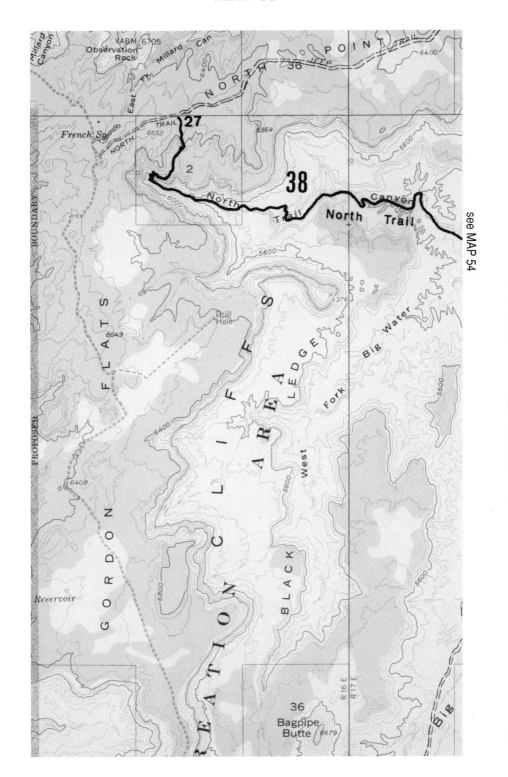

see MAP 54

# MAP 54

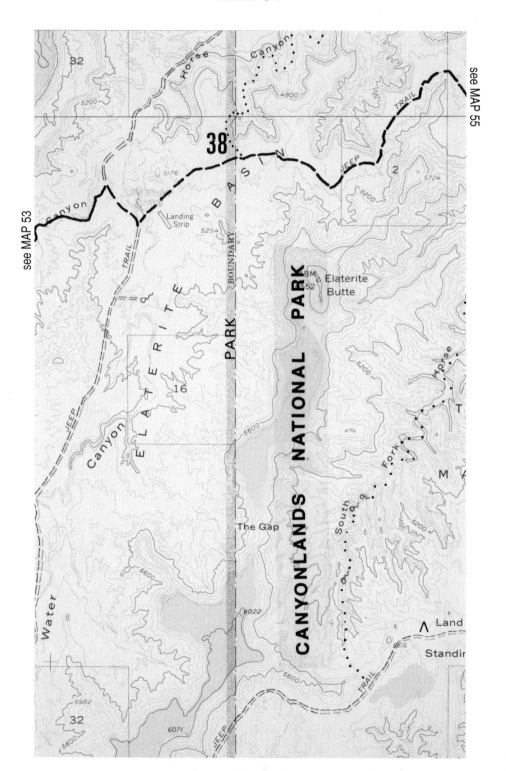

see MAP 55

see MAP 53

32

5200

Horse

Canyon

4800

38

TRAIL

JEEP

2

5724

5200

5176

Canyon

Landing
Strip

5254

TRAIL

JEEP

BOUNDARY

PARK

CANYONLANDS NATIONAL PARK

ELATERITE

BM
52

Elaterite
Butte

5200

Horse

T

M

Fork

South

16

Canyon

5600

5200

5600

The Gap

JEEP

Water

5600

5600

6022

6071

5982

32

5600

Land

5816

Standin

TRAIL

JEEP

BASIN

# MAP 55

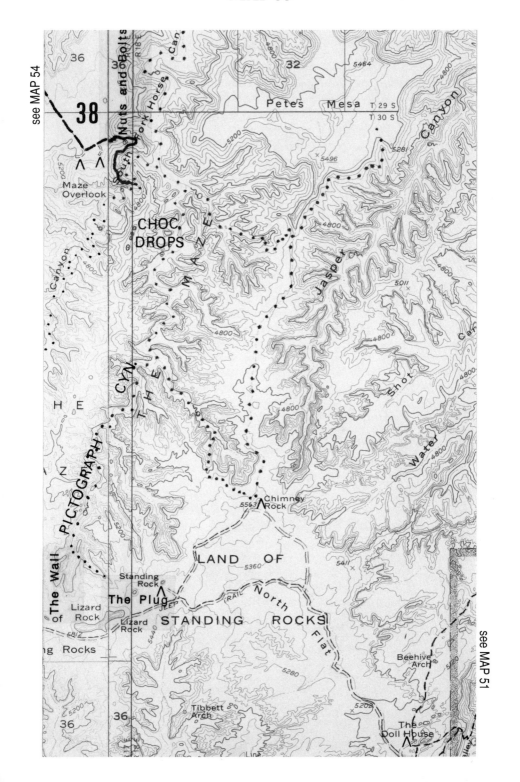

see MAP 54

see MAP 51

36

32

5464

**38**

Nuts and Bolts

South Fork Horse Can

Pete's Mesa    T 29 S

T 30 S

Canyon

5200

5281

5496

Maze Overlook

5200

**CHOC. DROPS**

4800

Jasper

5011

THE MAZE

4800

Canyon

4800

4800

4800

Can

4800

H  E

THE PICTOGRAPH CYN.

Z

Shot

4800

Water

4800

4800

4800

5563

Chimney Rock

5200

**LAND  OF**

5360

5411

The Wall

5200

Standing Rock

**The Plug**

RAIL

North

Beehive Arch

of

Lizard Rock

Lizard Rock

5440

**STANDING   ROCKS**

5280

Flat

g Rocks

5200

36

36

Tibbett Arch

5208

**The Doll House**

Line

# INDEX